The Economy of *Ulysses*

Richard Fallis, *Series Editor*

The Economy of *Ulysses*

Making Both Ends Meet

MARK OSTEEN

SYRACUSE UNIVERSITY PRESS

Copyright © 1995 by Syracuse University Press
Syracuse, New York 13244-5160
All Rights Reserved

First Edition 1995
95 96 97 98 99 00   6 5 4 3 2 1

This book is published with the assistance of a grant from Loyola College of Maryland.

Permission to quote from the following sources is gratefully acknowledged:
   Passages from *Ulysses: The Corrected Text*, by James Joyce, edited by Hans Walter Gabler with Wolfhard Steepe and Claus Melchoir (New York: Random House, 1986), are reprinted by permission of Random House, Inc.
   Quotations from *Finnegans Wake* (New York: Viking Penguin, 1939) and *Letters of James Joyce,* 3 vols.; vol. I edited by Stuart Gilbert; vols. II and III edited by Richard Ellmann (New York: Viking Penguin, 1957, 1966), are reprinted by permission of Viking Penguin, a division of Penguin USA Inc.

The paper used in this publication meets the minimum requirements of American National Standard for Information Sciences—Permanence of Paper for Printed Library Materials, ANSI Z39.48-1984. ∞™

Library of Congress Cataloging-in-Publication Data
Osteen, Mark.
   The economy of Ulysses : making both ends meet / Mark Osteen.
      p.   cm.
   Includes bibliographical references (p.   ) and index.
   ISBN 0-8156-2653-3 (cloth : alk. paper).—ISBN 0-8156-2661-4
   (paper : alk. paper)
   1. Joyce, James, 1882–1941. Ulysses. I. Title.
      PR6019.O9U6847   1995
823'.912—dc20   94-44601

Manufactured in the United States of America

For Leslie

Mark Osteen is associate professor of English at Loyola College in Maryland and has published a number of articles on Joyce and twentieth-century literature.

Contents

Acknowledgments

Anyone who undertakes to write about Joyce incurs debts to several generations of laborers who have gone before him. In addition to these general debts, I wish to acknowledge and thank others who have helped me in the research and writing of this book. My dissertation adviser, the late Richard Ellmann, made many insightful comments on the first several chapters that prompted me to clarify and sharpen my ideas, even while he was struggling with the illness that caused his untimely death. Ronald Schuchard graciously took over for him, and his support and constructive criticism inspired me to continue as if Professor Ellmann were still reading it. Jerome Beaty and Hank Harrington provided both general encouragement and specific editorial remarks. In addition, Michael J. O'Shea read and commented on the entire first draft, an arduous task for which he deserves my thanks and admiration. I owe thanks as well to Richard Fallis and Patrick McCarthy for their supportive and instructive readings of the draft I originally submitted to Syracuse University Press. Several other Joyceans, including Brandon Kershner, Garry Leonard, Derek Attridge, and John Bishop provided encouragement along the way. I also wish to thank Cynthia Maude-Gembler for her patience and understanding during the evaluation process, and my friends and colleagues at Loyola for their forbearance and advice.

A George Woodruff Fellowship from Emory University Graduate School and an English Department Doctoral Fellowship gave me uninterrupted time to devote to this study when it was a dissertation. At Loyola, I wish to thank David Roswell, Dean of the College of Arts and Sciences, and the Faculty Development Committee for their support in the form of a publishing subsidy and two summer research grants. The aid of a 1991 Junior Faculty Sabbatical from the Loyola Center for Humanities was indispensable in bringing the book to completion.

Portions of chapter 4 and chapter 6 were previously published in *James Joyce Quarterly*. An earlier version of chapter 7 was published in *Joyce Studies Annual* 1990, edited by Thomas F. Staley; a shorter version of chapter 10 appeared in *Modern Fiction Studies*. I am grateful to the editors of each journal for permission to reprint this material.

Of course, my greatest debts are to my son, Cameron, who helped me remember what is truly valuable, and to my wife, Leslie, for her unflagging emotional support and her willingness to sacrifice her own time for my work.

Baltimore, Maryland   Mark Osteen
January 1995

Abbreviations

The text of *Ulysses* used throughout is *Ulysses: The Corrected Text*, edited by Hans Walter Gabler with Wolfhard Steppe and Claus Melchior (New York: Random House, 1986). It is cited in chapter 1 by *U*, plus episode, followed by the line number, and in the rest of the book simply by episode and line number.

The other abbreviations and editions used in the text are the following:

CP	Joyce, James. *Collected Poems*. New York: Viking, 1957.
CW	———. *The Critical Writings of James Joyce*. Ed. Ellsworth Mason and Richard Ellmann. New York: Viking, 1959.
D	———. *Dubliners: Text, Criticism and Notes*. Ed. Robert Scholes and A. Walton Litz. New York: Viking, 1969.
Exiles	———. *Exiles*. New York: Viking, 1951.
FW	———. *Finnegans Wake*. New York: Viking Penguin, 1939. Cited by page and line number.
Hart and Hayman.	Hart, Clive, and David Hayman. *James Joyce's* Ulysses: *Critical Essays*. Berkeley: Univ. of California Press, 1974.
JJ	Ellmann, Richard. *James Joyce: New and Revised Edition*. New York: Oxford Univ. Press, 1982.
JJA	Groden, Michael, et al. ed. *The James Joyce Archive*. 63 vols. New York and London: Garland, 1978—.

JJQ   *James Joyce Quarterly*

L   Joyce, James. *Letters of James Joyce.* 3 vols. Vol. I, ed. Stuart Gilbert. New York: Viking, 1957. Vols. II and III, ed. Richard Ellmann. New York: Viking, 1966.

LB   Joyce, James. *James Joyce's Letters to Sylvia Beach, 1921–1940.* Ed. Melissa Banta and Oscar A. Silverman. Bloomington: Indiana Univ. Press, 1987.

MBK   Joyce, Stanislaus. *My Brother's Keeper.* New York: Viking, 1958.

Notesheets   Joyce, James. *Joyce's* Ulysses *Notesheets in the British Museum.* Ed. Phillip F. Herring. Charlottesville: UP of Virginia, 1972.

OED   *The Compact Edition of the Oxford English Dictionary.* 2 vols. Oxford & New York: Oxford Univ. Press, 1971.

P   ———. *A Portrait of the Artist as a Young Man: Text, Criticism and Notes.* Ed. Chester G. Anderson. New York: Viking, 1968.

SH   ———. *Stephen Hero.* Ed. John J. Slocum and Herbert Cahoon. New York: New Directions, 1944, 1963.

The Economy of *Ulysses*

1

Miser and Spendthrift

I pick up your reproof, the horsegift of a friend
For the prize of your save is the price of my spend. . . .
We are Wastenot with Want, precondamned, two and true,
Till Nolans go volants and Bruneyes come blue.
                                        —*FW* 418.21–22; 31–32

—But this prying into the life of a great man, Russell began
impatiently. . . . Interesting only to the parish clerk. I mean
we have the plays. . . . Peeping and prying into greenroom
gossip of the day, the poet's drinking, the poet's debts.
                                        —*U* 9.181–2; 187–88.

In an August 1904 letter to Nora Barnacle, James Joyce confesses
that his father's household was a "middle-class affair ruined by spendthrift habits which I have inherited" (*L* II 48). To read Joyce's letters
and biographies is to recognize the accuracy of his assessment. Like
his father, Joyce devoted many hours to borrowing or begging money
from friends and relatives and then squandering it on drinks, gifts,
and travel. Yet, in a letter to Nora written about three weeks later,
Joyce acknowledges a contrary impulse: "My life has made me very
reserved in what I say" (*L* II 54). This verbal reserve contradicts his
financial extravagance. On the one hand, then, is Joyce the habitual
debtor and profligate spender; on the other is Joyce the formal and
reserved intellectual. Joyce valued and cultivated both tendencies—
the extravagant bohemian poet and the controlled craftsman—and
believed both necessary to his art.

1

This chapter examines a series of related oppositions—extravagance and reserve, spending and hoarding, generosity and meanness—to demonstrate how Joyce's economic attitudes and behavior illuminate his aesthetic philosophy and artistic practices. It will become clear that Joyce never reached a satisfactory compromise between two strong, conflicting impulses: his desire to be a solvent member of the European bourgeoisie and his contrary desire to remain separate from the middle class, to defy bourgeois values, to spend his money and remain on the fringes of this community. This conflict is expressed in Joyce's life by the inconsistency between his excessive spending and consequent financial insolvency, and his recurring vindictiveness and emotional and verbal stinginess. His art reflects these antinomies in the oscillation between an economy of verbal excess and expenditure and an equally strong impulse toward control.

Creating two alter egos in *Ulysses,* Stephen Dedalus and Leopold Bloom, who in many respects represent his internal division, Joyce charts the paths that their very different economies trace. In Stephen, Joyce invokes both his literary and financial debtors and, using his writing as currency, pays them. In Stephen he portrays his own youthful economic habits, but also demonstrates how those habits contribute to Stephen's artistic paralysis. In Bloom's vacillation between shrewd cost accounting and generosity, Joyce depicts his own ambivalence about bourgeois economic habits. Bloom's occupation as ad canvasser not only reflects Joyce's interest in popular culture but also synthesizes both Bloom's and Joyce's aesthetic and commercial impulses. When the focus of *Ulysses* broadens to scrutinize Dublin's social life, the novel critiques the economic extravagance and excesses that Joyce believed he had inherited from his father; but at the same time it reinscribes those habits by engaging in its own economy of excess. Unlike his father, however, Joyce uses the expenditure of words to transform loss into gain by arduous labor. The meeting between Stephen and Bloom represents an encounter between Joyce's own conflicting economies; it results in a provisional and temporary synthesis that is undone almost at the moment it is offered as a model of true reciprocity. The penultimate episode of *Ulysses* achieves a powerful sense of balance and closure that seems to affirm Bloom's bourgeois economy. Immediately, however, Molly Bloom's monologue supplants that restricted economy with a ceaselessly circulating system that manipulates the economy of gift exchange to undermine not only closure, but also the economic divisions that the novel has established.

SPENDTHRIFT HABITS

To understand Joyce's economic and social conflicts and ambivalences, we must briefly examine the sources of those conflicts in his family's and his city's economic histories. Joyce critics have recently begun to acknowledge that his writings document Irish political and economic conditions. But not all historians agree about those conditions. As Patrick O'Farrell shows, it is nearly impossible to find an unbiased report on Irish social and economic conditions from the 1880s to the 1920s. Analyses from that period fall into one of two stereotypical patterns: the Irish nationalist version, which tended to exaggerate economic problems in order to blame the British and excuse the Irish; or the British/Unionist view, which stereotyped the Irish as idle, overemotional, and thriftless, and hence culpable for their own problems (O'Farrell 1975, 119, 125). One reason for this contradiction is that the late nineteenth-century Irish economy was itself full of inconsistencies. Although in some respects "comparable . . . to a handful of highly developed nations" (Cullen 1987, 170), Ireland remained primarily an agricultural nation with a narrow industrial base. Eighty percent of its net industrial output was accounted for by three industries: spinning and weaving, brewing and distilling, and shipbuilding and engineering (Cullen 1987, 159). Nor were conditions uniform throughout the country. Not surprisingly, Belfast, the home of the Protestant Anglo-Irish Ascendancy, produced a third of the nation's industrial output in those three industries and was thus the wealthiest Irish city (Cullen 1987, 162, 164). In contrast, Dublin, impoverished, unhealthy, and industrially stagnant, exemplified the worst of Ireland's generally backward economic conditions.

Joseph V. O'Brien has shown in depressingly thorough detail how British hegemony had helped to stultify the city economically. "The paucity of manufactures, an insufficiency (or misdirection) of capital, and an inability to compete with the products of British industry stifled economic progress" throughout Ireland, but especially in Dublin (1982, 36). These conditions, exacerbated by "want of employment, prevalence of poverty and inadequacies in public health and housing," ensured the continued decline of the city's fortunes, which had been on the wane for nearly a century (O'Brien 1982, 36). The two most intractable problems, a high death rate and unsanitary housing, were in fact the same problem: squalid living conditions hastened the spread of disease, producing an inordinately high death rate. At the turn of the century the rate stood at 33.6 per thousand, exceeding

that of "any large city in Europe or the United States," and falling
only slightly below that of the infamous Calcutta (O'Brien 1982, 102).
Indeed, Dublin had "the worst slum conditions of the British Isles"
(Cullen 1987, 165), not only in terms of the quality of life (typhus,
typhoid, smallpox and tuberculosis were endemic), but also in sheer
numbers, since about one-third of Dubliners lived in tenements usually comprised of one-room abodes, in which families of up to eleven
people eked out a nasty, brutish existence (Cullen 1987, 166; O'Brien
1982, 131). Some 30,000 people (about one-tenth of the city's population) lived in 2,300 dwellings that inspectors had deemed unfit for
human habitation. Clearly, for the very poor, Dublin was a hellish
place, a good deal more dirty than dear.

But economic hardship was not restricted to the very poor. Even
steadily employed laborers drew wages that provided no more than a
bare subsistence. O'Brien cites the typical cases of two male laborers
supporting families of seven on a meager 18s per week—only a little
more than the underemployed and impoverished Stephen Dedalus
earns as a part-time teacher (O'Brien 1982, 165–66).[1] Of course,
pockets of abject poverty exist even in the most prosperous cities, but
in Dublin economic insuffiency was not the exception for the working
classes but the rule. The percentage of skilled labor was much lower
than England's: only 30 percent of all laborers were tradesmen or
skilled workers making as much as £2 per week, and unemployment
averaged between 15 and 20 percent in the first decade of the twentieth century (O'Brien 1982, 201–2; Cullen 1987, 165).[2] The result was
that "a majority of working-class employed was forever on the fringes
of poverty" (O'Brien 1982, 202). Workers had few alternatives other
than emigration or the workhouse. Wages were low, hours long, and
unions weak (conditions that eventually produced massive labor agita-
tion between 1910 and 1916). Circumstances were just as abysmal for
female workers. Shop girls earned a paltry 7s to 10s per week; the
lucky ones who held clerical jobs might make as much as 12s 6d a
week (O'Brien 1982, 205–6). All of these rates were 20 to 25 percent
below those for comparable positions in England. Even for educated
women, jobs were both scarce and unprofitable (Walzl 1982, 37).[3]

   1. Stephen earns £3 12s a month, which comes to between 16 and 17 shillings a
week.
   2. The Dublin Corporation (municipal government) set the minimum income
necessary to provide for a family of three at £1 per week, which O'Brien (1982, 166–
70) considers inadequate.
   3. The title character of "Eveline" thus earns a typical wage of seven shillings a
week (*D* 38).

Given these dismal employment prospects, it is not surprising that an estimated 3–4 percent of adult females in Dublin found steady work in the oldest profession (O'Brien 1982, 193).

A common tendency of the era was to blame much of this appalling situation on drinking. One great irony in this regard is that the largest and most profitable firm in Dublin was Guinness's brewery. However, as the statistics cited above suggest, the very poor scarcely had money to sustain life, let alone to indulge in drinking bouts. Neither is it clear whether drink was primarily a cause or an effect of poverty: a frustrated, ill-paid worker might well turn to drink as a temporary palliative for his misery (see the *Dubliners* story "Counterparts"). Often, the bourgeoisie merely used charges of excessive drinking by the poor to shore up their own moral complacency and excuse themselves for failing to improve housing and working conditions. The fact that one-fourth of the city council consisted of publicans and wine merchants may help to explain the local government's passivity with regard to temperance (O'Brien 1982, 80). But if the truly destitute had no money to buy alcohol, it is clear from Joyce's works that drinking contributed to the decline in economic solvency and morale, especially among the working- and lower-middle classes. Since, as we know from "Telemachus" (*U* 1.724), a pint of beer cost only twopence, a determined Dubliner could get quite drunk on a single shilling. Most social investigations of the period saw boozing as "the predominant cause of misery and destitution" in Dublin, as well as a principal contributor to child-abuse (O'Brien 1982, 188), a charge borne out by several *Dubliners* stories. No doubt drunkenness was widespread; for example, although arrests in Dublin for drunkenness fell from more than 5,000 in 1871 to just 2,000 by 1901, the latter figure is still almost three times the number for the much larger London and twice as high as Belfast's (O'Brien 1982, 188). Thus the stereotypical Irishman: a lazy spendthrift who devotes his days to spinning yarns with his drinking cronies in the pub. Although Joyce scorned such patronizing stereotypes, his own works depict many who fit the mold.

These facts seem to offer sound reasons for Joyce's "exile": not only could he not write in Ireland, but he would have been hard-pressed to earn a decent living. L. M. Cullen, however, argues that, despite its enormous slums, Dublin was "a relatively prosperous city" (1987, 166)—relative, that is, to itself. In fact, Dublin had a large and growing middle class, residing in the suburbs, who were insulated from the worst of its poverty. It is curious that these middle-class people rarely appear in Joyce's fiction, and when they do, it is to exemplify repellent tendencies: complicity with the British (the pompous civic leaders in "Wandering Rocks"), emotional and financial stinginess (the anal retentive Duffy of "A Painful Case"), or aggressive self-righteousness (Stephen's employer, Mr. Deasy; Farrington's employer, Mr. Alleyne). Joyce's people are for the most part neither the very poor nor the complacent bourgeoisie but rather lower-middle class or shabby-genteel figures like Simon Dedalus, who has fallen from the modestly well-to-do to a glorified mendicancy. These are the Dubliners—the dispossessed drinkers, debtors, and spendthrifts—with whom Joyce was most familiar, not least because his own father was one of them.

As Colbert Kearney notes (1989, 59), "in many ways, the history of the Joyces is the history of the Catholic middle class in Ireland." It is a history of economic decline and fall. Indeed, financial failure seems to have run in the Joyce family. James's grandfather, after inheriting a solid fortune from his father's salt and lime business, went bankrupt in 1852, despite having married an O'Connell who brought a decent inheritance to the match (*JJ* 12; Kearney 1989, 62, 69). Of course, the strongest influence on Joyce's economic behavior was his father, John Stanislaus Joyce. In 1870, at twenty-one, John Joyce inherited a thousand pounds from his maternal grandfather, supplementing the annual income of £315 from his property in Cork (*JJ* 15). He invested his inheritance in a distillery and, in a striking prediction of his lifelong expenditures on drink, lost it all. In 1880 he got a position as a rate collector in Dublin at a salary of £500 per year, excellent wages for the day. But he lost the job after Parnell, to whom he had tied his political balloon, fell from grace. Thus John Joyce's life, according to Kearney, divides neatly in two: before and after 1891. Before 1891 "he was a man of means, albeit diminishing means, who had inherited a considerable amount of property in Cork; not long after 1891 he had mortgaged his properties away and was the unemployed father irresponsible for the welfare of a wife and ten children" (1989, 57). In the 1880s and 1890s he "filled his house with children and debts" (*JJ* 21), constantly moving his troop of children from house to house, often only one step ahead of his landlords and creditors. Joyce conferred many of these traits onto Stephen Dedalus's father Simon, whose occupations Stephen sardonically lists in *Portrait:* "a medical student, an oarsman, a tenor, an amateur actor, a shouting politician, a small landlord, a small investor, a drinker, a good fellow, a storyteller, somebody's secretary, something in a distillery, a taxgatherer, a bankrupt and at present a praiser of his own past" (*P* 241). John Joyce's life was a chronicle of decline from respectability into poverty. This history helps to explain why the Dublin of Joyce's fiction lacks the middle class that in fact it did possess: Joyce himself never lived among such people after his father's downfall and was probably jealous of the continued prosperity of those who, in his eyes, must have been traitors to the Parnellite cause.

This heritage left Joyce with a conflicting set of economic images. Like his politics, which were molded in the 1880s by Parnell's heroic and tragic life, Joyce's views on Irish economics seem to have become fixed in the economically "grim" eighties (Cullen 1987, 150). Like the history of Ireland, two versions of the Joyce family saga emerge. The first is the one cultivated by Joyce's father, in which the Joyces "fell from grace due to the meanminded treachery of the Irish people." A second, more factual version, shows that the Joyces had lived "beyond their means for two generations"; John Joyce "had failed either to earn enough money or to marry a sufficiently rich woman to finance his life of genteel leisure. It was only a matter of time before he fell into debts which could not be sustained" (Kearney 1989, 65). The confluence of his country's and his family's history endowed John Joyce with incompatible economic attitudes: he retained the self-image of a gentleman and the Victorian attitude that gentlemen do not work but coupled it with an inability to hold onto the jobs or money that might actually have permitted such gentility. James inherited this contradiction, cultivating a bourgeois, even aristocratic, manner and values but also scorning the bourgeoisie and living in his father's hand-to-mouth manner. James Joyce conceived of himself simultaneously as a middle-class man and a prodigal son, as both a gentleman dispossessed of his rightful inheritance and a profligate bohemian poet.[4]

Deprived of his position as "rate collector," John Joyce instead became, like Shem, a "collector general" of stray debts (*FW* 192.5). Cadging loans became his career, and in loanship he found his true calling (*JJ* 410). His letters to his son display both his delusions of status and his denial of responsibility for the lack of it. In 1907, for example, he writes:

> I did all in my power to forward your every wish, and any money I could get by *any means* I gave you ungrudgingly. So you can well

---

4. Asked what his father had been upon his death in 1931, Joyce gave a simpler answer than Stephen's: "He was a bankrupt" (*JJ* 22). Both McGee (1988, 191) and Valente (1988, 60) note Joyce's ambivalence about class, although neither explains its economic sources.

understand *my feelings* when I discovered my dreams so ruthlessly
dispelled, my hopes—proud hopes—shattered. . . . This is possibly
the last communication you will ever receive from me. . . . If you
and Stannie can afford 8s/- a week . . . I will pay the balance. . . .
Perhaps in years to come . . . you may learn to feel some of the pangs
I have endured, and then you will appreciate the feelings of a Father
who loved his children and had high hopes for them, and spared no
money when he could afford it . . . but who when adversity came
and he could no longer gratify all these wants, was despised disre-
spected, jeered at, scoffed at and set at defiance. (*L* II 221–23;
emphasis in original)

The father plays expertly on the filial heartstrings ("pursestrings too,"
as Bloom might put it—*U* 11.715), sandwiching the money request
between appeals to duty and guilt. His blend of florid prose and
lugubrious poses is the equal of Dickens's Micawber. The "adversity"
he so delicately mentions is another eviction brought on by his drinking, spending and refusal to find work. If Simon Dedalus mirrors
Joyce's father, then these appeals also display a disregard for the
truth: in *Ulysses* Simon begrudges the pittances he gives his famished
daughters. Two years later, John Joyce again writes: "I fear the end
is coming in more respects than one. . . . My last shilling went on
Sunday dinner and since then we are entirely *without* food, coal or
light, nor do I know any means under Heaven of getting a penny as
I have exhausted all my friends" (*L* II 228–9). He has exhausted all
his friends, who provided what little cash he has. He goes on, of
course, to ask for money—not for himself, but for his poor children.
There is no doubt that Joyce's siblings suffered, but his father's melo-
dramatic excuses surely wore thin before long. And while the fall of
Parnell was at least initially to blame for John Joyce's financial difficulties, and while Dublin provided few employment opportunities he
would have considered worthy of him, his own irresponsible behavior
caused most of his economic problems.

   The only child to have experienced relative prosperity, James
Joyce was nonetheless well aware of his father's failings. But unlike
his brother Stanislaus, in many respects James trod in his father's
unsteady footsteps. His letters too are a virtual catalogue of loans
and debts. James never resorted to his father's histrionics but instead
developed his own techniques. For example, his letters home from
his first "exile" in Paris in 1903 and 1904 display an odd blend of
pride and supplication, as he oscillates between stoic acceptance of his
plight and a feverish optimism about the future. He would repeatedly

send his financial accounts and descriptions of his meals, as if attempting to justify his pleas for money. Here is a typical example:
"Dear Mother / Your order for 3s 4d of Tuesday last was very welcome as I had been without food for 42 hours (forty-two). Today I
am twenty hours without food. But these spells of fasting are common
with me now and when I get money I am so damnably hungry that I
eat a fortune (1s/-) before you could say knife" (*L* II 29). He calls
these foodless periods "fasts," as though he were starving himself
deliberately as a test of religious asceticism, rather than because he
simply has no money. Most noticeable in these letters is the sense that
his privations are required by his vocation. It is as if the artist must
disavow all material claims, his fasting being but a necessary preliminary to his ultimate triumph. Yet he carefully writes out "forty-two,"
as if concerned that his mother might fail to perceive the enormity of
his suffering. Designed to obtain maximum sympathy, Joyce's sense
of martyrdom merges pride and self-pity. Stanislaus attributed
James's later extravagance to this "season of fasting and meditation
in the desert" (*MBK* 231), arguing that James responded to privation
by resolving never again to forgo luxury. But it seems more likely
that Joyce already possessed spendthrift habits acquired from years
of observing his father and his cronies. Stanislaus himself wrote in
1904 that "the possession of money changes Jim very much for the
worse. His mind seems to go on fire for dissipation," and attributed
this penchant to their father: "both Jim and Pappie seem to be proud
of having spendthrift blood in them. . . . Jim rarely . . . acts on principle, yet some fixed ideas influence his life. I think that one of these is
an objection to constraint" (1971, 48, 38–39). In other words, James
spent freely in order to be free.

But freedom was seldom the result. Instead, Joyce had to depend
upon those who, aware of the risks involved, were still foolish or kind-
hearted enough to lend him money. Sometimes he would scrupulously repay his creditors, keeping track in his notebook of the sums
owed, only to reborrow the same amount the next day. Thus despite
his vaunted "exile" from Ireland, he remained financially dependent
upon Dublin friends and family. Moreover, rather than freeing him
from money concerns, his improvidence and poverty kept money
constantly on his mind. His loanship took diverse forms. He would
sometimes couch his requests in peremptory tones: "I am counting
for £1 between you [George Roberts] and Ryan. That is not exorbitant, I think, as it is my last" (*L* I 56). He counts on their relief from
his further importunities to open their wallets. Or he would order

Stanislaus to borrow for him, protecting his own pride by forcing his brother to "touch" others for loans. Thus Stanislaus believed that James "does not recognize such a thing as gratitude. He says it reminds him of a fellow lending you an overcoat on a wet night and asking for a receipt. . . . As he lives on borrowing and favours . . . he has availed himself of plenty of opportunity of showing ingratitude" (1971, 54). Instances abound. He sometimes repaid kindness with a snub, as when he reimbursed Lady Gregory for her financial help by writing an unfavorable review of her book *Poets and Dreamers* (*JJ* 121; see *CW* 102–5 for the text of this review). Or he would pummel friends and enemies equally in such broadsides as "The Holy Office" (*CW* 152). His friend J. F. Byrne commented in mock-Latin: *"Non possum tibit dare libram, quia maxima in impecuniosa conditione sum. Miro cur habes satirizatum amicos vestros, num pecunia eorum defuit?* [I cannot give you a pound because I am in an extremely impecunious condition. I wonder why you have satirized your friends; was it because they had no money?"] (Ellmann's translation, *L* II 47).

James seemed the most ungrateful to Stanislaus himself, who for several years served as his brother's critic, literary agent, banker, and accountant. While Joyce and his family were in Rome, where he was working, most unsuitably, as a bank clerk (1906–1907), he wrote to Stanislaus each month asking for money, promising that each request would be the last (see *L* II 155, 161). Stanislaus, in Trieste, would be directed to borrow money from friends there and send it to James. Once again Joyce carefully listed his expenses and menus, as if justifying his chronically empty wallet. But he also boasted of his family's consumption. "There is literally no end to our appetites," he writes beneath the menu for a day in which he has eaten six meals (*L* II 172). Finally Stanislaus protested that he was depriving himself to maintain his brother, who responded, "you are really a mumchance —living on bread and ham" (*L* II 155), and instructed him to borrow more money and keep a little for himself. During this period James played Gracehoper to Stannie's Ondt, a mime of opposites in which "Stanislaus [was] bent as fanatically on making ends meet as James was on keeping them apart" (*JJ* 291). In later years, however, Stanislaus was less complaisant. Thus in 1922 James wrote to his brother about his patron's large grants, and Stanislaus wrote back demanding repayment of ten pounds he had lent James some years before, angrily pointing out that "this seems to me only part and parcel of the careless indifference with which you have always acted in affairs that concerned me" (*L* III 59). James sent the money without mentioning his brother's injured tone, but also called attention to his own sacrifices and informed him of another large gift from his patron (*L* III 61).

Stanislaus's indignation notwithstanding, Joyce's treatment of his brother was probably not careless at all. He relied upon him as his foil and "whetstone" (*U* 9.977). As long as Stanislaus was playing Ondt, James was free to play the Gracehoper. He needed his brother so that he could have someone from whom to sponge and against whom to define himself. When the two grew further apart, others, especially Sylvia Beach and Harriet Shaw Weaver, took his place. Moreover, his ingratitude seems to have been purposefully designed to defy bourgeois ethics. The sociologist Georg Simmel observes that gratitude is a powerful force that "effects the return of a benefit where there is no external necessity for it," and thus is "one of the most powerful means of social cohesion" (1950, 389). It creates bonds of reciprocity not "guaranteed by external coercion"; without it "society . . . would break apart" (Simmel 1950, 387). In rejecting gratitude Joyce thereby rejected the society that demanded it. Given his sense of the artist's need for freedom, gratitude is dangerous because, according to Simmel, it is "irredeemable. It maintains its claim even after an equal or greater gift has been made" (1950, 394). That is, once you are grateful, you must remain so, even after you have repaid the original benefaction. An artist attempting to throw off the nets trapping him in his society must avoid the irredeemable debts of gratitude even more completely than contractual debts; while the latter can eventually be paid, the debt of gratitude is eternal. Thus if gratitude is "the moral memory of mankind" (Simmel 1950, 388), Joyce proclaimed himself an amnesiac.

In 1905 Joyce wrote that he lived the way he did to conform to his "moral nature," and to defy "people . . . who think that the whole duty of man consists in paying one's debts" (*L* II 99–100). At least in his youth, Joyce rejected this morality as a bourgeois caricature and tried to subvert it by reversing the normal power structure in the debtor-creditor relationship. It was they, the citizens, who owed him, the artist, because he sacrificed material prosperity to produce artistic currency. As Roger Kempf describes it, Joyce thus magically created a "kind of contra-charity in which the creditor becomes the debtor and the debtor sovereign" (1976, 145; my translation). The artist's debts are not IOUs, but "you owe mes" (*FW* 183.15). He is not only justified in being in debt; he *must* remain so to defy the social order.

Perhaps hoping that that social order might itself be changed, for a time Joyce sought in socialism a solution to the problem of the artist's economic freedom. He read Kropotkin, followed Italian socialism (*L* II 173–74), and in 1905 proclaimed himself "a socialistic artist" (*L* II 89). His allegiance to socialism was at least partially founded upon a hope that such a state might furnish him a livelihood and thus free him from money worries. "What I wish to do is to secure a competence on which I can rely, and why I expect this is because I cannot believe that any State requires my energy for the work I am at present engaged in" (*L* II 89). Thus, as he himself admitted, his socialism was "thin . . . and unsteady" (*L* II 187), probably prompted more by personal economics than by strong political beliefs.[5]

Joyce's early writings stress that economic concerns can only taint the sacred realm of art. In his early essay "The Day of the Rabblement" he asserts that there shall be no truck with what he calls the "idols of the marketplace" (*CW* 71). And yet the importance of economics to his aesthetic practice is apparent even in his first story, "The Sisters," when the boy-narrator repeats to himself the word "simony" (*D* 9), which becomes a prominent motif in the volume. Referring to the sin of Simon Magus, who attempted to buy from the apostles the power of healing (Acts 8:14–24), simony comes to denote a pattern in which the sacred is reduced to a commodity, and hence a confusion of the spiritual and commercial. In *Stephen Hero* the ur-Stephen Daedalus announces to Lynch that he "does not want to sell my poetical mind to the public. I expect reward for my verses because I believe my verses are to be numbered among the spiritual assets of the State. That is not a simoniacal exchange. I do not sell . . . the divine afflatus" (*SH* 202–3). His defensive tone suggests that the artist must always be vigilant, because he is constantly in danger of committing literary simony. Joyce resisted "material considerations" (*SH* 203) throughout his long battle to get *Dubliners* published, refusing to alter words or give in to his publisher's demands. "The appeal to my pocket has not much weight with me," he wrote. "I have very little intention of prostituting whatever talent I may have to the public" (*L* II 137). It is almost as though he wanted *Dubliners* to fail as confirmation of his integrity: one may have to forfeit publication

    5. Robert Scholes (1992, 165–72) has recently argued that Joyce's socialism was stronger and better informed than critics have previously believed. But Joyce abandoned socialism fairly early, and it seems doubtful that his adherence was ever very deep or theoretically rigorous. For an informative discussion of Joyce's interest in socialism and anarchism, see Manganiello 1980, 67–114.

altogether to keep the artistic spirit uncorrupted. Indeed, the commercial fate of the first edition was similar to that of many of its characters—a "discreet financial failure" (*L* II 357). For the early Joyce, in sum, "material victory is the death of spiritual preeminence" (*JJ* 446).

Although Joyce earned more in Rome than he had in Trieste, he also spent more. This pattern recurred throughout his life: no matter how vast his earnings, he managed to spend a little more. Not surprisingly, Joyce was less than brilliant in the banking business. But he tried to succeed, filling an entire notebook with notes on banking and commerce, carefully writing each term on the left and its definition on the right.[6] Probably because of his long hours at the office ("wurruk is more dissipating than dissipation"—*L* II 203), he did little creative work in Rome. While his body prospered, his "imagination . . . starved" (*L* II 182). Denied outlets for linguistic expenditure, in Rome he seemed compelled to spend his material resources even more extravagantly, consuming and losing in an ever-increasing cycle.

For several years the family muddled along in Trieste and, in spite of his aborted attempts to set up a Dublin cinema and a Triestine business in Irish tweeds, somehow survived on Joyce's meager teaching earnings. Once they moved to Zurich in 1915, however, "money began to flow towards him" more freely than in the past (R. Ellmann, "Zurich-Trieste," *L* II 345). In addition to his grants from the Society of Authors and the British Royal Fund, Joyce received his first gifts from two female patrons, Harriet Shaw Weaver and Edith McCormick, who would figure prominently in his economic life. Miss Weaver gave him £200, and then in early 1917 John Quinn bought the manuscript of *Exiles*. By October, Joyce managed to be again in financial difficulties (*L* II 407). Mrs. McCormick gave him 12,000 francs and, beginning in February 1918, a monthly stipend of a thousand francs, which lasted until October 1919. By this time his monthly income was about 1500 francs—very good for the time—and her largesse enabled him to remain poor only through "determined extravagance" (*JJ* 481). Nonetheless, in Zurich, Joyce "subtly changed social position" (R. Ellmann, *L* II 345), becoming economically more middle-class than he had ever been before. In Zurich he also wrote much of *Ulysses*, including episodes that, as we shall see, display both an increased sympathy for the prudent financial habits of the middle

6. These notes have been reproduced in *JJA*, vol. 3, as "Notes on Business and Commerce."

class and at the same time an economy of verbal excess that mirrors his increased cash flow. In the Zurich years he also brought Leopold Bloom into being, as if rejecting the penniless, spendthrift, narcissistic Stephen part of himself in favor of a new, economically solvent identity. Yet even as he embraced his new middle-class status, he also recoiled from it, just as he both mocks and admires Bloom's financial prudence in *Ulysses*. Still, now that Joyce had money, it was difficult simply to proclaim indifference to it; thus his economic attitudes grew more complicated with increasing affluence.

The move to Paris in 1920 exhausted the Joyces' funds. In a letter to Ezra Pound in June 1920, Joyce once again announces that he is penniless until he can get another advance on his royalties (*L* II 468). For the next few years he continued to receive generous grants from Miss Weaver, including £2000 in 1920, and continued to spend them quickly. His financial troubles seemed to stimulate his sense of humor. Upon receiving £10 from his agent James Pinker, he proposed newspaper headlines à la "Aeolus" advertising his good fortune: "Joyce Gets Large Haul. Prompt Pinker Saves Desperate Dedalus. Glut of Greenbacks for Poet in Poverty" (*L* III 12). Sylvia Beach, another one of Joyce's female patrons, witnessed his profligacy throughout the twenties and concluded that he "enjoyed spending the way some people enjoy hoarding" (Beach 1980, 196–97). Often his expenditures were designed to display his prosperity and hospitality. Dining out frequently, he would urge his guests to order something expensive and would tip extravagantly (Beach 1980, 198). Ernest Hemingway also observed this behavior with bemusement: "the report is that he and all his family are starving, but you can find the whole celtic crew of them every night at Michaud's where Binney and I can afford to go about once a week" (*L* III 55n). Given these habits, it is no wonder that Joyce's "expenses always exceeded his income" (Beach 1980, 201), no matter how large that income became.

And it did become large. By 1922 he had received a total of £8500 since 1917 from Miss Weaver alone (*L* III 61); by July 1923 the sum had reached £21,000, or about $50,000 at the contemporary exchange rate (*L* III 78). During this time Joyce was also earning a steady income from sales of *Ulysses,* which was selling well despite its higher than average price and the censorship it faced in England and the United States. By 1930 he was making about $470 per month on royalties from *Ulysses,* as well as another $350 per month from his investments (*JJ* 633). These were huge sums for a writer, and seemingly more than enough to support anyone—anyone but Joyce, who still made himself "sporadically poor" by extravagant spending (*JJ* 633).

The recently published letters from Joyce to Sylvia Beach reinforce a sense of what Phillip Herring (1989, 91) has called Joyce's "unsavory" and "cavalier" attitude towards financially exploiting his friends. Virtually every page contains at least one request for an advance, a favor or a loan and displays great skill at manipulating his correspondent's sympathies. In April 1924, for example, he writes to complain of the publisher Jonathan Cape's failure to pay him £130: "I expect he went away for a few days at Easter. In the meantime while he is quaffing Easter eggs in the country I am gnawing my fingernails as my wallet is empty" (*LB* 37). In July he received a gift of 47,000 francs from Harriet Weaver and cleared his debts to Beach; but by August he had to wire for 2,000 francs (*LB* 40, 45). Perhaps finally noting the strains his constant importunities were placing on Beach, by January 1927 Joyce began to evince some guilt, writing, "Please ring me up and tell me in good Amurrican what you think of me, my money, my plans, my birthday, my muddles, my loans, my promises, my soup sociables etc" (*LB* 115). In fact, Beach composed just such a letter in April of that year which complains of her own financial problems and his indifference to her concerns:

> I am afraid I and my little shop will not be able to stand the struggle to keep you and your family going from now till June, and to finance the trip of Mrs Joyce and yourself to London "with money jingling in your pocket." . . . I have already many expenses for you that you do not dream of, and everything I have I give you freely. . . . The truth is that as my affection and admiration for you are unlimited, so is the work you pile on my shoulders. When you are absent, every word I receive from you is an order. The reward for my unceasing labour on your behalf is to see you tie yourself into a bowknot and hear you complain (I am poor and tired too). (*LB* 209)

She never sent this letter. But in 1932 their association ended, no doubt in part because of Joyce's constant money problems. When the American ban on *Ulysses* was lifted in 1934, Random House paid Joyce $45,000 for the rights to it. Beach writes optimistically that this money "put an end to his financial troubles" (1980, 205), but in fact it did not. In later years, he was forced to spend much of his prodigious income on his own and his daughter Lucia's medical bills.[7] But Joyce did not change his way of life to accommodate these extra expenses, and in 1939 we again read his complaints about a lack of money (*JJ* 729). The fact is that Joyce never managed to attain even Bloom's modest solvency; even in the best of times he struggled unsuccessfully with his need to spend whatever money he had.

Thus the economic habits that were designed to free Joyce from money worries actually produced the opposite effect: since he borrowed so often, money was constantly on his mind. One can scarcely be free of material concerns if he or she is constantly hounded by creditors. As Stephen Dedalus also discovers, a chronic debtor confronts a past full of IOUs and cannot live in the here and now. Joyce's awareness of this problem conflicts with the antinomian air that surrounds his economic behavior, according to which the artist is not bound by ledgers. For a time in 1904 he signed some of his begging letters as "Stephen Daedalus," the same pseudonym he had used for the stories already published in the *Irish Homestead,* and the same one he had given his autobiographical character in his unfinished novel. In using his artist name as his mendicant name, he forges a connection between writing and debtorship, seeking at once to announce his vocation and his disregard for economic convention; at the moment he begins to achieve his artistic destiny, he also attempts to launch a new identity, one free from the bourgeois desire to earn a quiet living but at the same time dependent upon future readers to supply that livelihood. These demands on his readers form a crucial part of the aesthetic of reciprocal expenditure analyzed in greater detail in later chapters. The use of the name Daedalus, itself borrowed from ancient texts, reveals Joyce's awareness that an artist must be both a literary debtor—because he owes his own and his characters' existences to previous texts—and a financial debtor, because he cannot bring his work to fruition without the monetary aid of his present and future readers. In later chapters we will examine in greater detail Joyce's deployment of this connection between literary and financial debts, both of which place the debtor at the point of intersection between the future and the past; far from freeing him from memory and history, they locate him ineluctably within it. He may shelter in artistic grace, but art exacts a different penance for its gift to genius: "every

7. Richard Ellmann (*JJ* 687), citing Paul Leon, estimates that as much as three-fourths of Joyce's income in the later thirties was spent on Lucia's various hospital expenses.

moment of inspiration must be paid for in advance" (*SH* 33). Accumulating debts, Joyce uses writing as a medium of exchange that enables him not only to collect more debts but also to recognize and pay them.

Herring (1989, 92) suggests that it is "rigidly ethnocentric" to describe Joyce as an "irresponsible spendthrift." He is right that Joyce's economic attitudes cannot be fully explained by the bourgeois Western norms of prudence and scrupulous repayment: we have seen how his youthful economic behavior was at least in part a deliberate strategy to subvert those very norms. In fact, he deemed these spendthrift habits necessary for his art. At his father's death Joyce wrote a tribute in which he admitted that he had acquired from his father "an extravagant licentious disposition (out of which . . . the greater part of any talent I may have springs)" (*L* I 312). He bestowed this disposition upon Stephen Dedalus, who in *Ulysses* embodies the debtorship and spendthrift habits of the young James Joyce. Joyce also treasured and made use of these habits in another way, by cultivating them and converting financial prodigality into a homologous verbal economy of excess. Later in this study I attempt to explain the connection between Joyce's "extravagant licentious disposition" and his artistic practices by recourse to theories of gift exchange and particularly to Georges Bataille's notion of *dépense,* by examining labor theories with which Joyce was familiar, and by considering the penchant for verbal and physical proliferation that Joyce identified as characteristically Irish. These models illustrate how Joyce's economic behavior is inextricably linked to his habits of composition and to much of what makes *Ulysses* such a rich and difficult text. In the late episodes particularly, Joyce redirects the extravagant economics of excess and expenditure (the economy he "inherited" from his father) into a linguistic economy that enables him to translate loss into productive labor. And yet the profligate Joyce is only one side of the coin. There is another side, one perhaps less obviously expressed in his money habits, but equally important to explaining his financial, psychic, and textual economies.

SCRUPULOUS MEANNESS

Despite his apparent squandermania, Joyce was not merely a careless Gracehoper. His excesses were usually reserved for the evening, when the sober, hard-working daytime self gave way to the hard-drinking, hard-spending nighttime Joyce, as if the Ondt and the Gracehoper each had shifts in their daily tug-of-war. More importantly, while he spent money freely, he guarded his emotions fiercely. In his early letters to Nora, for example, he resisted giving himself to her, even in words. Like Stephen Dedalus, he was chary of using the word "love": "if to desire to possess a person wholly, to admire and honour a person deeply, and to seek to secure that person's happiness is to 'love,' then perhaps my affection for you is a kind of love" (*L* II 55). Rarely does a person disavow what he has so painstakingly defined. Although Joyce eventually overcame his formality with Nora, his personal relations were almost invariably marked by a detached politeness. He called everyone Mr. or Miss even after he had known the person for years (Beach 1980, 41). Generosity was reserved for those who had proven their loyalty. But even with close friends like Frank Budgen, Joyce rarely used his own first name and called his friend "Budgen," never "Frank." For Joyce words and love, unlike money, were subject to an economy of scarcity. Every lover is under a double pressure, on the one hand to express and yield to affection, and on the other to withhold its expression: the more frequently one expresses love, the less value each expression has, and the cheaper that love seems to become. Joyce's reserve demonstrates his recognition of the power that words of love could exert, a power revealed when Stephen Dedalus begs his mother to give him a gift of the word "love," the "word known to all men" (*U* 3.435; 9.429, 15.4191–92). By withholding affection, one increases its value.

And yet in *Exiles* both Beatrice Justice and Robert Hand are criticized for a similar inability to give themselves; Richard Rowan tells Beatrice, "You cannot give yourself freely and wholly" (22). Later, Bertha Rowan reads a note from Hand: *"There is one word which I have never dared to say to you.* What is the word?" He answers, "That I have a deep liking for you" (34). In a play much concerned with the economies of love and in which Joyce confronts his own possessiveness, this inability to give oneself to another in language or deed is depicted as a form of emotional paralysis. But while Joyce satirizes this tendency, he himself possessed it, claiming that "isolation is the first principle of artistic economy" (*CW* 61). This emotional reserve seems incompatible with his financial prodigality and discloses another side to his character.

Roger Kempf has argued that Joyce constantly spent all his money in order "to create occasions for redemanding" (1976, 149; my translation). In other words, he borrowed and squandered money so that he could get further attention from friends by borrowing again. He needed constant reassurances of loyalty and love; money was tangible proof of that loyalty. His spendthrift habits may also have generated the sociability that he resisted in other ways. Picking up the tab substituted for the intimacy that would have threatened his freedom; in controlling occasions for generosity, Joyce controlled his personal relationships. It seems again that Joyce's spending was not simply careless improvidence; indeed, his strict control of himself in so many other areas suggests that he squandered by design.

In his youth, as we have seen, Joyce proclaimed his indifference to money and bourgeois morality, freely squandered his cash, and rarely repaid debts. This apparent antipathy to money carries over into *Dubliners,* where it usually appears as a sign of betrayal or simony. In "Araby," for example, the narrator achieves a bitter epiphany of his self-delusion when he witnesses the "fall of the coins" into the salver at the Araby bazaar (*D* 35). Money and the marketplace contaminate the imagination, just as simony contaminates spiritual values. Money—or, more accurately, the lack of it—plays a significant role in several other stories: in "Two Gallants" the final coin revealed in Corley's hand symbolizes the betrayal of the servant girl and Ireland herself; Jimmy Doyle's sense of inferiority is finally exposed in his financial disaster at the end of "After the Race"; Farrington, of "Counterparts," spends the shillings he has obtained by pawning his watch, and his frustration mounts when he discovers that he has spent all his cash and is not even drunk; in "A Mother"[8] Mrs. Kearney reveals the limitations of her class pretensions by haggling over her daughter's fee.

Joyce wrote these stories when he had very little money, and their verbal economy reflects an awareness of scarcity. Thus, while his financial economy was excessive, the verbal economy of these early stories betrays an opposite tendency: the volume, he wrote, was composed in a style of "scrupulous meanness" (*L* II 134). This much-cited passage may be variously interpreted. In one sense it refers to the scrupulousness with which he has documented the actual conditions of Dublin. "Meanness" also describes the ironic, even cruel, tone of such stories as "Counterparts" and "The Boarding House." But I want to suggest that "meanness" also signifies the way that Joyce's condensed style mirrors the financial and emotional poverty of Dublin's denizens. According to this reading, Joyce conceives his art in

---

8. Two useful discussions of money in *Dubliners* are Benstock (1988) and Somerville (1975). For a detailed treatment of the political economy of "Grace," see Osteen (1991).

economic terms, with language as his currency. In many stories words
are doled out stingily, as if each one must be earned by hard labor,
both by Joyce and by the reader, who must endure Joyce's withholding of meaning until the final epiphany that sometimes clarifies the
story but sometimes only complicates it. Indeed, like money, which is
generally defined by being absent or withheld (for example, the coin
withheld until the final sentence of "Two Gallants," the narrator's
inability to buy a gift in "Araby," the refusal to pay Kathleen Kearney
her wages in "A Mother," or the absence of the canvassers' pay in
"Ivy Day"), words in *Dubliners* are subject to a rigorous conservation
of meaning, as the reader is forced to endure a deprivation of gratifi-
cation that parallels the characters' material and emotional depriva-
tions (cf. Kershner 1989, 88). This verbal parsimony reveals a
different side of Joyce's economic character from the extravagance
that seems so evident.

"A Painful Case" perhaps best exemplifies Joyce's understanding
and use of scrupulous meanness. James Duffy, a middle-aged bache-
lor who abhors disorder of any kind (*D* 108), epitomizes the "anal
retentive" personality. He is a member of that relatively prosperous
middle class so little depicted in Joyce's works and, as that class did in
real life, lives outside the city in Chapelizod. "Free from pictures," his
walls and his spartan furnishings embody his desiccated concept of
freedom, which to him merely means freedom from involvement
(*D* 107). His vocation connects his emotional and economic life: he
works as a bank cashier (*D* 108), disbursing money as scrupulously as
he controls his rigid personal life (and probably his own money). But
as his affair with Mrs. Sinico develops, his emotional life becomes
more expansive: "He lent her books, provided her with ideas, shared
his intellectual life with her" (*D* 110). Lending, providing, sharing:
Joyce's narrator inscribes Duffy's emotional emergence in tropes of
economic generosity. But, of course, Duffy cannot overcome his habitual meanness. "We cannot give ourselves," his soul says, "we are
our own" (*D* 111). After he reads of Mrs. Sinico's death, Duffy has an
epiphany of his utter loneliness and asks himself why he had "withheld life from her" (*D* 117). But he soon regains his equanimity. It
would thus appear that Joyce is severely taxing Duffy for his stinginess, indicating that such "meanness" eventually only redounds on
the miser himself.

And yet the style of the story mirrors Duffy's own mind, as if
the author has borrowed Duffy's habit of composing sentences about
himself in the third person (*D* 108). The opening description of

Duffy's room is virtually uninflected, its neutrality capturing the detachment Duffy strives to achieve. In the opening pages Joyce seldom varies the syntax from the flat, subject-verb-object word order that renders Duffy's "adventureless tale" of a life in suitably expressionless prose. As the affair becomes more serious, the style becomes more lyrical, its syntactical structures more varied, an evolution that culminates in the passage in which Mrs. Sinico passionately presses Duffy's hand to her cheek (*D* 111) and thereby prompts Duffy's withdrawal. After they break off, the prose, like Duffy, regains its detachment. Thus the newspaper report of her death, with its careful "objective" neutrality and unwillingness to place blame, perfectly reflects his emotional condition. Nor does the journalistic idiom violate the previous tone or style; it is of a piece emotionally with the rest of the story's discourse. After Duffy's bout with his conscience, in which the narrator seems to work himself into a contempt that mirrors Duffy's own bitter self-loathing, the final paragraph returns to the disengaged style of the opening. Indeed, the final paragraph seems pathologically neutral, as if straining with Duffy to suppress self-contempt with a litany of Hemingwayesque "he's": "He turned. . . . He began. . . . He halted. . . . He could not feel. . . . He waited. . . . He could hear nothing. . . . He listened. . . . He felt" (*D* 117). While implicitly condemning Duffy's stinginess and the way he has "sentenced" Mrs. Sinico to death (*D* 117), the story sentences itself in a similarly Duffy-esque style. Joyce's own scrupulous meanness, apparent both in the stringent economy of the story and in its studied neutrality, thus reveals his understanding of and resemblance to Duffy.

Joyce's first book thus counteracts his monetary spending with verbal frugality and at the same time dramatizes the conflict in Joyce between the two tendencies, as he attempts to master his extravagance by shaping and channeling it into a rigorously managed artistic economy, one evidenced also in the careful structural economies of *Portrait* (its many lacunae and excisions). These compositional habits contrast with Joyce's economic habits during the years he was writing it. If his finances were in disarray from determined excess, his art was tightly controlled. This management of his verbal economy, then, paints a different picture of the artist than Joyce's self-portrait as a prodigal son and reckless squanderer.

Another manifestation of this "meanness" is the surprising vindictiveness Joyce could exhibit in money matters. Sometimes his personal reserve gave way when he believed he was being betrayed or swindled, a tendency that destroyed his friendship with Ottocaro

Weiss. Unjustly believing that Weiss had influenced Mrs. McCormick to cut off his stipend, he curtly demanded that Weiss repay a small debt and subsequently snubbed him (*JJ* 467–68). A similar form of "meanness," a kind of double-entry moral bookkeeping, often marks Joyce's artistic practice. Indeed, *Dubliners* is in one sense an act of revenge upon the people most likely to read his book—other Dubliners. In it Joyce returns to the source of his own economic habits, paying off his psychic debt with what Stephen calls his "cold steel pen" (*U* 1.153). The much-discussed term "metempsychosis" (*U* 4.341), a process by which a soul must be reborn endlessly to repay its sins, connotes a similar economy of justice. In his works Joyce subjected people he had known to metempsychosis, recreating them to transfer to the credit side the debits they had exacted from him, hoping to turn his losses into artistic gains. He revealed this intention in a letter to Stanislaus: "if I don't sharpen that little pen and dip it into fermented ink and write tiny little sentences about the people who betrayed me send me to hell" (*L* II 110). At once verbal and penal, his "little sentences" mimic Duffy's "sentencing" of Mrs. Sinico.

Scholes (1992, 169) suggests that Joyce may have borrowed the idea of "scrupulous meanness" from Guglielmo Ferrero, who describes love in French novels as being rendered with "scrupolosa esatezza di analista." Scholes shows that *esatezza* is a cognate of *"esatore,"* which means "tax collector, one who exacts payment" (1992, 169). If so Joyce verbally usurps his father's erstwhile occupation as rate collector; but in the son's economy those taxes are repayments for betrayal intended to stir the "moral conscience" of his country and shake the city out of its paralysis. In his satirical broadsides, "The Holy Office" (1904) and "Gas From a Burner" (1912), for example, he used poetry as a cudgel to give his perceived betrayers tit for tat, to "adequate the balance sheet" of his moral ledger ("Holy Office," in *CW* 152). In these pages Dubliners receive his "taxation of contempt" (*CW* 152).

Ulysses is also a partial record of Joyce's losses, a tissue of these "little sentences," in which the slights and grudges of life are reciprocated in art. Many of these offenders were unfortunate enough to have been involved in financial quarrels with Joyce, although some were actually benefactors. For example, Oliver Gogarty, whom Joyce resented and to whom he owed money, becomes Malachi Mulligan, to whom Stephen also owes money, and who is depicted as a quintessential materialist, an insensitive snob who borrows Stephen's creativity and claims it as his own. When Stephen sends him a condemnatory telegram indicting him as a "sentimentalist" who enjoys reality without "incurring the immense debtorship for a thing done" (*U* 9.550–51), Joyce is simultaneously repaying Gogarty for similar behavior. George Russell (AE), who lent Joyce a pound in 1904 but valued his art too slightly, receives his payment in the form of an unflattering portrayal as the stuffy pseudosage in "Scylla and Charybdis," despite (or because of) his dismissing "the poet's debts" as an unworthy subject for literary investigation (*U* 9.188). Perhaps the worst Dublin offender was Joyce's former friend Vincent Cosgrave, who once refused to help him during a skirmish in which he received a black eye. Worse, Cosgrave boasted about his attempts to win Nora away from Joyce when they visited Dublin in 1909 (*JJ* 160–61; 278–82). Joyce punishes him by turning him into Lynch, whose very name indicates his role as stereotypical false friend and who deserts Stephen in Nighttown and allows the British soldier, Carr, to knock him out (*U* 15.4730). Since AE and these other "convicts" might be supposed to have been readers of *Ulysses*, Joyce is exacting vengeance on his own readers, repaying with negative reciprocity those who have offended him, but who have also provided his livelihood by lending him money or buying his books.

Private Carr is based upon one Henry Carr, with whom Joyce battled in Zurich. He was an amateur actor in the English Players, a troupe that Joyce helped to finance. At first a petty squabble over a few francs, their quarrel eventually escalated into suits and countersuits far exceeding the damages done.[9] Carr got what Joyce believed to be his just deserts in *Ulysses*, where he is also demoted from an embassy official to a private. In the real-life Carr affair, Joyce appealed to Percy Bennett, the British consul, who unfortunately supported Carr. In return, Bennett's name is given to the English boxer knocked out by the Irish fighter Keogh in one of the parodic

---

9. The Carr suits were ruled in Joyce's favor. The judge ruled that Carr had to pay Joyce 25 francs (about £1) plus 5 percent interest in the first suit; he disallowed Carr's counterclaim, so Carr also had to pay Joyce £2 in court costs (*L* II, 422–23). However, Joyce lost the second suit, and the judge ruled that he owed 59 francs in court costs plus 120 francs in damages (*JJ* 452; according to Budgen, this amounts to £4 16s). But Joyce either never paid it, or paid only 40 francs (£1 12s). Although Joyce should have come out in the red (by paying £4 16s, he would have ended up losing the £3 1s he won, plus another £1 15s), he emerged with a balance in his favor of £1 9s, but only because he failed to pay the full tally of his "immense debtorship for the thing done." See *JJ* 426–28 and Budgen (1960, 198–200) for more detailed accounts of this affair.

insertions in "Cyclops" (*U* 12.960–87). Joyce makes his enemy take the beating he could not physically inflict. Rumbold, another official to whom Joyce appealed in the Carr case, is transmuted into the near-illiterate hangman whose letter of solicitation (*"five ginnees"* per hanging) appears in "Cyclops" (*U* 12.419–31). Rumbold is strung up by his own noose. For every debit, a credit.

The Carr case has a precedent in Shakespeare's life, as recounted by Stephen in "Scylla and Charybdis." Shakespeare "sued a fellowplayer for a few bags of malt and exacted his pound of flesh in interest for every money lent" (*U* 9.745–46). Throughout his discussion Stephen depicts the artist as usurer of old texts and jealous hoarder of old slights who repays both accounts in his art (see chapter 5 below). Thus Joyce who, like Shakespeare, seems to draw "Shylock out of his own long pocket" (*U* 9.741–42), exacts *his* pound of flesh, and Carr plays his part eternally, trapped in Joyce's artistic purgatory. All events bring grist to Joyce's mill. Like Stephen's Shakespeare, he carries "a memory in his wallet" (*U* 9.246), and rarely fails to collect on these bills. "Scrupulous meanness" thus describes Joyce's moral economy as well as his verbal one. Through such double-entry justice, Joyce attempted to turn life's losses into art's gains, using art to pay the debts of life.

In his Shakespeare disquisition Stephen delineates the problem with this scrupulous moral accounting. He likens this need to repay psychic debts to jealousy and incest, which he calls an "avarice of the emotions" (*U* 9.781). Since, as Stephen later says, the artist is "all in all" and inhabits all his characters (*U* 9.1020–21), he becomes his own villain, inhabiting his enemies so that he can repay them, but in the process reenacting their crimes. Thus "his unremitting intellect is the hornmad Iago willing that the moor in him shall suffer" (*U* 9.1023–24), and the artist penalizes himself when he carries out negative reciprocity (*U* 9.788–89). Retribution becomes self-punishment, as the artist's attempts to balance his ledger merely create another loss, and the blow recoils back upon himself. When Shakespeare depicts his own cuckolding again and again, he reinflicts the wound each time. He thus remains "untaught by the wisdom he has written," an "old dog licking an old sore" (*U* 9.475–77). Here, at least, loss becomes a gain for art, but not for the artist. In rewriting his injuries, the artist is "always meeting" himself (*U* 9.1046) as victim and moral miser. Ironically, then, this desire to make artistic profit at the expense of others who have allegedly caused his misfortune actually fetters Joyce to the bourgeois value system that his financial expenditures aim to subvert. In this moral accounting the economics of life are balanced, but not overcome, by the economy of art. Thus, despite condemning this avarice of the emotions, Joyce sometimes permitted the emotional miser to overwhelm the financial spendthrift.

How to explain this oscillation between meanness and extravagance? Simmel's writings on the personalities of financial extremists indicate that Joyce's opposite tendencies may stem from the same root. Simmel discovers two stages that precede the possession of an object: one first possesses money and then spends it on the desired object (1971, 183). The miser finds satisfaction in "the complete possession of a potentiality with no thought whatsoever about its realization" (Simmel 1971, 180); that is, he makes the possession of money an end in itself. The miser withdraws money from circulation, attempting not only to stabilize his existence but also to live in an ideal future of unlimited resources. He lives for imaginary fulfillment. If the miser fetishizes the first stage, the spendthrift makes the second stage an end in itself: he wishes to spend money but cares little about the goods it buys and thus makes apparently senseless purchases. Neither the miser nor the spendthrift can make ends meet; to be either selfish or frivolously generous is to inhabit only one side of the debit-credit ledger. Ironically, as John Vernon points out (1984, 39), it is not the spendthrift but the miser who is always short of money. But neither is ever truly fulfilled; both in fact live according to the same "demonic formula" in which "every pleasure obtained arouses the desire for further pleasure, which can never be satisfied" (Simmel 1971, 185). Simmel demonstrates that the spendthrift's apparent carelessness is not careless at all.

We may refine Simmel's analysis by means of Jean-Joseph Goux's insights into the three functions of money, functions homologous with those of other symbolic economies. Money serves first as a measure of values, as a kind of ideal gold; Goux calls this its Imaginary function. Gold as money also functions as a circulating medium; in this mode it can be replaced by materially worthless symbols of itself. This is the Symbolic function of money. Finally, as gold or silver coins money may also be a means of payment or a real store, a genuine material hoard of cold, hard cash. This is its Real function (Goux 1990, 47–48). The miser and the spendthrift each fetishize one or two of these functions. The miser craves money for its Imaginary qualities (as potential future purchases) and for its Real function as material store; in contrast, the spendthrift values only the Symbolic function of money as a circulating medium, and especially desires that moment of "transposition" in which money is translated into other forms of value (Simmel 1978, 248). Thus, it is clear that both the miser and the spendthrift value money. As Simmel observes, "the indifference about the value of money which constitutes the essence and the charm of prodigality is possible only because money is actually treasured and assumed to be special"; therefore, "the conscious and strongly negative stance toward money has the opposite sentiment as its basis" (1971, 183). The spendthrift spends because he recognizes the power of money; contrary to appearances, he loves money as much as the miser.

Given their close relationship, it makes sense that these seemingly opposite traits are often found in the same person. "Constricting or expansive moods are expressed in miserliness or prodigality, as though the impulse were the same and merely the valence differed" (Simmel 1971, 186): a person might shift from craving the Symbolic function to the Real function of money in different circumstances. It appears that Joyce's profligacy arises from the same source as his reserve and that his seemingly opposed economies are really part of a single continuum upon which he moves from one extreme to the other but rarely occupies the middle ground or synthesizes the extremes. His reserve manifested itself in extravagance, his extravagance in his reserve. Far from demonstrating indifference to money, Joyce's prodigality displays his attraction to it. Unlike his father, whose improvidence resulted from his alcoholism and personal weakness, Joyce's spending was merely the obverse face of his obsession with authority and control: he carefully cultivated it as a path to power. Joyce's miserliness is manifested more in his writing—literary currency—and personal relationships than in his economic habits; nonetheless this scrupulous meanness emerges strongly as the necessary countersign to his spendthrift habits. Both impulses suggest that Joyce cared a great deal about money and was fully aware of its symbolic, real, and imaginary power.

Joyce's changing ideas about the economic value of his art demonstrate how his financial impulses shifted in valence. From the *Ulysses* years on, he struggled to reevaluate his labor both by gauging the amount of sacrifice he had experienced and by assessing the economic value of his works. He would thus carefully calculate the expense of time and "expense of spirit" (*JJ* 598) he had sacrificed in writing his books. Both were prodigious. He figured that *Ulysses* cost him some 20,000 hours of work (*JJ* 510), the equivalent of almost two and one-third years at twenty-four hours a day. Indeed, that Joyce even completed *Ulysses,* given his constant changes of address and multiple debts, testifies to a great fund of will and energy. Had his finances been calculated as punctiliously as his hours of work, perhaps he would have had fewer money problems. As I will argue in more detail in later chapters, Joyce's arduous and extravagant labor becomes one means of recuperating his financial and psychic losses, of transforming his national and familial history of debt and expenditure into an aesthetic principle that makes loss a form of gain.

His assessments of the economic value of his works varied widely. He once wrote that *Ulysses* should be sold for "3/- which is about its value, I think" (*L* I 130). In keeping with this atypical humility, he published the modestly titled *Pomes Penyeach* between the gargantuan efforts of *Ulysses* and *Finnegans Wake*. He meant his title literally: thirteen poems, selling for one shilling (a baker's dozen, and thus actually less than a penny each). In this mood he said that he wanted his books sold "at low prices that those he considered his real readers could pay" (Beach 1980, 175) and answered his Marxist critics by protesting of his sympathy for the poor, maintaining that all his characters belonged to "the lower middle classes, and even the working class, and they are all quite poor" (quoted in Manganiello 1980, 225). Likewise, he would often protest that he was merely a "simple middle-class man" (*JJ* 595), an unassuming craftsman, a mere "crabapple-seller" (*LB* 120). Indeed, *Ulysses* was in a sense piecework done for hire: John Quinn bought the manuscript as it was produced, providing Joyce with both immediate recompense for his labor and a sense of its monetary value (*JJ* 489). The total paid for it, however, was the unkingly sum of 20,000 lire (*L* III 22). At times, then, Joyce not only did not scorn the petit bourgeoisie, but announced his solidarity with its concerns and forms of labor.

His justifications to his relatives, however, show a less humble sense of the economic worth of his work. To his aunt Josephine Murray the former scorner of the marketplace defends himself in financial terms: "In a few years copies of the first edition [of *Ulysses*] will probably be worth £100 each. . . . The entire [second] edition of 2000 copies at £2-2-0 a copy was sold out in four days" (*L* I 190–91). To that old debtor, his father, he also speaks the language of money: "It may interest you to know that a copy of the first edition (the one you have) was sold in New York City for £135" (*JJ* 540). Following that sentence are estimates of his latest gift from Harriet Shaw Weaver and protestations of his indifference to finances: "I am so careless in these matters . . . that I don't know the exact sum." He wants his father to admire his success, but is embarrassed to talk about it crassly. Likewise, he expressed dismay over John Quinn's sale of the *Ulysses* manuscript to A. S. W. Rosenbach for $1975, and his anger increased when he discovered that two poems by Meredith had been acquired at the same auction for $1400. He considered this sale "a grossly stupid act which is an alienation of valuable property (*L* I 211). From such events Joyce learned to view his works as commodities.

He also learned to become his own salesman. Thus, for example, he sometimes compared *Ulysses* to other novels strictly by size, as if he were dealing in grosses of fabric: "It is an extremely cheap . . . edition of the equivalent of 8 English novels of standard size (75,000 to 80,000 words) at the normal price today or less, as 8 10/- novels would sell at 270 francs a copy," whereas *Ulysses*, despite its bulk, cost only 350 francs (*L* I 196). Appropriately for a novel about an ad canvasser, Joyce became a literary adman, pitching his novel to potential subscribers as if peddling a suit of clothes. In response to George Bernard Shaw's crotchety refusal to subscribe and contention that no Irishman would pay 150 francs for uninscribed copies of the first edition (*L* III 50), Joyce jocularly countered that *Ulysses* was a steal: "there is now a special cheap edition 565,423 words = 8 × 70,877 [actually 70,677] = 8 novel lengths, slightly shopsoiled, a genuine bargain going for 60 francs = 60/86 = 30/43 = about 3/4 × 20/- = 15/- ÷ 8 about 1[s] 11 1/4d per normal novel suitlength real continental style—you can't beat it for the money" (*L* I 221). While feigning nonchalance, he carefully calculates the number of words and their financial equivalents. The author here becomes his own advertising agent, although, like Bloom's, his arithmetic is imprecise. He demonstrated this penchant for self-promotion at other times, too, as when he proposed placing slips with the story of his publishing problems with *Dubliners* inside copies of it, maintaining that these would be "a great advertisement for it" (*L* II 323). Sometimes this newfound commercial awareness led him to embarrassingly extreme measures, as when he urged Mrs. McCormick to renew her stipend by offering her a portion of the *Ulysses* manuscript (*JJ* 468).

Joyce's difficulties in articulating the value of his work thus begin at the point where, according to Kurt Heinzelman (1980, 166–67), most such conflicts occur: "precisely at the moment when labor has to . . . represent itself in its money form, as an exchange value." Joyce's widely oscillating views of his art present no problem until he must objectify aesthetic value into economic value; then he must face the material consequences of his aesthetic. But these instances at least

show Joyce's growing reconciliation with the realities of the marketplace: that books are, and must be sold as, commodities, and that the
artist must dirty his hands with commerce, because if he does not,
someone else will, and the artist will be the loser. *Ulysses* shows both
this recognition and his continuing ambivalence about it, primarily
through the contrast between Stephen Dedalus and Leopold Bloom.
It is Bloom, commercial man and ad canvasser, who receives most of
Joyce's attention and who emerges as the novel's hero; Joyce's newfound accommodation with the marketplace is reflected not only in
this choice, but also in his careful charting of the ways that Stephen's
economic beliefs reflect his artistic paralysis.

SELFISH GENEROSITY

We have seen how Joyce repaid psychic debts in his work. He also
used the texts themselves as materializations of his labor and thus as
means of payment; they become his money and as such have both
Symbolic and Real value. For example, in return for what he called
Sylvia Beach's "present of the ten best years of her life" (quoted in
Scott 1984, 99), he gave her the manuscripts of *Dubliners, Stephen
Hero, Chamber Music,* and the original sketch of "A Portrait" (Beach
1980, 89–90; *LB* 117–18). To Harriet Shaw Weaver he presented
copy number one of *Ulysses* (*JJ* 525), the manuscript of *Portrait*
(*SL* 241), and an autograph manuscript of *Finnegans Wake* (*L* III 409).
Upon completing the latter book he wrote to her: "with reference to
a commission given to me some time ago by your good self I have
pleasure in informing you that the order in question has now been
duly executed as per instructions. . . . I have therefore this day deliv-
ered the goods and trust that the same will be found satisfactory"
(*JJ* 722). His books are his currency, remittances to his most patient
and sympathetic patrons and readers. But these textual "payments"
may be better described as return gifts. Herring (1989, 92) suggests
that the economy of gift exchange helps to explain Joyce's apparently
irresponsible financial habits and attributes them to a "preference for
communalism," arguing that he "demanded much of his patrons and
friends, but his generosity was also great." As we have seen, however,
Joyce was not always so generous; nor was his sense of communalism
without reservations and complications. Thus I would alter and am-
plify Herring's suggestion and propose that the economy of gift
exchange provides a model that subsumes Joyce's apparently contradictory roles as spendthrift and miser.

   In his landmark study, *The Gift: Imagination and the Erotic Life of Property*, Lewis Hyde argues that gifts and gift exchanges are a "female property": that is, gift giving and receiving are female properties (gender-specifically feminine behavior) in many cultures and the process is itself feminine because gift exchange grows from a sense of fluidity and enables the establishment of communal and kinship ties (1983, 103). This association of women and gift exchange is manifest in Joyce's economic affairs. While, as we have seen, his commerce with other men was often marked by debt accumulation and sometimes bitter accountings of slights, with women he engaged in gift exchange. In giving his texts to them, Joyce gave himself, both because, as Stephen argues in "Scylla and Charybdis," the writer weaves his image into his texts (*U* 9.377–78), and because, according to Hyde, all gifts carry the donor's identity. Unlike mercantile exchanges, which stabilize and reify interpersonal boundaries, gift exchanges involve the identities of both giver and receiver in the act of giving and in the gift iself (Hyde 1983, xiv). In selecting and giving a present, the donor projects both his or her sense of the recipient and his or her self-image onto that present; in accepting it, the recipient sanctions those projected identities. Thus in giving to another the texts in which his identity is imbricated, Joyce also renews that identity; he may fully become himself as artist precisely because he gives himself away in his works. His sacrifices to his work repay both himself and those females who gave him material and spiritual support.

   This identification of self and gift is most clearly articulated in Joyce's gifts and letters to Nora, to whom he gave his most personal textual presents. For example, in 1909 he gave her a necklace with a small engraved tablet, on which was written a two-sided epigraph from *Chamber Music* ix: "Love is unhappy / When love is away" (*L* II 246–47). Later the same year he fashioned for her a Christmas present, a hand-copied parchment manuscript of *Chamber Music* scripted in indelible ink, and wrote that it was "the best thing . . . that I am able to offer you in return for your sincere and true and faithful love" (*L* II 277). He presents the best part of himself in his love letters, offering an embrace in words through postal return. These literary gifts, invested with the body of the donor, are attached to the body of the recipient. Such gifts unite donor and recipient and move back toward the giver, who thus gives and keeps at once. Ideally, in this formulation, gift exchange can become what Hyde calls "erotic commerce" (1983, xiv), the implications of which I examine in greater detail in chapters 8 and 9. Through the erotic commerce of gifts with

Nora Joyce aimed to repay the woman he claimed was one of the sources of his art: "Everything that is noble and exalted and deep and true and moving in what I write comes, I believe, from you" (*L* II 248). Of course he also asked for less "exalted" gifts in those famously scatological love letters of the same year. Their erotic-excremental content is congruent with their condition as gifts, as Freud's analyses of the relationships between money and feces suggest (Freud [1908] 1959, 49). Freud also argues that even before the child's feces become associated with "filthy lucre," they are "the infant's first gift, a part of his body which he will give up only on persuasion by a loved person, to whom, indeed, he will make a spontaneous gift of it as a token of affection" ([1916] 1959, 168). Both Joyce and (as we shall see) Leopold Bloom request this "gift" from their wives and use the gift of writing to do so. More importantly, Joyce's conception of his writing as part of a gift economy helps to explain the intersection of meanness and generosity that characterizes his economic and aesthetic practices. The child who is encouraged to give his feces to his parents nonetheless perceives this production as loss. Joyce's early economy of meanness implies a similar perception: if writing is a fecal loss, then it should be given sparingly. His later textual economy of extravagant expenditure testifies to a shift in this valence; if production is first conceived as loss, perhaps loss may also be conceived as production. For Joyce writing is an excremental gift, and thus announces itself as simultaneously waste and transcendent value; texts may therefore be hoarded, or given away, or used as currency.[10]

Hyde further contends that whereas mercantile exchanges—barter, buying and selling, debts—seek to establish balanced reciprocity and therefore stasis, gifts "must always move": they must be used up, passed on (1983, 4). A gift is only fully a gift, and therefore fully the property of the donor, when it is given to someone else, and hence becomes the property of the recipient. It is my gift when I give it, but yours because you receive it. A gift therefore belongs to both parties —and neither party—at once: to give away is also to own. Gifts are thus "anarchist property" (Hyde 1983, 84), or "property that perishes" (1983, 8). A strikingly similar dynamic is charted in *Exiles*, when Richard Rowan explains the idea of giving to his son: "Do you know what it is to give a thing? . . . While you have a thing it can be taken from you. . . . But when you give it, you have given it. No robber can

---

10. For Freudian readings of Joyce's excremental vision, see Shechner (1974, 133–39), Tucker (1984, 109–118), and Brivic (1980, 145–46, 155–59).

take it from you. . . . It is yours forever when you have given it. It will be yours always. That is to give" (56). The "thing" alluded to here is both love in general and Rowan's wife Bertha in particular, whose fidelity he tests by offering her to Robert Hand. This paradox is related to yet another sense in which gifts are "female property": the fact that women themselves have historically functioned as gifts, as exchangeable goods, to be owned and exploited by men in prostitution, marriage, and other institutions.[11] For Rowan to relinquish Bertha is actually to own her more completely.

Likewise, Joyce's gifts demanded the return gift of fidelity or loyalty. To give is to retain the recipient's obligation. Like Rowan, Joyce struggled with his own "avarice of the emotions," a possessive jealousy for which his letters to Nora were meant to compensate. Thus, while he first tells Nora that "I would like to give you everything that is mine," he also insists that she must give herself "all, all, when we meet. All that is holy . . . you must give to me freely" (*L* II 256, 259). Joyce's gift giving, then, dramatizes both his generous impulse to expend valuable currency and his scrupulous care to get back a value equal to what he has given; it involves both the miser and the spendthrift in his psychic economy. His textual gifts thus derive from a conflicted condition that he acknowledged when he confessed to Nora that he was "a poor impulsive sinful *generous selfish* jealous dissatisfied kind-natured poet" (*L* II 278; my emphasis). This selfish generosity may be behind his insistence upon having *Ulysses* and *Finnegans Wake* published on his birthday, as though his texts were birthday gifts to his own genius. In giving up his texts, he may more fully own them. In his gift exchanges we see the desire for control manifest in generosity, and generosity expressed in jealous reserve. As gifts, Joyce's texts participate in an economy that synthesizes his two impulses.

A similar economy pertains to the act of reading his works. Reading *Ulysses* involves the reader in a demanding reciprocal relationship: the more the reader gives, the more the text demands that we give, know, and remember. Joyce requires that the reader's labor mirror his own extravagant expenditure of words, his own arduous labor.

11. Hyde briefly notes this less positive role of females in gift exchange, but glosses it over in the remainder of his discussion. This tendency is prevalent throughout his book, which generally elides the ways that gift exchange may express uncharitable or antagonistic impulses that are quite apparent in the ethnological evidence. Chapter 7, below, analyzes such hostile gift exchanges.

Reading Joyce's texts may thus produce a more creative and more industrious reader, and yet one who spends the currency of attention prodigally. This contract between author and reader imitates the economic relations Joyce cultivated in his life. If the artist must be both a financial and an intellectual debtor, so must his readers—he demands that we pay what he has paid. Joyce rejects the economy of scarcity for one of evolution and extravagance that pays dividends for those willing to expend themselves. This economy of literary gifts may generate what Hyde (1983, 153) claims that gift exchanges create: "a copula: a bond, a band, a link by which the several are knit into one." If Joyce rejected the bourgeois community for much of his life, he founded an alternative through his texts—the community of readers whom he shaped. He is therefore indebted to his readers, as well: they form the community in which he can make both ends meet, can combine the miser and the spendthrift, can turn loss into gain. Situating Joyce's economic relations within a gift economy may thus free us from our own bourgeois prejudices while at the same time enabling us to accept Joyce's less attractive qualities as vital to his artistic practice.

For the rest of this study we shall explore how *Ulysses* exemplifies Joyce's opposing impulses: how it inscribes his desire for control in its careful charting of characters' social and economic fates, in its web of motifs, in its schemas and correspondences; how it appropriates and adapts his economic extravagance in its extraordinarily rich texture of narrators, styles, and characters, in its seeming waste of words in episodes such as "Cyclops," where the textual practice defies the conventional realistic economy. Like his financial economy, Joyce's artistic economy reflects both the miser and the spendthrift; his economics and aesthetics fuse in what I call his "Irish" verbal economy, a blending of the spendthrift and the diligent laborer. If Joyce never synthesized the two powerful economic impulses in his actual economic life, his writing permitted him to merge "Wastenot with Want," to make both ends meet, by replacing monetary with artistic currency. Through his literary economy, Joyce turns economic losses into artistic gains.

The novel's main characters dramatize the collision of his conflicting economies. In Stephen Dedalus, Joyce embodies the economic attitudes that characterized his youth: defiance of bourgeois economic norms; self-destructive and compulsive spending and drinking; a scorn for material life; a contempt for the economic and moral paralysis of Dublin, which paradoxically leads him to repeat the same patterns. Joyce's ironic sympathy for Stephen suggests his own partial repudiation of these notions, and his creation of the economically prudent ad canvasser Leopold Bloom displays his attraction to those middle-class attitudes he had formerly spurned. As Bloom circulates through the city, he becomes an embodiment of its economic life, while also starkly contrasting with its dominant economic habits. The crucial exchange of selves and money between Bloom and Stephen inscribes Joyce's economic ambivalence upon a backdrop of economic depression and failure that mirrors his own history. The protagonists' reciprocal exchange emerges from exploitation: each moves from a relationship of unequal power to more balanced exchanges that reflect and generate a temporary and partial synthesis of Joyce's conflicting economies. That balance, however, is immediately undone in "Penelope," where Molly Bloom offers an erotic economy that synthesizes the opposed strains into a single infinitely circulating system. But we begin, as does *Ulysses,* with Stephen.

2

Dedalus Dispossessed

The regulation of the purse is, in its essence, regulation of
the imagination and the heart.

Ruskin 1905, 17:94

Stephen Dedalus embodies many of the young Joyce's economic habits and philosophies. But while Joyce himself eventually evolved a
complicated, even paradoxical, attitude towards money, Stephen remains a spendthrift throughout his fictional existence. In *A Portrait of
the Artist as a Young Man* and the first three episodes of *Ulysses*, Stephen seeks to discover not only his vocation as an artist but also the
value of words themselves. I have detailed elsewhere how in *Portrait*
he passes through a series of stages that may be described as steward-
ships in the houses of various Authorities: his father, God and the
Church, and language itself (Osteen 1995). He rejects each one in
turn, finally accepting his vocation as the steward or economist (he
who sets the *nomoi*, or rules, for the *oikos*, or household) of the treasure house of language. This final stewardship, he believes, endows
him with the authority to speak the voice of his community, or what
he calls his "race." In learning to manage symbolic economies, Stephen progresses toward possession—of himself, of his destiny, and
of his language. By the end of *Portrait* he appears to have acquired
what an earlier Stephen calls his "spiritual assets" (*SH* 202): his linguistic and artistic patrimony.

And yet Stephen's identity remains negative, defined by his *non
serviam*, by what he "will not serve" (*P* 239, 246). His attempts to free

himself from the nets of material obligation by squandering his money and talent have left him homeless, impoverished, and paralyzed both economically and artistically. Indeed, he has unwittingly imitated the familial and national histories he has been attempting to flee. Thus when *Ulysses* opens he has returned to Dublin; dispossessed once more, he must discover those assets all over again. His development in the novel charts his quest to restore the artistic and economic assets that may permit him to attain artistic authority. His related economic and artistic failures, however, can be remedied only through encounters with his oppressors (including his own conscience) and finally through his meeting with Leopold Bloom and, vicariously, with Molly Bloom.

USURPERS

The Linati schema for *Ulysses* lists the "sense" of "Telemachus" as "The Dispossessed Son in Struggle," and indeed Stephen is here engaged in a power struggle with his roommate Buck Mulligan and Buck's guest, the Englishman Haines.[1] Unfortunately, Stephen is losing. An examination of the financial and social exchanges between Stephen and his coresidents of the Martello Tower (originally a military installation), illuminates this struggle for sovereignty. Stephen has been dispossessed both voluntarily and involuntarily: voluntarily dispossessed of his family ties and religious beliefs (as charted in *Portrait*); involuntarily dispossessed of his linguistic patrimony and faith in his artistic destiny. "Telemachus" also portrays the dawning of another, more positive, dispossession: the abandonment of false friends.

Two of Stephen's epithets for Mulligan "frame the chapter" (Benstock 1974, 3): "Chrysostomos" (1.26) and "Usurper" (1.744). The first refers to Mulligan's "golden mouth," in which his white teeth glisten with gold points (the Linati schema describes the episode's colors as white and gold). Mulligan is golden-mouthed in several senses: those gold teeth embody the financial resources and class position that enable him to visit the dentist regularly (Stephen's "threadbare cuffedge" [1.106] and rotting teeth contrast with Mulligan's foppish dress and expensive dental work); their brightness betrays his meretricious, deceptive materialism—his ability to remain "wellfed"

---

1. Both the Linati and Gorman-Gilbert schemata are reproduced in R. Ellmann 1972, appendix.

(1.107); and he is a brilliant talker, capable of sudden shifts in tone and lively witticisms as well as biting ironies. His shiftiness is displayed throughout the episode. Like Proteus, he is extremely difficult to battle because he is nearly impossible to pin down. For example, "Mercurial Malachi" (1.518) evades responsibility for his cutting remarks about Stephen's mother by claiming to have no memory ("I can't remember anything" 1.192). Without a memory, he would lack a consistent self and thus could incur no debts. Mulligan thus represents character and consciousness as a mere succession of roles; for him all behavior is "mumming." These protean qualities both attract and oppress Stephen. With his charm and strength of personality, Mulligan has temporarily usurped Stephen as hero, just as he parodically usurps the role of priest in the novel's opening lines (1.62).

Like the Greek Sophists, Mulligan believes wisdom can be sold, but only covertly. He also argues both sides of an issue, another Sophistic strategy.[2] "Do I contradict myself?" he asks, quoting Whitman. "Very well then, I contradict myself" (1.517). Thus when Stephen bitterly quips that Irish art is "the cracked lookingglass of a servant" (1.146), Mulligan urges him to repeat the epigram to Haines and "touch him for a guinea" (1.155).[3] He has no qualms about using Stephen's words to flatter and extract money from Haines but reproaches Stephen for blatantly requesting payment ("Would I make any money by it?" [1.490]). Stephen responds that, since "the problem is to get money," it little matters from whom one extorts it (1.497). Using Mulligan's own assumptions to rebut him, Stephen plays Socrates to Mulligan's Protagoras.

"Touch," Mulligan's word for borrowing money, was used in like fashion by the Joyce brothers. In October 1904, James wrote to Stanislaus, directing him to "go about the highways of the city but not to any of my touched friends and make up £1 before Saturday which send me on that day without fail" (*L* II 66). Another time Stanislaus wrote back, complaining, "I haven't a 'touching' manner" (*L* II 104). *Ulysses* consistently connects such financial "touching" with physical touches, both of which are associated with mock-paternal advice and illicit exercises of power. When Stephen is physically touched, it generally means that the toucher wants to exploit him under the guise of

---

2. Stephen, however, also plays the Sophist in his apparent cynicism about making money and owning up to his ideas here and in "Aeolus" and "Scylla and Charybdis."

3. Neither Mulligan nor Haines realizes that Stephen's remark is itself borrowed and adapted from Oscar Wilde (Adams 1962, 124).

friendly advice. The major exceptions are the genuinely helpful touches that Bloom offers in "Circe" (15.4922; 4937), "Eumaeus" (16.1721—although even this one is tinged by exploitation) and "Ithaca" (17.1222). These touches accompany Stephen's only positive financial exchanges in the novel, the only ones in which balanced reciprocal exchanges take place. The other, minor, exception is the touch of Stephen's teacher, Almidano Artifoni (10.356). Otherwise, when someone physically touches Stephen he is usually being "touched" in the other sense as well—bilked, bullied, or given bad advice.

The first physical touch between Mulligan and Dedalus immediately precedes Mulligan's directive to Stephen to "touch" Haines: "Buck Mulligan suddenly linked his arm in Stephen's and walked with him round the tower" (1.147–48; this moment also foreshadows Stephen's and Bloom's linked arms in "Eumaeus"). Mulligan pretends to take Stephen's side against Haines, saying confidentially, "It's not fair to tease you like that. . . . God knows you have more spirit than any of them." But this intimacy is spurious. Although Mulligan disguises his commands as friendly advice, his real objective is his own gain: he hopes to butter up Haines, and to borrow his money and prestige. Mulligan's "advice" is designed to further his own self-interest. Stephen recognizes the betrayal in his touch by recalling the touch of Cranly, another friend he believes has betrayed him: "Cranly's arm. His arm" (1.159; cf. *P* 238). But Mulligan's pseudo-friendly badgering and patronizing tone towards Stephen recall no one so much as Simon Dedalus himself. Indeed, the whistle with which Mulligan summons Stephen at the opening of *Ulysses* echoes Simon's whistles at the opening of chapter 5 of *Portrait* (1.24; *P* 175. Bloom repeats them at the beginning of "Eumaeus" [16.29–30]). It is a critical commonplace that Bloom plays surrogate father to Stephen in the late episodes. Mulligan's role is similar: he is not only a mock Father in the opening lines but also a mock father. Thus when Bloom later links Stephen's arm and shakes his hand he is both mimicking Mulligan and usurping him.

This falsely familial relationship between the two is borne out by their exchanges of money and commodities. Mulligan is established at the outset as a borrower *par excellence*. His first words borrow those of the mass, as he usurps the role of priest; in proposing to "Hellenise" Ireland, his first idea is to borrow twenty quid from his aunt (1.43); he then asks to borrow Stephen's "noserag" (1.69). Throughout the chapter he urges Stephen to imitate him—that is, to borrow money, influence, clothes, and quotations from others. Of course, Mulligan also lends Stephen his "secondhand breeks" and shoes (1.113) in an ostentatious display of generosity and has lent him large sums of money in the past (see 2.255). But the motive behind his largesse is to keep Stephen under his thumb. As Peter Blau writes, "the supply of services inevitably generates power" (1964, 119): the more he gives Stephen, the more he can control him. Thus Mulligan's current loans are designed specifically to keep Stephen in his debt, so that Stephen will have no choice but to give Mulligan whatever he has. Hence, we see Stephen broodingly serve his housemates breakfast and respond to Mulligan's brisk orders (e.g. 1.388). The "server of a servant" (1.312), Stephen recognizes, but does not yet resist his servitude. Meanwhile Mulligan seems hyperactive, even violent: he "lunges," "impales," "hacks," and "hews" (1.363–64; 349; 355), and his words leave "gaping wounds" in Stephen's heart (1.216–17). Learning that Stephen is to receive his teaching wages today, Mulligan immediately demands that he "Lend us one" of his pounds (1.293–94) for a "glorious drunk." (Mulligan also believes Stephen's wages to be larger than they actually are, alluding to "four shining sovereigns" [1.296], when his salary is actually eight shillings less than that.) Virtually penniless at this moment, Stephen responds passively: "If you want it" (1.295). Indeed, throughout the episode Mulligan acts as though Stephen's wages were already his own to spend, urging him to "Hurry out to your school kip and bring us back some money. Today the bards must drink and junket" (1.466–67).

The question of who owes how much to whom is crucial, because it involves one of the most basic ways that human beings maintain kinship and power relationships. As Nietzsche writes, the debtor-creditor relationship is "the oldest and most primitive relationship between human beings" ([1887] 1956, 202). But the details of the financial relationship between Stephen and Buck are not entirely clear. After leaving the tower for Mulligan's swim, Haines asks, "Do you pay rent for this tower?" Mulligan answers, "Twelve quid," to which Stephen adds, "To the secretary of state for war" (1.538–40). But who pays the rent? During one of Stephen's interior monologues, he thinks: "He wants that key. It is mine. I paid the rent. Now I eat his salt bread. Give him the key too. All. He will ask for it. That was in his eyes" (1.630–32). Stephen appears to be assuring himself that he has indeed paid the twelve quid rent in preparation for Mulligan's demand for the key. Kenner, however, argues that Mulligan paid it, which explains why Stephen remains under his thumb. Stephen's "It is mine, I paid the rent," are allegedly Mulligan's words, in "invisible quotation marks." He continues: "it is unlike Stephen to assert ownership in consequence of payment—that is the way of the Mulligans and Deasys. Moreover, when Haines asks whether rent is paid for the tower, it is Mulligan who promptly answers with the exact amount, twelve quid. And this is a preposterous amount for us to think of Stephen getting together at any time. . . . On his wage of £3 12s 0d [2.222] he could have amassed twelve quid (hardly eating) in four paydays, but there has been only one payday before this one—the first of 'three times' was a bargaining session—and his acknowledged debts to 10 people [2.255–59] total £25 17s 6d (of which 9 is owed to Mulligan)" (1987, 55-56n). Kenner's interpretation would indeed answer some difficult questions: Why does Stephen owe Mulligan nine pounds? It is part of the twelve quid he owes him for the rent. Why does Stephen act as his servant? Because he is so deeply in his debt. Joyce's biography appears to reinforce Kenner's view, since "in humble fact Gogarty paid it, not Joyce" (R. Ellmann 1972, 8). According to this reading, Stephen merely relinquishes the key to its rightful owner, Buck Mulligan. Having paid the rent, Buck rightfully possesses the key and the power it symbolizes. By this interpretation Mulligan would have earned his power in the usual way, through superior wealth, and would thus be executing the classic description of power as that which enables one to "compel others to provide services without offering a fair return" (Blau 1964, 105).[4]

And yet Kenner's solution raises more questions than it answers. First, if we are going to use biographical evidence, let us observe that the real-life rent on the Martello Tower was paid quarterly, and so might the fictional rent be. If so, Stephen would have had to find only £3, which is not out of his reach, given his earnings and facility in cadging loans.[5] Of course, Joyce could have changed the facts as he

---

4. Adams (1962, 45) also argues that "the Stephen we encounter in *Ulysses* has not seen twelve unencumbered quid in a long time." This is no doubt true; however, whether the twelve quid are unencumbered is irrelevant to the question of who pays. Other critics who have concluded that Mulligan paid the rent include Benstock (1991, 42), Arnold Goldman (quoted in Kenner 1987, 55), and Brook Thomas (1982, 158).

5. Pearl (1969, 82) reproduces the receipt for the actual Martello rent, dated June 24, 1904, which states that it is to be paid in "four equal quarterly payments." Since Stephen has been paid three months' wages, he must have been back in Dublin for at least three months. It is therefore possible that the rent was paid once three months ago and is due again or that each inhabitant has paid it once. It is also interesting to note that the rent on the tower has been increased from the actual figure of £8 to £12. Whoever paid it, the higher rent raises the stakes in the fictional power struggle.

saw fit. Thus neither whether the real-life rent was paid yearly or quarterly, nor the fact that, in real life, their relations always "involved the flow of money from Gogarty who had it to Joyce who didn't" (Adams 1962, 47), should provide the sole basis for interpreting the text. But what about the fictional life outside the dramatized events? Here Kenner's argument seems weak. If we are willing to resort to Stephen's imaginary life, we could easily also supply the twelve (or three) quid from a combination of Stephen's other creditors. He could have gotten together even the larger figure by borrowing from others, since we know that he has debts of more than sixteen pounds besides what he owes Mulligan. In any case, Stephen has already earned £10 16s at his teaching job—not so much less than twelve quid.[6] Perhaps more significantly, Kenner's argument ignores the most important word in the episode—"usurper." Why would Stephen apply this epithet to Mulligan if indeed the latter had paid the rent? There would be no usurpation involved, since Mulligan would rightfully own the key by virtue of having leased the tower; hence Stephen's epithet would be, as Stanley Sultan puts it, both "inaccurate and a touch whining" (1987, 274; Sultan weighs in on the "Stephen pays" side). Moreover, the key element in their relationship—Mulligan's abuse of power over Stephen—would be erased.

As to whether it is out of character for Stephen to assert ownership in consequence of payment, one must admit that he does seem nonchalant about his expenditures later in the day and readily lends money to Corley and gives his cash to Bloom. But one must remember that in the latter cases he is quite drunk; many people become less capable of counting pennies after a night on the town. In any case, Stephen is not indifferent to money; on the contrary, his mental calculations after receiving his wages demonstrate that he knows precisely how much he owes. Like Joyce's, Stephen's spendthrift habits mask a high regard for money and its power, a power he uses to buy drinks and gain attention throughout the novel. This Stephen who asserts ownership (and only to himself, after all) is the same Stephen who requests payment for his impromptu lectures; he is surely capable of reminding himself what rightfully belongs to him. Indeed, since Stephen never returns to the tower, his paying the rent and

6. *Pace* Kenner, the text never suggests that the first of Stephen's and Deasy's encounters was a "bargaining session." When he receives his wages in "Nestor," Stephen thinks, "The same room and hour, the same wisdom: and I the same. Three times now" (2.233–34): this is the third time he has received wages. That is how I have arrived at the figure of £10 16s.

then deserting his residence is very much in character, and even more significant as a statement of his distaste for Mulligan: he dislikes him so much that he forfeits the rent along with the key.

Now let us look at the passage itself. First, in regard to the "invisible quotation marks" around "It is mine. I paid the rent": if they were Mulligan's words, surely they would *follow* Stephen's prediction that "He will ask for it," rather than preceding it. To place the prediction after the request makes no sense. Second, as Sultan observes, "Stephen's 'now' " signifies "a rueful contrast of his present reliance on Mulligan for his very food with a time when he had enough money to pay the rent on the tower; it is a familiar human sentiment" (1987, 275).[7] Other questions arise: why would Stephen contrast "now" with an implied "then" if the financial relationship had always been the same? And why would he think "too," if to give up the key is merely to give Mulligan what belongs to him? The word implies that Stephen has previously yielded to Mulligan other important things (money, his autonomy) as well. Stephen willingly gives up the sovereignty he paid for, just as he willfully spends much of his wages for the rest of the novel. This "general resignation," as Sultan terms it (1987, 275), is again quite characteristic. Finally and more generally, to place "invisible quotation marks" in the text without compelling evidence that they belong there opens the door to all kinds of attribution problems, and needlessly complicates an already difficult text. A critic might simply add them wherever it seemed convenient. In conclusion, textual, biographical, and characterological evidence all strongly suggest that Stephen paid the rent.

But even assuming that Stephen has paid the rent, some of our questions about the money relations between Mulligan and Dedalus cannot be answered. We cannot know precisely how Stephen obtained the twelve (or three) quid, given only what the text tells us. And even if Stephen did pay the rent, nevertheless he is now nearly flat broke, wearing shabby clothes, and in debt to Mulligan for nine pounds (2.255)—more than twice his monthly earnings. If his own calculations are accurate, the rent question has been superseded by another debt, and thus any money that Mulligan now receives from Stephen is only a partial repayment of Stephen's outstanding debt. If so, Mulli-

---

7. "Salt bread" is not merely a reference to food but an allusion to Dante's *Paradiso,* in which Dante's ancestor Cacciaguida predicts the bitterness of his future exile (Gifford 1988, 24–25). "Salt bread" is thus a symbol of the unpleasant "taste" of being forced to depend upon others. Sultan's point nevertheless remains valid.

gan is technically, if not morally, within his rights to attempt to recoup his losses by garnisheeing Stephen's wages. Thus, when Stephen gives Buck the key, he also throws in two pennies "for a pint" (1.724). Mulligan pays the milkwoman but, typically, hedges. He slides a florin along the table, with Stephen acting as middleman, but underpays her by twopence (they owe "two and two": 1.445; 458). While Mulligan's bad faith is characteristic, nevertheless he does pay for the milk, and hence increases Stephen's debt by eightpence—his share of the florin (a coin that appears throughout the novel as a sign of bad faith or incomplete circulation). We can now add an extra sixpence that Stephen owes for the morning's activities to the £9 principal: eightpence for his share of the milk, minus the twopence he gives Mulligan at the end of the episode. But because the rent question remains clouded by the other debt, one must ultimately agree with Adams (1962, 46) that "as an accounting statement . . . the novel contains contrary indications."

The fact, however, that interpretations such as Kenner's are at all plausible demonstrates an important characteristic of Joyce's narratives. Vincent Pecora has written in a different context that "language in Joyce . . . is often *dispossessed* discourse—thought, feeling or inner speech that may be attributed to a particular character or speaker but that never completely belongs to that speaker" (1986, 235; emphasis his). In other words, Joyce's techniques blur the boundaries between narrative commentary and the thoughts and spoken words of the characters, so that it is often difficult to know the source of the words. Here is an example from "Telemachus": "putting on his stiff collar and rebellious tie he spoke to them, chiding them, and to his dangling watch chain. His hands plunged and rummaged in his trunk while he called for a clean handkerchief. God, we'll simply have to dress the character. I want puce gloves and green boots. . . . Mercurial Malachi. A limp black missile flew out of his talking hands" (1.513–18). Does "Mercurial Malachi" (to note just one problematic phrase) issue from Stephen's mind, from the narrator, or from Buck himself? Upon closer examination, one discovers it is Mulligan's phrase, but Joyce seems intentionally to make attribution difficult. Indeed, the chapter stages a struggle for the dominance of voice that replicates the power struggle depicted in the action, as if Joyce's narrator must constantly fight the characters for speaking time and control of the discourse. Not only does brilliant Buck outshine dour Dedalus, but his personality dominates the chapter and threatens to usurp even the narrator himself. Dubbed the "Uncle Charles Principle" by Kenner (1978, 18), this widely acknowledged tendency of Joyce's narrative "to borrow the pace and diction of the characters' language" (Lawrence 1981, 41) involves the narrative consciousness and the consciousness of the characters in exchange: the narrator lends them life in exchange for their linguistic idioms.

The language of "Telemachus" thus displays a trait that distinguishes novels from other forms of writing: the tendency, defined and explored by Mikhail Bakhtin, to become sites of dialogism between speech zones. Not only do the voices of Stephen and Mulligan collide and interpenetrate, but the character zones also constantly encounter the voice of the author. In this sense there can be no truly "dispossessed" discourse, because language is always "shot through with intentions and accents" (Bakhtin 1981, 293); if one speaker disowns or is dispossessed of his discourse, it is because another speaker or consciousness has appropriated it. Novelistic language always lies "on the borderline between oneself and the other"; it is always "populated—overpopulated—with the intentions of others" (Bakhtin 1981, 293–94). Like other writers, then, Joyce does not "speak in a given language . . . but . . . as it were, *through* language . . . that he merely ventriloquates" (Bakhtin 1981, 299). Like Buck Mulligan, the narrative voice is a mummer. Ultimately, the battle for supremacy enacted on the material levels of money and power is also a fact of linguistic life: "within the arena of almost every utterance an intense interaction and struggle between one's own and another's word is being waged, a process in which they oppose or dialogically interanimate each other" (Bakhtin 1981, 354). It might be more accurate to say, therefore, that Stephen and the narrator are not dispossessed, but rather *struggling against* dispossession, as the financial borrowings detailed in the chapter are mirrored in the narrator's borrowings and lendings to and from his characters. It is as though the narrator too is a "dispossessed son in struggle," caught between the inheritance of Stephen as protagonist and the allure of the lively Buck, between the need to own and authorize his language and the need to borrow it.

Another tension between inheritance and dispossession is manifest in the first episode. Many critics have pointed out the parodic quality of the writing in "Telemachus." Repeated phrases such as "cried thickly," or "said contentedly" seem more typical of clumsy popular fiction than of the premiere prose writer of the century. The narrative consciousness seems to evoke and parody his own inheritance of novelistic conventions by explicitly echoing some of the worst of them. This tendency is congruent with what the Gorman-Gilbert schema lists as the episode's technic—"narrative young"—which implies that the narrator is himself a youthful consciousness struggling for mastery of the intertextual patrimony he has been left. Thus while the Linati schema speaks of dispossession, the Gorman-Gilbert schema lists the episode's symbol as "heir"; this conflict between ownership and dispossession is manifest throughout the Stephen chapters. Just as Stephen wants both to control his possessions and to disown them, so the narrative presence is divided between the inheritance of literary conventions and the need to dispossess oneself of them through irony and parody. In this regard, the narrative of "Telemachus" is not so much dispossessed as *collectively possessed,* both in the Bakhtinian sense of dialogic competition or interpenetration of voices, and because any author must share the authority and the ownership of his text with previous writers: his linguistic capital has always been previously produced. The so-called initial style is therefore already collective, although the separate presences do not cooperate, but instead vie for authority. This narrative agon continues throughout the novel, but the episodes in which Stephen shows gains in confidence and creativity—"Aeolus" and "Scylla and Charybdis"— also display a more intrusive narrative presence. Thus the narrator's authority and expenditure of energy seem to mirror Stephen's, and perhaps represent, as James Maddox contends, "the very voice that Stephen desires for himself" (1987, 147).[8]

Umberto Eco's claim that *Ulysses* "begins in a lack of relations" (1972, 49) is thus true for the narrative discourse. It is also true for the characters: although Stephen and Mulligan live in the same household, their economic relations are far from those of kinsmen. Despite (or because of) their physical proximity, economically they are at war. In his study of preindustrial economies, Marshall Sahlins demonstrates that in economic relations among kin, "the reckoning of debts outstanding cannot be overt and is typically left out of account" (1972, 194). Normally, the economics of a household occupies this "solidarity extreme," which tends toward sharing and gift giving. But while Mulligan pretends to share and offer free loans, in fact the economics of the Martello Tower belongs to the opposite, or "unsociable extreme," characterized by "the several forms of appro-

---

8. Both Maddox (1987, 147–48) and Mahaffey (1988, 7–8) ascribe a univocal model of authority to the Stephen sections of *Ulysses.* I would argue that the narrative presence oscillates between univocality and dissemination or collectivity from the beginning of the novel.

priation" in which "participants confront each other as opposed interests" (Sahlins 1972, 195). In such relationships, financial resources do
not flow in a single direction but instead spur a continual battle for
the unearned increment. Thus, in fleeing from his consubstantial
family, Stephen has found refuge in a household that pretends to
offer friendship and fraternal feeling but instead strips him of his
resources and uses them against him. Seeking a brother, Stephen has
found an enemy. Instead of the economics of kinship, he faces the
economics of power: usurpation rather than communal sharing, chicanery rather than generosity. As in *Portrait,* Stephen's *oikos* (and his
economy) is disrupted. Thus he tells himself, "I will not sleep here
tonight" (1.739) and begins to move from this false family and from
the economics of hostility, imbalance and unpaid debts, toward a
relationship of balanced reciprocal exchange and genuine kinship
with Bloom. The meeting with Bloom, then, marks a highly significant step in Stephen's social and material growth, and dramatizes the
convergence of the two economic strains in Joyce we explored in
chapter 1.

But Mulligan is not Stephen's only tyrant. If Mulligan has
usurped the role of priest, the Englishman Haines represents the
other, more material tyranny—England's over Ireland. Like Mulligan, Haines is financially better off than Stephen: according to Buck,
Haines is "stinking with money" his father made in some "bloody
swindle or other" (1.155–57). Moreover, Haines not only speaks Irish
but also wants to collect Stephen's sayings for a chapbook containing
examples of Irish wit. Haines's appropriation of the Irish literary
heritage exemplifies England's usurpation of Irish cultural life. Even
as the British control the Irish economy, so they govern the commerce
in ideas by running not only the major industries but also the channels of information. Thus Irish sayings will be published under an
English imprint by an English author. Stephen's conversations with
the English spokesmen Haines and Deasy thus recall his meeting with
the Dean in *Portrait,* where he acknowledged English dominion over
the language, especially in such words as "*home, Christ, ale,* [and] *Master*" (*P* 189). Here he comments to Haines: "I am a servant of two
masters, . . . an English and an Italian. . . . and a third . . . there is
who wants me for odd jobs" (1.638–41).[9] The third, Ireland, is herself

9. Stephen once again revises Wilde, in this case *The Soul of Man Under Socialism,*
which contains a passage describing "the despots," the Prince, the Pope, and the People
(Wilde 1969, 282). Stephen combines this with an allusion to Christ's words in Luke

a servant of England, a role dramatized by the aged milkwoman who speaks no Irish; like her, Stephen serves his "conqueror and gay betrayer" (1.405). Stephen's domination by Mulligan (Rome) and Haines (Britain) is thus wholly Irish, in that he lets himself "be milked by England and yet increas[es] Peter's pence" (*CW* 190). Like Mulligan, Haines refuses to take responsibility, commenting pompously that "history is to blame" (1.649).

This material tyranny is represented by a kind of immateriality: Haines's invisibility. He first emerges as a "voice within the tower" (1.227) and is described as merely "a voice" (1.322) even when he is onstage. (Mulligan, too, seems to have the magic power of invisibility in the same passage: his head "vanishe[s]" but his voice drones on— 1.237; cf. Mulligan's anecdote about Haines in "Oxen of the Sun": 14.1011–12; 1025–27). Marc Shell (1978, 30) has demonstrated how in Greek thought "the concepts of visibility and invisibility involve definitions of political orders . . . and of economic forms . . . upon which political orders are often founded." The coining of money replaced more direct methods of political and economic exchange with symbolic representation and was thus believed to permit greater exploitation because it removed the necessity of taking immediate responsibility for transactions. Money and its control were thought to enable tyranny and bad faith, because actual goods were not exchanged but only symbolized in coins, which themselves replaced human witnesses of such transactions.[10] Invisibility signals the alienation of matter and spirit, of signifier and signified, of ruler and subject through an impersonality that more easily generates exploitative relationships. Removed from personal connections and thus from the consequences of the abuse of power, the tyrant is invisible to his subjects, but they remain visible and hence exploitable to him. Haines's invisibility resembles the alienation of ruler from ruled,

---

16:13: "No servant can serve two masters. . . . Ye cannot serve God and mammon." These words follow the notoriously difficult parable of the unfaithful steward, which is a key text for interpreting the *Dubliners* story "Grace" (see Osteen 1991, 83–89). Like the characters in the biblical text, Stephen is again wrestling with the nature of stewardship.

10. Shell employs Plato's and Herodotus's tales of Gyges and Candaules to demonstrate the connection between tyranny and invisibility (1978, 11–45). Hornik reads Stephen's relationship with the Blooms (Bloom as King Candaules and Stephen and Boylan as Gyges) as a modern instance of the Ring of Gyges tale. He claims that Joyce may also have been familiar with Andre Gide's play *Roi Candaule* (1900), which also adapts the ancient story (Hornik 1959, 9-18).

again exemplifying how the British exert political, economic and cultural tyranny in palpable but sometimes unobtrusive ways. Stephen's dispossession and servitude are thus Irish oppression writ small.[11]

Stephen must combat another invisible tyranny in "Telemachus" and throughout the novel: the tyranny of his own conscience, the agenbite of inwit. As Nietzsche shows, conscience is itself a form of debtorship, since it arises from making oneself one's own creditor by internalizing the burdens of economic and social indebtedness ([1887] 1956, 194–95). Religious guilt, moreover, is a projection of the debtor/creditor relationship into "the relationship between living men and their forebears" (Nietzsche [1887] 1956, 221). Stephen is mortified by just such an unremitted debt to his mother, which he has transformed into an internal conflict. This dilemma involves him in a Charybdean cycle of self-punishment, with his ghostly mother projecting his past misdeeds and personifying the rejected Catholic church, "a crazy queen, old and jealous," a "church militant" defending itself with its angels' lances and shields (1.640; 655). He cannot get his mother to forgive him in person because she is dead; he cannot forgive himself because he has yet to confront the source of his indebtedness. To his mother he sang the song from the pantomime *Turko the Terrible*—"I am the boy / That can enjoy / Invisibility" (1.260–2)— but now she is the ghost who lurks invisibly (to others, if not to him) behind his guilt.[12] Stephen is both debtor and creditor— and hence tyrant—to himself. Only when his mother becomes fully visible in "Circe" does he purge himself of this psychic debt and perhaps begin to usurp his mother's control. To do so, he must undergo mortification and sacrifice (a ritual contract that generates value), and kill his old self in order to gain a new one. Like other Irish, Stephen has internalized both spiritual and material tyranny and, as he finally realizes in "Circe," it is these internal priests and kings that he must kill (15.4436–37).

Stephen can be dominated until, like Gyges, he discovers a way to create his own brand of invisibility and power. Like Joyce, Stephen

11. For a complementary interpretation of Haines's political and ideological functions, see Trevor L. Williams 1991, 43–48.

12. The words to this song, recently published in Bauerle (1993, 26–29), reinforce the relationships between invisibility and financial chicanery: Turko sings of hiring an attorney but being able to "Disappear when he speaks of fees" and of vanishing when the landlord calls for his rent or the gas bill comes due. In the same volume, Henriette Power argues that the plot of the panto reveals that "neither visibility nor invisibility is a consistent and reliable source of power" (1993, 59).

aims to earn it through the currency and commerce of words. Language is already his mode of defense: he hopes to "pierce the polished mail" of Haines's mind with his turns of phrase (2.43), and believes that Mulligan "fears the lancet" of his art just as he fears Mulligan's piercing words (1.152). Thus the aptness of "usurper," the final word in "Telemachus" (1.744), is demonstrated throughout the episode: Mulligan usurps the religious stewardship of the priesthood and control of the household; the voices of characters (especially Mulligan's) threaten to usurp narrative authority from the narrator; Haines and the English usurp political and linguistic sovereignty; Stephen's mother usurps control of his conscience; soon Stephen will be usurped by Bloom as protagonist of the novel. But in an agonistic and threatening world like the one Stephen inhabits, the reacquisition of assets of any kind requires that one join the fight. Stephen must himself become a usurper in order to consolidate his economic and artistic assets, just as he usurped his father's household role in the second chapter of *Portrait*. He must wrest control of his linguistic patrimony from those who have stolen it. To do so Stephen believes that he must expend the material assets that fetter him to his masters; he must spend his money and sever all material ties. Thus for the rest of *Ulysses* he becomes a kind of living expression of the force of expenditure.

Ultimately, however, Stephen can advance toward sovereignty and balance only by integrating the material and spiritual; this in turn will come about only through an acceptance and transformation of the material world in his art, and thus through attainment of the kind of invisibility he ascribed to the artist in *Portrait* (215). But for this atonement he needs to encounter Bloom, confront more balanced economic models, complete Bloom's equally incomplete *oikos,* and thereby move from unequal relations of power to the reciprocal relations of surrogate kinship.

ON BORROWED TIME

Early in "Nestor," while desultorily giving a history lesson, Stephen meditates on Aristotle's view of history as a series of usurpations: "Time has branded [events] and fettered they are lodged in the room of the infinite possibilities they have ousted" (2.49–51; Gifford 1988, 31). Different versions of history, all of which view it as a trap, revolve in Stephen's mind throughout the episode. But he is tyrannized most by his personal past: his psychic debts seem as unremittable as his financial ones. The "graceless" and "bloodless" (2.126) student Sargent reminds him of his younger self and represents his own history as a series of futile repetitions. "My childhood bends beside me," Stephen thinks. "Secrets, silent, stony sit in the dark palaces of both our hearts: secrets weary of their tyranny: tyrants, willing to be dethroned" (2.169–72). Usurpers that he must oust from his conscience, secrets represent the tyranny of the past in Stephen's conscience; indeed, they are tyrants *because* they remain unshared. "Graceless" financially because he does not repay loans, Stephen is also psychically graceless because he cannot remit the debt to his dead mother. Although he seeks a consistent self behind constant flux and serial usurpation, this consistent self, manifested in memory as repetition, traps him in debtorship. This repetition is represented by snail figures: a blot resembling a "snail's bed" smears the bloodless cheek of Sargent, who himself has the potency of a "squashed boneless snail" against the march of history; his signature of "blind loops and a blot" mimics a snail's concentric shell (2.127; 140; 130). The spiral pattern of the snail's shell embodies the seemingly futile and oppressive repetition of history. Although Stephen feels compassion for the boy's ineptitude and dutifully performs his own pedagogical offices, he feels almost equally powerless, and Deasy soon usurps him as teacher and master.

"Nestor" dramatizes power and exchange straightforwardly when Stephen receives his teaching wages. This is the only scene in the novel in which Stephen receives money rather than spends it (until he meets Bloom) and the only occasion in Stephen's entire existence in which he receives pay for labor (the money he wins in *Portrait* is a prize, not earnings). Gazing at Deasy's collections of Stuart coins and Apostle spoons, he equates them with the master's other collection, shells: "whelks and money. . . . An old pilgrim's hoard, dead treasure, hollow shells" (2.213–15). The coins and spoons again symbolize his British and Roman masters. Coins "of the tribute," they tell him to render "to Caesar what is Caesar's, to God what is God's" (2.85–86). Both masters demand more than he is willing to give. Just as an earlier Stephen had vowed not to "be frightened into paying tribute in money or in thought" (*SH* 141), this Stephen aims to resist paying any tribute to his masters, to escape from history by spending money as fast as he earns it. He thus sees his employment as another form of servitude and his financial settlement with Deasy as another form of oppressive repetition—"The same room and hour, the same wisdom: and I the same. Three times now. Three nooses round me here"

(2.233)—and plans to quit. While Deasy believes the adage that "money is power" (2.237), that possessions give potency, Stephen feels dominated by money; although he needs cash, he holds it uneasily. Material assets merely usurp spiritual assets and signify the tyranny of history over Ireland and over his own identity. Of course, all money has both a symbolic and a material component; metal disks are not coins unless engraved with the emblem of the "authority of the state which mints them" (Mauss [1925] 1967, 93), an authority palpable even in the names of the coins. As Deasy digs for the money, "a sovereign f[alls]" on the table (2.217), the pun on "sovereign" invoking the political institutions behind minted money. An icon of power, the sovereign coin (£1) bears the British monarch's portrait on its obverse face, and its fall symbolizes both power and its loss. But Stephen fears mostly the "fall" of his own sovereignty and his inevitable contamination by these "symbols soiled by greed and misery" (2.227).

For his last month of teaching Stephen receives £3 12s: two pound notes, a sovereign, two crowns, and two shillings (2.209–21). Gifford claims that, given the standard of living in Dublin in 1904, this sum is not as paltry as it seems, although it is certainly not large. He calculates Stephen's wages as equivalent to about $388 per month in 1985 U.S. dollars (Gifford 1988, 7; in 1990 U.S. dollars, this comes to about $400 per month). But Gifford's conclusion that "Stephen could live quite comfortably within his income" (1988, 7) is far too sanguine, if "comfortably" implies his having any money for luxuries or even new clothing. In any case, Stephen has no intention of living economically, no matter how much he earns. His financial behavior on June 16, 1904 is wildly extravagant. By the end of the day he will have spent more than two pounds—well over half his month's wages —on drinks and whores for himself and his friends, on unwise loans, and on a bitter telegram to Mulligan. This is equivalent to spending over $200 for a single day and night's debauches. (See Appendix A for Stephen's budget.).

Responding to a pointed question from Deasy, Stephen mentally lists his outstanding debts: "Mulligan, nine pounds, three pairs of socks, one pair brogues, ties. Curran, ten guineas. McCann, one guinea. Fred Ryan, two shillings. Temple, two lunches. Russell, one guinea, Cousins, ten shillings, Bob Reynolds, half a guinea, Koehler, three guineas, Mrs MacKernan, five weeks' board. The lump I have is useless" (2.255–59). All told, his acknowledged debts (there may be others) come to £25 17s 6d, which does not include the unspecified amount of his five weeks' board. As Gifford points out (1988, 7), Stephen's debts amount to more than he could earn in seven months of teaching, and so the prospects for repayment anytime soon look quite dim. At least two of these debts, those to Russell and Ryan, were also Joyce's. It as though Joyce were acknowledging, and hence repaying in literary currency, some of the money that allowed him to reach the point of writing the novel that we are reading (and that presumably they would also read).[13] In short, Stephen is in dire financial straits, and neither doing anything to ease his burden nor giving any sign of readiness to repay his debts.

One of the bank notes that Deasy gives to Stephen is made of "joined halves" (2.209). Its shape recalls the original, ancient Greek *Symbola*, which were "pledges, pawns, or covenants from an earlier understanding to bring together a part of something that had been divided specifically for the purpose of later comparison" (Shell 1978, 32–33). Often a ring or coin was broken in two as token of a financial agreement, and since the two halves had to fit together, the possession of these tokens identified the parties for later repayment. That the very word "symbol" derives from financial exchanges indicates that what is at stake in discussing Stephen's economic behavior is his attitude towards all symbolic economies, including language. In *Ulysses* this *symbola,* the broken and reconnected bank note, represents the idea of reciprocal exchange, and more specifically embodies the central economic exchange in *Ulysses*—the one between Stephen and Bloom. Stephen tenders one of his two bank notes to pay Bella Cohen in the brothel (15.3531); since he has only two bank notes to begin with, there is a 50 percent chance that this is the one exchanged. Bloom takes the note, instead giving Bella a half sovereign (15.3583–90); Stephen allows Bloom to hold the bank note and the rest of his money for him (15.3604); finally Bloom gives it back to Stephen just before they part in "Ithaca" (17.957–58). The broken bank note represents not only each character's incompleteness but also the mutual self-interest served by their exchange and the temporary fusion that results from it.

The broken bank note is a material equivalent of Stephen's witty description of a pier as a "disappointed bridge" (2.39), a remark with bitter significance for his life. His exile to the Continent has been a

---

13. The debts to Russell and Ryan come up again in Stephen's mind in the library. Curiously, however, there the debt to Russell has decreased from a guinea to a pound (9.192).

disappointment, and the epiphanic bridge crossing in *Portrait* where he felt his destiny (*P* 166–67) now seems illusory, because he has failed to reconcile past and future through the bridge of his present. Because of its function of linking opposed entities, the bridge symbolizes the operation of metaphor: a bridge is designed to allow crossing or transfer, which is the etymological origin of the word "metaphor" (Heinzelman 1980, 10). These two figures, the broken bank note and the disappointed bridge, are symbols of symbolization, of consciousness moving outside itself to forge reciprocal exchanges with the material world; their disjunctions signify Stephen's impairment. Stephen must reappoint his disappointed bridge and bring together the sundered halves of his identity—matter and spirit, individual fulfillment and social connection—to achieve the destiny that now eludes him. Bloom may provide him with this bridge when they meet. But in the meantime, the severing signifies that Stephen's failure of imagination is homologous with his failure to carry out exchange: his economic and aesthetic problems are inextricably related.

Whereas Stephen piles up debts, Deasy collects spoons, coins and dusty facts. His vision of history is similarly linear and accumulative. "All human history moves toward one great goal, the manifestation of God" (2.380–81), he announces, his words punctuated and parodied by the cry and whistle from the students' field hockey game— "goal" (2.378). Stephen rejects this optimistic and mechanistic teleology as "the hollow knock of a ball" (2.154), and responds with the provocatively cynical statement that God is "a shout in the street" (2.386). Deasy's remarks on Ireland's demise, however, indicate that he actually subscribes to a vision of history as repetition, in which women cause every fall. In response to Deasy's linear, teleological model, Stephen offers a sardonic one—"History . . . is a nightmare from which I am trying to awake" (2.377)—as illustrated by the portraits of horses that ring Deasy's study. Looking at them, Stephen remembers a visit to the track with Cranly prompted by a vision of trying to "get rich quick" (2.307) and thereby defeat the oppression of history and England. For Stephen history is a horse, a night*mare* running endlessly around an elliptical track, seeking a final victory but instead merely retracing the same prints again and again and again (cf. Cheng 1991, 106). History as repetition is the "back kick" the nightmare gives (2.379). Thus the sovereign coin bears upon it an equine emblem of historical oppression: its reverse face carries an engraving of the patron saint of England, St. George, astride a rearing horse, slaying a dragon (Reinfeld 1969, 180). It is precisely this

historical convergence of military and economic power that England
represents to Stephen and from which he tries to awaken by living
solely in the present.

Richard Ellmann comments that "the evidence of [Stephen's]
wakefulness [in regard to history] is his debts, which testify to his
attempt to live in the present, unconscionably it may be, but desper-
ately. Better debts than battening upon past and future. An I.O.U. is
an act of moral defiance" (1972, 21). But a more defiant act would be
to forgo IOUs altogether, and simply to borrow without promising to
repay. Without some token such as a *symbola* or IOU, the existence of
the debt depends solely upon the conscience of the debtor. If Stephen
could lose his conscience or his memory, he could assert, like Mulligan, that he is responsible for nothing. But he does acknowledge
them, at least to himself, and in scrupulous detail. In incurring and
acknowledging debts, one accepts the existence of an identity that
remains consistent over time. The acknowledgment of a debt creates
a connection between two moments; thus it does not free the debtor,
but rather attaches him to past and future. Indeed, a debt is a means
of "living on borrowed time" (Vernon 1984, 110). As we have seen in
his relationship with Mulligan, Stephen's debts only give his creditors
power over him, and remind him that there is no absolute escape
from history, and that he, too, lives on borrowed time.

Yet Ellmann is correct in suggesting that Stephen's debts cannot
be ascribed simply to carelessness. In fact, they are only a by-product
of his actual aim: to spend wastefully. His extravagant spending announces a defiance of economic norms designed further to separate
him from bourgeois characters like Deasy. As Vernon writes, "the
spendthrift spends as quickly as possible to hasten the moment when
he has nothing and the future takes on the character of the unknown"
(1984, 38). To live in the unknown is to live free from constraint. If
debts bind one to the future, squandering places one in the indeterminate present. It may be argued, in fact, that Stephen represents in
Ulysses one expression of what Georges Bataille calls *dépense* (expenditure). Bataille contends that in such rituals as the potlatch, in which
rivals compete by giving larger and larger reciprocal gifts, expenditure reconstitutes power as the power to lose (1985, 122). Prestige is
established by overwhelming rivals with one's generosity; in a twist
on conventional economic relations, the greatest loser establishes the
greatest prestige. Similarly, Stephen means to defy his perceived rivals by spending the money that they value, money that represents
the institutions that give them authority. It is thus not coincidental

that most of his expenditures occur where others can witness them: he spends money on drinks after "Aeolus," buys rounds in "Oxen," and pays for the whores in "Circe" not only to impress his friends but to proclaim his autonomy and prestige. Like Joyce's, Stephen's expenditures demonstrate that he actually treasures money as much as a miser does, and for the same reason: for the power it gives him, defined here as the power to lose. His spendthrift habits, like Joyce's, are thus a form of selfishness.[14]

Stephen's expenditures again demonstrate the relationship between his economics and his aesthetics. He seems to view his squandermania as necessary to his poetic efforts, apparently agreeing with Bataille that "poetry can be considered synonymous with expenditure; it in fact signifies . . . creation by means of loss" (1985, 120). Stephen spends prodigally for the same reason that Joyce did: to free himself from obstacles to his art. Conceiving of production as extravagant loss, he aims to purge himself of contaminants, to prepare himself for the sacrificial transformations—the exchange of flesh for words—which language must undergo to become art. But he cannot escape indebtedness through mere expenditures of language or money. By spending, he accumulates debts; rather than freeing him, they fetter him to the nightmare of national and personal history. If Stephen begins *Ulysses* in a state of dispossession and alienation even from his own body (the Linati schema says that "Telemachus does not yet bear a body"), the key to regaining his power lies in some form of repossession. He is inevitably attached to the material history represented by objects such as coins and bank notes; he must learn to manage these exchanges to produce art that is both aesthetically satisfying and politically potent. He must accept indebtedness without allowing it to enslave him (cf. McArthur 1988, 96).

Deasy gives Stephen more than money; he also offers him Nestorian advice about it. Like Mulligan, Deasy oppresses Stephen with "authoritative discourse" that seems to be "located in a distanced zone, organically connected with a past that is felt to be . . . higher. It

---

14. Herring (1989, 89) asserts that "while Stephen represents the gift exchange system, his ludicrous adversary Garrett Deasy . . . represents commerce." But Stephen doesn't represent gift giving in any systematic way; his spending is designed to benefit himself more than others. Nor does Stephen's system foster, as Herring claims, "humane feeling and mutual trust." He is motivated more strongly by hostility and defiance than by trust or humaneness.

is, so to speak, the word of the fathers" (Bakhtin 1981, 342–43).
Leaving his spuriously familial relationship with Mulligan, Stephen
meets another false father in Deasy, who pontificates: "You don't
know yet what money is. Money is power. . . . what does Shakespeare
say? *Put but money in thy purse.* . . . He knew what money was. . . . He
made money. A poet but an Englishman too. . . . Do you know what
is the proudest word you will ever hear from an Englishman's mouth?
. . . *I paid my way*" (2.236–51). To refuse to borrow, says Deasy, is
to be free. Unlike Stephen, Deasy sympathizes with this "English"
materialistic philosophy, just as he proclaims his loyalty to Ulster and
the English side in the Anglo-Irish conflict. Deasy ventriloquizes the
master's voice.[15] Joyce and Stephen's seeming disdain for Anglo-
Saxon commercialism notwithstanding, the hero of *Ulysses* is a commercial man. That Leopold Bloom assumes center stage implies that
Stephen needs some of this "Anglo-Saxon" materialism, both to make
ends meet and to integrate Irish art with English literary history.

The exchange between Stephen and Deasy forecasts in other
ways Stephen's encounter with Bloom. In both encounters, Stephen
receives money and fatherly advice, and while their symbolic and
emotional significance differs, the words of the scenes echo one another (see 2.229; 15.641). Unlike Deasy, however, Bloom's advice is
reinforced by deeds, as his generosity prevents Stephen from losing
even more of his money. Deasy admonishes Stephen not to waste his
money, "We are a generous people but we must also be just" (2.262),
to which Stephen answers, "I fear those big words . . . which make us
so unhappy." Such "big words," he fears, contribute to linguistic and
political oppression. But he listens to them: when Stephen hands
over his cash to Bloom in Bella Cohen's, he echoes Deasy, mockingly
advising Bloom to "be just before you are generous" (15.3605). Deasy,
of course, is neither generous nor just, as his anti-Semitic comments
reveal: "England is in the hands of the jews. In all the highest places:
her finance, her press. . . . Wherever they gather they eat up the nation's vital strength. . . . As sure as we are standing here the jew merchants are already at their work of destruction" (2.346–50). Like

15. Joyce similarly argues in "Ireland, Island of Saints and Sages" that Anglo-
Saxon civilization is "almost entirely a materialistic civilization" (*CW* 174). In his monograph on Daniel Defoe, he also depicts the English as quintessential consumers whose
economic behavior is typified by Falstaff, for his corpulence—an image of consumerism—and Robinson Crusoe, because he turns a profit from imperialism (Joyce 1964,
7, 27). Later Stephen borrows Deasy's description of the English artist for his portrait
of Shakespeare as Shylock in "Scylla and Charybdis."

Mulligan associated with the sun and brightness (Epstein 1974, 25), Deasy claims that the Jews have "sinned against the light" (2.361), a phrase that prompts Stephen's recollection of Jews in the Paris Stock Exchange: "goldskinned men quoting prices on their gemmed fingers. Not theirs: these clothes, this speech, these gestures. . . . Vain patience to heap and hoard. Time surely would scatter all. A hoard heaped by the roadside: plundered and passing on" (2.364–70).

These nominally "Jewish" economic habits (heaping and hoarding) contrast with Stephen's "Irish" ones (spending and drinking) throughout the novel. And yet Stephen regards the Jews as his comrades in dispossession. Forced to adopt foreign habits, languages and gestures, they keep money as insurance against further appropriations. But even this money is plundered, and again history appears as a thief who constantly disperses their money and destroys their carefully laid plans to defeat its tyranny. Since time scatters all treasures, Stephen thinks, why save money? Ironically, the anti-Semitic Deasy possesses precisely those stereotypically "Jewish" values that he claims to despise. But his joke that Ireland never persecuted the Jews because she never let them in, although factually false, is true in a sense; as Bloom's treatment by other Dubliners demonstrates, even Irish-born Jews remain outcasts in Ireland. While Deasy attributes England's decay to Jews, Stephen asserts cynically that "A merchant is one who buys cheap and sells dear, jew or gentile, is he not?" (2.359–60), and later modifies this point (16.737) to suggest that the real whores are they who sell not material but "spiritual assets" (*SH* 202), which are the ones he hopes to regain. The prostitution of spirit, he claims, is more damaging than that of the flesh.

Stephen's conversation with Deasy also predicts the meeting with Almidano Artifoni in section 6 of "Wandering Rocks" (10.338–66), itself a foreshadowing of his encounter with Bloom. If Deasy is Stephen's "English master," Artifoni is literally an "Italian master," but with him Stephen is affable and respectful.[16] Like Deasy (and like Bloom), Artifoni gives Stephen advice about art and economics and urges him to use his voice as a source of income (cf. 16.1659; 1820–25). Stephen does not scoff at Artifoni but says he'll "think about

---

16. Joyce borrowed Artifoni's name from his master in the Berlitz school where he taught in Trieste. The real Artifoni thus occupied the same position with respect to Joyce that Deasy does for Stephen. Joyce's financial relationship with the real Artifoni typically consisted chiefly of Joyce's importunities for loans. See *JJ* 60, and *L* II 149, 153, 155–56, 161, 178, 180-81, and 215–16.

it." Then Artifoni's "heavy hand t[akes] Stephen's firmly," and his "Human eyes" meet Stephen's (10.356). These visual and physical touches, exceptions to the less friendly touches Stephen receives from most of his advisers, are reenacted when Stephen leaves 7 Eccles Street (17.1183; 1222–23). Stephen's exchange of thoughts with Artifoni thus serves as a transition between his soon-to-be-abandoned relationship with Deasy and his impending one with Bloom. While Deasy's words are mainly concerned with himself and his own projects, Artifoni and Bloom seem genuinely to care about the financial and artistic plight of the young poet, although Bloom's concern is certainly self-interested as well. But as he departs Stephen calls Artifoni "maestro" (he too is an "Italian master"), and shows an untypical gratitude when he thanks him respectfully (10.361). All of these encounters with father figures, however, seem to bear out Stephen's view of history as repetition: all three offer the same wisdom, with the same lack of effect.

But Stephen also gives Deasy something, delivering his letter about a treatment for the foot-and-mouth disease threatening Irish cattle to some of his "literary friends" in the newspaper office and thus reciprocating for the master's money and words. That Stephen does agree to help Deasy suggests that he has some respect for this master, as does his assumption of the Deasyan role in "Proteus," where he admonishes himself to "go easy with that money like a good young imbecile" (3.59), but follows this advice about as well as he does Deasy's other advice. Like Mulligan, however, Deasy figures his encounter with Stephen as a duel, saying that he "likes to break a lance" with Stephen (2.425), upon which heraldic words and images of knighthood intrude upon the narrative and Stephen's thoughts (2.429–30). The next episode indeed portrays Stephen as a knight who, fortune and mission in pocket, sets out on his own version of the grail quest. But his journey is not to find religious redemption but rather to discover the source of his own artistic knighthood and eventually to repossess the crown that signifies his desired artistic identity and authority ("Stephanos" means "crown"). In "Proteus" Stephen once again returns to the treasure house of language he built in *Portrait,* hoping to rediscover the source of his poetic power, a universal equivalent that may yield renewed linguistic capital.

DIGGING FOR BURIED TREASURE

Although the action of "Proteus" is mostly internal and therefore without financial or social exchanges, Stephen's dialogue with himself is highly emblematic of a shift in his economic attitudes. Since the end of *Portrait*, where he assumed management of the treasure house of language and wore the mantle of linguistic authority, he has fallen from grace and potency; he has lost both his anchor and his capacity to carry out the verbal exchanges necessary for art. Thus, while walking on the strand, he considers both stability and flux, and acknowledges the threats and values in each condition. In seeking the origins of language, he attempts to rediscover the key to his word-hoard and thereby to rediscover the heroic identity that treasure had defined. He must find a universal equivalent, an entity that, like money, stabilizes and measures exchanges and also mediates their circulations. By the end of "Proteus" he has found the linguistic key that enables him to take some necessary, though tentative and halting, steps toward reconnecting himself with the material world. The episode ends with Stephen writing a poem and depositing his material signatures on the shore. These spiritual and material deposits become his currency, a means to link origins and ends and thereby transform the decay of matter into a cycle that makes both ends meet.

Stephen wrestles with two opposed threats in "Proteus." The first is flux and total dispossession, represented by the ceaseless movement of the ocean and the ever-shifting sands. The waters of the sea eternally circulate throughout the globe; no wave slapping the shore contains the same drops of water as the one before it. Like the water in the sea are the cells of human bodies: if everything is constantly changing, a person owns nothing, not even his own physical being. As we have seen, Stephen hopes to escape from the oppression of historical repetition by submitting to an economy of flow and circulation in financial expenditure, believing that he can thereby counteract decay. But in fleeing from the heritage of "dead shells," he encounters the opposite danger, that of anchorless, ceaseless circulation, as language and money, like water and sand, seem always to elude Stephen's grasp. Lacking a foundation for tropic exchanges, language becomes merely a series of displacements, and money sweeps its possessor along in its flow. As in *Portrait*, Stephen immerses himself in the economy of flows but risks drowning in it like a poor swimmer in the sea. Lacking an anchor, he wanders, like Ulysses, homeless.

According to Vico, Proteus is actually Menelaus's own reflection in the water; hence his struggle is really a confrontation with himself (1968, 261). Likewise, in submitting to ceaseless circulation, Stephen is wrestling with the Protean changes in his own image, as reflected in his memory and language. That is, since Stephen defines his identity linguistically, the instability in symbolic forms like language threatens him with the loss of self. Such dispossession is liberating but also alienating; thus Stephen both fears and desires it. Looking ironically upon his earlier writings and aesthetic postures, he addresses himself as "you" and encounters versions of himself everywhere: in his "consubstantial father's voice" (3.62), in his imagined visit to his uncle's house, in his memories ("you bowed to yourself in the mirror, stepping forward to applause earnestly, striking face"; 3.137), in the dying exiled Irishman Kevin Egan, in the cocklepickers he encounters, and even in their dog. Splitting himself into a Janus-faced figure —one face looking forward, the other backward—he still lacks a way of unifying his past and future. He now recalls the affectations of his Parisian exile: "Other fellow did it: other me. Hat, tie, overcoat, nose. *Lui, c'est moi.* . . . Whom were you trying to walk like? Forget: a dispossessed. With mother's money order, eight shillings" (3.182–84). To forget is to be dispossessed, but even the memory that should unify identity is only a recollection of dispossession. Indeed, Stephen's willful dispossessions have merely mirrored those of other Irish exiles like Kevin Egan; like them, Stephen remains "loveless, landless, wifeless" (3.253).

By dispossessing himself of the symbols of wealth he has tried to prevent eternal recurrence, to liberate himself from history as quicksand or nightmare. The ocean also symbolizes this danger through its constantly returning tide and in the flotsam it deposits. The sea and the shore leave traces of old lives, "[h]uman shells" (3.157), those dark, cunning "nets" of familial and national history he hoped to escape. In this guise the "heavy sands" bear the burdens of material history, appearing as "language tide and wind have silted here" (3.288). The physical world becomes a text and the strand a library, so that "when one reads these strange pages of one long gone one feels that one is at one with one who once . . ." (3.145). In this light, the very reflections of himself that marked the dissemination of his identity now appear as oppressive repetitions. Even his dispossession is incomplete: impoverished in Paris, he was forced to carry his mother's money order, which bound him to family and Ireland. The estates bequeathed to him by his family—his name, his body, his linguistic and financial heritages—are "houses of decay" (3.105), and he again urges himself to "come out of them" (3.106). In fleeing one danger, Stephen is swept up by its polar opposite; "Proteus" traces his attempts to defeat both repetition and flux.

To do so he becomes a forager on the shores of time, a scavenger for buried or lost semiotic jewels: "Signature of all things I am here to read, seaspawn and seawrack, the nearing tide, that rusty boot. Snotgreen, bluesilver, rust: coloured signs" (3.2–4). Such "wild sea money" (3.19), that debris of history, litters the beach beneath his feet. Stephen wants to discover both the sources of symbolic thought in matter and the origins of matter in language: the world becomes words, and words as signs reveal the world. Musing on birth and death, he imagines that "The cords of all link back, strandentwining cable of all flesh. . . . Aleph, alpha: nought, nought one" (3.37). The umbilical cord trails, not back to flesh, but to primal signifiers, just as Stephen's walk on the strand excavates both material and symbolic origins. Thus the "sense" of "Proteus" according to the Linati schema is "Prima Materia," and the Gorman-Gilbert schema describes its art as "philology." Both demand a search for origins; thus, in confronting physical exchanges, Stephen also considers the nature of symbolic exchange. Philology follows linguistic cords back to their sources, hoping to resurrect dead signifiers and promote their reemergence into and recirculation in the linguistic marketplace. It aims to discover buried linguistic treasure that will enrich the language and its users. Stephen's philological expedition is therefore a quest for a kind of semiotic holy grail, itself thought to be the "source of all things," a cornucopia holding all things of value, at once source and symbol of all gifts (Shell 1982, 41). Stephen's linguistic grail not only represents the world and measures its wealth but also participates in its own circulating economy, as words acquire, lose, and regain meaning and value over time. However, as Shell observes, "money, which refers to a system of tropes, is also an 'internal' participant in the logical or semiological organization of language, which itself refers to a system of tropes" (1982, 3). The material exchanges in the cosmos are recapitulated in the exchanges in language and money, which are simultaneously material and symbolic; hence, Stephen's exploration of material exchange, flux, and repetition leads him to investigate several symbolic economies, including that of money.

The economies emerged nearly simultaneously in ancient Greece, one of whose philosophers Stephen (wittingly or unwittingly) invokes. His consideration of cosmic flux echoes Heraclitus, who wrote that "Everything flows and nothing abides; everything gives way and nothing stays fixed," and its corollary: "You cannot step twice into the same river, for other waters and yet others go ever flowing on" (Wheelwright 1966, 70, 71; Frag. 20 and 21). The instability that Heraclitus describes also infects his language, which is full of puns and proliferating verbal exchanges.[17] Like the cosmos, Heraclitus's language is elusive and ever-changing; thus "instead of equality between substantives of performance, we find reciprocity between verbs of change" (Vlastos 1947, 165). Reciprocity signifies *ex*change, and so, because it both describes and inscribes physical exchanges, Heraclitus's verbal economy reflects not merely chaotic flux but rather an ordering principle: it is not a chaos but a *cosmos*, and an economy—a cosmic economy.

In reflecting upon "the activity of metaphorization itself," Heraclitus implicitly reflected and analyzed the economic changes occurring in Greek culture (Shell 1978, 51). Indeed, his description of the cosmos as subject to indiscriminate flux captures a historical moment in which "the extended form of value" was the predominant economic mode (Goux 1990, 15). In this economy all commodities may be exchanged for one other; no standard (such as money) exists to mediate exchanges or stratify value. Every commodity is "caught in the interminable contradictions of a relativism in which no one component prevails" (Goux 1990, 15). Eventually economies evolve from this condition to a "generalized form" in which a single commodity becomes an equivalent that measures all others. This in turn develops into a money economy, in which gold functions as a "universal" or "general equivalent" of all commodities (Goux 1990, 16–17). Heraclitus describes cosmic commerce in terms of just such an equivalent: "There is an exchange of all things for fire and of fire for all things, as there is of wares for gold and of gold for wares" (Wheelwright 1966, 71; Frag. 28). Like fire, gold functions as a universal equivalent or medium of exchange and yet also participates in exchanges. It is both a measure of values (an Imaginary function) and a circulating medium (a Symbolic function). The Heraclitean cosmos is therefore based upon the unchanging principle of exchange itself, a principle reflected in the fragment's own modulating terms. Tropic exchange reflects physical and economic exchange (Shell 1978, 52–54). For Heraclitus, language both partakes of *and* symbolizes the exchanges and transformations in the cosmos; it both participates in exchanges and acts as a substrate or medium for them. It is thus homologous to gold as money, which may act both as a measure of exchange value and as a commodity to be exchanged.

17. Joyce was acquainted with the Heraclitean fragments as early as 1903, when he referred to him in his review of Lewis McIntyre's book on Bruno (*CW* 134). For a discussion of the language of Heraclitus and its relation to the money form, see Shell 1978, 51–62. My numbering of the Heraclitean fragments follows Wheelwright's.

Similarly, when Stephen reads the "signatures of all things" in the physical artifacts he finds on the beach, and when he contemplates the eternal changes in the commerce between ocean and sand, he is ineluctably led to reflect upon both this physical economy and the economies of language and money. If for Heraclitus the general equivalent is symbolized by fire, for Stephen it seems to be represented by water. His urination near the end of the episode therefore marks his attempt to enter into exchange with the world, to become a site of physical commerce and transformation: "Listen, a fourworded wavespeech: seesoo, hrss, rsseeiss, oos. Vehement breath of waters amid seasnakes, rearing horses, rocks. In cups of rocks it slops: flop, slop, slap" (3.456). Water is identified with language, as it both reflects the exchanges in matter and undergoes exchanges of its own.

And yet mere exchange, even through a universal equivalent, still presents the danger of infinite or ceaseless flux. Language must be brought to refer to something outside itself—to ideas, objects or concepts—in order to acquire meaning, and hence value, and thereby conquer absolute flux. In this sense, a concept may be analogous with a coin, since both are "universal equivalents, resulting from similar dialectical processes. They represent 'essences' " (Goux 1990, 96). Such entities stand outside the circulation of commodities, becoming the sovereigns that govern all other exchanges, even as they incite them. Thus Heraclitus's fragment 28 describes universal exchange, beneath which lies the unity of gold or fire, a symbol of the *logos*, or Word, which is the standard of value that gives order to the seeming randomness of exchange. Like the grail, it is a signature or source of all things, a rock around which the waters of eternal flux circulate, a sameness beneath differences. Like gold, the *logos* is a fixed standard that transforms the chaos of ceaseless exchange into a cosmos, an economy. Stephen seeks just such a universal value, an "anchoring point that moors the floating chain of signifiers" (Goux 1990, 103). Such a norm would function as a linguistic gold standard, as the "umbilical or gravitational anchor that ensures the consistency of a system of conventional or signifying marks and prevents them from drifting or floating in relation to the valences they are meant to signify" (Goux 1990, 114). A *logos* would both moor him (and his language) to the here and now and provide a philological "strandent-wining cord" trailing back to essences, and thereby anchor him to history through the linguistic treasury of past meanings. As in *Portrait*, here Stephen turns to language as his currency, hoping it will generate unity while still enabling creative metamorphoses. His philology therefore proceeds by borrowing old words and texts, halting their circulation and fixing their meaning, and then redepositing them into history with interest added. Philology—the search for buried linguistic treasure—may reconnect him to history and thereby reconstitute his identity. In reconciling transformation and identity, he may generate, like Heraclitus, a set of cyclic economies that will enable him to link origins and ends, to make both ends meet.

Throughout the episode both Stephen's thoughts and Joyce's narration are full of archaic or unusual words—"lourdily," "lollop," "grike," "eely," "dislove," "bing," and so on—drawn from the Anglo-Saxon and Romance heritages that constitute his linguistic patrimony.[18] In the recollection and use of ancient words, Stephen and Joyce metaphorically imitate the quest of the cocklepickers Stephen encounters (3.342); the writers seek lost shells, "tough nuggets" of language that may patter in one's pockets (3.388). The cocklepickers seem to exist only through the prism of Stephen's language, which constantly reconstitutes and transforms their activities as the woman "trudges, schlepps, trains, drags, trascines her load" (3.392–93). Near synonyms, each of these words has a different philological origin, and as each is exchanged for a new one, the characters and actions depicted subtly change (Gifford 1988, 62). Later Stephen peers through a lapidary's window, recalls the cocklepickers, observes dust sleeping on the gems and imagines that he wrests "old images from the burial earth" (10.802–4; 814). Like miners digging for gems, so poets, philologists and orators extract old images, words and phrases from the past. This intertextual "treasure," as Stephen calls it in *Portrait* (*P* 166), necessitates that one dig like a crab through shifting linguistic sands to find a "home" for words. Conceiving of language as the detritus of history, Stephen seeks to turn this flotsam into treasure and thereby discover the *logos* beneath transformation.

The cocklepickers' dog represents the threat Stephen perceives in protean reality, as well as his enslavement to Mulligan ("panthersahib and his pointer" 3.277–78). Vowing not to be "master of others or their slave" (3.295), Stephen pledges not to return home to Mulligan: "He has the key. I will not sleep there when this night comes. . . . Take all, keep all" (3.276–79). In the dog's apparent transformations into a hare, buck, bear, fawn, fox, pard, and panther (changes

18. McArthur (1988, 82) estimates that roughly 1400, or one-quarter, of the words or signs in "Proteus" are directly borrowed from written or spoken sources. In this regard, philology is related to history as intertextuality, an issue considered in chapter 6.

by metaphoric transfer), Stephen sees himself as "poor dogsbody. Here lies poor dogsbody's body" (3.351; cf. 1.112, 137). Like Stephen, the dog seems to be "looking for something lost in a past life," perhaps "something he buried there, his grandmother" (3.333; 360). Looking both forward and backward, Stephen sees the dog's corpse as evidence both of an old self he has lost or transcended, and of his ultimate goal—death. The dog digs, but it is unclear whether it is unearthing or burying, just as Stephen seems simultaneously to be burying and digging up his past.

The dog's protean qualities also represent Mulligan himself, who is both what Stephen would like to become and what he would like to leave behind, and whose heroic rescue of a drowning man prompts thoughts of Stephen's other home: "Would you do what he did? . . . I would want to. I would try. I am not a strong swimmer. . . . Do you see the tide flowing quickly in on all sides, sheeting the lows of sands quickly, shellcocoacoloured? If I had land under my feet. I want his life still to be his, mine to be mine. A drowning man. His human eyes scream to me out of horror of his death. I . . . With him together down . . . I could not save her. Waters: bitter death: lost" (3.320–30). In this passage the drowner changes from the man drowned nine days ago, to his father (whose inundation is detailed in later chapters), to his mother and sister Dilly, whom he meets in "Wandering Rocks": "She is drowning. Agenbite. Save her. . . . She will drown me with her, eyes and hair" (10.875). The "shellcocoa" color of the sand likewise derives from Stephen's recollection of how his sisters wait for "some weak Trinidad shell cocoa," a thin beverage that embodies their poverty (16.271). Stephen has the choice of sacrificing himself for his family or letting them sink and saving himself. To rescue someone from drowning makes one responsible for that life; thus, while Stephen's refusal to save his father and family from drowning in debts and poverty fosters guilt, it also saves him from drowning with them.

Ultimately, then, Stephen rejects both his Martello home and the home of the Dedalus family, instead seeking in language an *oikos* or home that will both stabilize the transformations that threaten him and enable more manageable transformations. The identity and authority he seeks in the anchoring logos of artistic language is nevertheless homologous with fatherhood. As Goux writes, "the existence of a signifier intended to define all effects produced by the signifier and to prevent arbitrary, floating, slipping signs . . . from losing their convertibility . . . [is] globally indicated by an axis linking phallus and

father" (1990, 115). As I have argued elsewhere in regard to *Portrait,*
what Stephen seeks in language is a fixed standard that mimics the
father's privileged position both inside and outside of the economies
of metaphoric transfer (Osteen 1995). Money (gold), father, and
meaning are symbols of the *logos* in the registers of economics, ego-
formation, and language, respectively. Just as one's father establishes
one's identity and social position, so language may stabilize the alter-
ations and exchanges in reality. In rejecting his father, Stephen rejects the identity and the political and economic impoverishment that
Simon represents, in favor of another economy, in which words both
moor and "float him" (Tucker 1984, 33). Language must be his anchor and his buoy; it must enable him to father himself.

At one point Stephen briefly imagines himself burying treasure
in the sand: "Hide gold there. Try it. You have some" (3.290). But
though he does not literally hide his money in the sand, he does make
other deposits that signal his acceptance of material reality and his
(tentative) reattachment to a productive linguistic economy. As the
cocklepickers pass, he begins to compose an erotic poem about vam-
pires: "Here. Put a pin in that chap, will you? My tablets. Mouth to
her kiss. No. Must be two of em. Glue 'em well. Mouth to her mouth's
kiss" (3.399–400). The "gluing" of the mouths together dramatizes
how words, deposited on paper, may arrest flux and decay. Searching
his pockets, he mistakes his bank notes for writing paper ("Paper.
The banknotes, blast them") and then scribbles on the bottom of
Deasy's letter (3.404–5). Money and writing are identified here as
currency subject to transformation, decomposition, and proliferation.
For Stephen, as for Joyce, writing replaces money and functions as
his medium for social and material exchanges. Stephen's momentary
conflation of money and writing paper symbolizes his Berkeleyan
recognition of the arbitrary value and meaning of his own signs, and
their tenuous relation to the material world (see Goux 1990, 106–9).
But by writing he rejects Berkeleyean immaterialism and begins to
reconsider his own avoidance of materiality.

The full text of Stephen's poem does not appear until he thinks
of it in the newspaper office (7.522–6): *"On swift sail flaming / From
storm and south / He comes, pale vampire, / Mouth to my mouth."* As Gifford
(1988, 62) shows, the poem is a slightly modified version of the last
stanza of Douglas Hyde's poem, "My Grief on the Sea." Appropriately, it embodies its own indebtedness, the spectre of intertextuality
rearing its head like a vampire in Stephen's consciousness: the poem
is about the persistence of the past, and at the same time enacts it.

But although Stephen's poem is largely borrowed, it is not merely a "poetic defeat" (Kenner 1987, 57). In fact, Stephen is only doing on a small scale what Joyce himself does in such episodes as "Aeolus," "Scylla and Charybdis" and "Oxen": borrowing the words of another writer and adapting them for his own production (McArthur 1988, 83). His composition instead demonstrates his recognition of history as materiality and his awareness of the unavoidable indebtedness that binds him by the "strandentwining cord" of intertextuality to the stock of language already written. Just as debtorship is a fact of social life, intertextuality is a fact of literary life; Stephen's recognition of both kinds of debtorship is a necessary first step to a renewed acceptance of materiality that will reattach him to history.

His poem acknowledges the presence of the past but, as a material deposit, also marks his movement toward linguistic mastery. It combines creation and philology, at once exhuming an old text and giving birth to a new one. And yet it remains incomplete because Stephen does not share it. Therefore, although it constitutes an exchange with the past, it remains isolated from the contemporary linguistic marketplace, from the commerce of response and consumption, from that social circulation that enables texts to influence both their own age and succeeding times. The deposit is thus only the beginning; it must now be circulated by other speakers and writers to acquire enhanced value through interpretive transformation. Writing that remains outside this cyclic economy of production and consumption will fail to fulfill to the Symbolic function in the linguistic economy and remain only a dead shell.

Stephen makes other material deposits that moor him to the physical world. First, his urination indicates his acceptance of circulation, as he adds his flow, his currency, to the flow of matter. Second, at the end of the episode, Stephen gropes in his pocket for a handkerchief and, failing to find one, carefully wipes his snot on a rock (3.500). Joyce's juxtaposition of Stephen's writing and his excremental productions is significant: a forager or miner, the artist must take what has been discarded as having exhausted its value and transform these substances into artistic gold (see Gose 1980, 133). The poet's imagination creates exchanges that synthesize flux and repetition, turning coal into more valuable forms of the identical element: carbon becomes coal, which is mined from the "burial earth" and then transubstantiated by imaginative fire in the "smithy of [his] soul" (*P* 253) into a precious gem. Stephen's poem and snot move in opposite directions: the poem is spirit becoming matter, words becoming buried treasure, while the snot is offal, living matter becoming dead shell. Both, however, issue from Stephen and then circulate in a material or verbal economy. Both embody Stephen's submission to exchange and catalyze his verbal deposits in the rest of the novel.

Stephen's movement toward accepting physical reality helps to cancel his earlier extreme alienation. This movement is shown in his rumination on the drowning man, as he imagines pulling the corpse up from the ocean and meditates on material transformations: "God becomes man becomes fish becomes barnacle goose becomes featherbed mountain. Dead breaths I living breathe, tread dead dust, devour a urinous offal from all dead" (3.477–80). The notion that God becomes matter again recalls Heraclitus, for whom "God is day and night, winter and summer, war and peace, satiety and want. But he undergoes transformations, just as ——— when mixed with a fragrance is named according to the particular aroma which it gives off " (Frag. 121, Wheelwright 1966, 79). Beneath the flux is a universal solvent or equivalent; Heraclitus's God, like Stephen's, lies at the source of metamorphoses. Although the missing word in the fragment is not literally "gold" (it is probably "water"), nevertheless it functions again as a universal medium of exchange or *logos* and thus is metaphorically linked to the fire in Fragment 28 and to the gold that is exchanged for all things (see Shell 1978, 53–54). That Stephen places God at the source of transformation implies that he now acknowledges a *logos,* a standard behind all exchanges.

Heraclitus depicted the cosmos as a cycle or circle. There is a downward path for metamorphoses, through which fire becomes water and finally inanimate stone; but there is also an upward road which leads back to the divine fire (Wheelwright 1966, 82–83). Unlike Heraclitus's, Stephen's road is downward only. It is not a cycle, but a fall: God ends by becoming an inanimate featherbed mountain (R. Ellmann 1972, 24). Stephen's inability to connect the ends of the cycle of transformation implies that, despite his provisional acceptance of materiality, he still conceives of the material world as corrupt. He has not yet linked origins and ends; he does not make ends meet. Remaining ambivalent and rebellious, his acceptance of materiality is incomplete. Many critics have discussed Joyce's tendency to make the end and beginning of his texts flow into one another. For Joyce, the artistic process simultaneously initiates destruction and creation, brings loss and redemption, links birth and death (Riquelme 1983, 4). This ability to "make both ends meet" is an essential quality that Stephen lacks and that Bloom possesses; Bloom's cyclic and redemptive view of the cosmos will ultimately replace Stephen's linear one. Stephen's artistic currency may one day enable him to fuse originality and intertextuality, debtorship and expenditure, and create himself as a kind of linguistic capitalist. But as yet this redemptive labor remains only potential, and his anxiety about money and his obsession with expenditure parallel his ambivalence about his literary production.

Even though Stephen is still alienated and increasingly irrational in his later chapters, nevertheless he is more the center of attention, more assertive and more confident. Still, the acts of deposition he performs in "Proteus" are necessary but not sufficient. He remains psychically and economically out of balance, and his squandering of money symbolizes in the economic register his squandering of artistic talent and unfulfilled capacity for love. Although, as we have seen, Joyce deemed his spendthrift habits necessary for the preservation of his genius, *Ulysses* now moves away from Stephen, and also from the implicit affirmation of the principle of expenditure he represents, and toward Bloom, whose more balanced economy forms a highly significant element of Joyce's new portrait of the hero. Even in Stephen's next two episodes, Bloom is present in the background as a shadowy presence or silent critic of Stephen's behavior. And while Stephen begins to rediscover the key to his word-hoard and hence to renewed verbal power, his triumph, if it ever comes, is never dramatized. The movement from Stephen to Bloom to the larger canvas of Dublin thus inscribes Joyce's growing fascination and reconciliation with bourgeois economic norms and his awareness of the wider and more complex social and economic world—a world of household finance, advertising, and popular culture. Indeed, the rest of *Ulysses* becomes both a critical document of Irish social life and a kind of encyclopedia of the economic behaviors that enrich and impoverish Joyce's and Bloom's Dublin. When Joyce begins to reinstate the principle of expenditure, he does so through an artistic economy of extravagance that confirms his superiority to Stephen by the very fact of his enormous labor and productivity.

3

Economic Man

A Merchant sitting at home in his Counting-house, at once converses with all Parts of the known World. This, and Travel, makes a True-bred Merchant the most Intelligent Man in the World, and consequently the most capable.
—Defoe, 1702, 8

THE ART OF HUSBANDING

Odysseus' travels in the *Odyssey* challenge his capacity for flexibility. As James Redfield has argued (1983, 226), Homer's hero is constantly faced with the problem of "necessary means": the need to balance and synthesize opposite and extreme forces. The adventures oscillate between violence and passivity, between an excess and a deficiency of civilization. Thus Odysseus is "the victim, alternately, of hypo-entertainment and hyper-entertainment. In hypo-entertainment the stranger is treated as a creature of another species, a beast or fish . . . to be incorporated into . . . another. Hyper-entertainment, by contrast, threatens cultural incorporation: the traveller is to be transformed by his host and so perfectly socialized that he can never leave" (Redfield 1983, 237). The same might be said of Leopold Bloom's adventures, although his episodes do not alternate so mechanically. Bloom is threatened by violence in "Lestrygonians," "Wandering Rocks" and "Cyclops"; in contrast "Lotus-Eaters," "Sirens," and "Nausicaa" show his imminent seduction. Hypo-entertainment operates by the negative reciprocity that menaced Stephen in "Telemachus," in which economic exchanges disguise hostility; the antidote lies in generosity and gift exchange. Hyper-entertainment promises leisure, bountiful presents, and the welcoming arms of a surrogate family. Since the danger in such spurious generosity is the loss of identity and intellectual distance, here the traveler must be shrewd, hardheaded, mercenary. Of course, both extremes are similar in that they threaten to absorb the voyager: decadence and barbarism are two sides of a single coin (Redfield 1983, 242). These opposed threats are alike in requiring a resilient psychic economy and a flexible economic philosophy, both of which Bloom possesses. Like Odysseus, Bloom must find a balance between extremes: he must respond to seduction with skepticism and cost-accounting, to violence with charity and mildness. Throughout *Ulysses* Bloom shuttles between a shrewd, sometimes mercenary, analysis of economic benefits and a generous willingness to offer gifts to the needy. The challenge for Bloom, as for Odysseus, is to "husband his resources, not consume, or not too much, or too soon" (Redfield 1983, 239): he must practice the art of husbanding.

It is clear from the first sentence of "Calypso"—"Mr Leopold Bloom ate with relish the inner organs of beasts and fowls" (4.1–2)— that we have entered a world much different from the highly intellectual universe of Stephen Dedalus. Whereas Stephen, according to the Linati schema, "does not yet bear a body," Bloom delights in the one he bears. Of course, Stephen really does have a body, as his rotten teeth prove; but they also prove his alienation from it. Thus while Stephen's mind dwells upon religion, literature, and history, kidneys are in Bloom's mind. The "organ" of the episode (and of Bloom's breakfast), kidneys provide his palate with a "fine tang of faintly scented urine," signifying his intimate connection to the most ignoble and least valuable matter of all—excrement. Bloom appears to reside in a strictly material universe, and hence a straightforwardly economic one. While Stephen seems pathologically antipathetic to money (although, as we have seen, this fear also masks his appreciation of its power), Bloom, a man who sells newspaper advertisements, handles it as confidently as he handles the breakfast implements. In fact, Bloom is financially more solvent and more secure than most of the Dubliners in *Ulysses*. When Joyce, in his schema, described the "art" of Bloom's first episode as "economics," he was not merely being whimsical or cryptic: thoughts of money and economics permeate Bloom's consciousness at breakfast and throughout Bloomsday. His economic philosophy conditions his family life, his social encounters, his modes of expression, and extends even to his most far-ranging philosophical meditations. Bloom's activities, indeed, exemplify the classic definition of economics: "the study of mankind in the ordinary business of life" (quoted in McCloskey 1990, 148).

Despite his materialism, however, Bloom's economic life remains somewhat troubled. While prices seem to offer reassurance and stability in a world of perilous flux, they fail to furnish authentic security, precisely because money itself plays several contradictory roles. Money not only represents a standard of value (Imaginary function) and a real quantity that may be stored—signs of stasis—but also functions as a medium of circulation and hence a symbol of motion (Symbolic function). Similarly, Bloom vacillates between the merchant's model of balancing accounts and paying debts (a static model that seeks stability through repayment and stays aloof from personal and sexual claims) and the more personal, fluid gift-exchange model, in which persons and things are inextricably related through circulation. Because the reassurance he hopes to gain from constant contemplation of economic value remains problematic, the challenge for his economy is to find a balance between contrasting qualities.

Bloom's sense of balance is exemplified in the mercantile desire to equalize debits and credits. But his first balancing act is a physical one: "righting [Molly's] breakfast things on the humpy tray" (4.7–8).[1] Literally, of course, it means that he is balancing objects by upending them, but it also represents his economic philosophy. In contrast to Stephen, who willfully tries to remain out of balance, for Bloom all debits must be compensated by credits. Freud ([1924] 1959) argues that such a "tendency to stability" governing mental processes constitutes a psychic economy in which the pleasure principle and the reality principle strive for dominance but in healthy psyches reach an equilibrium (cf. Shapiro 1964, 3). Although this psychic balance is only figuratively economic, it is reflected in Bloom's seemingly constant concern with money and prices: both processes seek stability (cf. Maddox 1978, 49).[2] And yet Bloom's balancing act is also evidence of a generous nature: in bringing Molly breakfast in bed, he is practicing

---

1. Bloom's habitual "righting" has been pointed out by Senn (1984, 61), who goes on to argue that this "righting" characterizes the novel's presentation of alternative viewpoints, its "ameliorative diversity," in which each viewpoint is allowed to "correct" the others. Finally, he argues, the novel "develops a Bloomian type of consciousness" that "counteracts or compensates [for] whatever it is that it has been attempting so far" (1984, 66). Hence, the reader must also "right" (and write) the text by constantly revising his or her expectations and interpretations.

2. Bowen (1989, 2) notes that the tendency to create balance identifies both *Ulysses* and Bloom as fundamentally comic.

the art of husbanding his wife. Still, his generosity is clouded by a self-perceived lack of power and his anxiety over her impending adultery, which brings with the gift of attention an implied obligation.

Like Odysseus, in many ways Bloom is the epitome of *homo economicus*, a "facer of choices, a spurner of options known as 'opportunity costs' " (McCloskey 1990, 143). His cost accounting appears often in "Calypso." A commercial man, he respects anyone who is good at making money, even Molly's father, Major Tweedy, whom he otherwise gently mocks. "Wonder what her father gave for [the bed]. . . . Bought it at the governor's auction. Got a short knock. Hard as nails at a bargain, old Tweedy. . . . Still he had brains enough to make that corner in stamps. Now that was farseeing" (4.61–65). He is always on the lookout for bargains. Like Stephen's, his clothes are "secondhand" (4.67), but unlike Stephen, who is forced to borrow clothes from the usurper Mulligan, Bloom finds clothes at the "lost property office," and thus gets something for nothing. Possessions are more valuable if obtained at no charge: "Astonishing the things people leave behind them in trains and cloakrooms. . . . Unclaimed money too" (8.57–60). Both Stephen and Bloom seek to recover "lost property," but Bloom reclaims others' as well as his own; his economies are also generosities. More generally, Bloom attempts to recoup what he perceives as his lost "property"—his home, wife, and dead son—in the course of the novel, but also loses some property—money, keys, dignity—in the bargain. His quest to recover lost property is just one of his many methods of seeking renewal, as if by owning the previously owned one may reclaim both the property and the person who owns it.

The price of things is never far from Bloom's mind, and he recognizes how property values are all related in a market economy. For example, when he thinks of a plan for a new tramway along the North Circular road, he predicts that the value of O'Rourke's pub would "go up like a shot" (4.110). Prudently musing on the rising wealth of pub owners, he disapproves of the characteristic improvidence of Dublin's drinkers:

> Where do they get the money? Coming up redheaded curates from the county Leitrim. . . . Then, lo and behold, they blossom out as Adam Findlaters or Dan Tallons [two successful businessmen]. . . . General thirst. Good puzzle would be cross Dublin without passing a pub. Save it they can't. Off the drunks perhaps. Put down three and carry five. What is that, a bob here and there, dribs and drabs. On the wholesale orders perhaps. Doing a double shuffle with the

town travellers. . . . How much would that tot to off the porter in
the month? Say ten barrels of stuff. Say he got ten percent off. O
more. . . . Fifteen multiplied by. The figures whitened in his mind,
unsolved. (4.126–35)

The circulation of liquids and money are usually related in *Ulysses*, as
many of Joyce's male Dubliners spend too much money on booze,
seemingly striving to keep their cash flowing as freely as drinks.[3]
Excessive drinking draws money out of the customers' pockets and
puts it into the pub owners'; although the amounts are small, they
add up, and the publicans get rich. In contrast, Bloom drinks and
spends moderately: here too he husbands his resources, and his cash
flows less freely than his water. Thus his calculations of the relative
costs are characteristic of Bloom: when he sees waste, he seeks ways
to economize, either by conserving or by recycling, hoping to stabilize
the economy and his threatened psyche.

    This pursuit of balance and equilibrium identifies Bloom as Ulys-
ses. Like Homer's hero, Joyce's is "wise at profit-turning" (Shapiro
1964, 3; cf. Homer 1961, 285–89), in both the psychic and monetary
economies. Redfield even argues that "Odysseus does a kind of cost-
benefit analysis of everything, weighing present expenditures against
hoped-for utilities" (1983, 228). Although Bloom's commercial mentality is supplemented and sometimes threatened by a competing impulse toward generosity, his concern with costs links him to Homer's
hero; moreover, it indicates a healthy, pragmatic skepticism that
shields him from the economic and emotional extremism ubiquitous
in Dublin. In this respect, Bloom is a quintessential realist and uses
what Stephen Shapiro has called a "psychic profit-motive" to transform "unpleasurable experience into pleasurable or at least 'safe'
states of mind" and thus to retain psychic balance (1964, 5–6). In
some ways, then, the shift from Stephen to Bloom is a shift from
idealism to realism.

Economies of Realism

    Bloom's devotion to materiality and the episode's celebration of
the grit of real life seem to mark "Calypso" as a return to a more

    3. See, for example, Bloom's portrayal of Stephen's uncle Richie Goulding, a
prototypical Dubliner whose false economies disguise his improvidence: "Fecking
matches from counters to save. Then squander a sovereign in dribs and drabs"
(11.620–21).

conventional literary realism. This movement is also economic: as Vernon notes, "in the realistic novel all objects have price tags" (1984, 67). To a significant degree, this is true of Bloom's world: he subjects every activity to economic analysis and calculates the cost of all properties. Returning home after his kidney purchase, for example, he notices that "Number eighty [is] still unlet. Why is that? Valuation is only twentyeight" (4.235). Regarding his picture of the *Bath of the Nymph,* he immediately recalls paying "three and six" for the frame (4.371). Property, for Bloom, is identified by its price, and virtually all objects can be bought and sold. Bloom's world is thus a commodified world of objects whose use-value is often secondary to their value as exchangeable merchandise. Vernon's point suggests that prices reflect the semiotic relationship in the episode's language as well; that is, when we enter Bloom's cosmos, we reenter a stable and reliable world where the text transparently describes a recognizable reality and lodges in a homely domain of kidneys, cats, and outhouses. Moreover, just as Bloom relishes matter, the narrator of "Calypso" seems to delight in words—"nutty gizzards," "dung," "bloodgouts"—that graphically describe the most banal and unsavory material objects. Indeed, "Calypso" seems more realistic than even nineteenth-century fiction, since for the first time the reader is allowed to accompany a character to the jakes: no action is too mundane, too merely sensual, to escape imaginative description.

"Calypso" is an "economical" chapter in another sense: the prose style suppresses the tendency towards excess displayed already in "Proteus" and overwhelmingly apparent in later episodes of *Ulysses.* Mimicking Bloom's own thriftiness, Bloom's first episode describes his thoughts in economical prose: "Heaviness: hot day coming. Too much trouble to fag up the stairs to the landing. A paper. He liked to read at stool. Hope no ape comes knocking just as I'm." (4.463–66). If Stephen embodies the principle of expenditure, Bloom appears to represent its opposite, the conservation of money and meaning. In more than one respect, both the narrative and Bloom's thoughts exemplify an important principle of literary and moral realism: minimizing excess (Michaels 1987, 38). The author of a realist fiction fulfills an ideological function: to embody what Foucault calls "the principle of thrift in the proliferation of meaning" (1979, 159), restraining the free play of signification and binding it to representationalism and transparent reference. In fact, "Calypso" appears to employ most of the tactics ascribed to realism by recent theorists: it accepts "the riches of the world" (Stern 1973, 28); it assumes that language copies the material world but remains secondary to it; it presents a relatively transparent style that hides the author's presence.[4]

But upon closer examination, it is clear that the language of "Calypso" is not merely transparent; rather, it constantly calls attention to itself, even as it portrays mundane events in earthy terms. Both words and objects are ceaselessly transforming themselves and constantly endangered by decay and dissolution. As H. M. Steele points out, one of the strongest threats to the realist aesthetic is "fluidity at the level of meaning (e.g., puns, metaphors)" (1988, 6). Thus, in one short passage, Bloom and his breakfast kidney undergo numerous metamorphoses. Smelling it burning, Bloom hastens down the stairs with "a flurried stork's legs." The smoke from the kidney now seems "angry"; then Bloom turns the kidney "turtle on its back" and finally eats the "toothsome pliant meat" (4.384–91). Bloom becomes a bird, the smoke is personified, the kidney becomes a reptile and then seems to exchange qualities with the person consuming it ("toothsome"). These transformations (mostly conventional—albeit striking—poetic devices) announce themselves as metaphors, as both substitutions for, and representations of, a stable world. Such extravagant tropes both reflect and produce exchanges, as they simultaneously proclaim the presence of an author and subvert the author's function as a principle of thrift. Meanings shift and proliferate as such tropes remind us that reference is constantly subjected not only to self-reflexivity but to the dual forces of decay and multiplication.

Even objects, like the name of Bloom's "high grade ha," decay. Still others, such as Bloom's soap and potato, take a variety of forms throughout the day. Like the kidney, which both transforms food and undergoes transformation when eaten, words and things reciprocally process and transmute each other. These transformations and decompositions reach their culmination in "Circe," but a sense of the inherent instability of matter and language is present from the beginning of the novel. In contrast, literary realism, like the gold standard,

---

4. I have drawn this list of features from H. Meili Steele (1988, 5–6), who cites Philippe Hamon as her source. Steele's introduction (1–9) provides a useful summary of realist conventions. Among the critics who read *Ulysses* as a realistic novel are Raleigh (1977, 6), Gordon (1981 and 1991), Chace (1991), and Lawrence (1981, 11–12), who, despite her astute recognition of the surplus of detail in the novel, interprets the stylistic excesses as reflecting reality rather than as contributing to its (de)construction. I would argue that the excesses of *Ulysses* aim to subvert this conventional economy of meaning.

attempts to provide that "anchor" that prevents signifiers from "drift-ing" into new significations (Goux 1990, 114). Thus, just as realism offers a fixed relationship between language and reality that merely disguises both its own transformations and those in matter, so Bloom's cost accounting and price fixing are responses to the (sup-pressed) recognition that the material world is in constant flux. Bloom's price fixing is a reaction to anxiety: when threatened by thoughts of death, cuckoldry or loss, he finds comfort in reckoning costs. Hence his concern for the valuation of the number eighty (a neighbor's house) is an attempt to suppress his "morning mouth bad images" of desolation and horror, to combat the decay of things into "dead names" (4.222), and to fight his sense that his own house is being appropriated; the recollection of his picture's price diverts him from uneasiness about the definition of "metempsychosis." Price fix-ing is aimed at arresting flux and decay by freezing matter into stable, reassuring, and knowable shapes. Money seems to moor him firmly to earth.

As Vernon (1984) and Michaels (1987) have shown, realism offers a transparent medium for the exchange of words for things, just as money supposedly represents the quantified exchange value of ob-jects based upon a stable gold standard. Realism also attempts to efface its own origins, to elide its conventionality (DiPiero 1988, 12); it thereby becomes reified into a fetish that suppresses the social rela-tions behind its invention, like commodities in Marxist thought. Simi-larly, the addiction to price fixing as a stabilizer of circulation and change amounts to a kind of economic fetishism; that is, it erects prices as an attribute of things, rather than as a social relationship involving fluctuations, human subjectivity, and market demands (Goux 1990, 158). This "goldbug" aesthetic, as Michaels terms it (1987, 162), is doomed to fail because it ignores the nature of money. To see prices as stable reflections of value is to recognize only part of the function of money, just as referentiality is only one of the func-tions of fictional language. The stabilizing functions of money as a quantity one may hoard or keep (the "Real") and as a standard of value (the "Ideal" or "Imaginary") are supplemented by its function as a medium of exchange. Thus, although in its role as real quantity money "seems to avoid relativity," in its symbolic function, on the contrary, it "expresses nothing but the relativity of things that consti-tute value"; indeed, money is "interchangeability personified" (Sim-mel 1978, 121, 124). To perceive prices as evidence of stability, then, is to blind oneself to the fact that prices actually prove exchangeability, flux, circulation. Moreover, prices do not even arrest the decay of commodities, because commodities are not simply objects, but entities symbolically coded with the changing social relations embedded in their exchange-value. Far from establishing fixity and arresting perilous flux, then, Bloom's price reckoning actually involves him ineluctably in a world of shifting values, and of circulation and exchange.

"Calypso" subverts the conventions of realism even as it mimics them in virtuoso fashion. In turn, its antirealism, even in the early episodes, exposes Bloom's price fixing as an anxious response to potential change. Just as the objects in "Calypso" only seem to be stabilized either by their names or by their exchange values, so the language of the episode actually demonstrates the conventionality of both realism and reality. Just as prices are only agreed-upon valuations and their stability only apparent, so realism is revealed to be only one historical alternative, one method of perceiving and using both language and matter. And yet, as I have noted, *Ulysses* also tries to be more realistic than most nineteenth-century novels, as is suggested by Joyce's famous words about being able to reconstruct Dublin from his novel (Budgen 1960, 69). However, the "reality" it depicts is not the stable, secure one of many nineteenth-century fictions; it is a world constantly transforming itself, in part through the symbolic economies used to portray it. Returning to the nineteenth-century novel's concern with money and property, *Ulysses* historicizes the conventions of realism, simultaneously affirming and subverting them, as Bloom's economic mentality is placed within a world of fungible commodities. Like money, *Ulysses* has different signifying functions at different moments; it demands that the reader be a complete economist and respond to its shifting operations. Likewise, my critical method sometimes resorts to calculating prices, treats Bloom and Stephen as realistic characters, and traces Joyce's Dublin and Dubliners back to their real-life models; at other times it recognizes (and celebrates) the ways that *Ulysses* discourages such responses. Such a flexible approach, even though it aims to challenge and refine the economies of realism, is itself simply realistic.

Restoration

Bloom does sometimes recognize and even embrace the Symbolic function of money as proof of circulation; it is the other half of his economy, the portion that permits generosity, gift giving, and the cyclic movements he undergoes both mentally and physically. For

example, after reading an ad for Agendath Netaim (a plan for reclamation of farmland) Bloom has a vision of the Holy Land as "a barren
land" of utter sterility, immobility, and death (4.219–30). But he reclaims himself by following the cycle from a "sunken cunt" to Molly's
"ample bedwarmed flesh," from age to youth, and from sterility to
fertility. Then he makes another substitution, saving himself from
these cloud-borne images by envisioning the returning sun as a "girl
with gold hair on the wind," dressed "in slim sandals," running to
meet him (4.241–42)—these are pictures of his daughter Milly.
Bloom finds the antidote to deathly stasis in motion, in the sun's cyclic
return every morning to revivify the earth, and in his daughter's
symbolic repetition of the youth of her mother (cf. 14.1086–87;
1101–3, where a similar moment occurs). Bloom's psychic economy
here copies the cyclic exchanges in the phenomenal world to recover
lost psychic property. If at one stage the metamorphoses in the world
seem horrifying, at other times their continued motion rejuvenates.

Bloom likewise rescues himself from depression over Boylan's
letter to Molly ("Bold hand. Mrs. Marion" [4.244–45]) by reading
Milly's letter. In fact, their father-daughter relationship is defined
almost entirely in terms of gifts given and received, bearing out
Freud's connection between gifts and children outlined in chapter 1.
Perusing the letter for the first time, Bloom fills his "moustachecup,
sham crown Derby, smiling," a "birthday gift," for which his return
gift was an amberoid necklace that she later broke (4.283–84). The
letter thanks her "papli" for the lovely gift of a new tam (4.398–99).
Bloom's satisfaction with her epistle (he reads it twice) implies that the
letter itself functions as a gift sent by postal circulation and embodies
recycling and return both in its geographic journey and in his renewed perusal. (This association of letters and the gift economy is
extended in "Penelope.") Even Bloom's lessons (verbal exchanges)
with Milly are figured in "Ithaca" as reciprocal gift exchanges. There
we learn that he used his and Molly's wedding gifts (an owl and a
clock) to "Interest and instruct" Milly and that she "reciprocated" by
remembering to give him the moustachecup; that she "provided" for
his needs; and that she "admired" his knowledge (17.909–28). His
image of her is encoded in the gifts given, and she returns that image
and his own image reborn; this is the same rejuvenating trajectory
that, according to Stephen, Shakespeare experienced with his grand-
daughter (9.422–32). As gift receiver and giver, Milly is indeed his
"lookingglass from night to morning," bringing a sunny mood even when
she is only imagined (4.288). If Mauss is right that in gift exchanges

"things . . . are to some extent parts of persons, and persons . . . behave in some measure as if they were things" ([1925] 1967, 11), then
it follows that Milly's letter and gifts contain her essence and also
signify the theoretically limitless circulation of gifts. In these exchanges, Bloom experiences the regenerative power of circulation.

But Milly is away in Mullingar, trying to imitate her father by
earning money. She has turned fifteen the previous day, for the first
time spending a birthday away from home. This separation and her
budding sexuality cause Bloom intermittent anxiety, which prompts
him to calculate some reassuring prices and consider a circular journey—"Might take a trip down there. August bank holiday, only two
and six return"—by obtaining free passage "through M'Coy" (4.452–
54).[5] The business where Milly works as a "photo girl" (she is also
mentioned in "Telemachus") is "getting on swimming," a phrase that
reiterates the connection between economic and aquatic behaviors
developed below. Like her father, Milly is keeping her head well
above water financially: with a salary of "twelve and six a week"
(4.425) she makes a bit more than £2 14s per month; by comparison,
Stephen, a male seven years her senior with a college degree, earns
just over 16s 6d per week. Thus she earns about three-fourths as
much as Stephen (£2 14s vs. £3 12s per month): not that much, but a
fifteen-year-old girl indeed "might do worse" (4.425).[6] Also like her
father, Milly seems to be a water-lover: she likes Boylan's song about
"those lovely seaside girls"; during a holiday voyage on the ship *Erin's
King*, Bloom got seasick but she was "not a bit funky" (4.435); and she
is symbolically associated (through her language, her clothing, and
her relationship with Bloom) with another seaside girl, Gerty Mac-
Dowell. More generally, Bloom's thoughts about Milly's earnings are
an attempt to comfort himself about the death of his infant son Rudy.
Price reckoning (for stability, the 'Real" function of money) and
Milly's presence (a symbol of circulation, the "Symbolic" function of
money) work in tandem here to reassure Bloom. Milly is the gift that
was not lost, the child who did not die, the investment that can be
recovered. Her image thus saves him from drowning in melancholy,

----

5. In "Eumaeus," Bloom says he "figure[s] on going there" but the price has
increased from two and six to five and six (16.509). In any case, he forgets to "work"
M'Coy when he encounters him.

6. We recall that Eveline Hill ("Eveline") gets by on only 7s per week (*D* 38).
Ironically, at the end that story, she fears that Frank "would drown her" (*D* 41),
even though she is already drowning financially.

pulls his emotions back into equilibrium, and renews him by mirroring his own financial habits. Paradoxically, her value as gift to him is partly a result of her economic pragmatism.

Home Economics

Bloom's feeling of security is fragile, in part because, like Stephen, albeit more willingly, he is a servant in his household (his service of breakfast in bed is apparently habitual). Given the typical domestic roles of the time, this seems unusual, if not exactly sinister.[7] Molly's apparent mastery of the home parallels Greek precursors. According to Helene Foley, in the Homeric world "women's control over [the domestic] sphere is seen as natural, unproblematic" (1984, 66); Odysseus' travels merely help to demarcate the division of labor and to separate realms of economic and social dominance by clarifying "the nature and range of female power over the inner sphere of household production, and of the male power over the external world of agriculture, diplomacy and exchange" (Foley 1984, 68). Whether the same holds true of *Ulysses* depends not only upon one's definition of "control" but upon where one looks in the novel. After all, Molly does work outside the home at singing and Bloom labors to produce breakfast. Their economic and power relations are complicated; as we shall see in my discussion of "Penelope," Molly exerts some control over Bloom's earnings, but this dominion is also constrained by powerful social and economic forces.

What is most important is not the actual condition but the perceived one: Bloom believes that the *nomoi* (rules) of his *oikos* (home) are out of balance. In the etymological sense, the "economy" of his household is disrupted, if not by Molly's power, then by the author of the letter addressed to "Mrs Marion [not Mrs Leopold] Bloom" (4.244), as if Bloom were dead. Like Stephen, Bloom is threatened by usurpers, and the letter underscores the sense of dispossession they share. Stephen relinquishes his latchkey and likewise yields control over the tower; Bloom forgets his latchkey, unconsciously enacting his loss of domestic potency and his ambivalence about his cuckolding. As with Stephen, Bloom's loss of his key is a synecdoche of his larger sense of dispossession, his lack of "home rule," a condition that typifies all of Ireland. Bloom's insecurity also derives from his many ad-

7. For a discussion of Molly's dominion over Bloom that presents it in a more threatening light, see Glasheen 1974.

dress changes; a man who has moved as often as Bloom has is likely
to value domestic stability but feel threatened by dispossession.[8] Nevertheless, Stephen and Bloom are different: while Stephen's motion
through the novel is a linear progress toward an uncertain destiny
that may reward him with power, Bloom's motion is a return, not
only because he seeks balance in the economic sense of a return on
expenditures but also because he seeks to return to and reclaim his
own household, to reassume a more secure, husbandly role. He does
not seek to dominate his wife, but merely to feel that his home is his
own. An economic analysis of "Calypso" reveals that Bloom constantly
seeks to restore both his financial resources and his marriage: he
wants to husband both money and his wife. Bloom's enterprise—
righting—parallels Odysseus'; like the Homeric hero, Bloom's chief
goal is to "recover and reconstruct his own *oikos*" (Redfield 1983, 230).
Bloom's adventures are straightforwardly economic inasmuch as he
carries out a variety of exchanges; but they are etymologically economic because they emerge from his desire to reclaim his domestic
economy.

Yet Bloom remains ambivalent about his usurpation, vacillating
between a desire to interrupt it and confront Molly and a voyeuristic,
secret relish of his cuckolding. Likewise, he is ambivalent about his
lack of power, enjoying domination and its concomitant freedom
from responsibility and at the same time resisting this impotence.
Molly appears as "Calypso," the nymph who in book 5 of the *Odyssey*
holds Odysseus captive until Hermes tells her to set him free. Since
"Calypso" means "I hide" or "veil" (Glasheen 1974, 63), the connection between invisibility and power operates here as in "Telemachus."
Returning from his kidney purchase, Bloom enters the bedroom,
"halfclose[s] his eyes and walk[s] through warm yellow twilight" towards Molly (4.247). Then he lets the blind up, revealing two con-
cealed nymphs—Molly and the picture above his bed. Just as Stephen
was tyrannized by his invisible guilt and the gradually visible Haines,
Bloom is dominated by invisible presences: the concealed Molly and
the as-yet-unseen Boylan.[9]

---

8. According to Raleigh (1977, 273), Bloom has had at least eleven addresses in
his life, and at least nine since he was married.

9. Bloom also thinks of Turko the Terrible, represented here by Boylan, who
remains only partly visible throughout the novel, appearing instead as fragmented
body parts, clothes, and accessories. Of course, when Bloom does espy Boylan, he
quickly averts his eyes.

An Economy of Souls

Bloom uses the nymph in a more pragmatic way, to exemplify his definition of that much-discussed term, "metempsychosis": "Reincarnation. . . . what the ancient Greeks called it. They used to believe you could be changed into an animal or a tree for instance. What they called nymphs, for example" (4.362; 375–77).[10] The term has a myriad connotations. In one sense it explains why Milly repeats Molly's traits: metempsychosis is genetics. In another commonly understood sense, it is what critics invoke to assert that Bloom is Ulysses, Stephen is Telemachus, and Molly is Penelope or Calypso, and to explain the parallels between other Dubliners and other Homeric characters listed in the Linati schema. Here metempsychosis denotes intertextuality.[11] More importantly, it provides a model for Bloom's notions of cosmic repayment and conservation through cyclic repetition and denotes the process by which Joyce revives characters from his life and from his earlier works and awards them grace or damnation. In this sense metempsychosis reflects an economy of retribution.

Bloom first defines it (inadequately) in response to Molly's query about the meaning of a word in *Ruby: the Pride of the Ring*. After failing with "transmigration," he tries again, after rehearsing to himself: "Some people believe . . . that we go on living in another body after death, that we lived before. . . . That we all lived before on the earth thousands of years ago or some other planet. They say we have forgotten it. Some say they remember their past lives" (4.362–65). The classical version of metempsychosis depicts a cyclic cosmos in which exists "a wheel of life, divided into two hemicycles of light and darkness, through which the one life or soul [*zoë*] continuously

10. Although Bloom seems to confuse metempsychosis with metamorphosis, in fact his definition echoes that of Empedocles, one of the earliest Greek exponents of the philosophy, who wrote that he had "been a boy and a girl, a bush, a bird, and a dumb water-dwelling fish" (Wheelwright 1966, 141). Bloom's many transformations— into a woman, into a "cod," into various alter egos—are themselves metempsychoses of Empedocles' metempsychoses.

11. Metempsychosis may also be used to refer to Joyce's method of repetition and recurrence, as when Stephen and Bloom undergo similar experiences and entertain similar thoughts. Certain female characters also seem to be reincarnated versions of each other. For example, Molly asks "Is she in love with the first fellow all the time?" (4.355), a question repeated almost verbatim by another "nymph," Miss Dunne, in the seventh section of "Wandering Rocks." She asks herself, "Is he in love with that one, Marion?" (10.371). Both women utter the same words, even though they do not know each other, and both want vocabulary lessons.

revolves" (Cornford [1912] 1957, 161). The narrative that surrounds Bloom's definition defines it more graphically in the cream's "curdling spirals through [Molly's] tea" (4.366). The metamorphoses Bloom and his kidney undergo follow directly his attempt to define metempsychosis and thereby exemplify it: in a past life, perhaps Bloom was a stork and his kidney a turtle. Just as seemingly solid objects are subjected to decay and alteration, because of metempsychosis bodies are only vehicles for immortal souls and hence merely provisional containers subject to alteration even after bodily death. In another sense, however, metempsychosis offers security: beneath the metamorphoses lies an essence that never passes away.

Metempsychosis fits more straightforwardly into the economics of "Calypso" because it creates a universe governed by economic laws. In Pythagorean theology metempsychosis permits souls to pay for sins committed in a past life. The soul goes through "an ordeal of purification" and is reborn "into some other human or animal shape, in which it is given a new opportunity to meet the challenges of bodily circumstance" (Wheelwright 1966, 209). This pattern is economic because it demands reciprocity: existence is a process of payment that balances moral and cosmic ledgers. Although it is usually conceived as a negative reciprocity wherein losses are disgorged, nevertheless metempsychosis achieves its balance by means of a cycle "wherein Nature returns upon herself" (quoted in Cornford [1912] 1957, 166–67). Moreover, because metempsychosis requires and permits the conservation of energy and souls, it is also "the most economical way of preserving psychic energy through the ages" (Knuth 1976, 119). That is, since the same soul is reborn again and again, nothing is ever lost—only recycled. Metempsychosis thus entails cosmic price reckoning: each sinful or failed existence is paid for by a commensurate penalty, so that "what you lose on one you can make up on the other" (6.218). Like Christian grace, metempsychosis offers an economy of salvation that is also a form of cosmic husbanding. It too makes reparation, a "righting" based upon payment. Finally, metempsychosis involves a quest similar to Bloom's; its primary motive is the soul's "recovery of its lost estate, the return to its source" (Moore 1921, 66), the same motive that propels Bloom's economy. Such restitution and renewal may connect origins and conclusions and thereby make "ends meet." Although it presumes a harsher view of human existence than Bloom's, metempsychosis nevertheless conforms to his belief that the cosmos ultimately produces balance and renewal through an economic process of cyclic circulation.

Prize Titbits

If "Calypso" presents metempsychosis as a means of managing the economy of souls, it also delineates an economy of matter that moves from the cultivation of crops, to the cooking and consumption of food, to its excretion and subsequent reuse as fertilizer that helps grow more food (cf. R. Ellmann 1972, 32). "Calypso" begins with breakfast and ends with defecation, moving from house to outhouse. Entering the jakes, Bloom takes an old copy of *Titbits* to read at stool, and we see him peruse Philip Beaufoy's "prize titbit: *Matcham's Masterstroke*," for which the author has been paid "at the rate of one guinea a column." Bloom compares his own participation in the excremental economy with Beaufoy's monetary prize and calculates the author's earnings: "Three and a half. Three pounds three. Three pounds, thirteen and six" (4.502–5; his price reckoning is philologically mandated, since "prize" derives from the same root as "price"). At almost the same moment he takes account of Beaufoy, Bloom deposits his stool, his own "prize titbit," in the vault of his "countinghouse" (4.499). But first he "keep[s] it a bit," as he might resist spending all his money. The scene again recalls Freud's pioneering explorations of the connections between financial and bowel habits ([1908] 1959, and 1916). Unlike Freud's subject, however, Bloom is not anal retentive—he "keeps it" only for "a bit"—just as his economic habits reflect a moderate philosophy of equilibrium and balance rather than miserly hoarding. At first he seems to envy Beaufoy's earning power and in similarly retentive fashion withholds his feces. Then, "yielding," he reads the story, by the end "kindly" envying Beaufoy's authorial and economic skill (4.516). Just as Bloom's bowel movement progresses from retention to yielding, his mood shifts from an anal-retentive "avarice of the emotions" to a more charitable generosity. This is the economy of the outhouse. Beaufoy's titbit also depicts Bloom's ideal domestic economy: the end of the story, when Matcham repossesses the "laughing witch" he had once lost, stages Bloom's desire to regain his wife and repossess his *oikos*.[12]

Reading and defecation occur simultaneously:

---

12. Brivic (1980, 155) contends that Bloom's "anal control represents a key pattern of [his] relation to the world." Shechner, on the other hand, calls Stephen a "more or less closed or 'retentive' character, and Bloom more or less an open one" (1974, 136). But Stephen's economic habits are far from "retentive," and Bloom is more regular and balanced than either of these extreme positions recognize.

quietly he read, restraining himself, the first column and, yielding
but resisting, began the second. Midway, his last resistance yielding,
he allowed his bowels to ease themselves quietly as he read, reading
still patiently that slight constipation of yesterday quite gone. Hope
it's not too big bring on piles again. No, just right. So. Ah! Costive.
One tabloid of cascara sagrada. Life might be so. It did not move or
touch him but it was something quick and neat. . . . Begins and ends
morally. *Hand in hand.* Smart. He glanced back through what he had
read and, while feeling his water flow quietly, he envied kindly Mr
Beaufoy who had written it and received payment of three pounds,
thirteen and six. (4.506–17)

At first resisting, he eventually yields to the movements of both story
and feces. "Costive" (constipated) describes his bowel problems but
also aptly describes Beaufoy's "neat" prose, which nonetheless has a
laxative effect on Bloom. The "tabloid" (i.e., medication) that expe-
dites his relief is *Titbits*, which was indeed a tabloid—a digest of news
and bits from around the world—although as far as I know it was not
printed on sacred bark.[13] Reading and excreting are in fact related
both etymologically and psychoanalytically. "Excrete" comes from the
Latin *ex + cernere,* meaning "to separate or sift," which is what a
careful reader does. Similarly, Freud contends that both the "desire
for knowledge" and the anal instinct are sublimated forms of the
possessive instinct ([1913] 1959, 130–31). Thus a reader comes to
possess a text by incorporating its information; it passes through him
or her and becomes something else, sometimes even being expelled
as more writing, more excrement. In this passage Bloom acts as the
ideal resisting reader, appreciating the craft of the story but also
recognizing its artistic and ideological limitations: "It did not move or
touch him but it was something quick and neat" (4.511). The ideal
reader of *Ulysses* performs similarly: he or she reads "patiently," first
resisting then yielding, but always looking back over what has been
read. Bloom's movements here exemplify what Wolfgang Iser calls
"retention," in which a reader moves both linearly and back and forth
through a text, while also recalling what he or she has read (Iser 1978,
111; cf. Bell 1991, 212, 47–48). Of course, Joyce habitually connects
writing and excrement, as readers of *Finnegans Wake* know, and as I
have noted in chapter 1. Bloom comically makes this connection more

13. The *OED*'s first citation for "tabloid" as a form of journalism dates from
1898 and therefore antedates the action here. The earlier definition was coined by
Burroughs, Wellcome & Co. to denote a pill.

palpable when he tears off part of the prize story and wipes with it: while Beaufoy values the story for its exchange value, for Bloom it has use value. But the contents of Bloom's "critical" act are congruent with the contents of *Titbits:* both "titbits" are digests. The matched beginning and end of Beaufoy's story also mimic the structural economy of *Ulysses,* in which Bloom begins his day by eating and defecating, and ends it with his face in Molly's rump. In all these economies, conclusions match beginnings: both ends meet.

Let us read in Bloomian fashion for a moment and trace the movements of Mr. Beaufoy, who reappears in "Circe," an episode that collects and purges all of the text's previously unpurged matter (McGee 1988, 131). In "Calypso," Beaufoy's titbit prompts Bloom to contemplate writing a "sketch. By Mr and Mrs L. M. Bloom," as if he could recoup his fecal and spousal losses with a profitable tale (4.518–19). And so in "Circe" the imaginary Beaufoy accuses him of plagiarism: "it's perfectly obvious that with the most inherent baseness he has cribbed some of my bestselling copy, really gorgeous stuff, a perfect gem" (15.823–25). It seems odd that a person engaged in producing "copy" (a word that implies a lack of originality) would be upset about someone's copying him, but it is not surprising that an author of tales about "love and great possessions" would protest lost profits ("we are considerably out of pocket"—15.836). Beaufoy also wants to retain his prize titbits. Bloom's fecal comment on Beaufoy's writing is also an act of creation in which Leopold defaces Beaufoy's titbit with his own—Bloom's masterstroke. Bloom makes his mark on Beaufoy's text and in "Circe" pulls from his treasure house a final critical and financial comment on Beaufoy's titbit—"Overdrawn" (15.840).[14]

Most significant in the Beaufoy/writing/excrement/money nexus, however, are the affiliations between creation and excretion and between origins and ends. Money and its symbolic analogues—dirt, feces, gold—are consistently linked in *Ulysses* to creativity and birth. Freud explains this association: "in the products of the unconscious . . . the conceptions *faeces* (money, gift), *child* and *penis* are seldom

14. Stanislaus Joyce recalls that, in the 1890s, James submitted a story of his own to *Titbits,* and notes that the description of the "laughing witch" was found in his brother's manuscript (*MBK* 91). Stanislaus claims that the story was merely an experiment in "raising the wind." Kenner reproduces a typical *Titbits* story called "For Vera's Sake," which is indeed about love (although it lacks great possessions); for the record, it too begins and ends morally (Kenner 1986, 12–18).

distinguished and are easily interchangeable" ([1916] 1959, 165–66). This interchangeability of excretion and birth, of feces and babies, may explain Bloom's habitual substitution of the name Beaufoy for that of the pregnant Mrs. Purefoy (see 8.276; 13.959). Bloom unconsciously associates Beaufoy's production of "perfect gems" of stories and the Purefoys' mechanical production of "hardy annuals" (8.362). Mrs. Purefoy's delivery of "prize titbits"—babies—mimics Beaufoy's churning out of lucrative copy. Bloom counts up Beaufoy's earnings on the story, which also has a useful function in Bloom's outhouse/countinghouse (after Bloom makes his deposit there); likewise, Mr. Purefoy works in a "countinghouse" (14.1417), where he labors to generate interest through usury from the deposits of others. The Purefoys try to use their children as a form of interest-bearing capital. Like offspring, money offers a kind of immortality, but one gained through production rather than reproduction. To cite Norman O. Brown, "money inherits the infantile magic of excrement and then is able to breed and have children: interest is an increment" (1959, 279). Buried here is an intertextual pun (developed, along with a more detailed discussion of usury, in chapter 6) that links monetary interest and offspring. The connections among children, money and excrement are further dramatized when in "Circe" Bloom bears eight gold and silver children, all adorned with "expensive plants" (they are Blooms, after all, engendered by his fertilizers), and all of whom grow up to be bankers and financiers (15.1821–32). Through the identification of Beaufoy and Purefoy, feces and babies, money and offspring, the issue of the vagina and the anus converge: once again "both ends meet" (6.760).

Because he has just reread Milly's letter, children are already on Bloom's mind. Thus his attention to his feces may be related to his sense of loss over Milly and Rudy; as Freud argues, "the interest in *faeces* is carried on partly as interest in money, partly as a wish for a child" ([1916] 1959, 169). Perhaps by husbanding and reclaiming both his feces (through cultivating a garden) and his money (by saving) he might symbolically reclaim his child, his other "prize titbit," and the only one he has left.[15] Both children are part of the gift

15. This oblique and unconscious connection between Beaufoy and Rudy might help to explain the similarities between the clothes of Rudy (15.4957–67) and of Beaufoy (15.814–17), as noted by Fogel (1990, 48). In a different context Levine (1979, 111) also remarks on the circular but progressive alimentary cycle and its connections to reproduction.

economy, which, we recall, must always circulate; a gift is property that always perishes but yet can always be reconstituted. Like money, which represents pure exchange value and, according to Marx, is always "the excess above and beyond necessary use-values" (quoted in Goux 1990, 27), so excrement is an excess. Its value lies less in the fact that it can be deposited in a storehouse like gold (its "Real" value, or rather its lack of value), than that it can be recycled, and can therefore represent the possibility of circulation itself (a "Symbolic" value, like that of money as a medium of circulation). Excrement as a medium of circulation thus mimics the economy of the gift. This economy and Bloom's attraction to cyclicity are therefore integrally related, and their resemblance is inscribed both in Bloom's spatial movements through Dublin and in his thoughts about the natural function of excrement.

Since Bloom's movements are habitually circular or cyclic, he might well believe that excrement functions organically the same way. Thus as he walks to the jakes he notes the paradox that excrement is also fertilizer (a useful recognition for a person named for a flower), and imagines he might "manure the whole place over. . . . The hens in the next garden: their droppings are very good top dressing. . . . Mulch of dung. . . . Reclaim the whole place. . . . Always have fresh greens then" (4.477–83). This is a concise description of the function of manure in what Wendell Berry calls "the Great Economy" of nature (1987, 56). As we have seen, feces also fertilize Bloom's imagination, allowing him to bloom (or rebloom) himself in imaginary sketches. Through the art of husbanding (cultivation), the ends of matter in excrement and dirt are reclaimed and become edible plants, thus beginning the cycle all over again: "being humus the same returns" (*FW* 18.). Though at this point Bloom only stores his "prizes titbit," eventually it will be recycled into the soil; similarly money, even when deposited in a "countinghouse," eventually gets circulated. The parallels between money and feces and the importance of excrement as fertilizer also help to explain why Beaufoy's earnings on his excremental titbit (three pounds thirteen and six) are exactly the same as the amount Bloom imagines as the price for the decaying corpse of William Wilkinson, auditor and accountant: both feces and decomposing bodies can be recycled to "give new life" (6.771–75). Furthermore, like the decay and reconstitution of organic matter, Bloom's motion around Dublin and back is a "commodius vicus of recirculation" (*FW* 3.2), a circulation also economic: the Latin *vicus,* or "village," is etymologically related to the Greek *oikos* (house), the root of "economics" (Singer 1958, 30; Senn 1989a, 51). "Vicus" also puns on "feces" (both are commodious), suggesting that the house and the outhouse may equally be sites of reclamation. Defecation is thus to the health of a body as monetary circulation is to the health of a city. Just as food is absorbed and circulated through the body, then becomes feces, and then is eventually redeposited into the soil, so money is exchanged from hand to hand, never halting, even when someone stores it in a countinghouse. Thus, in "Calypso," excrement, like money, serves three functions—Imaginary, Symbolic and Real. It is a representation of uselessness when Bloom wipes with Beaufoy's story, as if to comment on its lack of aesthetic worth (the "Imaginary" function—a measure of value—here a metaphor for lack of value); it functions as a medium of circulation in Bloom's meditation on its powers of reclamation ("Symbolic"); and it is simply itself, pure waste, when he deposits it in the outhouse "vault" ("Real" function, like money as stored wealth or payment). Excrement is the universal equivalent in the economy of matter.

Bloom's movements through the vicus of Dublin function similarly, as he becomes a kind of universal human equivalent. Moreover, his geographic, monetary and physical economies operate by the same principle: ends meet. We can see this pattern even in his first financial transaction in "Calypso," when he pays threepence for the pork kidney and returns home, a commercial excursion that adumbrates his larger trajectory on Bloomsday: Ulysses leaves home, makes transactions, and then returns to the place where he began. His circular movement in the novel represents an attempt to overcome the scarcity of means through economy of motion but embodies also the pattern of an ideal gift economy, in which the gift always returns to its source. Bloom envisions traveling around "in front of the sun, steal a day's march on him. Keep it up for ever never grow a day older technically" (4.84). Stealing time is saving time—a method of economy and potential immortality. According to John Locke, humans find a similar potential in money, which he describes as "something that men might keep without spoiling" (quoted in Vernon 1984, 33–34). That is, humans keep money because it is a commodity that cannot decay, unlike, say, the food it purchases, but also so that we ourselves might stave off death and decay by passing the money on to our heirs. As we have seen, Bloom's calculation of prices often serves a similar preservative function. However, Bloom's predominant economic motive is neither miserly hoarding nor capitalistic generation of surplus value, although both are sometimes present.

Rather, his world is always cycling and recycling itself; matter and money are conserved and renewed by circulation. The man who travels around the earth and never grows a day older is always renewed by the new dawn. It is in this sense that the phrase "making ends meet" refers not only to a financial balance but also to the capacity and desire for cyclic renewal: in the circumference of a circle, ends meet (cf. Seidel 1976, 28). Because Bloom's motion in *Ulysses* is a return, it makes ends meet and is therefore fundamentally economic.

A Man of Means

Both the organic cycle and the circulation of money may conserve scarce resources and stave off death or sterility. Ideally, in either cycle a good husband can make ends meet. Bloom does so. Despite having held a variety of fairly uninspiring jobs since reaching adulthood and in none of them having attained real wealth, he is financially solvent. Most of his jobs have been commercial: he helped his father sell trinkets (14.1050–60); sold something door-to-door (17.54; this may be the same job); managed sales accounts at Thom's (13.1126), and worked for Wisdom Hely's as a "traveller for blottingpaper" (6.703; cf. 8.131–42), but got fired from both positions (the first for a mistake in valuation and the second perhaps for insubordination); was an actuary or clerk for Joe Cuffe, a cattle merchant (17.484), where he was again dismissed for overstepping his authority (12.837); and worked for Drimmie's insurance (8.939; 18.1112), before assuming his present position as a freelance ad salesman for the *Freeman's Journal*.[16] The leanest period seems to have been after he was fired from Hely's, when the Blooms were "on the rocks" and Molly was forced to sell clothes and sing in "the coffee palace" for very meager wages (18.561; 11.485–97). Despite this checkered career, acquaintances like Nosey Flynn believe Bloom to be a financial wizard, probably because of his membership in the Masons (8.955–63).

Two recent critics have argued that Bloom's economic position is marginal at best. T. C. Theoharis contends that Bloom has changed jobs and addresses too many times to be economically healthy, notes that he "has never had enough capital to buy a house," and goes on to describe Bloom as an "industrious but perpetually unsuccessful provider of middle-class comfort" (1988, 158, 160). In one respect

16. Raleigh (1977, 274–75) provides a more detailed catalogue of Bloom's occupations.

Bloom is indeed less than a true "husband": the word originally referred to a peasant who owned his own home, and Bloom does not.
More persuasively, Edward Ahearn explains Bloom's habitual cost
accounting as a response to his precarious financial condition: he has
to watch every penny because he is so close to insolvency (1989, 88).
But the fact is that Bloom, although far from wealthy, is better off
than almost every other Dubliner in *Ulysses.* His success has little to
do either with his Jewishness (as Theoharis claims) or with magic; it
is the result of prudent saving and investing—the art of husbanding.
The running budget he compiles in "Lestrygonians," for example,
shows that he has at least five guineas of prospective income, if he
can nail down the Keyes and Prescott ads (8.1059). This is quite a
respectable sum, given that an average manual laborer supported a
family on little more than a pound a week (O'Brien 1982, 166–67;
201–7). In Bloom's final budget we also learn that he has received a
commission of £1 7s 6d today, evidently from selling an ad not listed
in his mental compilation (see 7.113, where Bloom refers to having
tapped the cashier). By itself this is almost exactly the same as the
average *weekly* wage for a skilled laborer in the building trades, or a
journeyman tailor, and more than almost all railway workers (O'Brien
1982, 204–5); it is precisely one and two-thirds times Stephen's
weekly earnings. No, Bloom does not own a home; but he does have
a considerable nest egg: a £500 life insurance policy, a savings account
of £18–14–6, and £900 worth of Canadian government stock at 4
percent, free of stamp duty (17.1856–65). His stock earns him £36
per year, and his savings account (at the same bank where Mr. Purefoy works), although apparently quite modest, could pay Stephen's
wages for more than five months (Gifford 1988, 597). Further, as
Gifford points out, "if Bloom's annual rent was £28 as his house was
valued, [the savings account] would pay for almost eight months of
rent" (1988, 597). All told, Bloom possesses almost £1500 in assets.
Although he could not quite "buy and sell most of the people he deals
with on Bloomsday" (Kenner 1987, 44), nonetheless he is not in any
immediate danger of going under, despite his spotty employment
record, Molly's complaints, and his humble position as an ad canvasser. Bloom has less difficulty than most of Joyce's Dubliners in
making ends meet.

   He does so, however, according to two competing economies.
Believing both in the static principle of balance and in the cyclic,
dynamic concept of reclamation, Bloom constantly oscillates between
the two. These conflicting models are analogous to the competing

economic models of market exchange and gift exchange. In the former, the desired result is balanced reciprocity: equal value taken for value given (Sahlins 1972, 194–95). Such transactions yield stasis, a zero-sum resolution that balances debit and credit. By contrast, gift exchanges can theoretically go on forever. A gift truly exists as such only by perishing as property—by being given—and is then reconstituted as new property for the donee. Gift exchange both produces and results from constant exchanges, whereas market exchanges aim to produce stability, at least temporarily. Since gifts are invested with the essence of the persons giving and receiving them, their exchange actually flows in two directions at once: both to the donee, who now possesses the gift, and back to the donor, who now possesses what might be called a "spirit" of the gift, a kind of incorporeal interest. Thus, although a gift must be given or lost, something intrinsic to the process of gift exchange makes the gift "seek to return to its origin" (Sahlins 1972, 150, 153; both models are present in the idea of metempsychosis, which offers recirculation as well as balance of payments). Bloom is constantly jostled between these alternatives: as a businessman he tries to earn commissions for himself and profits for his clients, and believes in paying only what an item is worth; as a compassionate citizen he recognizes imbalances and injustices and attempts to right them through generosity and charity. When threatened by flux, he returns to the stability of prices and mercantile cost analysis; when faced with the ultimate stasis of death, he resorts to recycling and renewal. Often the patterns overlap, but both are necessary for an individual and for a society. However, it is not always easy to select the appropriate model for a given circumstance or relationship. Gifts tend to be restricted to families, and debts to friendly but businesslike relations; to confuse the two economies is often to produce hostility or exploitation.

Bloom seeks the complementary realms for these competing ideals—to discover the necessary means—and therefore his economies embody both the cyclic motion of gift exchange and the drive toward balance and equilibrium. As Wendell Berry observes, the qualities that make for good soil husbandry are also moral acts that are sometimes "conditioned by the ability not to act, by forbearance or self-restraint, sympathy or generosity" (1987, 66). Sometimes Bloom must restrain himself; sometimes he must give himself. His ultimate aim, however, is to replenish his barren *oikos*. This return is also a result of the art of husbanding, which aims to conserve matter by uniting origins and ends, and to rebalance the psychic ledger, to repossess what one conceives as lost property. Bloom's attempt to bring these models together, to maintain himself as a man of means, and thereby to comprehend both the great economies of nature—birth, death, decay, the revolutions of celestial bodies—and to facilitate satisfactory exchanges on the smallest human level, is the subject of the next section.

GREAT AND SMALL ECONOMIES

Whereas "Calypso" concerns itself with household economics—a small economy—"Hades" and "Lestrygonians" concern themselves more explicitly with the great economies of birth and death, national politics, the universe. Bloom's thoughts repeatedly circle from the small to the great economies and back again, as if the greater ones merely reinscribe in broader terms the principles of household economy. "Hades" and "Lestrygonians" once more display Bloom's belief in husbanding, elaborating upon and augmenting the economic ideas introduced in "Calypso." Both episodes dramatize the problem of the necessary means, and in both Bloom meditates upon the menacing or comforting qualities of cycles. But whereas in "Hades" he finds renewal and redemption within the movement of the cycles, in "Lestrygonians" the cycles themselves seem threatening. Thus he first strives to arrest them through balancing and cost accounting, and finally to circumvent them through the cyclic movement of his memory and through genuine acts of generosity—literal or figurative gifts. In each case he discovers the necessary means: stasis and decay are conquered by growth through recycling; mechanical repetition is defeated by the gift of oneself.

Canvassing Death

In "Hades," Bloom confronts death during the funeral for his nondescript friend Paddy Dignam. His meditations typically employ economic terms to illuminate and translate religious or ethical concepts, and he usually prefers practical measures to prayer. His economic pragmatism functions as his cost accounting does elsewhere, counteracting depression and making the incomprehensible concrete and manageable. Thus, his compassion for the plight of Dignam's children is expressed as a concern about insurance (6.535): resurrection seems more manageable if it can be transformed into a business transaction. After all, "the hell idea and the lottery and insurance . . . were run on identically the same lines" (16.641–43). Insurance is a better policy than hoping for rewards in the afterlife. Thus, several hours after the funeral, Bloom helps Mrs. Dignam get her money from the insurance company, a good turn that combines generosity and practical knowledge of the insurance business (12.760–74; 13.1227). He also contributes five shillings for the children to help get them through in the meantime (10.975; 17.1462). Bloom does not merely express concern; he acts, and his economic agency here is both shrewd and charitable.

Moreover, Bloom's turns of phrase are often economic as well as humorous, not least because they make the mysterious seem mundane. For example, when considering the deaths of children in plagues and epidemics, he deftly eludes depression by thinking of diseases as "canvassing for death," and of death as a grim salesman exhorting his customers, "Don't miss this chance" (6.124–25). Near the end of the episode, while watching a large rat wriggling itself into the grave, he thinks "good hiding place for treasure" (6.975–76—the treasure image creates a parallel between Bloom's third episode and Stephen's). Musing on priests' antipathy to cremation, he jokingly turns heaven and hell into competing companies. Cremation is "devilling for the other firm" and Satan is an agent for "Wholesale burners and Dutch oven dealers" (6.984–85). Bloom's mind follows a policy of compensation in these passages, his commercial shrewdness and skeptical humor disarming death by making it seem just another economic matter.

The death chapter is also littered with the dead language of cliché. When confronted by the incomprehensible, humans often resort to the anonymous, soothing language of commonplaces. As Jennifer Levine has pointed out, in a cliché "it is precisely its lack of originality that is a comfort, holding the unknown at bay" (1979, 116). But Bloom seldom accepts them at face value. Instead he performs witty turns on this verbal flotsam, revivifying dead language by unexpectedly taking platitudes literally, or exposing their absurdity by expanding on their ramifications. His wordplay recycles language as metempsychosis recycles souls: both reanimate the dead. In cataloguing euphemisms for death, he unearths their buried metaphors and offers his own revisions: "Near death's door. Who passed away. Who departed this life. As if they did it of their own accord. Got the shove, all of them. Who kicked the bucket. More interesting if they told you

what they were. So and So, wheelwright. I travelled for cork lino.[17] I
paid five shillings on the pound. . . . Entered into rest the protestants
put it. Old Dr Murren's. The great physician called him home. Well
it's God's acre for them. Nice country residence. Newly plastered and
painted. Ideal spot to have a quiet smoke and read the *Church Times"*
(6.935–45). Bloom satirizes clichés by accepting their literal denota-
tions, so that "God's acre" becomes a "nice country residence." Typically, his obituaries focus on the economic and vocational identities of
the deceased; the idea is that the deceased still have an economic
function, although in a different economy. Bloom recycles and restores these commonplaces through skeptical revisions that couple
economic ideas with verbal wit, thereby recirculating the obsolete
coins of discourse and making them original again.

Just as his sense of the ridiculous deals well with clichés, his materialism cuts through and undermines the mourners' postures and
platitudes. When Simon Dedalus and Martin Cunningham wax sentimental about Dignam ("as decent a little man as ever wore a hat"
and "Breakdown. Heart"), Bloom inwardly comments, "Blazing face:
redhot. Too much John Barleycorn. Cure for a red nose. Drink like
the devil till it turns adelite. A lot of money he spent colouring it"
(6.307–9). Like most of Bloom's friends, Dignam lacked Bloom's frugality and temperance. Tom Kernan, another notorious tippler, expounds on the relative virtues of the Protestant funeral service,
pompously intoning: *"I am the resurrection and the life.* That touches a
man's inmost heart." Bloom responds, "Your heart perhaps but what
price the fellow in the six feet by two with his toes to the daisies? No
touching that" (6.670–73). Again, it is the economics of salvation
that concerns Bloom, and his metaphoric reference to "what price"
deflates both Kernan's pomposity and his own fear of death. Kernan's
idea of "touch" seems as suspicious to Bloom as Mulligan's does to
Stephen. Death is simply an arrested economy in which "circulation
stops" (6.434). Bloom also scoffs at the idea of physical resurrection:
"Once you are dead you are dead. That last day idea. . . . Come forth,

---

17. This line unwittingly (for him, not for Joyce) describes the occupation of
Gerty MacDowell's father (who travels for cork lino) and thus foreshadows his encounter with her. Gerty helps out by carrying the letters for him while he is laid up with
gout (10.1207; 13.321–23). She also knows the Dignams, but it is not clear if Bloom
knows MacDowell. Given MacDowell's drinking and illness, it may not be long before
he too is listed in the obituaries.

Lazarus! And he came fifth and lost the job" (6.678–79). Resurrection comically becomes an unemployment line.

Both Ends Meet

Bloom's management and revision of the small, verbal economy nevertheless leads to consideration of the greater economy—the human place in the material cosmos. Thus he accepts the Great Economy of natural laws to combat his fear of death. His philosophy springs from a recognition of the propinquity of birth and death, of origins and ends. Both passages are managed by doctors and women (see 6.14–18; 14.392–93), who are able to move "From one extreme to the other" (6.382). The economy of *Ulysses* follows the same route, as the death episode ("Hades") and the birth episode ("Oxen of the Sun") offer nearly identical formulations. Bloom's thoughts also traverse this path, typically moving redemptively from death to life, or from ends to origins. For example, upon seeing Stephen, whose father's pride in him prompts depressing thoughts about Rudy, Bloom recalls the moment when Rudy was conceived: "My son. . . . Must have been that morning in Raymond terrace she was at the window watching the two dogs at it by the wall of the cease to do evil. . . . She had that cream gown on with the rip she never stitched. Give us a touch, Poldy. God, I'm dying for it. How life begins" (6.76–81). The erotic commerce signified by "touch" turns death into life; "dying for it" is stripped of its morbidity and becomes an expression of lust and the "little death" of sexual intercourse; conception starts the cycle again. The memory of the body's pleasures counteracts the body's inevitable decay. Here, as in "Lestrygonians," memory is a gift that allows renewal through recirculation; Bloom rescues himself from death by returning to the scene of conception. Whereas "touch" for Stephen usually disguises exploitation, for Bloom it usually represents the genuinely redemptive power of the body and the sexual touch in which each party gives up the self in return for the reciprocal gift of the other's self. This touch is gift exchange in its purest form.

Surrounded by death, Bloom seeks renewal. Just as he recognized the uses of excrement for fertilizer, he also discovers the possibility of reclamation in the fertilizing properties of corpses. Observing that cemeteries nourish magnificent flowers, he imagines using this fact in a business enterprise: "Every man his price. Well preserved fat corpse, gentleman, epicure, invaluable for fruit garden. A bargain.

By carcass of William Wilkinson, auditor and accountant, lately deceased, three pounds thirteen and six. With thanks" (6.772–75). Again practicing the art of husbanding, he recognizes that soil is not simply dirt, but "a graveyard, a place of resurrection, and a community of living creatures" (Berry 1987, 66); it constantly creates life out of death. In this passage, Bloom again transforms a cynical economic cliché—"every man his price"—by taking it literally, so that a body becomes a commodity used to fertilize new life. The commodification of persons engineered by advertising is made comically innocuous here, as Bloom's imaginary classified ad converts physical decomposition into a profitable enterprise. Presumably, an epicure's corpse would be more valuable than others because it would be fatter and hence could produce more food for the garden for others to fatten on—good husbandry again. Since Wilkinson was an "auditor and accountant," it only seems fitting that his worth is accounted in pounds sterling. This price reckoning also deflects Bloom from a threatening train of thought about anti-Semitism and decay. Wilkinson's price is of course the same as Philip Beaufoy's fee for his prize titbit story: Wilkinson's own epicurean consumption has made his body a prize titbit. Once again Bloom renders grace and resurrection as a material and economic pattern: just as the body contributes to new life, so physical reclamation produces profits both for the seller of the body and for the buyer's garden. As in the Beaufoy/Purefoy nexus, the ends of matter—waste and rot—become associated with growth and life. Whereas Wilkinson once sought the balance of account books, he is now part of a cosmic cycle; the small economy has given way to a greater one. In Wilkinson, notions planted in "Calypso" bear fruit.

Bloom expresses his economic philosophy most concisely as he respectfully observes John O'Connell, the cemetery caretaker who, according to the Linati schema, plays the role of Hades. In this passage Bloom again offers sex as the answer to death but recognizes that their proximity lends resonance to both oppositions. He imagines how O'Connell must have wooed his wife: "Come out and live in the graveyard. Dangle that before her. It might thrill her first. Courting death. . . . Want to keep her mind off it to conceive at all. . . . Love among the tombstones. Romeo. Spice of pleasure. In the midst of death we are in life. Both ends meet" (6.747–60). Bloom revises another cliché, giving it a new meaning with multiple significances; as I have suggested, his final phrase succinctly describes both the economic balancing that Bloom manages again and again and his geographic motion. Here it also incorporates the idea that death and life interpenetrate and that neither is complete without the other; if so, it is only proper to call Dignam's coffinband his "navelcord" (6.914). Moreover, in this context the phrase also captures the motions of sexual intercourse, in which ends meet and remeet. Finally, the formula demonstrates his ability to condense complex ideas into miniature, economically expressed capsules, an invaluable talent for an ad man. In the Great Economy, "Both ends meet" refers to a universal power of compensation, a double-entry ledger on which debits and credits are entered and balanced, and to a cyclic universe in which the ends and origins always encounter each other, repeating and doubling back upon themselves, like Bloom's own physical and mental motion. These passages display that formula, showing how Bloom encompasses oppositions not only by his flexibility in moving between images of static materialism and cyclicity but also by disclosing the interrelationships between the small economies of words and the greater economies that govern the universe.

Joyce illustrates Bloom's principle with numerology. The number eleven has long been recognized as Joyce's integer of resurrection in *Finnegans Wake,* denoting a fresh start after the completion of a group of ten. Combined with thirty-two, the number of the fall (shorthand for the rate of acceleration of falling bodies, 32 feet per second per second), 11 becomes 1132, an emblem of the essential human trajectory, the descent which is also an ascent, the "phoenix culpa" of the *Wake.* Eleven acquires similar significance here. Bloom's infant son Rudy died eleven days after his birth (17.2282) and, had he lived, would be almost eleven years old now (4.420; cf. 15.4957); Bloom's memories of Rudy acknowledge the convergence of birth and death. Moreover, 11:00 A.M. is the hour of Dignam's funeral and the novel's hour of death. But it is also the hour of birth: "Oxen of the Sun," during which baby Purefoy is born, ends at around 11:00 P.M. Origins and ends coincide, birth and death becoming opposite points on a circular clock. But because, as we have seen, Bloom's ruminations on death lead him to birth and the birth chapter also contains intimations of mortality, their opposition is only apparent. As a number on a clock face, eleven is nearly the end of a cycle; in a base-ten number system, it is the beginning of a new cycle. In short, eleven is the numerological equivalent of "both ends meet."[18]

18. For a brief discussion of some other instances of eleven in *Ulysses,* see Kenner 1983, 244–5.

The inextricable link between birth and death is implicit even in the word Joyce used to describe his technique in "Hades": *incubism*. It derives from the Latin *incubo* (nightmare), suggesting that Stephen's nightmare of history encompasses Bloom's episodes too. Just as Stephen is haunted by memories, Bloom is beset by dead heroes, dead language, memories of the dead. In one sense, "incubism" connotes the dead's oppression of the living, the kind of psychic incubi seen in such *Dubliners* stories as "The Sisters," "Ivy Day in the Committee Room" and, of course, "The Dead." But the word from which *incubo* stems, *incubare* (to lie upon), also connotes birth, because from this root comes the word *incubation* and its connotations of warmth, nurturing, and birth. Lying upon eggs hatches them: incubism becomes incubation; both ends meet. As in the number eleven, and as in Bloom's conversion of Rudy's death into the moment of his conception, the same sign may signify both death and birth.

Like Odysseus visiting the underworld, Bloom encounters the spirits of numerous dead heroes: Smith O'Brien, O'Connell, Parnell. But another sort of reincarnation is at work here, inasmuch as Bloom's economic cosmology reaffirms, by metempsychosis, his identification with ancient Greeks such as Empedocles, Heraclitus, and Alcmaeon, who wrote that "men perish because they cannot join the beginning with the end" (Wheelwright 1966, 30). In other words, humans who deny their participation in the Great Economy, who fail to acknowledge their own primary existence as bodies partaking of natural cycles, also fail to be renewed by that economy. Bloom's philosophy is thus profoundly ecological as well as economic, recognizing that mankind is part of nature and endures the same round of birth and death, of eternal exchanges, as other beings. In such recognitions he both accepts the possibility of rebirth and embodies it, restating the philosophies of early Greek codifiers of reincarnation and thereby dramatizing it.

Reincarnations of a different kind, of course, occur throughout *Ulysses*, especially in "Oxen of the Sun," which also reiterates the philosophy of ends meeting. But whereas in "Hades" death seems to lead inexorably to life, in "Oxen" birth leads to death. Thus the tenth paragraph after the opening invocation admonishes readers to "look to that last end that is thy death and the dust that gripeth on every man that is born of woman for as he came naked forth from his mother's womb so naked shall he wend him at the last for to go as he came" (14.107–10). This dire equation of birth and death echoes the Malthusian doctrines the episode ostensibly condemns, as I shall discuss in greater detail in chapter 6. Although these passages do assert that both ends meet, here the formula seems disheartening.

Eleven paragraphs after the "everyman" passage, Bloom's formula is restated, though much less economically, by Stephen: "as the ends and ultimates of all things accord in some mean and measure with their inceptions and originals, that same multiplicit concordance which leads forth growth from birth accomplishing by a retrogressive metamorphosis that minishing and ablation towards the final which is agreeable unto nature so is it with our subsolar being" (14.387–92). Whereas "Hades" offers conception ("give us a touch") as the antidote to death, Stephen sees death as the result of conception; obsessed with his mother's death and his artistic sterility, he views birth through morbidly fixated lenses. But the numerological parallels are striking: the second warning comes eleven paragraphs after the first, as if proving that the same number that provides hope of regeneration can also give evidence of morbidity. The principle is again restated twenty-two paragraphs later (14.1222–1309) in a passage, mimicking Victorian science writing, that contains a discussion of obstetrical problems and infant mortality, into which Lynch inserts his idea that both "natality and mortality" are "subject to a law of numeration as yet unascertained" (14.1268, 1272–73). With his attention to elevens, Joyce seems to offer his own "law of numeration" beneath the discussion.[19]

Stephen views the natural order with despair and offers a chilly account of the natural economy. While the narrator invokes Darwinian law to explain infant mortality, Stephen blames the hangman God, who digests equally "multifarious aliments as cancrenous females emaciated by parturition [i.e., his mother, and] corpulent professional gentlemen [e.g., William Wilkinson, auditor and accoun-

---

19. This paragraph also contains the only explicit reference to Empedocles of Trinacria (14.2132), the early Greek writer responsible for perhaps the first coherent philosophy of the coincidence of origins and ends. Since Homer's "Oxen of the Sun" adventure takes place in Sicily (Trinacria), it is appropriate that he appear here. For him, too, birth and death coincide: "Double is the birth of things and double their demise. For the coming together of all both causes their birth and destroys them" (quoted in Lambridis 1976, 55). Ends meet. Although for Empedocles nature may be economical in its recycling of souls through metempsychosis, it is also "a spendthrift, creating many unfit creatures, until some succeed in surviving in suffient numbers" and producing equally adaptable progeny (Lambridis 1976, 101). Empedocles' early version of evolution science is thus obliquely linked to the Huxleyan science of the passage (Lambridis 1976, 104). Like Joyce and Bloom, however, the philosopher sees in cosmic cycles as much evidence for hopelessness as for hope.

tant]" (14.1289–90). A "morbidminded esthete and embryo philosopher" (14.1295), Stephen argues that God is crueler than evolution.
Having recently composed a poem about a vampire, he still envisions
sex and death as inextricably linked. Thus the message about origins
and ends changes slightly with each recapitulation. Whereas the medieval passage finds evidence of Divine Providence in the ineluctabil-
ity of death, the second passage offers cyclicity as a paradigm for
human weakness and ignorance, and the third explains these phe-
nomena by empirical science yet finds no evidence of meaning in the
cycle of births and deaths.

Bloom sometimes shares Stephen's pessimistic cosmology. This
vision is adumbrated in "Hades," where Bloom sees death as a Great
Consumer, a voracious organism with chronic dyspepsia (the cemetery "looks full up of bad gas" [6.607]) but an unslakeable appetite:
"Every mortal day a fresh batch: middleaged men, old women, children, women dead in childbirth, men with beards, baldheaded businessmen, consumptive girls with little sparrows' breasts" (6.623–26).
Reproduction only feeds mortality, especially in the inexplicable
deaths of young women and infants, which serve a mechanical and
monstrous deity resembling Stephen's description of the gluttonous
God in "Oxen." As we have seen, Bloom usually counteracts such
dejected rumination by transforming the cycle into one of renewal
and rebirth. But, by the time of "Lestrygonians," under the influence
of an empty stomach and rebuffs in the newspaper office, Bloom
displays a more pessimistic stance toward the Great Economy.

Charitable Compensations

"Lestrygonians" depicts Bloom attending to numerous small
economies—the price of lunch, the cost of oysters, the likelihood
of profiting from gambling, his forthcoming commissions—that lead
inexorably to ruminations on the greater economies of birth and
death, of eating and excreting, of memory, and of the repetitive consumption of a predatory universe. Once again he attempts to counteract threatening forces by conjuring up compensatory examples.
Painful memories are displaced by the memory of touch, and negative
reciprocity is replaced by the positive reciprocity of gift exchange.
Unlike Stephen, too paralyzed by debts to act, Bloom behaves effec-
tively in the human social world, generously reaching out to provide
charity for babies, birds, blind boys—the throwaways of society.

Early in "Lestrygonians" he sees Dilly Dedalus outside Dillon's auction rooms, where the family is selling off some furniture: "Fifteen children he [Simon] had. Birth every year almost. That's in their theology or the priest won't give the poor woman the confession, the absolution. Increase and multiply. Did you ever hear such an idea?" (8.31–33). Bloom believes that the church's admonitions against contraception contribute to the misery of its devotees, who seem to reproduce mechanically, without sufficient planning for the provision of those babies. The result is grinding poverty: "Good Lord, that poor child's dress is in flitters. Underfed she looks too. Potatoes and marge, marge and potatoes" (8.41–42). The debate about proliferation and economy continues throughout the novel on many levels, culminating in "Oxen." But here Bloom recognizes that, as Mary Lowe-Evans puts it, "the Church is guilty by valuing celibacy and paradoxically encouraging fertility" (1989, 73). Elsewhere Bloom makes more explicit and more general the connection between economics and Catholicism, asserting that "in the economic . . . domain the priest spells poverty. . . . Because if they didn't believe they'd go straight to heaven when they die they'd try to live better" (16.1127–30). But while he is sympathetic to the Dedaluses' plight, he seems to think that he cannot do much to ease it for now, although his later aid to Stephen may derive from this sympathy. Instead, he transfers his nurturing impulse to "those poor birds," the Liffey seagulls (8.73). Buying two Banbury cakes for a penny (a gift that appears in his final budget), he tosses the food to the gulls, who nonetheless fail to appreciate his bounty: "Lot of thanks I get. Not even a caw" (8.84). A penny expenditure is therefore "quite enough." Bloom's instinct is a typical, though ineffectual, attempt both to circumvent poverty and misery and to offset his dejection by using a very small expenditure on a gift as a token of much larger concerns.

The economy of childbearing and -rearing appears after Bloom discusses the Purefoy pregnancy with Mrs. Breen. With a "houseful of kids at home," Mrs. Purefoy is in labor again, and has been for three days. Bloom expresses sympathy, but after she departs, he considers Mr. Purefoy's compulsive behavior: "Methodist husband. Method in his madness. . . . Eating with a stopwatch, thirtytwo chews to the minute" (8.358–60). His mechanical fetish is matched by his compulsive reproduction: the Purefoys seem to reproduce as if by stopwatch, their fecund husbandry yielding "hardy annuals" (8.362; not all are hardy, Frederick Albert having died in infancy [14.1329]). Birth now seems no more than "life with hard labour," a punishment for both mother and child (8.375–78). Bloom disapproves of their

blind fertility not only because it is painful but because it is uneco-
nomical, a squandering of limited means, and a debasement of
human worth. In fact, Bloom's assessments of the high birthrate,
infant mortality, and childhood poverty accurately reflect conditions
in turn-of-the-century Dublin. Though the Dublin infant mortality
rate had been lower than that of comparable British cities, and
though it fell in the first decade of this century, its rate remained
higher than that of the rest of Ireland, and "child mortality in general
and infant mortality in particular were by far the most pressing problems of public health" in this period (O'Brien 1982, 109, 107). Moreover, the Dublin birthrate remained about a third higher than
Ireland's as a whole. These trends produced two effects: first, a high
dependency rate that exacerbated the poverty of the largest (and
generally the poorest) families; and second, the creation of a dispro-
portionately large part of the population in the age groups most
vulnerable to epidemics (Cullen 1987, 166). Indeed, if Bloom had
wandered into other sections of the city, he would have seen far
more severely destitute and hungry children than the relative few he
notices in *Ulysses*. In any case, what Bloom perceives is not a mirage:
the economic state of Dublin's working families in 1904 was dismal,
and for their children, even worse. Ironically, the accelerating birthrate, far from producing prosperity, actually increased childhood
deaths from disease and hunger.

Though these bleak reflections haunt Bloom, they prompt a
movement from the small economy (the Purefoys in particular) to an
analysis of the greater mortal and moral economy: "Dignam carted
off. Mina Purefoy swollen belly on a bed groaning to have a child
tugged out of her. One born every second somewhere. Another dying
every second. Since I fed the birds five minutes. Three hundred
kicked the bucket. Other three hundred born, washing the blood off,
all are washed in the blood of the lamb, bawling maaaaaa" (8.477–
83). The balanced ledger of deaths and births in the cosmic economy
now seems cruel and redundant. Natality and mortality merely turn
on a wheel that mechanically revolves but makes no progress, and the
pangs of birth seem indistinguishable from the throes of death. But
just as in "Hades" Bloom advocated spending "the money on some
charity for the living," instead of wasting it on the dead (6.930), he
characteristically contrives a practical economic solution:

> Time someone thought about it instead of gassing about the what
> was it the pensive bosom of the silver effulgence [quoting Doughy

Dan's speech in "Aeolus"]. Flapdoodle to feed fools on. They could easily have big establishments whole thing quite painless out of all the taxes give every child born five quid at compound interest up to twentyone five per cent is a hundred shillings and five tiresome pounds multiply by twenty decimal system encourage people to put by money save hundred and ten and a bit twentyone years want to work it out on paper come to a tidy sum more than you think. (8.380–88)

If each child were given five pounds at birth, at 5 percent the interest would be 5 shillings the first year (five pounds = 100s. Five percent = 5s.) In twenty-one years the interest on £5 alone would add another £5 10s. This is how Bloom arrives at "hundred and ten and a bit." According to his calculations, the total sum would reach £10 10s by age twenty-one. But he forgets that the amount of interest would also increase with the principal. With interest compounded, the total comes to £13 18s 7d: a tidy nest egg, equal to almost four months' wages for Stephen, and not that much less than Bloom's own savings account (Gifford's figures [£13.18s; 166] match mine approximately). The precise amount is less important, however, than the impulse behind its conception: Bloom again attempts to compensate for the pain of childbirth through economic planning. Again he finds solace in reckoning prices, in the concrete value of money, and its perceived capability to stave off time and permit humans to possess something to "keep without spoiling." To counteract the accretion of pain by entering life, Bloom envisions a gift for every child. The amount is not fixed, but incremental; thus he answers the problem of human proliferation with the proliferation of interest. Though the generation of interest is often viewed as immoral, it performs a moral function here, as the "illicit" offspring of money produces a bounty for human progeny.

Bloom's plan implies a political philosophy that resembles welfare socialism. Indeed, his savings scheme is just one of the plans he espouses in the novel, which culminate in his Circean fantasy of himself as "the world's greatest reformer" (15.1459). In his conversations with Stephen in the cabman's shelter, he advocates "all creeds and classes having a comfortable tidysized income . . . something in the neighbourhood of £300 per annum" (16.1133–35). But the income depends upon labor—"Where you can live well, the sense is, if you work" (16.1139–40)—and thus contradicts the welfare socialism he espouses in "Lestrygonians." During his mayoral fantasies in "Circe," he preaches a similar gospel (15.1687–88). Typically, however, Bloom believes that reforms must come gradually: "I resent violence or intolerance in any shape or form. . . . A revolution must come on the due instalments plan" (16.1099–1101). Characteristically, his socialism is presented as part of the newly burgeoning economy of bourgeois credit ("due instalments"), as if one pays for revolutions the same way one pays for a new sofa. Always nonviolent and devoid of class antagonism, Bloom's ideas are not truly Marxist (Manganiello 1980, 113). Moreover, in his reformist schemes, his two economic principles collide: on the one hand, his compassion for the oppressed (children, workers, cattle) leads him towards welfare socialism; on the other hand, his prudent bourgeois values prompt him to require manual labor and to propose technological solutions that would have negative effects on those same laborers he wants to help. But beneath his sometimes contradictory political and economic schemes lie a few solid ideals: "a classless, humanitarian, pacifist and cooperative society, devoid of all forms of hatred and sentimentality" (Manganiello 1980, 113). Typically, too, in Bloom's mind the small economies —the Purefoys' and Dedaluses' economic problems, the embarrassment and inconvenience of cattle herds interrupting solemn occasions—invariably send him to the greater issues of civic reforms, national politics, and cosmic justice.

The confrontation between justice and mercy occupies Bloom's mind a good deal in this episode and eventually produces a vision of history as nothing more than a cycle of oppression and empty serial replacement, in which a cityful of houses changes hands but "Landlord never dies they say. Other steps into his shoes when he gets his notice to quit. They buy the place up with gold and still they have all the gold. Swindle in it somewhere. Piled up in cities, worn away age after age. . . . No-one is anything" (8.484–93). All fades, but it does so repetitiously, so that even what replaces the faded is not new. Architecture (the "art" of "Lestrygonians") merely attests to the nightmare of history: structures remain, but nobody owns them. Although the domination of an individual landlord or landlady is limited to the length of his or her life, the idea of landlordship never changes, nor does the oppression that results from it: the rich will always take from the poor. Even gold, usually a comforting and stable element for Bloom, now provides succor neither to him nor to the human souls in transit; though appearing to be a stable, real quantity, it is merely a symbol of endless, futile circulation. Given Ireland's long history of dispossession and usurpation by foreign landowners, it is no surprise that Bloom would extrapolate from Irish usurpation and economic

oppression and perceive injustice even in the economy of metempsychosis: just as a landlord never dies, a soul, occupying a body as a
landlord occupies a piece of real estate, simply repeats its occupancy
again and again but never achieves transfiguration or genuine ownership. In Bloom's vision of the cosmic economy, landlords, not tenants,
get "notice to quit"; thus landlords are just disguised tenants. Nobody
owns his body; he only rents it. Lacking even the ownership of his or
her own body, a human being is nothing, and so the conservation of
matter through the ages instead becomes merely scrupulous meanness on a cosmic scale, and existence becomes a struggle for power
that is lost time and again.

Eventually Bloom's movement from small to great leads him to
meditate upon the cyclic movements of the planets, which now seem
like empty shells (8.581–84) whose cycles end in frozen stasis. Like
the people he encounters, the planets circle one another but do not
exchange; there is no justice because nothing cares for anything else.
Similarly, ruminating on the *General Slocum* disaster, he asks, "Where
is the justice being born that way? All those women and children
excursion beanfeast burned and drowned in New York. Holocaust.
Karma they call that transmigration for sins you did in a past life the
reincarnation met him pike hoses. Dear, dear, dear" (8.1145–48).
Metempsychosis is no longer redemptive, but just another instance of
cosmic injustice in a world of strife. He rejects the mechanical quality
of metempsychosis, in which every sin must be paid for by a quid pro
quo, sans mercy or mitigation. The balancing mind-set now seems
heartless and insufficient, merely reenacting the blind retaliation of a
cruel universe, and no longer suffices as a model for human behavior.

The last rendition of this horrifying vision (and most appropriate
in this food-filled episode) is manifest in the cycles of consumption.
When he enters the Burton hotel dining room for lunch, he is re-
pelled by the human role in this Darwinian equation. The men there
stuff and gobble without thought: "Every fellow for his own, tooth
and nail. Gulp. Grub. Gulp. Gobstuff. . . . Eat or be eaten. Kill! Kill!"
(8.701–3). He decides that a universe of eternal predation is chaos,
not cosmos. The food chain, rejuvenating in "Calypso," now seems
merely mechanical, as we stuff "food in one hole and out behind"
(8.929–30). Everything eats everything else, but nothing is nourished,
and nothing is saved. Bloom's antidote to this perception is again both
economically and morally prudent: he eats lunch somewhere else,
abandoning the Burton's brutal munchers for Davy Byrne's "moral
pub," where he once was allowed to cash a check (8.733–34), and

where he can get a 7d lunch of gorgonzola sandwich and burgundy that is both lighter and cheaper than the fare at Burton's.

Bloom is equally incapable of remaining dejected over the cosmic economy and again practices charity in the small economy as compensation. Near the end of "Lestrygonians," he sees that a "blind stripling" wants to cross the street. "He touched the thin elbow gently: then took the limp seeing hand to guide it forward" (8.1090). An instance of generous physical touch counteracts the cruel economy of justice. His act proves that, as Davy Byrne conceded a few moments before, Bloom is willing to "put down a hand to help a fellow" (8.985). Though embarrassed, he still observes the boy closely, feeling that his hand is "Like a child's hand," specifically Milly's (8.1096). The blind boy's association with Milly brings him into the fold of the family, the realm of generalized reciprocity where gifts may be freely exchanged. Bloom's beneficence to the blind boy, as has been noted many times, presages his rescue of Stephen, not only because of the motive but also because the stripling—blind, with a "bloodless face like a fellow going in to be a priest" (8.112)—resembles the myopic Stephen, who pretends to be blind during his walk on the beach, briefly considered becoming a priest and later comments that giving up singing is a "bloodless sacrifice" (in Italian [10.348]). Finally, Bloom repeats the helpful touch that he gives to the blind boy when at the end of "Eumaeus" he passes his arm through Stephen's and leads him to his home (16.1721–72). Bloom's good turn here is a rarity in *Ulysses:* an act of charity neither undermined nor mocked by another character or narrator. But Bloom also gains something from it—he is pulled further out of his mood of dejection. Thus, his generosity functions according to the model of generalized reciprocity in gift exchange, which benefits both giver and receiver. The spirit of the gift is given to himself even as it is shared with another; it returns to its source, renewed.

While this encounter suggests that personal charity can rectify cosmic injustice, other conditions remain oppressive. For example, Bloom is depressed by the nature of time. Recalling his early sexual life with Molly, he laments that one "Can't bring back time. Like holding water in your hand" (8.610). But his mind is more earthly, as he constantly churns up the soil of memory to bear new mental fruit. Thus his rescue from this more personal despair issues from an unlikely source. As he finishes his sandwich in Davy Byrne's, he spots two flies copulating on the windowpane. Prompted by the savor of wine and the sight of sex, Bloom rescues himself with a memory. A linked recollection of sex and food engenders a return to a moment of pure erotic commerce. The sun's heat "seems to [be] a secret touch telling me memory. Touched his sense moistened remembered" (8.898–99): once again for Bloom "touch" symbolizes a fruitful and healthy exchange, the kind that Stephen lacks and craves. He recalls lying with Molly in the grass on Ben Howth: "O wonder! Coolsoft with ointments her hand touched me, caressed: her eyes upon me did not turn away. Ravished over her I lay, full lips full open, kissed her mouth. Yum. Softly she gave me in my mouth the seedcake warm and chewed. . . . Joy: I ate it: joy. Young life, her lips that gave me pouting. . . . Flowers her eyes were, take me, willing eyes. . . . Wildly I lay on her, kissed her. . . . She kissed me. I was kissed" (8.904–16). Instead of the vampire kiss that Stephen conceives, Bloom remembers a kiss of love, an exchange that transfers the shared "goods" of love not hand to hand, but mouth to mouth. The text carefully stresses the transactive, reciprocal quality of the exchange: "I . . . kissed her. . . . She kissed me." We know that the emotion is shared, too, since Molly ends her monologue with a memory of the same scene (18.1572–1609). As in "Hades," the antidote to death is erotic commerce. If Stephen's vampire poem depicts incubism, Bloom's sexual reverie offers incubation, as he borrows from his own memory the wealth of love he has stored. Once again, it is a positive return, in this case to an earlier moment in memory, that provides an alternative to negative reciprocity. In contrast to the touches that menace Stephen with sycophancy, mistrust, and chicanery, Bloom's memory projects the possibility of an uncontaminated touch, an exchange of gifts that brings each party a costless reward.

Although this erotic transaction is dressed in the same terms— food—as the rest of the episode, instead of each consuming each other, Bloom and Molly exchange half-eaten seedcake, each blending his or her spittle into a new consistency, as though they share a single meal, a single digestive tract. And it is *seed*cake: not only does the cake contain the germ of their marriage, since Bloom proposed marriage this same day, but it refertilizes him upon his return to it in memory. Bloom husbands memory to recycle the moment of gift exchange and to bring forth new blooms. In this exchange of gifts, Bloom received his own image reborn ("Flowers her eyes were") and receives it again now, displacing the sterile exchanges of bodies, houses, and babies that have beset him throughout the episode; the vision of universal negative reciprocity is balanced by evidence of a past exchange of gifts. As a gift the memory functions paradoxically: although the moment is "potted" and can now never change, Bloom can recall it anytime. Hence it is both static and constantly circulating. Here Bloom combats perilous flux and decay with the memory of an exchange that, though fixed forever, symbolizes the endless revolutions that constitute gift exchange. Past and present come together as male and female merge: both ends meet.

It is clear now that Bloom's recurrent capacity to make ends meet designates far more than a cost accountant's obsession with balancing ledgers. It signifies his resilience in discovering methods of renewal, his ability to make the small economies coincide with the great economies, his constantly circulating thoughts, as well as his restless body. Bloom is economic man, a pragmatic person attempting to solve large problems with shrewd practicality, but also one who recognizes the economies that underly the macrocosmic structures in human existence: the recycling of food, bodies, and souls. Sometimes mercenary and shrewd, at other times charitable, Bloom encompasses both poles of the economic spectrum. In his myriadmindedness, he makes ends meet. Moreover, Bloom's two impulses constitute the major principles of the economy of *Ulysses:* on the one hand, it is a tightly controlled, realistically economical novel; on the other, it contains passages of excess that seem to issue from a bottomless purse of styles. *Ulysses* is scrupulous, satirical, pointed; it is also extravagant, comic, excessive. It both moves linearly and constantly recycles itself; it is founded upon nearly endless circulation; it is based upon Bloomian cost accounting; it is based upon Stephen's sense of expenditure. Joyce's hero, in short, exemplifies the impulses that ultimately (if briefly) fuse when he meets Stephen. If Bloom makes ends meet, then so does the novel in which he lives.

4

Bloom and the Economies of Advertising

Promise, large promise, is the soul of an advertisement.
—Johnson, 1963, 125

Joyce seemed to possess an almost superstitious faith in the power of classified ads (see *L* II, 197). In addition, the "Notes on Business and Commerce" he made while working in Rome include a glossary of advertising terms and techniques that testify to an early and broad, if probably superficial, knowledge of the advertising strategies of his day. A tantalizing note appears near the end of that section, where he writes, "Institute of Advertising would be open to educated men" (*JJA* 3:610), as if he were contemplating pursuing the career he later gave to Bloom. In a sense, he did pursue such a career: as we have seen, he was not above energetically advertising his own books, preparing press clippings for inclusion in review copies or presenting *Ulysses* as a real steal to recalcitrant purchasers. Thus, in making his hero an ad canvasser, Joyce was not setting him up for easy ridicule. On the contrary, Bloom's sophisticated advertising designs graphically synthesize aesthetic and commercial sensibilities. More generally, Joyce's attention to and respect for the details of popular culture reveal his recognition of advertising's key role in the social and economic life of Dublin and turn-of-the-century Europe. I want to show in this chapter that detailed analysis of advertising in *Ulysses* opens important avenues for interpretation not only of the novel's economic patterns and Bloom's character, but also of the social life of Dubliners, the ideologies that surround them and Joyce's own artistic methods.

We will see that Joyce's treatment of advertising is ambivalent, combining a healthy skepticism about its complicity with exploitative power structures with a pragmatic recognition of its rhetorical sophistication and potentially positive economic effects.

The revolution in aesthetics that we call Modernism was but one of several revolutions occurring at the turn of the century. Thomas Richards and Jennifer Wicke have persuasively demonstrated how the culture of commodities became predominant in part because of the crisis of overproduction in late capitalism: more goods were being produced than were consumed, and hence much more sophisticated advertising techniques were needed to distribute those goods.[1] Advertising was a burgeoning industry: in 1905 one advertising manual called the period a "golden age in trademarks" (quoted in Haug [1971] 1986, 24). Most texts agree that advertising underwent a revolution in the early twentieth century. Thus Joyce selects a profession for Bloom that places him squarely in the mainstream of the economic changes of the period, even though, as Wicke notes, Bloom's advertising career is decidedly small potatoes (1988, 127). Nevertheless, Bloom's occupation is in its way as typical of the economic sensibility of its era as Stephen's vaunted artistic vocation is of the period's aesthetic sensibility.

One result of Bloom's intercourse with popular culture is the increased presence of the subliterary in the novel's texture (Lawrence 1981, 52). Advertising is one method whereby Joyce subjects *Ulysses* to heteroglossia: to a dialogue between the "literary" and the "marketplace" traditions that Stephen distinguishes in *Portrait* (*P* 188), one that discovers nearly equal value in each. Thus when Stephen and Bloom consider intellectual originality during their conversation in "Ithaca," Stephen constructs an epiphany of loneliness and paralysis in which a woman writes to her lover, while Bloom remembers a rejected advertising idea (17.606–20). Although their aims differ, their epiphanic methods are quite similar, as our investigations will

---

1. Wicke overstates the case, however, when she claims that advertising was somehow responsible for the Modernist revolution (1988, 123). Although the economic and aesthetic revolutions are homologous, since both involve new forms of symbolic currency and revolutionary strategies in presenting them, their relationship is too complex to assign causality to one or the other. The Modernist revolution in the treatment of language is also related to a shift in the methods and structures of banking and finance that took place at about the same time (see Goux 1988, 17, 23). Nevertheless, I am indebted to Wicke and Thomas Richards for their valuable work in laying the foundation for the study of advertising in *Ulysses*.

show. In general Joyce uses advertising to add to the novel a chorus of voices virtually unheard by Stephen, voices that enrich the surface of the text while adding one more entry to the socioeconomic encyclopedia that is *Ulysses*. At the same time, Joyce spurs his readers to become "active participants in social dialogue" (Bakhtin 1981, 276) through a heteroglossic method that transforms his authorial presence into a kind of traveling salesman of discourse who moves from *topos* to *topos* bearing a bag of linguistic samples. He thereby turns the novel into what Franco Moretti calls a "mad clearance sale of literary styles" (1983, 206). To create Bloom and depict his professional praxis, Joyce too had to become an ad man; "Joyce" is thus the name we give to the ad man who designed both *Ulysses* and the ads within it, the authorial consciousness becoming more Bloomian as it foregrounds Bloom's advertising enterprises.

MASS PRODUCTS

The first ad Bloom encounters is the flyer for Agendath Netaim that he picks up in Dlugacz's (4.191–99). The prospectus asks for subscribers to purchase sandy tracts in Zion and reclaim the soil by planting new crops: a scheme for restoration and renewal, it is a prototype for most of the ads that follow. The "idea behind" the Zionist flyer—a faith in renewal, restoration, and cyclicity—demonstrates how advertising enacts the Bloomian economic philosophy outlined in chapter 3. The flyer also promises to found a new community of believers, in this case Jews; similarly, throughout *Ulysses* a strong connection—perhaps even an identity—is forged between the discourse, rituals, and products of advertising and religion. Both promise redemption, both encourage a (perhaps false) sense of community, and both satisfy basic human needs. Neither Bloom nor Joyce implies that one is more efficacious or more valid than the other. The similarity between the effects of commodities and those of religious rituals is also suggested in the schema for "Lotus-Eaters," the first episode in which advertising plays a prominent role. The episode's symbol is described as Eucharist and its art as chemistry. The relationship between the two has already been jokingly established in Mulligan's mock-communion at the very outset of the novel; for him transubstantiation is a matter of chemistry and corpuscles. Joyce extends this association, especially in "Lotus-Eaters" and "Lestrygonians" (the originals of which also deal with consumption), to scrutinize the nature of physical and commodity consumption.

Transubstantiation

Advertising plays a crucial role in capitalist economies. Ads are intended to lubricate the circulation of goods; in this sense the circulation of advertising messages imitates the exchanges between money and commodities that those ads aim to instigate. In order for an economic transaction to take place, some mediator between production and consumption must exist—an additional sign system must be operating (Rossi-Landi 1975, 133). Money is this mediator, acting both as a measure of value and as medium of circulation. In simple exchange, a transaction between buyer and seller is diagrammed as M—C, C—M: from the buyer's point of view, money is exchanged for a commodity; from the seller's, the commodity is exchanged for money (Marx 1978, 329). Money permits the smooth circulation of commodities, because as a universal equivalent it enables the exchange of unlike things: real objects for bills or coins. The seller receives money (embodied exchange value) in return for the commodity (embodied use value) given to the buyer. But because buyer and seller view the commodity differently, a mystery inheres in it (Marx 1978, 320). For the buyer, the commodity satisfies a use value —for example, the satisfaction of hunger. For the seller, however, the same transaction is viewed in terms of exchange value: he or she wants to make money and is thus concerned solely with the economic value of the commodity, not with its use. Thus buyer and seller not only seek different goals when they enter a transaction; they also perceive the commodity in completely different terms. How can one object fulfill both aims? This contradiction inheres in capitalism. When the seller goes on to use that money to purchase something else, the transaction outlined above becomes C—M—C. But in capitalism, a merchant always wishes to earn more from the transaction than he or she had to pay in production costs, and a buyer goes on to sell the commodity for more than he or she paid for it. In both cases the party is no longer concerned with use value but with exchange value. Now the circuit becomes M—C—M′, the latter symbol referring to the augmented value the seller receives for the second sale; this is surplus value (Marx 1978, 332). Money is given material shape as a commodity, which is in turn transformed into more money, as though the process of exchange has magically supplemented the value of the commodity, or as though the commodity can shape itself to fit its user's wishes. In such exchanges, the commodity acts as the medium between use value and exchange value, because it both embodies the buyer's use value and enables the transformation from object to money. At the point of exchange, it is as if exchange value, "trapped in the body of the commodity, yearns to be rescued and released into monetary form" (Haug [1971] 1986, 23). This metamorphosis constitutes a "miracle of . . . transsubstantiation [*sic*]" (Marx, quoted in Haug [1971] 1986, 23) from commodity back into money. Through money the physical commodity acquires added value, just as the wafer and wine become spiritually mutated and charged with the blood and body of Christ, thereby generating a form of surplus value. The commodity is both itself and an embodiment of the invested desire of its communicants; in the process of exchange, its substance is at once simple and complex.

For the buyer to want to engage in the transaction, however, the merchant must always give the appearance of use value, and this is where advertising enters the picture (Haug [1971] 1986, 15–16). A commodity is a commodity rather than simply a useful article insofar as "it operates as a message" of some kind (Rossi-Landi 1975, 127); purchase thus becomes consumption when it involves the exchange of messages. Ads therefore promise use value in a wide variety of shapes: better health, convenience, sexual or emotional satisfaction, security, and so on. We can now see that consumption actually involves two related activities: the consumer ingests the messages about the product along with or before actually purchasing the product; these exchanges of messages permit and accompany the exchange of commodity for money. Advertisements thus act as intermediaries between producers and consumers, and between commodities and value. Just as economic exchange takes place when commodities are transformed into money and vice versa, so advertising performs a similar transubstantiation, operating as medium of circulation that mirrors the role of money in simple exchanges. Advertising turns purchase into consumption by attaching messages to commodities: object + message = commodity; purchase + exchange of messages (assumption of use value) = consumption. Just as money functions as a host enabling the transubstantiation of one commodity to another commodity (C—M—C), and just as commodities mediate the transformation of exchange value into surplus-value (M—C—M'), so ads function as a host that changes simple purchase into consumption through an exchange of messages or signs. Through advertising, the body (commodity) is loaded with spirit (meaning). In this sense, advertisements constitute both a medium of circulation and a standard of value, or what Judith Williamson calls a "currency of signs" (1978,

20). Thus in "Lotus-Eaters," an episode in which Bloom both encounters many ads and observes a communion ceremony, the transformation in the Eucharist seems homologous with the transformations in the market economy instigated by advertisements.

The specific nature of these exchanges can be demonstrated better not through theoretical forays but through a detailed analysis of the praxis—specific advertisements—by which Bloom mediates "between the economic base of Dublin—its manifold shops, pubs, and private services, and what could be called its superstructure, i.e. its newpaper offices, cultural productions and social rituals" (Wicke 1988, 128). Thus in his economic agency Bloom too becomes a medium of circulation, encouraging both economic exchanges and the exchanges of signs that constitute advertising. He stands as human currency who constantly remakes his identity as a nexus of exchange, so that by the end of "Lotus-Eaters" he becomes a host, an embodiment of both economic and semiotic transubstantiations: foreseeing himself in the bath, he thinks, "this is my body" (5.566). What he advertises, and what he ultimately exchanges with Stephen Dedalus, are in two senses "massproducts" (17.369), a pun that serves as the linchpin for both Joyce's equation of religion and advertising and for my own discussion.

Wonderworking Power

Let us begin with two advertisements that paradigmatically represent both the claims of advertising and Bloom's relationship to them. The first comes not from "Lotus-Eaters," but from "Ithaca": the prospectus for "The Wonderworker, the world's greatest remedy for rectal complaints." Probably copied from an extant ad,[2] the prospectus claims that the medicine or device "assists nature in the most formidable way, insuring instant relief in discharge of gases, keeping parts clean and free natural action, an initial outlay of 7/6 making a new man of you and life worth living. Ladies find Wonderworker especially useful, a pleasant surprise when they note delightful result like a cool drink of fresh spring water on a sultry summer's day. Recommend it to your lady and gentleman friends, lasts a lifetime.

---

2. See *Notesheets* 468. Though there are a few variations from the *Notesheets* (for example, the notes ensure that users will be "free for natural action," whereas in the text the preposition is deleted to create an ungrammatical sentence), the length of the note and the minimal changes from notes to text suggest a separate original source.

Insert long round end. Wonderworker" (17.1827–33). Pledging to make a "new man of you and life worth living," the ad seems to answer Bloom's habitual desire for renewal. It comically makes "both ends meet" by likening a rectal remedy to a drink of water (but don't drink it, folks!), and in so doing paradoxically employs an image of nature to draw attention to its "scientific"—and hence unnatural— effects. Nature is "assisted" and then supplanted by a product that announces itself as artificial. Wonderworker thus both conceals and celebrates its origin as a mass-produced object.[3] Once Wonderworker has finished its improvements, we may not be so sure if "this is my body" or not, since the product wants not only to improve the body, but to appropriate it. The testimonials that follow imply that Wonder-worker can improve the body politic as well: it is so democratic that everyone, from absentminded beggars to officers, may benefit from its potent thaumaturgy. Equality is as easy to achieve as inserting "long round end." The testimonial from the "wellknown author" (17.1835) is probably that of Philip Beaufoy, whose productions work their own magic on Bloom's bowels; like Wonderworker, his "Master-stroke" also enabled Bloom to "assist nature." With its London ad-dress, however, even the Wonderworker prospectus alludes to the subservient condition of the Irish economy. The absentminded beg-gar (alluding to a Kipling character who may indeed need such a remedy, having "left a lot of little things behind him!" [Bowen 1974, 329]) offers patriotic testimony that the remedy would have helped British troops in South Africa, a war in which Irish sympathies were generally with the Boers. British products, virtually the only ones on the Irish market, were, like Wonderworker, designed to "afford a noiseless, inoffensive vent" (15.3276) to Irish political activism by de-flecting their explosive political frustrations into private consumer-ism.

Ultimately, however, its strongest appeal is neither sociopolitical nor natural but magical: the results of use are disproportionate to the effort needed, and the consumer must follow a prescribed ritual to reach his (pardon the expression) ends (Williamson 1978, 141–42). Indeed, since the prospectus is addressed to "Mrs L. Bloom with brief accompanying note commencing (erroneously): Dear Madam" (17.1822), Wonderworker has already made a "new man" of Bloom by giving him a new gender and thereby turning him into "the new

3. For an extended analysis of advertising and its commodification of "the natu-ral," see Williamson 1978, 123–37.

womanly man" (15.1798–9). More importantly, this phrase makes overt what other ads only imply: that the consumption of commodities will produce renewal, in this case, physical (and by implication, emotional) health. Regeneration is available for only 7/6.[4] The buried promise of most ads—that the true value of human life is achievable only through consumption—is merely more explicit here. But despite the ad's comic hyperbole, the product does fill a genuine need: since Bloom has used it, that "slight constipation" of yesterday is quite gone (4.509), and he wishes for it just before his farting episode in "Sirens" (11.1225). Perhaps it will not make anyone a new man, but life *is* more worth living without rectal problems or gas pains. Bloom does not blindly buy the ad's ludicrous claims; but empirical evidence has proven to him both the power of the words and the efficacy of the medicine. Thus Bloom uses words that echo the Wonderworker ad to encourage Stephen to eat a roll in the cabman's shelter ("you would feel a different man": 16.814) and to lean on him while walking to Eccles Street ("you'll feel a different man": 16.1719). Even Molly, who is often skeptical of advertising claims, buys a certain kind of face lotion because it "made my skin like new" (18.459; this is the same brand of lotion that Bloom buys on credit at the end of "Lotus-Eaters"). The similarity between advertising and religion is clear, and not only because one of the testimonials that succeeds the prospectus is from a "clergyman": Wonderworker's pledge to provide miraculous restoration juxtaposes, and ultimately equates, commodity kitsch and religious transformation, and Bloom borrows its words to attempt to forge a connection to a person he conceives of as a surrogate son.

Abodes of Bliss

Patent medicines ads like Wonderworker were pervasive at the turn of the century (as Stephen announces, apropos of nothing, "This is the age of patent medicines" [15.4470]). Richards shows that such ads told consumers that "the only way they could sustain a secure sense of selfhood was to consume more and more commodities" (1990, 196). Thus the claims of Wonderworker lead directly back to the opening of "Lotus-Eaters," where Bloom peruses ads for tea and

---

4. This amount is the same as that in the title of one of the "world's worst books," *50 Meals for 7/6*, situated right next to *Expel That Pain* (15.1579). The ad's comparison to a drink of water notwithstanding, Wonderworker would be one of the world's worst meals at any price.

temperance beverages and where everything appears as a sedative or patent medicine, as if all advertised products (and the ads themselves) are lotus blossoms. The second prototypical ad appears early in that episode, as Bloom chats with Charlie M'Coy and scans the paper:

> *What is home without*
> *Plumtree's Potted Meat?*
> *Incomplete.*
> *With it an abode of bliss.* (5.144–47)

The constant recurrence of this jingle-like slogan produces an annoying effect on Bloom that belies its claims to bliss. M'Coy's question, "Who's getting it up?" (reiterated by Nosey Flynn [8.773]), concerns Molly's upcoming tour, but of course we and Bloom know that Boylan is "getting up" his own potted meat as well. In this committee "Part [Bloom] shares and part [Boylan] profits" (5.163); but Bloom also profits, since Molly will earn money. Although any reader could recognize the sexual innuendoes in "meat" that leads to "bliss," this ad seems aimed specifically at Bloom, its promise to produce an "abode of bliss" forcefully reminding him of the disruption in his own domestic economy: his *oikos*, his own abode, is incomplete, missing Milly, Rudy (Bloom dreams of hearing "his voice in the house" [6.76]), and satisfactory sex. The ad even uses the same word as the "Ithaca" respondent, who tells us that the Blooms' sexual relations have been "incomplete" since Rudy's death (17.2283). The erotic connotation of the ad becomes a trope of incompleteness whenever Bloom thinks of it, leading him to conclude that Boylan "gets the plums, and I the plumstones" (13.1098–99).[5] What is disturbing about the ad, then, is that it reminds Bloom not only of his missing children, but of Boylan, whose meat is formidably present, and who makes 7 Eccles Street far too blissful for Bloom's comfort.

In fact, Plumtree's Meat functions as a metonymy of Boylan throughout the novel. We see him buy a jar of it at Thornton's in his section of "Wandering Rocks," while eying the sales clerk and deeming her an appropriately carnal "young pullet" (10.327). Then he presents the meat—along with some fat peaches and pears, metonymies of Molly's body—to her as a prelude to sex. This identification of persons and products is perfectly in line not only with Boylan's sexism, in which women are no more than meat, but with the ideology

---

5. For actual ads for Plumtree's Meat, see Pearl 1969, 67, and Pierce 1992, 127.

of advertising, where everything carries a price tag in a currency that mediates exchanges between persons and commodities by endowing them with equal exchange value. When Bloom returns home, he notes the empty pot in the cupboard and, upon getting into bed, brushes aside some "flakes of potted meat, recooked," as if symbolically ousting Boylan (17.304; 2125). Boylan's presence also explains why Bloom enters the bed "With circumspection, as invariably when entering an abode (his own or not his own)" (17.2115–16): in providing bliss, Boylan has temporarily appropriated the abode as well as Bloom's wife. Indeed, Molly's recollection that "it had a fine salty taste yes" seems to conflate Boylan's and Plumtree's meat (18.132). In any case, Boylan and Molly have enacted the ad's narrative, both becoming potted meat in the process. The ad goes further: it implies not that the commodity accompanies sexual fulfillment but that it replaces it. Sexual desire is transformed into the "need" for consumer goods; reproduction becomes mass production, as the ad's narrative is enacted innumerable times by countless consumers.

The Plumtree's ad thus offers meat as an intermediary between money and happiness and thereby creates its own economy of meaning, with the meat as universal equivalent. Moreover, it performs transubstantiation by appealing not to material happiness but to the spiritual well-being that is magically attached to the product. Professing to rehabilitate the domestic order, the ad exemplifies what Sut Jhally calls "Black Magic" claims, which use a before-and-after format to dramatize how "before [the product's] use [social] relations were incomplete and with its use they are complete" (1987, 163). But this ad does not even require that one eat the stuff: its mere presence in the home triggers its marvelous transformation, its masterstroke. Carnal and spiritual presences, flesh and word, are exchanged. In this sense the religious appeal of the ad—its use of a pseudocatechism and movement from the material to the transcendent—does demonstrate the meat's condition as a "massproduct": not only is it directed at individual consumers in the mass, thereby mimicking its mode of production, but it also offers itself as the host in a sacred ritual that induces spiritual renewal.[6] Hence its comic placement near the obituaries is congruent with its depiction of a commodified afterlife: what is heaven but another "abode of bliss"?

6. Fritz Senn (1980, 23) suggests that the ad's question imitates familiar contemporary adages, such as "What is home without a Bible? / 'Tis a home where daily bread / For the *body* is provided, / But the soul is never fed." On advertising as a "magic system," see Raymond Williams 1980, 170–95.

Bloom is thinking economically, however, when he ridicules Nannetti's unfortunate insertion of the ad under the death notices and speculates about the meat's ingredients: "Lord knows what concoction. Cauls mouldy tripes windpipes faked and minced up. Puzzle find the meat" (8.749–50). In his view, the product is pure surplus value, since it is made of inedible by-products that have no use value and hence costs very little to produce. By suppressing the facts of the meat's production, the ad engineers a kind of surplus value of consumption—waste becomes meat becomes bliss—as well as a metamorphosis that imitates the one Bloom considers in "Calypso," in which excrement is made into food, or even (in Agendath Netaim) into a symbol of Judaism. Under the obituaries the ad implies that human bodies are also potted meat and therefore need both processing and reconstitution. This association simply exposes the buried claim in the ad that as consumers we cannot decay: forever warm and still to be enjoyed, Plumtree's Potted Meat (in its advertised form), poises consumers eternally on the brink of bliss, like the lovers on Keats's urn. Once again advertising's litany identifies persons and commodities. Just as the ingredients have been divorced from their original digestive functions and potted, so human beings may be suspended forever in an abode of potted bliss.

But the word "abode" connotes far more than merely a happy home. Indeed, the ad's narrative seems directed at specifically Irish consumers. If, as Bloom notes, "the Irishman's house is his coffin" (6.822), then the door of domestic life also opens directly into the political avenue. Forced to entertain British "strangers in [their] house" (12.1151, 15.4586), and separated from their Northern cousins, Irish consumers—gnomons all—would instinctively respond positively to the picture of a blissfully secure and complete home. For an Irish reader the single home synecdochically represents the homeland; thus the Plumtree's ad manipulates Irish political anxiety and nostalgia through its promise to reconsecrate the domestic order. With the proper consumer items, Ireland may become an abode of bliss. In this respect, Bloom's incomplete home and disrupted domestic economy is characteristically Irish, though he has probably had more abodes than most. Of course Plumtree's Meat doesn't provide real completeness, just as the ad's question is not a real question. The satisfaction it offers is not communal but private, and the very picture of the secure "home" urges consumers to forget politics and concentrate on rehabilitating the domicile. Purchase of this commodity therefore merely opens up another gap to be filled by the next product, especially when the consumer who eats the meat discovers that

his or her reward is a less political feeling of fullness. Still, the allure-
ments of "home" are so magnetic for the Irish that, as we shall see,
even Bloom's ads play upon this pervasive sense of dispossession and
incompleteness.

And yet, despite the ad's silliness and bad faith, the meat itself
seems to fill a need. Molly and Boylan do renew themselves sexually
after (or before) sharing it, and in so doing enact a consumerist transubstantiation, with the meat as host for erotic commerce. When presented as an erotic gift, at least, Plumtree's Meat does serve the useful
function it claims to fulfill; its use value of generating bliss is authenti-
cated at 7 Eccles Street, despite Bloom's suspicion that it isn't even
real meat. The role of Plumtree's Meat then, suggests that although
the claims of advertising may be spurious, nonetheless advertised
mass products can stimulate genuine human interaction and even
produce a certain satisfaction.

Consuming Christianity

This affiliation of advertising and communion is further extended when Bloom enters All Hallows church. His observations on
religion and the communion ceremony recognize disturbing affinities
with commodity culture that move in both directions: religions use
advertising, and advertising appropriates the promises and rituals of
religious belief. Bloom's assessment of Catholic rituals strips them of
their abstract and spiritual connotations to suggest that the ceremonies mask an underlying materialism. Observing communion as an
ironic outsider, Bloom watches the priest administering the wafers:
"Shut your eyes and open your mouth. . . . Good idea the Latin. Stu-
pefies them first. . . . Rum idea: eating bits of a corpse. Why the canni-
bals cotton to it" (5.349–52). Although his anthropological instincts
are sound, most Catholics would find his interpretation blasphemous:
Carnivorous Christians Eat Nazarene's Potted Meat![7] In Bloom's eyes
the communicants are lotus-eaters, and the ceremony provides precisely the same sedative sense of solidarity induced by Plumtree's
Potted Meat: "Now I bet it makes them feel happy. . . . There's a big
idea behind it, kind of kingdom of God is within you feel. . . . Hoky-
poky penny a lump. Then feel all like one family party, same in the

---

7. As Restuccia points out (1984, 330), Bloom's materialistic reading of the Eucharist exemplifies the "sensualist heresy," whose advocates believed that "the recipient of
the host actually bites the body of Christ." Mulligan is guilty of the same heresy.

theatre, all in the same swim. . . . Not so lonely. In our confraternity. . . . Lulls all pain" (5.359–68). "Eat this and you'll be saved" is the formula of both consumerism and communion (cf. Wicke 1988, 148). And the wine? Merely another mass product that "makes it more aristocratic than for example if he drank what are they used to Guinness's porter or some temperance beverage Wheatley's Dublin hop bitters or Cantrell and Cochrane's ginger ale (aromatic)" (5.387–90). The choice of wine draws a better class of communicant but could be replaced in a pinch by any other advertised beverage. Under Bloom's scrutiny the word becomes flesh, and communion is but a light repast.

Even more troubling are Bloom's remarks on the Church's organizational structure. He detects the commercial aims just beneath the pious surface. "Wonderful organisation really, goes like clockwork. . . . Salvation Army blatant imitation. Reformed prostitute will address the meeting. How I found the Lord. ["I found him to be an excellent lover"?] Squareheaded chaps those must be in Rome: they work the whole show. And don't they rake in the money too?" (5.424–25; 433–36). Christianity and prostitution emerge as similar institutions, both using similar seductive techniques and offering similar rewards. Hence the "sense" of the episode is "the seduction of the faith": Christianity both seduces its believers and has been seduced by commodity culture. The introduction here of the name of Father Vaughan (5.398)—who called himself "God's advertising man" (Torchiana 1986, 219) and was the model for the corrupt Father Purdon in "Grace"—only solidifies the connection; Purdon's name was taken from a street in Dublin's red-light district (*MBK* 227–28).[8] Houses of worship and houses of prostitution both appear as sites of exchange that are at once sexual and commercial.

In later episodes Bloom extends the kinship of religion and commodity culture to the shared structure of their litanies. In "Nausicaa" he masturbates to the accompaniment of the Litany of Our Lady; when both ceremonies have concluded, he remarks, "Mass seems to be over. Could hear them all at it. Pray for us. And pray for us. And pray for us. Good idea the repetition. Same thing with ads. Buy from us. And buy from us" (13.1122–24). Advertising uses several kinds of

---

8. Many late nineteenth- and early twentieth-century ads exploited the authority of the Church and tried to transfer it to their products. In one famous ad, the Pope is pictured drinking a cup of beef tea. The ad's caption reads, "Two infallible powers. The Pope and Bovril" (de Vries 1968, 22). For an extensive treatment of Purdon's commercial theology, see Osteen 1991, 84–89.

repetition, two of which Wicke discusses (1988, 162–65).[9] In the passage cited from "Nausicaa," however, Bloom is referring to a third form, which consists of repeating the name of the product or slogan several times within a single ad, a technique he employs in his own ad designs. As for the litany, Bloom seems to be echoing Joyce's cynical entry in his "Notes on Business and Commerce": "Repetition. A liar believes a lie he has repeated" (*JJA* 3:605).

An episode exploring consumption in all its forms, "Lestrygonians" further expands the association between religion and advertising, as it depicts Bloom's comments on sandwichboard advertising, recollections of his own rejected designs, and assessments of other ads. In this episode Christianity (both Protestant and Catholic) appears as a "system of cruelty" that demands blood sacrifices (Nietzsche [1887] 1956, 193). Observing the white-smocked sandwichmen advertising Hely's stationers, Bloom remarks, "Bargains. Like that priest they are this morning: we have sinned: we have suffered" (8.124). A more significant parallel is introduced when a YMCA young man places a throwaway (i.e., flyer) in his hand. "Bloo . . . Me? No. Blood of the Lamb. . . . Are you saved? . . . Elijah is coming. Dr John Alexander Dowie restorer of the church in Zion is coming. Is coming! Is coming!! Is coming!!!" (8.8–15; this repetition contains its own sexual double entendre). The throwaway hints at the original meaning of "advertise," which was "to give warning or notice"; in this sense all evangelism advertises the Day of Judgment, and all preachers are ad men. Bloom's momentary confusion between his name and blood again confirms his role as host of the exchange between advertising and the divine, and implies parallels between the circulation of his blood and that of the throwaway.

Like the Agendath Netaim flyer and the Wonderworker ad, Dowie's throwaway promises restoration. But Bloom is typically skeptical of his "paying game" (8.17), in which Dowie seems more interested in saving profits than in saving souls. Dowie reappears as an American frontier snake-oil peddler at the end of "Oxen of the Sun," where Stephen or Lynch glosses one of his throwaways.[10]

9. The first is the mass-produced repetition of the ads themselves. The second is the repetition of the ad message over time; this is what Bloom means when he tells Hynes that "for an advertisement you must have repetition" (12.1147) and why he pursues the renewal of Alexander Keyes's ad. On the varieties and uses of repetition in advertising, see Bogart 1967, 162–79.

10. The pastiche must be spoken by either Stephen or Lynch, since they are the only two speakers remaining here. Lynch asks, "Christicle, who's this excrement yellow gospeler on the Merrion hall?" (14.1579). The rest of the passage may be his follow-up

Elijah is coming! Washed in the blood of the lamb. Come on you winefizzling, ginsizzling, booseguzzling existences! Come on, you dog-gone, bullnecked, beetlebrowed, hogjowled, peanut-brained, weaseleyed fourflushers, false alarms and excess baggage! Come on, you triple extract of infamy! Alexander J Christ Dowie, that's my name, that's yanked to glory most half this planet from Frisco Beach to Vladivostok. The Deity ain't no nickel dime bumshow. I put it to you that He's on the square and a corking fine business proposition. . . . Shout salvation in King Jesus. . . . He's got a coughmixture with a punch in it for you, my friend, in his backpocket. Just you try it on. (14.1580–91)

In Dowie's sermons as in Vaughan's, God is an entrepreneur, religion a slightly seedy commercial enterprise, and salvation a patent medicine.[11] When "Elijah" speaks in "Circe," his rhetoric is less threatening but equally hortatory, urging listeners to "Rush your order and play a slick ace. . . . Book through to eternity junction. . . . Florry Christ, Stephen Christ, Zoe Christ, Bloom Christ, Kitty Christ, Lynch Christ," he urges. "Be on the side of the angels. Be a prism." The "higher self" is invoked in language borrowed from American advertising argot: "You once nobble that, congregation, and a buck joyride to heaven becomes a back number. You got me? It's a lifebrightener, sure. The hottest stuff ever was. . . . It's just the cutest, snappiest line out" (15.2192–2203). Christ becomes "everyman and noman" (17.2008), a consumable mass product. If religion is a quack medicine, advertising is the evangelism of commodities; there is no God but business, and Dowie earns His profit.

Throwaways

The Elijah throwaway is used to comment on the possibility of a redeemer for Ireland and eventually becomes identified with Bloom's own recuperative powers. Throwaway is, of course, first of all the

---

or the rejoinder of Stephen, who is earlier called "Parson Steve" (14.1451; cf. 15.65, 67), doubtless because of his black clothing. A parson is usually a Protestant preacher of humble station—someone like Dowie. Given his names and the cleverness of the parody of Dowie, the words at the end of "Oxen" are probably Stephen's.

11. Voelker and Arner show that Dowie's style of "bullying exhortation" (1990, 284) was no less intimidating than the words of the poster burlesque. Their phrase is quoted from the *Evening Telegraph,* March 11, 1907. According to their humorous factual account of the real Dowie's travels and reception in England and Ireland during 1904, Dowie "violated every principle he ever espoused" (1990, 285) and was ridiculed mercilessly in the British and Irish press as well as by Joyce.

name of the surprise winner of the Gold Cup horse race; the race motif is introduced near the end of "Lotus-Eaters" when Bloom's offhand comment to the grimy Bantam Lyons is interpreted as a tip. The race and the throwaway have affinities: the desire to gamble resembles the desires engendered by advertising, inasmuch as both offer hope of bliss without labor and promise economic salvation as a parody of the economy of grace. In both economies one's just deserts are displaced by an undeserved bounty. Bloom is identified with the horse, especially in "Cyclops," where the belligerent drinkers believe Lenehan's story that Bloom has won money and refuses to spread his winnings around. Like Throwaway, Bloom is a "rank outsider," at least in Kiernan's. During one of his fantasies in "Circe," Bloom is treated as a horse when Bella/Bello (who has also lost money on the Gold Cup), *"throws a leg astride"* the feminized Bloom and mounts him (15.2943–49).

The other throwaway, now a crumpled paper ball, circulates through Dublin on the Liffey, reappearing three times in "Wandering Rocks," each time obliquely commenting upon the absence of— and the need for—economic and religious grace. It first turns up in the fourth section, as the destitute Dedalus girls complain about their father's indolence (this appearance also connects the throwaway back to its initial occurrence just after Bloom sympathetically spots the ill-dressed Dilly Dedalus). Cursing "our father who art not in heaven" (10.291), the Dedalus daughters must rely instead for their provisions on the charity of nuns. Simon's improvidence is an earthly economic equivalent of the absence of Divine Providence in their lives, as well as a dramatic manifestation of the Irish economic condition. The throwaway rides lightly down the river, its pledge of redemption ironically revealing that no Elijah is forthcoming to rescue them from destitution. They need financial redemption far more than Dowie's empty promises of spiritual restoration.

In the twelfth section (10.752) the throwaway again exposes an absence of grace, for this is the section devoted to Tom Kernan, the drunken subject of his friends' misbegotten reforms in Joyce's story "Grace." The throwaway's evangelism seems as useless as the ministrations of Cunningham and Purdon, who also fail to give Kernan spiritual grace. The simoniac equation of grace and cost accounting in that story is reiterated in the parallel between advertising and Dowie's attempts at revival. Finally, the throwaway reappears in the sixteenth section, as Haines and Mulligan take tea and scones at the DBC while smugly discussing Stephen (10.1096–99). Stephen's usurpers remark on the absence of hell in Irish myth, where "the moral idea seems lacking, the sense of destiny, of retribution" (10.1082–84). But, as I have noted, Joyce mercilessly subjects them to his own economy of retribution, exposing their complacency and bad faith. In sum, these sections are linked through the absence of grace: the Dedaluses need economic salvation, whereas both Kernan and Mulligan need to learn charity. The throwaway's sections also climb the ladder of class, rising from the Dedaluses' hopeless poverty; to Kernan's fragile, bourgeois commercial world; to Mulligan and Haines's well-fed complacency. Perhaps we ought not blame Mulligan too much for failing to help the Dedaluses, since Stephen himself resists doing so. Nevertheless, the throwaway's futile circulation comments upon the economic and spiritual gracelessness that permeates Joyce's Dublin.

As we have seen, it is Bloom who acts as the economic and moral conscience of Dublin. And it is Stephen, rescued by Bloom, who most needs both sorts of grace; Bloom ben Elijah provides it. Thus the thrownaway Elijah descends at "thirtytwo feet per sec" (8.57), the formula for the velocity of falling bodies. But when the gulls will not swallow it (no fools they, unlike those who swallow Dowie's promises), Bloom compensates by buying Banbury cakes and feeding the hungry birds. The throwaway falls, but Bloom rises to generosity. Like the throwaway, Bloom circulates through Dublin, revealing the economic and moral failings of those he encounters; in a sense, he circulates like the blood of the lamb, his circulation also triggering redemptive transformations. Like the throwaway, he floats on the tides of senti-ment and debt that wash through the city and escapes drowning in either flood. Thus Bloom's positive economic agency contrasts with the throwaway's spurious promise of redemption. Espousing love and charity (admittedly, not without hedging), Bloom gives genuine gifts. Perhaps more importantly, his ability to earn a living by his wits estab-lishes him as an economic countermodel not only to Simon Dedalus but to most of the characters he encounters on Bloomsday. Himself a kind of throwaway ("it'd be an act of God to take a hold of a fellow of the like of that and throw him in the bloody sea," exclaims the barfly in "Cyclops" [12.1661]) and a target of missiles thrown by the Citizen and nameless shopkeepers (15.1764–66), Bloom still manages to res-cue thrownaway people and give them grace. Subjected to humilia-tion (in "Cyclops") but eventually ascending to greatness as "ben Bloom Elijah" (12.1916), Bloom falls only to rise.[12]

---

12. Wicke (1988, 152) arrives at similar though less positive conclusions, observ-ing that through this throwaway, "the religious vocabulary of incarnation, grace, and communion . . . is mapped onto advertisement."

"Once More That Soap"

Throughout *Ulysses*, Bloom is identified less with a specific commodity than with the shared premises and redemptive rhetoric of
both religion and advertising. The end of "Lotus-Eaters" reinforces
his association with Christ (ironically, of course) when he foresees his
bath and thinks "this is my body." He is the host of advertising's
transubstantiation in *Ulysses* from throwaway into significant discourse. He becomes a chemist or alchemist who not only combines
commercial and spiritual discourses but exchanges one for the other.
Moreover, Bloom sometimes finds a genuine source of renewal in
commodities themselves. The best example of the power of such mass
products is the soap he purchases for 4d from Sweny the chemist just
before his bath and eventually takes with him into that Eucharistic
immersion. Since he must wait for Sweny to make up the lotion, he
agrees to come back later and pay 3s 1d for both items (the lotion
thus costs 2s 9d). He never does return to pay for them, even though
he recalls the debt guiltily during "Nausicaa" (13.1048–50). While he
temporarily ignores its exchange value, the use value of the soap is
nevertheless important to him, since he bathes with it (the "lemonyel-
low" color of Bloom's skin in his dream of the bath [5.569] means that
he will use the soap there). The soap is first of all just soap, a product
with an established use. But it eventually metamorphoses into a talis-
man, like his famous potato, which several times protects him from
danger and emotional ruin. The soap's transformation from commodity to magical fetish exemplifies how commodities metamorphose
into mass products with wonderworking powers.

The soap is not immediately used up; like other commodities in
Ulysses, it "decay[s] through a series of use-values, as if possessed of a
radioactive half-life" (Law 1989, 199). In fact, the soap both shrinks
and grows in the novel: it literally shrinks from use and from its
placement in Bloom's sweaty pocket; but as Moshenberg (1988, 345)
points out, it also grows into THE SOAP, an entity capable of providing
emotional succor at key moments to the depressed Bloom. Since it is
neither actually bought nor completely used, by the time Bloom
washes his hands with it at the end of the day, the soap is still only
"partially consumed" (17.231). Along the way, he sits on it (6.22),
transfers it from pocket to pocket (6.494–96, 7.229), and removes its
adhesions from his skin (11.1127).[13] Its grandest appearance occurs

---

13. Sims (1989, 239) wittily suggests that pockets, such as the one holding the
soap, represent "the world of work, labor and economics, where one thing is produced

in "Circe" when, after conjuring up the threatening apparition of "Marion," Bloom envisions *"a cake of new clean lemon soap aris[ing], diffusing light and perfume."* Here THE SOAP sings its own advertising jingle: "We're a capital couple are Bloom and I. / He brightens the earth. I polish the sky" (15.336–40). Sweny's face, asking for money, emerges from the soapsun, upon which Bloom claims both products are "For my wife. Mrs Marion" (15.345). Strangely, this explanation —factually untrue, since only the lotion was intended for Molly— drives the intimidating spectre away. Transubstantiated into THE SOAP, the lemony cake has become a host with magical powers to dispel threatening phantoms.[14] But THE SOAP appears as if prompted by Molly's presence; this association of Marion and soap is borne out several times in *Ulysses* and seems partially responsible for the saving powers Bloom finds in it.

First identified with Milly's "tubbing night" (8.170–72), soap also acquires the salutary powers of Milly's image discussed in chapter 3. Eventually, however, this soap becomes invested with Molly's essence, as though Bloom's muddy recollection of the debt and his failure to pay it have turned both items into presents for her. Indeed, because it is both a gift and a purchase, the soap combines the person/object identifications characteristic of gift economies and the commodity fetishism of capitalist economies in which "a definite relation between men . . . assumes . . . the fantastic form of a relation between things (Marx 1978, 321). The soap and Molly become identified through a pun on *moly*, that mysterious herb that saves Odysseus from Circe's threatening transformations. Joyce was much concerned to develop this parallel. In a letter to Budgen, he described *moly* as "the gift of Hermes" and "the invisible influence (prayer, chance, agility, presence of mind, power of recuperation) which saves in case of accident" (*SL* 272). Thus the soap as *moly* saves Bloom from the Marion apparition in the passage just cited. More pertinent is Joyce's description of

---

and exchanged for other things." But although the soap is clearly a mass-produced object, its mode of production is suppressed; nor is it exchanged for money, though it should be. However, Sims is correct that the soap epitomizes the role of pockets as places of exchange.

14. Moshenberg's ingenious analysis of this passage claims that the soap exemplifies Marx's description of commodity fetishism and surplus value through Bloom's perception of his "reciprocal relation with the soap" (1988, 338). However, his discussion of how it accrues surplus/value is flawed by his contention that its price has somehow been inflated into 3s 1d (1988, 345). When Sweny appears in "Circe," he is reminding Bloom of his total debt, including the price of the lotion. The guilty Bloom has merely lumped both items together; hence there is no inflation.

moly as a "milky yellow flower" (*JJ* 496), because yellow is Molly's color. For example, when Bloom first met her at Mat Dillon's, he was struck by her "yellow knees" and yellow dress (11.726); when he brings her breakfast, the room is bathed in "yellow twilight" (4.248); in "Circe," "Marion" wears a "yellow cummerbund" (15.299); when Bloom returns home, her yellow gloves rest upon the piano (17.1304); at the end of the day, he kisses the "mellow yellow smellow melons" of her rump (17.2241). Given these associations and the similarity in sounds between *moly* and Molly, it seems clear that the soap is both Bloom's Molly and his *moly*. This identification is made clear at the end of "Lestrygonians," when Bloom spies Boylan and, seeking any means of suppressing his thoughts about being cuckolded, pretends to search his pockets. After rejecting the Agendath Netaim flyer, his handkerchief, the paper and the potato, he discovers "Ah soap there I yes. Gate. Safe!" (8.1191–93). Though he may not be sure of his hold on Molly, he is comforted by knowing that he still possesses that *moly*, his soap, and his feeling of security is signaled by his use of her word, "yes."[15]

Bloom seems temporarily renewed by his bath at "11 Leinster Street" (17.339), as eleven signals a moment of regeneration in *Ulysses*. Thus the soap is less a narcotic than a genuine remedy for depression and anxiety. Its purchase nudges Bloom towards a self-sufficiency that counteracts the temptations of lotus-land, the threat of being consumed by Boylan, and the perils of Circe's cave. Whereas he often sees transformation as dangerous, here the transformative powers of soap-as-*moly* are genuinely salvific. Bloom's belief in the powers of such mass products is thus another gift of Hermes, god of commerce, who protects Bloom by giving him frequent contact with commodities as buyer and seller and as ad man. During his bath Bloom sees himself as the host of a commodity-impelled transubstantiation; later, when entertaining Stephen, he acts as host in a different sense. Inviting Stephen in for a chat, Bloom serves "Epps's massproduct, the crea-

15. Other associations solidify this connection. For example, in "Aeolus," O'Madden Burke dubs Molly "Dublin's prime favourite" (7.610); "Dublin's Favourite" was a brand of soap advertised in the *Freeman's Journal* for June 11, 1904. In contrast to Molly's ambiguous reputation, however, the soap is alleged to be "Absolutely Pure." Elsewhere in "Circe" the soap is part of the litany of the Daughters of Erin, who chant "Wandering Soap, pray for us" (15.1946), as if it had magical powers. In the litany the soap takes the place of the Blessed Virgin Mary, a pure woman.

ture cocoa" (17.369–70). Now the pun on "massproduct" completes the equation between mass-produced commodities and spiritual properties; indeed, Bloom washes his hands with it before serving, as a priest cleanses himself before administering the wafers and wine. Epps's ad called its cocoa "the greatest invigorator for the fagged" (Gifford 1988, 558), a claim which Bloom takes seriously and proves true. Here, at least, commodities do have magical powers. Bloom's secular communions using advertised mass products replace both the bankrupt and inefficacious rituals of the Church and the bad-faith claims of false advertising. Indeed, through Bloom, commodity culture may provide a new model for the spiritual and economic rehabilitation of fagged-out Dublin.

Everyman and Noman

Another connotation of "massproduct" concerns consumers themselves. Advertisements appeal to the individual and the mass simultaneously; more accurately, they reconstitute the consumer as an entity defined by acts of private consumption that are reproduced by other consumers. As Jean Baudrillard puts it, in advertising "we can imagine that each individual feels unique while resembling everyone else," since the discourse of consumption "aims to transform the consumer into the Universal Being, the general, ideal and final incarnation of the human species" (Baudrillard 1988, 11, 53). In short, advertising turns consumers themselves into mass products, into the hosts of its transubstantiation. Commodities are given human traits, and humans become commodities. The interchangeability of people and advertised goods is dramatized in Bloom's correspondence with Martha Clifford. Martha has answered a want ad Bloom placed in the *Irish Times* for a "smart lady typist to aid gentleman in literary work" (8.326–27). One of forty-four responses, she now "aids" Bloom by writing vaguely sadomasochistic replies to his letters. Their erotic commerce is indeed "work" for her, since Bloom gives her money for the letters (in "Sirens" he sends a money order); indeed, the entire exchange is a commercial transaction, once again preceded by the exchange of signs in the ad and their letters. (Thus when Bloom writes his return letter in "Sirens" and tells Richie Goulding that he is "answering an ad" [11.886], he is not lying.) Though he calls his money order a "little present," their exchange is to real gift exchange as Martha's letter is to Milly's: rather than reflecting and reinforcing genuine identities, their correspondence exchanges aliases.[16]

In one sense, the correspondence "makes a new man of" Bloom by rewriting him as Henry Flower, the sensitive swain depicted in "Circe" strumming a dulcimer and wearing a sombrero. The Henry/Martha correspondence indeed exemplifies what Judith Williamson calls the "appellation" of the consumer by advertising, in which an exchange occurs between the consumer and the person figured as the reader of the ad. Ads constitute us "as one of the objects in an exchange that we must ourselves make, thereby appropriating *from us* an image which gives us back our own 'value' " (Williamson 1978, 50, 64; emphasis hers). In other words, consumers of ads are also the commodities advertised: in creating structures in which we and commodities are interchangeable, ads are "selling us ourselves" (Williamson 1978, 13). Thus Martha reflects Bloom's image by enclosing a flower (yellow!) with her letter; in this exchange Bloom is first advertiser, then consumer, and finally commodity. But because Henry Flower and Martha Clifford are probably false names, the entire correspondence is a form of false advertising in which each responds to the illusions engendered by the other's pseudonym. For Bloom, "Martha" conjures up a picture of Christ and the sisters of Lazarus. Jesus is "sitting in their house, talking"; he can just "loll there: quiet dusk: let everything rip. Forget." (5.290–93). Their hospitality creates for Him an abode of bliss. Similarly, this Martha permits Bloom, like a commodified Lazarus, to be reborn. For Martha, "Henry Flower" is the "beautiful name" of a "naughty boy" who gives her vocabulary lessons (5.246–48); he is a "lost one" she will show the way home (15.753–54). Bloom recognizes the pretenses but plays the game anyway.

This correspondence implies that Bloom's pseudonymity and anonymity are closely related to his condition as advertising man and advertised man. As authors, ad designers are almost always anonymous, because advertisements suppress the name of their authors and replace them with the product's name, as if the commodities are self-made. The designer of an ad is subsumed into the identity of the mass product. Moreover, the reception of the ad induces a similar feeling in the viewer. Fredric Jameson argues that advertising is the most basic manifestation in modern society of what he calls *seriality,* a

---

16. Similarly, in Flotow's opera, *Martha,* "Martha" is really Lady Harriet Durham in disguise (Gifford 1988, 129).

mode of activity in which "the uniqueness of my own experience is undermined by a secret anonymity, a statistical quality. . . . I feel that I am no longer central, that I am merely doing what everybody else is doing. But . . . everybody else feels exactly the same way" (1970, 76). Ads individuate each consumer, paradoxically, as part of a mass; thus the reception of an ad is always simultaneously collective and unique; each viewer is configured separately as a mass product. In this sense, ad designers and ad consumers become "everyman and noman" (17.2008).

But Bloom's pseudonyms generate an anonymous, collective self that transcends mere lying or bad faith. His anonymity is personalized through a series of "trademarks," false selves that transfigure and free him from his usual role as outcast and his new role as cuckold. Just as Odysseus went in disguise as a strategy to determine loyalties, so Bloom's name changes are part of his shrewd tactics of self-preservation. Thus when he enters the post office to pick up the letter and when he reads it, he thinks "No-one" (5.53; 230), assuring himself that nobody sees him, but also repeating his Odyssean name, Outis (Noman). Indeed, in calling him a "naughty boy," Martha unwittingly names this very namelessness. "Naughty," according to Skeat, Joyce's source on such matters, derives from *naught,* nothing, which in turn comes from the Old English *na* + *wiht:* either "not a whit," or "no wight"—i.e., no man (Skeat 1935, 396, 715). Bloom is indeed a "naught"-y boy, a person simultaneously anonymous and universal. Henry Flower is a brand name, like Mermaid cigarettes, a sobriquet for a sombrero-doffing Lothario. At other times and places Bloom can be Virag, Poldy, Mackerel, Old Ollebo M.P., Herr Luitpoldt Blumenduft, L. Boom, and so on. Henry Flower, a name with "no fixed abode" (15.733), a free-circulating agent, can therefore be discarded as easily as tearing up a check (5.303): thus when accused as Henry Flower of "unlawfully watching and besetting," Bloom claims the flower was "given me by a man I don't know his name" (15.733; 738). Henry Flower allows Leopold to bloom into "everyman and noman." Paradoxically, then, precisely because of his capacity to be many selves, Bloom becomes more singular, more unique, a "myriadminded man" (9.768), a "massproduct" as polytropic and polyonymous as Odysseus himself. As we shall see in the next section, he is also a man of many turns, a master of tropes, in his advertising designs. Indeed, Joyce's choice of occupation for Bloom may itself suggest Bloom's aesthetic and commercial polytropism, since, as Knuth observes, "advertise" derives from the Latin *vertere* (to turn) (1976,

82). Advertising is thus an appropriate occupation for the reincarnation of Homer's man of many turns; Bloom serves as the host for his own transubstantiations of identity.

Bloom's spurious identities serve important use values. Moreover, his position as ad designer and consumer enables him to exercise his economic agency in a variety of positive ways. Bloom's correspondence with Martha allows him to reinvent his domestic economy by imagining two keys: Martha, who fills a gap in Henry, and Henry, who fills a gap in both Martha and Bloom. As Flower, ironically enough, Bloom is quite Boylanesque. In this way his reconstitution of self enhances his self-worth; the exchanges he carries out by advertising himself and by working through the connotations of other ads he encounters add surplus value to the mass product that is Leopold Bloom. Ultimately, there can be little doubt that the life of commodities in *Ulysses* is complexly related to the promises of religious belief and practices of magic, as well as to the transformative abilities of authors. Advertising may work upon bad faith, but the commodities it speaks about often fulfill important needs, not the least of which is the need to transform the self and to believe in the possibility of transcendence. If this is the substance of advertising's transubstantiation, is it so much different from the metamorphoses that Stephen hopes to achieve through the priesthood of art?

AGENCIES OF ADVERTISING

Stasis and Motion

Since Bloom is a recycler, it is characteristic that his want ad recycles one of his earlier ad ideas. Watching Hely's poor sandwichmen trudging through Dublin, he is reminded of his own employment there and his idea of "a transparent showcart with two smart girls sitting inside writing letters, copybooks, envelopes, blottingpaper. . . . Smart girls writing something catch the eye at once. Everyone dying to know what she's writing" (8.130–36). Bloom exploits his own attraction to "smart" writing females in both the showcart idea and the want ad. It is scarcely an original strategy: even in 1904 traveling showcarts were hackneyed promotional gimmicks (see Richards 1990, 48–50). Nevertheless, Bloom's design adumbrates the position of females throughout *Ulysses* as writers whose output is designed to attract the male gaze. Clearly, much of Martha's erotic allure lies in her role as writer/typist, "Martha" becoming the generic name for a writing female. The showcart's greatest strength, however, is motion; though it promotes stationery, it would not be stationary. Circulating constantly through the city, it would presumably draw male (and perhaps envious female) attention, renewable in each locale. Its reappearance in "Ithaca" after so many hours thus dramatizes the ad's effect upon spectators. In any case, the showcart notion, if not very original, still seems more promising than either the ink bottle with a false stain of black celluloid, or the trite Jones/Robinson dialogue about *Kansell*, the only reliable ink eraser, both of which Bloom also proposed for Hely, and both of which were mercifully rejected (8.137–42).

A savvy salesman, Bloom also admires the floating ad for Kino's eleven-shilling trousers, both because it costs Kino's nothing ("how can you own water, really?" 8.93–94) and because, like the showcart, it conforms to his own aesthetic of advertising, as delineated in "Ithaca": it is "vertically of maximum visibility (divined), horizontally of maximum legibility (deciphered) and of magnetising efficacy to arrest involuntary attention, to interest, to convince, to decide" (17.582–84). Here Bloom's commercial aesthetic recalls Stephen's description of the aesthetic rhythm in *Portrait:* good ads, for Bloom, involve "a stasis called forth, prolonged, and at last dissolved" (*P* 206). But because it is displayed on water, the Kino's ad is not stationary; its power to arrest attention, to make the viewer pause, paradoxically depends upon its wavelike motion. Up and down, back and forth—the ad is anchored yet always moving, its magnetism resulting from its imitation of the "stream of life" that constantly repeats yet always changes. Kino's ad prompts Bloom to recall a certain billsticker (probably not Boylan) who placed ads for a Dr. Hy Franks in all the public urinals —a felicitous location, since he claimed to be able to cure the clap. One of these flybills ("pusyellow" for gonorrhea) speaks words in "Circe" that blend the trouser ad and the quack's poster: "K.11. Post No Bills. Strictly Confidential. Dr Hy Franks" (15.2633). The proximity of Franks and Flower here (Franks also has Henry's initials), suggests that Bloom's sexual anxiety is at work again, along with his guilt about writing to Martha; both Henry and Hy are "strictly confidential," and both offer respite from the pain of love.[17]

---

17. K.11 recurs when Bloom remembers the Kino's ad at the end of the day, although here it seems to be his own condensation of the original (17.586). Elsewhere in "Circe," Bloom responds to Chris Callinan's astronomical poser with "K.11" (15.1658); the question leads again back to Lenehan's story about feeling Molly's "milky way" while returning with Callinan from Featherbed Mountain (10.552–74). Here again the phrase reflects Bloom's sexual anxiety.

Eventually, however, the K.11 motif leads indirectly to a motif of redemption through the significance of the number eleven. In "Circe," George Mesias, Bloom's tailor, appears with other Jewish acquaintances and presents Bloom a bill for "alteration one pair trousers eleven shillings" (15.1911), the same price as Kino's new ones. Of course, Mesias is also Boylan's tailor and has fitted him with the indigo blue serge suit in which he woos Molly (11.880–81). Apparently not a Messiah, Mesias has aided in altering both Bloom's trousers and his marriage, a fact that helps to explain why K.11 appears with gonorrhea remedies: "Some chap with a dose burning in him. If he . . . [Boylan were afflicted]? (8.101–2). But eleven has the regenerative connotations already discussed, and as a numerical amount (eleven shillings) figures prominently in Stephen's financial exchange with Bloom: it is the total sum—ten shillings for whores, plus a shilling for the lamp—that Bloom tenders for Stephen's expenses at Bella Cohen's, a generous deed that initiates their further exchanges in the Nostos and that saves Stephen from further Circean perils (15.3583– 90; .4312). Monetarily, at least, Bloom is Stephen's mesias. Eleven shillings will buy you new trousers, or alter your old ones; it might also save you from Circe. Despite these redemptive associations, Kino's trousers exemplify the economic dispossession that Dubliners must struggle against daily: J. C. Kino was a London clothier who had a Dublin outlet for his English-made products (Gifford 1988, 159), the profits for which doubtless ended up back in English coffers, eleven shillings at a time.

Bloom himself is subjected to the power of good ads to arrest and magnetize attention when, in "Oxen," he stares abstractedly at a bottle of Bass Ale. Mesmerized, he imagines a horde of grotesque creatures trooping through a dead land, until he is rescued by a vision of Milly "shod in sandals of bright gold" (14.1078–1109). "Alpha, a ruby and triangled sign upon the forehead of Taurus" (14.1108–9) is of course the famous red triangle ("England's oldest registered trademark") centrally displayed on bottles of Bass. The Bass Ale logo certainly "catches the eye," although it is not "triliteral," as his ideal ad should be (17.581), but trilateral (three-sided).[18] It fits another of Bloom's criteria as well: it is "monoideal" (17.582)—producing "monoideism," a "concentration of the mind, or fixation of the attention, upon one

18. Triliterality is the quality of having three letters, specifically referring to Hebrew words, in which three letters equal three consonants and hence three syllables. In one sense, the trisyllabic "House of Keys" fits this description.

idea, especially as a form of . . . hypnotic condition" (OED). Since Bass Ale is a British product consumed in large quantities by the Irish (if *Ulysses* is reliable evidence), one might argue that the drink produces a monoideism—paralysis—engineered by British manufacturers, in which consumption of British products deflects political unrest and elicits stasis in consumers.

When Mulligan and Lenehan poke fun at Bloom's abstractedness, the "Macauley" narrator comes to his defense, claiming that he is merely "recollecting two or three private transactions of his own" (14.1189). In one of them Bloom recalls his labor for his father and his own lack of a son (14.1076–77). While the memory of Milly makes him feel less incomplete, these unpleasant thoughts probably spring from the resemblance between the red-labeled bottle of beer and the "redlabelled bottle" of aconite with which Bloom's father committed suicide (6.359). Thus he remains painfully aware of his condition as son. The second "transaction" is Bloom's memory of his first sexual encounter with Bridie Kelly, who would not bear "the sunnygolden babe of day" (14.1074). Both memories, then, circle around Bloom's sense of his home's incompleteness, his sexual anxiety, and his wish for a son. But "wonder of metempsychosis" (14.1099): when he looks up from the Bass bottle, he sees Stephen eyeing it; "both their eyes met," and Bloom pours some out for him (14.1191). The Bass Ale bottle thus also magnetizes the first reciprocal encounter between Bloom and Stephen; like the cocoa they share at chez Bloom, the bottle of beer instigates a moment of sympathetic exchange. The red label compensates for Bloom's lost children by provoking the attention of a possible surrogate son.

As I have implied, ads themselves circulate and repeat in *Ulysses*, mimicking Bloom's own cyclic trajectory. Likewise Bloom's ideal ad would "cause passers to stop in wonder" but remain "congruous with the velocity of modern life": it would fuse stasis and kinesis in a renewable pattern of recirculation. His advertising aesthetic thus both revises Stephen's "applied Aquinas" and rehabilitates paralysis by offering a theory of movement and circulation that also allows reflection. Indeed, the reappearance of minor motifs such as K. 11 or the resurfacing of the Elijah throwaway demonstrate how Joyce uses the same techniques Bloom admires in ads: each time K.11 or the throwaway appears, our attention is arrested and we are momentarily jostled out of the "stream" of reading and thrust backwards in our memories and forward to predict possible future appearances. Joyce has adapted his epiphanic technique to fit Bloom's categories, just as

Bloom's theory is itself based upon Joycean practice. The ad logos in
Ulysses thus function as a *logos*—an anchor beneath its "stream"—or a
series of charged particles that alternate in announcing themselves to
our attention.

Catching the Eye

The showcart, Kino's ad and Bass bottle all "catch the eye." But
Bloom would better achieve that goal if he could institute his proposed improvements on the bicycle poster he sees near the end of
"Lotus-Eaters": "College sports I see today. He eyed the horseshoe
poster over the gate of college park: cyclist doubled up like a cod.
Damn bad ad. Now if they had made it round like a wheel. Then the
spokes: sports, sports, sports: and the hub big: college. Something to
catch the eye" (5.550–54). As figure 1 shows, Bloom's proposed circular design would catch the eye in a dual sense: it would not only *attract*
the viewer's eye—it would mirror it. A synecdoche of the bicycle, the
hub-and-wheel design would magnify and reflect the eye that reads
it, thereby becoming a synecdoche of the viewer as well. Recon-
structed as an eye, the organ of sign consumption, the spectator
merges with the bicycle: consumer and ad converge. The poster stares
back as though watching the spectators, who are already watching
themselves watching the bicycle wheels. The ad appropriates the act

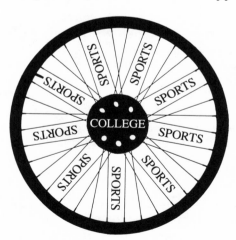

Fig. 1. Bloom's proposed poster for the Trinity College bicycle race
(see 5.550–54).

of viewing the race and returns it to the viewer, thus implicating the viewer in the action it depicts. Like the showcart idea, the poster fuses stasis and motion, first freezing the viewer's eye on the hub and then generating movement as one reads "sports, sports, sports" around and around the wheel. The spectator circulates like a commodity or coin. Reduced "to its simplest and most efficient terms not exceeding the span of casual vision and congruous with the velocity of modern life," the bicycle poster exemplifies Bloom's ideal ad.

Self-consciously and ingeniously "catching" the eye of would-be spectators, the poster stages the very process of consumption, in which purchase is preceded or accompanied by the consumption of messages, an exchange of signs. But because it neither pictures a purchasable commodity nor urges purchases, it seem to be an atypical ad, one that escapes the capitalist economy even as it exemplifies the capitalist mode of signification.[19] More generally, however, the poster epitomizes what all ads aim to do: figure the consuming subject (Richards 1990, 58). It reimagines the viewer as incomplete, with desire remaining to be satisfied. Graphically represented as an eye or wheel, the viewer attempts to complete the picture by filling the open spaces; the consumer is present (and absent) only in this space (Wicke 1988, 160; Williamson 1978, 44). The spectator must complete "the circuit of meaning through which the current of meaning flows" (Williamson 1978, 41), as the ad draws that spectator into and back out of its semiotic economy. That circuit is always both complete and incomplete, as the viewer's eyes range around and around the wheel, in a circuit that, unlike the race, could continue interminably, driven by a desire for completion that remains unfulfilled.

Currents and circuits and wheels: Bloom has long been fascinated by circular shapes and movements. In earlier years, for example, he used to take Dante Riordan out in her wheelchair to watch, often through binoculars, "roadster bicycles equipped with inflated pneumatic tyres," and loved to observe "the spectacle offered with continual changes of velocipedes, vehicles, passing slowly, quickly, evenly, round and round and round the rim of a round and round precipi-

---

19. One might argue that in advertising Trinity College the poster promotes the image of the elite (Anglo-Protestant in sympathy if not in fact) students who attend the school. Furthermore, since the operating funds of Trinity came from its Irish land holdings (Gifford 1988, 147), the bicycle race may be helping to generate funds that perpetuate the landlord system. Both the poster Bloom sees and his hypothetical one suppress this political message, although Gerty MacDowell seems unconsciously to register it by associating bicycles with gentlemanliness.

tous globe" (17.493–94; 499–502). The magnification produced by
binoculars, as well as the dual effects of this observation of motion,
are now captured in the blowup of the wheel. Bloom again uses the
third form of repetition in which the message is reiterated within a
single ad. More importantly, the viewer's eyes here limn the cyclic
trajectory of Bloom's geographic movement through the novel. The
ad makes both ends meet and invites readers to do the same. Expressing his devotion to circulation and cyclicity as modes of producing
renewal by repetition, the poster displays Bloom's economic philosophy for all eyes to see and reproduce. Nevertheless, its returns are
merely repetitive cycling to reproduce the status quo.

The germ for the poster probably dates back to Joyce's 1906
"Notes on Business and Commerce." In the section on advertising,
under the heading "Illustration," he writes, "Bicycles: all the same:
better to draw attention to one feature [such as a wheel] pictorially"
(*JJA* 3:605–6). Just above that, under "Attention" he notes that "in-
tensity [is] obtained by movement. . . . Ex. Smoking Cigarettes, Riding
Bicycles" (605). In reducing the bicycle to a wheel, and in designing it
to produce movement, Bloom follows Joyce's examples. They were
well chosen, since bicycles were not only heavily advertised commodities in this era, but were also used to lend their aura of health and
strength to other products.[20] This youthful mystique also affects
Bloom, since his poster obliquely foreshadows his encounter with
Gerty MacDowell, who loves "the boy that has the bicycle," Reggie
Wylie, brother to one of the racers (12.1494; cf. 13.130–36). The eye
of the bicycle poster thus adumbrates the voyeuristic eye Bloom trains
on Gerty, as well as the eye she trains on the Wylies; through these
eyes both Bloom and Gerty try to complete their unfulfilled domestic
economies. Bloom, would-be designer of bicycle posters, is sexually
rejuvenated by an ocular exchange with a consumer of such ads.

In those advertising notes, Joyce describes posters as "primitive"
ads because the advertiser has "no control of result because not
'Keyed' " (*JJA* 3:608); that is, posters advertise to all who pass by

---

20. See, for example, Hindley 1972, plate C.4, which depicts a young woman
resting after a bicycle ride, drinking Stower's Lime Juice Cordial, "THE ONLY HEALTHY
BEVERAGE THAT CAN BE SAFELY TAKEN AFTER CYCLING OR OTHER EXERCISE" (incidentally,
it is also "excellent for the complexion"). Milly Bloom's emergence into commodity
culture (and adolescence) is represented by the same two accessories. In "Penelope,"
Molly recalls that Milly was "riding Harry Devans bicycle at night," and "getting out of
bounds wanting to go on the skatingrink and smoking their cigarettes through her
nose" (18.1026–29). For a complementary treatment of woman, bicycles, and cyclicity,
see Scott 1991.

rather than to a selected market and thus are not an economical way to spend advertising funds. Furthermore, a poster "can only invite attention" (*JJA* 3:608), rather than magnetize it, and is therefore less effective than, say, a newspaper ad. Bloom proves this axiom wrong with his ingenious design, but Joyce's earlier assessment may help to explain why Boylan is called a "billsticker": his clumsy techniques betray a less sophisticated mind and aesthetic philosophy than Bloom's. Probable examples of Boylan's bills appear in "Wandering Rocks," where Young Dignam scans a boxing poster (10.1133–37) and an ad for Marie Kendall, charming soubrette (10.1141–42). As if to imply his responsibility for the posters, Boylan walks by as young Dignam gazes at the hoardings (10.1150).[21] The posters attract the boy's interest, although he soon learns that the match has already been fought. But he is unlikely to be allowed to attend either event, and so, as Joyce's notes suggest, neither poster is keyed to the proper audience: Marie "smiles daubily" and pointlessly on everyone equally (10.1221). Anyone who has seen a boxing poster knows what this one probably looks like; such flyers (as Joyce notes, "developed from 'fly posting' on houses" [*JJA* 3:608]) are as hackneyed and formulaic as the sportswriting parody that describes the match in "Cyclops" (12.960–87). Neither placard matches the ingenuity of Bloom's proposed poster. Thus although Bloom has contrived some weak ads in his time (the inkblot comes to mind), his strategies have improved a great deal (judging from the bicycle poster and from the Keyes ad, analyzed below), while Boylan, "prosperous rival agency of publicity" (17.2207), seems satisfied with promiscuously catching everyone's eyes. Boylan's lack of skill may bode ill for the success of Molly's upcoming tour; nevertheless his prosperity proves Bloom's contention that "originality, though producing its own reward, does not invariably conduce to success" (17.606–7).

Houses of Key(e)s

Although Bloom spends much of his day pursuing less profitable activities, eventually we do see "THE CANVASSER AT WORK" (7.120),

---

21. Boylan allegedly earned "a cool hundred quid over it" by rumoring that Keogh was a drunk to run up the odds (8.800–2, 12.947). But he kept Keogh sober "down in the county Carlow" for "near a month" to ensure a victory (8.802–6). If, as is also implied, Boylan was promoting the fight, this amounts to fraud. His connection to Marie Kendall is implied by the presence of a duplicate poster on the wall of his office (10.380–84).

attempting to renew two ads, one for the firm of Alexander Keyes, and one for Prescott's dyeworks. Like most ads in *Ulysses,* both promise restoration and therefore fit Bloom's characteristic economic aesthetic. They both surface in Bloom's cogitations in "Lestrygonians," as he calculates prospective earnings: "Keyes: two months if I get Nannetti to. That'll be two pounds ten about two pounds eight. Three Hynes owes me. Two eleven. Prescott's dyeworks van over there. If I get Billy Prescott's ad: two fifteen. Five guineas about. On the pig's back" (8.1057-60; see also 13.920–21 and 18.1342–43; the actual amount would be £5 6s, just over five guineas). Here Bloom's cost accounting provides a real sense of financial renewal, since his income from these two ads alone amounts to £5 3s, a decent month's earnings. An ad for Prescott's dyeworks actually appeared on page 1, column 2 of the *Freeman's Journal* for June 16, 1904, and is shown in figure 2 along with my version of the completed ad for Alexander Keyes.[22]

Proclaiming that lace curtains can be cleaned and "finished" (i.e., restored) in only three days at a shilling per pair, Prescott's ad offers to refurbish a household accessory in the time it took Christ to be resurrected. But is the ad Bloom's? It is certainly less sophisticated than his other designs, focusing only on use values—benefits actually resulting from the product—rather than changes in fortune or sexual

22. A facsimile of the Bloomsday *Freeman's Journal* has recently been published in which a number of "business card" ads for Prescott's also appear on p. 8, col. 9. Because advertising rates are listed on the front page of the newspaper, we can calculate the cost of these ads for the merchants. At 42 words, Prescott's ad would cost the firm at least 1s 2d per day for insertion in the *Journal* alone; adding it to the *Telegraph* would cost another 7d, for a total of 1s 9d per day. Three insertions costs 2s 4d, with the *Telegraph* adding another 1s 2d, for a total of 3s 6d for three insertions in both papers. Prescott would probably take the cheaper, three-day rate, and so for the firm to spend £2 15s (Bloom's projected earnings) on the ad, it would have to run more than 23 times at the three-insertion rate in the *Freeman's Journal* (71 days), or just over 15 times (47 days) in both papers. Keyes's ad, at fewer than 27 words (excluding the "little par" Keyes hopes to add to the *Telegraph* [7.973–74]), would cost 1s 6d for three insertions in both papers. For the amount to reach £2 8s, it would have to appear 32 times, three days for each. It would therefore take 96 days for the total to reach £2 8s. The "little par" would need to expand the ad to 42 words in order for the total cost to come to £2 8s (48 shillings) in two months (60 days, divided by three for the three-day insertion rate; the cost per three-day insertion is 2s 4d). Given these advertising rates, it seems impossible for Bloom to earn as much as he reckons on these two ads in only two months, especially since his commission is probably a small percentage of the total fee. In calculating Bloom's income from the ads, then, Joyce departs from documentary realism and augments Bloom's projected earnings.

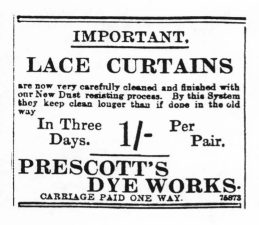

ALEXANDER KEYES, TEA, WINE
& SPIRIT MERCHANT
HIGHCLASS LICENSED PREMISES.

Satisfies your longfelt want.

Fig. 2. Bloom's ads for Prescott's Dye Works and Alexander Keyes as they would appear on the front page of the *Freeman's Journal* (see 8.1057–60; 7.126–58).

potency. Nor does it possess Bloom's characteristic visual cleverness. Gifford claims that "Bloom has sold Prescott's an ad" (1988, 97), but his thoughts about it are conditional—"*if* I get," and "that ad I must"—implying either that he hasn't yet renewed it or that it is not his design at all. Because, aside from its message of rehabilitation, it lacks Bloom's design signatures, I would suggest that Bloom earns commission by selling the space for the ad but did not design it.

Since Bloom's job consists primarily of selling advertising space to merchants, he is essentially a salesman. As the bicycle poster shows, however, he is also a graphic designer of decided sophistication. The Keyes ad, Bloom's magnum opus, demonstrates how his job exploits both his commercial and his artistic skills, while synthesizing nearly all the strains of meaning circulating around advertisements that we have so far considered. Here is Bloom describing the design to Joseph Nannetti, printer and politician:

He wants it changed. Keyes, you see. He wants two keys at the top.
. . . Like that, Mr Bloom said, crossing his forefingers at the top. . . .
Two crossed keys here. A circle. Then here the name. Alexander
Keyes, tea, wine and spirit merchant. So on. . . . Then round the top
in leaded: the house of keys. . . . The idea . . . is the house of keys.
You know, councillor, the Manx parliament. Innuendo of home
rule. Tourists, you know, from the Isle of Man. Catches the eye, you
see. . . . and just a little par calling attention. You know the usual.
Highclass licensed premises. Longfelt want. So on. (7.126–58)[23]

Nannetti gets the pun on keys and agrees to print the design, stipulat-
ing that Bloom ensure a "three months' renewal" (7.160), which he
fails to obtain, although he does get Keyes to agree to two months
(7.973). The ad not only fits the atmosphere of oratory and begging
that pervades the episode but also exemplifies both its "art," rhetoric,
and its technic, enthymeme (buried premises). More significantly, because a version of it has appeared in a Kilkenny paper (and in the
Journal) and because it depends upon a sophisticated knowledge of
the iconography of Irish religion and politics, it forms an important
strand of the intertextual web encompassing the episode that is considered in detail in chapter 6. Indeed, its symbolic significance may
surpass that of Stephen's tale. Because it is partially borrowed and
because Bloom allows Nannetti to supply "the usual" copy, the ad
must be seen as a collaborative production, even though Bloom is the
primary author, just as Stephen's parable draws from the oratory that
precedes it and from his auditor's recent words. Moreover, the Keyes
ad emerges from the intertextual network of all the ads—indeed, all
the cultural and political discourses—circulating in Dublin; therefore,
the ad, inasmuch as it exemplifies the conditions circumscribing Irish
consciousness, can also be said to author Bloom. The Keyes ad resides
in "Aeolus," in short, both to demonstrate that advertising is as legitimate (or illegitimate) a form of cultural discourse as legal argumenta-
tion, political oration, or Dedalian epiphanies, and to show how all of
these discourses depend upon citation, borrowing, and credit.

The surface of the ad is an allegory of power, both spiritual and

23. According to Tomkinson (1965, 104), Bloom uses the term "leaded" incor-
rectly, because leaded type is used to create spaces between lines, and this ad had only
one line of copy at the top. Thus he must mean letter-spaced type. My version of the
ad uses a bit of license in adding bullets between the letters of the slogan for a more
spaced effect. I am indebted to the art department of W. T. Quinn Advertising, Inc.,
and to my wife, Leslie Gilden, for help in desiging the Keyes ad and the bicycle poster.

temporal (Wicke 1988, 146). It is no accident that Keyes bears the same first name as Dowie, especially when one of the ad's primary signifers, keys crossed saltire (like an *X*), is an emblem of St. Peter, holder of the keys "of the kingdom of heaven" (Matthew 16:19). Both Dowie and Keyes are "spirit merchants" offering spiritual regeneration through a consumerist communion (Wicke 1988, 147). Just as Dowie promises to restore the church in Zion, this ad implicitly promises to restore the houses and souls of consumers. Indeed, the crossed keys reiterate in different terms the promise of Plumtree's Potted Meat: heaven, an abode of bliss, can be entered through the cup. St. Peter possesses two keys, one gold and one silver, the first representing absolution and forgiveness, the second excommunication (Webber 1971, 168–70, 194). Likewise the ad appropriates an aura of selectivity—not everyone is worthy of entering Keyes's house—to lend the firm an elite image and thus translates spiritual and moral judgment into matters of class or money. The economy of grace is reduced to material consumption: suppliants must pay to enter Keyes's abode of bliss.

Keys are almost always seen crossed in *Ulysses:* Bloom makes a cross with his fingers as he demonstrates the design; when Stephen relinquishes the huge tower key to Mulligan, he lays it "across his heaped clothes" (1.722); in "Circe," John Howard Parnell (himself politically keyless) gives Bloom the keys to the city, *"crossed on a crimson cushion"* (15.1520). The crossing of the keys may again identify Bloom with Christ's sacrifice, or may connote a betrayal, a double cross in which advertising cloaks its pursuit of customers in the symbols of religious redemption. In this latter sense, Bloom himself may be a betrayer as Peter was, complying with both the "Italian" master's subjugation of the Irish and the Church's own collusion with the exploitative economy of the British Empire. Or it may suggest that Bloom is himself betrayed and scapegoated, as were both Christ and Parnell, and as he is later in the episode, when the journalists and hangers-on in the office laugh at the boys who imitate his walk (7.440–52), and Crawford rudely tells Bloom that Keyes can "kiss my royal Irish arse," damning Bloom for his diligence. Like Peter, Crawford, himself a keyholder (7.459), denies the scapegoated Jew three times (7.672; 981; 991).

Other spiritual powers are metonymized in keys. For example, John O'Connell, the cemetery caretaker, is seen during Dignam's funeral "puzzling two long keys at his back" (6.716). Bloom admires him because he is a "good sort" but also because of his power: "Keys:

like Keyes's ad: no fear of anyone getting out" (6.740–41). O'Connell's keys are the terrestrial analogue to St. Peter's; the former controls access to the kingdom of the dead (the schema identifies him as Hades), just as the latter controls access to heaven. The keys here symbolize both real power, since the caretaker can prevent funerals from taking place, and the metaphoric power of "seeing all the others go under first" (6.785–86). Thus, speaking in "Circe" as a kind of landlord, O'Connell guides Dignam to his plot: "Burial docket letter number U.P. eightyfive thousand. Field seventeen. House of Keys. Plot, one hundred and one" (15.1249–50). He rules this house of keys, an abode of oblivion, if not bliss. The conflation of the parliamentary name and the burial plot again reminds us that the Irishman's house is his coffin, his land a graveyard from which only the elect receive "passout checks" (6.741).

Bloom emphasizes the larger political connotations of the ad because of the interests of his interlocutor, the councilman and future lord mayor Joseph Nannetti, a man who already possesses keys to political power and doesn't need Bloom to "teach him his own business," either politics or printing (7.144). J. H. Parnell's bestowal of keys on Bloom in "Circe" dramatizes the ad's political message, as does Keyes himself when he asks "When will we have our own house of keys?" (15.1683). A good question: unlike the Isle of Man, whose parliament is metonymized by the keys, Bloom's nation is keyless, lacking the home rule such keys represent. Like Plumtree's jingle, this ad leads ineluctably to both Bloom's and Ireland's domestic economy: once again the image of a unified and secure Ireland is used to entice citizens to consume. Ironically, however, the ad also plays upon this gap between the Manx and the Irish, ingratiating itself with "tourists" from the Isle of Man by selling them back their own image. In any case, the political and the personal coalesce in the ad's implication that Bloom's domestic economy is typically Irish. Indeed, his sense of inadequacy, symbolized by his keylessness, is a synecdoche for the complicity of the Irish in their own political and economic powerlessness.

For a man who has had as many addresses as Bloom, his current keylessness merely adds another layer of anxiety to the chronic insecurity betrayed by his "ultimate ambition": to own a place like "Flowerville," a "thatched bungalowshaped 2 storey dwellinghouse" with all the modern conveniences, and to have it "protected against illegal trespassers" (17.1498; 1505; 1560; 1580). But Bloom's forgetting his key suggests other motives: he both wants and does not want Boylan to "trespass" and cuckold him. Does he leave the key as a (conscious or unconscious) excuse for a return that would interrupt the liaison? Or does his loss of it imply a submission to the inevitable? It is clear that keys are emblems of sexual intercourse as well as of hospitality and power. For example, during a painful moment in "Circe," Bloom pimps for Marion and Boylan, while the usurper directs him to "apply your eye to the keyhole and play with yourself while I just go through her a few times" (15.3788–89): Bloom gets the keyhole, Boylan the key, and Bloom's eye treats their rendezvous as a consumable spectacle. Even more explicitly phallic is the description in "Ithaca" of Bloom's opening the door to let Stephen out by "inserting the barrel of an arruginated male key in the hole of an unstable female lock" (17.1215–16). Of course, "key" is also a musical term and used as such frequently in "Sirens," where Bloom himself puns on its phallic connotation (11.1198) and on keys' dual significance as door openers and pitch determiners (11.1241). Both meanings of keys converge in the souvenirs of Boylan's visit, at once a musical rehearsal, business meeting, and erotic rendezvous. Bloom notes the piano's "exposed keyboard" and the open sheet music to "Love's Old Sweet Song," in the "key of G natural" (17.1303; 1306). The lovers were properly keyed up. In contrast, Bloom's wandering is keyless ad libbing. Curiously, since keys are the symbol of St. Martha, patroness of good housekeeping (or good husbanding [Gifford 1988, 375]), the key symbolism admits the name of Bloom's erotic correspondent, as if the instrument of his cuckolding also opens the door to a compensating liaison. With Martha he sings his version of "Love's Old Sweet Song" (his virtuoso performance on "her heartstrings" [11.714] coming, appropriately, in "Sirens"), though not in the original key. No saint, Bloom's Martha nonetheless provides a momentary abode of bliss.

As we have seen, Ireland's economy had been disrupted and impoverished by centuries of British rule. Ironically, in selling tea, the ad markets a product originally made available by the same British colonialist commerce that dominates Ireland. The political appeal is thus built on the same (unlicensed?) premises that have created the conditions that oppress the very consumers it targets. Far from enlisting consumers in "the service of a subversive politics," as Herr argues (1986, 71), the ad exploits a vague innuendo of home rule and then transforms it into a plea to satisfy "longfelt wants" through consumption. Wicke is right that "no one will be mobilized to agitate for British removal after seeing the Keyes ad" (1988, 147). I would go further: the ad first stresses and then suppresses its political content by deflecting political *ressentiment* into the urge to consume. This suppression is not a matter of some vast conspiracy between government and the press; it simply means that the ad ingeniously reads itself first, its economy of meaning demanding a response framed in terms directed at specifically Irish consumers. In so doing, it suppresses both the causes of and the remedies for the colonized condition that it vaguely promises to remedy.

The ad's design is based upon a rebus (O'Shea 1986, 78), or visual pun. Viewing the ad, a reader would first notice the keys and the slogan but then remark the altered spelling ("Keyes") at the bottom. This movement would then trigger a rereading of the top of the ad, in turn prompting the reader to supply the missing letter to the original caption. As in the bicycle poster, here again the viewer slips into the gap provided by the ad; the reader is enticed into the space between competing signifiers and thus becomes the medium for the circulation of its economy of meaning (see Williamson 1978, 14, 77). Indeed, the ad insinuates that Keyes's mass products perform a similar completion: to consume Keyes's drinks is not only to make one's own home more secure (with keys) but also to restore security to the homeland. Bloom's ad thus slyly exploits Ireland's pervasive sense of dispossession and incompletion, an incompleteness that is also the source of the consumer's desire. Hence the ad offers on the ideological level its own spurious fulfillment of Ireland's "longfelt want" —political and economic home rule. Attracted simultaneously as a patriotic Irishperson and a British subject, the consumer is remade as a schizophrenic subject with radically conflicting allegiances. While unconsciously imbibing the patriotic implications, the Irish consumer would also ingest both the ideology of empire (through the economy that makes tea available) and the ideology of consumerism.[24] The ad shows how the British had wrested control not only of the products sold in Ireland but also of the messages about those products. That is, an Irish consumer could not help but read the ad according to codes already conditioned by the imperial political economy. In this ad, as in the economic relations between the countries, England plays

24. Richards (1990, 40) persuasively shows how Victorian England successfully sold "the culture and ideology of England, its plans for commercial dominance, its dreams of empire, its social standards, and its codes of conduct" when it sold its products abroad. Tea, a product originally taken from the Orient but then strongly associated with Britain, beautifully exemplifies how Britain dissolved foreign cultures into its own identity through these ideological ingredients.

Egypt to Ireland's Israel, the ad comprising another example of how, to quote Bloom's version of the Haggadah, the English have brought the Irish "out of the land of Egypt and into the house of bondage" (7.208–9). Since the English hold the keys, few "passout checks" are issued.

The ad also shows how consumerism and imperialism can cooperate to efface consumers' political consciousness. It steals its audience's sense of history by removing the signifiers of autonomy from the political register and making them a function of consumer desire; in place of a history lesson about English-Irish relations, the ad enshrouds the facts and moves them into the eternal present of consumption, in which one is forever on the brink of satisfaction. Moreover, in pledging to satisfy communal and collective "longfelt wants," the ad diverts political activity into private acts of individual consumption. The social subject is transformed into an isolated, consuming subject, whose future holds not political freedom but only more drinks. Thus when Keyes sells tea and spirits as remedies for physical or emotional malaise, those products are cleverly transubstantiated into panaceas for Ireland's political and economic illnesses: the body and the body politic are identified. In Ireland the signifiers of capitalist economics are invariably freighted with the codes of the imperialist political economy. Perhaps most importantly, Bloom's role in designing the ad demonstrates that he too is implicated in the English master's control over Irish exchanges—both linguistic and economic.

But if England plays Boylan to Ireland's Bloom, this fact also suggests that the Irish may be as complacent or complicit in their usurpation as Bloom is in his. And indeed, the Irishmen depicted in "Aeolus" (and elsewhere in Joyce), show few signs of actively resisting their oppression. Instead they wax sentimental about their lovely land and patronize the local pubs, their rhetoric conjuring up a misty feeling of nostalgic well-being about the past and future of Ireland, even as their idleness disables them from producing genuine home rule. Like Bloom, who will benefit financially from Boylan's intervention, some Irish talk about economic freedom but take advantage of its absence. Part shares and part profits: the Irish get a payoff from their colonized condition. Bloom's mixture of complicity and resistance thus makes it clear that Ireland is his country (7.87).

Keyes is scarcely a revolutionary; indeed, he profits well from his merchandising, as is implied by his presence at Dillon's auction rooms (7.431), where he can buy at a discount the shabby possessions of families like the Dedaluses, who must auction off their belongings to earn temporary provision (see 10.645–50).[25] The real Alexander Keyes was a member of the jury on the Childs murder case (Adams 1962, 174), also mentioned in "Aeolus." Thus he would have heard Seymour Bushe's speech on the law of evidence, so orotundly quoted by O'Molloy a few pages before Bloom's plea for renewal (7.768–71). Just as Stephen attempts to win credit from his audience by metaphorically echoing O'Molloy's pleas for money, so Bloom's importunities to Keyes echo Bushe's pleas for mercy. Both Bushe and Bloom seek renewal. Bushe's speech woos Stephen; it must have wooed Keyes, too, since Childs was acquitted (Gifford 1988, 115).[26] Likewise, Keyes grants Bloom a partial renewal of two months—not the three he asked for, but better than nothing. Bloom's pleas thus again demonstrate his resemblance to the other Irishmen whose words waft through "Aeolus" to borrow, beg, or beseech. Like their fates, the fate of Bloom's ad remains up in the air, since he is unable to confirm the transaction and lists it as an "imperfection" in the day upon retiring (17.2074).

Despite (or perhaps because of) this inconclusiveness, the design of Bloom's ad, with its circular shape and sophisticated symbology, once again embodies his obsession with renewal and regeneration. Of course, the ad works upon him, too, conditioning his response to his cuckolding—even as it expresses his anxiety about it—and demonstrating his dependence upon preexisting texts and cultural codes. But the crossed keys may presage a later, more hopeful, "crossing": the meeting between two keyless citizens, Stephen and Bloom. They cross paths several times before their final encounter, including near-misses here and in "Wandering Rocks," and an encounter at the end of "Scylla and Charybdis" in which Bloom crosses between Stephen and Mulligan (9.1203). Though their final meeting is also crossed by thoughts of exploitation (Bloom's), by hostility and indifference (Stephen's) and characterized by talking at cross-purposes (both), each character gains something from this encounter, which fortifies each against oppressors and arms each for future battles. Their ex-

25. The fictional Keyes is much wealthier than his real-life model, who was probably only the manager, not the owner of the firm (Gifford 1988, 128–29).

26. Coincidentally, the case against Samuel Childs, who was alleged to have murdered his brother, rested chiefly "on the fact that only Samuel had a key to the house, and that there was no evidence for the murderer's having entered by force" (Gifford 1988, 115). Apparently Childs was not keyless.

change of money and power is graphically represented by their valedictory handshake, in which their arms meet and form an angle that
inverts the crossed keys in Bloom's ad (17.1222–23), as if their own
keylessness is made less hopeless by sharing it. Each experiences a
brief feeling of security, domesticity, and a sense of power; each also
gets a reminder of his own incompleteness and lack of power, and
therefore of the need for others to abet any movements toward domestic or artistic authority. Each begins to move towards new power
with the creations depicted here in "Aeolus," the site of their first
crossing. Like a home without Plumtree's meat, the "home" they temporarily make at Eccles Street is incomplete; nevertheless, it may yield
a "new lease of life" (16.547). If this is the book's central exchange,
and if each character becomes (however briefly) a "new man," then
does the argument of *Ulysses* differ so much from that of the Wonderworker?

Seeking Renewal

Bloom's theory and practice of advertising testify to a lively and
sophisticated mind at work on enterprises that he deems significant.
The central tropes in his ad designs harmonize with the tenor of his
entire discourse, which, as David Lodge has argued, is "essentially
metonymic" (1977, 140), and which, as I have argued, reinscribes his
attachment to figures of circulation, exchange, cyclicity and renewal.
His bicycle poster condenses both bicycle and the spectator into twin
synecdoches; his ad for Keyes appropriates the political and religious
metonymy of keys and reanchors it to another semiotic register. Both
stimulate the refiguration of the viewer and instigate an exchange of
symbolic currency; both thus again render the novel's and Bloom's
redemptive economic formula—both ends meet. In addition, Bloom's
theories of motion—that good ads should arrest attention, convince,
and decide, and that an ideal ad should stop time and yet remain
"congruous with the velocity of modern life"—echo the axioms of
real advertising strategists (including the young James Joyce).[27]
Joyce's own ad notes contribute to Bloom's expertise, and his lessons
about attention, motion, and repetition have been transferred almost
directly to the ads in *Ulysses*.

27. One recent advertising textbook describes a good ad in terms strikingly similar to Bloom's: it should attract *attention* and then *interest*, then stimulate *desire*, and
finally spark *action* (Mandell 1984, 441–43).

These ads not only express Bloom's anxieties and moor their signifiers to a specific place and time but also universalize his desires. Michael Schudson has argued that advertising, which he dubs "capitalist realism," characteristically operates in that way. Like socialist realism, advertising simplifies and typifies its characters, shows lives worth emulating, celebrates the march of progress, aids the masses in assimilating new social and technological features, and privileges the present over the past (1984, 215–16). Both forms also share the same weaknesses, rewriting history with a teleological and progressive bent, reducing human consciousness to the satisfaction of needs and thereby narrowing the channels of desire, and presupposing the normalcy of the idealized lives they present. Like literary realism too, capitalist realism masks the history of its production, presumes a transparent semiotic relationship between signifier and signified that collapses upon close examination, and presents an allegedly credible speaker whose reliability is usually spurious. Thus Baudrillard (1988, 20) is at least partially correct that the price of commodity culture's "radical simplification" of needs and desires is an impoverishment of the language of value, as human beings are described solely in terms of objects.

Overall, however, Joyce's treatment of commodity culture is less dark. Bloom, for one, genuinely believes that the consumption of commodities can satisfy important needs, and *Ulysses* demonstrates that he is right: Boylan and Molly use Plumtree's Meat as an aphrodisiac that produces temporary bliss; Bloom figuratively and literally adheres to the soap and believes in the salvific powers of Wonderworker; Bloom's ad-soaked exchange with Gerty (examined in chapter 8) regenerates both characters; Bloom shares mass-produced cocoa with Stephen in a secular communion. One must concede John Kenneth Galbraith's point that advertising sometimes creates false needs and influences consumers against their own best interests, while preying most upon the ignorant, powerless, and dissatisfied. But it does not follow that a need stimulated by advertising is necessarily false; nor do consumers always blindly buy what ads urge them to buy.[28] Moreover, in a market economy advertising provides indispensable help in moving products and thereby contributes to the health of that economy, even as it increases the range of choices and information available to the consumer. On the other hand, advertis-

28. My summary and rebuttal of Galbraith's argument are drawn from Draper 1986, 15–16.

ing also implies that all needs can be satisfied through consumption and thus deters consumers from finding other methods of rectifying wrongs or satisfying needs, such as politics, religion, or human intimacy; it also creates "needs" as avenues to sell already manufactured goods with questionable use values (patent medicines are good examples). Given these mixed motives and the inconsistent results of Bloom's advertising practice, we are warranted in seeing a good deal of ambiguity in Lenehan's remark that Bloom has a "touch of the artist" about him (10.582): he exercises a sophisticated form of art in the school of capitalist realism, but like Odysseus he is also a con-artist with a touch of the trickster. In his advertising practice as in his larger economic life, Bloom is both mercenary and altruistic, selling goods and the ideas of goods both to make money and to help others gain renewal.

For the most part, however, the lives of Joyce's Dubliners are not dominated by consumption; it is merely one of many rituals that enable them to "make sense of the inchoate flux of events" (quoted in Jhally 1987, 7), the same function served by Bloom's price fixing and Stephen's search for linguistic treasure. *Ulysses* at least demonstrates Joyce's understanding of advertising theory and praxis as well as his profound comprehension of the rhetorical power and economic force of commodity culture. More importantly, Joyce's own artistic practices mirror those of advertising, and he bases the structural economies of *Ulysses* upon principles that mimic Bloom's aesthetic-commercial philosophy. Bloom insists, for example, that "for an advertisement you must have repetition" (12.1147–48), a dictum that certainly applies to *Ulysses,* a text that "makes itself with repetitions" (Wicke 1988, 164), particularly that second form, in which a message or motif is repeated with a difference over time. For a novel like *Ulysses,* you must have repetition.

Likewise, according to Bloom, a good ad stops time momentarily and then lets it continue renewed; "life is a stream" (8.95), but advertising (like Stephen's moment of aesthetic apprehension) permits pause for refreshment and reflection. This belief in the complementarity and eventual fusion of stasis and motion brings together Bloom's and Stephen's (and Joyce's) aesthetic philosophies. Indeed, Bloom's aesthetic philosophy is more practical than the one Stephen expounds in *Portrait,* because it moves away from the paralysis that the younger Joyce saw as Dublin's typical posture. Ultimately, the philosophy of balance, repetition, and circulation that Bloom formulates as "both ends meet" and practices in his ad designs underlies

Joyce's own principles of construction, as motifs introduced in the novel's opening (e.g., keys) return at its close. This is not to say that Joyce learned his aesthetics from advertising. It does mean that, when one reads *Ulysses,* one observes another ad man at work, one who boldly advertised his own works as commodities, and who unapologetically weaves discourses and figures from popular culture and into his texts—James Joyce. His agency subsumes Bloom's, and his novel contains the products of that agency.

For Joyce, advertising involves agency in two respects: it is an active mode of relation to goods in which consumers make choices based upon perceived needs and use values, and it mediates between consumers and products. Reading *Ulysses* also demands a dual agency. The reader of *Ulysses* also frequently halts in his or her journey through the novel, arrested by an image, a moment, a memory. Likewise, the efficacy of repetition requires readers active enough to recognize its existence and to bring together discrete moments. As when reading an ad, a reader sees each instance emerge from an intratextual web of references that can be woven only with his or her collaboration. In Joyce's economy of reading, as in the theoretical economy of advertising, consumers contribute to their own refiguration by filling the gaps of meaning that the text leaves open. This economy of meaning is not determined by a mastermind advertiser, whether it be Joyce or some anonymous copywriter, though it does revolve around a limited number of alternatives. Rather, it is collective as well as active: we invest our memory in its economy of meaning, creating a currency that is not given to us but that we earn. Thus it would be more accurate to say not that *Ulysses* makes itself, but that readers constantly remake it by engaging in transactions with its signs and thereby generating a circulating medium of exchange between the text's tropes and our revisions of them. Joyce's advertising agency depends, finally, upon our own activity.

If the economy of *Ulysses* owes much to ads, so does the economy of Dublin. As an exemplary reader and designer of ads, Bloom's occupation is inseparable from his general economic agency. While Bloom's ads identify him as Irish, they also inscribe his geographic, financial, and aesthetic philosophy of cyclicity, enabling him to transcend the Irish (and Jewish) economic identities he has inherited— identities comprised of nostalgia, victimization, and despair—and replace them with an optimistic belief in the possibility of regeneration through imagination. Advertising gives Bloom a means to envision domestic, political, and erotic renewal, as well as a practical means of improving his own economic condition. His remedy for dispossession and incompleteness is to make returns—as in a circle, and as in a functioning economy. After all, he does ultimately reclaim his *oikos*, even achieving a modicum of bliss as he drops off to sleep. It is clear that Bloom's economic agency—his instigation of genuine material exchanges in charity, payment of debts, and prudent financial management—is a positive force in the Dublin economy. As a nexus of exchange, he embodies a powerful and highly functional textual and financial force. In this respect he becomes a model for the regeneration of the Irish economy: transformation is possible only if consumers remain alert to the exchanges they carry out with commodities and their messages. If Ireland could make ends meet as Bloom does, reclaiming her own products and messages (including the image of Ireland herself), and sell them at home and abroad—using advertising!—perhaps she could also renew her domestic economy as a prelude to genuine home rule.

5

Circulation and Exchange

The circulation of wealth in a nation resembles that of the blood in the natural body. There is one quickness of the current which comes of cheerful emotion or wholesome exercise; and another which comes of shame or fever.
—Ruskin 1905, 17:48

ECONOMIES OF GRACE

The economy of *Ulysses* extends beyond Stephen and Bloom into the network of debts and exchanges in Joyce's Dublin. I have shown elsewhere how Joyce's story "Grace" analyzes this network, exposing the collusion of Ireland's "two masters"—the British empire and the Catholic church—and charting ways that their lines of power intersect in a shared economic ideology (Osteen 1991). Church and state inculcate a bourgeois economism based on cost accounting while at the same time barring most Dubliners from attaining a secure bourgeois position. This complicity between spiritual and secular powers and the economic effects of their mutually reinforcing ideologies are also glaringly apparent in *Ulysses*, perhaps most obviously in "Hades" and "Wandering Rocks," the episodes that also resuscitate the "Grace" characters. However, in both *Dubliners* and *Ulysses*, Joyce blames not only the institutional powers that oppress the Irish but also Irish citizens themselves for their passive acceptance of failed ideologies and for their inability to discover alternatives to the cult of patriotic sacrifice that paralyzes them and prevents them from shaping a more positive definition of Irishness.[1] Joyce wrote that he aimed in *Dubliners* to write "a chapter in the moral history" of Ireland (*L* II 134): those bleak and sometimes bitter stories were designed to alter Ireland's political and economic conditions by reflecting them in the mirror of art. By unflinchingly documenting its social ills, Joyce hoped that Dubliners could, if not cure those ills, at least repudiate the illusory remedies that had so long held out false hope. Similarly, in *Ulysses*, Joyce administers a moral economy of grace and redemption with the scrupulousness and control of a priest operating a "great cash register" (*P* 148), thereby not only completing the arcs of the *Dubliners* characters and deciding their fates but also completing his moral history by documenting the economic conditions of his city. In these sections the author acts as moral arbiter, as Cosmic Economist.

In returning to the moral economy that shaped *Dubliners*, Joyce also temporarily reassumes the aesthetic of "scrupulous meanness": whereas many of the late episodes embrace an economy of excess, "Hades" and "Wandering Rocks" manifest an aesthetic of control in which Joyce spends words frugally and exacts upon his characters a stringent economic morality. The moral and verbal economies reflect each other. Thus, in these parts of *Ulysses*, the meaning of "economist" traverses the same route as the original word. Originally referring to the office of steward, *oikonomos* broadened its meaning to denote "every kind of . . . regulation . . . and arrangement, including divine dispensation" (Singer 1958, 53). As the *oikonomos* of his text, a Dispenser of rewards or punishments situated above the action, Joyce repudiates the irresponsible economic behavior of his Dubliners and at the same time supplants the economic control of the two masters with his own authorial control and power; in so doing, he aims to provide a model through which the Irish may break the patterns of the past. Whether he judges his characters with or without grace, at least the economy remains in Irish hands.

To expose the conditions that have produced Dublin's economic stultification, Joyce documents virtually the entire range of social and economic exchanges that comprise the life of the city. If, as Simmel writes, "exchange is the objectification of human interaction" (1950, 388; cf. Homans 1958, 606), we may best understand the social life of Joyce's city by analyzing its exchanges. We can chart this network

---

1. As McMichael (1991, 171) reminds us, a critic or author who strips characters of individual will and responsibility merely mimics the operations of the colonizing forces.

according to Marshall Sahlins's outline of the exchange continuum,
which ranges from the ideal of pure charity (generalized reciprocity
and gift exchange), to the pragmatic medium of balanced reciprocity,
in which each party gets equal value from the other, through the
negative extreme of economic exploitation (1972, 193–95). Although,
as one might expect, little genuine charity is present, in Dublin other
economic norms have been distorted by poverty, centuries of political
oppression, institutional hypocrisy, and citizens' willingness to exploit
each other.

Ulysses revives some characters "Grace" had left in purgatory. Indeed, although "Grace" ostensibly concerns a redemption and
"Hades" a funeral, the underlying movement of the two pieces is the
reverse: "Grace" deals with damnation and "Hades" with reincarnation. Their economic subtexts also mirror each other, as Joyce uses
literary metempsychosis to permit his characters to reenact or repay
their moral and financial debts. Some are given (qualified) grace;
others seem damned by an author who, like Shakespeare, carries a
memory in his wallet and always pays his grudge debts. In exhuming
these dead—both from *Dubliners* and from the real Dublin—Joyce
achieves partial reconciliation with his past and the economic conditions that molded his own behavior. In this sense Joyce's moral economy operates by a kind of usury: just as Aristotle's usurer generates
monetary offspring out of money itself, so Joyce generates more
words out of the encounter with his own texts, as if the value of the
original deposits in his verbal treasury increases by being withdrawn
again. Debtorship again dominates both form and content, as Joyce's
moral economy is presented through Dubliners' economic habits and
attitudes, which, ironically, include a nearly universal condemnation
of usury.

An enormous system of reciprocal debts underlies the novel like
the submerged mass of an iceberg. As in "Grace," where the hidden
parts of characters' lives—their gnomons—are usually economic
problems, so the absences in "Hades" define the dramatis personae
by revealing their social and economic interactions and failures. In
this regard, the idea of incubism carries even more connotations. It
refers most obviously to the oppression of the living by the spirits
of the dead. Thus everyone in "Hades" is haunted by invisible or absent beings: Bloom by his dead father, Simon Dedalus by his wife,
all of the Irish by Parnell, Stephen by the ghost of his mother, and so
on. But as a symbol of the nightmare of history, incubism signifies
other invisible influences upon the characters that are drawn from

their individual fictional histories, from the troubled histories of the real people upon whom the characters are based, or from the incubistic and oppressive memories of financial creditors in the text. In this last sense, incubism signifies the hidden but oppressive conditions of debtorship: obligation and poverty. Like Stephen, most other Dubliners are oppressed by the personal history—both fictional and real—latent in their debts. And just as Stephen fears the tyranny of invisible beings—his mother, Haines, his creditor Buck Mulligan—other Dubliners are haunted by secret economic problems. In a wider sense, of course, Britain and Rome are the incubi, spectres whose massive historical weight continues to bear down on the Irish, demanding tribute that can never be fully paid. Ultimately, however, Joyce replaces them as the powerful but invisible presence who governs the social life of his fictional world.

Relics of Old Decency

The first half of "Hades" reprises the characters and sense of enclosure of the sickroom scene in "Grace." Martin Cunningham, Jack Power, Bloom, and Simon Dedalus ride together in one funeral carriage while Kernan rides in another. But those who are not present are as important as those who are. Chief among these missing persons are Stephen and Boylan, both of whom Bloom glimpses along the route (6.39;199), and both of whom prompt his uneasy musings on mortality and sexuality. The cortege passes statues of dead Irish heroes, as the passengers prepare to mourn the dead Irish nonhero Paddy Dignam, the most obviously absent person. This movement from the heroic to the banal mirrors the routes of decline traced by most of the Dubliners in the episode, which are dramatized by Bloom's recollection of the lyrics of a song, "The Pauper's Drive": "Over the stones. Only a pauper. Nobody owns" (6.333; Gifford 1988, 111). Though not precisely a pauper, Dignam was on the downward slide from drinking done, ironically, with those who now mourn him. As we have seen, Bloom recognizes how much money Dignam spent to get the way he is now. But though Dignam's decline is exemplary, he has at least escaped his economic condition: while he owns nothing, nobody owns him either.

Another song, "The Hat Me Father Wore," comes to Bloom as he contemplates the decline of one Tweedy, an erstwhile lawyer now reduced to selling bootlaces: "Has that silk hat ever since. Relics of old decency" (6.234; Gifford 1988, 109). The latter phrase epigrammatically sums up the condition of a majority of the male Dubliners in *Ulysses,* including Dignam, who was fired from his job with John Henry Menton for drunkenness—"many a good man's fault," according to Simon (6.573). He should know: himself a relic of old decency, he still possesses the once-handsome clothes and manners of a gentleman without any of the concomitant economic or social clout. Thus Molly Bloom's later description of Simon captures his sham gentility: "such a criticiser with his glasses up with his tall hat on him . . . and a great big hole in his sock" (18.1088–89).[2] The song introduces a minor but intriguing motif. Hats figure metonymically here and elsewhere as emblems of the characters' shifting social and economic identities; sitting visibly atop the head, a hat is an unmistakable sign of one's social position or aspiration: Stephen's poverty and pretension are represented by his "wide hat" (6.40), a badge of bohemianism; Boylan's sham gallantry by his "white disc of a straw hat" (6.199); Martin Cunningham's pomposity by his tall silk hat (6.1); Bloom's false address is hidden in his "high grade ha" (the omitted letter suggesting his own condition as a gnomon); Lenehan's sporting interests and spurious sophistication by his yachting cap (10.579); the begging sailor's destitution by his begging cap; Lynch's sterility by his cap/condom. Thus, as the cortege passes through Dublin, it is saluted by a series of doffed hats, gestures repeated when the viceregal cavalcade passes through the city in "Wandering Rocks." When the mourners listen to the funeral ceremony, they take off their hats and assume properly grave manners; when they replace them, they return to their public identities, and Bloom is able to inform his enemy, John Henry Menton, that he has a "dinge" in his hat, as if to remind him that his public identity is less imposing than he thinks it is (6.1015–23). This haberdashic motif itself reprises "Grace," where Kernan's sartorial splendor belies his economic impotence but bears witness to his moral trajectory: he loses and besmears his hat when he falls down into the lavatory filth (*D* 150–51), but it is "rehabilitated" by the time he visits the retreat, thus experiencing the grace Kernan himself fails to achieve (*D* 173). Like O'Madden Burke's umbrella, hats represent the characters' desperate attempts to mask their real financial condi-

---

2. Simon says Dignam was "as decent a little man as ever wore a hat" (6.303). But while charitable in his expressions, he is less generous with money, probably because he doesn't have any: when asked by Ned Lambert to give "a few bob a skull . . . to keep [Dignam's family] going till the insurance is cleared up," Simon rudely brushes him off (6.565–67).

tions by maintaining the appearance of respectability; minor but telling symbols, they betray the characters' hidden economic problems.

The sartorially splendid Tom Kernan, the object of rehabilitation in "Grace," is absent from Bloom's carriage. His sobriety has evidently been short-lived, for Cunningham tells the others that "Tom Kernan was immense last night" (6.142), and he has already imbibed some gin by the time he appears in "Wandering Rocks" (10.724) and is later seen drinking in "Sirens." "Immense"— like the "retrospective arrangement"—is a Kernanesque term suggesting his inebriated pomposity. But like the latter phrase, the word "immense" is woven into the structural connections of the novel. Here it presages Stephen's telegram to Mulligan about incurring *"the immense debtorship for a thing done"* (9.550–51), and links Kernan's "immensity" and his indebtedness. Addicted to retrospective arrangements and Ben Dollard's trenchant rendition of the sentimental song, "The Croppy Boy," Kernan is undoubtedly a sentimentalist. Just as the epigram prompts us to scrutinize Mulligan's immense debtorship, so the word "immense" suggests a connection between sentimentality and debt. Thus we learn that he still owes money to his "friend" Fogarty, a presence in "Grace" who is also absent from the cortege: Kernan has "left him weeping," never paying the bill for groceries he has owed for some time now (6.456; cf. *D* 166). Simon jokes that "though lost to sight," Fogarty is "to memory dear," and his invisible presence follows Kernan, even though he pretends to be debtless. Kernan's sentimentalism thus implies not just a failure to pay but an eagerness to "enjoy without incurring" debtorship, a forgetfulness of whatever is inconvenient that recalls Mulligan. Despite his devotion to "The Croppy Boy," Kernan swears allegiance to Protestantism and the English (*D* 157; 10.788–92); but if his religious and political affiliations differ from most Dubliners', he epitomizes the "Irish" failings Joyce exposes throughout his work—sentimentalism, drunkenness, and economic failure. Kernan remains a gnomon, his afterlife in *Ulysses* merely extending the lines of incompleteness depicted in "Grace" without granting him economic or moral grace.

Even he has his redeeming moments, however, in his relations with Bloom. Though at first he and Bloom are "related in a simple buyer-seller relationship" (Dick 1981, 148) in which Bloom plans to get some tea from him (5.19–20) but never completes the transaction, their relations are primarily social rather than economic exchanges. The difference is that in social exchanges obligations remain unspecified by financial calculations; such exchanges "generate trust in social

relations" and constitute an intermediate case between pure calculation of advantage and pure expressions of charity (Blau 1964, 93,
112): each party receives something from the encounter. Thus during
the funeral Bloom is observing Simon's histrionic mourning when
Kernan approaches him as a fellow outsider to the Catholic ceremony: "Mr Bloom nodded gravely looking in the quick bloodshot
eyes. Secret eyes, secretsearching. Mason, I think: not sure. . . . We
are the last. In the same boat. Hope he'll say something else" (6.660–
63). Kernan obliges with a sentimental phrase ("that touches a man's
inmost heart"), unwittingly providing Bloom with fodder for the
skeptical comment about hearts quoted in chapter 3. Their social
exchange enables Bloom to rediscover his humor and repudiate the
sentimentality that paralyzes other Dubliners, just as their reciprocal
gazes and knowledge of each others' secrets permit them to share
emotional currency. This moment may explain Kernan's helpful role
during Bloom's Lord Mayor fantasy in "Circe" when Kernan tells
Bloom that he deserves the keys to the city (15.1523); Kernan's presence here is in keeping with his love of pomp. But they are "in the
same boat" only momentarily, and Kernan's primary function, as Dick
observes (1981, 153), is to shine a reflected light on Bloom's better
qualities, not the least of which is his unsentimental and prudent
economic mentality. Joyce thus accords a modicum of grace to Kernan but also exacts a fee, a kind of interest that Kernan must forever
pay simply by existing: just as memory insures debtorship, so Kernan's previous existence prevents him from changing dramatically. If
his economic condition remains the same, his encounters with Bloom
reveal a slightly more graceful side, if only because his foolishness
gives Bloom a moment of release.

Another "Grace" character absent from the carriage is Charlie
M'Coy, whom Bloom has already encountered during "Lotus-Eaters."
Initially the two seem to have much in common: both have been ad
canvassers, both have singing wives, both are half-outsiders to the
Cunningham-Power circle, and once again there is a moment of doubling in their reciprocal gazes (5.150). M'Coy habitually uses such
friendly gestures as excuses to exploit his acquaintances with his "valise tack": he "borrows" his friends' valises to "enable Mrs M'Coy to
fulfill imaginary engagements in the country" (*D* 160), in exchange
promising free tickets to her nonexistent performances (16.523–24).
Apparently M'Coy then pawns the valises for a modest profit—typical
tactics of a man who "levanted with the cash of a few ads" and thereby
lost the job that Bloom now holds (6.887). But Bloom is on guard:
when M'Coy says "My missus has just got an engagement," he deftly

eludes him by mentioning Molly's upcoming tour. And when he leaves, Bloom puts mental distance between them by comparing their wives: "Reedy freckled soprano. Cheeseparing nose. . . . You and me, don't you know: in the same boat. Softsoaping" (5.184–86).³ M'Coy, in short, disrupts the reciprocity of friendly social exchanges by attempting to pilfer his friends' possessions.

Despite M'Coy's chicanery, Bloom does him a favor. When M'Coy asks him to "shove in [his] name" to the list of those present at the funeral (5.171–72), Bloom answers "that will be done," echoing the "Lord's Prayer," which contains that significant clause about debts and debtors. At the funeral Bloom discharges his promise to M'Coy, who was probably afraid to show up because of having embezzled money from the *Journal,* whose representative, Joe Hynes, is sure to be present. Yet Bloom seems to perceive his generous act as a debt: "I saw to that M'Coy. Thanks, old chap: much obliged. Leave him under an obligation: costs nothing" (6.888).⁴ If contracting a debt is oppressive because the degree of indebtedness is made both specific and contractual, in contrast, doing a favor leaves the reparation indefinite, both in amount and in time. Bloom considers trying to get a free pass to Mullingar as repayment (5.321—he forgets to do so), although why and how M'Coy would be capable of such perquisites remains a mystery. In any case, Bloom will now be able to use M'Coy's small indebtedness to him as a "capital of willing compliance" (Blau 1964, 28) he can call in whenever he wants. But despite his mercenary interpretation of the favor, Bloom seems unlikely to call in the debt anytime soon: his moral economy is generally gracious, and he is usually above such mean cost accounting. In M'Coy's eyes, at least, Bloom's favor is a gift that establishes Bloom's prestige and generosity as a model for others to follow (Blau 1964, 108).

Indeed, M'Coy does repay it, albeit indirectly, and at the same

---

3. See also 11.972–76: "M'Coy valise. My wife and your wife. Squealing cat. Like tearing silk. Tongue when she talks like the clapper of a bellows. . . . Want a woman who can deliver the goods" (cf. 18.1267–68). The M'Coys seems to be rough drafts for the Blooms: M'Coy is Bloom without his imagination or honesty, and Mrs M'Coy is Molly without talent.

4. French (1976, 86) notes Bloom's "mercenary interpretation of his own kindness" and calls it "distressing." But such moments merely demonstrate Bloom's vacillation between generosity and prudence. Given M'Coy's checkered history, one can hardly blame Bloom for contemplating some repayment. In another sense, Bloom's favor might be said to counteract the effects of Hades himself, who wore the helmet of invisibility: if Hades creates invisibility, Bloom here makes the invisible M'Coy "visible," at least in name.

time imitates Bloom's good deed. When M'Coy appears with Lenehan in "Wandering Rocks," his affiliation with that voyeur and sponger seems to confirm his disreputability. But M'Coy performs surprisingly well here. First he pushes aside a banana peel on the sidewalk, thinking that a "Fellow might damn easy get a nasty fall there coming along tight in the dark" (10.513–14). This Bloomian act—which might save someone from the kind of drunken tumble Kernan takes in "Grace" —contrasts with both Lenehan's behavior and with M'Coy's own history. His act has a kind of retrospective efficacy: although he furnished no grace to Kernan in the earlier story, at least he tries to save someone else from a similar fate. Perhaps more significantly, when Lenehan finishes his sophomoric tale about trying to fondle Molly in the carriage, M'Coy barely smiles, thereby puncturing Lenehan's hilarity. His refusal to participate in mocking Bloom thus indirectly reciprocates for Bloom's favor to him: the ledger balances, M'Coy's stature rises perceptibly, and he is allowed an interior life and even some redeeming qualities. Through Bloom's example, even M'Coy is given a form of grace. Both Kernan and M'Coy double momentarily with Bloom, who mentally registers their secrets, and M'Coy, at least, seems to profit from the social exchange. "What you lose on one you can make up on the other" (6.218): this phrase describing Molly's tour also sums up the social and economic relations in Bloom's circle.

Bloom's example seems to have little effect on Joe Hynes, the die-hard Parnellite from "Ivy Day in the Committee Room" whose loyalty contrasted with the crass and mercenary machinations of the other election canvassers. Hynes has changed. In "Hades" he and Jack Power visit Parnell's grave, and when Power mouths the superstitious hope—incongruously, since he is not a Nationalist—that "one day he will come again," Hynes, whose poem proclaimed that the chief would "Rise, like the Phoenix from the flames" (*D* 135) now retorts, "Parnell will never come again. . . . Peace to his ashes" (6.924–27). Whereas Parnell's ghostly presence was once palpable amid the living, now he too is fading into invisibility, represented only by legends—for example, Bloom's memories of returning his fallen hat (16.1334; 1523)—and by his spectral brother, an incubistic figure in "Wandering Rocks." Hynes's flame is fading with Parnell's. If in "Ivy Day" he is merely sentimental, in *Ulysses* he is a debt-denying sentimentalist: although he has owed Bloom three bob for three weeks (7.119), he has to be reminded both of Leopold's "christian" name at the funeral (6.880) and of the debt. Bloom hints at the debt (for the third time) in "Aeolus" by telling him that it is payday, but Hynes conveniently forgets it, even though he later has enough money to buy three pints and brags that "there's more where that came from" (12.209).

If Bloom seems invisible to Hynes, he nonetheless does get something from their transaction: Hynes's promise to speak to Crawford about the House of Keyes ad (12.1143–54). Hynes's debt is dramatized and perhaps psychically purged in "Circe," when, during his "trial" Bloom appeals to Hynes for help: "You know me. That three shillings you can keep. If you want a little more . . ." Peter to Bloom's Christ, Hynes replies "(coldly) You are a perfect stranger" (15.1192–95). But after his rehabilitation in the Bloomusalem fantasy that follows, Bloom magnanimously *"refuses to accept three shillings offered him by Joseph Hynes, journalist"* (15.1611) and releases him from the debt. If, in the naturalistic depiction of the debt, the long grace period testifies to Bloom's impotence and mildness, in the fantasy his leniency signifies the power that his elevated position permits him to use justly, replacing the unjust steward in "Grace" (Fr. Purdon) by giving economic grace to "children of this world." Even in the fantasy, however, Bloom is not so saintly as to defer payment forever without feeling a touch self-righteous.

While Kernan and M'Coy are at first missing from this metempsychosis of "Grace," Jack Power and Martin Cunningham are clearly present. But even they are haunted by the incubus of debt. In Power's first incarnation, he was on the rise, and "the arc of his social rise intersected the arc of [Kernan's] decline" (*D* 154). With his yellow ulster coat, job with the hated Royal Irish Constabulary (*D* 152), and association with the respected Cunningham, the allegorically named Power embodied the way that some Irish gain political power by colluding with the English master. In both texts his power is evident in the "small, but opportune loans" he provides to people like Kernan (*D* 155): whereas closed or fully symmetrical exchanges tend to be self-contained systems that allow the debtor to cancel out and thereby deplete the creditor's power, maintaining a debt reinforces the creditor's power (Sahlins 1972, 222; Blau 1964, 135). Extending long grace periods makes Power seem more generous, when in fact he is merely solidifying power by maintaining others' obligations. On the other hand, a loan to Kernan is scarcely safe, and he probably benefits socially from associating with more respected men like Power. Power's loans, then, both signify his stature and entrap him in reciprocal relationships with bad credit risks, such as in his ill-advised two-shilling loan to Simon (10.698). With these lending practices, it is no wonder that Power has "inexplicable debts" (*D* 154).

Power's once-ascending arc is in decline; indeed, he seems to be fading into impalpability, as though the missing section of his gnomon is spreading and overwhelming the remainder. Habitually depicted as "collapsing" (6.257) in laughter, emitting a "stifled" sigh or a "choked" laugh (6.288), shading his face (6.292), or speaking in a "blank" voice (6.922), Power is rapidly becoming a shade—both Bloom and Molly comment on his rapidly graying hair (6.242; 18.1274)—and receding into the penumbra of Martin Cunningham's arc of power (when both enter Kiernan's, only Cunningham's presence is noted [12.1621]). Though he suggests activities, Cunningham carries them out. Power also has an incubus—a mistress, to whom he has turned because "there is no carnal" intercourse with his wife. Merely a "Barmaid in Jury's. Or the Moira," she is far beneath him socially (6.244–47; cf. 18.1272–73), and her invisible presence provides another explanation for Power's inexplicable debts.

The name of the Moira hotel invests Power's gnomonic debtorship with a cosmic significance that further illustrates Joyce's role as artistic Providence and reveals another connection between the Greeks and the Irish. A copy of Roscher's *Ausführliches Lexikon der Griechischen und Römischen Mythologie,* which Joyce had in his Trieste library, could have led him to another meaning of the word *moira,* the early Greek term for destiny (R. Ellmann 1977, 13, 136). Thought to apportion provinces or fates, and thus to "define the limits . . . of social customs" (Cornford 1912 [1957], 51), *moira*'s moral power resembles Joyce's position as cosmic economist. A person's *moira* is allotted at birth and defines "the span or limit of his vital force, the negative and repressive aspect of his fate" (Cornford [1912] 1957, 110). Power's *moira* thus necessitates his incurring "inexplicable debts" as compensation for his compromised position in Dublin Castle and thereby balances his moral debits and credits. It is appropriate that Joyce describes Power's social status as an arc, because *moira* was originally a spatial concept that circumscribed an individual human's or god's domain in terms of territorial boundaries. As in "Grace" and "Wandering Rocks," here Joyce employs spatial and geometrical figures to chart the effects of institutional and individual powers on characters' economic and social lives. Power's "secret mistress" is indeed his *moira,* an invisible incubus that circumscribes the limits of his social and economic power.

There may be an earthbound motivation for Joyce's subtle punishment of Jack Power. The character is based on Joyce's friend Tom Devin (*JJ* 705), who, in a rare turnabout of the usual arrangement, twice borrowed money from Joyce when he returned to Dublin in 1909 but never repaid him (*L* II 275, 279–80). Devin's debts are transformed into Power's, perhaps as retaliation for Devin's failure to repay his loan. The author with a memory in his wallet imitates Stephen's scrupulously mean Shakespeare and becomes a cosmic creditor, exacting payment from Devin/Power by burdening him with an unremittable negative *moira*. As Providence, Joyce, like Stephen's priestly economist of souls, gains control over his real-life debits and credits by replicating them and managing them in fictional Dublin.

The most respected member of the carriage cartel, Martin Cunningham, enters and exits first, consistently leads discussion, and generally remains the authoritative presence he was in "Grace." H. Porter Abbott demonstrated years ago that *Ulysses* slightly improves the earlier ironic portrayal of Cunningham as a "subtly bullying" pontificator (1967, 47). As we have seen, in *Ulysses* he organizes a fund for the Dignam children while their insurance is being worked out (6.536; 564) and later enlists Bloom to contribute. This charitable project is consistent with the aggressive do-gooding that he imposed on Kernan in "Grace": "a good practical catholic," according to Father Conmee, he is "useful at mission time" (10.5–6). During the carriage ride he tries to protect Bloom from Power's unwittingly damaging remark about suicide as "the greatest disgrace to have in the family" (it literally dis-graces a Catholic) by saying "we must take a charitable view of it" (6.338–40). He even offers a legalistic explanation of Divine grace: "Better for ninetynine guilty to escape than for one innocent person to be wrongfully condemned" (6.474; cf. Luke 15:7). Later he defends Bloom (tepidly) from the vicious rumors that circulate in Kiernan's pub, admonishes the others to show "charity to the neighbour" (12.1665), and then helps to rescue Bloom from the angry Citizen. If he does not quite merit Abbott's hyperbolic description as "Dublin's moral caretaker" (1967, 49), nonetheless Cunningham stands morally above most Dubliners, just as his position in Dublin Castle signifies a superior social status.

Bloom registers his appreciation for Cunningham's sensitivity by initiating another moment of social exchange through reciprocal eye contact: "Martin Cunningham's large eyes. Looking away now. Sympathetic human man he is. Intelligent. Like Shakespeare's face. Always a good word to say" (6.344–49; but cf. his comments on Bloom in "Cyclops" [12.1635]). Cunningham's connection with Shakespeare and his similarities to Bloom are reaffirmed in a climactic scene in "Circe," examined below. But this glowing portrait is dimmed by

Bloom's recognition of his friend's shameful secret, his invisible punishment: the drunken wife who has pawned their furniture "six
times" (*D* 157) and leads him "the life of the damned" (6.351). Cunningham's domestic problems diminish both his status as paragon and
his financial solvency, and his inability to cure his wife casts doubt on
his capacity to convert Kernan or to solicit sufficient contributions
for the Dignam children. If Cunningham's personal authority is a
synecdoche of the institutional power he represents, his disrupted
domestic economy seems typically Irish. Joyce balances Cunningham's ledger by repaying him economically and morally for his complicitous position in Dublin Castle. If Cunningham's "secret sources
of information" (*D* 159) illustrate the incubistic tyranny wielded by
the Castle, Bloom's knowledge of Cunningham's secret—his incubus,
his gnomon, a "tyrant, willing to be dethroned" (2.172)—places them
on equal footing and reveals Cunningham's equivalent impotence.
Ultimately, then, the social exchanges between Bloom and Cunningham yield a balanced moral and economic budget.

Drowning Men

In "Hades" the motif of the drowning man, introduced in the
Telemachiad, is woven into the network of debtorship and obligation.
This nexus not only complicates Cunningham's character but also
reveals a crucial set of relationships between physical salvation and
economic grace in *Ulysses*. The model for Cunningham was the Joyces'
acquaintance Matthew Kane, Chief Clerk of the Crown Solicitor's
Office in Dublin Castle (*JJ* 133). Adams notes that Kane suffered a
stroke and died while swimming from a boat off Kingstown Harbour
on July 10, 1904, and that much of the material of "Hades" derives
from Joyce's observations at Kane's funeral (1974, 92–93; 1962, 62).
Since the drowning-man motif is so prominent in *Ulysses*, it seems
curious that Joyce "blithely deleted from the novel a death by water"
(Adams 1962, 64). But in fact he didn't: in "Ithaca" Kane drowns
under his own name in the list of Bloom's deceased companions:
"Matthew F. Kane (accidental drowning, Dublin Bay)" (17.1253). In
a sense, then, Kane/Cunningham dies twice in *Ulysses*, once as Kane
and once as the quietly suffering Cunningham/Sisyphus. In a fitting
and ironic punishment, Cunningham is present at his own funeral.

He might even be said to drown a third time. In Johnny the
Gospeller's narrative in *Finnegans Wake* we read of "poor Merkin
Cornyngwham, the official out of the castle on pension [as was Kane
at the time of his death], when he was completely drowned off Erin

Isles . . . and thank God . . . there were no more of him" (*FW* 387.28–32). The gospeller Matthew adds, "Poor Andrew Martin Cunningham!" (*FW* 393.5). In spite of his ostentatious knowledge and authority, Cunningham too bears an immense debtorship for which his drowning is both evidence and repayment. Because of his wife's pawning, Cunningham's financial state is far less solvent than his occupation and social position would lead one to expect. His portrayal as a drowning man thus represents the spectre of economic ruin that lurks behind most bourgeois respectability in Joyce's Dublin.

Joyce used the metaphor of drowning when writing to Ezra Pound about his own troubled finances: "if [the exchange-rate] reaches 50 [francs per pound] I cannot swim any more but disappear under the surface" (*L* II 468): he is unable to stay afloat on the economic tides. Likewise, as we have seen, Stephen envisions his alcoholic, debt-ridden father as a drowning man in "Proteus" (3.328; 471), and worries that his sisters are drowning with him in "Wandering Rocks" (10.875). Most of Simon's acquaintances are similarly drowning in debts and drink; indeed, more money and time is spent drinking in *Ulysses* than on any other activity, except perhaps playing the horses. In many cases—Kernan, Simon, Richie Goulding, Mrs. Cunningham, Ben Dollard, Bob Doran—alcoholism is both a cause and a result of economic failure. Although they are drowning because of their own flaws, they nonetheless believe that it is the usurer Reuben J. Dodd who keeps them submerged. With our knowledge of Kane/Cunningham's death, Cunningham's tale about the near-drowning of Dodd's son seems doubly ironic.

When the mourners spot Dodd, "a tall blackbearded figure, bent on a stick," during the funeral ride (6.252), Cunningham says, "We have all been there." But his eyes meet Bloom's and he qualifies it with, "Well, nearly all of us" (6.260–61). Cunningham's pointed glance raises the possibility—difficult to substantiate—that Dodd and Bloom share Jewish ethnicity as well as their stereotypical economic behaviors.[5] At any rate, Bloom is singled out here either because "[Cunningham thinks] Bloom as a Jew is in some sort of complicity

---

5. Although McCarthy has made a persuasive case that Dodd is not Jewish at all but rather, like his real-life counterpart, an Irish Catholic (1984a, 174), the evidence remains inconclusive. Statistically, Jews were a small minority in Dublin: only 2,048 resided in Dublin in 1901, and thus comprised less than 1 percent of the population, a fact that would suggest that Dodd is not likely to be a Jew (O'Brien 1982, 96). As Robert Boyle noted many years ago, Dodd's forerunner is the moneylender Harford, of "Grace," who "never embraced more than the Jewish ethical code," but, like Dodd, is still called a Jew by his fellow-Catholics (Boyle 1965, 65; *D* 159).

with Jewish money-lenders like Dodd" (Adams 1974, 97) or because
he is seen as "someone who is prudent enough to be able to avoid
money lenders altogether" (McCarthy 1984a, 174). For whatever reason, Bloom starts to tell the tale of Reuben J's son's near-drowning,
but is thwarted by Cunningham, who tells it better. Young Dodd,
distraught over a failed relationship, tries to commit suicide by jump-
ing into the Liffey. He is rescued by a boatman, to whom his father
ungenerously tenders a florin as reward (6.286); Simon drily adds,
"one and eightpence too much." Dodd's only begotten son may be
redeemed physically, but his father offers no economic grace to his
redeemer. The significance of the tale increases when one compares
it to the real-life event. Young Dodd actually jumped into the Liffey
on Aug. 26, 1911, and was rescued by a man named Moses Goldin,
probably a Jew (Adams 1974, 97n), who "during the last twenty years
saved some twenty lives" (quoted in *JJ* 38–39). Ironically, then, the
Irish "Jew" Dodd relied on a Jewish savior (named, appropriately
enough, *Gold*in) to rescue his son: the usurer's son makes his father
part with some of his money.

Dodd's appearances elsewhere in the novel prove his stinginess.
For example, in "Wandering Rocks" we learn of his attempts to serve
a writ for nonpayment on Simon's friend Bob Cowley (10.890–94).
The personal motive behind Reuben J's negative portrayal was probably the financial exactions of the real Dodd, who owned the mortgage
on Joyce's father's house (*JJ* 37–38), and "was in bad odour because
he had loaned money to John Joyce and, curiously, expected repayment" (Adams 1962, 105). Joyce makes Dodd pay, drawing a Shylock
from his own long pocket and charging moral interest, thus carrying
out a kind of moral usury that metaphorically duplicates the usury
for which he damns Dodd. In becoming an artistic father, Joyce tries
to balance his books, generating a miserly replica of the real Dodd in
order to pay off in art the debts incurred in life. Dodd also appears
in "Circe" carrying the *"drowned corpse of his son"* over his shoulder
(15.1918–20). As "Reuben J. Antichrist" (15.2143) he is the antithesis
of both Christ, who promised to bring grace for all mankind's moral
debts, and of Bloom, the Jew who refrains from taking usury and
who is in Nighttown out of paternal feelings for Stephen. As I will
argue below, Dodd and his son implicitly invoke the Aristotelian pun
on *tokos* ("interest" and "offspring"): the suicidal son is as "unnatural"
as the monetary offspring his father breeds through usury, his near
death becoming a brilliantly appropriate punishment for his father's
unfriendly financial activities.

Viewing the matter objectively, however, it is difficult to see how Dodd merits being dubbed an *"Iscariot"* (15.1918). Indeed, his scapegoating dramatizes Old Testament admonishments about usury. Deuteronomy 23:20 forbids usury in dealings with kin but tolerates it in transactions with strangers. As Thomas Aquinas reads the passage, "The Jews were forbidden to take usury from their brethren, i.e., from other Jews. By this we are given to understand that to take usury from any man is simply evil, because we ought to treat every man as our neighbor and brother" (quoted in Hyde 1983, 119).[6] Thus, whether or not he is religiously a Jew, Dodd's usurious practices announce to other Dubliners that he is not their kin and is not bound by "blood"; he proclaims his "Jewishness" against the Christian brotherhood of debtorship. If the symbols of "Hades" and "Wandering Rocks" (heart and blood, respectively) imply that citizens are unified by circulation and exchange, Dodd's usury demonstrates his attempt to halt circulation, to stand "in the stream where surplus wealth flows toward need" (Hyde 1983, 124): to them he is not blood but bloodsucker. The history of usury also helps to explain Bloom's vacillation about economic motives. As Hyde shows, one result of Christianity's ambivalent attitude about usury is an internal division within every citizen, so that "each man has a civil and a moral part, [and] the brother and the stranger live side by side in his heart" (1983, 125). Thus, though Bloom feels himself a true Dubliner, his economic behavior alienates him from his fellow citizens, and he can never truly enter their interlocking network of mutual indebtedness.

In reality the boatman Goldin received a half-crown for his trouble—six shillings more than the fictional boatman but still a puny reward. The fictional florin, however, is connected symbolically to Bloom, who once sent out a marked florin to circulate and thereby test "the waters of civic finance" (17.983–84). It never came back, thus proving that circulation does not always lead to returns. Nonetheless, the florin, serving as payment for a son's redemption and as a symbol of circulation, yokes the two senses of liquidity. If in the Dodd story the florin symbolizes "Jewish" meanness, for Bloom it represents for the impossibility of perfect circularity; in both cases the coin stands for the unlikelihood of perfect economic grace. Originally displaying a flower on its face (Somerville 1975, 116), the florin is also

---

6. Hyde's brief history of usury (1983, 109–40) demonstrates how uncertain and contradictory Christian attitudes about the practice have been, partly because of the conflict between Old and New Testament writings.

a bloom, thus suggesting that Bloom/Flower is a Jewish "florin" who sometimes redeems the debts of drowners.[7] A "waterlover" (17.183), Bloom is sometimes associated with fish: his childhood nickname was "mackerel" (8.405;15.3331), and the "Cyclops" narrator describes his "cod's eye" (12.214). This association among Bloom, florins, and liquidity is borne out by the florin itself. In 1904 florins in circulation bore on their reverse face a picture of Britannia standing above the waves (Reinfeld 1969, 181). Like Britannia and Odysseus, Bloom is not a drowner but a swimmer (18.960). Thus while the son of the putatively Jewish Reuben J. Dodd nearly drowns, Bloom, an actual (if lukewarm) Jew, both resists drowning and later metaphorically saves from economic drowning the son of the debt-ridden Simon Dedalus. While Bloom may see himself in Dodd (Theoharis 1988, 169), for the most part he traverses the middle way between "Jewish" usury and Irish improvidence, mediating between the extremes of negative reciprocity and gift giving in his circulation through debt-inundated Dublin.

But florins are also associated with less charitable rescuers. Mulligan, we recall, once saved a man from drowning but exacts moral and emotional usury from Stephen, borrowing both his witticisms and his money in compensation for Stephen's financial debt. Buck produces a florin in "Telemachus" to pay for the milk, crying, "a miracle!" as though performing a Christlike act of resuscitation or redemption (1.451–53). In this scene he seems to generate money out of itself, like Aristotle's exploitative usurer or chrematist. In this sense, Mulligan too is a "Jew," Stephen's Dodd, a usurer who masks exploitation as salvation, a moneylender who pretends to be helping while charging exorbitant interest.

Mulligan's real-life model, Oliver Gogarty, jumped into the Liffey on June 23, 1902, to save a bookmaker named Max Harris (Adams 1962, 171). Tom Rochford, the bookie in *Ulysses*, performs a similar act of heroism. In the ninth section of "Wandering Rocks," M'Coy and Lenehan visit Rochford, after which Lenehan recounts how the bookie rescued a man who had fallen down a manhole into the sewer: "Down went Tom Rochford anyhow, booky's vest and all, with the rope around him. And be damned but he got the rope around the poor devil and the two were hauled up. —The act of a hero, [M'Coy]

---

7. I am indebted to Professor Hank Harrington for pointing out the connection between Bloom and the florin.

said" (10.500–3).[8] Rochford seems to be Mulligan's thinner alter ego: both rescue others from death by immersion; both are called heroes; both wear gaudy waistcoats (Mulligan's is "primrose" [1.550] and Rochford's "claret" [10.465]). Moreover, each character's heroism is associated with a florin, Mulligan's as noted above, and Rochford's when in "Circe" he puts "a hand to his breastbone, bows," and says, "Reuben J. A florin I find [Dignam]" (15.1262). The latter passage associates Rochford's act with that of the anonymous boatman who saved the son of Dodd: in the Circean world, Rochford gets paid the same amount for a similar act, even though he has (so far) failed to raise Dignam from the dead. Rochford's last appearance in the novel, however, implies a less heroic role in Dublin's social life. During the "burning of Dublin" in "Circe," he leads the populace in leaping *"into the void"* (15.4672–74); rather than salvaging people, he incites mass suicide. Indeed, this "hallucination" merely translates into religious terms his economic agency as bookie: he promises economic provi-dence and salvation without effort but more often leads his customers closer to the economic void. The bookie, indeed, reenacts Father Purdon's interpretation of grace as bookkeeping.[9] Enacting both physical rescue and economic ruin, Rochford, like Mulligan, com-bines the offices of priest and profiteer.

Caretaker

If Bloom seems exempt from drowning and debts, nonetheless he too has his incubi, his invisible oppressors: Molly, barely visible for most of the novel; Boylan, reduced to a series of synedochic fetishes; and the memories of his own father, which haunt him throughout the novel because he scoffed at Jewish rituals (17.1894–95). The shadowy figure of Rudolph Bloom again yokes fatherhood and finances. The nameless narrator of "Cyclops" intimates (probably falsely) that Ru-

8. M'Coy might well remember Rochford's act on this day: he has told Bloom that he must miss Dignam's funeral because he has to attend to "a drowning case at Sandycove" (5.170–71). For an account of the real-life incident upon which this is based, see Adams 1962, 92–93.

9. Adams claims that Rochford's role is to lead "mankind in the act of throwing away his life and thereby saving it" (1962, 92). But this reading ignores both the economic effect of Rochford's occupation and the fact that the religious ritual in "Circe" is not a redemption but a black mass. Given the Church's role in Joyce's fiction, it is more likely that Rochford is associated with the Church's illusory promises of salvation.

dolph Bloom was, if not a Dodd-like usurer, at least a swindler: "perpetrating frauds, old Methusalem Bloom, the robbing bagman, that poisoned himself with the prussic acid after he swamping the country with his baubles and his penny diamonds. Loans by post on easy terms. Any amount of money advanced on note of hand" (12.1580–84). But Rudolph's financial and physical offspring are more "natural" than that. Although he was not an Irish native, and somehow had enough money to purchase the Queen's Hotel in Ennis, Bloom's father exemplifies the financial failure that follows Joyce's Irishmen around like a dark cloud. Rudolph's suicide is probably attributable to dejection over economic ruin, rather than to his purchase of a "new boater straw hat, extra smart" on the day of his death (17.629; although Rudolph became a "relic of old decency," at least his hat was not).[10] Molly recalls her husband's unfinished plan to start "Blooms private hotel" and is worried that he'll "go and ruin himself altogether the way his father did down in Ennis" (18.981–83); when Leopold remembers the day of the coroner's inquest, his mind again reverts to "The Pauper's Drive" ("No more pain. Wake no more. Nobody owns"), which implies that his father was a financial failure (6.365). Nevertheless, Rudolph gave his son prudent financial advice—"having taken care of pence, the pounds having taken care of themselves" (17.1910–11)—which Leopold habitually follows. Bloom's guilt is expressed in similar economic terms in "Circe," where Rudolph appears as a scolding Jewish stereotype warning Bloom against losing money (15.253; money is the major topic of fatherly advice in *Ulysses:* witness Stephen's encounters with Deasy and Artifoni). A dutiful son, Leopold visits his father's grave every June 27, bringing "ten shillings for the gardener" (6.934), and carries out his father's last wishes: "Thy will be done" (6.126). The phrase from the Lord's Prayer again articulates Bloom's sense of obligation to his father in terms of money and debt.

This consideration of Bloom's filial offices brings us back to the symbol of "Hades"—caretaker. Referring most obviously to the cemetery keeper, the word also describes Bloom's role as the caretaker of his father's grave and, more generally, as the character most willing

---

10. His suicide note is inconclusive, suggesting that his final depression might also have resulted from his wife's recent death (17.1884). It says that he will be "with your dear mother" but also that "Tomorrow will be a week that I received," which could refer to a notice of some unpayable debt, the news of his wife's death, or some other event. For a list of Rudolph's appearances, see Raleigh 1977, 70–75.

to offer a helping hand to people like the Dignams. If Joyce's management of the economy of grace imitates Divine powers, Bloom's participation as a steward of that grace fulfills a priestly role. A good economist, Bloom resembles St. Paul's description of the bishop who, as a just steward *(oikonomos)* of God, must be not "self-willed, not soon angry, not given to wine, no striker, not given to filthy lucre; But a lover of hospitality, a lover of good men, sober, just, . . . temperate" (Titus 1:7–8; King James Version). In a less pious vein, Molly characterizes Bloom's differences from the rest of his circle: "he has sense enough not to squander every penny piece he earns down their gullets and looks after his wife and family" (18.1277–9). While many Dubliners are, as Cunningham later declares, "still waiting for their redeemer" (12.1644), battening upon debts that actually wrap them in an ever-tightening chain of economic failure, Bloom tries to do some redeeming of his own. He stands as an example of successful economic activity amidst Dublin's economic losers, and indicates that, although Joyce recognized the social determinants of his Dubliners' problems, he also believed that they could transcend these conditions if they tried. Bloom's generally positive agency also suggests that Joyce finds Dublin to be less hopelessly paralyzed by serving two masters than he did in *Dubliners:* perhaps grace is possible here after all. For all of his peccadillos and occasional ungracious thoughts, Bloom does practice *charis,* the biblical word for *grace* and the root of *charity.* To a significant degree, he is Dublin's just steward, the moral and economic caretaker of its social life. Thus, in returning to *Dubliners* in "Hades," Joyce both relives and relieves their economic tribulations through Bloom's graceful stewardship.

And yet, in the wider scheme of Irish economics and in Joyce's broader portrayal of the city, Bloom's effect is small. Though he often acts charitably, Ireland's economic condition can improve only through the unified efforts of the community: they must throw off the oppression of the two masters and abandon the lifelong habits cultivated to combat such domination. Like Stephen, other Dubliners must also "kill the priest and king" in their consciousnesses and banish their apathy along with them. The lines of power and exchange charted in *Ulysses* imply that Joyce conceived of his text both as a means of retaliation against his personal and political enemies through double-entry moral bookeeping and as a redemptive political instrument. Thus it is Joyce who remains the most potent incubus, the largest invisible presence of all, the Providential artist who stands over his own Dublin, judging and dispensing—the Cosmic Economist of his creations. His re-creation of Dublin thus becomes an assertion of ownership over both his personal past and his city, an act that usurps institutional authorities through the invisible power of authorship. If, in "Hades" and "Wandering Rocks," Joyce approximates the aesthetic of scrupulous meanness and the economy of realism that he adopted in *Dubliners,* he remains the caretaker of his Dublin, though his stewardship is often harsh and demanding. In "Wandering Rocks" he uses the artist's divine powers to chart in even greater detail the interlocking economic lives of his Dubliners; closer scrutiny reveals even more plainly how those lives are mastered by the institutions that control the power and money and by Dubliners' acquiescence to that power.

THE BLOOD OF "WANDERING ROCKS"

"Wandering Rocks" documents the social life of Joyce's Dublin from three o'clock to about four on a weekday afternoon. During an hour when most people would presumably be at work, few characters are doing gainful labor. Nevertheless, economic exchanges are the central events in virtually every one of the nineteen sections. As we have seen, many social and economic theorists view exchange as the most essential and typical activity in social life, because exchanges create a sense of community by constructing a system of mutual dependencies (Gouldner 1960, 168). Exchanges rest upon the norm of reciprocity, a principle established as far back as Aristotle's *Nicomachean Ethics,* in which he argues that "reciprocity is necessary if the state is to be held together, for it is held together by exchange of services, and people will not exchange services unless they get as good as they give" (1980 [Ross, Introduction], xiii). Well-versed in Aristotle, Joyce would have been familiar with his notion of reciprocity as an ethical and economic norm; indeed, despite his violations of the norm in his own economic dealings, he uses it as a significant ordering principle in the middle episodes of *Ulysses.*[11]

Reciprocity dictates that exchanges should be balanced so that

11. Hartsock (1983, 19) argues that, in viewing all exchange as voluntary, the exchange model "leads to the conclusion that competition in exchange results in relations of domination and at the same time legitimizes this domination either by denying it or treating it as inevitable but unimportant." Though I find her critique persuasive, I think the exchange model can be employed to analyze Joyce's depiction of Dublin's economic life.

each party receives equal value. But in practice the ideal is difficult to achieve. Thus many of the theorists who view reciprocity as a norm also recognize a conflicting strain in social behavior. As Blau observes, people are interested in "maintaining a balance between inputs and outputs and staying out of debt; . . . hence the strain towards reciprocity. Their aspirations, however, are to achieve a balance in their favor and to accumulate credit" that endows them with superior status; "hence the strain toward imbalance" (1964, 26). Moreover, reciprocal balance in one exchange may create an imbalance in another (Blau 1964, 314). Even Simmel, perhaps the most influential exchange theorist, admits that there is probably "not a single interaction in which the things that go back and forth, in the reciprocity of giving and taking, are exactly equal" (1950, 390). Like charity, balanced reciprocity is a "norm" breached as often as it is followed. Not surprisingly, balanced reciprocity seldom occurs in Joyce's Dublin. Most characters either try to get something for nothing or are the victims of such exploitation. An even more troubling phenomenon emerges here: in the classical models the antidote to such exploitation and coercion is charity and gift giving, but in Joyce's Dublin even gift giving has been distorted by inequities in power. Thus virtually every one of the sections in "Wandering Rocks" details an economic exchange—begging, borrowing, purchasing food, pawning, gift giving, gambling, auctioning—in which one party receives more than the other. There are multiple reasons for these distortions, but they must be partially attributed to the economic deformations produced by the imperial presence in Ireland. Dubliners seem to have grown so used to the unequal exercise of economic power that they can no longer even conceive of equal relations. The norm of reciprocity seems to be viewed as a bourgeois—and therefore English—ideal, and the citizens willfully resist paying debts. Instead they gamble, pawn, or beg to defy the British master. Unfortunately, the habits aimed at flouting the British merely exacerbate the economic inequities they are meant to resist. Rather than expelling the "invaders," they exploit each other. What emerges is a picture of a city disrupted and warped by the two masters whose collusion induces economic paralysis and social fragmentation.

The Linati schema for "Wandering Rocks" lists its "organ" as "blood," which most obviously refers to the circulation of characters in overlapping scenes. The interpolations from other sections that intrude upon each section represent the social strands that unify the community. Yet each section is also separated on the page from the others, so that the composition of the chapter produces as strong a sense of alienation and estrangement, of a city whose "blood" is breaking apart into separate cells, as it does of a unified community. What really unifies the episode—the thread through its "labyrinth" (the episode's "technic")—is the circulation and exchange of financial and social currency, as the Dedalian artificer traces the paths of Dubliners seeking lost objects (Knuth 1976, 126, 155).[12] Thus "Wandering Rocks" may be fruitfully analyzed using what Heinzelman calls "poetic economics," which studies "the way in which literary writers use . . . economic discourse . . . as an ordering principle" (1980, 11–12). That is, the episode's seemingly random and whimsical organization can be made coherent by scrutinizing the economic and social exchanges that provide its patterning; in this way the reader too participates in mapping the labyrinth. We can catalogue the characters' economic behaviors not only according to their levels of reciprocity, but also according to their success or failure at providing economically for themselves and their dependents. The concepts of provision and providence are laden with historical significance derived from the memory of famine, still strong in Irish culture: the ability to feed one's family is a primary measure of economic and moral health. In most cases the Dublin pattern is an improvidence that is, paradoxically, managed by an Authorial Providence who scrupulously controls and evaluates his city. Yet that pattern is often crystallized in linguistic exchanges that seem to elude full authorial control.

Figuring Exchange

Although books are prominent in the episode, the authorial figure does not write books; rather, he is a game player, a plotter, a minor political figure. In section sixteen "a longfaced man" hangs intently over a chessboard in the D.B.C (10.1046): John Howard Parnell, brother of the "uncrowned king," whose family has been reduced from national to civic politics, and now to the metaphorical wars of chess. This Parnell does not even look up when the viceregal cavalcade passes (10.1226), but does manage to "translate a white bishop," enacting on the chessboard what his brother could not do with Irish Catholic bishops, a failure that ultimately doomed him. As

---

12. Wright notes that "Money often appears in 'Wandering Rocks' as a particular sign of social relationships that have gone awry" (1991, 48). McArthur likewise calls the city a "constantly flowing network of circulations" and notes that "money flows through arteries of a city in an unbroken if discontinuous movement (1988, 89, 93).

in "Grace," chess here provides one organizing structure for the episode (see Osteen 1991, 77–78). Like a chessmaster planning strategic
moves, Joyce carefully plotted the movements of his characters in
"Wandering Rocks" according to actual routes that could be covered
in the time allotted (Hart 1974, 199). Moreover, all kinds of games
and gaming pervade the episode. Playing his labyrinth like a game (it
was the name of a game Joyce played while composing the episode),
Joyce fills the episode with reader traps to trip up the unwary (Hart
1974, 188). Aware of such dangers, I shall nonetheless assign piece
names to many of the figures here, both by analyzing their socioeconomic positions and by scrutinizing their geographical routes. In this
game of mastery the players' allegiances seem to shift: sometimes
Joyce simply lays bare the operations of the real game players,
Church and State; sometimes he appears to be playing against Dublin; sometimes he seems to be playing for Dublin against the masters.
In the last case Joyce assumes a Parnellian role as the advocate for
the Irish against the conditions and powers that oppress them. But
ultimately the image of J. H. Parnell as author is self-mocking: neither
powerful nor respected, he seems to be playing chess against himself.
Whereas Stephen Dedalus imagined himself as Parnell's successor,
the authorial presence here settles for Parnell's less impressive
brother. In any case, most of Joyce's Dubliners are not players but
pawns dominated by political and economic power structures, just as
they are controlled by the Joycean chessmaster who narrates and
arranges the episode.

Besides the geometrical movements of chess pieces, other geo-
metric figures enable us to chart some of the episode's exchanges and
near-exchanges. For example, the bicycle racers round the curve near
the college library as they near the finish line, just as Simon Dedalus
rounds the corner of Williams's row (10.653–55): both are approaching their "last lap" (Hart 1974, 209). Lenehan tells his story
about feeling Molly Bloom's "curves" (10.564) just after spotting
Bloom, who is about to read a passage from *Sweets of Sin* in which a
character feels for a woman's *"opulent curves"* (10.612). A more important figure in the episode—the arch—can be read either as geometrical or architectural. Arches are places to seek something
valuable, liminal sites where sexual or commercial seductions are attempted. They are locations for begging: J. J. O'Molloy's attempt to
borrow money from Ned Lambert begins "among the flickering
arches" in the old council chamber (10.402); Corley first accosts Stephen for money from "under the arches" of the railway bridge
(16.112). Often arches signal the intersection of sexuality and com-

merce. Thus Bloom under Merchant's arch seeks a sexy book to bring home for Molly (10.520), just as he tore up Martha's seductive letter under a railway arch (5.300); Stephen imagines whores plying their trade "from an archway where dogs have mired" (3.376; cf. 15.578–79). Less architecturally, "arches" constantly appear in seductions: Boylan eyes the barmaid-siren Miss Douce as she passes by a "gilded arch for ginger ale" (11.421–22); in "Circe" the nymph tempting Bloom "arches her body in lascivious crispation" (15.3392–94); while he reads the pornographic book, Bloom's nostrils "arched themselves for prey" (10.621). Thus the color of "Wandering Rocks" is "rainbow," an arch that represents the spectrum of exchanges; but the rainbow of Joyce's Dublin is a less hopeful one than Noah's, and here its hues are exploitation and insincerity. Typical locales for financial seductions, arches thus signify actual or metaphorical prostitution.

Through Parnell's brother, who symbolizes Joyce's management of the economies and geometry of the text, Joyce figures another crucial structural principle in "Wandering Rocks." Earlier, spying him on his way to the D.B.C., Bloom recalls, "his brother used men as pawns" (8.511), linking Charles's management of men with John's control of chess pieces. In 1904, J. H. Parnell was also the city marshal and registrar of pawnbrokers (Gifford 1988, 172): he is thus a master of both pawns and pawning. Unable to wear his brother's crown, he manipulates miniature kings and queens.[13] The homophony between the two forms of "pawn" exposes an underlying economic connection between the words. Pawns of the British Empire and the Roman Catholic Church, Joyce's Dubliners, like those in real turn-of-the-century Dublin, frequently resort to the pawnbroker, the "poor man's banker" (O'Brien 1982, 162), from whom they get less money for their valuables than they are worth. An episode full of pawns and pawning, "Wandering Rocks" illustrates Stephen's description of Ireland as "a pawnshop" (2.46–47).[14] Like J. H. Parnell, the chessmaster

13. J. H. Parnell's official function may explain why his face and chessboard intrude upon section 8, where O'Molloy attempts to borrow money from Lambert. The barfly narrator of "Cyclops" tells how he has seen O'Molloy "pawning his gold watch in Cummins of Francis street where no-one would know him" (12.1026–27). The appearance of the registrar of pawnbrokers thus comments on the falling fortunes of the chronic pawner O'Molloy.

14. O'Brien (1982, 162) tells us that in 1906 "over 4.5 million pledges [in pawnshops] were taken in Dublin, almost double the rate for Belfast." The two words spelled "pawn" have different etymologies. The chess piece derives from the Old French word for footsoldier (a variant of peon); the other word comes from the Old French *pan*, meaning "pledge" but also "booty."

of "Wandering Rocks" marshals his fictional city, registering both the pawnbrokers and pawns who live in it.

"Pawn" is only one of the many significant homophones Joyce deploys in "Wandering Rocks." Indeed, the Linati schema gives "Homonyms" as one of the episode's symbols, along with "Christ and Caesar." Some of the homophones—the similarity in names between Leopold Bloom and Mr. Bloom the dentist, or between Mrs. M'Guinness the pawnbroker and Mr. Maginni the dancing master—are false similarities, distorted mirrors, reader traps that recall the wandering rocks that endangered Greek ships. Such random concurrences of sounds demonstrate how language frustrates attempts to manage its economy: since words create odd and unpredictable juxtapositions that human users cannot control, language seems to be having a private joke at our expense. But Joyce accepts these coincidental exchanges, using them to illuminate both the economy of language and the economy of his city (cf. Mahaffey 1988, 187). Homonyms such as "pawn," meaning both a chess piece and a pledge or surety, demonstrate how Joyce's playfulness—his willingness to turn errors into "portals of discovery"—enables him to discover and construct passages through the labyrinth that reveal the shared foundations of the linguistic and financial economies.

Many writers have noted how often economic terms creep into discussions about language. Because they are metaphors about metaphors, economic terms enable language to talk about itself.[15] Like metaphors, homophones constitute what Shell calls "tropic exchanges": crystallized linguistic exchanges that posit a hidden identity between unlike things (1978, 7). Joyce employs such figures of exchange to expose more plainly the homologies between the linguistic and economic registers. As I will argue more explicitly in chapter 6, Joyce's characteristic punning constitutes a kind of verbal usury whereby excess meanings are generated without creating additional signs, a practice that seems ironic considering the condemnation of usury that he depicts and with which he seems to concur. In another sense, puns are the "most economical of linguistic transactions in

15. Derrida, for example, observes that "in signifying the metaphorical process, the paradigms of coin, metal, silver and gold have imposed themselves with remarkable insistence" (1982, 216). Goux even claims that the history of Western philosophy insistently compares "money and language in what is not merely a surface phenomenon but a localized, isolated perception of a real sociohistorical coherence. The monetary metaphor that haunts discussions of language . . . betray[s] an awareness . . . of the correspondence between the mode of economic exchange and the mode of signifying exchange" (1990, 96).

which verbal value may be exchanged" (Heinzelman 1980, 74–75), because they engender extra meanings without producing more words. But homophones do more than merely assert identity; because we must hold multiple meanings in suspension, they also exemplify difference. They produce temporary junctures—exchanges—that figurally replicate the temporary conjunctions of human actors carrying out economic exchanges. As Allen Hoey writes in another context, tropes, like commodities, "hinge at the exchange." What they "mean" is "a suggestion of a relation. . . . Tropes invite us to recognize the fundamental operations of language and thought, the relations of signifier and signified, in each textual transaction, as money, denuded of privilege, reveals the sweat behind every exchange" (1988, 36). Words circulate like money and thereby figure exchange in several registers at once.

Let us look briefly at two other important homophones before turning to a detailed analysis of the episode. The first is introduced when Father Conmee remembers that his purse holds "one silver crown" (10.11). A metonymy of the institutional authority engraved upon it, the crown coin and its financial equivalent (5 shillings) repeatedly signal failures of providence or charity and distortions of reciprocity: it is the amount that Conmee refuses to give to the beggar; it is the amount that Dilly Dedalus believes her father has "borrowed" but won't give to her (10.680); it is the amount bid for the curtains the Dedaluses must auction off to get the money Simon will not earn (10.648). As if to prove the rule by his exception, it is also the amount that Bloom contributes to the Dignam fund (10.976). The crown in Conmee's pocket thus symbolizes the power—both political and economic—that the Church shares with the British and refuses to share with the Irish (cf. Gordon 1981, 60–63). Representing money "impersonalized, detached from any relationships with moral collective or individual persons other than the authority of the state which mints them" (Mauss [1925] 1967, 93), crowns symbolize how money exchanges supplant exchanges of personalized objects in barter and gifts. The various crowns that appear (either as coins or as emblems of monarchy) in *Ulysses* signify a loss of sovereignty, and by this metaphoric displacement an actual displacement of power: the headgear of sovereignty, a crown is what Stephen seeks (see 14.1540; 15.896, and 15.3823) and in so doing also seeks his own identity; it is also what Parnell failed to win and, metonymically, what the viceroy represents. Indeed, because the economy of Joyce's Dublin is a colonized economy, metaphorically the crown influences all of the exchanges in

Ulysses. As for Conmee, his crown is a silk hat, the mitre of a man more concerned with social class than spiritual redemption, who doffs it only to nobility, real or spurious (10.30). Like the hats and the economic sermon in "Grace," Conmee's crowns represent the superficial and spurious "grace" that the Church's stewards offer to Catholic Dubliners.[16]

The second homophone emerges mainly by implication. In section 9, Tom Rochford shows his invention for counting music hall turns to Lenehan and M'Coy, who have presumably placed bets for the Gold Cup race with him. After Lenehan mentions Bantam Lyons, who was going to back Throwaway because of Bloom's "tip," on cue the men spot Bloom scanning books under Merchants' arch (Lyons's bet was also going to be five shillings—a crown; see 8.1016). Here a resemblance between Rochford and Bloom is posited through a pun on "book": while Rochford "makes book," Bloom wants to buy or rent one. Indeed, inasmuch as Bloom's inadvertent tip helped Lyons spot the winner, Bloom too is a bookie, and today, at least, a better one than Rochford. The third sense of "book" (as a verb) emerges when strutting Tom Kernan appears after having "booked" an order with a Mr. Crimmins (10.719). Rochford's "book" consists of the odds he sets for gamblers to win a great prize; Kernan's "book" provides future income; Bloom's "book" is the object of a quest to find the right gift for Molly, a product of his penchant for bargains. All three senses of the word converge in section 7, as a call from Boylan interrupts his secretary, Miss Dunne, who is reading a book (10.368). He asks about the dates the tour he has booked for Molly (10.389–90) and finally is reminded that he is supposed meet Lenehan, with whom he has made book on the Gold Cup (10.394). The discrete meanings of "book" are circulated and combined in Joyce's linguistic economy.

In sum, the most important puns and homonyms in "Wandering Rocks"—*pawn, book, crown*—are economic both in content (they denote exchange or power) and in form (they generate and undergo tropic exchanges in the linguistic economy); therefore they elucidate ways that linguistic and political conditions mirror each other. Almost in spite of themselves, homophones demonstrate that words are products of human labor and history. Their constant recurrence in "Wandering Rocks" also shows how the linguistic capital of Ireland—the English language brought by the English—has been invested in

16. My analysis of this pun on "crown" resembles that of Wright (1991, 49–54), whose book became available as I was completing this study.

games of power and how the linguistic economy in Dublin bears the
economic and political history that continues to oppress the Irish.
Dubliners are the "linguistic workers" (Rossi-Landi 1975, 48) whose
labor has been exploited by English rule; but one Dubliner, James
Joyce, attempts to revise this history by accepting the economies of
language and laboring to generate new economic exchanges.

Divine Stewards

Since Christ and Caesar are the two banks of Joyce's labyrinth,
the first section is appropriately devoted to "the superior, the very
reverend John Conmee, S.J." (10.1). We recall him as the rector of
Clongowes who helped young Stephen Dedalus rectify (as his title
implies) an unjust pandying in the first chapter of *Portrait*. Always
named by his titles, Conmee's identity seems to consist solely of official
functions; his thoughts are similarly superficial, orderly and self-satisfied. Although he is ostensibly on a mission of mercy to help Paddy
Dignam's son get into Brother Swan's institute for destitute boys,
Conmee's charity never extends beyond such official functions. That
he represents the Church's unjust stewards—priests who fail to provide either spiritual or material aid for the needy—is suggested in the
second paragraph, as a onelegged sailor holds out to him "a peaked
cap for alms" (10.9). The mock-genteel narrative neutrally notes that
Conmee refuses to part with any of the money in his purse, which
holds "he knew, one silver crown" (10.11). Instead, he gives the sailor
a blessing—it is free.[17] His failure of stewardship is also inscribed
geographically: he departs from the Jesuit church in Gardiner Street,
the same church where, in "Grace," Father Purdon delivers his hypo-
critical and inaccurate sermon about spiritual accounting, using as his

---

17. In contrast, Gordon argues that Conmee cannot be blamed for holding onto
the crown because "he needs it to complete a charitable mission—he can hardly ask the
beggar for change" (1981, 63). But he scarcely needs the entire crown to ride the tram
to Artane (the fare is a penny); and he could easily pop into a shop for change if he
truly wanted to give alms. As Wright notes (1991, 49), the reverend father seems to
have chosen this large coin precisely to avoid having to give alms to the ubiquitous
beggars in Dublin. McMichael contends that Joyce's narrator is "picking on" Conmee
(1991, 62), but the mildly satiric tone merely replicates Conmee's own habits of
thought. The narrator's refusal to penetrate beneath the surface is thus itself revealing.
Others who, like me, blame Conmee include Wenke (1980, 103) and Herring (1989,
89), who observes that most of the privileged men in "Wandering Rocks" are equally
derelict in this regard.

text the Parable of the Unjust Steward (Gifford 1988, 260; *D* 172). Conmee apparently follows Purdon's dubious doctrine. Engaged in an official mission of charity (which will cost him little: Cunningham will do the hard work, although the priest does speak to Brother Swan about helping young Dignam), Conmee has no time for spontaneous generosity. Like *Dubliners'* Purdon, Flynn, and Keon, Conmee is one of Joyce's unjust divine stewards.

Though he is always aware of how much money he has, Conmee's imperturbable comportment barely notices the poverty and misery around him. He thinks, "but not for long, of soldiers and sailors, whose legs had been shot off by cannonballs, ending their days in some pauper ward" (10.12–14): the qualifying clause condemns his lack of compassion for people like the sailor. Because Conmee is so oblivious, the reader must piece together the connections that he fails to make. For example, when he meets and patronizes "three little schoolboys" from the Christian Brothers school at Belvedere, he seems unaware that they are the sons of those who exploit others financially. Adams has pointed out the ironies here: young Lynam is probably a bookie's son (10.506) and Jack Sohan a pawnbroker's son (Gifford 1988, 261; Adams 1962, 15). On the same page Conmee admires the "queenly mien" of Mrs. M'Guinness (who, like Mulligan, is "stately"), but finds it remarkable that "she was a pawnbroker!" (10.62; 66–67). Conmee's (and by extension, the priesthood's) veneration of nobility reveals a snobbish allegiance to the status quo. Moreover, the juxtaposition of pawnbrokers, bookies and priests identifies their offices: pawnbrokers of souls, Irish priests "redeem" them with the mercenary indifference of pawnbrokers redeeming cast-off goods, or bookies redeeming betting tickets, with as little profit for the customer. The association of pawnbrokers with queenliness and stateliness becomes equally significant when we later learn that queenly Mrs. M'Guinness has refused to give the Dedalus girls any money for Stephen's books (10.267–69). The Dedaluses thus represent the disenfranchised Irish whose land and possessions have been both appropriated and deemed valueless by history's pawnbrokers: both the English who own Ireland, and the spiritual pawnbrokers of the Roman church. In this sense Mrs. M'Guinness is indeed a queen on Dublin's chessboard, a stately symbol of English rule. If she is a queen, the self-satisfied Conmee deems himself a bishop, and his route traces a diagonal path away from the center of the city, imitating the bishop's moves on the chessboard (see Gifford 1988, 258–59).

Conmee neglects the bishop's spiritual offices. As a priest, he has a special charge to be a steward, *oikonomos* (economist) of the faith; to administer grace to all believers, as he himself has received it (I Peter 4.10); and to "convince the gainsayers" (Titus 1.9). But though Conmee reminds himself that "one should be charitable" to Protestants, his superficial faith seems unlikely to convince nonbelievers of anything but the Church's hypocrisy. Seeing a bargeman with a grimy straw hat, he reflects "on the providence of the Creator who had made turf to be in bogs whence men might dig it out and bring it to town and hamlet to make fires in the houses of poor people" (10.104– 6). Just as he gives the maimed sailor a blessing instead of a penny, he blandly accepts this meager comfort as adequate provision, never wondering why Providence permits poverty, the landlord system, and British agricultural policies to decimate the devout rural Irish. His version of Providence seems as "unlabouring" as the men he salutes (10.94). Musing about the millions of souls who have never received Christian baptism, he does manage to find it "a pity, that they should all be lost, a waste, if one might say" (10.151–52). This is less a serious consideration of a theological problem than a complaint about waste-fulness by a man who always keeps his hands on his loose change. The consummating censure of Conmee's self-absorption comes when, moving "in times of yore," he fails to recognize that the "flushed young man" and woman he blandly blesses have been interrupted during sex (10.199–205). The man is, of course, Lynch, who typically raises his cap (10.201—slang for a type of contraception that the Church has never sanctioned), while his "queen" (14.1143) brushes off her skirt. The portrayal of Conmee explains the interpolation of the dancing master Dennis Maginni: both are concerned more with deportment than devotion. The episode opens, then, with an indict-ment of the Irish priesthood presented from the inside: all the things Conmee misses or ignores define the failings of the institution. Al-though Conmee husbands his money and reveres God's providence, he is ineffectual as a steward *(oikonomos)* of grace.

Along his way Conmee passes Corny Kelleher, manager of O'Neill's funeral parlor, whom we have previously seen working at Dignam's funeral. Kelleher reappears in section 2 chatting with Con-stable 57C, confirming Bloom's suspicion that he is a police informer (5.14; 6.685). Kelleher's compromised role becomes useful later, how-ever, when he uses his clout to rescue Stephen and Bloom from Nighttown: "Providential you came on the scene," says Bloom (15.4858). This invocation of Providence (repeated in 16.69) suggests that Corny Kelleher serves as one distributor of *moly*, the "invisible influence" and "gift of Hermes"—himself an "accident of providence" (JJ 497)—that saves Odysseus from Circe. In addition to providing Joyce with a means of getting Stephen and Bloom out of Nighttown (he is "providential" for the author, as well) Kelleher "provides" both knowledge (for the police) and prostitutes (for the businessmen he escorts). These roles depict Kelleher as a Dublin analogue to Homer's Hermes: as undertaker, he fulfills Hermes' role as escort of souls to Hades (Wheelwright 1966, 225); as police tout, he parallels Hermes' position as the messenger or steward of the gods and master of "lies and deceitful words" (N. Brown 1947, 13); finally, just as Hermes protects travelers, thieves and merchants, Corny coincidentally protects the ad canvasser Bloom. Both Kelleher and Conmee are thus divine stewards. Moreover, Kelleher's providential appearance in "Circe" occurs because he is acting as a pimp, a mediator between *eros* and commerce; together with his police connections, this indicates that Kelleher plays Hermes' role as "amoral connecting deity" (Hyde 1983, 247), a kind of impersonal Providence or divine gossip. In "Wandering Rocks" his connective function is shown both by his ability to "connect" with policemen and by the synchronization of his "arching" jet of spittle with Molly's gift to the one-legged sailor (10.221–22): the arch motif not only presages Molly's impending liaison but also graphically illustrates Kelleher's ability to connect with "arch girls." In an episode full of missed and made exchanges and connections, the appearance of this Hermes figure seems not only appropriate but necessary.

"Generous" Gifts

Although Molly Bloom appears here only synecdochically as a "plump bare generous arm" (10.251) providing a coin for the beggar, her presence is suggested by the economic activities of several other characters.[18] "Generous" modifies "arm" in two senses: her arm is generously fleshed and represents by association her generosity in flinging the coin (scarcely extravagant, since it is only a penny [18.346]). But even her generosity has an ironic component, since later these generous arms embrace Boylan. If, unlike most other

18. That the sailor begs in Ireland by appealing to England is plainly ironic, as is his appealing to the destitute Dedalus girls (10.233–34). As the daughter of a British soldier, and a woman whose first two lovers were in the military, Molly might well respond to such a plea, no matter how formulaic.

Dubliners, she is a provider, her providence is more indiscriminate
than her husband would wish. As she flings the coin, a "card *Unfur-
nished Apartments* slipped from the sash and fell" (10.250–51): the
Bloom home is not only metaphorically "incomplete" in the way I
have already discussed; it is also literally "incomplete" because a room
stands empty.

While Molly gives a gift to the sailor, Boylan purchases a gift for
her. In the fifth section we see him buying Plumtree's Potted meat,
port wine, peaches and pears—choices that exemplify his ad man's
version of communion via mass products (like Conmee, Boylan fingers his change, rattling "merry money in his trousers' pocket" during
the transaction [10.324]). His gifts of food embody his view of Molly
as a consumable item and are thus congruent with his sole moment
of interiority: looking into the salesclerk's blouse, he thinks of her as
a "young pullet" (10.327). Similarly, in the past he bought the Blooms
a "fish supper" (18.1421), and in "Circe" he announces to Lenehan
that he has been "plucking a turkey." Sniffing his fingers, he comments lewdly, "Up to sample or your money back" (15.3747–51);
women can be purchased after being fondled like plump red toma-
toes (10.608). For Boylan, in short, women are consumable flesh,
although the menu may vary from time to time. Molly's appearance
as a generously fleshed arm thus reflects Boylan's ideology, in which
the "blood" of Dublin is merely the liquid that flows from animal
tissue. Even the flower he sticks between his teeth carries this carnivorous connotation: a carnation, its name derives from the Latin *carnis,*
or "flesh" (Restuccia 1989, 82). In Boylan's purchased presents we see
enacted the primitive erotic commerce voiced by the spectral Virag,
an expert on such matters: "Woman, undoing with sweet pudor her
belt of rushrope offers her allmoist yoni to man's lingam. Short time
after man presents woman with pieces of jungle meat. Woman shows
joy and covers herself with featherskins" (15.2549–51). Boylan tries
to buy Molly's flesh with other flesh. Smiling "gallantly" when he
accepts the flower (10.329), Boylan, a sham knight on Dublin's chessboard, is merely a more polished version of Lenehan and Corley, the
"gallants" of *Dubliners.* Thus Kershner's elucidation of the ethos of
gallantry accurately describes Boylan's erotic economy as well: a "conspicuous consumer whose public consumption of food, drink, ap-
parel, and ornaments validates his masculinity," the gallant practices
"a variety of objectification and depersonalization that is especially
pernicious because it mimics and parodies romantic devotion, while
replacing the interpersonal element with impersonal economic ex-

change" (Kershner 1989, 85–86). And yet Molly seems to accept his gifts and even feels that she gets something in return. As I have argued, their exchange is an erotic communion lubricated by food and carried out with a good deal of relish, one in which Molly accepts Boylan's corporal assets in return for her own. As I will argue in more detail later, her acceptance of Boylan's gifts permits her to manipulate the gift economy for her own profit.

At the end of this section Boylan makes a phone call, a social exchange completed in section 7 by his secretary, Miss Dunne (10.388). If, as some critics have suggested, she is the real identity of Martha Clifford, then Boylan's phone call demonstrates that he has a more significant relationship with her than Bloom does: he pays her salary. While Bloom writes her suggestive letters, Boylan determines when she is allowed the time to write them. Thus if Boylan usurps Bloom erotically with Molly, he also usurps him economically with Martha. The phone call concerns Molly's tour, and Miss Dunne answers his unrecorded question with, "Only those two, sir, for Belfast and Liverpool" (10.390). Boylan then mentions a figure, "twentyseven and six" (£1 7s 6d), which may refer to Boylan's bet on the Gold Cup (since Lenehan's name is mentioned immediately after), to Molly's fee for the concerts, or to the price of the presents he has just bought for her (he has just asked the fruit girl the price and may be informing his secretary of his bill so she can send a check, although the amount seems too large for the purchase). It most likely refers to the concert fees and thus reminds us again of that crucial economic element in their relationship: as her manager, Boylan negotiates for her fees, and thus determines part of the Bloom finances, so that Bloom does have a financial stake in encouraging their engagements. Boylan's sections thus expose the threads linking *eros* and commerce: he controls his client—also his lover—by purchasing gifts for her and controlling her earnings.

Like Conmee and Boylan, Bloom is on a quest; unlike most of the other characters (but like Boylan), he wants to give the object of his quest to someone else. Bloom may be called the chief provider of the episode because, as Hart notes (1974, 187), he finds what he is looking for, a smutty book that he rents for a shilling.[19] The shabby environment where Bloom is reading—the bookseller's "phlegmy coughs" and his own thoughts about "armpits' oniony sweat" (10.632; 622)—

---

19. Bloom's budget contains an entry for a one-shilling "renewal fee" for a book (17.1465), and he exchanges *Ruby: The Pride of the Ring* for this one.

contrast ironically with the book's florid prose. Moreover, the interpolation in section 5 (Boylan's section) to the "darkbacked figure" scanning books under Merchant's arch identifies the "gallant" activities of Boylan and Bloom, both of whom are spending money on gifts for Molly. Appropriately, the passages Bloom reads from *Sweets of Sin* concern commodities purchased as gifts for lovers: *"All the dollarbills her husband gave her were spent in the stores on wondrous gowns and costliest frillies. For him! For Raoul!"* (10.608–9). Curiously, Bloom selects a book that mirrors his own erotic triangle. Like Boylan's gift of potted meat, Bloom's gift inscribes a relationship between commerce and sex; in the book, the woman's clothes—e.g., *"sabletrimmed wrap"*—are fetishized in place of the woman beneath them.

These fetishes textualize some of Bloom's previous gifts: he once bought her violet garters (18.457–58) and, years ago, three pairs of gloves that he loved to kiss (18.186). Thus whereas Boylan's gifts embody his carnivorous view of Molly and sex, Bloom's gift of a book depicts her as *"heaving embonpoint"* and *"sabletrimmed wraps";* for him she is not the meat but the wrappings. Just as the gifts the woman in the book buys are not for her but *"for Raoul,"* so Bloom's gifts seem designed to fulfill his own sexual fantasies more than his wife's. Thus, both Bloom's and Boylan's gifts to Molly conform to a recognized pattern wherein males "tend to confirm their own identity by presenting it to others in objectified form" as gifts (Schwartz 1967, 2). Therefore "to accept a present is to accept the giver's image of yourself implied by the gift; and to reject the gift is to reject the image" (Schwartz 1967, 3). Like Joyce, who gave books to Nora and other females in his life, Bloom presents himself in his gift. While Molly may or may not accept either of these gifts as her looking glass—she is neither meat nor something written or read—there is less difference between Boylan's and Bloom's gifts than we might hope. Both males expect a return from their presents, and both express through the commodities they offer that, in some sense, Molly is herself a commodity. In this light, neither gift seems particularly generous. And even if Molly possesses *"queenly shoulders"* like the woman in the book (see 16.1448), here she seems less a queen than a pawn of male desire, a purchasable commodity metonymized in, or even replaced by, consumer goods. It almost seems as if Bloom, like Richard Rowan, is attempting to declare ownership of his wife by his willingness to "give" her (*Exiles* 56).

A line in Joyce's *Notesheets* for "Nausicaa" reads, "Merchant's Arch: conjugial love" (132). This note disturbingly stresses the mercenary nature of marriage and, through the arch figure, even yokes marriage and prostitution. Indeed, the men's competition is as much commercial as erotic, as suggested in "Ithaca" when Bloom identifies Boylan's "commercial ability" as "a bester" (17.2145–46), and connects his economic role—"a prosperous rival agency of publicity"—with his "moral" role as a "successful rival agent of intimacy" (17.2207–8). Molly becomes a medium of exchange between the two ad men, although only she can determine when and to whom she gives herself. Their gifts carry accompanying obligations. Boylan expects, and gets, Molly's flesh in return for his meat, and Bloom, in spite of her infidelity, expects a deeper loyalty and bond. She resists their control over her and manipulates both the gift economy and the market economy in an attempt to manage her corporal assets herself. In any case, the circulation of gifts, like that of blood, here binds together the exchanging parties; again economic exchange lies at the heart of the episode's portrayal of Dublin.

If Bloom's generosity seems a bit suspect here, elsewhere he is portrayed as a charitable provider. John Wyse Nolan, no friend of Bloom, notes that "Bloom put his name down" for a five-shilling contribution to the Dignams' children's fund. After Martin Cunningham adds, "and put down the five shillings too," Nolan quotes, "I'll say there is much kindness in the jew" (10.974–80). Unfortunately, his allusion contaminates the compliment, because the line he quotes from *The Merchant of Venice* is spoken by Antonio as he swears to forfeit a pound of flesh if he fails to pay his debt to Shylock (1. 3. 147–48). Shylock's "kindness" consists in taking Antonio's flesh, a less valuable surety than other bonds he might take; however, since forfeiting that bond would also take Antonio's life, the attribution of "kindness" is at least ambiguous, if not bitterly ironic. Thus in "complimenting" Bloom, Nolan is ungenerously identifying him as a Shylock. Nevertheless Bloom's contribution—five shillings, a crown —contrasts favorably with the stinginess of these representatives of the Crown. As these castles on Dublin's chessboard depart from the Castle yard (10.956), Cunningham takes the arm of Jimmy Henry, the town clerk, in an attempt to touch him for a contribution (10.987). When subsheriff Long John Fanning is approached, he suddenly has a lapse of memory about Dignam's identity (10.1017). At the end of the section, the viceregal cavalcade passes them without acknowledgement: just as the British governor ignores his charges, these men pretend ignorance of the children for whom Cunningham labors. Thus although John Wenke is right that "simple acts of charity are at the very heart of Joyce's vision of social felicity" (1980, 113), he neglects to note how rare such "simple acts" are and how complex their ramifications. The city fathers' complacency demonstrates how Dublin's privileged classes disregard the needy; unlike Bloom, whose contribution confirms his "blood" kinship with other Dubliners despite his economic differences from them, these men deny their own membership in the community they govern. While they too may be pawns of the British Empire, these castle pieces show allegiance only to one another, not to Dublin's other pawns.

Knights and Pawns

Tom Kernan, refugee from "Grace" and one of the few characters who actually works in this episode, does not concern himself with charity; he is returning from a successful business transaction with Mr. Crimmins, which he has also used as an excuse to have a "thimbleful" of gin. The preening salesman views all business dealings as exploitation, and his comments about the *General Slocum* disaster show that he thinks the world is run on equally corrupt lines. His cynicism, a belief that "all things may be decomposed and broken into fragments" (Hyde 1983, 128), is inimical to the charitable spirit and thus to the "blood" that unifies a community. Perhaps Kernan cannot be blamed for it, since he himself is a victim of "modern business practices" and of the foreign ownership of his business (see *D* 153–54): British rule had stifled economic progress and inhibited the growth of competing industries, so that the Irish merchant class had constantly to scrabble for marginal success (O'Brien 1982, 36). Nevertheless, Kernan remains proud of his sartorial dash, gazing at himself in the mirror like the self-important Fanning (10.1027): "Stylish coat, beyond a doubt. . . . Well worth the half sovereign I gave Neary for it. Never built under three guineas" (10.742–45; a half-sovereign is a ten-shilling piece, worth twice as much as Conmee's crown). Kernan's half-sovereign signifies his political confusion: just as the gold coin (a sovereign or half-sovereign) Corley reveals at the end of "Two Gallants" represents Irish complicity with British exploitation (Torchiana 1986, 105), so Kernan, a Protestant and Unionist who also waxes nostalgic over past Irish heroes, is himself a "half-sovereign," a divided man whose allegiance to Britain actually works against his own economic interest. A look at the map of Dublin (Gifford 1988, 258 and frontispiece), shows that Kernan strolls just to the spot where James's Street becomes Thomas Street and then turns north: his perpendicular path imitates the moves of a chess knight.[20] He also thinks of himself as a "knight of the road" (10.748), an illusion reinforced by the military nomenclature he attaches to his profession (*D* 154) but contradicted by his unheroic socioeconomic functions. Despite his knightly self-image, Kernan must rely on the charity of his acquaintances; thus he is actually a pawn, not only of the English merchants who own his business (17.2075–77), and of the kings, queens, and bishops who control Ireland, but even of his own friends.

Linked to Kernan by the circulation of Bloom's throwaway, the Dedalus girls, dependent upon charity and the grace of pawnbrokers, are the most obvious pawns in the episode (10.294–97; 752–55). They have tried to pawn Stephen's books but could get no money from the "queenly" Mrs. M'Guinness. The girls tend two pots, one of shirts and the other of pea soup obtained through the charity of a Sister Mary Patrick rather than through any effort of their improvident father. Even if, as Kenner notes, their poverty is "genteel squalor indeed compared to what might have been found a few blocks away" ("Foreword" to O'Brien 1982, viii), hunger is never genteel. Thus the section's first interpolation, to Father Conmee, suggests an affinity between fathers—Catholic priests (and Providence Himself) and Simon, "Our father who art not in heaven" (10.291)—all of whom fail to provide adequately.

Dilly's attempts to wheedle money from her father are detailed in section 11. She waits outside Dillon's auction rooms as curtains (probably theirs; Van Caspel 1986, 148) are sold for five shillings (another crown)—far less than the two guineas they brought when new (10.647). Like pawning, auctioning property is often the last resort of the truly destitute. Simon tries to put her off by claiming that "There is no-one in Dublin would lend me fourpence" (10.669–70): like John Joyce, he claims to have "exhausted all his friends" (*L* II 229). But Dilly persists and Simon relents, giving her a shilling. "I suppose you got five. . . . Give me more than that," she persists, as if to compensate for the curtains by demanding the same amount bid for them (10.680). Simon curses, threatens her, admits that Jack Power has lent

20. His movement recalls Mrs. Kernan's comment in "Grace" that he would "walk to the end of Thomas Street and back again to book even a small order" (*D* 156). Joyce places Kernan where his wife imagines him, but makes him avoid Thomas Street. Her compliment seems less impressive when we look at the map and discover that Thomas Street is only three blocks long! He probably turns off because it skirts the edge of the Liberties, a dismal slum. Addicted to surfaces, Kernan cannot bear to have his complacency shattered by views of Dublin's poverty.

him two bob, reluctantly doles out another twopence, and walks away cursing. Power's two-shilling loan reprises the florin motif and recalls the amount Reuben J. gave for his son's rescue; ironically, although Simon joked that Dodd's florin was "one and eightpence too much" for his son's life, he gives his own drowning children even less. Hence, while Simon threatens to give them "short shrift," it is difficult to see how it could get much shorter than it already is.[21]

The Dedaluses mirror their real-life counterparts in this scene: in 1904, John Joyce was forced to pawn much of the family furniture. Although Margaret ("Poppie") "became fairly adept at wheedling shillings from her father to support the family [which was still large], . . . sometimes there was nothing to eat" (*JJ* 143). That Joyce is critical of Simon is suggested by the placement of this section: coming immediately after Bloom's bookhunt, it juxtaposes Stephen's consubstantial and transubstantial fathers and proves the latter's superiority. Bloom provides, Simon does not; Bloom gives gifts to his family and to others, while Simon is not only constantly in debt but even begrudges his daughters the money they need to live. Although Simon is not to blame for the political changes that cost him his rate collector's job, and although Joyce documents the larger conditions that conspire against Irish families, Simon, like John Joyce, is culpable for his family's poverty. Like the priests he condemns, he is an unjust steward who repudiates his own blood by failing to provide for them; rather than circulate his money among his kin, he spends it on liquid refreshment for himself and his cronies.

Stephen, in the meantime, pursues his own profligate ways. He listens tolerantly to—but rejects—Artifoni's paternal advice that he should use his voice to make money. Though he has inherited "his father's voice" (16.1659), the power and sentimentality of which are dramatized in "Sirens," Stephen means to dispossess himself of that inheritance along with the others Simon has left him. He thus considers the loss of income from a vocal career to be merely a "bloodless sacrifice"—i.e., no loss (10.348). His words allude to Christ's bloodless self-sacrifice through transubstantiation into bread and wine, and therefore to Stephen's belief that art must be eucharistic. Stephen sacrifices his vocal career, and hence his material assets, for the blood-

21. Gordon (1981, 63) contends that Simon is actually giving Dilly most of what he has (if he is not lying, he has only eightpence left) and hence should not be condemned for his behavior. But Simon's veracity is suspect: he has enough money to booze it up shortly after this scene.

less (immaterial) assets of poetry. As we have seen, bloodlessness is its weakness: lacking material substance, it fails to carry out transformation or symbolic exchange. In the context of the episode, Stephen's words also repudiate Dublin: the circulation of money and language among Dubliners proves their blood kinship, and Stephen resists such exchanges. If money, scored with the symbols of Ireland's English master, is blood, Stephen vows to remain bloodless.

Nevertheless, his debtorship proves his blood ties. In section 13 he broods on his dilemma: "Your heart you sing of. . . . Between two roaring worlds where they swirl, I. Shatter them, one and both. But stun myself too in the blow" (10.822–25). Wandering between Dublin and his private destiny, Stephen hears the roaring of the blood uniting him to community and family. He fears that by alienating himself from Dublin, he will also lose his inner direction: Dublin's "blood is in me, their lusts my waves" (3.306–7). And yet, because exchanges of objects and money create bonds that may become nets, he must fight the guilt that prompts him to give money to the drowning Dilly: "She is drowning. Agenbite. Save her. . . . She will drown me with her, eyes and hair" (10.875–77). Though he does show sympathy for her, he refuses to help financially; perhaps, after all, his father's blood courses through his veins.

Stephen's wavering between the roaring worlds of commerce and art is dramatized, like Bloom's vacillation about Molly's infidelity, through a bookhunt. His joke that he might "find here one of my pawned schoolprizes. *Stephano Dedalo, alumno optimo, palmam ferenti*" (10.840–41) proves his financial and artistic dispossession. Like Dilly, who asks for five shillings from her father, Stephen seeks a crown; but it is the sovereignty of art, as forecast by his own name—"*Stephanos*, my crown" (9.947). However, his crown is unfilled, as lost as his latchkey; indeed, Stephen has not even a "plais whear tu lay crown of his hed 2 night" (14.1540). Despite Dilly's brave attempt to assert the value of book learning by spending her pennies on a French primer, books have greater value as commodities that can be sold to get the financial crowns needed for subsistence. For all his vaunted talent, Stephen is not yet a king, nor even the knight that he seemed earlier in the day (2.425; 3.503) and that his right-angled path through Dublin suggests. A pawn between armies, he is trapped between the ties of blood and the desire to be bloodless.

In this sense Stephen resembles the dawdling and directionless young Dignam, depicted in section 18 carrying home a "pound and a half of [probably bloody] . . . porksteaks he had been sent for"

(10.1122–23). Like the Dedalus children, Master Dignam must find a substitute for an improvident father who, unlike Simon, is truly dead. Like Stephen, young Dignam is haunted by the memory of a dead parent: like Boody's, his father "art not in heaven." At once comic and pathetic, young Dignam is at least attempting to take his father's place, to provide for his family by buying their food. Young Dignam also bears the blood of Dublin males within him: he reads Boylan's posters, sees him speaking to Doran, and, like Boylan, buys meat; he speaks Bloom's name (his favorite expression is "blooming"); he is the object of Cunningham's and Conmee's charitable missions; he is Stephen's younger, dimmer mirror image—just as Stephen's crown is lost, so young Dignam's cap is "awry" (10.1140). An absolutely ordinary boy, he is given just enough interior life to prove that the charity extended to him has nothing to do with intellectual merit. Judging from this heir, the Dignams seem destined to remain pawns dependent upon charity for their livelihood.

Trespassers

The counterpart to Lenehan's and M'Coy's discussion of Bloom occurs in section 16, where Haines and Mulligan talk smugly about Stephen. Haines's "newbought book" both recalls Bloom's and Stephen's quests and demonstrates his economic superiority to them: while they browse at secondhand stalls, he can afford to buy new ones. This section follows directly after the one detailing the stinginess of Dublin's city officials; Mulligan and Haines are equally well fed, their relative wealth setting them apart from families like the Dedaluses and demonstrating their obliviousness to the history of hunger. Haines, who demands "real Irish cream" because he does not want to be "imposed on" (10.1094–95), and Mulligan, his well-pleased pleaser, patronize Stephen as the wealthy classes patronize and criticize the poor. Like Conmee, whose priestly functions Mulligan parodies, they are blind to the irony of feeding themselves on Irish products. "History is to blame," says Haines, who disregards it; indeed, he is associated in this episode with other characters who try to rewrite, and thereby master, Irish history.

Haines, Conmee, the smug priest who has written a book about "old times in the barony" (10.159), and the Unionist Kernan are all devoted to questionable accounts of Irish history. But the most significant character in this regard is another bishop on Dublin's chessboard, the Rev. Hugh C. Love, who first appears in section 8 with

Ned Lambert and J. J. O'Molloy. Lambert shows Love the ancient council chamber of St. Mary's abbey, "the most historic spot in all Dublin" (10.409). Like Kernan a Protestant and Unionist, Love is fascinated by the FitzGeralds. And like Haines, who also appropriates things Irish for English use, Love is at first invisible, entering the text merely as a "refined accent" (10.415); his invisibility represents the economic and political tyranny analyzed in chapter 2. Love's expropriation of history also links him that other Unionist, Garrett Deasy: Love says he "won't trespass on your valuable time" (10.426–27); Deasy asks to "trespass on your valuable space" (2.324).[22] But as representatives of the Anglo-Protestant usurpers, they cannot help but be trespassers. Love's economic and symbolic contrast to other Dubliners becomes more pronounced in his absence: once he leaves, O'Molloy is free to ask Lambert for a loan.

Love is profoundly implicated in Irish economic history and in the problems of other *Ulysses* characters. Section 14 introduces two of Simon's derelict cronies, the failed fathers Bob Cowley and Ben Dollard: Cowley is a spoiled priest and Dollard, a failed ships' chandler with a *basso profundo* and a prominent male member, symbolizes sterile virility. Hounded by Reuben J. Dodd for unpaid debts, Cowley has enlisted Dollard (a kind of lesser Cunningham) to urge the subsheriff to restrain Dodd's men. But Cowley's more crippling problem is that his landlord, the same Reverend Mr. Love, is distraining him for nonpayment of rent (10.943–44). Objectively, one cannot fault the landlord for trying to get his due. Symbolically, however, Love represents all those Protestant landlords who populate Irish history, a fact that places him firmly with the usurpers—the bishops and castles—not the pawns. Not only, then, does he want to rewrite Ireland's history; he embodies it by playing the part of the absentee landlords who have victimized Irish tenants over the centuries.[23] Of course, Joyce was quite familiar with the conditions of evicted *urban* tenants, since he had been one many times. Moreover, as Adams shows, Joyce's personal history is germane to the portrayal of this cleric, since a Reverend Mr. Love was in 1900 either the Joyces' landlord or

22. Restuccia (1989, 110) also notes that Love echoes Deasy, though she does not develop the political and economic similarities.

23. Moshenberg (1991, 814) cleverly describes this situation: "the Catholic priest (Cowley) is saved from paying his debt to the 'jewman' moneylender by the rent he has failed to pay to the absentee Protestant cleric landlord." The only thing wrong with this formulation is that Cowley is not a priest, though he is probably Catholic.

his agent when they lived in Windsor Terrace (Cowley lives at 29 Windsor Avenue, which may or may not be the same property; see *MBK* 75). Hence as Cosmic Economist or Dublin's Providence, the author carries a memory in his wallet: "in putting Hugh C. Love in *Ulysses* as a hard-hearted landlord, [Joyce] is evidently paying off an old family score" (Adams 1962, 32). Love's dual roles as landlord and cleric converge when in "Circe" he becomes "Hugh C. Haines Love," a celebrant of the Black Mass (15.4695): while Haines (French for "hates") usurps Stephen's home in the Martello Tower, so Love duns his tenants and threatens to evict them, just as the Protestant Ascendancy class appropriated the lands and drove out Irish Catholic landowners. Though the intemperance and improvidence of Cowley and Simon remain the primary causes of their destitution, Love's association with Haines, Mulligan, and the Protestant ruling classes symbolize how the collaboration of political and economic forces have historically oppressed the Irish as well.

As in chess, the king, represented by the viceregal cavalcade, is given the final move. The cavalcade receives a series of salutes that double those Conmee receives, suggesting their complementary positions as Ireland's two masters (although Stephen, Bloom, Gerty MacDowell—she of the "queenly *hauteur*" [13.97]—and Joyce's surrogate, John Howard Parnell, do not salute). Here to "inaugurate the Mirus bazaar in aid of funds for Mercer's hospital" (10.1268), the viceroy seems to provide for his dependents. But his uncomprehending passage through poverty and improvidence demonstrates the vanity of his authority and the inadequacy of his charity. Indeed, the enclosure of his carriage typifies the blindness and patronizing attitudes that created the "Irish problem." Thus Conmee's and Dudley's missions of charity are similar: merely doing "public duty," they do not show real compassion or understanding (Wenke 1980, 102). Neither the Church nor the State offers lasting economic redemption; though they resemble the other pieces on the chessboard, ultimately they stand for the two masters who manipulate the pieces. Framing the labyrinth, the viceroy's progress illustrates the wall between the Irish and their masters. Unlike the Dubliners who enact their dependence on one another through social and economic exchanges, the viceroy, in spite of his official mission, engages in no genuine exchanges.

Reciprocity, Circulation, and Community

The episode's chiastic structure, noted by several writers (e.g., Knuth 1976, 137, and Seidel 1976, 187), finds a visual analogue in the prevalence of mirrors. The mirror produces a reciprocity of gaze (see 17.1340–60) and thus may seem to represent the norm of economic reciprocity, in which parties receive what they give. But only the most self-absorbed characters—Fanning, Kernan, Mulligan (in "Telemachus"), Boylan (in "Sirens"), the dim Master Dignam—look into mirrors. Thus mirrors figure not reciprocity but the narcissism and selfishness that defeat social consciousness and community. Likewise, in "Wandering Rocks" (and throughout the middle episodes of *Ulysses*) reciprocity is distorted: instead of exchanging mutual benefits or genuine gifts, the characters gamble or beg, borrow money without returning it, give and accept gifts tainted with ulterior motives, deny charity, pawn or auction their belongings, or undertake exploitative business transactions. If they provide for one another, it is unwillingly, inadequately, or sporadically. With few exceptions (Bloom's charity, for example), this systematic distortion of reciprocity denotes a deformation of the entire range of Dublin's social and economic relationships. Moreover, if, as Simmel remarks, "the feeling of personal security that the possession of money gives is perhaps the most concentrated and pointed . . . manifestation of confidence in the socio-political order" (1978, 179), then Irish improvidence proves Irish political anxiety. Stripped of self-determination and economic independence, Dubliners exploit each other and so mirror the masters' disregard for reciprocity and economic provision.

The circulation of blood—money and social currency—knits together the community so that what affects one character or group of characters necessarily redounds upon others. Ideally, such circulation takes the form of gifts, which act as agents of social cohesion. Hyde argues that the "perfect gift is like the blood pumped through its vessels by the heart. Our blood . . . distributes the breath throughout the body . . . [and] moves freely to every part but is nonetheless contained, a healer that goes without restraint to any needy place in the body" (1983, 138). In other words, blood is the body's internal Providence, a medium for charity that demands no compensating payment. But in Dublin, as in most modern communities, the exchange of gifts is supplanted by the circulation of money, the primary medium of economic exchange and hence the chief means of creating unity. In this sense, even the atmosphere of obligation that seems to trap some characters may be a powerful unifying force, one of "those 'microscopic' but infinitely tough threads which tie one element of society to another, and thus eventually all of them together in a stable collective life" (Simmel 1950, 395). But as Marx observes, money can be both the "bond of all bonds" and the "the universal agent of sepa-

ration" (1978, 104): while it may create economic ties, its use in market relations generates conflict between parties, thereby alienating
and sundering kinship relations. Thus, in Dublin, money is laden
with signifers of oppression and fragmentation, as Joyce's cracked
looking glass reveals that the "blood" of Dublin is always on the verge
of dissolving into separate cells. The surface of the episode, with its
discrete, fragmented sections, threaded by interpolations and exchanges, illustrates this deep tension in the city between the forces of
unity—represented by the circulation of "blood" in all its forms—and
forces of fragmentation. The circulation of money and gifts in Joyce's
Dublin thus illustrates and generates both unity and anxiety, both
love and hostility, but more often the latter. If Providence is charity,
or perfect gift exchange, then Dubliners' improvidence demonstrates
both the limits of charity and the disintegration of the "blood" kinship
of its citizens. And if Joyce's Dublin is a city united by its resistance to
and hatred of British oppression, it is also a community on the verge
of disintegration, one in which persons remain fundamentally isolated from one another, in part because of the economic relations
fostered by centuries of that hegemony.[24]

The political and moral design of Joyce's economic aesthetic is
thus inscribed in "Wandering Rocks." This order is not immediately
apparent, however, but must be pieced together by the attentive
reader, who still always seems to be playing the game a few moves
behind Joyce's clever and sometimes hostile narrator. Like the gaming male Dubliners, Joyce's narrator is a game player, a plotter, a
chessmaster who subjects both his text and his readers to a rather
frustrating ludic skill. Moreover, the narrator seems strangely distant
emotionally from the material. Indeed, if the later episodes often
manifest an economy of comic excess that parallels the characters'
tendency towards extravagance and profligacy, this one seems to critique that economy by employing a stringent economy of strict control
by a singular and dominant authorial presence (cf. Hart 1974, 190).

---

24. Hartsock argues that such a vision of community is inherent in the exchange
model of social behavior, which necessarily sees humans as "fundamentally isolated
from each other" in pursuit of "deeply conflicting interests," and able to associate
"only on the basis of complementary (but conflicting) desires." A society based upon
commodity exchange is thus a "society of strangers" (Hartstock 1983, 27, 98). Such a
community, "leveled by an economic reality which made all things equivalent through
the mediation of money . . . consists entire of meaningless uniform surfaces, and the
men and women who live in it engage in the endless manipulation of objects—a category that now includes themselves" (Knapp 1988, 137).

This is perhaps an appropriate stance since, according to Simmel, metropolitan life demands adherence to "punctuality, calculability, exactness" (1950, 413), qualities displayed in the narrator's charting of movements and times. Instead of excess, we find the scrupulous meanness of a *Dubliners Revisited,* governed by an Authorial Providence who metes out punishments, salvations, and grace on his great cash register with the power and implacability of Divine Providence.

And yet, this narrative economy is subsumed by a larger struggle within the narrative discourse of *Ulysses:* the conflict between control of the text by a single dominant authority and the dissemination of that authority into a collective authorship, as if the characters themselves are writing it. The narrator places us within the minds of characters like Kernan, young Dignam, Boylan, and Conmee, at once inviting and defeating our sympathy and his own. Thus while the narrator controls the characters' movements, he also relinquishes control and lets them speak for themselves. The movement from "Hades" to "Wandering Rocks" is thus a movement from a singular to a collective authority, as the text widens to become a virtual catalogue of economic behaviors. Moreover, the illusion of total control can be maintained only by constantly patrolling the text to guard against the accidental (and redemptive) linguistic exchanges that nonetheless occur, just as Ireland could be controlled only by its authorities' constant patrolling of its moral and political life. Rather than standing outside the tides of separation and unification charted in the text, Joyce and his narrators stand directly within them. Again Joyce uses the mock-realism of documentary facts but undermines it by permitting the text to smuggle in tropes, homophones, and tricks that demonstrate how the linguistic economy of realism—one meaning per word—always eludes its encirclement by the forces of authority. These puns and homonyms also permit the reader to discover threads between the linguistic economy and the economic life of Dublin, threads that both reproduce the tensions in Dublin's economy and draw the reader into that community. The text challenges the reader to play its games, to gamble along with it: as we perform and observe linguistic exchanges, we too are implicated in the "blood" of "Wandering Rocks." In this sense, reciprocity becomes the (distorted) norm not only for evaluating the events of the episode but also for the narrator's relationship with his readers: he demands from us a reciprocal commitment to game playing, a capacity for scrupulousness and excess that mirrors his own and his citizens'.

Thus though the narrator seems to lack charity, and though this trait reflects the economy he depicts, at the same time he invites readers to work hard enough to find a path through the labyrinth. If Joyce himself is the ungenerous Providence of "Wandering Rocks," that role is essential to his moral history. As author, he illustrates the economic blood of Dublin with the currency of language. By manipulating tropic exchanges—puns, homonyms, synchronicities, mirrored characters—that expose the distortions and eccentricities in both economies, the author may restore that reciprocity, so that the depiction of Dublin's economic failure may engender a new order, a new community united by the currency of words. The weaving of the text is therefore political labor that also invites political engagement with the text; in its diligence it embodies an alternative to the idleness of Dubliners and to the Divine Providence who seems to scorn them. Joyce attempts to redress equilibriums that have been upset by reproducing them in an art that is not bloodless but an embodiment of the blood of Dublin. This new currency becomes a gift that may restore the broken unity inscribed by the text. Joyce similarly writes elsewhere that "nationality . . . must find its reason for being rooted in something that surpasses and transcends and informs changing things like blood and the human word" (*CW* 166): nationality is affirmed by the reproduction of the "blood" of Dublin in literary currency. In presenting the economy of Dublin, Joyce also participates in it by offering the text itself as both commodity and gift, both blood and bloodless sacrifice. If one may master a text, such mastery might displace the mastery imposed by Church and State. And if the reader can donate his or her own labor in response, that reader may achieve a similar mastery.

6

The Intertextual Economy

> He who will not work . . . gives birth to wind, but he who is willing to work gives birth to his own father.
> —Kierkegaard 1954, 39

SPIRITUAL ASSETS

When we left Stephen alone on the strand, he had tentatively begun to renegotiate both his material and artistic economies. The next three episodes in which he plays a major role—"Aeolus," "Scylla and Charybdis," and "Oxen of the Sun"—find him amidst the Dubliners he formerly scorned. "Aeolus" dramatizes his encounter with and rejection of the stereotypes of Irish patriotism, through a rhetorical contest with elder male Dubliners; "Scylla and Charybdis" stages his confrontation with the ghost of Shakespeare, the greatest single English literary father; "Oxen" marshals the entire history of English literature to catalogue Stephen's and Joyce's debts to English literature and to illustrate Joyce's own labor theory. All of these relationships are marked by an ambivalent mixture of hostility and complaisance. In these episodes Stephen faces the past; in all of them he spends financial assets to gain credit and an audience for his literary creations—spiritual assets that he hopes will replace financial assets; in all of them his productions challenge his interlocutors and progenitors. In all of them, too, Joyce develops homologies between literary and financial debtorship to chart both the pathways and the barriers to Stephen's difficult encounter with the intertextual economy. If earlier his spending symbolized a more general dispossession, here he spends his money (mostly on drinks) to help generate creative gains: that is, he ingests spirits to help create, expend, and share his spiritual assets.

Raising the Wind

"Aeolus" locates us again "IN THE HEART OF THE HIBERNIAN METROPOLIS" (7.1–2), amid barflies, hangers-on and employees of the *Freeman's Journal*. The newspaper office is one of those "nodal points at which . . . pathways and trajectories meet," a point of "totalisation" where information is stored and exchanged (Jameson 1982, 133). Like the nearby post office and tramlines, the newspaper office is a hub for the circulation of words—most of them borrowed (Lawrence 1981, 64)—and those who generate them (McArthur 1988, 90). "Aeolus" establishes and explores homologies between the verbal borrowings that the characters use to gain favor and the financial borrowings with which they attempt to support each other. Both forms of currency—linguistic and economic—implicate them in what McArthur (1988, 93) calls a "culture of debt," a distorted economy that both produces them and that they produce.

Many critics have noted that the pervasive wind references in the episode point not only back to Homer but to the words that flow through the office, which is headquarters for the windiest discourse available, best exemplified by the three quoted speeches that highlight the episode. Just as the lungs (the episode's "organ" in Joyce's schema) process the oxygen in air, send it into the bloodstream, and then receive and return carbon dioxide back to the outer world, so the newspaper office processes events and turns them into news—allegedly valuable printed currency—that it then transmits back to the citizens. But the occupants here exchange little news; instead, they circulate borrowed rhetoric and money, the rhythm of respiration paralleling the economic rhythm of income and outgo. Today is payday, and so those with nothing better to do gather here hoping to tap one of the newly flush employees. Thus as Stephen enters the office he encounters MacHugh, a *"ponderous pundit"* (7.578) and putative professor; Lenehan, the sponge from "Two Gallants"; Myles Crawford, editor of the newspaper; and J. J. O'Molloy, the unsuccessful lawyer introduced above. Whereas Hynes, onstage, and Bloom, off-stage, receive payment (and Hynes, for the third time, fails to repay the three shillings Bloom lent him three weeks ago [7.119]), Stephen enters with his wages in hand, hears some speeches, thereupon decides to treat for drinks, and leaves the office, leading the thirsty troop to Mooney's pub. As the employees' money flows in, Stephen's flows out.

In the *Odyssey*, Odysseus' men scheme to release Aeolus's bag of winds, believing that it contains treasure (1961, 166). When they open it, the winds are released and blow them back to Aeolia. Admirers of oratory and bombast, Joyce's Aeolians resemble Odysseus' men. They believe that the bags of wind gusting through here contain genuine wisdom, verbal treasure. But the linguistic economy of the episode is inflated, and just as inflation results from an excess of printed money without an accompanying increase in the stock of gold on which it is based, so discourse here proliferates without augmenting wisdom. It is spirit without matter, currency without substance. As in the dichotomy Stephen develops in *Stephen Hero*, words are devalued by circulation in the marketplace. The result of this proliferation of verbiage is the depreciation of relative value. In place of the missing substance that would lend real value to their words, the characters exchange forms of credit: they act as though they believe in each other and in so doing further distort the verbal economy, since their "credit" merely sinks them deeper into debt. Even the narrator participates in this linguistic inflation, using mock-heroic descriptions of trivial actions in some of the interpolated headings (a cigarette becomes "THE CALUMET OF PEACE" [7.464]), and headlining the most trivial incidents, as if all words and events have equal importance, and hence none has much. Like the characters, the narrator "raises the wind."

These "spiritual" assets—*spirit*, from the Latin *spiritus* (breath)— lack material authority. Even the characters seem to recognize this "Irish" condition, as MacHugh's words simultaneously expose and excuse it: "Success for us is the death of the intellect and of the imagination. We were never loyal to the successful. We serve them. . . . I speak the tongue of a race the acme of whose mentality is the maxim: time is money. Material domination. *Domine!* Lord! Where is the spirituality?" (7.553–57). Though the Anglo-Saxons dominate because of their commercial expertise, they lack spiritual assets; the Irish, Greeks to England's Romans, are paralyzed by excessive spirituality and material ineptitude. As we have seen, Joyce sometimes similarly claimed that material failure was necessary for artistic success.[1] But what of nonartists? Material failure leaves merely an empty pocketbook. Hence virtually all of the Dubliners in *Ulysses* are lost causes, devoted to a legendary history of ever-foggier facts. These characters use this "spirituality" to excuse indolence and alcoholism; to defy British materialism, they ruin themselves. In this sense, the newspaper office is peopled by speakers lacking both financial and "spiritual" credit.

Thus, in Joyce's Dublin, "those rigid constraints imposed by imperialism on the development of human energies account for the symbolic displacement and flowering of the latter in eloquence, rhetoric and oratorical language," talents more highly prized in precapitalist societies (Jameson 1982, 134). In this reading, British imperialism has barred the Irish from employing their abilities in more profitable activities. Yet this assessment condescends by ascribing to the characters too little responsibility for their failings, unlike Joyce, who never refrained from criticizing them. For example, Stephen enters accompanied by Mr. O'Madden Burke, a man seemingly without fixed occupation who was last seen in "A Mother," where he is described as "a suave elderly man who balanced his imposing body, when at rest, upon a large silk umbrella. His magniloquent western name was the moral umbrella upon which he balanced the fine problem of his finances. He was widely respected" (*D* 145). In that story he kibitzes at the concert in progress, hanging at the fringes, waiting for someone to offer him a drink. His goal here is the same. Still possessing his material and moral umbrellas, Burke uses his suaveness and sartorial elegance to disguise his poverty and emptiness. Using his full name each time he is mentioned, the narrator ironically emphasizes the gap between his title and his real worth. Burke's precarious financial balance applies to most of the characters here, Stephen (of the magniloquent name) included; Burke's umbrella unfolds symbolically as the excuses they make to cover their lack of ambition.

Like Burke, Myles Crawford ("Incipient jigs. Sad case" [7.366]) is out of balance both physically and financially, as shown by his ram-

---

1. In 1918, for example, about the time he was composing this episode, he asserted that "material victory is the death of spiritual preeminence. Today we see in the Greeks of antiquity the most cultured nation. Had the Greek state not perished, what would have become of the Greeks? Colonizers and merchants" (*JJ* 446). Elsewhere Joyce describes the Irish as "strange spirits, frigid enthusiasts, sexually and artistically untaught, full of idealism and unable to yield to it, childish spirits, ingenuous and satirical," and Anglo-Saxon civilization as "materialistic" (*CW* 173).

bling, inaccurate history of the Phoenix Park murders (he dates them from 1881, when any Dubliner of the day would know it was 1882 [7.632]). Likewise, before Stephen appears, Simon Dedalus and Ned Lambert share a laugh at Dan Dawson's orotund periods on Irish landscape. But neither of them is doing anything better. Lambert, taking a day off from his job at a grain store, is idle; in any case, his job is merely a way of passing time as he waits for the "windfalls" that will appear when his wealthy granduncle breathes his last (7.266). The notorious welsher Simon is seen "welshcomb[ing]" his hair. Both use Dawson's words as an excuse to get an early drink (7.351). Lenehan, as usual, laughs and leeches, contributing occasional bad puns. None of these characters seems excessively spiritual, but each lacks the ambition to rouse himself to remedy his circumstances. Although the imperialist economy can be held partly responsible for their paralysis—by impeding the progress of Irish industry and causing unemployment—Joyce again indicts Irish idleness and complacency. Despite their scorn for Dawson's speech, these characters exemplify negative stereotypes at least as damaging as Dawson's stultifyingly clichéd language. Like Dawson's discourse, they have been reduced to "compilations of received fictions" (Herr 1987, 32). Stephen recognizes this pattern as a fact of history, now a "Nightmare from which you will never awake" (7.678). Indeed, that he is in their midst suggests his complicity with that history. Moreover, his ambivalent response to the two examples of "received fictions" he hears dramatizes his indebtedness to this Irish verbal and economic heritage.

The first speech is presented by O'Molloy, who quotes the lawyer Seymour Bushe's defense during the Childs murder case, in which Samuel Childs was indicted for murdering his brother. Of Michelangelo's statue of Moses, O'Molloy's Bushe says: *"that stony effigy in frozen music, horned and terrible, of the human form divine, that eternal symbol of wisdom and of prophecy which, if aught that the imagination or the hand of sculptor has wrought in marble of soultransfigured and of soultransfiguring deserves to live, deserves to live.* His [O'Molloy's] slim hand with a wave graced echo and fall" (7.768–71). Enough a Dubliner to feel "his blood wooed by grace of language and gesture," Stephen blushes; such rhetoric is his blood inheritance (7.776). But the "grace" in the passage has nothing to do with religious redemption. It is rather the kind of superficial grace exemplified by Burke when he falls "back with grace on his umbrella" (7.593), the same kind we traced in Kernan's character in the preceding chapter. Another relic of old decency, O'Molloy is seeking financial grace. Bloom earlier summarizes his plight: "Cleverest fellow at the junior bar he used to be. Decline poor chap. . . . Touch and go with him. What's in the wind, I wonder. Money worry. . . . Practice dwindling. A mighthavebeen. Losing heart. Gambling. Debts of honour. Reaping the whirlwind" (7.291–94; 303–4). O'Molloy attempts to conceal his incipient bankruptcy by borrowing words—and hence authority and verbal credit—from a more successful lawyer. But his discourse is inflated currency; rather than buttressing his authority, his verbal borrowings are devalued by being severed from their judicial context. In his mouth the speech is designed not to invoke justice but merely to prop him up in his friends' eyes. Although his paradoxical condition as an "Irish practitioner of British law" (Herr 1986, 73) may be difficult, Bloom suggests that his improvident habits are to blame for his economic difficulties. In fact, he is here to borrow money as well as words—to raise the wind—and doggedly pursues this quest throughout the novel, later carrying his importunities to "Wandering Rocks" and "Cyclops." Thus the words he borrows are perfectly appropriate: just as Bushe pleads for leniency, O'Molloy asks for grace from those he attempts to touch for a loan. His borrowed verbal credit is designed to earn financial credit. It is indeed "touch and go" with him: touch a friend for money, then go.

MacHugh counters by quoting the words of the Fenian lawyer John F. Taylor. An even more skillful speech, it too compares the Irish with an ancient race, the Israelites. The speech is situated amid several layers of literary borrowings, each one a further example of the kind of verbal metempsychosis upon which *Ulysses* is based. Taylor's speech actually took place on October 24, 1901, and followed that of the antinationalist Gerald Fitzgibbon, who had defended English against the Irish language movement.[2] In part of MacHugh's version of his speech, Taylor quotes the words of an Egyptian priest (a stand-in for Fitzgibbon), who attempts to persuade the Jews to accept an Egyptian culture that is as superior to the Jews' in wealth and strength as England's is to Ireland's (7.845–59). In short, Joyce borrows from an account of an actual event, placing his version of the real man's words in the mouth of a fictional character, who quotes the fictional version of the real orator, who himself cites the words of an imaginary priest. We might chart the intertextual layers of appropria-

---

2. Richard Ellmann (1977, 35–36) quotes the colorless newspaper account of the speech, and reproduces the pamphlet from which Joyce apparently borrowed his version. For a different rendition of Taylor's speech, see Yeats (1965, 64–67).

tions and borrowings as follows: (1) Real-life Taylor [quotes Egyptian priest as Fitzgibbon], quoted by (2) James Joyce, who becomes the "Aeolus" narrator, who quotes (3) MacHugh, quoting (4) fictional Taylor [quoting Egyptian priest]. Joyce creates the fictional Taylor, based upon a real-life character who quoted an imaginary Egyptian, and then wraps an ironic narrator around the next layer; then the fictional MacHugh quotes the fictional Taylor, who himself quotes a fictional priest. The speech thus acknowledges and embodies the condition of history as verbal debtorship, demonstrating the dependence of Joyce's texts upon the linguistic capital or fund of all previously spoken (or written) words. Indeed, the passage itself is about borrowing, since the priest asks Moses to borrow Egyptian culture in order to make the Jews richer. Such intertextual layers typify *Ulysses*, itself a revision of an epic borrowed from a group of folktales and collected by "Homer," who placed some of the tales in the mouth of Odysseus, within a larger frame tale told by a third-person narrator. Like Homer and Odysseus, the teller of *Ulysses* is a ventriloquist and borrower *extraordinaire;* like O'Molloy and MacHugh, he depends upon loans for his artistic livelihood.

The relationships among the quoted speakers are, however, filled with tensions. Although MacHugh, like O'Molloy, is attempting to "raise the wind"—borrow authority to gain prestige and to be included if any drinks are to be awarded—his windy belch undercuts the stirring message he delivers (R. Ellmann 1977, 36). Ironically, too, the priest's disparaging description of the Jews as *"Vagrants and daylabourers"* (7.858–59) is an all-too-accurate picture of the idlers who hear it now. Unlike O'Molloy, who quotes Bushe to reinforce his own dubious credit, Taylor borrows the words of an authority figure with the aim of subverting that authority, just as Stephen does later with his parable. Thus the conflict between the law and the outlaw reflects both an intratextual and intertextual tension between the speaker and his creditor: MacHugh's (like O'Molloy's) poverty and lack of credibility ultimately infects and undermines the words of his source. These speeches "FROM THE FATHERS" (7.841), though seeking to become "authoritative discourse" (i.e., words from "the fathers") actually display what Bakhtin calls "double-voicedness" (1981, 343, 324), so that within every utterance "an intense interaction and struggle between one's own and another's word is being waged, a process in which they oppose or dialogically interanimate each other" (1981, 355). The linguistic capital these speakers have inherited is tainted not only by their current dispossession, but by the fact that they bor-

row out of desperation; far from generating surplus value, they leach
value from their borrowed assets.

This struggle for possession of the language becomes even more
complex when we consider that Joyce chose this speech for his only
sound recording of *Ulysses* (Joyce, *Readings* I). When spoken by Joyce,
the speech acquires both additional authority and an additional intertextual layer. When Joyce utters MacHugh's version of Taylor's
speech, does he own the sentiments in that speech? André Topia
argues that in such cases the voice that delivers the words "cannot
prevent itself from taking them over," because the spoken word is
"always identified . . . with the voice which utters it" (1984, 121). Thus
when Joyce, "all in all" in all his characters, delivers the speech, he is
acting successively as author, professor, orator, and priest. But he
does not merely quote the speech; he also improves the style, adding
his own interest to the loan. Moreover, on the recording Joyce clearly
distinguishes between Stephen's mental comments and Taylor's
words, and assumes a supercilious tone for the Egyptian priest, thus
distancing himself from these borrowings. The recording suggests
that, by placing the speech within multiple frames and showing how
it has been circulated among so many speakers, Joyce at once accepts
and denies his authorship of it. If, as Bakhtin notes, language is
always "populated—overpopulated—with the intentions of others"
(1981, 294), then Joyce's voice here is less "his" than a composite of
voices gathered from his cultural inheritance. Like his characters,
Joyce cannot avoid debtorship (nor does he want to); like them, he
must "raise the wind" and borrow words. But unlike theirs, his borrowings paradoxically affirm his authority: by disseminating it, he
more fully acquires it. Like the narrative discourse of "Telemachus,"
that of "Aeolus" is multipossessed, undermining through intertextuality the notion of private authorship and redefining it as the ability
to create interest from borrowed linguistic currency.

Thus whether Joyce and Stephen use English or Irish makes little
difference; both Irish and English words are already freighted with
the meanings and values previous speakers have attached to them.
Indeed, the speakers in the episode seem to believe that the value of
discourse increases through recirculation and try to borrow some of
that surplus value for themselves. But the words they speak are no
more owned by the English than MacHugh's words are his sole property. Despite Stephen's argument in *Portrait* that his using English
bespeaks his colonized condition, the accompanying fact of intertextual debtorship complicates that condition and provides a way out:

the Irish can appropriate these verbal assets and make them their own. Stephen's task (and Joyce's) is to solidify this appropriation through Irish artistic labor, to turn English assets into Irish "spiritual assets," adding interest and value to the borrowings through recirculation. In this sense, Moses is Stephen's counterpart both as auditor of the Egyptian's speech and as potential deliverer of his people.

Parabolic

Stephen's first reaction to the speech is to wonder, "Could you try your hand at it yourself?" (7.836–37). But his final response is telling: an internal proclamation, "I have money" (7.884). Though he is referring primarily to his remaining wages, the episode's constant play with the homologies between money and language imply that he also means verbal currency. The two economies are identified as Stephen reciprocates for his reception of borrowed words by offering to spend both financial and verbal currency. That currency is his "parable." It is much more a product of social dialogue than his poem in "Proteus," since it takes the Mosaic theme from MacHugh's and O'Molloy's speeches for the title, the women he watched on the strand for its characters, and the Dublin environment in which he now resides for its setting. Offering to spend his money to buy the attention of his audience, Stephen tells a story that draws from the words of others. His parable thus implicates him in a transaction with other Dubliners and shows that, like them, he is a debtor. Despite his disdain, the parable proves that he shares their "blood."

Stephen presumably hopes that his story will touch his auditors. They, in turn, are preparing to touch him for free drinks. He has already been physically touched in the episode, when Crawford urges him to write something for him "with a bite in it. You can do it. . . . Put us all into it, damn its soul" (7.616; 621), and lays a hand on Stephen's shoulder. Later, as Stephen proposes that they adjourn for drinks, Crawford touches him again, slapping him on the shoulder and shouting "Chip of the old block!" (7.899): Stephen is replicating his consubstantial father, who has just responded to an even more florid quotation by departing for drinks. Like Mulligan, Crawford wants to appropriate Stephen's words for his own purposes. Interrupting Stephen's story to pester Crawford about Keyes's ad, Bloom recognizes the dynamics of the situation: "All off for a drink. Arm in arm. Lenehan's yachting cap on the cadge beyond. Usual blarney. Wonder is that young Dedalus the moving spirit. . . . Careless chap"

(7.983–87). As Bloom accurately perceives, they are both following Stephen's lead and exploiting his desire for an audience. They touch him for money, while he hopes to touch them with words: all of them are involved in the system of debts.

Although Crawford does not realize it, Stephen does take his advice to produce something that "puts us all into it." Ultimately entitled *A Pisgah Sight of Palestine or the Parable of the Plums,* Stephen's contribution to the rhetorical contest portrays two women viewing Dublin and is itself a view of Dublin that simultaneously confirms and repudiates his identity as a Dubliner. To summarize, it tells the story of two "elderly, pious" virgins who want to see views of Dublin from Nelson's pillar. They take out their savings and buy brawn, panloaf, plums, and tickets to the monument. When they get to the top after an exhausting climb, they eat the brawn and bread. Too tired to look up or down, they go near the railings and eat the plums, spitting the seeds out between the railings onto the people below. As he begins the parable, Stephen thinks, "Dubliners" (7.922), and certainly its apparently neutral but scathingly ironic tone would fit well with the economy of "scrupulous meanness" that Joyce manages in *Dubliners,* a meanness also displayed in Stephen's careful attention to the characters' finances.[3] This uncharacteristic scrupulousness indicates Stephen's current preoccupation with money and debts as well as his recognition of his listeners' financial worries. The anticlimactic and sardonic conclusion—spitting on Dublin—dramatizes the youthful bitterness Joyce often felt towards his home. Indeed, Joyce also used a parable to powerful effect in "Grace," where a misinterpretation of Christ's parable of the unjust steward is used to indict the Irish Catholic church for its collusion with the imperium. Nevertheless, the naturalistic theme and terse style of Stephen's parable contrast with the high-blown rhetoric offered by the other characters: they inflate but he deflates, as though aiming to restore value to words by using them sparingly, to rejuvenate the Irish by reflecting their faces in his cracked looking glass. Stephen the creator is thus also Stephen the editor (the episode's symbol), borrowing from recent experiences to editorialize on the windbags he has just heard.

---

3. They set out with 3s 10d (2s 3d in silver and 1s 7d in coppers [7.932–4]) and spend 1s 4d on brawn, buy four slices of panloaf (price unknown), spend 3d on plums (which are 8 for a penny: see 6.294) and 6d on their tickets. The total expenditures are 2s 1d plus the cost of the panloaf, and thus well over half of their savings. Like many characters in *Dubliners,* they spend their money but get little out of it (e.g., "Counterparts").

As he begins, Stephen goads himself to "Dare it. Let there be life" (7.930). To create is to risk, to gamble by expending imaginative energy in the production of something that may not be reciprocated. For Stephen, as for Bataille, poesis entails the willingness to lose (1985, 119). Stephen's verbal expenditure is his form of gambling. He gambles to create, forfeiting financial assets to generate spiritual ones, although the latter may also be sacrificed to incomprehension or artistic failure. This devotion to expenditure and loss identifies him as a Dubliner, even though his parable mocks them, and even though they gamble on the Gold Cup rather than on literary currency. He also hopes his verbal and financial expenditures will help him establish authority and credit. As in the potlatch ceremony, which allows participants to create prestige through the radical destruction of wealth, Stephen's "gift" of a tale proclaims his power to lose but does so both to gain credit with his audience and to defy them by placing himself as far above them morally as the virgins are physically. The economies behind Stephen's parable are therefore as ambiguous as his motives and implicate him simultaneously in an economy of debt and in a subversive economy of gifts.

Still, the prevailing wind in "Aeolus" smells of debt and credit, and so Stephen asks for credit from his audience when presenting his parable. They must tender their belief in him and in the story, lending their attention in return for his narration and promise of spirits. This homology between verbal and financial credit is further implied when, as Stephen narrates his parable, O'Molloy attempts to borrow money from Crawford: both are "RAISING THE WIND" (7.995). The editor replies to O'Molloy that he is too broke himself to lend any money (7.996–98); unfortunately for O'Molloy, both his and Crawford's chief asset is wind. Bloom, too, interrupts the story with a request, again to Crawford, to agree to run the Keyes ad in exchange for a "little puff" calling attention to it (7.978). Bloom is also asking for financial credit, his request therefore paralleling Stephen's: neither can succeed in his artistic enterprise without a reciprocal promise of credit from someone else. Stephen's parable thus frames the end of the episode as Bloom's House of Keyes ad, with its innuendo of home rule, framed the beginning. Both comment cryptically and obliquely on Dublin's political and economic condition, in contrast to the inflated language that issues from the other speakers. But all of them are rebuffed: Crawford tells Bloom to tell Keyes to kiss his arse, O'Molloy is denied his loan, and Stephen's story is met with incomprehension. Although Crawford earlier professed his belief in Stephen, now he withholds it.

Stephen's desire for credit and attention from his audience, then, reenacts the other Dubliners' need for financial credit. All of them are debtors, both verbal and financial, as evinced by the borrowed speeches they offer as the currency of social prestige. But Stephen's parable is also an act of revenge and a statement of repudiation: the virgins' final spits dramatize his own views of Dublin while also obliquely indicting Ireland's submission to her conquerors through the virgins' sexually "submissive posture" between Nelson and his pillar (Weir 1991, 658–59). Thus, if Stephen's parable borrows from his Dublin audience, what he "DONATES" (7.1021) in return, a critique of their adherence to the myths of patriotism and exploitation (Weir 1991, 661), is as unwelcome as the plumstones spit by the virgins. He first involves them in the parable, and then spits or throws that involvement back at them. Since "parable" derives etymologically from *para* (beside) + *bole* (to throw), his title suggests that the Irish are the throwaways of history, sedated by their ingestion of the discarded "seeds" of both Britain and their own heritage. But insofar as Stephen himself is a Dubliner, a man wooed by myths of the past and battening upon debts to save him, his parable is also self-mocking. As MacHugh comments, Stephen is like Antisthenes the sophist, of whom "none could tell if he were bitterer against others or against himself" (7.1036). In throwing away the parable while walking to a pub, Stephen seems to recognize both his own complicity and his own absurdity; as the narrator observes, Stephen is at once wise and foolish—a "SOPHOMORE" (7.1053). Indeed, by buying drinks for his auditors, Stephen partially undercuts his own moral aims, because the intoxication that will result from his expenditures will blunt his blows and weaken the audience's capacity to understand his parabolic indictment. Stephen's parable thus constitutes literary *lex talionis*, an act of negative reciprocity against his past, his audience, and himself.

Finally, then, Stephen's act of creation is a self-conscious recognition of his own paralysis and an attempt to conquer it. His acts of expenditure acknowledge his resemblance to the debtors of Dublin and his indebtedness to them but also symbolize his rejection of that identity. In promising to spend his money on them, he participates in their self-destructive behavior; but in his expenditure of imagination, he attempts to bear the seed that will destroy this pattern. Stephen raises the wind, promising to spend money on alcoholic spirits, in hopes that the spiritual assets he creates in his parable will balance the expenditure of money their creation requires. Perhaps these spiritual assets will replace his diminishing financial ones. For the rest of the novel, Stephen continues to squander his money on a rotating collection of spongers but always obtains attention and credit from them in exchange. Even if Stephen spends his money to retain his talent, as Joyce suggested that he himself did, the significance given to his meeting with Bloom indicates that Stephen's way is not sufficient. As we have seen, Stephen's squandering, far from freeing him from his Dublin inheritance, repeats its impoverishing patterns of improvidence and debt. And if he believes that self-sacrifice, in the form of art, may turn loss into gain, he has yet to effect that transformation. His parable suggests that he remains bitter against himself, his self-destructive tendencies evidenced both by his compulsion to lose his money and by the harsh tone of his parable. But Stephen's disquisition on Shakespeare not only demonstrates Joyce's own brilliant apprehension of the homologies between the literary and financial debts; it also demonstrates Stephen's recognition of his debtorship and a tentative attempt to pay.

THE POET'S DEBTS

In "Scylla and Charybdis" Stephen develops a theory about Shakespeare's life and art that borrows Shakespeare's words to describe an intertextual economy based upon economic terms and metaphors. Out of the relationship between Stephen as embryonic poet and Shakespeare as literary progenitor emerges a complex demonstration of the convergence of literary and financial debts. Dialectic, listed in Joyce's schema as the technic of the episode, is the engine that generates Stephen's theory. But ultimately the concept of generation, both sexual and financial, underlies the method and content of the theory by linking usury and reproduction through an intertextual pun that is itself a form of verbal usury.

Stephen confronts both forms of debtorship in the library. After listening to AE dismiss all such prying into "the poet's debts" (9.188), the incipient poet considers his own: "How now, sirrah, that pound he lent you when you were hungry? Marry, I wanted it. . . . Do you intend to pay it back? O, yes. When? Now? Well. . . . No. When, then? I paid my way. I paid my way. . . . Wait. Five months. Molecules all change. I am other I now. Other I got pound. . . . But I, entelechy, form of forms, am I by memory because under everchanging forms. . . . I, I and I. I. A. E. I. O. U" (9.192–213). Memory ensures one's stable identity but also therefore the fact of debtorship, and the vowels of AE's pseudonym prompt Stephen's pun fusing linguistic and economic debts. In one sense, the "other I" who got the pound was Joyce himself, who borrowed a pound from Russell in 1904 (*JJ* 178; *L* II 58).[4] By means of Stephen's recollection, Joyce pays his debt to AE with literary currency through his fictional progeny. But the fictional AE, while he asks for no interest on his loan to Stephen, also evinces little interest in his theory, leaving before Stephen gets well launched and omitting him from the poets' gathering scheduled for that evening. And if Stephen mentally acknowledges his debt, he makes no attempt to repay it, although we know that he has received £3 12s from Deasy earlier this day. What is important, then, is not the money itself, but rather the acknowledgment of debt; indeed, Stephen's entire theory amounts to such an acknowledgment. AE's view that literature should reveal "formless spiritual essences" and lead to Plato's "world of ideas" (9.49; 53) represents the Platonic pole of the episode's dialectic, but he also represents one of its economic polarities—the creditor who takes no interest.[5]

Stephen's other monetary creditor in the episode is Buck Mulligan, who enters halfway through. No matter who paid the Martello rent, we know that Stephen owes Mulligan nine pounds (2.255). As we have seen, Mulligan uses this debt to exploit Stephen, lending him his boots and breeks but in return appropriating Stephen's ideas and money. Indeed, Mulligan is a kind of spiritual usurer, defined by the church fathers as one who turns an originally interest-free loan into an excuse for indefinitely prolonged favors and gratifications (quoted in Shell 1982, 75). The Buck demands both monetary and personal compensation, milking Stephen's debt for all it is worth and compiling usurious interest for himself.

In response, Stephen indicts Mulligan with a telegram sent earlier from College Green. Itself borrowed (or plagiarized, since Stephen fails to acknowledge his source) from Meredith's *The Ordeal of Richard Feverel,* the wire accuses Mulligan of failing to pay his debts: *"The sentimentalist is he who would enjoy without incurring the immense debtorship*

---

4. But cf. 2.257, where the debt is listed as a guinea, not a pound. Stephen's reduction of the debt here may be part of his own sentimentalism, his refusal to incur full responsibility.

5. Moshenberg similarly argues that "Both Stephen's art and his economic activity are debt-production" but does not develop this point; he also mistakenly lists the debt to AE as two pounds (1988, 335, 337). Rabaté (1991, 159) and McGee (1988, 66) observe that Stephen's acknowledgment of his debt to AE is more significant than the amount because, in the Ulsterman AE, Stephen is admitting his debts to imperial England as well.

for a thing done. Signed: Dedalus" (9.550–51; Meredith 1961, 196). The missive, condemning Mulligan's evasion of responsibility for his damaging remarks to and manipulation of Stephen, marks the sundering of their exploitative relationship. Although Mulligan extorts payment from Stephen for his debt, when Stephen claims that Mulligan owes *him* something, Buck claims forgetfulness ("I can't remember anything" [1.192]). No memory means no debts. In Meredith's novel the narrator accuses a character of "moral usury" (1961, 409), which means accepting an error with such pride that it begins to seem a virtue. Mulligan is guilty of such moral usury as he blithely boasts of his own irresponsibility. In a sense, Stephen wishes to carry out a similar transformation by abstracting his financial condition into a literary theory and then into a spur for artistic creation, thereby turning errors into "portals of discovery," and loss into gain (9.229). But if AE is a creditor who takes no interest, Mulligan is sometimes a usurious friend and sometimes a bad debtor whose views about debtorship constantly shift, depending upon which side of the balance he finds himself on. Stephen's cost to expose Mulligan's failure to pay is the price of the telegram, which I have discovered to be a shilling and a halfpenny.[6] Ironically, however, Stephen might be accused of sentimentalism according to his own plagiarized definition, since he owes more than twenty-five pounds to various people and shows little likelihood of repaying any of it (2.259). Moreover, his failure to acknowledge that his epigram is cribbed makes him a literary sentimentalist as well. (Mulligan reminds him of his cribbing in "Oxen" [14.1486].) But Stephen is not merely a sentimentalist: he does not claim he doesn't have debts (in which case the signature on the telegram might be read "debtless," rather than "Dedalus"); he simply fails to pay them, and the remainder of his disquisition demonstrates his attempt to confront both his literary and his financial debts.

Stephen's discussion tries to address both literary sentimentalism

---

6. According to *Thom's Directory* for 1904 (1051), a telegram sent to anywhere in the U.K. cost 6d for the first twelve words and a halfpenny for each additional word, including the names and addresses of the sender and recipient. Thus Stephen's wire of sixteen words, plus "Signed: Dedalus" and Mulligan's "address"—"Malachi Mulligan, The Ship, lower Abbey street"—would cost a shilling and a halfpenny. (I've counted "Signed" because it is written in capital letters in the text; if Mulligan were merely saying it rather than reading it, it would probably not be capitalized, since a listener cannot distinguish between written letters.) In a typical instance of Joycean symmetry, Stephen's extra debtorship begins to be incurred just after the twelfth word of the telegram, which happens to be "debtorship."

—unacknowledged borrowing—and the textual and economic usury of the great progenitor, Shakespeare. However, to call literary borrowing "debtorship" or, indeed, to develop any parallel between economic and literary debts depends upon "syllepsis," which Michael Riffaterre defines as a pun that consists in understanding a word in "two different ways at the same time, one being literal and primary, the other figurative" (1980, 629). The concept of syllepsis involves apprehending the same word simultaneously in its contextual meaning and in its intertextual meaning (Riffaterre 1980, 629n, 637), though it specifically refers only to words that signify in mutually incompatible ways (Riffaterre 1990b, 131).[7] Certain writers have labeled such punning verbal usury, because puns generate new meanings without generating new words, just as interest produces money out of money without producing more goods.[8] But the concept of usury figures in several senses, because an intertextual pun on "interest"—an instance of syllepsis—underlies both Stephen's discussion of intertextual economy and mine.

The intertextual economy in "Scylla and Charybdis" in fact exemplifies Riffaterre's definition of "mediated intertextuality," in which a reference from one text to another is understood by reference to a third (or fourth) text functioning as the interpretant (1980, 629). We may better understand the convergence of literary and economic debts in this episode by an intertextual trail that leads not to the usually cited sources in *Hamlet* but to *The Merchant of Venice*, and from there back to Plato and Aristotle. In turn, these literary debts themselves depend upon syllepsis—verbal usury—coined from the concepts of debtorship, interest, and usury and their homologies with physical reproduction.

Joyce's schema implies that the dialectic of the episode evolves from the opposition between Plato and Aristotle. This has been much noted. Less well known is Plato's yoking of the dialectic to the generation of monetary interest. In the *Republic,* Socrates states that the seminal ideas of dialectical discourse are partial deposits ("hypothesis" derives from *hypotheke,* meaning "deposit") of truth produced from

7. A good example is Derrida's term *iteration,* which designates both repetition and alterity (1982, 315). Aristotle's word *tokos* is also a true syllepsis because it refers both to legitimate and to illegitimate offspring.

8. In using this term, Shell (1982, 22, 50) cites Francis Bacon's *Advancement of Learning,* Book 6, Chapter 1. Bacon does not actually use the phrase "verbal usury," though he does draw an analogy between words and coins in that passage (1944, 164) and develops the analogy throughout that work.

the idea of the Good, which cannot itself be attained. Since one cannot speak of the Good itself, Socrates offers instead to speak of the "offspring" of the Good. "I could wish," he says, "that I were able to make and you to receive the payment and not merely as now the interest. But at any rate receive this interest and the offspring of the good" (1961, 742). Socrates is a kind of banker of ideas who distributes the "interest" of the Good; through these dialectical deposits his interlocutors may eventually approach true knowledge by generating interest on the principal (Shell 1978, 46). The sense of this passage depends upon an etymological pun: the same word, *tokos*, means in Greek both "offspring" (children) and the "offspring" or interest on a loan. This example of syllepsis thus reveals homologies between financial and physical generation. In his Shakespeare discussion Stephen plays Socrates, who learned from Xanthippe the art of dialectic and from his mother "how to bring thoughts into the world" (9.235–36). Like Socrates, Stephen hopes to produce the truth (in this case, about Shakespeare) through dialectical generation from half-truths, to approach the principal through its offspring or interest. He thus aims to use dialectical logic as verbal currency, or as what Marx calls "the mind's coin of the realm" (1978, 110). To do so he depicts Shakespeare himself not as the grand ideal of AE's Platonism but as a usurer, a producer of both financial interest and physical offspring.

Stephen's Shakespeare "drew a salary equal to that of the lord chancellor of Ireland. His life was rich" (9.624–25). "[A] capitalist shareholder, a bill promoter, a tithefarmer . . . , [h]e drew Shylock out of his own long pocket. The son of a maltjobber and a moneylender he was himself a cornjobber and a moneylender. . . . He sued a fellowplayer for the price of a few bags of malt and exacted his pound of flesh in interest for every penny lent" (9.711–12; 741–47). Stephen then develops the idea of Shakespeare's "Jewishness," accusing the bard of both financial stinginess and a homologous "avarice of the emotions" (9.781)—jealousy and a kind of emotional incest. (As we have seen, Joyce carries out a similar double-entry moral bookkeeping in his texts; like Shakespeare, he carries a "memory in his wallet" [9.246].) A man, argues Stephen, "who holds so tightly to what he calls his rights over what he calls his debts will hold tightly also to what he calls his rights over her whom he calls his wife" (9.788–90). A husband and father, Shakespeare eventually devises the "mystical estate" of fatherhood upon his son, yet his most important offspring are not those of his body but those of his mind and pen (9.835). When he writes his plays, he becomes "the father of all his race, the father of his own grandfather, the father of his unborn grandson who, by the same token was never born" (9.867–70). Shakespeare "weaves and unweaves" his own image in his texts; ultimately, like the Agenbuyer, his "onlie begetter" is himself, and he creates himself as both father and son (9.378; 838–39; 493). Like Socrates, then, Stephen brings together the generation of physical and fiscal offspring to expose the nature of both forms of production.

To unravel the intertextual threads determining the relationship between self-generation and economics, we must now follow the strand back to Aristotle, the other bank of Stephen's dialectical stream.[9] Whereas for Plato the dialectic uses interest to approach the great principal and is therefore analogous to natural generation, albeit inverted, for Aristotle the production of interest is condemned precisely because it does not participate in a dialectic and is therefore seen as unnatural. In the *Politics*, Aristotle admonishes against usury, which he describes as illicit generation of financial offspring (*tokos* again means both "children" and "interest") that are homogeneous with the parents: that is, money reproduces itself as money rather than as exchangeable commodities (1940, 51). Money begets more money in a kind of Oedipal reproduction in which father and son are identical. Aristotle thus describes usury as chrematistic—unnatural and exploitative, a kind of incestuous or narcissistic practice—and distinguishes it from the truly economic, which involves the exchange of goods.[10] It lacks the dialectical properties of "true" economics, because money is generated from itself rather than from labor. Paradoxically, however, Aristotle employs the currency of language in a way he defines as illicit when applied to money: in his pun on "interest" (*tokos*) no new goods (words) are created, only new wealth (meanings). In condemning monetary usury, he employs a syllepsis that brings together mutually incompatible meanings and thus commits verbal usury.

9. Joyce's interest in Aristotle is well documented: he alludes to "a short course" in Aristotelian political theory as far back as the fall of 1904 (*L* II, 71). Stephen's discussion implies that he has completed a similar course. In "Of Usury," Bacon (1937, 118) alludes to Aristotle's condemnation of usury.

10. Marx also condemns this form of money-making. For him, capitalism inverts the "normal" economy of C—M—C (a commodity is exchanged for money, and then for another commodity of equal value), into M—C—M' (money becomes commodity, which becomes more money) and hence into surplus value. Usury distorts this system even further by eliminating the commodity altogether; its formula is M—M'. Marx echoes Aristotle when in volume 1 of *Capital* he calls interest-bearing capital "money which begets money" (1978, 335).

As an artist Joyce is always a verbal usurer because he bases his art upon puns. "Scylla and Charybdis," like other Joycean texts, is full of puns and other wordplay. Like metaphors, these tropes bring about exchanges or transfers (the root of *metaphor* means "to cross or transfer") and thus reveal how a form of commerce or exchange underlies both linguistic and economic symbol systems. But a more Aristotelian sense of usury lies at the heart of Stephen's theory of intertextual economics. According to Stephen, Shakespeare, guilty of the avarice of the emotions, generates himself out of his own self-investment, like money in Aristotle's description of chrematistics. He is his own only begetter, at once interest and principal. Stephen's Shakespeare (and, by analogy, every author) is therefore necessarily a usurer or chrematistic economist. Typically, Mulligan parodies this self-begetting with his mocking "I have an unborn child in my brain. . . . Let me parturiate!" (9.876–77); thus if AE symbolizes the abuses of Platonism, Stephen's other major creditor mocks his Aristotelian borrowings. But Stephen's key point is that in drawing Shylock from his own long pocket (a phrase that makes Shylock a bill or coin), Shakespeare himself becomes a Shylock (cf. Rabaté 1991, 169–70).

Interestingly, Shylock himself voices this connection between usury and physical generation in act 1, scene 3, of *The Merchant of Venice*. As he and Antonio dicker over his loan, Shylock extends Antonio's pun on "ewes" and "use," identifying the "work of generation" (1.83) in sheepbreeding with his own generation of interest, saying "I make [gold and silver] breed as fast" (1.97).[11] After his daughter Jessica disappears, Shylock again brings the two kinds of progeny together when he cries, "My daughter! Oh my ducats! Oh my daughter!" (2.8.15). Like Aristotle, the Venetian Christians condemn Shylock's usurious generation of money as illicit and unnatural chrematism. But insofar as Shakespeare is himself a Shylock, his usurious financial practices and his chrematistic literary production are woven together. Moreover, Stephen suggests that Shakespeare's family relationships were equally unnatural: when he was living richly in London, his wife had to borrow forty shillings from her father's shepherd, a man who evidently exemplified Shylock's equation of economic and zoologic husbandry (9.680–81).

11. I am indebted to Shell (1982, 48–55) for pointing out this connection between Aristotelian and Shakespearean versions of usury. As he observes, Shakespeare also links sexual generation and the generation of interest in *Measure for Measure*, 3.2.5–7: " 'Twas never merry world since, of two usuries, the merriest [sex] was put down, and the worser allowed by order of law a furred gown."

The Shylock of *Ulysses*, Reuben J. Dodd, embodies in Joyce's Dublin this homology between usury and fatherhood. A tightwad and a usurer, Dodd is also an unnatural father who values his silver more than his son; in both senses he practices chrematistic economics. But whereas Shylock makes money breed as fast as sheep, Dodd, as we have seen, is a "bad shepherd" whose son is not just unnatural but (in Circe) dead (15.1918). In the terms of Christ's Parable of the Good Shepherd, another pertinent intertext (John 10:7–18), Dodd is the "hireling" who abandons his fold when threatened.[12] In contrast, Stephen thinks in "Proteus" of AE, the creditor who takes no interest, as a "good shepherd of men" (3.228). Other Joycean fathers solidify the conjunction of interest and offspring. Theodore Purefoy, the "remarkablest progenitor" in "Oxen" and father of eight children, works in a "countinghouse" multiplying the interest on the "ingots" of others (14.1411; 1417). Despite prolifically begetting both interest and children, Purefoy, unlike Shylock or Dodd, fails to profit from either kind of progeny. If Dodd, a "bad shepherd," earns interest, Purefoy's finances are inadequate even though his "fleece is drenched" (14.1419).[13] And Leopold Bloom, a Jew although not a usurer, gives birth in "Circe" to eight gold and silver children who grow up to be bankers and financiers (15.1821-32), and sketches in "Lestrygonians" the plan for the generation of interest for every child born that we examined in chapter 3: he wishes that money could be bred as fast as babies. On the other hand, Simon Dedalus, Stephen's consubstantial father, is not a usurer but is a sentimentalist who refuses to pay his debts, a bad shepherd who breeds prolifically but fails to beget the financial offspring needed to provide for his children.

Stephen's theory also implies that Shakespeare is a usurer of literary currency for those writers who follow him. The great progenitor is a textual moneylender in that all later writers must borrow from him, and what they create generates interest on his great principal.

---

12. The Bible gives mixed messages about usury. In Matthew 25:27 (the Parable of the Talents), Christ employs usury as a metaphor for making the most of one's goods and seems to sanction it; in Deuteronomy 23:20, usury is permitted when dealing with "strangers" (i.e., non-Jews). In this latter sense literary usury would necessarily subvert the filial or paternal relationships among writers: in borrowing and practicing usury on their forebears, writers alienate themselves from those ancestors. But the Old Testament contains several injunctions against usury: see, for example, Proverbs 28:8.

13. Gifford (1988, 440) cites this phrase as an allusion to Judges 6:36-37, where God gives a sign to Gideon that he will deliver Israel from false gods by drenching his fleece and leaving the ground around it dry.

All latecoming writers are indebted to Shakespeare for their language; they must be borrowers before they can be creditors, readers before writers.[14] The borrowers augment the value of Shakespeare's literary assets, enhancing the currency of his reputation through their indebtedness. Given this fact of intertextual debtorship, how does one avoid sentimentalism? By foregrounding those loans, by giving explicit credit, as Joyce and Stephen do in "Scylla and Charybdis": its discussion of intertextual debts to Shakespeare is fabricated from dozens of Shakespearean quotations, rather like the famous Ireland forgeries of Shakespeare.[15] To fail to credit is to commit plagiary. Thus in discussing Shakespeare, they boldly appropriate his words, using his own threads to weave and unweave his image. In this sense, "Scylla and Charybdis" is the Irish writer Joyce's own "Ireland" forgery, an appropriation of Shakespeare that "forges" him for both Joyce and Stephen. In so doing, the latecoming authors capitalize on the debts and make the words part of their own textual images, while also spending those words, as if purging them from their literary economy. But Joyce is not only a clever plagiarist; he adds interest of his own, so that his literary offspring are not simply homogeneous with Shakespeare's.

Another way to escape oppressive indebtedness is by massive ap-

14. McArthur (1988, 94–96) also points out the analogy between Stephen's two kinds of debts and briefly discusses Shakespeare as a usurer but does not develop the theme as I do.

15. William Henry Ireland forged a series of "Shakespearean" documents in the 1790s that culminated in two "lost" plays, which he fabricated by spatchcocking his own words to hundreds of lines from actual Shakespearean plays. As Mallon puts it, his forgery was "based on borderline plagiarism" (1989, 136). Coincidentally, his initials were W. H.; thus he fancied himself the "onlie begetter" of some of Shakespeare's plays, like the mysterious dedicatee of the sonnets. Ireland's motives for his forgeries/plagiaries were as Oedipal as Stephen's theory: he was trying to impress his bardolater father (Mair 1938, 24). Indeed, Ireland's forgeries were designed to make Shakespeare resemble precisely the kind of "rich country gentleman" portrayed by Stephen (Mair 1938, 38). The Ireland family is mentioned in "Scylla and Charybdis": Shakespeare's "house in Ireland yard" (9.710) was originally the property of the Ireland family (Mair 1938, 52), a fact that William used to forge a deed from Shakespeare to his own ancestor that awarded him sole title to all the Bard's holdings. Why would the business-like bard do such a thing? Gratitude. In a truly Mulliganesque turn, the progenitor Ireland had allegedly saved Shakespeare from drowning (Mair 1938, 49–50)! This Ireland was a sentimentalist who hoped to enjoy the benefits of rewriting Shakespeare without incurring the immense debtorship for the things done. Such forgeries lie behind Stephen's theory, as do allegations that Bacon or somebody else really wrote the plays.

propriation of the progenitor's currency. Joyce does so, challenging the condition of texts as the property of a single author by wholesale borrowing in "Scylla and Charybdis" and especially in "Oxen of the Sun." In these episodes the borrower assumes the usufruct, or right of temporary possession and use, of the property of the lender. If an author can usurp authorship of the precursor's texts, then he or she comes to share their production and hence their ownership. Thus, through Stephen, his own literary offspring, Joyce reweaves the image of Shakespeare, and thereby, like Shakespeare in Stephen's theory, gives birth to his own progenitor. The borrowers become usurers insofar as they can appropriate the earlier author's words and use them to depict him anew. If a usurer is one who generates off-spring, then the later author is now a usurer of both him- or herself and his or her literary parent.

Stephen's production of interest on Shakespeare implies that all authors are usurers in both senses: they create literary currency that others must borrow and the interest of which accrues to them; and they generate their texts out of self-involution, through chrematistic generation in which the product of the investment—the author's image—is homogeneous (but not identical) with the progenitor—the author's image. In both cases, Stephen's theory turns disadvantage into advantage, loss into gain, by a transformation similar to that in Meredith's moral usury. If, however, Stephen uses the dialectic as does Socrates, to generate the principal (truth) out of its interest (half-truths) as a kind of banker of ideas, then he escapes mere chrematism. Stephen's theory dialectically engages both Plato's and Aristotle's no-tions of usury: he takes from Plato his Socratic role as generator of ideas as interest; from Aristotle he borrows the definition of usury as self-begetting. He thereby creates a kind of verbal credit by announc-ing his own indebtedness, and through the "interest" on the idea of Shakespeare as usurer, generated dialectically, demonstrates that the artist is at once borrower and usurer. Yoking the two kinds of usury through Shakespeare's life and his literary offspring Shylock, he at-tempts to weave himself of threads borrowed from several lenders. The foundation of both kinds of usury is discovered in a third kind, the verbal usury of a syllepsis on *tokos* as both progeny and interest, both natural and unnatural offspring. Stephen thus tries to make himself a verbal capitalist, both by creating his theory dialectically and turning a philosophical profit in Plato's sense, and by transmuting the fact of his own literary debtorship into a method of generating sur-plus value for his own potential art: he borrows and capitalizes on Shakespeare's assets.

Stephen ends by saying that the artist, an "androgynous angel," ultimately becomes a "wife unto himself," as in the "economy of heaven"; that is, he provides his own dialectical opposite (9.1051–52).[16] If so, Stephen's artist contains in himself the antithesis necessary for dialectical generation, and hence his production of literary offspring is not merely chrematistic in Aristotle's sense. The female principle lies in that famous image of weaving and unweaving, itself an intertextual strand plucked from the *Odyssey:* Penelope unweaves by night what she weaves by day. Her labor generates neither a product nor a synthesis but rather an equilibrium, a zero sum, a balanced budget. Like Penelope's garment, Stephen's Shakespeare is deconstructed—both newly created and torn apart—by the operations of Stephen's intertextual weaving; his theory at once glorifies Shakespeare and demystifies him. But Stephen proves that no artist weaves his image without the aid of shepherds, good and bad, who lend him the raw materials that become his finished woven products through the labor of creation that itself depends upon borrowing.

After all his witty effort, however, Stephen disavows belief in his own theory (9.1067). He might at first seem to agree with Francis Bacon (to whom some attribute Shakespeare's plays), that such chrematistic labor of the mind is ultimately worthless (1944, 17). It may appear that he also disavows the intertextual economy I have outlined. But even his denial is dialectical. To begin with, Stephen "beg[s] with swift glance" the hearing of his interlocutors; in return, they must lend ear and tender their belief (9.154–55; Moshenberg 1988, 336). That is, he needs their credit, "the very ground of aesthetic experience, and the same medium that seems to confer belief in fiduciary money (banknotes) . . . and in literature" (Shell 1978, 7). Once they have given him their credit, he withdraws his own, forcing the listeners to labor to produce their own interest on his dialectical deposit. In denying his own belief, he defines himself dialectically: if they now credit it, he must reject it. Stephen's theory has become logical currency, a money of the mind. But now his disavowal forces his auditors to become usurers themselves, to discover some truth through their own generation of interest and to generate capital from his mental coin. And while Stephen's verbal deposits have made him

16. The intertext behind this phrase is as Victorian as Meredith: in *Unto This Last,* Ruskin argues that the conventional political economy of self-interest is the one that "brought schism into the Policy of angels, and ruin into the Economy of Heaven" (1905, 17:105). In *The Merchant of Venice* the condemnation of usury is carried out by an "androgynous angel," Portia, cross-dressing as a male judge.

a usurer, financially he remains committed to the squandering he began earlier in the novel. If Shakespeare is a good businessman, Stephen must be a bad one; this purgative pattern, which Harold Bloom calls *kenosis*, is yet another means for Stephen to define himself dialectically against Shakespeare, simultaneously to flout the law of debtorship and to pay his debts.[17]

In fact, Stephen's denial does not refute the economic content of his dialectical theory but only makes it explicit. Eglinton says that "Fred Ryan wants space for an article on economics" for the next issue of *Dana*. Stephen thinks "Fraidrine. Two pieces of silver he lent me. Tide you over. Economics," and tells Eglinton that "For a guinea . . . [he] can publish this interview" (9.1082–85; Ryan's two-shilling loan is mentioned in "Nestor" [2.256]). In other words, the theory he has just generated like interest on the Platonic ideal of Shakespeare is worth a guinea: a pound (not a pound of flesh, but a pound sterling), with an extra shilling added. If Ryan needs an article on economics, Stephen could give him the one he has just presented. Had AE stayed to hear the end, he would have received Stephen's only repayment for his pound loan: a pound's-worth of argument, with interest (one shilling) added. In sum, Stephen's denial allows him to adopt the mercenary attitude he has demonstrated as necessary to Shakespeare's textual production. His apparently sophistic recantation actually affirms his belief that his theory, like those verses described in *Stephen Hero*, has become a "spiritual asset." He now offers his words as compensation for his financial debts, thus coming full circle to yoke by metaphoric transfer both kinds of debts and then to liberate himself from them (cf. Mahaffey 1988, 11). If Shakespeare is a usurer and his texts currency, then Stephen's own productions make him a creditor as well (cf. McArthur 1988, 96; Moshenberg 1988, 337) and endow his speech with both spiritual and economic value.

"Scylla and Charybdis" depicts the convergence of economics and aesthetics, of literary and financial debts. For Stephen, and by implication for Joyce, all authors must be usurers, chrematistic creators of indebtedness. In throwing off sentimentalism and simultaneously defying and repaying his literary and economic creditors, Stephen attempts to beget himself through the verbal usury of puns and to

---

17. In *kenosis*, the later poet is thrown into a repetition which he soon understands "must be both undone and dialectically affirmed, and those simultaneously" (H. Bloom 1972, 83). This tendency towards self-emptying also characterizes Stephen's financial habits: he is trying to purge himself of money tainted by history.

weave together Shylock and Shakespeare, Plato and Aristotle, usury and debtorship through intertextual labor. Joyce, in turn, pays off his debts through his own literary offspring Stephen and begins, like Shakespeare, to generate interest in overplus.

But Stephen's labor, grounded upon both the recognition of the debt that characterizes Dubliners and the excessive spending that brings it about, recapitulates the pattern of debt that characterizes Irish history; in that sense it is Irish labor. His Shakespeare theory, at once a payment and a rejection of Shakespeare, takes another step towards appropriating the English language and her literature for Ireland, an enterprise brought to culmination in "Oxen." Stephen's Shakespeare, the figure with whom he has brought about a paradoxical reconciliation and sundering, also resembles Leopold Bloom, a good businessman plagued by infidelity who comes between Stephen and his usurer Mulligan at the end of the episode. But despite his brilliant exploration of the intertextual economy, Stephen's ledger will remain unbalanced unless he can engage in social and financial exchanges with a creditor like Bloom, someone who exacts no financial interest for his loans but does take a paternal interest in his surrogate offspring, someone who may help to bring his spiritual assets to maturity, if only by offering himself as another creditor against whom he can rebel.

CRIBS IN THE COUNTINGHOUSE

The third movement of Joyce's exploration of the intertextual economy occurs in "Oxen of the Sun," which mimics the fathers of English prose style to present, on several levels, a debate about human proliferation and its relation to political economy and the quality of life. The episode also confronts the inescapable fact of literary debtorship and again demonstrates how Joyce both acknowledges his debts to his predecessors and makes literary capital from them. These two thematic planes intersect in Joyce's adaptations of nineteenth-century writers, particularly John Ruskin, whose writings on value, labor, and political economy reveal the same tensions displayed in "Oxen." Like "Scylla and Charybdis," "Oxen" employs homologies between physical and artistic generation to translate the debate about human proliferation into a self-reflexive examination of Joyce's own artistic practice. As it explores parallels between Mr. Purefoy's work in a bank and Joyce's management of the intertextual economy, the episode also discloses relationships between the Purefoys' reproduc-

tive excesses and Joyce's verbal proliferation. In a famous letter to
Budgen, Joyce claimed that the episode's theme was "the crime committed against fecundity by sterilizing the act of coition" (*L* I 139),
which has usually been interpreted to apply to Stephen and his cronies, who fail to show proper respect for Mrs. Purefoy's labor. The
letter goes on to say that Bloom is the "spermatozoon" and Stephen
"the embryo"; thus the theme of generation again exposes the economic conditions behind Stephen's delayed literary birth. By juxtaposing the intertextual and political economies, "Oxen" ultimately
illustrates how Joyce privileges artistic labor—an Irish labor of excess
—over both the female labor of childbearing and the male labor of
begetting physical and financial offspring.

The Last Word in Stolentelling

"Oxen of the Sun" catalogues the history of English prose style,
beginning with Anglo-Saxon, proceeding through the styles of Carlyle and Ruskin, and ending with a mélange of slang and street patter.[18] Rewriting old texts is hardly new to "Oxen"; as Richard Ellmann
observes, "inspired cribbing was always part of [Joyce's] art" ("Introduction" to *MBK*, xv). The dual meanings embedded in "cribbing"
punningly embody Joyce's achievement: it refers both to plagiarism
and to a baby's bed. Another syllepsis, the word refers to both illicit
and licit creation and bears both textual and extratextual significance
in the episode. The word is used in both senses in "Oxen," first in the
"Ruskin" section to describe the bed of the Christ-child (14.1383),
and later when (presumably) Mulligan comments that Stephen's telegram was "cribbed out of Meredith" (14.1486; a crib is also a bed
for young oxen). But Joyce's cribbing is both more subtle and more
systematic than Stephen's; throughout the episode he kidnaps the
literary offspring of his forebears and places them in his own textual
crib. Indeed, because he borrows not only the styles of his predecessors but also their words, his strategy may be described as bold plagiarism, a term that is especially appropriate since a "plagiary" was
originally a word for one who kidnapped a child (Mallon 1989, 6).[19]

18. Joyce names his models in the letter cited above; Janusko (1983) and Atherton
(1974) have previously explored some of these intertextual patterns.

19. Both meanings of the word were in use in the seventeenth century. The first
use of the word in its current sense is attributed by the *OED* to Ben Jonson and dates
from 1601; as *kidnapping*, the term was still in use for much of the century. Other early
users of the word to mean literary theft include Browne, one of Joyce's models in
"Oxen."

By appropriating others' textual progeny and becoming their foster father, Joyce aims to beget his own literary progenitors in the manner Stephen describes in "Scylla and Charybdis."

These syllepses on "crib" and "plagiary" invoke the problem of intertextuality, two versions of which have gained prominence since the 1960s. The first, the more radical, describes an infinite and irrecoverable citationality that affects not only texts but also the consciousnesses of authors and readers. According to Roland Barthes, the self who approaches a text is "already a plurality of other texts, of infinite, or more precisely, lost codes" (1974, 10). Even the protocols of a single reading are derived from the innumerable readings that have preceded it. Derrida employs another syllepsis, "iterability," to describe the linguistic condition in which repetition and alterity operate simultaneously (1982, 315). For him intertextuality means that "every sign . . . can be *cited*, put between quotation marks; thereby it can break with every given context, and engender infinitely new contexts in an absolutely nonsaturatable fashion" (1982, 320; emphasis his). An "iterable" text is thus an original tissue of citations. But to search for specific intertextual sources is to miss the point: the intertextual citing of a text in relation to the discourses of others is both ongoing and irrecoverable; even those passages and words not consciously cited are subject to general citationality. These other discourses impose an intertextual determinant onto language, without which texts are unreadable.

Iteration permits tropic exchanges to be forged between the past and present and thereby to fling the text, author and reader into the future (Bazargan 1985, 272). By invoking intertextuality as the basis for artistic practice, "Oxen" undermines the barriers between text and context, because it envelopes within its frame precisely those historical discourses that have produced the conditions for reading it. It deconstructs the difference between borrowing and original creation by making the latter a function of citationality: an original author is one who cribs successfully and extravagantly. According to this reading, Joyce proclaims himself a literary criminal and heretic, a plunderer of copyrights and sacred literary archives, a Shem-like forger armed with a "pelagiarist pen" (*FW* 182.3) who studies "how cutely to copy all their various styles of signature so as one day to utter an epical forged cheque on the public for his own private profit" (*FW* 181.15–17). Citationality thus destroys the boundaries that allow us to determine whom a text "belongs to"; it places words into the same condition as the pauper in the song Bloom recalls in "Hades" —they are that which "nobody owns." This view of intertextuality challenges notions of literature as property and shatters the linear version of literary history in which the earlier writer influences the later. It also violates the conventional author-reader contract, according to which the reader's labor is rewarded with original literary currency. If Joyce commits a "crime against [literary] fecundity" by stealing words and reneging on his contract, he cannot be prosecuted, because all authors are guilty of plagiarism; some are just better at it than others. Indeed, in this view there are no authors, only circulating and recirculating texts.[20]

The other school of intertextuality, by contrast, argues that tracing specific intertexts is not only helpful but, according to Michael Riffaterre, its most systematic theorist, compulsory (1990a, 76). For him, the intertext consists only of those texts the reader may "legitimately connect with the one before his eyes" (1980, 626). His use of "legitimately" is telling: Riffaterre's theory seeks to sanction authorial power and ownership—the same powers overturned by theories of general citationality—by recognizing the author's ingenuity and restoring the texts to their rightful "owners." This school, which would read "Oxen" as the "last word in stolentelling" (*FW* 424.35), would aim to recover the stolen merchandise and provide restitution. Riffaterre regards intertextual stock as a kind of fund and the author's role as bank manager or notary. He claims that an author is "a guarantor, witness to a verbal contract. Intertextuality is to the hypogram [i.e., the precursor text] and its palimpsest what escrow is to the lender and the borrower" (1978, 85–86). The writer may take interest on these deposits by borrowing the words of others, but this operation, like financial usury, is subject to regulation. Where does "Oxen" fit into these competing models? Although it exemplifies general citationality, the episode is also consciously allusive and bears the stylistic signatures of its originals: Joyce wants us to recognize his sources (he named them to his friends) and invites us to try to recover the historical conditions of the discourses he imitates. Unless we recover these specific intertexts, the full historical import of the debate on proliferation and the nature of Joyce's intertextual economy remains undeveloped.[21]

20. Joyce's "Notes on Business and Commerce" include an entry on literary copyright, which ends "A copy of a copy not protected" (*JJA* 3:615).

21. Joyce criticism has analyzed "Oxen" according to both schools; sometimes the same critic has argued both positions. Lawrence, for example, observes in her book that Joyce "plays down the idea of the general citationality of language in favor of the

But we cannot truly recover them, just as the styles reproduced cannot seem modern. Instead, the borrowed styles impose upon the events a moral universe alien to them, revealing less about the characters than about the ideological grounding of discourse. For example, the Bunyan pastiche (14.429–73) allegorizes the characters (Lenehan is "Mr False Franklin," Costello is "Mr Ape Swillale," Stephen becomes "Young Boasthard" and Bloom "Mr Cautious Calmer") and castigates them for using contraceptives and for abuses and "spillings contrariwise to his word which forth to bring brenningly biddeth" (14.465–68; 472). Although these reproaches echo the praise given early in the episode for proliferation at any cost, they are irrelevant to the characters' existences elsewhere in the novel. To urge these impoverished, unmarried men to bring forth babies violates both their own fictional histories and the moral parameters already established in such episodes as "Nausicaa," where Bloom himself masturbates. Not only, then, does each style redesign the characters according to its own ideological pattern; each one is also deaf to its own ideology and to other voices, and thus each resembles Bakhtin's monologic, "authoritative discourse" (1981, 342–43). The styles ultimately demonstrate the irrecoverability not of sources but of the entire sociohistorical framework within which each style operates; though an historical style can be imitated, imitation cannot restore to power the ideology into which it fits.

Therefore we must historicize the idea of plagiarism. According to Thomas Mallon, the concept of plagiarism was virtually unknown until the seventeenth century, when factors both economic (writers' new ability to live by their pens) and aesthetic (the new premium on originality) led to the portrayal of words as property (1989, 2, 39). Thus the "crime against fecundity" we call plagiarism became a crime only when it was perceived to violate a law; until then, citationality was neither a crime nor a particularly significant fact. Because the

---

narrower idea of literary models" (1981, 144). But in a later essay she asserts that here "pater texts are . . . ransacked, vandalized" and thus that "the prodigal word cannot be pinned down" (1987, 94). Intertextuality can be distinguished from source criticism because the former rejects linear causality in favor of explorations of the cross-fertilization of the texts and attempts to show how later texts both subsume earlier ones and revise them (see Frow 1990, 46). As Jonathan Culler argues, the citationality model almost always gives way to the recognition of sources whenever one begins doing practical criticism. For helpful discussions of intertextuality, see Culler (1981) 100–18 and Worton and Still (1990).

theft of words becomes plagiarism only when the robbed see themselves as victims, texts began to have authors only when, according to Foucault, "authors became subject to punishment" for illicit appropriation (1979, 148). That is, the "crime" of plagiarism defines the modern idea of authorship as much as authorship defines plagiarism. Only when texts are implicated in the "circuit of ownership" or "system of property" (Foucault 1979, 148–49), does their circulation become subject to legal and economic regulation, and become a restricted economy of appropriations rather than a general economy of infinite citations. Thus, everything preceding the "Milton-Taylor-Hooker" passage (around line 333) is public domain, since the "authors" of these passages would not have conceived of themselves as authors—owners—in the modern sense. The early sections are therefore a kind of public fund or freely circulating collective capital available to all linguistic laborers, rather than a series of signed investments.

In "Oxen," plagiarism and originality are the poles around which the intertextual economy circulates. To be true to the historical definitions of authorship, we must see the episode's words as both (or first) freely circulating in a general economy of citation and also (or then) manifesting the restricted economy of ownership and authorship erected later. It recognizes that any style is both product and producer of the economic, legal, and aesthetic ideologies that coexist with it. This recognition extends even to Joyce's own technique of borrowing styles and demonstrating their relativity: relativism itself is merely a modern ideology as historically conditioned, and therefore provisional, as any other. Invoking both versions of intertextuality, "Oxen" weaves and unweaves itself, its catalogue of plagiarized authors at once constructing the system of authority and tearing it down. It thus invites us to examine the economic and legal foundations of authorship in order to reveal what both models of intertextuality share: a recognition that authors are readers before they are writers. In foregrounding the relationship between authorship and the appropriations necessary to reading, "Oxen" valorizes the labor of reading, ultimately suggesting, as I will argue in more detail below, that readers are cocreators. The redefinition and redistribution of authorship Joyce performs here thus undermines the ideology that grounds the "crime" of plagiarism even as it seems to canonize those who have created it. Ultimately, it suggests, authorship is always collective. The cataloguing of the "fathers" of English prose style actually deconstructs the patriarchal authority upon which such lists are based by implying that authorship and cribbing are themselves historical constructs. In place of ownership, it proffers a paradoxical intertextuality in which originality and authority are functions of the proliferation and dissemination of plagiarism.

Proliferation and Prosperity

That the overt subject of "Oxen" is human proliferation is announced in its opening Latinate paragraphs. In the most facile sense, the episode displays how Mina Purefoy's difficult labor produces further abundance and suggests that the fear of death—so prominent in the passages discussed in chapter 3—can be conquered by fertility. But the question of whether the Purefoys' fecundity enhances or impairs their quality of life has too often been glossed over by critics deaf to the episode's ironies. Indeed, the Purefoys' prolific fecundity may have economic ramifications that belie both the narrators' praise for Theodore Purefoy's virility and the sense of abundance that one might expect from such a large family. The "crime against fecundity" may describe the results of coition and thus suggest that the Purefoys' reproductive excess paradoxically sterilizes sexual reproduction by robbing it of its life-enhancing sacredness. By producing more and more children without increasing their provisions or considering the increasing suffering of the mother, the Purefoys reduce coition to a mechanical madness; their procreation may not be fecundity but merely proliferation, an excess that weakens both the household economy and the economy of the state. As in monetary inflation, so in excess proliferation: there are more lives, but less value in each one.

The relation between proliferation and economy is illustrated by the textual economy of the opening paragraphs, which announce that "by no exterior splendour is the prosperity of a nation more efficaciously asserted than by the measure . . . of its solicitude for . . . proliferent continuance" (14.12–15). Thus (to paraphrase the rest) citizens should obey God's command to "be fruitful and multiply," because "except with proliferent mothers prosperity at all not to can be" (14.32–52). But because the passage embodies its content, its periphrastic style and tortured syntax dramatize the dangers in permitting linguistic proliferation and, by implication, undercut the praise for physical proliferation. Mere abundance enhances neither quality of life nor clarity of style. The subject of the episode, "proliferent continuance," thus refers not only to reproduction but also to literary production.²² The dual definitions of "labor"—both obstetrical labor and arduous, spirit-killing work—crystallize the tensions in the episode: the final product of labor (in both senses of the word) is death.²³ I want to develop this pun a little later in connection with Joyce's own labor to bring forth this episode; but for now it is enough to observe that the syllepsis on "labor" (one form of which seems to bring life, the other death) already tempers the episode's praise for proliferance.

In contrast to the Purefoys' devotion to procreation, the medical students and hangers-on seem both to advocate sterility and to represent it. Unlaboring, unlike Mina, they are metaphorically associated with infertility, as if to suggest that procreation and prosperity are united in labor. In the "Defoe" passage, for example, Lenehan is described as "mean in fortunes" and as fraternizing with con-men and criminals (14.535–37). Both his purse and his scrotum are "bare testers" (14.542).²⁴ Likewise, Costello is a "donought" (14.554), but also a kidnapper and hence a "plagiary" (14.562), though he has only "naked pockets" to show for his criminal enterprises (14.564). These characters' sterility and poverty converge in their aversion to profitable labor. In contrast, Mulligan's hilarious scheme for a "national fertilising farm" appears to represent fertility itself (14.684–85). Believing sterility to derive from "a parsimony of the balance," he plans to revivify the nuptial couches of "agreeable females with rich jointures" ("jointures" referring both to a wife's property and to her crotch, as if the only female riches worth mentioning lie between their legs). Aiming to be democratic, he claims that "money was no object" (14.689). This passage parodies not only the opening paragraphs' language—even using the same word, *opulent* to refer to the wealthy [14.47]—but also their ratification of reproduction and their description of Irish maternity hospitals. In retrospect, Mulligan's scheme

---

22. Mary Lowe-Evans's monograph helpfully analyzes the terms of the debate about contraception, but her contention that "language itself is guilty [of a crime against fecundity] because it obscures truth" (1989, 73) ignores how the episode's form self-reflexively dramatizes the tensions it discusses.

23. Earlier Bloom thinks of Mrs. Purefoy's pregnancies as "Life with hard labour" (8.378); here Crotthers, one of the medicals, comments ironically on "women workers subjected to heavy labours in the workshop" (14.1258).

24. The precursor text here is Defoe's *Colonel Jacque*, which relates the exploits of a kidnapper and kidnappee (Janusko 1983, 67). If we recall the earlier meaning of "plagiary," this intertext seems strikingly appropriate, as does Lenehan's later accusation of Bloom as a plagiarist (15.1734).

renders the opening passages ironic by representing human sexuality as no more than livestock production, an equation that "sterilizes" the act of coition by removing its spiritual component; it reveals the excesses and inadequacies to which any blanket endorsement of proliferation is subject.

The debate about proliferation is most apparent in the first two passages adopted from nineteenth-century writers. This too is historically mandated since, as Lowe-Evans has demonstrated in detail, nineteenth-century culture was much concerned with the problems of population and prosperity. Both passages describe the Purefoys and their children and ostensibly applaud their fecundity. The first parodies Dickens, announcing that "the skill and patience of the physician had brought about a happy *accouchement*" for the suffering Mina Purefoy (14.1310–11).[25] It praises her for "manfully" helping, congratulates Mr. Purefoy (called "Doady," caricaturing *David Copperfield*) for fighting "the good fight," and ends with "well done, thou good and faithful servant!" (14.1313; 1320; 1342–43). Unfortunately, "Doady" is not present to help his wife endure her pain; moreover, the ironies of describing Mina's labor as "manful" or as merely "helping" are excruciating. "Dickens" represses and sentimentalizes Mina's agony while aggrandizing Theodore's labor; but it is difficult to see what Theodore has done that is so worthy of praise. The narrator's articulation of patriarchal values emerges plainly in his assumption of the voice of Christ-as-master in the final lines, which are quoted from the Parable of the Talents. In it a master praises his good servants for multiplying what they have been given and condemns the bad servant for failing to increase his store by trade or "usury" (see Matthew 25:14–30). When the Dickens passage reveals that Purefoy works as the "conscientious second accountant of the Ulster bank" (14.1324), Joyce's multiple intertexts converge brilliantly: like the good servants in the parable, Purefoy labors to earn interest, to multiply what he has been "given." Like Shylock, Purefoy breeds money as well as children, but unlike Shylock and Christ's good servants, he gains nothing from his chrematistic generation.

25. Bakhtin defines parody as "double-voiced" discourse that implies an authorial intention at odds with the one being parodied (1981, 360, 364). As others have noted, however, most of the other "Oxen" sections are closer to pastiche than to parody. It is ironic to note that Dickens played a major role in getting British copyright laws improved and thus inhibiting plagiarism of the kind Joyce is doing to him here (Mallon 1989, 39–40). For an illuminating discussion of Joycean parody and pastiche, see Caesar 1989.

The passage also informs us that the baby will be christened "Mortimer Edward after the influential cousin of Mr Purefoy in the Treasury Remembrancer's office, Dublin castle" (14.1334–35). The parents will use the baby—like the others, named for British nobility or members of the Anglo-Protestant elite—to ingratiate themselves with wealthier and more respectable relatives. The Purefoys' mercenary reason for giving the child his name clearly conflicts with the cloyingly sentimental tone of the passage. The cousin's position, treasury remembrancer, an officer responsible for collecting debts, is also significant (Gifford 1988, 438), because it again links physical offspring and the interest from debts. Most disturbing is the Purefoys' use of children as their medium of exchange, as their ladder of social mobility. Ironically, however, by producing more children than they can easily provide for, their efforts yield the opposite result.

The fact that Joyce disliked Dickens also leads one to believe that he is parodying both his style and his sentiments (*MBK* 61, 79). Indeed, because the specific intertext for the passage is chapter 53 of *Copperfield,* where the important event is not a birth but a death (Janusko 1983, 153–54; Atherton 1974, 332), the saccharine sentimentality merely masks the recogition that Mina's labors are bringing her ever closer to death. Joyce's intertextual debt thus exposes not only the falseness of the ideology behind the narrator's complacency but also his contempt for the Purefoys' methods. Like the elder Mortimer, Joyce acts as debt collector in this episode, but in acknowledging his debt to Dickens he aims to pay with negative interest and thereby decrease the value of the progenitor.

The last of the historical pastiches and the only one that violates chronology mimics Carlyle (who follows "Ruskin" rather than preceding him). Praising Mr. Purefoy for doing a "doughty deed and no botch," it names him "the remarkablest progenitor . . . in this chaffering allincluding most farraginous chronicle" (14.1410–12). This narrator puns on "labor," calling Purefoy's impregnation of his wife "man's work," and exhorting both to "labour like a very bandog" (14.1414). Because I will be scrutinizing this passage and its intertexts in detail, it merits quoting at length:.

> [L]et scholarment and all Malthusiasts go hang. Thou art all their daddies, Theodore. Art drooping under thy load, bemoiled with butcher's bills at home and ingots (not thine!) in the countinghouse? Head up! For every newbegotten thou shalt gather thy homer of ripe wheat. See, thy fleece is drenched. . . . Copulation without pop-

ulation! No, say I! Herod's slaughter of the innocents were the truer name. Vegetables, forsooth, and sterile cohabitation! Give her beef-steaks, red, raw, and 'bleeding! She is a hoary pandemonioum of ills, enlarged glands, mumps, quinsy, bunions, hayfever, bedsores, ringworm, floating kidney, Derbyshire neck, warts, bilious attacks, gallstones, cold feet, varicose veins. . . . Twenty years of it, regret them not. . . . Thou sawest thy America, thy lifetask, and didst charge to cover like the transpontine bison. (14.1415–31)

"Malthusiasts" are accused of encouraging "copulation without population," and thus of sterilizing the act of coition.[26] Malthus's famous doctrines were based upon the supposition that "the power of population is indefinitely greater than the power in the earth to produce subsistence in man. Population, when unchecked, increases in a geometrical ratio. Subsistence increases only in an arithmetical ratio" (quoted in K. Smith 1951, 5). The only products of unbridled procreation are "misery and vice": "vice" yields more children and promotes the breakdown of marriages, but "misery," in the forms of starvation and poverty, might eventually curb procreation (K. Smith 1951, 6, 37). Only want or fear of want can bring population under control.[27] In general, Joyce borrows Malthus's implication that "economic laws of commercial production have an allegorical relation to the economy of human (sexual) production," a relation in which "the prosperity expressed by the biblical injunction, 'be fruitful and multiply,' belies and ultimately impoverishes any economic prosperity." Hence "production and reproduction contradicted each other" (Heinzelman 1980, 92, 93, 94). Unchecked proliferation leads not to vitality but to stagnation and starvation, and Malthus's harsh recognition that "man labors blindly toward his own extinction" (Heinzelman 1980, 93) reverberates here and throughout "Oxen."

26. Neo-Malthusians advocated contraception, but Malthus himself did not. Even though his writings clearly point to the need for contraception, Malthus was strongly against it, instead calling for "moral restraint," which included postponing marriage and avoiding sex after it (K. Smith 1951, 42, 320). On the Malthusian debate, see Lowe-Evans 1989, 58–74.

27. Joyce's *Notesheets* prove that he was familiar with Malthus: an entry reads "Malthus in Irel. food decreases arithm population incre geometrically" (282). This is, however, a misreading of Malthus, who wrote not that subsistence decreases, but only that it increases more slowly than population. The allusion to America in the "Carlyle" passage may also contain a Malthusian intertext, since he used the rapid American increase in population in the eighteenth century as the (virtually only) evidence for his theories of population. Both of his ratios were later discredited (K. Smith 1951, 326).

The Carlylean intertexts that circulate here are also pertinent. Janusko (1983, 99, 126–27, 155) shows that Joyce's chief stylistic model here was Carlyle's *Past and Present* (of which he had a copy in his library [R. Ellmann 1977, 104]). *Past and Present* (an apt title for "Oxen," too) condemns the Gospel of Mammonism and the Gospel of Dilettantism, both of which are on display in the hospital: whereas the idle and dissolute medicals follow the latter creed, the Purefoys seem to worship Mammon, bearing children with the goal of rising in class (see Carlyle 141–49). But unlike Joyce's "Carlyle," the real Carlyle condemned laissez-faire economics for leading to precisely what Malthus predicted: "such world ends . . . in 'over-population;' in howling universal famine, 'impossibility,' and suicidal madness" (179). While borrowing Carlyle's style, Joyce inverts his views on political economy. Carlyle's antidote for all misguided credos is, of course, labor, which he praises indiscriminately (and redundantly), particularly in the section entitled "Labour" which, I submit, was Joyce's primary Carlylean intertext. One excerpt from the section typifies both the real Carlyle's style and his ideology: "Doubt, Desire, Sorrow, Remorse, Indignation, Despair itself, all these like hell-dogs lie beleaguering the soul of the poor dayworker, as of every man: but he bends himself with free valour against his task and all these are stilled" (190).[28] Ironically, however, the narrator praises as "man's work" only Theodore's "labor" of sexual intercourse, not his banking job (highly ironic, given Carlyle's evangelical Christian ideology), but although her labor is virtually ignored, it is Mina who is tortured by Sorrow and Pain. Thus, although Carlyle valorizes work above all— "labour is life" (191)—his endorsement is shown to be limited by a patriarchal ideology that values only male labor.

"Carlyle's" words actually owe more to Ruskin's economic ideas than to Carlyle's. Joyce's familiarity with Ruskin has been long established.[29] Indeed, it appears at first that Joyce borrowed Ruskin's definitions of value and positive labor as the foundation for the chapter's anticontraceptive pronouncements. The cornerstone of Ruskin's political economy is laid in *Unto This Last* (1862), where he defines

---

28. The "Labour" section also alludes to Gideon's fleece (Carlyle 192), the same biblical passage alluded to in the "Oxen" passage. At the end of "Labour," Carlyle exhorts his readers to make the world bear them to "new Americas" (193), a metaphor that Joyce also borrowed for the "Carlyle" passage.

29. Joyce acknowledged his debt, once writing to Stanislaus that he had been taught "by Father Tommy Meagher and Ruskin" (*L* II 108).

value as that which "avails toward life" (17:84). Thus he divides all labor into positive and negative kinds: "the positive, that which produces life; negative, that which produces death; the most directly negative labour being murder, and the most directly positive, the bearing and rearing of children" (17:97). Specifically addressing Malthusians, he argues that "there is not yet, nor will yet for ages be, any real over-population in the world," but only local overpopulation caused by lack of foresight and planning (17:73). For Ruskin, as for "Carlyle," "the final outcome and consummation of all wealth is in the producing as many as possible full-breathed, bright-eyed, and happy-hearted human creatures" (17:56). In sum, Ruskin boldly states, "THERE IS NO WEALTH BUT LIFE" (17:105).

But his definitions of key terms—especially "life" and "labor"—complicate these axioms. Ruskin immediately qualifies his distinction between negative and positive labor by noting that he means "rearing not begetting," and remarks how profusely we praise a person who saves a life (someone like Mulligan) but not someone who "by exertion and self-denial prolonged through years, creates one" (17:97): the implication is that a person is not truly created until he or she is grown. Merely begetting or bearing a child is not particularly worthy of congratulations. In *Munera Pulveris* (1866) he further refines his definition of "life" and qualifies his scorn for Malthusianism.[30] Now advocating the increase of population only "so far as that increase is consistent with their happiness" (17:148), he defines the goal of political economy as "the multiplication of human life *at the highest standard* (17:150; emphasis mine). Dunned for butcher's bills, "drooping" under the load of children and work, and with Mina chronically ill, the Purefoys have surpassed the number of children consistent with this standard, and with their own happiness. The Ruskinian intertexts, then, both reinforce and qualify the chapter's accolades for the Purefoys' proliferation.

As for labor, Ruskin believed its most troubling characteristic to be "what is mechanical about it" (Anthony 1983, 157). If, as Bloom observes, the Purefoys produce "hardy annuals," mechanically and methodically (they are Methodists) making children as a factory produces manufactured goods, then for Ruskin their methods sap their labor of its positive qualities. Moreover, if, as the passage states, Theodore multiplies "ingots (not thine!) in the countinghouse" (the Ulster

---

30. For discussions of Ruskin's responses to Malthusians, see Sherburne (1972, 69, 84), and Anthony (1983, 94).

Bank—where Bloom has his savings account), then his main labor is usury; similarly, Purefoy has made his own home a countinghouse for children and seeks wealth thereby. While financial depositors earn interest, his deposits generate babies. His employment would also disappoint Ruskin who, drawing from both Aristotle and the Bible, condemns all taking of interest as illicit, and would thus define Theodore's labor as negative (34:417; cf. Anthony 1983, 83; Austin 1989, 211). Theodore's negative labor thus offsets Mina's apparently positive kind. In making children his medium of exchange, his ticket to class mobility, he has become a paternal chrematist whose methods of physical production are as illicit as his generation of interest. Thus, when in "Circe," Bloom himself parturiates, giving birth to the same number of children as the Purefoys, his inversion of fertilities imitates theirs. Like Shylock, Purefoy equates ducats and daughters, although he produces more of the latter than the former, at least for himself. The narrator's description of the bank as a "countinghouse" recalls Bloom's use of the word for the outhouse in "Calypso" (see chapter 3) and Freud's explorations of the psychic economy ([1908] 1959, 49; [1916] 1959, 169). Equated with money, the Purefoy children are "ingots" that are simultaneously precious and worthless, at once jewels and waste. All the family's energy is directed toward the labor of birth rather than toward labor as provision. In replacing money with children, the Purefoys' prize titbits have become as worthless as Beaufoy's. They perversely make ends meet by identifying vaginal and anal products.

But what of Mina's labor? It is certainly arduous enough: even the "Carlyle" passage acknowledges her suffering on the way to dismissing it, and portrays her as a living encyclopedia of disease. Moreover, this birth is not only the most difficult one that Mina has endured; it is also the most difficult that the experienced maternity nurse Callan has ever witnessed (14.116). Thus Mina may be forgiven if her attitude towards this pregnancy is rather less joyful than the Carlyle narrator's. In this respect, Ruskin's definition of labor is highly pertinent: it is "the quantity of 'Lapse,' loss, or failure of human life, caused by any effort. . . . Labour is the *suffering* in effort. . . . In brief, it is 'that quantity of our toil which we die in' " (17:182). True labor, he goes on to say, is not life-preserving but life "spending" (17:184). Mina's childbearing, earlier presented as entirely positive, has produced illness and horrible pain and thus exemplifies Ruskin's definition of labor as loss and suffering. Joyce's own views about childbearing may be ambivalent, but as Lowe-Evans notes, he had observed the effects of excessive childbearing upon his own mother, who "experienced seventeen pregnancies and died at the age of forty-five" (Lowe-Evans 1989, 26). Indeed, Joyce attributed her early death at least in part to her exhaustion from childbearing (ironically, this is the same letter in which he acknowledges his inheritance of his father's "spendthrift habits": *L* II 48). Mrs. Purefoy's labor in fact fits Marx's description of the worker in capitalist production, who remains alienated because he or she owns "only [the] capacity for depletion . . . because the capitalist has purchased his [or her] capacity for production" (Heinzelman 1980, 175).[31] Marx's "Juggernaut of capital" is homologous to Theodore's juggernaut of procreation, which begets babies as a capitalist creates surplus value—at the cost of his laborer (the mother), who in this case is also the factory. In this light, the praise for the father's virility at the expense of the mother's health merely echoes the insensitivity of the medical students. In short, the result of Mrs. Purefoy's labor is not wealth but, to use another of Ruskin's coinages,"illth" (17:89).

Ulysses elsewhere condemns proliferation at the price of prosperity and quality of life not only through Bloom's comments on the miserable Dedalus children but also by casting Mrs. Purefoy as the "goddess of unreason" and sacrificial victim in "Circe" 's Black Mass (15.4693). Nonetheless, many critics have accepted the repeated encomiums to proliferation without recognizing the text's deconstruction of this ideology.[32] But while the Purefoys may be a bit better off than some other large families in Dublin, even the passages that seem to laud their fecundity covertly acknowledge the problems this proliferation has brought about. "[B]emoiled with butcher's bills," the Purefoys have trouble feeding their offspring, despite Theodore's soul-killing labor. By producing more and more children without increasing their provisions or considering the mother's suffering, the Purefoys subject the act of coition to a mechanization that imitates the depredations of

31. Cf. Goux 1990, 233: "the position of labor within the capitalist 'act of production' reproduces in its specific domain the position of female reproductive labor within a pateralist [i.e., patriarchal and philosophically idealist] reproduction. The value produced (children, goods) is a lost positivity, a 'surplus' that becomes estranged from the producer. The relation between mother and offspring, under the father's control, is like that between worker and product under capitalist domination. There is an *inversion of fertilities*" (emphasis his).

32. See, for example, Gordon (1991, 244), and Janusko (1983, 13) who seem to accept the putative argument of the episode; recent critics such as Bell (1991, 147) and Thornton (1987, 258) reject it, each for very different reasons.

capitalism. As in monetary inflation, so in physical proliferation: there are more lives, but less value in each. Taken together, then, the inter-textual, contextual and textual evidence collaborate to undermine the episode's ostensible praise for proliferation by exposing the eco-nomic, physical and spiritual effects it brings upon laborers both male and female. Just as the episode appears to sanction (male) definitions of authority and authorship but actually challenges them by a plagia-ristic proliferation that affirms the labor of reading over that of writ-ing, so it appears to applaud the patriarchal values behind excessive reproduction (in which more children equal more possessions and greater proof of male ownership), but actually subverts them.

"Proud possessor of damnall"

Like "Scylla and Charybdis," "Oxen" also highlights parallels be-tween physical reproduction and artistic production. But whereas in the library episode Joyce uses Stephen, his own literary offspring, to develop his theory of artistic debtorship, here the intertextual econ-omy seems to proliferate without Stephen's participation. Stephen himself seems much less impressive than he did there, despite Joyce's obstetrical implication that his artistic delivery is imminent. One rea-son for Stephen's apparent regression is that the "embryonic poet" has spent most of his day drinking in "Mooney's *en ville,* Mooney's *sur mer,* the Moira, [and] Larchet's" (15.2518–19). As a result, the Malory narrator tells us, he is "the most drunken that demanded still of more mead" (14.194–95). His coffers have shrunken accordingly. Of the £3 12s he received this morning he now has "coins of the tribute and goldsmith notes the worth of two pound nineteen shilling that he had, he said, for a song which he writ" (14.286–88). If this sum is accurate, so far he has spent thirteen shillings (the halfpenny change from the telegram seems forgotten), mostly to buy drinks and atten-tion from newspapermen, literati, and medical friends. Those in the hospital expect him to continue to treat and, since they are broke (14.287–88), he must if he is to get any drunker. Of course, Stephen is lying about the source of his money, no doubt because artistic labor is more prestigious than earning money by teaching (cf. 11.263). In fact, Stephen's only artistic product has been the minor "black pan-ther vampire" poem composed on the strand, a "song" for which he borrowed the words of others and for which he is unlikely to receive any payment, and his parable, for which he actually paid off his audience. Unlike Joyce, who uses literary "coins of tribute" and

"Goldsmith notes" (some borrowed from Goldsmith) to earn profits, Stephen's money still seems to trap him in history.[33] Frustrated and drunk, he orates grandly about his artistic philosophy, as if to undam his blocked creativity by sheer force of will; but his ingestion of spirits inhibits his production of "spiritual assets." Stephen's obliviousness to the cataloguing of literary debts here thus implies that these debts remain as unpaid as his financial ones. The apparent progress he had made in "Aeolus" and "Scylla and Charybdis" now seems to have dissipated; if anything, Stephen has regressed.

He still propounds a eucharistic aesthetic based upon a vision of the artist as medium of exchange, as both god and sacrificial victim (14.292–94) and deems his sacrifices of money and physical well-being necessary to his transubstantiation as an artist and to the transubstantiations that art promotes. His sacrificial aesthetic sketches an economy in which flesh is exchanged for word in a pattern of reciprocal exchange that mirrors the priest's powers. Like the priest and Christ, Stephen portrays himself as a redeemer of bad and doubtful debts, an "Agenbuyer" who trades his physical being for artistic immortality in an operation that mimics the economy of grace. And if he claims to have given up the priesthood because it demanded "involuntary poverty all his days" (14.337), for this priesthood he must live in voluntary poverty, his expenditures of money freeing him from "flesh" so that he may devote himself to the transformations of the Word.

Further asserting that his recreation of his past through memory will lend it properties beyond the merely personal, Stephen boasts that he can revivify ghosts and claims that as "Bous Stephanoumenos, bullockbefriending bard" he is "lord and giver of their life" (14.1113–16). His grandiloquent gesture announces that he has fulfilled the destiny of his name, "stephanos"—the crown. But Lynch, always prepared to deflate his friend's pretensions, notes that so far only a "capful of light odes can call your genius father" (14.1119). Associated and even identified with caps throughout *Ulysses* (his cap even speaks for him in "Circe"), Lynch adapts Bannon's and Mulligan's euphemisms for contraceptives, cloak and umbrella (14.772; 785), to

33. Joyce defines Goldsmith notes (or Goldsmiths' notes) in his "Notes on Business and Commerce" as "acknowledgements of deposits passed from hand to hand as currency" (*JJA* 3:476). Since Oliver Goldsmith is one of Joyce's models in "Oxen," his texts are also deposits passed down from hand to hand as currency. The term clearly links the financial and literary economies.

suggest that a fitting hat for Stephen would be not a crown, but an emblem of artistic infertility—a cap. While Stephen gives himself the name of the sacrificial bull, the "oxen of the sun" are his stillborn literary works. And although Stephen's failure of artistic fatherhood contrasts with Theodore Purefoy's fertility, both are similar in that they produce and redundantly expend everything—except the one thing needful. Unlike Joyce's, Stephen's expenditures remain financial rather than literary or "spiritual"; he still cannot garner the interest on the capital of his predecessors nor pay his debts, despite his elaborate theorizing about these operations in "Scylla and Charybdis." The episode's extravagant marshaling of English literary history thus merely highlights Stephen's artistic paralysis.

The "Ruskin" passage proclaims the "utterance of the word" (14.1390)—"Burkes!"—typically and anticlimactically the name of a pub, to which Stephen now leads the others. Another syllepsis, the word captures Stephen's condition. In nineteenth-century slang, "to burke" meant "to murder," especially by suffocation or strangulation, after a notorious criminal who smothered his victims and then sold the parts for dissection. It was soon extended to denote all kinds of suppression, but particularly the suppression of a book before publication *(OED)*.[34] Stephen's artistic birth is indeed burked, and part of what has stifled it is his diversion of energy from literary work to extravagant drinking and spending at places like Burke's. This "embryonic" poet is in danger of being strangled by his own umbilical cord; his artistic birth is burked. In uttering "Burke's" as the word of birth, Stephen ironically makes both ends meet, substituting death for birth and identifying himself as a self-strangler who tries to rechristen himself even as he chokes.

And so the medicals, led by Stephen, trailed by Bloom, adjourn for a "buster," or drinking spree (14.1440). Once again the drinks are on Stephen, since all the others plead poverty: "Proud possessor of damnall. Declare misery. Bet to the ropes [probably Lenehan]. Me nantee saltee [Mulligan doing his "chinless Chinaman" routine]. Not a red at me this week gone" (14.1465–67). But they order anyway: "five number ones" (Bass ales) followed by prudent Bloom's request

---

34. In the *OED* (to which Joyce had access through the letter *T*) the example for this last definition comes from 1880. Joyce performs similar surgery on his predecessors: the episode involves a form of graverobbing and dismemberment of previous authors' "parts," from which Joyce then strives to profit by re-presenting them as his property.

for a "ginger cordial" (14.1468). Someone else orders "absinthe for me, savvy?" and the other three want "Two Ardilauns. Same here" (three Guinnesses; 14.1470, 1476–77). This comes to ten drinks for ten drinkers.[35] All defer to Stephen, who has "got the chink": "Seed near free poun on un a spell ago a said war hisn" (14.1499–1501). Stephen pays; total: 2s 1d, "two bar and a wing" (14.1502–3; Gifford 1988, 445). If he has £2 19s at the beginning of "Oxen" (give or take a halfpenny), his coffers now stand at £2 16s 11d. But the spree is not finished. After running into the newly shaved (in two senses) Bantam Lyons, Bannon recognizes Bloom as the father of his "photo girl" (14.1521; 1535), and he and Mulligan slink off. Stephen buys another round, despite protests (14.1528–31). Bloom asks for "Rome boose" (wine); otherwise it is "absinthe [for] the lot" (14.1533–34). According to my calculations, this round comes to 2s 4d (fewer drinks, but costlier ones), bringing his expenses for drinks in "Oxen" to 4s 5d. If this is accurate, Stephen departs for Nighttown with £2 14s 7d in his pockets, having spent almost a pound on drinks and his acerbic telegram since getting his wages. A young man who earns only £3 12 per month, Stephen has so far spent the equivalent of a week's pay—prodigal behavior indeed.[36]

The Stephen we leave at the end of "Oxen," then, is a good deal drunker, but otherwise about the same as the one we met this morning. His excess expenditures have neither forgiven him his debts nor paid them. Thus while Joyce demonstrates his mastery of literary history and his discharging of literary debts, Stephen seems paralyzed

---

35. Benstock (1991, 195–96) offers a different account of both rounds. He contends that Dixon declines because of his "pectoral trauma" (14.1472) from a bee sting, and that therefore only nine drinks are ordered. But the drinks clearly add up to ten, so nobody is abstaining yet. He also speculates that the second round consists of only five drinks, because Mulligan, Bannon, and Lenehan have departed and Bloom declines. But the text is relatively clear here: Bloom gets wine, although he may not have ordered it himself (14.1534–35) and may not drink it. In any case, I am less concerned with the number of drinks than with determining how much Stephen pays for them.

36. He earns about 16s 7d per week and has so far spent between 17 and 18 shillings: roughly a week's pay. Efforts to determine exact expenditures must remain indeterminate, however, because we never learn how much money Stephen has left at the end of the day. Nor do we know for sure if the halfcrowns he discovers in "Eumaeus" are part of this amount or separate from it. I have arrived at the sum here by calculating how many halfcrowns his pocket holds in "Eumaeus" before he gives one to Corley, and by assuming that all of the money must be subtracted from the £2 19s. See the notes to chapter 10, below, for a more detailed accounting of those expenditures, and Appendix A for Stephen's entire Bloomsday Budget.

by the same historical burden. Attempting to throw off his oppression by the monetary tokens of the nightmare of history and remain defiantly a "proud possessor of damnall," Stephen continues to squander his money and his talent. Failing to use literary history productively for artistic birth, he fails to make ends meet in either history or economics. Unlike Theodore or Mina, Stephen is neither laboring nor in labor. As with them, however, an extravagance aimed at liberation actually produces the opposite effect.

Bloom seems to recognize Stephen's prodigality; he acknowledged paternal feelings for him earlier in the episode, and "grieved he also . . . for young Stephen for that he lived riotously with those wastrels and murdered his goods with whores" (14.271–76). The cadences and the words are borrowed from the Wyclif Bible's version of the Parable of the Prodigal Son, whose role Stephen now plays. This son does not return home, but instead accompanies Bloom to Eccles Street; this "father" also contemplates further exploitation of the "son," though he does not carry it out. Nevertheless, the redemptive pattern of the parable resonates beneath their encounters in "Circe" and the Nostos, as their reciprocal exchanges—money, filial feelings, conversations—ultimately, if temporarily, balance their psychic (and in Stephen's case, financial) ledgers. Bloom's economic stewardship provides the balance through which the book makes both ends meet, and his example may help Stephen learn how to pay his debts or turn them to profits.

Irish Labor

Although, as we have seen, Joyce was often as much a spendthrift and debtor as Stephen, he was not as idle. Stephen's expenditures occasion more dissipation, but Joyce's verbal expenditures are the medium of his labor. Moreover, Joyce's labor is homologous with the Purefoys' labors. Like Theodore, Joyce works in a countinghouse in "Oxen": not only does he laboriously construct the episode arithmetically so that both he and his readers must count the number of paragraphs and stages of gestation, but he treats the history of English prose as a kind of bank vault, as "a vast repertoire of examples," an "immense repository" or linguistic clearinghouse from which the author can draw at will (Topia 1984, 103; Lawrence 1981, 143). The capital of his predecessors is Joyce's currency; through the literary usury described in "Scylla," he manages to turn a profit from their deposits so that their capital becomes his. In storing, borrowing, and then expending this hoard, the author at once increases his own stock and augments the value of his forebears' deposits. If, like Theodore Purefoy, Joyce labors in a "countinghouse" with the "ingots" of others, unlike Purefoy, who redundantly produces children as compensation for his lack of authority and prosperity and who never profits from the generation of financial offspring, Joyce makes capital from his literary progeny and not only pays his debts but turns his "fathers" into his own offspring.

Moreover, Joyce's artistic labor must depend upon female principles, or it merely duplicates the patriarchal ideology that, I have argued, it deconstructs. Indeed, the failure to recognize and show compassion for female labor is one of the "crimes" the episode indicts. Thus if Joyce's labor sets him apart from Stephen, it brings him closer to Mina. Joyce's and Mina's labor have in common an economy of excess. Joyce estimated that this episode cost him "1000 hours of work" (*L* II 465)—less than Mrs. Purefoy's forty weeks, but still an enormous expenditure of energy. At times Joyce too felt abused by his labor, writing that he worked at "Oxen" "like a galley-slave, an ass, a brute" (*L* I 146)—"like a very bandog" (14.1414–15). Just as this child is Mina's most difficult to bear, so "Oxen" was "the most difficult episode" to execute (*SL* 249). Joyce hoards the linguistic capital of his male predecessors, but then, in a concentrated and willful catharsis, expends it, purging himself of indebtedness like a woman delivering a child. Once again Joyce mimics the "economy of heaven," in which the author is at once male usurer and female laborer, both begetter and bearer of literary offspring, to bring forth his intertextual text. Moreover, by legitimizing cribbing as artistic labor, the episode both unweaves Joyce's "image" as original author and reweaves it as a female principle of collective or antiauthoritarian authority. Like "Cyclops," "Oxen" eschews the scrupulous authority and accounting we have traced in "Wandering Rocks" in favor of a more communitarian model.

Paradoxically, even though the episode covertly critiques the excess proliferation that impoverishes Irish families like the Dedaluses, its own artistic principles imitate that proliferation. Like many of the other later episodes, "Oxen" proliferates wildly, seeming to waste words and thus violate the sacred principles of artistic economy Joyce used in *Dubliners*. This excess labor yields comedy, in part from the disparity between the bulky apparatus of the episode and the minor events it depicts, but also from the reader's (unsuccessful) attempts to integrate this excess into the conventional economy of reading, in

which each word or phrase is meaningful and not redundant.[37] In
fact, the debate about proliferation and economy presented in the
episode is staged on another level throughout the second half of
Ulysses, where Joyce practices an economy of excess that adapts Irish
economic behavior as a model for his expenditures of words. If, as
Foucault writes, "author" is the word we give to "the principle of
thrift in the proliferation of meaning" (1979, 159), Joyce redefines
the nature of authorship. Challenging the fear of proliferation that
Foucault describes as the function of authorship, Joyce authorizes
textual excess. In so doing he imitates Stephen's sense of abandon
and his equation of creativity and loss. As in "Cyclops," here Joyce
replaces Henry James's "sublime economy of art"—an economy that
"saves, hoards and 'banks' (1908, vi)—with one of splendid waste. But
even this excess can be seen as banking: if chrematism is a form of
uncontrolled and illicit proliferation, then in that respect "Oxen" (like
many of the late episodes) is chrematistic, replicating the operations
of usury defined both here and in "Scylla" as the artist's labor. In
short, "Oxen" critiques the ideology of proliferation on one level only
to reinstate it on another level as an economic principle of artistic
composition; it also questions Purefoy's usury only to replicate it.
Once again Joyce's practice reinscribes the conflict between control
and expenditure, between miser and spendthrift, that his economic
habits betrayed time and again.

If, as we have seen, the culture of Dublin is founded upon debt
(both verbal and financial), and the economic behaviors of its inhabitants are characterized by excess expenditure, then Joyce's artistic
labor here and for the rest of the novel is identifiably Irish. That is,
the very excessiveness of Joyce's verbal expenditures and labors to
bring forth the episode replicate in another register the economy of
Dublin. In this way Joyce's artistic praxis is inherently political: by
exposing the historical contingency of English style, by extravagantly
cataloguing the English "fathers" and creditors who have bequeathed
him their literary capital, he pays off these debts, as Ireland could not
do to England. In rewriting English literary history in extravagant

---

37. Bell (1991, 150) similarly points out that the concept of "proliferent continuance" is both a social and artistic credo for the episode, but he is concerned primarily
with the comic effects of this dissemination, rather than with tracing its homologies
with Joyce's economy of composition. I concur, however, with his contention that the
phrase refers to the episode's own "fecundity" and dissemination of meanings (1991,
10, 22) as well as its overt discussion of the problems of procreation.

Irish fashion, he appropriates the language and the history for those excluded from that history: the female, the Irish.

Several kinds of offspring are produced (or not produced) in "Oxen," including Joyce's own monster child—the grotesquely abundant catalogue of prose styles that increasingly emphasizes the contingency of all styles while inflating and distorting the naturalistic scene almost beyond recognition. But what is ultimately celebrated in "Oxen" is Irish labor—the labor of excess—not of procreation but of textual production. Joyce's own exemplary labor reveals his similarities to and differences from not only Stephen and his unlaboring friends, but also from the Purefoys. If we mimic this Irish labor based upon debtorship and excess, it will be possible to bring forth the text, which will nonetheless always be a kind of monster child. If the catalogue of styles in "Oxen" shows that all authors are readers before they are writers, then it must also encourage—even demand—a Joycean expenditure of labor on the reader's part. The reader must revise his or her relationship to the textual and intertextual economies; we too must perform "heavy labour" in the countinghouse to bring forth *Ulysses*. Despite our best efforts, some parts will always elude that conventional economy of meaning in which every part fits the whole; an excess remains. The reader too must labor and spend in excess; the reader too must become more Irish, more female. We can no longer fear the proliferation of meaning; we must embrace it. Collaborating with the labor of writing, the labor of reading permits us to become coauthors. It is this extravagant, arduous, and proliferating labor of reading and writing—Irish labor—that "Oxen" ultimately affirms.

7

"Cyclops" and the Economy of Excess

For living matter in general, energy is always in excess; the question is always posed in terms of extravagance. . . . To give is obviously to lose, but the loss apparently brings a profit to the one who sustains it.

—Bataille 1988, 23, 70

Although the announced "art" of the "Cyclops" episode is politics, its content and form revolve around economics. We have seen how the "Wandering Rocks" episode maps the tensions in Dublin's economic life between solidarity and disintegration caused by distortions of reciprocity. Economic behaviors that should establish and strengthen the sense of community instead tear it down. Similarly, in "Cyclops" economic exchanges that should reinforce communal solidarity instead foster hostility. As the tribal economy of gift exchange comes to dominate the economic relationships among the characters, the words and stories they exchange also become deceptive and extravagant gifts, so that their distorted economic exchanges correspond with distorted verbal exchanges. In "Cyclops," as in the other late episodes of *Ulysses*, Joyce's "spendthrift habits" are mirrored in those of his profligate characters. Through homologies between linguistic and material economies, "Cyclops" not only critiques the financial behavior of Joyce's Dubliners but again reveals how Irish economic paradigms underlie Joyce's compositional methods. Foregrounding gifts and gambling, "Cyclops" examines the excesses of Dubliners and at the same time imbricates them in its structural economy.

While comically detailing the political and economic excesses of the drinkers in Barney Kiernan's pub, "Cyclops" also exemplifies the kind of textual excesses that characterize the second half of *Ulysses:* proliferating narrators, long catalogues, absurdly inflated diction, incongruous descriptions of banal activities. In short, the extravagant verbal economy of "Cyclops" both mirrors and satirizes the economic activities of its characters. Ultimately, however, Joyce's economy is most fully expressed neither in the episode's examination of political economy nor in the opposition it depicts between hostility and charity, but rather in the comic dialogue that takes place between Joyce and his readers. Through this liberating comic economy, the episode redefines the personal and ethnic identities of Joyce and his Irishmen and again generates a revolutionary economy of reading that invites readers to engage in extravagant exchange with the text and hence to become spendthrifts and gift givers themselves.

GREEK GIFTS

The economics of Homeric Greek culture, like that of many other archaic societies, was based upon gift exchange. The term *gift,* however, described a wide variety of activities now distinguished from one another, including "payments for services rendered, desired or anticipated; what we would call fees, rewards, prizes and sometimes bribes" (Finley 1954, 64). Even for loans, the Homeric word is always *gift.* The motive for these gift exchanges was not profit but "equality and mutual benefit": balanced reciprocity. Nevertheless the return gift was essentially obligatory (Finley 1954, 66). Fittingly, then, in the *Odyssey* both the frame narrative of the Cyclops episode and the tale itself revolve around gifts and reciprocity. This tale (book 9) is the second adventure that Odysseus himself narrates to the Phaiakians, who have rescued him from the sea and hospitably entertained him according to Mediterranean norms. Following custom, Odysseus' hosts demand that he tell a story as his repayment for the food and drink they have provided him. Odysseus' narrative is thus his means of repaying his hosts, his medium of exchange (Homer 1961, 141–42); his story *is* his return gift. In typically shrewd Odyssean manner, however, his tale concerns a failure of hospitality and an exchange of spurious gifts and thereby challenges the very norms on which it is based.[1]

Odysseus tells how, after being captured by Polyphemus, he offered the giant the wondrous wine of Maron as a gift (Homer 1961, 155). But the Cyclopes live in a primitive world without Greek norms of hospitality and gift exchange: Polyphemus is so barbaric a host that he literally has his guests for dinner. Thus he responds to Odysseus' offering by giving him a return "gift," which turns out to be the dubious favor of eating him last (Homer 1961, 156). Of course, Odysseus' wine is designed to intoxicate Polyphemus so that Odysseus can destroy him, and thus itself violates the norm, since his return gift is also hostile. This exchange gains more resonance from what precedes it: just before embarking on his tale, Odysseus (still incognito) had asked the Phaiakian bard to retell the story of the Greek conquest of Troy by means of the Trojan Horse and to describe the legendary cunning of Odysseus (Homer 1961, 139–40). Clearly Odysseus' "gift" to the giant is meant to remind both his and Homer's audience of the Trojan Horse: both wine and horse are spurious gifts that lead to the destruction of their recipients.

As a preface to his tale, Odysseus announces his name, responding to the Phaiakians' request that he identify himself. Since Odysseus' story also identifies and describes him, it contains and exemplifies his identity. He offers himself as a kind of narrative gift by telling his tale. Because the tale relates how he gave himself the pseudonym Outis—noman—to deceive Polyphemus, Odysseus identifies himself by slyly boasting of his disguises. Just as the gift he gave to the Cyclops was not a gift, Outis is not really a name (M. Ellmann 1982, 85). When his hosts ask, "Who are you?" he narrates a story in which the same question led to the blinding and humiliation of the questioner and in which his final defiant announcement of his name to Polyphemus led to many of his later troubles. Thus his response to the demand to identify himself is disturbing: it identifies him by demonstrating his skill in misidentifying himself. By boasting of his mendacity, Odysseus casts doubt on both the veracity of his tale and on the identity that his tale reveals. His audience cannot be perfectly

---

1. Redfield (1983, 234) argues that Odysseus proceeds by the principles of cost-benefit analysis, and that his behavior to the Phaiakians is pure exploitation, since he will never have to reciprocate for their gifts. This view, however, ignores the value that the hosts place on Odysseus' narrative gifts: they, at least, seem to accept his narrative as reciprocation.

sure who he is—perhaps "Odysseus" is another alias. His pseudonym becomes a "Greek" gift both to Polyphemus and to his audience, a trick that recalls the Trojan Horse. Odysseus thus emerges as a double consciousness, a narrator simultaneously authoritative and untrustworthy. Moreover, within the frame tale Odysseus' return gifts of name and story seem equally eccentric, at once violating and fulfilling the gift-exchange norm: he reciprocates for his auditors' gifts by telling of false gift exchange and conforms with the rule of hospitality by telling of its violation.

Ironically, the Phaiakians respond to Odysseus' tale by showering even more gifts upon him. Odysseus' problematic tales have enhanced his prestige. Narrative is his gift, and the audience recognizes its value. Nevertheless, Odysseus is presented in the Cyclops tale as an elusive narrator who simultaneously reveals and conceals himself beneath pseudonyms and disguises and whose "gifts" may camouflage hostility. This interchange of spurious and compulsory gifts, both commodities and narrative, also characterizes Joyce's reworking of the tale: the spenders and speakers in Kiernan's pub resemble Polyphemus, exchanging "gifts" that are at once obligatory and oppugnant. By their lights, Leopold Bloom, the Dublin Odysseus, breaks the rules of hospitality and reciprocity; according to Bloom, they are barbaric and their gifts destructive. Like Odysseus, Bloom is capable of creating pseudonyms; unlike Odysseus, his anonymity is dictated in part by his peers' refusal to recognize him as one of them. In this sense he is Odysseus as Outis. Moreover, Joyce's identity is, like Odysseus', buried in the anonymous voices of his competing narrators. He exists inside the tale only in these pseudonymous personae, these Outises. As the episode unfolds in the digressive and extravagant discourses of these unreliable narrators, narrative again becomes a Trojan Horse: a gift that conceals hostility. In sum, both Homer's and Joyce's "Cyclops" concern and contain "Greek gifts": verbal and financial presents that conceal threats and challenges. By adapting the narrative exchanges of Homer to depict a Dublin economy of expenditure, Joyce suggests that narrative language is a Greek gift: an apparently charitable present that may undermine the very ground of narrative—credit and belief—while also subverting the traditional relationships between signifier and signified.

Joyce's "Cyclops" projects an agonistic world where competition infects the narrative surface. Two voices alternately narrate and interrupt the action. The first is that of an unnamed raconteur and barfly ("I"); the second issues from an anonymous compendium, a depersonalized collection of borrowed, clichéd or archaic public discourses. While the first narrator sees everything with a jaundiced eye, the second wears rose-colored glasses: both are Cyclopean in that neither has fully binocular vision. Both are infected by what Joyce's schema calls "gigantism," a form of linguistic inflation that imitates the physical size of Homer's Cyclops.[2] The first narrator, a "collector of bad and doubtful debts" (12.24–25) named, paradoxically, "The Nameless One" later in the text (15.1144–45), exaggerates the defects of everything and everyone, offering rumors as gospel truth. As in Odysseus' tale, the time of Nameless's narration appears to be later than the events he narrates; he is recounting them to an anonymous auditor, presumably in exchange for more drinks (Hayman 1974, 243). Since we never see him buy a drink in Kiernan's, it seems likely that storytelling is his only form of currency: as long as he entertains his listeners, he can continue to drink. Just as Odysseus used his tale as a countergift with which to earn presents and prestige, Nameless's stories about the events in Kiernan's pub are his medium of exchange. As narrative exchanger, he is also Odysseus' alter ego, and hence the Linati schema dubs him "Noman."[3]

In part because of Nameless's current vocation, even apparently non-economic activities gain economic connotations: dying, for example, becomes paying the "debt of nature" (12.335). As usual in impoverished Dublin, the economy of debt permeates figures of speech. But economic concerns dominate the episode in a more straightforward sense. Nameless's first anecdote, for example, describes a lawsuit in which Moses Herzog sold £1 5s 6d worth of tea and sugar to Michael Geraghty, from whom Nameless has been charged to collect the unpaid remittance. A legal document describing the affair comprises the first aside in the second narrative zone (12.33–51), and thus the two zones offer competing versions—not a dialogue, since neither acknowledges the other—of a failure of dialogue and reciprocal exchange. This twistedly legalistic atmosphere pervades the episode, and indeed, Nameless's drinking, self-importance, and

2. To call the second voice a "narrator," is of course to ignore the collective nature of the voices in the insertions. For brevity's sake I have simplified the narratological complications in the episode. Lawrence 1981 and Riquelme 1983 offer useful discussions of narratology in *Ulysses.*

3. Given his loquaciousness as narrator, it seems odd that Nameless is relatively closemouthed during the events in "Cyclops." Just as he is collecting free drinks that will loosen his tongue later, he is also collecting material to spend in exchange for liquid currency at a later time in the day.

suppressed rancor recall Farrington, from Joyce's story "Counterparts," who was employed by a law firm and conversant with legal language.[4] If Farrington has no first name, this narrator has no name at all. Joyce's characters are counterparts in other ways as well: Nameless, with his monocular vision, is a counterpart of Polyphemus and a mirror image of the parodist/narrator, as well as an alter ego of Odysseus. As a collector of bad and doubtful debts, he is also the negative counterpart of Bloom, who does not hector debtors but instead— sometimes reluctantly—gives them grace. The narrator is thus depersonalized both by his namelessness and by his resemblances to other characters, just as Odysseus depersonalizes himself in his tale through his pseudonyms.[5] Nameless's stories, however, are deceptive in a more commonplace way—he spreads gossip.

A crude but hilariously energetic storyteller, Nameless displays wide knowledge of Dubliners' finances. Privy to secret information, he uses the power of the financial and legal institutions that support his debt collecting to buttress his narrative credibility. But in his eyes everyone is a con-man, thief or sponger: he mocks the pathetic drunk Bob Doran for "standing Alf [Bergan] a half one sucking up for what he could get" (12.486–87); Boylan is "Dirty Dan the dodger's son off Island bridge that sold the same horses twice over to the government to fight the Boers" (12.998–99); Bloom is censured for "trying to get the soft side of [Mrs Riordan] doing the mollycoddle playing bezique to come in for a bit of the wampum in her will" (12.506–7) and receives even severer treatment for failing to buy a round. Like Farrington, this mooching narrator damns anyone he suspects of resembling himself. A true parasite, he changes according to the way the wind seems to be blowing and panders to his listeners by telling them what, presumably, they want to hear. Ironically, while he acts as a

---

4. As Torchiana points out (1986, 142), a "counterpart" is a copy of a legal document, one of which Farrington makes during the story, and one of which appears here as the story of Geraghty and Herzog. Cf *D* 88.

5. "Ithaca" further suggests that Nameless is Bloom's counterpart when the catechist "reduces" Bloom through possible futures to a "dun for the recovery of bad and doubtful debts" (17.1937–38). In "Penelope," Molly gives us both the only information we have about Nameless's appearance and a clue as to how he gets *his* information. He is "that longnosed chap I dont know who he is with that other beauty Burke out of the City Arms hotel . . . spying around as usual on the slip always where he wasnt wanted" (18.964–66). His "nosiness" and intrusive eye are conventional but effective analogues for his knowledge of secrets. Nameless himself mentions his association with the ubiquitous Pisser Burke (12.1659).

hired representative of powerful institutions such as banks and courts, at the same time he undercuts the authority they lend him by reducing all economic activity to fraud. In this regard his narrative is subversive, as his nihilism and lack of character implicitly expose the economic and political institutions he represents as the parasitic and exploitative forces many Dubliners believe them to be. This irony also affects his authority as teller. Given his sources in the public domain of gossip, Nameless depends upon his audience for his authority—he tells only what "everybody" already knows—and presents himself as the collective voice of an allegedly homogeneous society. Yet he undermines that collectivity by refusing to grant credence to any speech but his own and thus tears down the communal values upon which his credibility rests. By submitting all economic activities to his levelling cynicism, he destroys the foundation of his own narrative authority by making his tales another form of exploitation: if all acts merely camouflage fraud and theft, then his own narrative must be yet another swindle. His roles as collective voice and collector of debts, then, are as problematic as Odysseus' crafty subversions of ritualized gift exchange and name giving. Like Odysseus, Nameless attacks his own authority even as he voices it, inadvertently revealing the ulterior motive behind his taletelling—to get something for nothing. Both of them present narratives as intrinsically untrustworthy, as Greek gifts that use the norms of narrative exchange only to subvert them. Nameless thus unwittingly represents a collision of opposite forces: he stands for legal authority but also subverts authority by mandating whatever the market will bear.

The second narrator or narrative zone interrupts Nameless's narration with expansive digressions often hilariously incongruent with the mundane events that inspire them: everyday social amenities become formal, archaic ceremonies; descriptions of objects balloon into mammoth Rabelaisian lists; a dog's growl becomes canine poetry.[6] Both zones draw from a vast store of received opinion and collective discourses: the Nameless One knows all manner of gossip, scandal, and secrets, while the parodies borrow from legal documents, travelogues, theosophy, Irish legends, newspaper reports, graffiti, and so on. Indeed, "Cyclops" is a kind of emporium for the collection and

6. For Bakhtin, a zone is both "a territory and a sphere of influence . . . [and a] locus for hearing a voice; it is brought about *by* the voice." These realms are attributable sometimes to characters ("character zones") and sometimes simply to an authorial or disembodied voice ("speech zones"). See Bakhtin 1981, 434, 316–20.

dissemination of discarded, twelfth-hand collective discourses. The second zone beautifully exemplifies Bakhtin's theory of "heteroglossia" (the tendency for novels to become zones of dialogical contact among various planes of social and historical languages), as *Ulysses* perfectly fits his description of the English comic novel as "an encyclopedia of all strata and forms of literary language" (1981, 270–73; 301). But although the parodies do present highly diverse languages, often within a single aside, the dual narrative zones are not "dialogized" in Bakhtin's sense, because Nameless cannot "regard [his] language (and the verbal world corresponding to it) through the eyes of another language (1981, 296). And though the insertions alternate with Nameless's narration, they do not merge or cooperate with it until the end of the episode. The effect is much closer to competition, as the Nameless One's excesses prompt greater extravagances in the parodies. This second zone transmits archaic, conventional, and institutional discourses, none of which acknowledges its relativity and some of which pretend to be "connected with a past that is felt to be hierarchically higher," as if speaking "the word of the fathers"; these insertions thus exemplify Bakhtin's "authoritative" (and hence monologic) discourse (1981, 342).[7] But the asides also display conflicting impulses, offering ancient languages as authoritative discourses while at the same time subverting that authority through an excess that sanctions licentiousness and verbal prodigality. These conflicting impulses of control and profligacy, but especially the latter, impel the verbal economy of the episode.

    Although ultimately Joyce's juxtaposition of these voices destroys the claims of each to sole authority, only the reader stationed outside the text recognizes the relativizing effect of this alternation. The dialogue does not occur within the narrative but only as a frame around it. In fact, this refusal to acknowledge alternative ideologies or points of view characterizes the entire episode: both the narrative structure and the action of "Cyclops" revolve around purblind antagonism. Just as the characters in the episode talk a good deal but have little actual dialogue, so the narratives fail also to carry out genuine exchange. Language, the most powerful vehicle for social exchange, instead becomes a bar to genuine reciprocity. In Kiernan's pub words are

---

7. See, for example, the second and third insertions in the episode. The second introduces the pub neighborhood as "the land of holy Michan" and then gives a long list of natural resources; the third describes the Citizen in archaic terms as an Irish hero.

weapons masquerading as modes of reciprocal exchange, and the verbal transactions that usually prevent aggression instead foster it. These distortions of verbal exchange parallel both the distortions in the Homeric tale and those of the Irish economy depicted in Joyce's. That is, like the "gifts" of Odysseus and Polyphemus, and like Odysseus' narrative gift to the Phaiakians, the gifts—both verbal and material—in Joyce's "Cyclops" are Greek gifts: deceptive, obligatory, and antagonistic. Only at the end, when Bloom confronts the prevailing mood of aggression and chicanery, do Nameless and the characters face an antithetical language and ideology, and only then is the language of the episode internally dialogized by Bloom's pluralistic identity and charitable economics (cf. McArthur 1988, 136).

IRISH ECONOMICS

Nameless's first drinking crony is Joe Hynes, himself a bad debtor who, we recall, has owed Bloom three shillings for several weeks. Instead of paying Bloom, Hynes buys rounds at Kiernan's. Nameless is aware of Hynes's financial problems—"decent fellow Joe when he has it but sure like that he never has it" (12.65–66)—but collects not money but free drinks, further disabling Hynes from paying those debts. Entering the pub, they encounter another nameless personage known only as the Citizen (modeled upon the Fenian Michael Cusack [*JJ* 61]), who is "waiting for what the sky would drop in the way of drink" (12.120–21). Hynes buys a round (three pints at twopence each), and Nameless professes wonderment: "begob the sight nearly left my eyes when I saw him land out a quid. . . . A goodlooking sovereign. —And there's more where that came from, says he" (12.207–9). The Citizen is described in a parodically excessive aside as a "broadshouldered deepchested stronglimbed frankeyed . . . sinewyarmed hero" with "rocklike mountainous knees" and nostrils so big a lark could nestle inside (12.152–61). Describing his "girdle" of seastones, the insertion soon digresses into the first of several gargantuan lists, a catalogue of "Irish heroes," many of whom are neither Irish nor heroic, including "Napoleon Bonaparte," "Captain Nemo" (noman), "Jack the Giantkiller," "Sidney Parade," and "The Man that Broke the Bank at Monte Carlo" (12.176–99). The insertion illustrates the Citizen's inflated view of himself, his stereotypical notions about Irish heroism, and his own dubious claims to represent the community. But although this set piece borrows "heroic" language to glorify him, its effect is finally parodic, overwhelming him with its own grandiosity. Nonetheless, the introduction of the Citizen (whose xenophobic, self-aggrandizing, spuriously authoritative discourse is itself "gigantic") prompts proliferating excesses of language in the parodic narrative zone. Such verbal excesses, to which I shall return below, also mirror the economic condition of the pub's patrons and the distortions of the Irish economy.

The Citizen bullies the other characters with his "authoritative" rhetoric. Like Nameless, he is monocular, viewing everything through jingoistic green spectacles—everything Irish is good, everything else is contemptible—and employing a simplistic either/or mentality that mimics the antithetical positions of the narrative voices. His discourse is exclusivist and monologic, and he attempts to instill a view of Irish homogeneity by depicting common foreign enemies: the French (12.1385), the English (12.1198–99), and the Jews (12.1811). He lives inside a national myth of the innocent and expoited Irish, a myth too strong to dislodge.[8] He also blends the traits of the two narrative zones, alternately cursing whatever he dislikes and sentimentally inflating all things Irish. Like Nameless's, the Citizen's discourse represents a spurious collectivity based on an antagonistic exclusion of all voices but his own.

Although some of his bluster is based on fact—for example, his laments about the depopulation of Ireland and the degeneration of her industries—his list of natural resources is undermined by the hilarious "marriage of the trees" pastiche that follows it (12.1240–79). His exaggeration of lost Irish wealth echoes the second insertion of the episode, which lists the "superabundance" of resources in "Inisfail the fair" (12.68–99): a land of abundance requires an overabundance of words to represent it, as "gigantism" affects both structure and content. Such hyperbole was commonplace in Ireland at the time, offering a Utopian vision of unearned bounty at odds with the actual poverty of the citizens and reinforcing the widespread Irish belief in their innocence and victimization. According to Cullen, because English colonialism had stultified the country's economic development, many Irish of the day "tended to overestimate Ireland's natural . . . resources, and hence . . . assumed optimistically that under altered

---

8. Ironically, the Citizen's rantings echo those of the British sympathizer Garrett Deasy, whose politics and economics he would abhor: the Citizen shouts that "We brought [the strangers] in. The adulteress and her paramour brought the Saxon robbers here" (12.1156–58); Deasy claims that "a faithless wife first brought the strangers to our shore" (2.392–93). Both are anti-Semites.

political arrangements much of the country's industrial recovery would be spontaneous" (1987, 164). Such beliefs provided an excuse for those unwilling to blame themselves for their economic insolvency, as if idle or spendthrift inhabitants would somehow magically change lifelong habits once the Sassenachs had left. On the contrary, the episode itself suggests a more straightforward, if also somewhat oversimplified, explanation: nobody, including the Citizen, is exerting himself to remedy the situation, either by working or by taking political action. England is an oppressor, but she is also a ready scapegoat.

As "Aeolus" also shows, many contemporary Irishmen were "political" in the same sense as the Citizen, diverting themselves from effective action with sentimental, histrionic oratory. As an Irish pundit wrote in 1907, "everyone shouts 'Die for Ireland,' but no one works for her" (Kenny 1907, 80). The emigration of these citizens was not so much spatial as temporal, for they envisioned and tried to occupy either a nostalgic past of tribal loyalties and simple barter (a past that never existed, and one reflected in the archaisms that dominate the asides) or an implausible future of a united, wealthy, and serene Ireland (cf. Valente 1988, 59). The Citizen's sacrificial politics are thus lampooned in the long aside describing the hanging of an Irish hero (12.525–675). But he does not sacrifice himself; indeed, his chief political activity is drinking at others' expense, as we see Hynes treat both him and the narrator to three rounds (12.147; 749; 1410). This is a typical day for a man whose life consists of "arsing around from one pub to another, leaving it to your own honour . . . and getting fed up by the ratepayers and corporators" (12.752–54). (Of course, Nameless's comment reflects ironically upon himself, since he drinks without paying whenever the Citizen does.) But the debt collector reveals that the Citizen is much worse than a sponger; by his own standards he is a traitor, compromising Ireland even as he glorifies it: "As much as his bloody life is worth to go down and address his tall talk to the assembled multitude in Shanagolden where he daren't show his nose with the Molly Maguires looking for him to let daylight through him for grabbing the holding of an evicted tenant" (12.1312–16). When it comes to personal finances, apparently the Citizen's political beliefs are more flexible. Not only, then, do some of Joyce's Irish blame the British for their own failures; they are accomplices in exploitation, sacrificing political freedom for short-term economic gain. The Citizen's economics are thus reflected in his drinking habits: in both cases, his aim is to get something for nothing.

Nevertheless, some of his declarations do reflect contemporary political and economic realities. As I noted in chapter 1, the economy of turn-of-the-century Dublin was in dreadful shape, with an unemployment rate of almost 20 percent, and the lowest average wage and worst slums in the British Isles (O'Brien 1982, 202; Cullen 1987, 165). Anyone looking outside the door of Kiernan's would have seen abundant examples of these conditions, since St. Michan's parish, where the episode takes place, was one of the poorest districts in the city (O'Brien 1982, 31). Moreover, some of the Citizen's statements echo Joyce's earlier writings on Irish political economy, although Joyce's analysis is more complex. Like the Citizen, Joyce argued that "Ireland is poor because English laws ruin the country's industries" (*CW* 167) and elsewhere deplored the same deforestation that the citizen laments (12.1256–57), setting the value of this "moral debt of the English government to Ireland" at "500 million francs" (*CW* 195). The economically exploitative relationship between England and Ireland is represented in the episode by the newspaper story concerning the visit of the Alaki of Abeakuta. The chief is given a "treasured" Bible by the "Royal Donor," Queen Victoria, a gift as spurious and cynical as the Greeks' "peace offering" to the Trojans (12.1522–26). This present merely purchases at low cost further colonial exploitation of the Chief's people.

Yet Joyce was ambivalent about the extent of British responsibility, in other contexts withholding blame from England—"I find it rather naïve to heap insults on England for her misdeeds in Ireland" (*CW* 166)—and recognizing Irish complicity in this exploitation: "individual initiative is paralyzed by the influence and admonitions of the church, while its body is manacled by the police, the tax office, and the garrison" (*CW* 171). Also like the Citizen, Joyce noted sadly how many Irish were emigrating (*CW* 190), but recognized that "no one with any self-respect stays in Ireland" (*CW* 171). What remained there was "a long parade of churches, cathedrals, convents, monasteries and seminaries" (*CW* 190), a procession embodied in the long lists of saints and clerics that decorate "Cyclops" (12.927–38; 1689–1712). While these insertions present Ireland as an island of saints and sages, the human resources that remain in Ireland—those clerics and saints—cannot replace the natural resources that have been depleted.[9] In-

---

9. While Joyce might applaud the Citizen's nationalism, he would scoff at his xenophobic notions of racial purity: "to exclude from the present nation all those who are descended from foreign families would be impossible, and to deny the name of patriot to all those who are not of Irish stock would be to deny it to almost all the heroes of the modern movement" (*CW* 161–62).

stead of trees and crops, Joyce would tell his Berlitz students, "the government sowed hunger, syphilis, superstition, and alcoholism there; puritans, Jesuits, and bigots have sprung up"; as a result, "the Dubliner passes his time gabbing and making the rounds in bars or taverns or cathouses, without ever getting 'fed up' with the double doses of whiskey and Home Rule" (*JJ* 217). Despite their jocoserious tone, these phrases attest to Joyce's recognition of the shared responsibility for the dismaying state of Irish economics.

The other characters in "Cyclops" bear out this picture of idleness, insolvency, and political schizophrenia. The debt collector is surrounded by bad debtors and economic failures: J. J. O'Molloy, with his "name in Stubbs's" (a register of bad debtors given to merchants), and "half smothered in writs and garnishee orders" (12.1025); Bob Doran, who blows his money on periodic benders; the sponging Lenehan, who lurks at the ege of the conversation, attempting, like Nameless, to wheedle free drinks after losing his money on the horses; Martin Cunningham and Jack Power, entering near the end, who are trying to collecting money for the Dignam children but exist within a very Irish network of bad debts and economic decline that we have already traced. Like the rest of the novel, "Cyclops" exposes Dublin as a city in dire economic straits, a community of bankrupts, swindlers, spongers, and gamblers.

AN ECONOMY OF EXPENDITURE

The economics of "Cyclops" demands still closer scrutiny. In Kiernan's (and, no doubt, other Dublin pubs), spending money on drinks is a means of establishing prestige. These boozy and economically insolvent characters enact a microcosmic version of the potlatch ceremony, an orgy of property destruction and gift giving found in many archaic societies (which is congruent with the language of many of the asides). Each participant in a potlatch attempts to outdo the others in generosity, which often takes the form of extravagant gift giving but may also involve actual destruction of property. Power and prestige accrue not through investing, saving money or acquiring goods, as in bourgeois economies, but through expenditures and loss of goods.[10] But the gifts in a potlatch only seem voluntary; actually

10. The conspicuous consumption that typifies the affluent in capitalist societies may seem similar, inasmuch as a person can acquire prestige by spending large amounts of money on goods imbued with social status. But the prestige comes *with*

there are three intersecting obligations—to give, to receive, and to reciprocate (Mauss [1925] 1967, 37–41). To fail in any of the three is to suffer social humiliation and loss of honor. The potlatch constructs the boundaries of the social group and solidifies its hierarchies: those who give or destroy wealth are included, and those who do not are cast out; those who cannot reciprocate by giving back a larger gift than the one they have received lose social status. The greater the loss, the greater the prestige, which is bound up with "the duty of returning with interest gifts received in such a way that the creditor becomes the debtor" (Mauss [1925] 1967, 35; cf. Blau 1964, 106). The *Odyssey* depends upon a similar economy, which Joyce has adapted for his revision of the tale. Like the gift exchanges in a potlatch, the treating in Kiernan's is actually compulsory and self-interested. The accepted behavior is to buy a round, accept another, buy another, and so on. When one is treated, he must reciprocate by buying for several people: one's loss is thus generally greater than the price of his own drinks, especially when, as here, some drink but never buy. Thus, the economy of "Cyclops" revolves not around balance but around loss. The impoverishing results of it can be seen in "Counterparts," when Farrington, after pawning his watch for six shillings, is left at the end not even happily drunk, and with only twopence in his purse (*D* 97). In "Cyclops" linguistic and economic inflation sometimes occur simultaneously when characters buy rounds: for example, Bergan can "ill brook to be outdone in generous deeds but [gives] therefor with gracious gesture a testoon of costliest bronze" (12.290–92)—but not that costly, since the testoon is only twopence.

Significantly for Joyce's adaptation of the model, the gift exchanges in potlatch ceremonies are usually interpreted as sublimated aggression. Although they seem sociable, "their sanction is private or open warfare," their effect is "essentially usurious," and their ultimate purpose is "to crush a rival with future obligations which it is hoped he cannot meet" (Mauss [1925] 1967, 3, 4; Levi-Strauss 1969, 53). In Sahlins's terms, the exchanges in "Cyclops" only appear to conform to the altruistic extreme of "generalized reciprocity," in which gifts are given freely, but actually resemble the opposite extreme of "nega-

---

the acquired object and thus remains the trace of an acquisitive ideology. To spend profligately on a useless item does not create prestige. In contrast, the power and rank in a potlatch come about *because* of the expenditure itself, not because of any goods received through such expenditure; the aim is not to gain, but to lose, whether or not these losses are ultimately recuperated in some symbolic fashion.

tive reciprocity," in which parties attempt to get something for nothing (1972, 193–96). Like the gigantic and deceptively informative stories of the two narrative zones, a potlatch gift must be extravagant, and although it seems to be given in a spirit of generosity, its motive is usually antagonistic; like both the action of the episode and the antithetical perceptions framed by the narrative zones, the potlatch is based upon a competitive relationship among parties. In this way, both the structure and content of "Cyclops" revolve around distortions of reciprocity. As in "Wandering Rocks," economic patterns that bind the community together do so perversely, and sometimes instead engender hostility and alienation.

This perverse economy is exemplified in the "Cyclops" characters' addiction to gambling. Since many of them have wagered on the Gold Cup horse race, gambling occupies a good share of the episode's conversation. Most writers on the potlatch describe gambling as its best modern instance.[11] Like potlatch gift exchanges, gambling takes on its full meaning when the risk of loss, or the loss itself, is as great as possible. Also as in the potlatch, the player who acquires the greatest prestige is the one who risks the most, and may even be the one who loses the most: Boylan, for example, actually wagers two quid but later tells Molly that he has lost twenty (18.424), in keeping with his image as a big spender. In gambling, economic failure occasions social unity: Lenehan, for one, uses this solidarity with other losers to get free drinks, and the losers here eventually find a common enemy in Bloom as a means of demarcating their social circle. But if betting seems to provide an easier alternative to gainful labor for such characters as Lenehan, ultimately it produces as much alienation as the most menial laborer's job. The gambler subjects the conventional economy of balance and gain to the conditions of play, which would seem to announce the gambler's freedom from constraint. But in placing a bet the gambler puts himself or herself at the mercy of chance—a force at least as powerful and inscrutable as corporations or the British government—and hence negates that freedom. The gambler's labor may be even more alienated than, say, the factory worker's, because it is rarely validated as labor by the larger culture. If he or she loses, the labor of wagering has been worse than fruitless; if the gambler wins, other gamblers see him or her as a cheat, and other

11. Lévi-Strauss, for example, writes that "gambling provides, in modern society, the most striking picture of these transfers of wealth with the sole purpose of gaining prestige" (1969, 56); cf. Mauss (1925 [1967], 101n.

laborers may envy that person, but will call the gambler lazy. Hence, playing the game according to the accepted rules of the gambling subculture—calculating odds, seeking tips, winning modestly at best —is more acceptable than winning great sums; indeed, winning is an affront, since a winner necessarily alienates himself or herself from the majority of players, who are always losers. Thus, as Vernon observes, "the inevitable desire of the gambler, just beneath the desire to win, . . . is the desire to lose" (1984, 127). While appearing to many Dubliners as a means of gaining large unearned gifts, gambling more often results in losses that, over time, resemble the extravagant losses in the potlatch. Issuing from a drive towards self-sacrifice, gambling both creates solidarity with other gamblers and enacts the larger culture's impulses toward self-destructive expenditure.

These forms of expenditure may be illuminated by the economic theories of Georges Bataille. Seeking an alternative to what he calls the "restricted economy" of acquisition and conservation, Bataille generalizes from the potlatch to discover a principle of expenditure and loss behind all social activities that defy the bourgeois economy of gain. This "general economy" holds that humans subsist not in order to save, but in order "to accede to the insubordinate function of free expenditure" (1985, 129). This economy of expenditure impels all moments of liberation from acquisitive labor—gambling, games, festivals, and the arts—and especially the drive for sacrifice. Potlatch resembles sacrifice in that it is "the complementary form of an institution whose meaning is in the fact that it withdraws wealth from productive consumption": that is, in sacrifice destruction acquires value. Since, according to Bataille, social rank is an economic exchange value as tangible as property, squanderers may gain prestige from their expenditures (Bataille 1988, 75–76, 72). Thus the apparently senseless losses of Joyce's Dubliners are recuperated as positive values in the social rank that accrues to the spenders, and, more importantly, in the sense of national solidarity against the bourgeois (read English) economy of acquisition. In sacrificing economic health, they gain the only quantities left for them—unity and the moral superiority of sacrificial victims. Even sponging, which seems to violate the economy of loss by allowing lazy people to get something for nothing, actually conforms to it, since spongers eschew profitable work in favor of mere subsistence: begging will never make one wealthy. And most of the spongers in *Ulysses* (Lenehan, Corley, O'Molloy) do so because they have spent more money than they earn and now request that other Dubliners give them gifts, thereby perpetuating the cycle of expenditure. In sum, both the Citizen's sacrificial politics and the drinkers' gambling and spending habits may be explained as an impulse towards liberation through loss, as the Irish define themselves in contrast to the British through their principle of expenditure.[12]

These inverted Irish economic practices are thus related to the economic disenfranchisement already discussed. Stripped of economic and political self-determination, Joyce's Dubliners respond either by accommodating the British and Roman masters and betraying their countrymen, or by contriving a perverse relish of their own poverty. It is as if they view losing money as a means of defying the British masters, as if the very possession of coins—those "symbols . . . of beauty and of power" (2.226)—engraved with the likeness of the monarch reminds them of their subjugation. To flout what even Joyce saw as English economic ethics—saving and acquiring—they spend and drink themselves deeper into poverty and paralysis, rebelling against oppression by making themselves unprosperous. Political *res-sentiment* is thus materialized in an economy of unproductive expenditure. As I have argued, Stephen Dedalus's rebellion against his masters takes a similar and characteristically Irish form: refusing to be dominated by either political or personal authorities, he squanders a good share of his meager earnings. The economy of "Cyclops" therefore represents the larger economy of Dublin, in which power is defined as the power to lose and destroy goods (and oneself), and Irishness as the willingness to spend unproductively.

But if Bataille approves of this impulse towards loss as a way of circumventing the limitations of classical economics, Joyce has reservations about it. He exposes the limitations of this economy in several ways. First, as to gambling, no character wins regularly on the horses,

---

12. Barbara Herrnstein Smith (1988, 134–49) argues that Bataille is unable to retain the original meaning of "loss," and that his theory does not, as a result, revolutionize traditional ideas of political economy. Instead, in pointing out the social benefits gained by losses, Bataille merely redescribes loss or expenditure as a positive form of value, and hence only reverses the valence of the most familiar terms of classical economics. Smith is correct that Bataille hedges on the nature of "loss," but in his later writings he is quite clear and unapologetic about claiming that reciprocity exists in the exchange of gifts for prestige. *Pace* Smith, Bataille's crucial insight about the drive away from acquisition of property and its replacement by the impulse towards expenditure remains a powerful explanation for the behaviors of certain minorities and for certain irrational moments in culture such as games and festivals. For a more sympathetic reading of Bataille, see Richman 1982.

and those most associated with betting are among the least attractive characters in the novel: Lenehan, Bantam Lyons, and the mucus-plagued Nosey Flynn (see 8.828–45). Second, although this economy of expenditure is meant to create solidarity and sociability, the hostility so prevalent in "Cyclops" demonstrates that it merely translates the Citizen's pugnacity into economic terms. Furthermore, these Irish celebrate their differences from the English by attacking other ethnic groups, making the Citizen's nationalism as authoritarian as the system he despises. Nor does this economy make the Irish happy. The denizens of Kiernan's, like most of Joyce's Dubliners, are oppressed by the poverty that has derived in part from their economy of spending. In them Joyce exposes the Irish penchant for martyrdom as a primitive and inadequate response to oppression, one that perversely inspires more self-destruction. As the faltering economy of Ireland demonstrates, their method redounds negatively on the participants, not only making the Irish poorer and inadvertently aiding the British but also reinforcing demeaning ethnic stereotypes. What restricts the Irish economy is not acquisition but the denial of it. In sum, by defying English imperialism through the economy of expenditure, the Irish exacerbate the destructive economic effects of that imperialism.

Joyce's reservations about such expenditure are perhaps best embodied in the one character who does not participate in the potlatch. A refusal to participate in ritual gift exchanges may imply either submission to the givers' powers of bestowal or defiance of them, and one may break the circle of gift exchange either by refusing to reciprocate or by giving an immediate quid pro quo, both of which proclaim one's unwillingness to enter into economic exchange and hence amount to a rejection of social bonds (Schwartz 1967, 6). Both acts defy the coercion of collectivity and are "equivalent to a declaration of war" (Mauss [1925] 1967, 11). A similar refusal characterized Homer's Cyclopes and made Odysseus' stretching of the norms seem eccentric in the Homeric context. In Joyce's tale it is Bloom who transgresses upon the prevailing economic rules: he neither drinks nor gambles. In refusing to buy a round, in effect he tells the others that they are not worthy of exchanging with him, which epitomizes again the deep distinction between his economic habits and the other Dubliners'. He refuses to participate in the drinking potlatch for several reasons. First, he knows that accepting one round means buying others for men who never reciprocate; second, he disapproves of insobriety as a waste of money ("General thirst. . . . Save it they can't" [4.129–30]); and third, he recognizes that chronic drinking and treat-

ing has ruined fellow citizens like Simon Dedalus and Ben Dollard
(whose plight is detailed in the next chapter). Bloom usually stays
sober and here takes only a cigar (12.437). His abstinence inflames
the others, but what is worse, he plumps for the antitreating league:
"Bloom putting in his goo . . . about . . . the antitreating league and
drink, the curse of Ireland. Antitreating is about the size of it. Gob,
he'd let you pour all manner of drink down his throat till the Lord
would call him before you'd ever see the froth of his pint. . . . Ireland
sober is Ireland free" (12.682–92). Bloom violates their rule of hospitality and symbolizes what they see as Jewish stinginess; unlike Odysseus, he fails to offer even a spurious gift to the Cyclopes, who view
his prudence as a judgment against them.

Bloom's indifference to gambling also distinguishes him from the
spenders. Lenehan spreads the rumor that Bloom has won on the
Gold Cup (12.1550–51) and soon inflates Bloom's alleged winnings
to a hundred shillings (12.1556). As Bloom's supposed miserliness
increases, so does the others' hostility: "Then sloping off with his five
quid without putting up a pint of stuff like a man. . . . your pockets
hanging down with gold and silver. Mean bloody scut. Stand us a
drink itself" (12.1663–64; 1759–60). Bloom's alleged gambling success defies their economy of loss, and the gamblers see this niggardli-
ness, like his sobriety, as evidence of his failure to be a good Irishman.
Not only does he have the gall to win on a dark horse, but to compound the crime, he refuses to spread his winnings around. Had he
actually won, this would be a double refusal to play the game properly. In any case, Bloom cannot win: if he wins, he makes the others
envious; if he refuses to play, his frugality makes the others' losses
look more futile. Either way, Bloom remains a "rank outsider"
(12.1219), a Trojan Horse in the Cyclops' cave.[13]

This animosity towards Bloom's "Jewish" economics demonstrates how gift exchanges may express hostility as well as kinship and
how the pressure to spend can become as coercive as the English
ideology of acquisition. In contrast to the others' unproductive expenditures, Bloom tries to balance losses and gains, and instead of partici-
pating in their "gift" exchanges, he quietly reminds Hynes about his
three shilling debt, in return getting Hynes's promise to intercede
with Crawford about Bloom's ad for Alexander Keyes (12.1144–54).

---

13. Nameless recalls a story about Bloom's unsuccessful attempt to sell tickets to
the Hungarian lottery, ("Royal and privileged Hungarian robbery"). According to
Nameless, then, Bloom's lottery was a Greek gift, or as the *Notesheets* to the episode
describe it, a "Wooden horse (Hungary)" (119).

But while Bloom refuses to join the circulation of expenditure, he is not merely an account balancer. In fact, his reason for being in the pub is the antithesis of the others'—he intends to meet Cunningham, whom he has promised to accompany to the Dignams' to help with the widow's insurance policy: "You see . . . Dignam . . . didn't serve any notice of the assignment on the company at the time and nominally under the act the mortgagee can't recover on the policy" (12.762–64). Bloom manages to muddy the waters as he continues, but he is trying to say that Dignam used his insurance policy as security for a loan but failed to notify the insurance company; under British law this technically invalidates the loan and allows the lender to collect on the value of the policy (Gifford 1988, 339). Kenner observes that they are actually "defrauding a moneylender named Bridgeman on a technicality" (1987, 103). But "defraud" seems an excessively harsh term, considering that they are trying to uphold the spirit over the letter of the law, to counter technical legality with charity, just the opposite of Nameless's legally sound but ethically questionable occupation. If the legal problem remains somewhat cloudy, Bloom's task seems fairly clear—to help persuade Bridgeman to relinquish his claim. He is never fully at ease with this charitable mission, perhaps because of its dubious legality, but also because of his habitual vacillation between mercantile shrewdness and altruism. Yet he fulfills the errand from a sense of mercy (see 13.1226–27). Although Lenehan says Bloom is "defrauding widows and orphans" (12.1622), in fact he is doing precisely the opposite—helping Dignam's widow and orphans to "defraud" Bridgeman, an act of charity in sharp contrast to the obligatory "gifts" that prevail in the pub.[14]

14. Bloom thinks little about this errand later, however, and the gap between "Cyclops" and "Nausicaa" remains the longest lacuna in the text. Several critics have speculated as to why Cunningham believes that Bloom would be able to help with this errand and why Bloom thinks so little about it. Kenner conjectures that Bloom has been deputized because he is Jewish, and so Cunningham believes that he has some "hereditary skills." He "has devised for Bloom a role modelled on Shylock's. Being cast in the stereotype of Semitic fiscal cunning, that seems to be what Bloom senses and resents; that is why he pushes the rendezvous out of his mind for nearly five hours after it is made" (1987, 103). This ingenious reading fits the episode's anti-Semitic undercurrent, but the textual evidence for it seems sketchy. Cunningham's reasons are probably more straightforward: Bloom was once in the insurance business himself and thus might know about such technicalities (see 13.1226–30, and 18.1113 and 18.1224). He also has a policy with the same company (17.1856), and hence may be familiar with both the agent and the company's practices. But any interpretation of motives here remains problematic, since this encounter is never dramatized, and Bloom seems reluctant even to allude to it. His reluctance fits a Bloomian pattern of giving gifts and then

Thus, while the others drink and spend in a downward spiral of
loss motivated by envy and masking hostility, Bloom tries to carry out
genuine charity. Later in the episode, he advocates brotherly love as
a universal philosophy. Against the Citizen's aggressive xenophobia
Bloom bravely points out that his "race," the Jews, is being "Robbed.
. . . Plundered. Insulted." Others, he says, are "Taking what belongs
to us by right" (12.1470–71), and he makes the famous assertion that
"it's no use. . . . Force, hatred, history, all that. That's not life for men
and women, insult and hatred. And everybody knows that it's the
very opposite of that that is really life. . . . —Love, says Bloom. I
mean the opposite of hatred" (12.1481–85). Of course, the others
see Bloom in their own image: "Beggar my neighbour is his motto"
(12.1491). In opposition to the extravagant expenditures of the other
Irish and to the compulsory gift exchange in the pub, Bloom here
advocates the freely given gift. Ironically, the Jewish Bloom voices the
Christian idea of charity ("Well, says John Wyse. Isn't that what we're
told. Love your neighbour" [12.1490]) and offers an alternative to
both the prevailing economy of "Cyclops" and to the bourgeois economy of acquisition and balance. His discourse also opposes both the
Citizen's and Nameless's, representing tolerance rather than authoritarianism, flexibility instead of rigidity. Moreover, in contrast to
the inflated bluster around him and to his own occasional long-
windedness, in this passage Bloom expresses himself quietly, economically, without rhetorical flourishes. His version of love echoes the
positive view of gift giving articulated by Mauss, who asserts that "by
setting up will for peace against rash follies . . . peoples succeed in
substituting alliance, gift and commerce for war, isolation and stagnation" ([1925] 1967, 80). In other words, the economy of love as creative altruism may displace both usury and extravagant loss. This
Bloomian expenditure demands no countergift. But Bloom's lovely
words are immediately undercut by comical graffiti that end with
"You love a certain person. And this person loves that other person
because everybody loves somebody but God loves everybody"
(12.1500–1501). The insert reduces "love" to another cliché, a euphe-
mism for sentimentality lacking any social connotation of charity or

---

finding mercenary reasons for doing so (such as in his rationalization for doing the
favor for M'Coy [6.888–90]). He also resists dwelling on this errand, feeling that
"houses of mourning are so depressing because you never know" (13.1226): i.e., it
reminds him of his own mortality. Joyce's own knowledge of insurance practices and
terms is shown by the twenty-three-page section in Insurance on the "Notes on Business
and Commerce" (*JJA* 3: 537–60).

gift giving. Such irony is characteristic: Joyce's texts often ridicule the same values that they profess. But the real objects of ridicule are trite expressions of love, worthless linguistic currency that transforms love into a valueless signifier. Nevertheless, as we saw in "Wandering Rocks," the ideal of charity—gift without reciprocity—is difficult to carry out in economically oppressed Dublin, and Bloom's own oscillation between charity and mercantile shrewdness testifies to its fragility. Moreover, Bloom's verbal and financial economies are at least partially subverted by Joyce's own economy of composition in "Cyclops" and the other late episodes of *Ulysses*.

LOSS IS HIS GAIN: JOYCE'S "POLITICOECOMEDY"

The competing impulses displayed by the narratives are also expressed in Joyce's economy of composition. At times, like Nameless and the Citizen, Joyce uses words as weapons, inscribing negative reciprocity in the names and behaviors of characters. As I argued in chapter 1, Joyce was sometimes a collector of unpaid debts, a vengeful, uncharitable Shylock who carried a "memory in his wallet" (9.246) to pay off those who slighted him. In "Cyclops" this is represented by the prizefight insertion, in which the British fighter knocked out by the Irishman Keogh is named Percy Bennett (12.960–87). Since Percy Bennett was also the name of a British official with whom Joyce clashed in the lawsuit against Henry Carr, Joyce is paying off an old score by making his enemy take the beating that he could not inflict. Here the text again resembles Odysseus' gift to Polyphemus: an offering that carries a burden of aggression toward certain possible future readers. Like Odysseus' tale, Joyce's narrative functions as a medium of exchange, here defined as linguistic payment to one's enemies. For every slight against him, Joyce gives tit for tat, balancing his ledger by a double-entry mental bookkeeping that turns losses into gains. While these blows fall upon British citizens, they seem to bear personal rather than political grudges, since Joyce carried out similar double-entry justice against such Irishmen as Gogarty and Cosgrave. This negative reciprocity, this "scrupulous meanness," certainly violates Bloom's words about charity and mercy, and more closely resembles the angry Irishmen than the mild Jew.

In the second half of *Ulysses*, however, this resentment gives way to the textual economy of proliferation and excess discussed already in regard to "Oxen of the Sun." The Cyclopean insertions likewise exemplify an economy of verbal excess that mimics the excesses of consumption and expenditure portrayed in the episode. The potlatch, or rather the larger concept that subsumes it, the notion of expenditure, now becomes the model for both the financial and linguistic economies in Joyce's writing. Michael Groden has argued that "Cyclops" was the point at which Joyce quit writing one kind of book, concerned with Bloom and Stephen, and began writing another, occupied with language and narrative strategies (1977, 126). After "Cyclops," Groden suggests, Joyce's habits of composition tended increasingly toward encyclopedism. In the late revisions, which began after "Cyclops" (and especially those made in the last six months of 1921), Joyce augmented many of the text's lists. For example, between the fair copy of "Cyclops" and its publication as part of *Ulysses,* he expanded the list of saints from twenty-one to eighty-four names and enlarged similar passages in "Circe" and "Ithaca" (Groden 1977, 158). In these extravagant digressions, Joyce establishes a linguistic economy of excess in which he spends words as his characters spend money. This verbal gigantism, which Fritz Senn has dubbed "provection," becomes the typical mode of discourse in the second half of *Ulysses,* which inscribes the Dublin economy of extravagant expenditure into the text itself, creating a verbal potlatch that parallels that "monster child of the gift system" (Mauss [1925] 1967, 41).[15]

The Rabelaisian voice of the parodies is also that of a collector in a different sense: one who heaps up names, discarded texts, and borrowed or anonymous discourses and then spends them in prodigal fashion. Several times the asides digress into colossal catalogues—of heroes (12.176–99), of mourners (12.556–69), of clerics (12.927–38), of names of trees (12.1268–78), of geographic features (12.1451–61), of those saints and their symbols (12.1689–1719)—that have no necessary relation to the events in the pub, to Joyce's life, to documentary facts about Dublin, or even to the beginning of the section in which they appear. These gargantuan series move the discourse of the episode toward the nonsensical, sometimes appearing to comment on the extravagances of the characters (for example, the list of saints follows a false moment of piety, and the list of heroes comments on the citizen's spurious Irish heroism), but more often overshadowing any parodic effect and calling attention to themselves as sheer excess.

15. Defined as "an excessive bias, a tendency to overdo, to break out of norms, to go beyond," *provection* is a useful name for Joyce's tendency to get "carried away" (Senn 1991, 171, 175). Useful as the concept is, it fails to account for the economic component of this practice and thus does not recognize how the form and content of this episode dovetail.

The asides are enlarged in at least four ways: extension (e.g., the size of the Citizen and Ireland), quantity (e.g., the absurdly large number of saints), importance (e.g., Garryowen's growls become Celtic verses, the bartender becomes a knight), and most significantly, value (e.g., twopence becomes a "costly testoon").[16] Many of the asides, but especially the lists, create value where none exists; like the tall tales of the characters, they lend the appearance of worth and abundance to an impoverished and idle environment, even as they themselves seem filled with excess or excrement. These passages adumbrate the catechistic voice in "Ithaca," which often "enlightens" us by giving both more and less than we wish to know. What seems to be generous informativeness actually makes absurd the enterprise of seeking definitive knowledge, as excess effaces distinctions between the trivial and the significant, the useful and the ornamental. Such overwhelming generosity again resembles a gigantic Greek gift: just as Odysseus subverted the gift exchange norm even as he used it, this economy subverts the conventional economy of reading in which each textual element can be fit into some organic unity, instead transforming the text into a huge verbal midden heap. Although they enrich the textual surface, in terms of signification these lists resemble the absurd engorgement of the hanged man's erection (12.473–78).

Joyce's defiance of organic unity and the economic relationship of words to meaning violates that Jamesian "sublime economy" of realism and replaces it with one of splendid waste. Here again Joycean practice recalls Bataillean theory, which locates art as one of the primary expressions of the impulse towards expenditure. As we have noted, for Bataille poetry is "synonymous with expenditure; it in fact signifies . . . creation by means of loss" (1985, 120). Joyce's willingness to risk the loss of meaning thus yokes his writing to gambling and the potlatch. The mammoth lists in their fully engorged shapes not only mirror the economic and verbal behavior of the non-Bloomian characters in the pub; they represent Joyce's own movement from a financial economy of expenditure to a verbal one. As we have seen, the young Joyce, like Stephen Dedalus, spent prodigally and accumulated large debts, as if determined to throw off the subjugation of materialism by squandering whatever money he earned.

16. These instances of gigantism thus exemplify Susan Stewart's description of the gigantic in literature as representing "infinity, exteriority, the public and the overly natural" as symbols of "surplus and licentiousness, of overabundance and unlimited consumption" (1984, 70, 80). Senn (1989b, 563–64, and 1991, 176–77) offers two slightly different, but compatible, descriptions of the gigantism of the lists.

But in contrast to Stephen's creative paralysis and his own distinct lack of economic prudence, Joyce's artistic economy in the later episodes of *Ulysses* allows him to achieve sovereignty and control, paradoxically, by relinquishing it, by challenging the limits of existing systems of representation and sacrificing meaning by subjecting it to expenditure. Joyce wrote that each time he finished writing an episode of *Ulysses* his mind lapsed "into a state of blank apathy. . . . The progress of the book is like the progress of some sandblast. . . . Each successive episode, dealing with some province of artistic culture . . . leaves behind it a burnt up field" (*L* I, 128–29). Joyce's verbal economy empties him as it fills the text, his expenditures of words paralleling his expenditures of money. Especially in such passages as the Cyclopean asides, this economy approaches what Derrida, discussing Bataille, calls the destruction of discourse, "a . . . potlatch of signs that burns, consumes, and wastes words . . . a sacrifice and a challenge" (1978, 274). This potlatch weaves the Irish economy into the fabric of the text, combining an impulse toward artistic control with a more Irish drive towards expenditure and loss.

In "Cyclops," then, we again see competing impulses at work. On the one hand, the drive towards authority and control is manifested not only in the monologic quality of the narrators' discourses but also in the skill with which Joyce manipulates these voices and in his obsessive labor on the episode. On the other hand, however, the extravagances of both zones testify to a powerful drive to relinquish control, to spend words as profligately as Joyce's characters spend money, to lose oneself in sheer excess. The result of this collision is again described in Bataille's general economy. "It is contradictory," he writes, "to try to be unlimited and limited at the same time, and the result is comedy" (1988, 70). Likewise, the comic economy of *Ulysses* displays a continual competition between rigid design and riotous exuberance. The recognition of Irish poverty and suffering, combined with the absurdity of Joyce's verbal extravagance, produces an anguished laughter that frees language from monologic signification but also permits communication in the shared experience of comedy.[17] As Freud notes, we laugh at "expenditure that is too large"

17. Richman further suggests that Bataille's laughter (and, I would argue, Joyce's) resembles that in Bakhtin's carnivalesque: it "purifies from dogma, from the intolerant and the petrified, liberates from fanaticism and pedantry, from fear and intimidation, . . . from the single meaning, from the single level, from sentimentality" (Bakhtin 1965, 123; quoted in Richman 1982, 151).

([1905] 1960, 191); thus, while we laugh at the sheer excess in the Cyclopean lists, our laughter is tempered by the suffering we experience when reading through them and attempting to fit them into our interpretive economies. Just as Joyce's comic economy of excess finally disarms the monologic discourses of Nameless and the Citizen, so it disarms our attempts to discover a single meaning or a single pattern in the episode. The comic excessiveness of the language of the second narrative zone produces a dialogic effect that undermines even its own claims to authority. Through extravagance, political economy metamorphoses into "politicoecomedy" (*FW* 540.26).

But this economy of expenditure sets up a large irony: while the episode satirizes the excesses of the characters and narrators and privileges Bloom's prudent economic behavior, it reinstates the value of excess by foregrounding its own exuberant linguistic energy. There remains, however, a crucial difference between his verbal economy and the financial expenditures of his characters. For Joyce, these losses become assets. Unlike the potlatch at Kiernan's and the Dublin economy in general, his expenditure is also productive labor that subverts the economy of balance and the discourses of authoritarianism. It is therefore the antithesis of the idleness of characters like Nameless and the Citizen and of their bullying rhetoric. While the characters shout and fume but do not otherwise work, the author exerts himself strenuously, as if to compensate for their idleness by adopting their verbal expenditure as his work. Paradoxically, however, at the same time he parodies that labor by carrying it to excess, turning artistic work into a kind of indulgence. Through his cramming of excess into the novel, Joyce himself becomes a kind of gambler, risking both loss of meaning and loss of readers by his verbal largesse. Yet ultimately his writing is also politically productive labor: the "superabundance" of description in the insertions reconstitutes the lost wealth of Ireland, not in money but in words. Language becomes the Irishman's true wealth, and it is this rich vein that Joyce taps in "Cyclops" and throughout the second half of *Ulysses*. Joyce was fond of quoting Oscar Wilde, who said that the Irish had "done nothing" but were "the greatest talkers since the Greeks" (*CW* 174). While such verbal gifts cannot make insolvent citizens successful, they do provide Joyce with the linguistic currency needed to turn the Irish habit of expenditure into literary capital. Finally, it is not Joyce's political writings but the political economy of his *artistic* writings that affirms and redefines his Irish identity. Joyce's "politicoecomedy" thus rehabilitates Irish political and economic identity, its verbal gifts turning Irish losses into gains.

THE COMMERCE OF IDENTITIES:
AN ECONOMY OF READING

As in Odysseus' tale, narrative is Joyce's medium of exchange. He uses art as verbal currency, as an embodiment of Irish labor that advertises its excessiveness. Joyce's gift is both Irish and Greek: his texts demand a large reciprocal expenditure of energy from the reader, a challenge that may be unwelcome, or impossible to recipro-cate, and which may inspire the reader's hostility or resistance. No matter how much the reader strives to integrate the heterogeneous elements of "Cyclops" into a restricted economy of reading (that is, to find a pattern that subsumes them all), laughter erupts because some of them resist integration. As Derrida writes, the laughter that *Ulysses* inspires both "laughs to know . . . and laughs at knowledge" (1988, 60).[18] In demanding extravagant reciprocity on the part of the reader, the text simultaneously binds together author and reader and en-gages them in comic competition. The depiction of potlatch creates a potlatch of reading, as the reader is challenged to match Joyce's exces-sive labor, to meet his gift with the gift of understanding that is, ironically, doomed to fall short. With its enormous range of voices, its daunting catalogues, and its competing excesses, "Cyclops" becomes a Greek gift to the reader, obliging a reciprocal gift of attention and knowledge. Still, the contest creates a dialogue, an engaged interac-tion absent from the Cyclopean characters' relationships. Moreover, it ideally moves the reader to generate an identity as flexible as those Odysseus offers in his tale. The focal point for this dialogue of identi-ties is Bloom.

"Cyclops" represents the point at which Joyce's competing textual economies engage each other through the economic oppositions rep-resented by Bloom (conservation and charity) and the other Dublin-ers (expenditure and excess). Its proliferating signifiers and multiple voices ultimately make all discourses seem relative, despite its speak-ers' claims to absolute authority. But the end of "Cyclops" forces these voices into dialogue, as Bloom becomes the center of both narrative

18. This laughter, according to Derrida, is simultaneously jubilant, "resigned," and cynical (1988, 58). Elsewhere Derrida (1984, 146) describes Joyce's demanding gift to his readers in terms similar to mine.

zones, and thereby constitutes the dialogical force in the episode, a third possibility against both zones' excesses. His economic ideologies of prudence and charity "break through the alien conceptual horizon of [the others]," and construct "his own utterance on alien territory, against . . . the listener's apperceptive background" (Bakhtin 1981, 282). Thus at the end, Bloom flees the Citizen, proclaiming that "Christ was Jew like me" (12.1808–9), while the Citizen flings a biscuit tin after him. Even here the parodist reinterprets the scene as a gift exchange: Bloom is said to be "presented" an "illuminated scroll of ancient Irish vellum . . . on behalf of a large section of the community," as well as "the gift of a silver casket" (12.1820–23), this passage obviously recalling the departing gifts Odysseus received from his hosts).[19] More importantly, the two narrative zones finally collaborate in this section, as the drinkers behold "ben Bloom Elijah, amid clouds of angels ascend to the glory of the brightness at an angle of fortyfive degrees over Donohoe's in Little Green street like a shot off a shovel" (12.1916–19): the second zone begins a sentence that Nameless finishes. Bloom's identificative departing shouts mimic those in which Odysseus reveals his true identity to Polyphemus, and he now flaunts the "Jewish" economic identity that the others hate. And yet, as we have seen, Bloom's economy is a far cry from the stereotypical Jewishness embodied by Reuben J. Dodd (who is probably not Jewish), and his philosophy of charity associates him with a Christian economy of unearned gifts. Curiously, however, relating the incident to Stephen later in the day, Bloom seems to recant his Jewishness (16.1083–85). There he resembles Odysseus as Outis, giving with one hand while taking away with another, answering the question of identity by complicating it. His triumphant announcement of his identity may be an Odyssean Greek gift, an alias that deceives even as it seem to reveal. In fact, Joyce suggests in the *Notesheets* to "Cyclops" that Bloom's very Jewishness makes him anonymous, and that this identity is a function of his economics: "Noman: <unnameless> & unrestless in Israel, attempters of many enterprises" (119). Bloom's enterprise in "Cyclops" is both an errand of charity and a battle for his identity,

---

19. Ironically, the biscuit tin is probably engraved, not with "Celtic ornament," as the parodist voice tells us, but with symbols of the British Empire. Boxes and tins of Jacob's Biscuits commonly carried such symbols as the Union Jack or redcoated soldiers (see, for example, Opie 1985, 39). With this touch, Joyce again subtly undercuts the Citizen's xenophobia: the nationalist proclaims his patriotism by deploying symbols of the very empire that he says oppresses his people.

an identity that nonetheless resists simple definition. Like Odysseus, the polyonymous Bloom is "Everyman or Noman," whose real name is "known to none," and who sometimes wins the "honour and gifts of strangers" (17.2008), but sometimes their animosity. As *andra poly-tropon* (man of many turns) Bloom is a kind of living dialogue, a place where names and ideologies intersect and create a dynamic interchange, enabling the text describing him to permit a cooperative dialogue of opposite points of view.

Bloom's ambivalent economic roles and cunning name changes give the text a shifting center made even more malleable by Joyce's changes in voice. The final passage in "Cyclops" blurs the boundaries between the two narrative zones, rendering each even more anonymous. Through this movement towards anonymity and collectivity, the implied author also becomes a kind of Odyssean Noman. As in "Oxen," here Joyce buries his stylistic identity in public and collective discourse, thereby becoming a composite, or "massproduct" (17.369). This dissemination of authority implies that authors are necessarily collectors and debtors who borrow or accept verbal gifts from the chorus of voices and ideologies in their culture. Like the narratives in the *Odyssey*, the language of "Cyclops" reveals itself as a medium of exchange that both prompts and responds to social interaction. Language becomes social currency, and as such it depends upon reciprocity and exchange; both linguistic and financial economies are distorted, but exchange does ultimately occur. Words no longer belong solely to any single speaker but become shared property, and authorship depends upon a commerce of selves and their discourses. Such exchanges make the language in "Cyclops" fully dialogical, "a living, socio-ideological concrete thing," inasmuch as its language is "populated—overpopulated—with the intentions of others" (Bakhtin 1981, 293–94). The author becomes a sponge who soaks up the linguistic gifts of others, and whose identity is redefined by these gifts. Like Odysseus, Joyce reminds his audience that narrative may be a Greek gift in which competing discourses offer competing claims to authority that paradoxically disseminate that authority. Adapting Homer, Joyce suggests that narratives ultimately engage all levels of society in their commerce and thereby challenge stable meaning, stable identity, and normal verbal economy.

If authors are "Intellectual debtors of society" (*Notesheets*, 81) who imitate Odysseus and Homer, then so are their readers, who are required to collaborate in the commerce of identity and authority. As in Odysseus' framing of his tale, Joyce's redefinition of identity forces his audience to participate in creating the narrative; by defining and assuming the author's identity, we also assume partial authorship. His narrative gift requires a return gift, which itself endows readers with the gift of authority. "Cyclops" forces its readers to engage in exchanges of words with the tellers, to give the gift of interpretation that revises the self who gives it. Conventional relations between teller and audience clearly demarcate who is speaking and who is listening. But Joyce's revolutionary economy of reading demands that the reader's role become simultaneously less clear and more expansive as the identities of the tellers become less clear and their words more excessive: we are at once readers and authors, receivers and givers. The reader must revise his or her economy of reading, substituting a dialogical movement back and forth that admits its own provisionality. Just as Joyce and Odysseus revise their identities as authors within their own tales, so the reader must revise his or her identity as reader while reading. From "Cyclops," then, an economy of reading emerges in which an extravagant text demands an extravagant countergift of attention but resists closing the cycle of reciprocity. By inscribing his version of the Irish economy of expenditure into the text, Joyce draws the reader into a compelling dialogue with its extravagant comic economy. The result is the growth of a new flexible identity in the reader, whose reading habits become more Irish—and more Greek—as he or she reads. In the end, it is the reader who must become the taleteller and thereby come to resemble a Cyclops or an Odysseus by reciprocating or refusing Joyce's Irish gifts. The reader must expand—must become, as it were, gigantic or composite, and thus, perhaps, more heroic. In sum, Joyce reciprocates his audience both negatively and positively, sacrificing economy of meaning but offering his collective textual identity as simultaneously a gift and a critique of gifts. Therefore, neither the agonistic economy of potlatch nor the economy of charity suffices to read "Cyclops." Just as Bloom is simultaneously Irish, Jewish and Greek, the reader's social identity is complicated by the necessity of requiting Joyce's linguistic gift and identifying himself or herself with Bloom; the reader must be both Irish and Greek, at once cunning and excessive. This redefinition may again achieve a kind of political revolution, not through political economy, but through politicoecomedy.

8

Erotic Commerce I

Jymes wishes to hear from wearers of abandoned female costumes, gratefully received. . . . His jymes is out of job, would sit and write. He had lately commited one of the then commandments but she will now assist. Superior built, domestic, regular layer. Also got the boot. He appreciates it. Copies. ABORTISEMENT.

—*FW*, 181.27–33

SENTIMENTAL SOLICITATION

On both sides of Bloom's halting proclamation of the virtues of love and charity are two episodes that test this philosophy. Both "Sirens" and "Nausicaa" explore the relationships between love and commerce, between eroticism and economics. In "Sirens" the audible economy and in "Nausicaa" the visual economy of perception engage Bloom. Just as what one hears in seashells as the roaring of the sea turns out to be the sound of the hearer's own blood, so in "Sirens" and "Nausicaa" characters perceive others as projections of their own desire. Yet these self-projections paradoxically lead to reciprocal erotic exchanges that resemble gifts.

Like "Wandering Rocks," these episodes dramatize the conflict between unification and disintegration, both on the narrative surface and in the economic and social relationships between characters. This conflict is expressed as the contrast between "Love and War," also the title of one of the songs in "Sirens." War sunders persons from others;

love brings them together. As Freud argues, the erotic drive acts to "combine single human individuals, and after that families, then races, peoples and nations, into one great unity" (1930, 59). In his study of gift exchange, Hyde similarly argues that the gift economy impels and is impelled by the power of love: "gift exchange is an erotic commerce, a joining of self and other" (1983, 163); that is, gift exchange differs from market commerce by creating bonds between parties. The exchanges in "Sirens" and "Nausicaa" are erotic, then, to the degree that they involve tangible or intangible gifts, and involve gifts to the extent that they forge bonds between characters and exemplify eros.

But excessive love is as threatening to Bloom as the rampant hostility of "Cyclops"; if, in the latter, Bloom is cursed and cast out by hostile xenophobes, in "Sirens" and "Nausicaa" the threat is absorption by sentimentality and the consequent loss of identity. He must adjust his psychic economy to counter such "hyperentertainment." Whereas in "Cyclops" he counters hostility, obligatory gift exchange, and excess with a simple expression of love, in "Sirens" and "Nausicaa" he responds to excesses of "love"—sentimentality, seduction, desire—by donning a mask of mercenary skepticism that exposes the commercialism beneath the seductions. Neither polarity exists uncontaminated by the other; both episodes demonstrate the eroticism of commerce and the commercialism of eros. By blending the ingredients, Bloom finds the necessary means to retrieve his balance; but only by undergoing these exchanges can he proceed toward his climactic reconciliations with Stephen and Molly. Thus in these episodes Bloom is temporarily absorbed by a sentimentality that erases individual identity; he exchanges with another character and emerges renewed.

"Sirens" explores sentimentalism as both an emotional and an economic condition. Emotionally, sentimentalism is the unearned feeling displayed in coy sexual games and nostalgic songs—an avoidance of genuine sentiment. Economically, sentimentalism is the bad faith suggested in that now familiar epigram Stephen cribs from Meredith: *"The sentimentalist is he who would enjoy without incurring the immense debtorship for a thing done"* (9.550–51). In "Sirens" sentimentalism denotes a moral and economic sophistry that offers bogus or shopworn merchandise as genuine valuables; it is unearned emotional or economic credit. Meredith's narrator comments that sentimentalism is "a happy pastime . . . to the timid, the idle and the heartless, but a damning one to them who have anything to forfeit" (1961, 196). A gallery of the "timid and the idle," "Sirens" is populated by sentimentalists who have, if anything, too much "heart": they sedate themselves with songs that seem to reflect deep emotion but actually never penetrate the surface. The relics of old decency—Simon, Dollard, and Cowley—who sing in the Ormond music room about loss and betrayal are male sirens who solicit sympathy from their auditors; but it is the singers who are drowning. These sirens have already forfeited not only their possessions but also their claim on their listeners' sympathy. Indeed, their songs actually prevent them from "feeling the pain that might create in them genuine compassion and generosity," or engender it in others (Sicari 1990, 484). To succumb to these sirens' solicitations is to be immersed in what Joyce called the "warm, comfortable fog" of sentimentalism and to drown in its murky "backwash" (quoted in Power 1974, 57). It is to become a relic oneself. Nearly succumbing, Bloom resists the solicitations of several sirens. The central exchange in the episode—the aural encounter between Simon and Bloom, Stephen's consubstantial and transubstantial fathers—demonstrates how Bloom uses sentimentalism without drowning in it. His temporary exchange of identities with Simon releases Bloom from sentimentality and steels him against further emotional temptations, while also endowing him with a metaphorical crown, a gift of fatherhood and authority that he later passes on to Stephen.

The most obvious analogues to Homer's sirens are the barmaids Mina Kennedy and Lydia Douce, who tempt wayward males, but without singing. Like Gerty MacDowell constantly aware of the male eyes upon them, they present their bodies as fields to display commodities: "They pawed their blouses, both of black satin, two and nine a yard . . . and two and seven" (11.110–11). Prices, those "wooing glances cast at money by commodities" (Marx, quoted in Crosby 1991, 5), embody several forms of exchange: the spurious and fleeting erotic relationship between cash and commodities, which come together in brief exchanges; the seduction of women by the fashion system and women's seduction of men through such consumption; and the general condition of women as commodities on the marriage market. Thus the barmaids' hair and skin become identifying synecdoches: bronze for Miss Douce, gold for Miss Kennedy (11.64); their bodies become precious or semiprecious metals, currency in the sexual marketplace. Despite earning but "eighteen bob a week," according to Bloom (11.1076–77), they must use their earnings to decorate themselves with finery and thus get men to "shell out the dibs" (11.1077).[1] But they are not really golden, and their flirting reveals through the veil of giggles a desperate longing to escape from their jobs and lonely lives. Since their worth can be proven only by their ability to prompt purchases from men—of alcohol or of themselves—their bodies are their most valuable possessions. Thus, as she flirts with Boylan and Lenehan, Miss Douce describes herself as "fine goods in small parcels" (11.368). Perhaps not so fine: beneath the satin she and her friend fear that they are more brass than gold, and thus that they cannot induce any male to purchase. In fact, the frowsy whore who appears at the end of the episode is an image of an all-too-likely future.[2]

Given this atmosphere, the presence of the sentimentalist Lenehan and the "gallant" Boylan is quite appropriate. In dressing themselves as commodities, the barmaids play into the hands of men like Boylan who exploit them without incurring the debtorship of emotional commitment. Identified by his fashionable "gay hat" (11.302), Boylan is as much a commodity as they. Thus the commerce of sex is potentially reciprocal: they hope he will "purchase" them, but he also offers himself as a valuable product by flaunting his conspicuous consumption. Indeed, Boylan and the barmaids *are* clothes; the sexual marketplace transforms them into synecdoches of themselves, as erotic desire becomes a commercial competition that reduces them to hats, blouses, and flowers in lapels.

The barmaids often appear as focal points of mirrored reciprocal desire. Miss Douce, for example, is seen "in the barmirror gildedlittered where hock and claret glasses shimmered" (11.118); when she serves a customer she glances sideways to observe herself (11.214); near the end of the episode, Bloom sees her looking in the mirror and wonders, "Is that the best side of her face? They always know" (11.1046). Boylan, "eyed, eyed" her: each eyes the other in reciprocal regard, but his eyes, reflected in Miss Douce's mirror, also gaze at himself (11.419). Just as Miss Douce reflects male desires and fanta-

---

1. If Bloom's estimate is correct, the barmaids earn a little more than Stephen Dedalus, who makes between 16 and 17 bob per week and would reach his monthly earnings of £3 12s in four weeks. Miss Kennedy's golden hair also foreshadows Gerty's "wealth of wonderful hair" (13.116).

2. Walzl illustrates how limited employment opportunities were for women in Joyce's Dublin (1982, 37–44). Of the most common occupations for women, the only one the barmaids have any chance of pursuing would seem to be "tavern owners" (Walzl 1982, 41). O'Brien estimates that between 3 and 4 percent of adult females in Dublin at the time were prostitutes (1982, 193), and so Lydia or Mina might conceivably be driven to that trade eventually.

sies, so Boylan reflects her yearning for financial security; if she has
come to look at herself as males do, Boylan also regards himself as a
third person might. As in "Wandering Rocks," mirror images signify
not true reciprocity, a dynamic and shared flow of income and outgo,
but narcissism: the characters desire their own images, reconstituted.
This spurious reciprocity finds an aural analogue in the shell Miss
Douce later shares with George Lidwell and foreshadows the mutual
projections that create a momentary unity between Gerty and Bloom.

Much of the verbal richness of the episode derives from its tropic
exchanges, its violations of the economy of realism. Words and
phrases leap free of signification to advertise themselves as music or
testaments to the narrator's playful spirit. "Sirens" subjects words to
almost ceaseless transformations, as if flouting the conventions of
realism by an excessive love of sound. One goal of literary realism
was to replace the "monstrously disproportionate role" played by love
in the sentimental novel "with a more balanced vision of 'human
feelings in their true proportion and relation.' " Realism thus valorizes the "natural economy of pain," instructing readers how to repudiate the unhappiness that results from false ideals (Michaels 1987,
38). If so, "Sirens" first mimics the sentimental novel as a prelude to
subverting it; its textual excesses satirize emotional excess. In demonstrating the dangers of sentimentality, "Sirens" uses its antirealist surface to evoke an emotional realism, just as Bloom embraces and then
moves beyond pain (Sicari 1990, 481).

One of Joyce's most significant tropic exchanges or puns here is
introduced with the lawyer George Lidwell. A "suave solicitor"
(11.562), Lidwell has a vocation that gains broader connotations after
Miss Douce entices him into the bar: "George Lidwell, suave, solicited,
held a lydiahand" (11.567). The rest of the episode rings changes on
the word, as the characters embody varieties of sexual, emotional, or
economic solicitation. Simon and the other singers solicit attention
and drinks; Lenehan solicits Boylan's money; the barmaids solicit the
males' sexual desire; Lidwell solicits in court and at the bar; Bloom
answers Martha's letter soliciting him to "tell me more" with his own
letter soliciting sympathy; the whore of the lane tries to solicit Bloom.
In "Sirens" sentimentality is fueled by solicitations, by attempts to
receive unearned emotional credit.[3] Lidwell solicits Miss Douce's attentions by various stratagems, including sharing a seashell with her:

---

3. The character most often referred to as a "solicitor" is John Henry Menton,
Dignam's former employer and Molly's erstwhile suitor. She identifies the two forms
of soliciting when she recalls Menton's dalliances: "Menton . . . and he not long married

"she bore lightly the spiked and winding seahorn that he George Lidwell, solicitor, might hear" (11.923–24). The reciprocity of this enticement is implied in the portmanteau formations "Lidlydia-well" (11.820) and "Lidlyd" (11.39); their encounter is mutual self-admiration.

The characterization of George Lidwell as a lecher probably owes something to the real John G. Lidwell's business dealings with Joyce. In 1912, Joyce tried to enlist his legal help to prevent George Roberts's censorship of allegedly offensive passages in *Dubliners*. Although Lidwell did not think that the censors would take much notice, he too objected to the "questionable taste" of the characters' references to the king in "Ivy Day" and was disgusted by the suggested masturbation in "An Encounter" (*L* II 306–7). After much coaxing by Joyce, Lidwell finally wrote to Roberts, advising him to proceed with publication. He never did; in fact, Lidwell ultimately took Roberts's side (*JJ* 331)! But Joyce repaid Lidwell for his squeamishness and ineffective advocacy by turning him into a man whose practice is restricted to soliciting barmaids. Scrupulous meanness again reaches from *Dubliners* to *Ulysses*, as Joyce's pun on "solicitor" enables him to litigate against Lidwell, to repay with paper currency —his book—those who attempted to litigate against his books.[4] Thus later in the episode Bloom passes Barry's legal offices and comments, "Twentyfour solicitors in that one house. Counted them. Litigation. Love one another. . . . Messrs Pick and Pocket have power of attorney" (11.1225–27). If solicitation is the sentimentalists' form of love, litigation is the legalists' form of war, a force that sets persons against one another for financial gain and breaks the community into fragments (cf. Sicari 1990, 484).

The chief "solicitors" in the episode, however, are those sentimental singers of Simon Dedalus's circle. Simon also flirts with Miss Douce, while chiding her for "tempting poor simple males," including "simple Simon" (11.202; 207).[5] Although he begrudges money for his children, he needs no coaxing to order himself "some fresh water and

---

flirting with a young girl at Pooles Myriorama . . . of all the big stupoes I ever met and thats called a solicitor" (18.39–43).

4. As Richard Ellmann notes, Lidwell was a poor choice in the first place, since his practice was limited to police court work (*JJ* 329). Joyce had to seek out Lidwell in the Ormond bar to solicit his help; now he fixes him there forever (*JJ* 330).

5. The sobriquet seems apt, since one verse of that nursery rhyme goes: "Said the pieman to Simple Simon / 'Show first your penny.' / Said Simple Simon to the pieman / 'Indeed, I haven't any' " (Gifford 1988, 296).

a half glass of whisky" (11.211), and Miss Douce with alacrity serves him "gold whisky" (11.215–16), the only gold that regularly flows through his life. Dedalus is joined in the music room by two other failures, Father Cowley and Ben Dollard, who are finishing their deliberations about Cowley's rent difficulties with the Reverend Mr. Love (11.437–38). Thinking of Cowley's landlord, Dollard sings the wrong part of *Love and War* and then comments "Love or money" (11.533–34). Neither he nor Cowley can claim much of either. Instead, Simon and his sentimental friends try to compensate for their economic insuffiency by circulating the more common currency of Joyce's Dublin—songs and booze.

The singers recall the Blooms' good turn in furnishing Dollard with a pair of pants for a concert, when the Blooms lived on Holles Street and Molly was forced to sell "left-off" clothes for extra money (11.487–97).[6] Bloom's version casts a more comical light on the incident. "Trousers tight as a drum on him. . . . With all his belongings on show" (11.555–57): Dollard's phallic "belongings"—his "corporal assets," along with his voice the only belongings he has—solicited (perhaps inadvertently) sexual attention. A decent soul, Dollard is a "bit addled now. Thinks he'll win in *Answers*, poets' picture puzzle. We hand you crisp five pound note" (11.1023–24). Like many other Dubliners, he wants to win money without working: he is definitely idle, if not heartless. Another relic of old decency, Dollard has drunk himself into bankruptcy: "Big ships' chandler's business he did once. . . . Failed to the tune of ten thousand pounds. Now in the Iveagh home. . . . Number one Bass did that for him" (11.1012–15). The Iveagh home for "impecunious commercial men" was founded by the heir of the Guinness brewing fortune, a company to whom many of the inhabitants owed their dissolution.[7] As Bloom observes, "Wreck their lives. Then build cubicles to end their days in" (11.1018–19). Dollard's business "failed to the tune" of ten thousand pounds, and now he substitutes nostalgic tunes of failure for business enterprises, a substitution that shields him from the necessity of paying the "im-

---

6. In "Penelope," Molly recollects the event from a slightly different perspective: "he said I could pose for a picture naked to some rich fellow in Holles street when he lost the job in Helys and I was selling the clothes and strumming in the coffee palace would I be like that bath of the nymph with my hair down" (18.560–63). Here Molly is used as a siren and solicitor.

7. This seems to be an anachronism, however, since the Iveagh home did not open until either 1905 (O'Brien 1982, 168) or 1906 (Adams 1962, 65). Of course, the symbolic appropriateness of the home makes this "error" unimportant. In 1912, Joyce's own father lived in the Iveagh home (*L* II 217).

mense debtorship" for his inadequacy. His accompanist, the spoiled priest Bob Cowley, has solicited Dollard's help but, like Ben, "stuns himself" with music; for him it is a "kind of drunkenness. . . . All ears. . . . Eyes shut. Head nodding in time. Dotty. . . . Thinking strictly prohibited" (11.1191–94).[8]

The singers do not know that Bloom is in the next room, eating dinner with Simon's brother-in-law, Richie Goulding, who resembles them more than he does Bloom. Indeed, drinking seems to have permanently damaged Richie's health: "Backache he. Bright's bright eye. Next item on the programme. Paying the piper. . . . Sings too: *Down among the dead men.* Appropriate" (11.615–17). Unlike Simon, Richie at least pretends to save money, but his economies are a spendthrift's mask. "Fecking matches from counters to save. Then squander a sovereign in dribs and drabs. And when he's wanted not a farthing. Screwed refusing to pay his fare" (11.619–22). His avoidance of debtorship marks him as an economic sentimentalist, just as his lugubrious response to Simon's song marks him as a emotional one. Thus, as Simon sings *All is lost now,* Bloom sees the song written on Richie's "Face of the all is lost. . . . Now begging letters he sends his son with. . . . Wouldn't trouble only I was expecting some money" (11.646–49). Like Simon, Goulding is reduced to soliciting money from acquaintances. In fact, each character is identified with a song: Goulding shows the face of "all is lost"; Dollard, apparently the "last of his race" (11.1065), is *The Croppy Boy,* "a bit of a natural" (11.1249) grown old and feeble, now exhorting his listeners to shed a tear for him; Cowley, who chides Dollard for singing the wrong verse of *Love and War,* is himself "absorbed" and paralyzed by sentimentality (11.530); Simon, similarly absorbed by the character of Lionel when he sings *M'Appari,* fills his time with "idle dreaming," while bemoaning "lost ones" (11.694; 740)—Parnell, his deceased wife, and his own departed gentility. Like the songs, these characters are variations on a single theme: they are lost ones all.

As we have seen, love and war are the antinomies around which Bloom's encounters in the middle episodes revolve.[9] The danger in

8. Cowley also seems to be a mark for other solicitors: he fell for M'Coy's "valise tack" and "never heard tidings of [his suitcase] from that good day [a year ago] to this" (5.180–82).

9. This shuttling between love and war may again recall the cosmology of Empedocles. For Empedocles (as for Joyce in "Sirens") Love is a synthesizing, unifying force, and Strife a force of disintegration. For extensive discussions of Empedocles' poetic cosmology, see Wheelwright (1966, 122–39), Cornford ([1912] 1957, 224–42), and Lambridis (1976).

love is absolute absorption, which is precisely what occurs during Simon's song—"Love that is singing" (11.681)—ending with a fusion of singer, song and hearer. But the erotic charge in Simon's song is also what enables Bloom to experience and purge himself of his dejection and jealousy. In turn, this catharsis allows him to marshal an ironic detachment that counteracts the sentimentality of the singers in Simon's circle. Bloom's exchange with Simon gives him a gift that compensates for his troubled love life, rectifies a deficit in his psychic economy, and again yields psychic balance.

Simon's rendition of *M'Appari* ("When first I saw that form endearing"), from *Martha,* is the loveliest and the most impressive performance in the episode. After being cajoled into singing, Simon announces that he is "most deeply obliged by your kind solicitations" (11.655–56) and then solicits his audience: "I have no money but if you will lend me your attention I shall endeavour to sing to you of a heart bowed down" (11.658–59). Just as his son solicited the belief and attention of his interlocutors in "Aeolus" and "Scylla and Charybdis," here Simon requests attention—and emotional credit— in return for his aural currency.[10] A master of financial solicitation, Simon touches his friends for money; likewise his voice gives and withholds, "touching their still ears with words" (11.676): the aural economy mimics the financial one. In spite of Bloom's skepticism, the song temporarily touches him deeply, and he contributes his own sense of loss to the song's emotional economy as, "Braintipped, cheek touched with flame, they listened feeling that flow endearing flow over skin limbs human heart soul spine" (11.668–69).

Few readers miss the song's sexual burden. Bloom himself muses that "tenors get women by the score. Increase their flow" (11.686). But the song is both more and less than a male seduction; indeed, its imagery is hermaphroditic, pairing pulsing phallic virility with feminine liquidity: "Tenderness it welled: slow, swelling, full it throbbed. . . . Ha, give! Take! Throb, a throb, a pulsing, proud erect. . . . flood of warm jamjam lickitup secretness flowed to flow in music out, in desire, dark to lick flow invading. Tipping her tepping her tapping her topping her. . . . Flood, gush, flow, joygush, tupthrob. Now! Lan-

---

10. The phrasing of Simon's announcement is a bit mystifying, however: why would he say that he has no money and then request attention? It would make more sense to assure the audience that it does not matter whether *they* have money, since they need only lend attention. But his preface does furnish an appropriately pitiful tone to his song.

guage of love" (11.701–2; 705–9). Simon's siren song entices his auditors to participate in an aural commerce of give-and-take that mimics
the reciprocal exchanges of sexual intercourse. It inspires Bloom to
remember when he first saw Molly's "form endearing" and, as it proceeds, lures him into the pulse of the music and the lyrics' lonely
pleas, until the final soaring note attains a rapturous height: "It
soared, a bird, it held its flight, a swift pure cry, . . . sustained, to
come, . . . long breath he breath long life, soaring high, high resplen-
dent, aflame, crowned, high in the effulgence symbolistic, high, of
the etherial bosom, high, of the high vast irradiation everywhere all
soaring all around about the all, the endlessnessnessness. . . . . . . —
To me! Siopold! Consumed" (11.745–53). Eros blends Lionel with
Leopold and Simon in a melding of selves that exemplifies the economy of gift exchange. Like gifts, the song erases boundaries, its erotic
commerce engendering a "copula: a bond, a band, a link by which
the several are knit into one" (Hyde 1983, 153). As in gift exchange,
the giver is embodied in his gift of song, and momentarily a kind of
collective self is generated (Hyde 1983, 17) that confirms and renews
the identities of the singer and auditors. In the merger of fathers and
lovers in the song, Simon, whose name means "hearer," transmits his
identity to Bloom, *his* hearer, who temporarily becomes a "simon."
For a moment Bloom is no longer himself, but everyman and noman.
Thus Hugh Kenner is surely wrong when he asserts that Bloom "undergoes rape by voice" (1987, 91); Bloom participates in the song's
reciprocal erotic commerce, as the blending of names implies. A total
failure in the financial economy, Simon briefly succeeds in the aural
erotic economy.

But the moment is fleeting, and the climactic words carry their
own satirical intimations. The narrator's description of the song borrows from Doughy Dan's speech in "Aeolus" (cf. 7.328), a gaseous
effusion that disgusted even Simon, and thereby suggests that Simon's song is a musical version of Dawson's sentimental rhetoric. Like
Stephen, who felt briefly attracted by the speeches in "Aeolus," Bloom
is pulled into the song's sentimental excesses. Like Odysseus, Bloom
is in danger of drowning in the siren song's sentiment. But not only
does he eventually regain his distance; in fact, he resists all along.
Even before his final fusion with Simon and his song, he comments
on the singer's absurdity: "Silly man! Could have made oceans of
money. Singing wrong words. Wore out his wife: now sings. But hard
to tell. Only the two themselves" (11.695–97). Although Simon can
still occasionally produce a "glorious tone," alcohol has damaged his

voice. Even Dollard tells him that with "seven days in jail . . . on bread and water" he'd "sing like a garden thrush" (11.772–73). Indeed, the song's aqueous imagery implies that, as Jackson Cope suggests, "Simon Dedalus is drowning," but not in "oceans of money" (1974, 224). Instead he wades in tides of foggy sentimentalism that draw him under and at the same time envelop him in a mist that prevents him from recognizing his condition. Still, the copious eroticism of Simon's voice does help Bloom to expel some self-pity about his impending cuckolding, and thus prompts a renewal of his sexuality that is further enhanced in "Nausicaa."

In any case, Simon is more attractive here than perhaps anywhere else in *Ulysses,* as Joyce balances his condemnation by demonstrating Simon's talent and humor. The man can sing! Thus we are more likely to excuse his "hysterical devotion" (Kaye 1957, 31) to the memory of his wife and his voluminous self-pity. An ambiguous figure, Simon is capable of grand emotion, but he is also drugged by false emotions and bad faith. Still, his "extravagant disposition" (the trait that Joyce recognized as crucial to his own art) remains a key element in the episode's verbal economy. Like Simon, Joyce solicits our attention, begs for our tolerance and complicity with his excessive verbal expenditure and playfulness. Just as Bloom responds to the song by mentally staging his own sexual drama, the reader here is asked to contribute his or her own ear, eyes and sympathetic attention. Such attention makes the reader an accomplice in both the characters' sentimental solicitations and in the narrator's expenditures of verbal currency; if one resists, then he or she is guilty of the self-absorption of Lidwell or the deafness of the waiter Pat. Even as it satirizes Simon's excesses, then, the text also valorizes them and recognizes his vigor and humanity. At the same time, however, Bloom's resistance provides a model for the reader, who must resist drowning in the narrator's playful solicitations just as Bloom must ultimately repudiate his absorption into Simon's nostalgia. Like Bloom, the reader must employ both sympathy and skepticism; he or she must give and withdraw, engaging the text fully and then disengaging in an economy that mimics the erotic commerce of sex.

The love about which Simon sings is also the magical verbal formula Stephen seeks in the "word known to all men." Here the word is given by a hermaphroditic father, and though the source seems to taint it, the message is received, as Bloom proves in "Cyclops." Identified by and through his voice as Stephen's father, Simon yields that mystical estate to Bloom in exchange for his active attention in their aural exchange (Cope 1974, 233). Through his penetration by Simon's voice, Bloom is "crowned" (11.747): the very symbol of sovereignty and fatherhood that Stephen seeks is Simon's vocal gift to Bloom, who will replace him. Now a king, Bloom is vested with Stephen's name, *stephanos*, which he later returns to him, not only through paternal solicitation, but by accepting Stephen's crown coins as surety for his debts. Bloom's gifts of sympathy and money thus help to restore Stephen's identity, and, thereby, perhaps his artistic destiny.

Once he has bestowed his gift on Bloom, Simon is no longer needed. Left behind like a snake's discarded skin, he disappears from the novel. Simon drowns; Bloom surfaces by a characteristic recourse to science: "numbers it is. All music when you come to think. . . . Musemathematics. And you think you're listening to the etherial. But suppose you said it like: Martha, seven times nine minus x is thirtyfive thousand. Fall quite flat" (11.830–37). His analysis removes him from the erotic community in the Ormond and returns him to his discrete, analytical self; whereas eros synthesized, numbers now tear asunder (11.804). Newly composed, Bloom begins to compose his letter to Martha. Nevertheless, the juxtaposition of Simon's song and Bloom's letter identifies both messages as forms of solicitation using the "language of flow" (11.298; both are also addressed to a Martha). But if Bloom's letter seems nearly as sentimental as Simon's song, it is also calculated to "Play on her heartstrings pursestrings too" (11.715). The mercenary aspects of the correspondence are underscored constantly by association with money. Before entering the Ormond, Bloom purchased for twopence (11.306) "two sheets cream vellum paper one reserve two envelopes" (11.295). At the same moment he espies Boylan crossing the same "Essex bridge" that he had earlier crossed (11.302): Bloom's letter partially compensates for Boylan's assignation with Molly, while responding to Martha's own solicitation ("tell me"), and to Simon's solicitation of "Martha."

As Bloom writes, he protects himself from Goulding's curiosity by pretending to be "answering an ad" (11.886), which, of course, he is. Along with the letter he sends a present, which substitutes for his inability to write the long letter that Martha asked for (11.714). Bloom has also regained enough presence of mind to calculate his budget: "Five Dig. Two about here. Penny the gulls. Elijah is com. Seven Davy Byrne's. Is eight about. Say half a crown. My poor little pres: p.o. two and six" (11.866–68). Typically, he resorts to price reckoning to quell anxiety and guilt and restore stability. Once again, however, these calculations suggest that his erotic commerce is as much commercial as erotic; like music, perhaps love may be reduced to juggling figures. Moreover, Bloom continues the liaison under a false name, clearly a case of failing to "incur the immense debtorship" for the thing done; in that regard this relationship is also an example of sentimentalism.

The shape of the letter contrasts with the syntactical flow of Simon's song; because of Bloom's mixed motives and emotions, the text comes out "in bits" (11.559), as if his identity has been disseminated by the songs. "Love" is now infused with pessimistic skepticism, as syntactical fragmentation suggests his newfound detachment. Here is how the letter reads, pieced together from broken words and phrases and with ellipses eliminated:

> *Dear Mady,*
>   *I got your letter and flower. But it is utterly* impossible *to write today. Please accept my poor little present enclosed. Do you despise me?*
>   *Your letter made me so excited. Why do you call me naughty? Are you naughty too? Bye for today. Yes, yes, I will tell you all. I want to. You must believe me. It is true. Write me a long letter. It will excite me. You know how. In haste,*
>
>   *Henry*
>
> *P.S. How will you punish me? Tell me I want to know. H.*
> *P.P.S. I feel so sad today. So lonely.* (11.861–94)

Although he recognizes its hyperbole—"Too poetical that about the sad. Music did that" (11.904)—Bloom's letter is his siren song, his sentimental solicitation, a description of a melancholy mood aimed at inspiring the reciprocal sentiment in her. As he writes, he thinks "Why do you call me naught?": the elided letter reiterates that in this correspondence he is a naught, an "everyman and noman." But this anonymity is liberating. Moreover, the fact that the half-crown gift follows immediately upon Simon's musical gift of a "crown" implies that Bloom acquires from Simon both the self-possession and the sentimentality needed to write the letter: Simon touched him, and now he touches Martha, while also giving her half a crown. The emotion is passed on like a circulating coin. But though the half crown is presented as a gift, the letter also contains a clear request for requital (emotional or sexual, rather than financial) in the postscript, where he echoes her letter by asking her to "tell me." Unlike Simon, Bloom retains a sense of his own absurdity, a self-consciousness that prevents him from fully crediting his own half-truth. The letter also purges his dejection, freeing him from the bonds of sentiment and enabling him to leave the dining room. Its mixture of eros and commerciality further helps to restore the balance to Bloom's psychic economy.

As he prepares to depart, Bloom views the flirting between Lidwell and Lydia more skeptically, noticing even the unromantic "fever [blister] near her mouth" (11.940–41). The shell they share seems only a mercenary ploy for sexual attention, spurious because it only magnifies the sound of the hearer's own blood; its communality and universality are mere narcissism. Bloom predicts the future of the Ormond's female sirens with a stringent skepticism that foreshadows his mood in the second half of "Nausicaa": "Virgin should say: or fingered only. Write something on it: page. If not what becomes of them? Decline, despair" (11.1086–87). But even in this mood he is fairly generous to Pat, the "bothered" (i.e., deaf) waiter. "One and nine. Penny for yourself. Here. Give twopence tip" (11.1002; according to his final budget, however, he actually leaves threepence, since his total for the dinner is given as 2s [17.1467]).[11] Leaving, he hears a part of Dollard's "*trenchant*" rendition (6.147) of *The Croppy Boy*. Whereas Simon sang of love, Dollard sings of war, of "unlove" (11.1007), but Bloom resists his song easily by recalling Dollard's economic decline. The song does, however, briefly induce melancholic musings: "I too. Last of my race. . . . No son. Rudy. Too late now. . . . Hate. Love. Those are names. Soon I am old" (11.1066–69). Because it is a landlord's name, "Love" now seems contaminated by political and economic tyrannies; it too is only a deceptive siren song. But whereas Simon's song resulted in a momentary fusion of singer and audience, Bloom's response to Dollard's "lugugugubrious" music illustrates his alienation from that circle of victims. When Dollard finishes, Bloom comments, "General chorus off for a swill to wash it down. Glad I avoided" (11.1144–45). His brief immersion in Simon's song has not only purged him of melancholy dejection; it has also steeled him against the magnetism of Irish sacrificial patriotism. "Popped corks, splashes of beerfroth, stacks of empties" (11.1111): these remnants of the swill recall the scene in "Ivy Day in the Committee Room" and represent a similarly exhausted world.

Now on his way to the unwelcome meeting with Cunningham at Kiernan's to help arrange the insurance for Mrs. Dignam, Bloom,

---

11. By many standards, however, even a threepence tip is not excessively generous, since it amounts to slightly less than 15 percent of his 21d dinner.

having resisted the sirens' sentimental solicitations, leaves them behind. But one siren still lurks—"a frowsy whore with black straw
sailor hat askew"—and approaches him (11.1252). Though he may
have sampled her wares in the past, this time he lets her pass. Identified by her black straw hat, this whore reappears in "Eumaeus" trying
to bring "more grist to her mill" (16.704–6). A synecdoche of identity
and mark of her economic condition (like her, it is a relic), the hat
foreshadows the newly bought hat worn by Gerty MacDowell, as well
as Molly's similar headgear (17.2103); sadly, the whore of the lane
may also be an image of Gerty's possible future. In fact, the black hat
has signified prostitution since *Stephen Hero,* where the ur-Daedalus
observes that "the woman in the black straw hat gave something before she sold her body to the State" and generalizes about the similarity between married women and whores (*SH* 202–3). In "Eumaeus,"
Bloom comments to Stephen that "it beats me . . . how a wretched
creature like that . . . reeking with disease can be barefaced enough
to solicit" (16.728–30). Here Bloom is more sympathetic to her condition and understands her role as both merchant and merchandise:
"Let her pass. Course everything is dear if you don't want it. That's
what a good salesman is. Make you buy what he wants to sell"
(11.1264–66). She is a bad salesperson not because she buys dear
and sells cheap, but because her merchandise has been devalued by
overuse. The shopworn whore fits the episode's atmosphere of seedy
emotional and sexual trafficking. Though easy to resist, she represents the underlying import of all the episode's solicitations—sirens
advertise great value where it does not exist.

Avoiding her eyes, Bloom looks into "Lionel Marks's antique
saleshop window" at a "battered . . . melodeon oozing maggoty blow-
bags. Bargain: six bob" (11.1261–64). Like the whore, barmaids and
singers, the melodeon is shabby, worn-out merchandise whose price,
its "wooing glance," advertises it as a bargain. The melodeon serves
as an objective correlative for all the sirens in the episode. Like the
singers, it can still produce music, but its songs seem cheap and tinny.
The north bank of the Liffey where Bloom now walks, a place of
"cast-off splendours" that Kenner has called "Dublin's Sargasso Sea"
(1987, 87), resembles the scene in the Ormond. Hence, the cast-off
splendours in the music room now raise their glasses again, their
broken names—"Lid, De, Cow, Ker, Doll" (11.1271)—illustrating not
only their personal economic disintegration but also the dissolution
of the fabric of the community. United only in their addictions, the
characters' fusion actually produces fragmentation. Bloom's final fart,

accompanying his recollection of Robert Emmet's stirring last words, also comments upon both the ersatz charms of the Ormond's sirens and the futility of the sentimental patriotism they peddle in songs like *The Croppy Boy*. As McArthur aptly notes, the episode's final siren is "the suffering soul of Ireland and the muse of self-destruction" (1988, 116). Emmet, that "gallant" hero (11.1274), has become a cheap kitsch item. Like the street where Bloom walks, the watery sentimental patriotism of Simon and company is exposed as "a backwash into which every kind of rubbish has been cluttered" (Joyce, quoted in Power 1974, 57).

While Lidwell, Dedalus, Cowley, Kernan and Dollard drown each other, Bloom surfaces, "undrowned" (Cope 1974, 224). His brief immersion has, however, revealed the close relationship between economic and emotional sentimentality: both traffick in bad faith, and both attempt to get something for nothing. In his temporary absorption by Simon's sentimental rendition of "love," Bloom exchanges selves with Simon, who now disappears from the novel, his paternity transferred to Stephen's surrogate father. Thus if, like "Wandering Rocks" and "Cyclops," this episode is structured around distortions of reciprocity and exchange, its ambience of deceptive "love" at least enables Bloom to carry out a significant exchange and thereby free himself from melancholy; he receives a gift from Simon and gives one to Martha. Moreover, if eros is unmasked as a form of commerce, this commerce is shown to be potentially erotic, capable of drawing individuals together to share and purge painful emotions.

TWICE NOUGHT MAKES ONE

Love for Sale

Worn out from his encounter with the hostile Cyclopes in Kiernan's and his long vigil in the house of mourning, Bloom is tempted at twilight by another siren, the "lovely seaside girl" Gerty MacDowell, in "a visual restaging" of the aural temptations of "Sirens" (Senn 1984, 176). The structure of the episode—a pair of barely overlapping monologues—implies a balance of opposed viewpoints. The Linati schema lists the episode's symbol as "The Projected Mirage," implying that neither one sees the other as he or she really is; instead both respond to a self-projection, a visual equivalent of the seashell in "Sirens." The discreteness of the sections again suggests that each character is gazing into a cracked looking glass. But in spite these distortions and their failure to achieve actual physical touch, Bloom and Gerty do engage in a reciprocal exchange mediated through the language of objects and the currency of signs that is advertising. By focusing on the body and its decoration, this currency becomes a "language of love," or at least of the erotic. Even though Bloom's and Gerty's concerns are often commercial, their encounter is also erotic: like a gift exchange, their erotic commerce yokes and renews them by engendering an eroticized self through the other's imaginative reading.

The opening paragraphs recall the glorifying parodic insertions in "Cyclops." This sentimentalizing narrator renders everything in excessively lovely terms: the day lingers "lovingly on sea and strand" (13.3); Jacky and Tommy Caffrey are "darling little fellows" with "endearing ways" (13.17–18); their sister Cissy is "lovable in the extreme" (13.37–38). It is also an eroticizing idiom: the phallic "promontory" of Howth guards the sea, as the evening embraces the world (13.4; 1). Like Cissy, the narrator is adept at "smoothing over life's tiny troubles," at coating with "golden syrup" the castor oil of the characters' flaws and economic struggles (13.57; 32). The style is saturated with advertising language, and indeed Joyce referred to this discourse as if he were an adman with a new campaign, proudly writing to Budgen of this "nambypamby jammy marmalady drawersy (alto la!) style with effects of incense, mariolatry, masturbation, stewed cockles, painter's palette, chitchat, circumlocutions, etc etc.," which he named "specially new fizzing style (Patent NO 7728S. P. Z. P. B. P. L. P.)" (*L* I, 135, 132). A prime example of Kenner's "Uncle Charles Principle" (1978, 17), Gerty's section appears to be another collection of bad and doubtful ingredients adapted from subliterary material: the scene is painted in the pastels of sentimental novelettes and the pages of women's magazines.[12] The first half of "Nausicaa" also exemplifies Bakhtin's "ennobled style": a discourse that presents a "pose of respectability" but remains static and inert, representing "the restricted world view of a man [or woman] trying to preserve one and the same immobile pose" and avoiding "associations with

12. In the "Uncle Charles Principle" the narrative vocabulary and manner are "pervaded by a little cloud of idioms which a character might use if he [or she] were managing the narrative" (Kenner 1978, 17). Several writers have discussed the influence of one major source, *The Lamplighter* by Maria S. Cummins, an 1854 novel whose heroine, Gerty Flint, shares many of Gerty MacDowell's aspirations, if not her destiny. For discussion of Joyce's debts to this source, see Richards (1990, 212–13, 219–22). As Benstock notes, however (1991, 162), Gerty's own reference to the book sounds suspiciously like the title page, which is probably as far as she has read.

crude real life" (1981, 385). Thus the painterly metaphors in the text demonstrate the attempt to freeze and reify the world's dangerous flux, just as its euphemisms suppress "crude real life" in favor of sweetness and light.

Permeated by commodity culture, the style also resembles Schudson's "capitalist realism," the typical discourse of advertising. As we have seen, this style "simplifies and typifies" the world by showing lives worth emulating, and presents the production of better goods as true progress (1984, 215). It represents as normative those rare moments of bliss or satisfaction derived from consumption, romanticizing the present and removing language and objects from their own and human history (Schudson 1984, 220, 218). The result is that social life is subsumed by private consumption. By suppressing unpleasant facts and processes that might disrupt its veneer, this discourse—like nineteenth-century realism—suppresses its own condition as representation. To use Michaels's terms, the first half of "Nausicaa" is grounded upon a "goldbug aesthetic" that stages Gerty's desire to make herself "equal to [her] face value, to become gold" (1987, 22): if Gerty can be what she dreams, then she will become what she seems, "good as gold" (13.34), rather than a copy of popular paper images. Thus the narrative, filtered through Gerty, turns processes into facts, the artificial into the natural, surfaces into substance. As in the realistic novel, in Gerty's world all objects have price tags, and not only because she must spend frugally; the prices seduce her into believing that all fantasies can be purchased. This section is a picture of Gerty's mind, a creative one constantly struggling to reshape the world into an ideal image; Gerty is thus an artist of capitalist "realism" who aims to transform the real into a collection of surfaces, objects and commodities—static entities that she can manipulate and control, unlike the threatening and unstable world of unsatisfied desire in which she really lives.

"But who was Gerty" (13.78)? The answer describes not so much Gerty as her clothes, cosmetics and cures. Moving without syntactic marking from the foggy clichés of sentimental fiction to the language of magazine ads to Gerty's own halting idiolect, the prose paints her as a "specimen" (13.81): "Her figure was slight and graceful, inclining even to fragility but those iron jelloids she had been taking of late had done her a world of good much better than the Widow Welch's female pills and she was much better of those discharges she used to get and that tired feeling. . . . Her hands were of finely veined alabaster with tapering fingers and as white as lemonjuice and queen of ointments could make them" (13.83–90). Buried in the lower-middle class, with limited education and little access to other sources of information about goods and services, Gerty is precisely the kind of person most susceptible to advertising. The careful delineation of her physical "improvements" implies that Gerty's labor is consumption, that she works diligently to make herself attractive according to the dictates of fashion magazines.[13] So of course her "silkily seductive" eyebrows are not strictly hers: "it was Madame Vera Verity, directress of the Woman Beautiful page of the Princess Novelette, who had first advised her to try eyebrowleine which gave that haunting expression to the eyes, so becoming in leaders of fashion" (13.109–12). "That tired feeling" and "that haunting expression": just as Gerty's self-image imitates a commodified femininity, so even her physical complaints seem less her own than a manufactured product of the patent medicine system. Thomas Richards and Garry Leonard have persuasively shown how Gerty's consciousness is a product of ads. I would argue, indeed, that the textual Gerty *is* an ad, a glorified version of the other Gerty MacDowell who offers this Gerty to enhance the value of the commodity she is attempting to market—that other Gerty, a limping, no longer adolescent, lower-middle class woman (cf. Barthel 1988, 150).

Gerty has bought not just clothes but the entire ideology of advertising, including its ontology of objects. A "votary of Dame Fashion," she wears "a neat blouse of electric blue selftinted by dolly dyes (because it was expected in the *Lady's Pictorial* that electric blue would be worn) with a smart vee opening down to the division. . . . She wore a coquettish little love of a hat of wideleaved nigger straw contrast trimmed with an underbrim of eggblue chenille and at the side a butterfly bow of silk to tone" (13.148–58). The "passive imperative" mood ("it was expected") gathers authority through anonymity (Barthel 1988, 39). If the earlier passage, with its "compassionate" concern for her health, imitates the nurturing, protective words of a mother, here the imperative mood, like the "scientific" terms (e.g., "discharges") and claims her medicines promote, resembles the authoritative pronouncements of a father, while the praise for her appearance sounds sororial. In short, the discourse of advertising has enabled Gerty to speak to herself ventriloquially in familial tones of concern

13. Cf. Wicke (1988, 159): "the 'feminine' is everywhere correlated with acts of consumption; either the woman figures in an advertising scenario, or she is implicated in *wanting* to buy something."

and love, tones she rarely hears in her own brutalized home.[14] The language of advertising thus appeals to Gerty in timbres of domestic love and kinship.

Her clothes speak a highly charged social language. Like Milly Bloom, she has a new hat, a virginal ("eggblue") straw one (the chaste counterpart of the black straw one worn by the whore of the lane), which both reveals and conceals her social and erotic identity: at once virginal and "coquettish," it covers a primary sign of sexuality, her hair, while also enabling her to peek at Bloom without his knowing it. Suggesting both Gerty's resemblances to and differences from the whore, her hat exemplifies her condition as a commodity, as *potential* exchange value among males that is fully realized in the whore (Irigaray 1985, 186). The blue blouse reveals a hint of décolletage ("the division"), just as her "chief care," her "undies," conflate the signifiers of virginity (they too are trimmed in blue) and sexual availability: she is "hoping against hope" that a man might see them (13.179–80) and partially exposes them to Bloom later in the episode. But even while they attempt to mask her economic status, her clothes and prose reveal it, as habitually she veers away from this mincing style toward a more genuine lower–middle-class vernacular: "All Tuesday week afternoon she was hunting to match that chenille but at last she found what she wanted at Clery's summer sales, the very it, slightly shop-soiled but you would never notice, seven fingers two and a penny" (13.158–61). The compulsive notation of the price suggests how care-fully she must parcel those pennies out to dress cheaply but still fash-ionably. Similarly, she would like to affect the "high" language of the *Lady's Pictorial,* but the clothes she can afford are, like her idiolect, "slightly shopsoiled," secondhand goods trying to pass as high-class originals. Blue-ribboned Gerty offers herself on the marriage market as both a bargain (Leonard 1991, 52) and as first prize.

Gerty's identity is both expressed and elided by consumerism. For her, ownership is not merely a "passive acceptance of objects but an acting with and upon them" (Simmel 1978, 321). Gerty's adornment by hats, colored underwear, and transparent stockings is an "articula-tion of the self" (Simmel 1978, 321) that "expands the ego and en-larges the sphere around [her] which is filled with [her] personality" (Simmel 1950, 344). She is more because she possesses more. In ex-hibiting her hat and stockings, Gerty positions herself at the intersec-

14. For an analysis of the familial voices in contemporary advertisements directed at women, see Barthel 1988, 40–49.

tion between social life and self-regard: her pleasure in clothes is designed for others, but she can enjoy clothes only insofar as they mirror her dreams and enable others to recognize and reflect them back to her. Similarly, she and the clothes reciprocate each other: she renders her adornment valuable by presenting it as an expression and extension of herself, but her value also depends upon others' recognition of the value of her clothes and accessories (Simmel 1950, 338–39). She needs her clothes, and they need her. In commodities Gerty seeks objects that do not resist her intentions, objects she can govern, unlike the people and larger conditions in her life. Thus for her commodities are religious icons that bring salvation. This religious parallel is reinforced by the voices issuing from the Star of the Sea Church reciting the Litany of Our Lady of Loreto and punctuating her narrative.[15] Unable or unwilling to distinguish between religious and commercial icons, between the "Queen of angels, queen of patriarchs, queen of prophets" (13.489) and the "queen of ointments" (Richards 1990, 224–25), Gerty conflates them with the Queen of England. An admirer of royalty and nobility, she is eager to observe the viceregal cavalcade at the end of "Wandering Rocks"; but her disappointment is mostly at failing to notice what Lady Dudley is wearing (10.1208–9). Indeed, Gerty's textiles and textual style recall the florid prose and fetishized fashions of *Sweets of Sin*, which is likewise impressed by "queenly shoulders" (10.616). Appropriately, her father's brand of cork lino claims to be "fit for a palace" (13.323): sometimes the Virgin Mary, sometimes the king's consort, Gerty imagines herself a queen.[16]

But Gerty's "queenly *hauteur*" (13.97)—like the "queenly mien" of the pawnbroker Mrs. M'Guinness so admired by Father Conmee—inadequately masks her real class status. Gerty is a pawn dressing up as a queen, and neither the Church's nor the State's borrowed images can change that. Only marriage might elevate her. Though commodities help her express herself, they are her sole means of expression and therefore also circumscribe her freedom and selfhood by limiting her to what can be said by commodities. Though all her efforts are designed to make her stand out, actually her devotion to mass

15. As several writers have noted, Gerty's white hands and golden hair imitate the description of the Blessed Virgin Mary that Stephen ponders early in *Portrait* as a "Tower of Ivory" and "House of Gold" (*P* 35).

16. Richards shows how the Queen's image in nineteenth and early twentieth-century ads "both legitimated consumption for women by offering them the queen's stamp of approval and lured even more women into department stores by leading them to believe that there they, too, would be treated like royalty" (1990, 104).

products depersonalizes her. The limitations of her brand of commodity fetishism are revealed in her language, which reduces processes to facts, concepts to things, and the body to its clothing (cf. Richards 1990, 218). Thus for Gerty a "brown study" is not a mood but a room decorated tastefully with only a single lamp (13.293–94); when the narrator asserts that Edy Boardman "never had a foot" like Gerty (13.166), we see not her foot but her footwear. Like the narrative discourse, Gerty paints herself as the static image of the kind of beauty "an artist might have dreamed of" (13.583)—a commercial artist. Even her memories are memories of commodities. Though Gerty does own a keepsake, her "girlish treasure trove" (13.638–39) was not given as a gift and does not contain sentimental objects without commercial value but is composed almost entirely of mass-produced items she has bought (13.639–42; Richards 1990, 221). Moreover, almost the only phrases Gerty clearly remembers are ad slogans. Stephen earlier argued that memory creates identity; thus Gerty's reified memory represents her commodified identity, because in a sense her memories are not even hers.

The intrusion of phrases from the Litany of Our Lady not only reiterates the homologies established earlier between advertising and religious discourse; it also demonstrates the shared patriarchal ideology of the Church and consumer culture. The Church has contributed to her fetishization by presenting icons of femininity that simultaneously celebrate virginity and make it seem supernatural. The coupling of the litany and ad language implies that Mariolatry is also a kind of commodity fetishism. It produces femininity as an exchange value under the sign of the universal equivalent—God— who, as the ultimate expression of Fatherly/phallic values, stands in the theological economy where money does in the money economy (Goux 1990, 54). If the Virgin Mary is important primarily because she helped to produce Christ, then she really signifies not female power but the "manifestation and circulation of a power of the Phallus" (Irigaray 1985, 183). Like the queenly image of the state proffered as her physical and economic ideal, the image of the Virgin is unattainable. In one regard the two ideologies conflict: while advertising images tell her to sell sex, the Church idealizes sexual restraint. No wonder Gerty seems confused. Her self-conception built out of mass-produced goods and half-understood products of the Mass, she is in two senses a "massproduct." Indeed, as a mere "specimen" of Irish girlhood, she is universalized to become a mass product in a third sense.

Gerty and Edy Boardman have been vying for the attentions of

Reggie Wylie, a boy younger than Gerty and the brother of the bicycle racer. But although Gerty has already conjured up a wedding notice in the society pages ("Mrs Gertrude Wylie was wearing a sumptuous confection of blue fox"), she knows it "was not to be" (13.198–99). The hackneyed phrases she has learned from sentimental fiction give her hope that "he might learn to love her in time," but the clichés cannot provide what is not there (13.138). Gerty admires "the way [Reggie] turned the bicycle at the lamp with his hands" and "also the nice perfume of those good cigarettes" (13.143–45). "Smoking cigarettes, Riding bicycles" (*JJA* 3:605): Reggie has modeled himself after the images of bicycling gentlemen in ads. His attractiveness depends upon the commodities in which his identity is invested; he too is a mass product she hopes to consume. Once again for Gerty human social relations bear "the fantastic form of a relation between things" (Marx 1978, 321). Indeed, with her straw sailor hat and ribbon, Gerty herself resembles the bicycling women in such ads, even though she claims to scorn these "unfeminine girls" who show "off what they hadn't got" (13.436–37).[17] Reggie, Gerty asserts, "would not believe in love, a woman's birthright" (13.200): in her reified consciousness love is not a dynamic, reciprocal exchange of selves, but an inheritance, a factual thing—property. But she seems as unlikely to inherit this birthright as she is to become "a gentlewoman of high degree" (13.99) or a queen.

Thus Gerty's visions of the future are both cloudy and self-contradictory. She dreams of making "brekky" for her husband (on the menu: the suitably regal "queen Ann's pudding" [13.225]), but her rosy reveries of a chaste honeymoon and a tall husband with broad shoulders are haunted by anxiety that she may not match the ideals she has consumed. Because she is unsure of her domestic abilities, Gerty's fantasies digress into a litany of sisterly instructions for insuring culinary success: "dredge in the fine selfraising flour and always stir in the same direction, then cream the milk and sugar and whisk well the white of eggs though she didn't like the eating part" (13.226). Disadvantaged by her age, class and physical handicap in a marriage market in which matches were increasingly few and late (Walzl 1982, 33; Leonard 1991, 52), Gerty compensates by contriving euphemisms and conjuring reveries that nonetheless betray her insecurity and naïveté. Envisioning a "beautifully appointed draw-

17. For some typical turn-of-the-century ads featuring bicycling women, see Opie (1985, 137, 139) and Scott (1991, 832–36).

ingroom" with "chintz covers for the chairs and that silver toastrack in Clery's summer jumble sales like they have in rich houses" (13.233–4), she is pathetically unaware that rich people do not buy their furniture at jumble sales. Gerty's sole medium of exchange is her own body, and so she cherishes her "wealth of wonderful hair" (13.116) as valuable currency she might exchange for love and marriage. In this sense Gerty possesses two bodies: her natural body (a use value) and the one she dresses for exchange among males (Irigaray 1985, 180). But unless she finds a wealthier lover, Gerty will never be able to buy the products to engender herself as a corporal asset and thereby win a husband with financial assets—a vicious cycle indeed. It is not surprising that her "revision" of the wedding vows transforms "for richer, for poorer" into a chance of "riches for poor" (13.216).

The description of her home life distressingly resembles a scene from *Dubliners:* "Had her father only avoided the clutches of the demon drink, by taking the pledge or those powders the drink habit cured in Pearson's Weekly she might now be rolling in her carriage, second to none. . . . But that vile decoction which has ruined so many hearths and homes had cast its shadow over her childhood days. Nay, she had even witnessed in the home circle deeds of violence caused by intemperance and had seen her father, a prey to the fumes of intoxication, forget himself completely" (13.290–300). Beneath the euphemisms—"deeds of violence" and "forget himself completely" —the MacDowell household seems a frightening and demoralizing environment, which surely explains Gerty's recourse to sentimental visions of a future marriage. Indeed, the very euphemisms testify to the squalor, as if she cannot bear remembering the events baldly; in her own mind they have been translated into pulp fiction formulae that universalize and distance her from the suffering. Typically, she believes that her father's addiction and her family's economic problems can be solved by purchasing the proper commodity, in this case a temperance powder.[18]

But ultimately her desperate consumption neither fills the "dull aching void in her heart" (13.136–37), nor enables her to transcend her socioeconomic limitations. Since she can find salvation only by continuing to buy more commodities, which are subject to the changing dictates of fashion, the cycle of consumption can never end. Each

18. Gifford (1988, 388) quotes an example of the kind of ad Gerty is thinking about: "TO CURE DRUNKARDS, with or without their knowledge, send stamp for Free Trial package of a wonderful powdered remedy that has saved homes."

desire demands another purchase, and each purchase demands another one, but the needs compelling these purchases are never satisfied by consuming. With her limited funds, she can purchase only
enough to whet her appetite for grander commodities. What she
really yearns for is an ideal self: dolled up in her carefully chosen
clothes, she smiles at "the lovely reflection which the mirror gave back
to her!" (13.162). This reflection is really a product of an ongoing
process of exchange between the hidden Gerty MacDowell and the
one spoken to by advertisements. Gerty wants to purchase that person, but because that self is a commodity she can never simply *be* that
person—she can, at best, only own it. The objects she loves and the
person she want to be are, in fact, not things but images of things.
Her very emotions contribute to the design; they are vented only
when properly framed: "She knew how to cry nicely before the mirror" (13.192). A portrait of the artist as a young consumer, Gerty's
narrative depicts not a materialist but an idealist who attempts, like
Stephen Dedalus, to recreate herself through images of spiritual and
erotic salvation. But her mirror image will never be she; only by
imagining a lover (modeled after ads and popular fiction) who is
Other can she eventually find fulfillment in erotic consumption. In
Bloom she temporarily discovers such an image.

As the litany of Our Lady proceeds, Gerty's erotic feelings about
priests and the confessional are translated into a desire to give the
priest a gift, perhaps "a clock but they had a clock she noticed on the
mantelpiece white and gold with a canarybird" (13.461). Gift exchange creates bonds of love as well as expressing them; Gerty's wish
to give the father a gift both reveals her erotic feelings and sublimates
them into the economic register, into a language of objects (white and
gold, like the body of the Virgin Mary) exchanged for purposes other
than self-gratification. Limited in her access to money, she turns to
the alternative economy of gifts, which also figures as part of the
idealized courtship ritual she imagines in her future. In the outhouse
at home, she has tacked a "picture of halycon days where a young
gentleman . . . was offering a bunch of flowers to his ladylove"
(13.334–36). Like Martha Clifford, she pictures flowers as ideal presents; but again the exchange is depicted not as a process but as a
tableau. If Gerty's picture bears out Hyde's contention that gift exchange is "female commerce" and gifts "female property" (1983,
103), nonetheless in her dreams men give gifts but women *are* gifts.
That is, Gerty really wants to give *herself* as a gift to a lover, as her

terms for her body suggest: her wealth of hair, her "little heart worth its weight in gold" (13.326), and especially her "flowerlike" face (13.764). Conditioned by a culture that turns the female form into merchandise, she translates herself into an offering to males that is coded both as a gift ("flowerlike") and as an exchangeable commodity ("gold" and "wealth"). She imagines erotic commerce as gift exchange, but since love is really property, she cannot help but also figure herself as female property.[19]

Both her troubled relationship with her father and her sexual feelings for priests explain why her "beau ideal" is not a dashing young man but an older man "who would understand, take her into his sheltering arms ... and comfort her with a long long kiss" (13.212–14). Bloom fits her image when he first appears, intercepting an errant ball (13.350). Hitherto she and Bloom have only "exchanged glances of the most casual," but now she looks at him from under her hat and kicks the ball, making sure to lift her skirt "a little but just enough" (13.367–68). While the men in the chapel perform Mariolatry, Bloom, she believes, is "literally worshipping at her shrine" (13.564). But her "Bloom"—a "foreigner," or double of Martin Harvey (13.416–17)—is as much an imaginative creation as her own image in the mirror. As her "dreamhusband," Bloom must be either someone outside the everyday marketplace in which she is a loser or else a photo. As such, he cannot help but act "gallantly," even when he is only picking up a ball (13.431; 350). Imitating the wooing glances cast at money by the transparent stockings Bloom likes so much ("three and eleven" from Sparrow's of George's street [13.499]), she advertises herself by unveiling her assets—legs and hair (she removes her hat [13.509]). Unlike her stockings, however, Gerty's commodified Bloom is valued not for his transparency but for his reflectivity, his ability to mirror her desire. Thus, although she wishes she had a box of paints to draw the scene because "it was easier than to make a man" (13.628–30), in fact Gerty is doing precisely that

---

19. Rightly rebutting Richards's contention that Gerty is "wholly circumscribed" by advertising (1990, 234), Leonard argues that she is "painfully balanced between a wholehearted effort to believe in the 'old time chivalry' of 'natural' attraction between 'men' and 'women' and a shrewder attempt to maintain her competitive edge in the sexual marketplace" (1991, 55). But she does not have an edge; nor was "old time chivalry" ever anything but an economic arrangement based upon the male exchange of females.

—making a loving and lovable man in an image borrowed from the popular culture that has also helped her create her own self-image.[20]

As Gerty begins to notice Bloom's attention, the namby-pamby narrative veneer cracks, and she becomes jealous and scornful of the other girls' attempts to do just what she is doing. Realizing she now has a viewer, she becomes focused and supercilious. Now the twins are "little monkeys common as ditchwater" (13.467); now Cissy is a "forward piece" always trying to show off, and Gerty hopes that "her high crooked French heels on her to make her look tall" will give her "a fine tumble. *Tableau!*" (13.481; 485); now myopic Edy is an "irritable little gnat . . . and always would be and that was why no-one could get on with her" (13.523–24). Gerty's sexuality blooms: she knows she has "raised the devil" in him and, translating the Sinn Fein slogan, wants him "for herself alone" (13.518; 441). Contrary to her conventional protestations that she "instinctively recoil[s]" (13.661) from indecency, she seems surprisingly guiltless about her exhibition. And although she claims to loathe prostitutes, her distaste is more social than moral: they are "degrading the sex and being taken up to the police station" (13.664). Beneath her facade Gerty is pragmatic and recognizes that marriage is as much a commercial exchange as an expression of love. Thus she does not disdain whores for selling themselves, only for doing it so overtly and cheaply.

The final movement of Bloom's and Gerty's visual intercourse begins when she decides she will "make the great sacrifice" (13.653–54)—offer her body as if in marriage. But like Stephen's sacrifice of his voice, hers is a "bloodless" one (no hymen is broken) that is more imaginative than physical. It is effected by means of reciprocal gazes: "The eyes that were fastened upon her set her pulses tingling. She looked at him a moment, meeting his glance, and a light broke in upon her" (13.689–91). Bloom's eyes, acting as his phallus, seem to "burn into her . . . [and] read her very soul" (13.412–13): he reads her as a text, writing his letter on the blank page of her virginity; conversely, she reads and rewrites him as a romantic hero. The climax of their exchange is counterpointed with the Mirus Bazaar fireworks, a juxtaposition that not only produces one of the great orgasm scenes in literature, but also recalls Gerty's first appearance (observing the

20. Both Richards's and Leonard's subtle and illuminating readings of the episode underemphasize the fact that Gerty also reads and imaginatively recreates Bloom. This reciprocal imagining is necessary in order for the exchange to be as restorative as both of them clearly believe it to be.

viceregal cavalcade's trek to the Bazaar) and suggests that their intercourse is itself a form of charity or gift. The breathless description
(echoing both Doughy Dan's speech and Simon Dedalus's song [cf.
11.745–50]) signifies by its simultaneously tumescent and precious
language the participation of both parties: "And she saw a long
Roman candle going up over the trees, up, up, and, in the tense hush,
they were all breathless with excitement as it went higher and higher
and she had to lean back more and more to look up after it, high,
high, almost out of sight, and her face was suffused with a divine, an
entrancing blush" (13.719–23). Even in her rapture Gerty's thoughts
are punctuated by an anxiety that demands recitation of a brief litany
of commodities: "and he could see her other things too, nainsook
knickers, the fabric that caresses the skin, better than those other
pettiwidth, the green, four and eleven, on account of being white,
and she let him and she saw that he saw" (13.724–26). At once ecstatic
and calculating, Gerty knows that she is an item on display; indeed,
she is a copy of those pictures of "skirtdancers" hoarded by the gentleman lodger (13.704; 732). The language accelerates as Gerty presents
her "wondrous revealment half offered" and holds out her "slender
arms to him to come"; it culminates in ejaculations of "O!" as "it
gushed out of it a stream of rain gold hair threads and they shed and
ah!" (13.731; 734–39). Gerty bestows her gold upon Bloom, as the
verbal spasms in Gerty's style give voice to Bloom's genital ones; the
language is their medium of erotic exchange.

But Gerty's discourse is incapable of rendering their erotic commerce in any terms outside its own conventional moralizing. Thus the
narrator quickly covers up, assigning blame to Bloom (13.745–47):
"What a brute he had been! At it again? A fair unsullied soul had
called to him and, wretch that he was, how had he answered?" Gerty's
sly and coquettish eyes are now "guileless." She must forgive *him*,
though her participation was equally avid. Because Bloom is viewed
only from the outside, as a function of Gerty's needs and dreams, he
remains fundamentally anonymous, an everyman and noman, and
hence her "all in all" (13.671). If both Gerty's existence and her narrative appear to exemplify seriality, that "secret anonymity," or "statistical quality" in which "the Other is secretly present at the heart of
my acts" (Jameson 1970, 76–77), it is precisely that anonymity, that
condition as a mass product, which both protects her and establishes
the ground for her erotic commerce with Bloom. They speak the
same language. And if, as I have been arguing, consumption is an
active mode of relations, then Gerty's consumption of his image is a

form of sign manipulation little different from that of Joyce himself (cf. Baudrillard 1988, 21). A prime consumer of the kind of commercial images that Bloom produces, Gerty also produces him as a consumable image.

Gerty is an artist who adorns and fictionalizes her world not only by shopping and consuming but by painting a man to whom she can give herself without guilt or blood. Her Bloom, like her other consumption, fulfills "diverse and even contradictory social and psychological needs" (Richards 1990, 212). Thus Gerty's sexuality becomes a "figure for capitalism's ability to imagine ways out of what appear to be biologically immutable limits" (Michaels 1987, 57)—her lameness. While Gerty's imagination is founded upon the dubious values of commodity culture, it nonetheless gives her some means of imaginatively transforming the world. As Senn observes, "To afford illusory gratifications is one of the legitimate functions of fiction, of highbrow literature no less than of Gerty's favorite reading matter" (1984, 162). Just as Bloom's aesthetic of advertising betrays a genuine artistic impulse, so Gerty's reception and revision of that aesthetic imply a poetic sense that belies the condescension of critics. Ingeniously writing "The Mystery Man on the Beach" (Benstock 1991, 202), Gerty possesses an artistic impulse as genuine as Stephen's; they are, Mahaffey points out, two reflections of "the impulse to inhabit a world of art" (1988, 153).[21]

Gerty has performed as an advertisement for herself, thereby separating her real existence from the iconic one she has fashioned. Her adherence to borrowed images has paradoxically freed her from them by temporarily allowing her to fulfill an ideal she cannot attain in any other way. As an emblem of the collective consumer decisions of Irish popular culture, Gerty's discourse shows how consumerism provides a lexicon of images and remedies through which lower–middle-class Dubliners can project their desire. Even if Bloom's and Gerty's erotic commerce is as much commercial as erotic, nevertheless something valuable has been exchanged, precisely because each of them has been made anonymous, composite, collective, and hence larger than life. In their "last lingering glance," Bloom's eyes "hung

21. As several writers have observed, the language during the climax echoes in both diction and rhythm Stephen's rhapsodic vision of the bird-girl in *Portrait* (171–73). This echo parodies Stephen's and Joyce's own earlier writings but also elevates Gerty's own aspirations to poetry and makes her "something of a young Stephen" (C. Smith 1991, 633).

enraptured on her sweet flowerlike face" (13.762–64). Figured as gifts both in Gerty's picture and elsewhere in the novel, flowers here represent Gerty's identity—now a gift—within this exchange. Imaged as a flower, her face signifies that the exchange with Bloom has renewed her, allowing her to bloom into sexuality; in becoming a "bloom" she simultaneously renews her own sense of herself and allows Bloom to write his fantasies upon her. Just as gift exchange is erotic commerce that creates bonds of kinship, so Gerty's gift has united the two flowers by enticing Bloom to give a gift of his own imaginary self in return. Gerty's gift of herself rejuvenates Bloom, providing another petal of *moly,* the flower (*JJ* 497) that protects him from Circe. As restorative erotic commerce their encounter exemplifies the positive elements of the gift economy. And yet this restorative, like the cures of patent medicines, can only be temporary, not only for the characters but also for the novel itself. "Up like a rocket, down like a stick": we immediately shift from Gerty's breathless romanticizing to Bloom's jaundiced cynicism, just as Gerty's real life will reassert itself, confronting her again with her lameness, her brutal father, and her dim prospects for future happiness.

"Thankful for small mercies"

At first Bloom's section seems utterly distinct from Gerty's, and his apparent detachment suggests an unbridgeable gulf between their interpretations of these events. While Gerty's discourse veils the unpleasant and the erotic, Bloom counters with a clipped, fatigued, and apparently callous reductivism. The two sections—one inflating, the other deflating—oppose each other like the dual narrative zones of "Cyclops"; neither sees itself through the eye of the other. Whereas, in "Cyclops," Bloom promotes love against hostility, here he plays the world-weary sophisticate for whom love is just an advertising trick. Once again, however, the oscillation is aimed at achieving balance. Ultimately, moreover, their zones do engage each other in dialogue through the reading consciousness who mediates and makes ends meet. The reader once again offers the gift of attention as a currency that permits narrative exchanges.

Unlike Gerty, Bloom recognizes the illusiveness of their reciprocal performances but believes such fantasies are necessary: "See her as she is spoil all. Must have the stage setting, the rouge, costume, position, music. The name too. . . . Curtain up. Moonlight silver effulgence" (13.855–58). Bloom immediately pierces the veil. And though he briefly preens and tells himself that she "Saw something in me. Wonder what. Sooner have me as I am than some poet chap with bearsgrease plastery hair" (13.833–35), he quickly resumes his other attitude, which depicts women as deceivers and himself as a handy object for their use (13.884). To ward off guilt for exploiting the youthful Gerty, he must paint women as self-absorbed, sexually knowing, and financially shrewd: "Sharp as needles they are. . . . Milly for example drying her handkerchief on the mirror to save the ironing. Best place for an ad to catch a woman's eye on a mirror. And when I sent her for Molly's Paisley shawl, . . . carrying home the change in her stocking!" (13.912–22). Bloom reverses Gerty's staging of the roles of seducer and victim, so that now women see only themselves, and men merely play to that narcissism. There are no reciprocal gazes, only reflections in the mirror. Trained to see each other from a male point of view, women compete vindictively: "the others inclined to give her an odd dig. . . . Barbed wire. . . . Sister souls. Showing their teeth at one another. . . . Wouldn't lend each other a pinch of salt" (13.809–21). As in Gerty's reified world, but much more overtly, love is just a disguise for property disputes, in which women vie ferociously to capture their male prizes. And since females are tough and mercenary males must be on "guard not to feel too much pity. They take advantage" (13.1095–96). Love is not a gift but a competition for scarce goods, a capitalism of the heart.

Thus if Gerty glamorizes eros by dressing it in commodities, Bloom economizes, using economics to strip eros of glamor. Although he is "Thankful for small mercies" that Gerty provided, these gifts merely camouflage a "cheap" prostitution (13.789). In postorgasmic dejection, all sexual solicitation is equivalent—"they like dressing one another for the sacrifice. . . . No reasonable offer refused" (13.798;806). In this mood Bloom recognizes no distinctions among virginal flirtation, marriage, and prostitution, and even considers Molly's adultery an acceptable variation on such exchanges: "Ten bob I got for Molly's combings when we were on the rocks in Holles street. Why not? Suppose he [Boylan] gave her money. Why not? All a prejudice. She's worth ten, fifteen, more, a pound" (13.840–42). Hair, Gerty's signifier of sexual availability, now becomes just another commodity for cheap sale, like the woman who wears it. Rewriting Gerty as a whore reduces her to a stereotype as unthreatening as the fatherly gentleman that she first imagines Bloom to be; rewriting Molly as a whore purges his jealousy and feeling of helplessness. They are no longer real women, but anonymous, clichéd examples of "woman."

Ironically, this apparently sexist and mercenary equation echoes feminist and Marxist theorists who contend that marriage passes through the merchant's arch to merge with prostitution.[22] For Marx, marriage inevitably makes prostitutes of women, and prostitution is merely the specific instance of the general prostitution of labor (1978, 82), an idea that the Stephen of *Stephen Hero* echoes: "A woman's body is a corporal asset of the State: if she traffic with it she must sell it either as a harlot or as a married woman or as a working celibate or as a mistress" (202). Such trafficking in sex is simony because it "revolts our notion of what is humanly possible" (*SH* 203): it turns women into commodities. But just as Stephen's analysis is more a response to his rejection by Emma Clery than a coherent social philosophy, so Bloom's equation of all forms of sexual contract is only a temporary defensive position meant to excuse his own lapses.

Nevertheless, Bloom's hard-boiled style is a refreshing breeze after Gerty's stifling, "sweet and cheap: soon sour" perfume (13.1010). Bloom's discourse amounts to a counternarrative, a competing fiction that willfully subverts Gerty's idealism with a grim realism. If Gerty insists that surfaces equal substance, Bloom argues that surfaces always deceive; if Gerty aims to turn herself into gold, Bloom contends that nothing is gold, but only its equivalent in the unconscious—excrement. His fiction is realistic—anti-idealist—but also founded upon a goldbug aesthetic that pretends nothing is what it seems. As in the realistic novel, here all objects (including persons) have price tags; but now price tags exhaust the value of persons and objects, reducing all value to exchange value. This discourse uses imagination against itself to empty out the symbolic domain. Thus Bloom's fictions of domestic life humorously countervail Gerty's honeymoon prose: "Sad however because it lasts only a few years till they settle down to potwalloping and papa's pants will soon fit Willy and fuller's earth for the baby when they hold him out to do ah ah" (13.952). But Bloom does acknowledge compensations and equitably metes out blame and credit: "Husband rolling in drunk, stink of pub off him like a polecat. . . . Then ask in the morning: was I drunk last night? Bad policy however to fault the husband. . . . Maybe the

22. One influential version of this theory is found in Lévi-Strauss (1969, 52–68) and has been analyzed by Rubin and Irigaray, among others. For a critique of Lévi-Strauss and his followers, see Hartsock 1983, 293–303. In Frank Budgen's illustrations for "Proteus" and "Nausicaa," an arch reaches down from the sky to connect the protagonist with the other objects on the beach. These drawings again use the arch to symbolize the intercourse of sexuality and commerce.

women's fault also. . . . Chaps that would go to the dogs if some
woman didn't take them in hand. Then little chits of girls, height of a
shilling in coppers, with little hubbies. . . . Sometimes children turn
out well enough. Twice nought makes one" (13.964–77).

Beginning with a knowing cynicism that baldly re-presents
Gerty's veiled memories of drunkenness, the passage ends in a mathematical impossibility in which the product of two nothings equals
something: through erotic commerce, twice nought makes one. Thus
while Bloom's scenarios remain disillusioned, his account yields a
credit balance by acknowledging that somehow people continue to
gain hope and renewal from sexual love. As the episode proceeds,
Bloom moderates his aggressive cynicism, just as Gerty could not
continue to suppress her ungracious and lustful thoughts. Near the
end of the episode, he voices a fatherly concern over children's games
(13.1192); considering Mrs. Dignam's insurance, he softens his severe
judgments about women's business acumen: "Buried the poor husband but progressing favourably on the premium. Her widow's mite.
Well? What do you expect her to do? Must wheedle her way along"
(13.1229–31). Moreover, their opposing discourses finally generate
dialogism on the narrative surface when, at the end of his section,
Bloomian sentences bleed into Gerty-like locutions (especially
13.1292–1305). Though the two discourses at first seem jarringly
dissimilar, by the end of the episode they betray some common
ground. Thus the episode ultimately balances debits and credits to
show that their encounter makes both ends meet.

At first a businessman, Bloom then plays scientist. Perhaps love is
really only a kind of physics: "Back of everything magnetism. Earth
for instance pulling this and being pulled. That causes movement.
. . . Little piece of steel iron. When you hold out the fork. Come.
Come. Tip. Woman and man that is. Fork and steel" (13.987–93). At
first this seems to be another reductionism, a physicist's explanation
of spiritual conditions. But it may just as easily be read the opposite
way, as a poetic projection of human emotions onto physical reality
that echoes, for example, the poetic-scientific formulations of ancient
philosophers. Although Bloom has pulled away from sentimentality
to find commercialism beneath love, nevertheless the eroticism that
binds persons together still seems to him a universal force and unites
the polarities of the episode. Their encounter does involve a kind of
electromagnetism: a "radiant vision" (13.511) in her blouse of electric
blue, Gerty emits waves and radiation from her eyes, clothes and
accessories, enabling her identity to expand outward like electromag-

netic waves and pull Bloom into its field.[23] Likewise Bloom's gaze sets her "tingling in every nerve" (13.514) as though she were shocked or magnetized. In fact, Bloom's discovery of magnetism beneath such influences is congruent with his aesthetic philosophy: he finds the same force at work in good advertisements, which possess "magnetising efficacy to arrest involuntary attention" (17.583). Gerty's body has indeed magnetized his attention; in becoming an advertisement for herself, she has embodied Bloom's commercial philosophy of attraction. In her, Bloom observes a subject constituted by his labor and thus finds his labor rewarded in her laborious self-making. He too gazes into a mirror that is also a shop window.

Reciprocity and Return

Like Stephen, Bloom contemplates the opposed dangers of repetition and flux while strolling on the strand. If historical repetition is merely a "Circus horse walking in a ring" (13.1111), flux means that for this Odysseus (as for the first) "Returning [is] not the same" (13.1103). While Bloom does not return home yet, the notion of return returns frequently for the rest of the novel, gathering significances that are at once geographic, ethical, structural, and economic. Return is manifested both by Bloom's memory and by the novel's memory of itself. From here to the end, *Ulysses* refers to itself more and more, rehearsing its own plot in various "retrospective arrangements" such as the one Bloom provides near the end of the episode (13.1214–16). Like the running budgets he keeps, these retrospective moments enable him to turn his experiences into a narrative: both his summaries and his budgets are "accounts" of his day. The economy of retrospection, like Stephen's awareness of debt, produces order; it is a fictionalization of experience based upon a philosophy of accounting, which assumes that the meaning of events can be determined by calculating loss and gain. These retrospections alternate with, and sometimes prompt, plans for the future, as when Bloom recalls his failure to pay for the soap and lotion for Molly and imagines that he will "call tomorrow" (13.1048). Forward and backward movements depend upon and motivate each other: today's credits presage tomorrow's debts, as the economy of retrospection never ends.

Bloom's recollective moments also encourage the reader to move

23. Cf. Simmel (1950, 342): "Adornment intensifies or enlarges the impression of the personality by operating as a sort of radiation emanating from it."

backwards, inducing a return (by memory and rereading) to earlier points in the text. These returns, in turn, occasion predictions, as the reader attempts to produce an account of the text. Wolfgang Iser argues that such moments of "retention and protension," in which the reader's memory oscillates with and prompts prediction or expectation, are primary processes in all reading and permit the reader to complete gaps of indeterminacy she or he finds in the text (1978, 111, 112). Just as Bloom rereads his experience, the reader rereads her or his experience of reading, revising her or his narrative account, as she or he proceeds, and thus compiles a kind of running budget balanced between the known and the unknown. But retrospection does not merely produce balance; it also engenders change. Thus for the reader as for Bloom, "returning [is] not the same" (13.1103): each returning movement both alters what has already been read and changes the reader's expectations of what she or he will read. The economy of reading demands both progress and regress, just as Bloom's eventual cyclic return to the rock of Ithaca will find it changed along with himself. Thus Joyce describes the episode as a "retrogressive progression": the reader's economy matches the novel's own structure. This paradoxical formula finally describes not only Bloom's nostalgia and his exchange with Gerty but also the continuing acts of shaping, storytelling, and accounting necessary for the reader to progress further in the text. Ultimately, however, this forward movement is itself a return: like Bloom, we end where we began, at the rock of Ithaca.

In this sense, it is the reader who becomes Odysseus, who constantly alters his or her reading self in a process that mimes Bloom's polytropic identity. Like Gerty and Bloom, the reader finds in the text as actual what is implicit within him or herself; yet although the reader sees as in a mirror, this reflection is not a static image, but a cinematic montage of reading selves that instigates further changes. Juxtaposing and attempting to integrate the mutually contradictory narrative voices of the chapter as well as his or her own identities, improvising a way to unite the beginning and end of the text, the reader, like Odysseus, tries to make both ends meet. In a sense, the Nostos of *Ulysses* begins here with Bloom's and the reader's returns, the latter through an economy of reading that mimics Bloom's economy of movement. This dialectic of reading underscores how reciprocity also governs exchanges between readers and texts and implies the social function of such imaginative reflections: they change readers through exchanges with challenging texts. In turn, these encounters open dialogues with a broad range of social voices, perhaps producing a "royal reader" (13.1066) who will show both compassion for and judgment on Queen Gerty and King Leopold. Like Bloom, then, we can be "thankful for small mercies"—these moments of textual self-reflection—that help us to balance our own reading budget.[24]

One striking example of history repeating itself within the text occurs at the end of the episode when, spying something on the strand, Bloom asks, "What's that? Might be money." Picking it up, he wonders if it is a "letter? No. Can't read. . . . Page of an old copybook" (13.1247–48). On the same strand where Stephen earlier wrote his vampire poem (not on the same paper: Stephen pocketed that [3.437–8]), Bloom also considers writing a message. He thinks of Martha's letter, writes "I. AM. A." and recalls her words—"I called you naughty boy because I do not like" and then rubs it out (13.1258–64). Bloom's effacement of the longed-for epithet seems to ensure the anonymity engendered by Gerty's fantasy and to embody the incompleteness of his domestic life.

Few critics have been content to leave the message incomplete, although it is probably one of those conundrums that can never be solved.[25] Bloom's message remains a permanent gap in the text that requires the reader's imagination and polytropism to complete, or better, the reader's negative capability and forbearance *not* to complete. That said, I too propose a solution. The most appropriate way of completing the message is with "naughty," a word Bloom thinks of between the subject and predicate of his sentence, and which derives from the last writing he did in the novel, his correspondence with Martha. In this epithet Bloom is revealed again as a "naught"—a noman, a Ulysses at once universal and anonymous. "Naughty" thus has the advantage of being both complete and incomplete, both spe-

---

24. French (1976, 3) argues similarly that "the reader . . . is in fact the Ulysses of the title." For further discussions of returns and the act of reading *Ulysses*, see Brook Thomas (1982, 40–55) and Iser (1978, 231–33).

25. For example, Henke (1978, 172) finds in it a sign of Bloom's dejection. On the other hand, Senn (1984, 163) reads it as a cryptic message praising love (*ama*, the Spanish word that appears on the previous page [13.1209]), and Brivic (1985, 93–95) sees it as an allusion to Jehovah (I AM THAT I AM) or Christ ("I am Alpha and Omega": Revelation 1:8). Other words recently submitted to complete the phrase range from "I AM A WRITER" (McArthur 1988, 12), to "I AM A CUCKOLD" or "FOOL PERHAPS" (Bell 1991, 43). As Benstock notes (1991, 220), one might also fill in the blank with "stick-in-the-mud," a name "Marion" gives Bloom in "Circe" (15.329), and which fits because, after writing, Bloom flings the stick, which falls "in silted sand, stuck" (13.1270).

cific and indeterminate. If the key point about the incomplete message is its incompleteness—it says "I AM ANONYMOUS" (cf. Benstock 1991, 220)—then "naughty" is still a good answer, because it captures Bloom's elusiveness. Refusing to pin himself down to a single, unchanging identity, Bloom is a bouquet, an anthology of flowers, including Henry, Poldy, Senhor Enrique Flor, Professor Luitpold Blumenduft (the theorist of magnetism?), the Mystery Man on the Beach (Gerty's dream husband, to whom she offers her own flower), and so on. Just as Gerty is a mass product, a composite of women's fiction, advertising and Mariolatry, so Bloom, like HCE, is "the mass product of teamwork" with himself and others (*FW* 546.15). As the "man of many tropes" (Joyce's favored translation of *polytropon*) whose identity mediates and undergoes many of the novel's tropic exchanges, Bloom's heroism is the heroism of exchange. Inasmuch as his exchange with Gerty both necessitates and contributes to this polytropism, it simultaneously affirms and alters his identity, thereby giving him back the gift of exchangeability.

As in his correspondence with Martha, the anonymity and deception Bloom recognizes here (13.946–47) actually facilitates their intercourse. Moreover, this anonymity makes him feel rejuvenated. "Twice nought makes one": because each is simultaneously nobody and everybody to the other, they are able to create a single entity out of the relationship. Such a paradoxical formula overflows the economy of balance, just as it expresses the real effect of reading the episode: despite their differences, the two—with the mediation of that third party, the reader—form a unity. Thus the episode's ledger yields not merely a balance but a new beginning; it is a reciprocal gift exchange in which each gains something and the whole is greater than the parts. Bloom is a new man because of having become a noman. The exchange with Gerty is possible only because each of them becomes a product of the exchange between the other's desire and his or her own. Each allows the other to remake him or her. Indeed, Bloom's recognition that "we meet what we feel" echoes Stephen's description of the artist's attainment of self-knowledge through self-objectifying narcissism (9.1041). As in "the economy of heaven" Bloom embodies and imagines "a wife unto himself" (9.1051–52). The exchange of fictionalized selves performed by Gerty and Bloom is thus an authentically imaginative creation, a collaborative tale. With the aid of Gerty's "touch of the artist" (Bell 1991, 72), Bloom has made himself a character in a prize "titbit" story. "Still it was a kind of language between us" (13.939–40): through advertising's "currency of signs" (Williamson 1978, 20), Bloom and Gerty have carried out an exchange at once erotic, semiotic and economic.

In spite of Bloom's cynical "realism," he admits that he has gained something valuable from the exchange. Just as Gerty's self-confidence has been reinforced and renewed by the feeling that she can attract such a man, so Bloom feels rejuvenated: "Did me good all the same. Off colour after Kiernan's, Dignam's. For this relief much thanks"; "Made me feel so young" (13.939–40; 1272–73). The exchange is a "eucharisto" (Senn 1984, 142), a transmutation of flesh through the "word" of imagination, generating a bloodless sacrifice as authentic as those Stephen aims to create through art. Moreover, their exchange closely resembles the classic model of gift exchange. In gift exchange "twice nought makes one": the gift must be used up—become nought —and perish as property in order to be reconstituted as the property of the other; it can then be passed back or onward to another. It becomes nought, but in so doing "makes one" of the exchanging parties (Hyde 1983, 8–9). Like the charitable narcissism in Gerty and Bloom's encounter, gift exchange combines self-interest and generosity, loss and gain: each giver offers something without demanding return but nonetheless receives compensation and renewal. Gerty and Bloom's exchange, like a gift exchange, transcends ego boundaries and knits them together (Hyde 1983, 163, 153). Thus, in her encounter with the mystery man, Gerty feels truly queenly for a few minutes; likewise, in his encounter with the Dublin Nausicaa, Bloom receives the "honour and gifts of strangers, the friends of Everyman" and "A nymph immortal, beauty, the bride of Noman" (17.2010–11).

This reading of their encounter as a gift exchange is borne out by Joyce's discussion of the episode. He wrote that *moly*, the plant that preserves Odysseus from Circe's transformations, has many leaves, one of which is "indifference due to masturbation" (*JJ* 497). *Moly* is "the gift of Hermes," god of thieves and merchants, protector of commerce and "giver of good things" (N. Brown 1947, 21). Thus the god's gift is masturbation, which comes about through Gerty's gift of herself to Bloom and his reciprocal gift of attraction.[26] Indeed, Hermes would seem to be the most appropriate patron for the erotic exchange of Gerty and Bloom, since it is provoked and propelled by

26. In a sense, then, Richard Ellmann's apparently exaggerated claim that Bloom's masturbation in "Nausicaa" is "heroic" (1972, 133) is indirectly correct: Bloom's masturbation enables his heroic actions later in the novel.

the language of commerce and commodities. However, gift exchange emanates from Eros and thus would seem to belong not to Hermes' world but to Aphrodite's. Because of its subversion of market exchange and its tendency to create a language of flow, gift exchange is often identified with the feminine (Hyde 1983, 103). And yet Gerty's narrative seems informed as much by a "masculine" calculation of economic value as by erotic attraction. In fact, Bloom and Gerty's exchange ultimately acts to blend genders, and "Nausicaa" depicts erotic commerce as precisely a melding of eros and commerce, of male and female, of Aphrodite and Hermes, two divinities "frequently associated in ritual and . . . combined in the figure of Hermaphroditus" (N. Brown 1947, 14). In sum, the episode engenders a *hermaphroditic* narrative: it first offers the stereotypical discourses of each gender as expressed through the polarities of eros and commerce but then blurs these distinctions and ideologies by demonstrating their interpenetration in a complex, restorative gift exchange. The episode is hermaphroditic not only sexually but also economically.

Moreover, by making himself into "Gerty," Joyce becomes a Hermes (himself hermaphroditic) who gives a bi-sexual gift to Bloom, Gerty, and his readers. This complex blend of economic, erotic and narratological ingredients thus generates a new kind of hero as well as a new kind of narrative and prepares us for an even more forceful celebration of the hermaphroditic in "Circe." Combining the masculine and feminine poles into a sexual economy that imitates the "economy of heaven," *Ulysses* becomes hermaphroditic, a transformation that in turn encourages the reader to throw off stereotypical gender associations and identifications. If we are to read the episode with full comprehension, we too must be (symbolically) hermaphroditic, capable of negotiating the full range of sexual and economic exchanges.[27] Perhaps in this way our heroism, like Bloom's, may become "heroticism" (*FW* 614.35): a synthesis of eros and heroism tempered in the fires of sexual, semiotic, and economic commerce.

27. MacCabe contends that Joyce's writing shows "an ineradicable and inexhaustible bisexuality" (1978, 151), but what the text valorizes is a flexibility of gender, not of sexual preference; it places readers in the mind of both genders, but does not (I assume) produce sexual feelings for both genders. Thus it is more accurate to call it hermaphroditic than bisexual.

9

Erotic Commerce II

> In . . . the economic realm, sacrifice is the condition of all
> value.
>
> —Simmel 1971, 49

PROSTITUTION AND PURGATION

Expanding upon the excesses and threats in erotic commerce presented in "Sirens" and "Nausicaa," "Circe" stages the transfers inherent in several economies. Set in a district where women's bodies are
sold, the episode adapts the economy of prostitution as the foundation for its textual economy. In this way, "Circe" illustrates "the capitalist assumption that every item—inanimate or human—can be
exchanged on a market that operates according to a single monetary
scale of value" (Herr 1986, 167). It portrays a prostituted domain in
which the Symbolic function of money—its role as a circulating medium—infects all social and psychic conditions and relations. Indeed,
the episode embodies Simmel's description of the intimate connection
between money and prostitution: "only money, which does not imply
any commitment, . . . is the appropriate equivalent to the fleetingly
intensified and just as fleetingly extinguished sexual appetite that is
served by prostitution." Thus when we deal with money, we experience "something of the essence of prostitution" (1978, 376–77). Just
as prostitution emphasizes the commerciality of erotic commerce, so
money reduces all values and relations to fleeting exchanges of material currency. Prostitution transforms erotic reciprocity into the im-

personal reciprocity of financial transactions and thereby declares that exchange value is the only value.

The episode's theatrical form demands that everything be dramatized; accordingly, mental conditions, memories, and words are animated and given material form, and inanimate objects speak. Just as in a whorehouse women become commodities and houseguests become customers, so in "Circe" intangible conditions become words, and words become palpable objects. Franco Moretti is thus close to the mark when he claims that "Circe" is the "unsurpassed literary representation of commodity fetishism" (1983, 185). Joyce's Nighttown is a fetishized realm in which social and spiritual values are reduced to prices. In fact, the episode universalizes fetishism beyond the economic register: if, as Robert J. Stoller comments, a "fetish is a story masquerading as an object" (1985, 155), then the materialist method of "Circe," in which processes become things and persons are merely clothes, also fetishizes the erotic and linguistic economies by freezing processes into material shapes. However, the episode also demonstrates the fragility and instability of fetishized reality. While its textual economy reifies persons by turning them into objects, at the same time it makes events and conditions seem provisional by constantly replacing one set of dramatis personae, costumes, and scenarios with another. Its fetishized objects and persons are continually disseminated and thrown back into circulation, as if to illustrate the Symbolic function of money as a circulating medium. The episode's linguistic economy thus discloses a materialist ethos in which conditions are things and only the purchasable are real; but it also resists reification in that its social encounters, linguistic exchanges, and ontological violations are all as "fleetingly intensified" and "fleetingly extinguished" as the financial exchanges in a brothel. The reader is jostled from reification to redistribution, as the episode oscillates between fetishization—which weaves processes into things—and a countermovement that unweaves objects back into mental processes and cycles. In this sense, "Circe's" circulating economy resists the reification inherent in prostitution and money, paradoxically, by replicating the very symbolic circulation that the money form certifies.

The last of the adventures, "Circe" recycles and exaggerates the more subtle tropic and material circulations of the first adventure, "Calypso." If its hallucinatory method typifies the late episodes' antirealist economy of excess, paradoxically this extravagance also reinforces one of realism's major principles—that the world is materially rich (H. M. Steele 1988, 6). Indeed, Joyce claimed that, by imaginatively depicting sensation, "Circe" "approached reality closer" than did any other episode (quoted in A. Power 1974, 75). Through its obsession with the purged, degraded, and marginalized portions of culture, moreover, "Circe" reprises the motifs of "Calypso": the inter-dependence of the excremental and the mental economies, of circula-tion and purgation, of textual and spiritual metempsychosis. One entry in Joyce's *Notesheets* for the episode, in fact, reads "Circe = Calypso" (393), which not only suggests similarities between Homer's female figures but also ratifies the underlying unity between the be-ginning and end of Bloom's adventures. "Circe" makes ends meet. Beneath its dizzying transformations lies a gold standard of realisti-cally portrayed economic events that advance towards the exchange between Stephen and Bloom that we have been awaiting. That ex-change both reflects and consummates the psychic exchanges and purgations they undergo on the way to fusion.

In reviving minor characters and the memories of major charac-ters, "Circe" dramatizes the classic descriptions (cited in chapter 3) of metempsychosis as a cycle of rebirth and judgment. As many critics have observed, the episode is a *ricorso* that recycles and transposes *Ulysses* itself.[1] Not only does it revive the memories of both the textual and extratextual past; it also offers internal schemas of the novel so far, in passages such as the lists of the World's Worst Books (15.1578–84), of Bloom's nine new muses (15.1707–10) and, most obviously, in the Litany of the Daughters of Erin (15.1940–52). Sometimes the symbolic motifs of a single episode are dramatized, as in the Dance of the Hours passage, which transmutes the symbols of history from "Nestor"—horses, bridges, snails—into choreographic commands (15.4098), suggesting that history is writ small in every day that pas-ses. Such metempsychosis in turn demands that readers make returns and thus also adumbrates the Nostos, or return, to which the episode ultimately yields. Like "Nausicaa," then, "Circe" embodies the "first entelechy, the structural rhythm" of *Ulysses* (15.106)—return. Incor-porating the first adventure and pointing to the final episodes, "Circe" functions as the "Interval which" [is] "Consistent with. The ultimate return" (15.2111–12); it acts as the musical dominant to the tonics of "Calypso" and "Eumaeus." It is the fulcrum upon which the novel balances.

Operating as a counternarrative or counterfeit of *Ulysses*, the Nighttown episode recirculates the events of Bloomsday and reflects

1. See, for example, Kenner 1974, 356, and Riquelme 1983, 149.

them in its cracked looking glass. Patrick McGee notes that "Circe" "dialogizes the whole book," and concludes that the episode is not "the place of retribution" but of "distribution" (1988, 116). But it *is* also a place of retribution, employing a dialectic of purgation and expenditure that yields balance, and which therefore conforms to the economy of metempsychosis. The reappearances of characters and the trials of the protagonists compensate—by exaggeration, reversal, and expansion—for the novel's previous events. The "excrement of the text" (McGee 1988, 131), "Circe" is its *part maudite*, its accursed portion, as bottled up energies are expelled and expended in a carnivalization of politics, psychology, and language in which Stephen and Bloom begin to pay their psychic debts by confronting their invisible tyrants. "Circe" thus typifies the aesthetic philosophy described in "The Holy Office," where Joyce names himself "Katharsis-Purgative" and vows to relieve "timid arses" as a "sewer" of society (*CW* 149). In this sense, "Circe" purges not only the characters but also the novel's own repressed social energies; it is the debit side of the book's ledger, the countermovement that balances its credits.

This purgation occurs not only through scenes of trial and ordeal but also through laughter. The humor of "Circe," one of the novel's funniest episodes, illustrates Freud's description of the comic economy, according to which "laughter arises if a quota of psychical energy which has earlier been used for the cathexis of particular psychical paths has become unusable, so that it can find free discharge" ([1905] 1960, 147). That is, laughter acts as a safety valve for the psychic economy, so that energy used to inhibit expression can now be given free vent; we "laugh this quota off" (Freud [1905] 1960, 149). Laughter is also a *part maudite*, an expenditure of excess energy sometimes prompted by visions of excess. Like other late episodes, "Circe" proliferates wildly (Bell 1991, 159), its textual extravagance mirroring Stephen's and Bloom's financial expenditures and physical transformations. Generating laughter by dramatizing excesses, "Circe" also reflects Joyce's obsessive investment of labor, his "wish to go beyond the previous limits of his novel, to push the exploration of perversity into another space of writing" (Rabaté 1991, 86). In this sense, "Circe" seems to violate the classical theater of catharsis: its excesses temporarily deflect our empathy with the characters and thus defuse our emotional purgation. As Bloom and Stephen undergo trials that express their shame, guilt, and anxieties as comic pantomimes, the reader's expectations about the characters are carnivalized and reshaped as in a funhouse mirror. The characters become grotesques, caricatures; our empathy, strongly engaged in previous episodes, is satirized. But the laughter that remains is the trace of that empathy: we place ourselves in their positions and laugh when the comparison reveals our shared absurdity. Their ordeals are so painful, so ridiculous, that we cannot help laughing at their agonies, at their clownishly exaggerated expenditures of energy, and at the difference between those expenditures and what we perceive as the normal (Freud [1905] 1960, 190, 195).[2] In absurdly staging the purgation of its characters' psychic debts, "Circe" also liberates the psychic economies of its readers, and at the same time balances the novel's structural and internal economies.

The proliferating economy of excess and the fetishization and circulation of inner conditions manifest themselves in diverse ways in "Circe." One significant symptom of these economies is the episode's series of what Marjorie Garber calls "transvestite effects" (1992, 16). Characters in "Circe" are costumed and recostumed in constant violation of gender and class categories. As Garber notes, theatrical transvestism generally marks a "crisis of category" repressed in other cultural registers and thereby permits the overthrow of binary oppositions that organize systems of logic and identity (1992, 32). Challenging the stability of identity and representing the space of theatricality, cross-dressing signifies the possibility of crossing or transgressing all boundaries and classifications. At once fetishizing the real and denying the fetish its ability to capture the reality of exchange, transvestite effects stage theatrically what money does in economics: each marks the entrance into representation, the place of the Symbolic (Garber 1992, 239, 356). Just as "Circe" translates all things and events into exchange value and thereby underscores the Symbolic function of money (its role as circulating medium), so cross-dressing shows that gender is merely a conventional representation capable of being exchanged for others. Transvestism is to identity what prostitution is to commodity culture: both announce that the body is merely an object to be sold, decorated or exchanged. Thus Bloom, Molly, Bella Cohen, Virag, and others change costume and even sexual organs. If, as Garber argues, "Excess, that which overflows a boundary, is the space of the transvestite" (1992, 28), then the gender transgressions of "Circe" are one of the most striking

2. As Sabin notes, Joyce's comedy here "subverts conventional pieties about psychic pain and psychic ordeal by turning both the action and the material of disclosure into laughable matters" (1987, 212).

manifestations of *Ulysses'* economy of excess. Bloom's changes place his identity in circulation and also adumbrate the episode's most significant crossing: his exchange with Stephen. In "Circe," even the prudent Bloom is subjected to the excess usually associated with Stephen; the protagonists' material exchanges signify an exchange of identities.

Bloom's ability to change even his sex, to mark himself as neither male nor female but both, liberates him from sexual jealousy. It also permits a temporary transcendence or fusion of the two economic paradigms that have propelled him all along: his generous acts to Stephen, motivated at once by self-interest and charity, by economic prudence and the spirit of the gift, move him into a third space between or beyond oppositions. Bloom and Stephen come to embody the Symbolic function of money: they become circulating mediums. Although neither character seems drastically different after the events and fantasies of "Circe," the staging of each one's guilt and anxieties enables their exchange to take place. Bloom's trials prepare him for his generous financial assistance of Stephen, and his economic concern for Stephen enables him to act out the motives of paternalism and possession that propel his fantasies. In another sense, Bloom's subjection to the economies of Circean excess initiate him into Stephen's own mode of behavior: in a sense, he becomes Stephen. Stephen moves toward sacrifice, for him the logical culmination of his habitual drive toward expenditure and abandonment; he aims to create value by giving up value. Yet, by giving his money to Bloom, he demonstrates that he recognizes the value of the "commercial traveller's" mentality. Their economic exchange thus symbolizes and occasions their psychic exchange.

THE COMMERCIAL TRAVELER ON TRIAL

Bloom enters Nighttown as a consumer: he is first seen *"cramming bread and chocolate"* he has just purchased into his pocket (15.143), and soon after buys a pig's crubeen and sheep's trotter (15.158–59). While he feeds the pork parts to the (imaginary?) dog that follows him throughout the episode (15.672–73), and thus seems to offer them as a gift, the chocolate implicates him in the economy of Nighttown: he later offers it to the whore Zoe (15.2700), but then she gives it back to him (15.2729), so that the chocolate transaction replaces his purchase of her sexual charms. Bloom remains ill at ease in this seamy district and, as usual, expresses his anxiety by worrying about money: "Be-

ware of pickpockets. Old thieves' dodge. Collide. Then snatch your
purse" (15.245). The apparition of Bloom's father, Rudolph, embodies his bourgeois concern about cash as well as his social and ethnic
alienation. Rudolph caricatures the "Jewish" economics of parsimony
Bloom himself violates later in the episode and reiterates the association between fathers and financial advice that we have already seen in
Stephen's encounters. Rudolph is a Jewish stereotype, a kosher Dodd,
complete with the *"caftan of an elder in Zion"* and "Jewish" accent:
"Second halfcrown waste money today. I told you not go with
drunken goy ever. So you catch no money" (15.253–54). Ironically,
although Bloom's paternal emotions motivate him to come to
Nighttown, he begins the episode by acting as an adolescent son endowed with Stephen's prodigality: "One night they bring you home
drunk as dog after spend your good money" (15.266–67). He is
marked as a Jew from the outset of the episode, and his ordeals of
glorification and degradation are partially results of that identification. As a "Jew," Rudolph Bloom comically dramatizes the economic
fetishism Leopold sometimes manifests, in which value is a matter of
fixing prices.

As for Bloom's mother, after a brief appearance as a stereotype of
Irish motherhood, she metamorphoses into the masculinely-named
"Marion," a "handsome woman" dressed in "Turkish costume"
(15.297–98), the first of the transvestite effects in "Circe."[3] Bloom
claims to be her "business menagerer" (15.325)—a meaningful slip,
since *ménagère* is French for "housewife"—thereby acknowledging his
"capture" by Molly-as-nymph in "Calypso." The verb *ménager* also
means "to save, to be thrifty"; it thus punningly denotes Bloom's
economic habits as well as his recognition of the disruption of his
oikos: he saves, while Marion is too generous with her gifts; he plays
housewife while she pursues sexual freedom. Once again, his sexual
shame is promptly translated into the economic register when the
Soap, associated with Molly, metamorphoses into the face of Sweny
the druggist, who reminds Bloom of his unpaid debt (15.337–43). In
these introductory sketches, Bloom's sense of alienation as a Jew and
his shame about his cuckolding become economic fetishes or mone-

---

3. Garber (1992, 311–52) traces the history of Turkish costumes, which were
often used to disguise females as males but also provided a modicum of sartorial
freedom to eighteenth- and nineteenth-century women used to the restricted garments
of the time. This transvestic element conforms with the other ambivalent gender markers attached to Marion's appearance.

tary amounts—his Jewishness is a "second halfcrown," and his cuckolding is "Three and a penny" (15.343)—as the Circean economy
reduces all conditions to prices.

Despite these distractions, Bloom manages to recall his original
reason for following Stephen, which he represents in economic terms:
"What am I following him for? Still, he's the best of that lot. . . .
Kismet. He'll lose that cash. Relieving office here. Good biz for
cheapjacks, organs [con-men and usurers]" (15.639–42). Bloom
hopes to act as a personal "relieving office," replacing with his own
financial ministrations the governmental bureau that in rare cases
doled out money to the poor (Gifford 1988, 461). He fears that Stephen will be swindled out of his cash, and indeed, before they leave
Nighttown, Bloom protects Stephen from just such a flimflam. But he
recognizes the absurdity of his mission ("Absurd I am. Waste of
money" [15.658]), and his charity is ridiculed when, after being ac-
costed by the Watch, he self-righteously stammers "I am doing good
to others" (15.682).

Bloom's first purgative trial, which stages his anxieties about
wealth, class, and citizenship, expands from this encounter with the
Watch. Appearing first as Signor Maffei (a character in *Ruby: The
Pride of the Ring*), then as Henry Flower, and then as a clubbable
"staunch Britisher" (15.794), Bloom "wears" the garments of other
professions and classes to ingratiate himself with the threatening con-
stables. Claiming to be an "author-journalist," he is confronted by
Philip Beaufoy, a "genuine" Englishman garbed in the signifiers of
his nationality and class. Beaufoy, as we have seen, accuses Bloom of
plagiarism (here a kind of linguistic transvestism), of pilfering his
stories of "love and great possessions" (15.826), tales that fit the prostituted economy of "Circe." Lacking even a university education,
Bloom could not have penned the works of this bourgeois "prosodite"
(*FW* 190.35): he belongs to the wrong class (Herr 1986, 167). He
must then defend himself against charges of abusing his own class
superiority over his former servant Mary Driscoll. The defenses given
by Bloom (15.900–922) and his attorney, the down-and-out O'Molloy, present him in turn as an "acclimatised Britisher" (15.909), a
poor immigrant (15.942–43), and an "Oriental" genetic degenerate
(15.951–54). For each role Bloom changes his clothes, becoming in
turn a disheveled householder, a befouled plasterer in a stained
frockcoat, and a pigeonbreasted, pidgin-speaking lascar. The appearance of the "Queens" of Dublin society, who allege that Bloom has
written them obscene letters, reaffirms his feeling of inferiority. As
Herr notes, Bloom's masochistic fantasy of abuse by these wealthy

matrons is a "perfect image for the lower middle and lower class's belief in its own inadequacy" (1986, 173). His curiosity about upper-class sexual behavior casts him as a masochist.

These "queens" are little more than fetishized garments. Thus this allegory of caste is confirmed by the females' cross-dressing (15.1058–56), which both implies the dominance of their social position and undermines it by suggesting that sexual and social roles are merely matters of costume. Bloom's costume changes, furthermore, signify that his Jewish, male, and Irish identities are themselves merely forms of transvestism in which he tries to assume the typical clothing, speech, and manners of the dominant group. Indeed, this scene suggests that Irishness itself has become a kind of forced transvestism in which the oppressed nationality must affect the clothes and language of the colonizer but never feels truly at home in them. As Irishman, Bloom is politically feminized; therefore the "queens" must be coded as upper class and as masculine to play out Bloom's crisis of personal and political identity. But since Bloom ultimately manages these fantasies and agrees to undergo them as a psychic contract (he'll get the most "unmerciful hiding a man ever bargained for" [15.1100]), his degradation permits him to emerge from the other side purged. Only by completing this series of exchanges and symbolically sacrificing himself can Bloom pay his psychic debts, expend his most paralyzing fears and desires, and generate new values to fill the void.

Bloom's social anxieties are further displayed when he is then tried by his friends and acquaintances as a "dynamitard, forger, bigamist, bawd and cuckold" (15.1159). But when he gives up his protective potato to the whore Zoe Higgins, he is launched into a fantasy of aggrandizement in which scapegoat and hero are presented as the obverse and reverse sides of a single coin. In return for his potato, he receives the information about Bella Cohen's son that rescues him at a crucial later moment: one *moly* is exchanged for another. Bloom gives the potato to Zoe, whose surname is the same as Bloom's mother's maiden name (15.2123; 17.536), and then gets it back from her. The loss of the potato allows him to expel his grief over his mother's death through a fantasy of glorification and degradation. His returning balance comes with the return of the potato from the girl playing the mother's role; thus the potato transaction embodies the psychic transactions he carries out in the episode. These structures illustrate the symmetry and balance of both the episode and of Bloom's psychic economy.

Having played son and cuckold, Bloom "becomes" Lord Mayor

of Dublin. Now his fatherly feelings for Stephen are expanded into a political paternalism that doles out worthless symbolic gifts ("temperance badges, . . . spurious coins," etc. [15.1568–84]) to the masses. He announces a vaguely socialist program in a speech laced with populist condemnations of industrialists and mechanization as "hideous hobgoblins produced by a horde of capitalistic lusts upon our prostituted labour" (15.1393–94). Since Bloom is crowned by the archbishop, his exaltation is also religious; in his fantasy Leopold brings Ireland's two masters under a single head, while also receiving a crown that symbolizes his impending exchange with Stephen. In compensation for his earlier spurning by the Citizen as insufficiently Irish, Bloom is now glorified as Irish. He proclaims a new political order: "Union of all, jew, moslem and gentile. . . . Free money, free rent, free love and a free lay church in a free lay state" (15.1685–93). With its secularized and socialized political economy, Bloomusalem would not have been a comfortable Utopia to most Irishfolk of the day. Thus, after Parnell's brother proclaims him the rightful "successor" to the uncrowned king (15.1513), Bloom retraces Parnell's swift fall; incited by the clergy (Father Farley [15.1712–13] and A. J. Dowie [15.1753–60], it seems prototypically Irish.[4]

Jew and Irishman: these are the Philip Drunk and Sober of Bloom's ordeal, the dichotomies he may bridge, expel or transcend by material transformations. If the first part of this fantasy emphasizes Bloom's Irishness, the second part again foregrounds his Jewish and sexual identities. Brini's reading of his genealogy clearly signifies his Jewishness, as does the appearance of his childhood friends Mastiansky and Citron, complete with earlocks (15.1855–69; 1904–5). Now Bloom's problematic Jewishness is translated into sexual terms: his condition as "new womanly man" (15.1798–99) is related to his alleged "degeneracy" as a Semite. Thus it is as a Jew that he delivers the *"eight male yellow and white children"* who take prominent positions in the financial world (15.1821–32). At once Irish and Jewish, Bloom can serve as ideal scapegoat for both nations. Because his glorification is presented as part of a larger structure of balance and compensa-

---

4. Joyce wrote in 1907 that the Irish "have given proof of their altruism only in 1891, when they sold their leader, Parnell, to the pharisaical conscience of the English Dissenters without exacting the thirty pieces of silver" (*CW* 196). In his fantasy the wealthy Bloom is able to decline presents from people like Larry O'Rourke (15.1677) and to refuse Joe Hynes's payment of his three-shilling debt (15.1611–12). This is true prosperity to a man who usually counts his pennies.

tion, his Jewishness is depicted as an economic configuration as well as a national, religious, or ethnic one. That is, the "Jewish" economy of parsimony and balance is parodied and enacted in the episode's structural and psychic economies, as Bloom's glorification leads inexorably to his degradation. If Bloom's transformation into a female bearing golden children dramatizes how both of his ethnic identities have been feminized by the dominant classes, at the same time it suggests his resilience, his ability to cross, circulate, and exchange identities when required.

GIFTS OF HERMES

The next phase of Bloom's trial is heralded by his grandfather Virag, another Jewish caricature. Possessing both the knowledge of a father figure and the cynical philosophy of a pimp, Virag embodies Bloom's "scientific" side and articulates the economic materialism beneath the "meretricious finery" of the brothel (15.2332). Thus if Bloom's father represents economic fetishism, his grandfather embodies erotic fetishism. Viewing the whores' clothing as false advertising, Virag shrewdly assesses the women as commodities: "those pannier pockets of the skirt and slightly pegtop effect are devised to suggest bunchiness of hip. A new purchase at some monster sale at which a gull has been mulcted. . . . permit me to draw your attention to item number three. . . . We can do you all brands, mild, medium and strong. Pay your money, take your choice" (15.2329–51). Virag's cynicism may help Bloom to resist the whores' siren songs: if prostitutes and their customers are merely animals, then feminine wiles are merely brute instincts, and their seductions can be defeated by ratiocination. Virag's naturalism is countered by the appearance of Henry Flower, whose sombrero and dulcimer cover the bald economics of prostitution with the trappings of lovelorn romanticism (15.2478). Flower permits Bloom to camouflage both his sexual attraction to the whores and his guilt over it.

Virag's role is complicated by his ambiguous gender: even as he articulates fatherly warnings and mouths sexist stereotypes of women, he also manifests feminine characteristics. Laughing in *"a rich feminine key"* (15.2432), Virag is a virago, at once womanly man and manly woman (cf. Herr 1986, 138; McGee 1988, 125). Melding the commercial know-how of Hermes and the erotic expertise of Aphrodite, Virag is another of the hermaphroditic figures in "Circe." Expressing Bloom's own ability to cross or transcend gender roles, he is also a caricature of the supposedly "degenerate" and "homosexual" Jew of nineteenth-century typologies, who could be identified by his squeaky voice and "feminine" hands (Garber 1992, 226). Virag's hermaphroditism thus again suggests both Bloom's ethnic and sexual alienation and his resilience. Virag also foreshadows the gender-violating encounter between Bloom and Bella/Bello: both are Jews in Nighttown; both view sex as a business. More importantly, Virag signals the importance and proliferation of exchange in "Circe," where the ability to change one's sex becomes the most radical form of theater or transvestic costuming, one in which exchange overflows its boundaries to encompass sexchange. The hermaphrodite Virag is thus a petal of *moly*, a gift of Hermes whose presence protects Bloom from these sirens' seductions; when he flutters away Bella/o takes his place.

The *"massive whoremistress"* Bella Cohen dominates the next and crucial phase of Bloom's ordeal. Because Bella's lines are spoken by her fan, even before she becomes a man she seems little more than a transvestite fetish, a costume uttering the words that the masochist Bloom enormously desires: "You are mine" (15.2775). At first glance, Bloom's masochism seems to present what Freud calls an "economic problem" because it violates the pleasure principle that seeks to minimize pain. However, the submissive role also allows the masochist to commit " 'sinful acts' which must then be expiated by the reproaches of the sinful conscience"; in this sense it again exhibits the "tendency to stability" that marks Bloom's psychic economy (Freud [1924] 1959, 266, 255).

At work in masochistic games is another economy, which depends upon what Michaels calls the "phenomenology of contract." In one sense, a person who plays a masochistic role or submits him- or herself to bondage actually affirms his or her ownership of the body: that is, one's freedom is complete enough that one can freely contract oneself into slavery. In this case the masochist paradoxically exerts self-ownership by giving it up. The masochist's desire, then, is simultaneously "to own and to be owned," both of which are made possible only by the "bourgeois identification of the self as property" (Michaels 1987, 123–24). Thus, ultimately "the masochist loves what the capitalist loves: the freedom to buy and sell, the inalienable right to alienate" (Michaels 1987, 133); he or she uses compliance as social and sexual currency. Moreover, it is the masochist who usually controls the operations of the dominant party (Michaels 1987, 118). Accordingly, it is Bloom who conjures up the fantasy of degradation he undergoes at Bella/Bello's hands. Perversely, his bondage expresses his freedom to submit himself to a masochistic contract, to circulate his identity and thereby undergo expenditure and achieve balance.

In this way masochistic scenes enact the capitalist economy that underlies prostitution. If everything is for sale, then everything and everybody is alienable; to own the self is also to recognize that the self can be owned or purchased by another. Bloom as masochist is thus Bloom as prostitute: he agrees to give up his freedom for a reward. At the same time, however, Bloom the masochist remains Bloom the customer: his very degradation is his payment, and this payment also embodies his ultimate power over the whore who dominates him. Indeed, because the economy of prostitution—a specific instance of capitalism in which the body becomes a commodity exchanged for money—enables the masochist to treat the body as currency or property, these scenes ultimately confirm the power of market economy, and of money as circulating medium and measure of value. Both customer and whore operate within an economy in which the body is purchasable; both become prostitutes. Underneath the apparent powerlessness of the masochist lies the freedom to submit to contract, beneath which lies the power of money itself. Thus it is no accident that Bloom's masochism further demonstrates his excremental obsession; in the bawdyhouse, sexual and excretory functions are inextricably linked by the operations of filthy lucre.

As Bloom becomes a woman, Bella becomes Bello: they exchange sexes. The whoremistress becomes both phallic mother and Jewish financial father; both personae illustrate the stereotypically "feminized" sexuality and mercenary attitudes attributed to Jews at the time (cf. Garber 1992, 232). Just as Bella/o blends Rudolph, Virag, and the whores, Bloom becomes both john and "molly."[5] These sex-changes produce stereotypical results, as each character is freighted with the signifiers of "normal" gender roles: Bella/o bellows, smokes a cigar, and reads the *Licensed Victualler's Gazette* (15.2897–99), while Bloom is all laced and "staysed" femininity. Like most male Dubliners, Bello has lost money on the Gold Cup won by Throwaway; in one sense, then, Bello embodies Bloom's guilt over his "Jewish" financial luck, and punishes him by mounting and riding him—here Bloom *is* Throwaway. But even before her transformation into a male, Bella, with her heavy olive face and *"sprouting moustache"* (15.2746–47),

5. In eighteenth-century England some homosexual males frequented clubs called "molly houses," where they dressed as women in order to be recognized as homosexual (Garber 1992, 30, 131).

bears masculine markers. There is another sense in which Bella is a man before her transformation: in operating a whorehouse, she already commodifies women and thus complies with the male-directed economy of prostitution. Hence her caricatured depiction as a male businessman merely dramatizes the implications of her profession. As "trick," Bloom too has already accepted those values. Thus Bloom's "transformation" makes explicit what the economy of prostitution does covertly: both the masochistic and the transvestic components of the encounter demonstrate how prostitutes are already female impersonators and how prostitution turns both prostitutes and customers into commodities.

In keeping with that economy, Bloom is given a new name— "Ruby Cohen"—and put up for sale (15.3092–3112). Making Bloom "mine in earnest, a thing under yoke" (15.2965–66), Bello gives him a ruby ring and says, "With this ring I thee own" (15.3067–68). A signifier of Bello's possession, this ring carries far-ranging connotations. The wedding vows again recall Marx and Engel's argument that marriage is no more than lifelong prostitution (1978, 82, 742). The relationship among marriage, money, and whoredom has earlier been suggested by the Nighttown appearance of Gerty MacDowell. Supposedly a virgin, Gerty has also been put up for sale as she mangles the wedding vows: "with all my worldly goods I thee and thou" (15.375). Her error suggests either that when given in marriage, "I" become the worldly goods of "thee" and "thou" (both husband and father), or that marriage is the marketplace in which she sells herself, and therefore the only way to acquire the "worldly goods" of "thee" and "thou." As a virgin, she is "pure exchange value. She is nothing but the possibility, the sign of relations among men" (Irigaray 1985, 186). Indeed, her virginity makes her more valuable: she can be sold at "Ten shillings a maidenhead" (15.359). Similarly, Bloom's auctioning parodies the institution of marriage. As Ruby Cohen, Bloom is identified with the ruby ring, just as Bella has become "Cohen" by marrying Mr. Cohen. Moreover, as if in compensation for his mercenary ruminations on Gerty, Bloom now "becomes" her as well as "his own wife" (Ungar 1989, 495). Nighttown thus confirms Stephen Daedalus's contention that a woman must sell her "corporal asset . . . either as a harlot or as a married woman . . . or as a mistress" (_SH_ 202). Likewise in "Circe" the wedding ring, usually a sign of erotic bonding, becomes a graphic emblem of the prostitution and possession of women in the male-dominated money economy.

Bloom endures—even relishes—his ill-treatment, but when one of his possessions, the "little statue" of Narcissus, is threatened, his ire is roused (French 1976, 194). Thoughts of the kitsch statue invoke another kitsch commodity and bring to life the Nymph from the painting that hangs over the Blooms' bed. Claiming not even to breathe, eat, or defecate (15.3392), the Nymph seems the opposite of the whore. But she too has been offered for sale amidst "ads for transparencies, trued up dice and bustpads," in *Photo Bits* (15.3249–50). The Nymph thus lies along the same continuum as the virgin, the wife, and the whore, her elevation being merely another commodification. The Nymph knows the secrets of Bloom's bedroom and prompts the return of repressed memories. Ironically, this return to the past saves him, as the Nymph's transformation into a nun causes Bloom's trouser button to snap, breaking his hallucinatory spell; a commodity again (indirectly) brings about temporary salvation. Returning to reality with a thump, Bloom seems as hard-boiled as he is in "Nausicaa" and views the whoremistress as mere shopsoiled merchandise.

Restored to his presence of mind, Bloom now asks for his potato *moly* back from Zoe. But he cannot ask for it until he has completed the fantasies of possession and commodification that will purge his psychic economy. Having given the potato to Zoe, he now gets it back: the potato traverses the gift exchange circuit. A gift of Hermes, this *moly* restores Bloom's prudence and paternal feelings and enables him to offer a gift to Stephen. The encounter with Stephen in turn triggers Bloom's final scene of degradation, where his passive complicity with Molly's adultery becomes active. The economic relationship with Stephen, then, occurs between Bloom's two scenes of degradation and thus itself functions as a *moly* that purges him of jealousy, humiliation, and shame.

The potato symbolizes on the naturalistic level other gifts of Hermes that Bloom receives in "Circe." Hermes is first represented by Dark Mercury, who appears several times during Bloom's trials: just before the apparition of Rudolph (15.213), as an adjunct to the appearance of Martha during Bloom's first trial (15.748), then as a "DARKVISAGED MAN" who bids "A hoondert punt sterlink" for the feminized Bloom at auction (15.3110), and finally in the figure of Corny Kelleher. Hermes' guardianship is appropriate for an episode in which all relationships are economic. But here Mercury seems more the amoral trickster than the beneficent patron of travelers, and his gifts seem as unwelcome as the Trojan horse. His most valuable gift, however, is not an object but the capacity for transformation and exchange, a capacity demonstrated in the encounter with Bella/o.

Since the object of degradation must become a woman and the abuser a man, the sexchange between Bella/o and Bloom simultaneously challenges and reinstates gender codes. The conventionality of their resulting gender roles suggests that male and female gender roles are to some degree always costumes or playacting. In this sense, even Bloom's acquisition of a vulva (15.3089) seems merely an exaggerated form of transvestism, and the female organ a detachable prop (Herr 1986, 152). But these sexchanges are ultimately more radical. Just before Bello penetrates Bloom's "vulva," Bello is seen riding his mount and squeezing "his" (Bloom's) testicles (15.2945). This scene, in which Bloom is a man, occurs after Bloom has been called "she" in the stage directions (15.2852). Possessing the organs of both sexes, Bloom is less a transvestite than a hermaphrodite. This conclusion is reinforced by one of Joyce's "*Circe*" *Notesheets:* "waters of Salmacis make hermaphrodite" (344). Hermaphroditus, the progeny of Hermes and Aphrodite, bathed in the waters of Salmacis, a nymph who fell in love with him; ultimately their bodies merged to create a dual-sexed being. This hermaphroditic condition or capacity, then, is another aspect of *moly,* and perhaps the most valuable gift of Hermes.[6]

Like the transvestite, the hermaphrodite constitutes a third phenomenon or space outside of the conventional sexual economy. Unlike the transvestite, however, the hermaphrodite both valorizes the phallic signifier and dramatizes its inadequacy. If the transvestite, according to Garber, symbolizes the entry into the Symbolic by representing theatricality as crossing or exchange, the hermaphrodite transcends that economy of representation by signifying an excess in which logical either/or binaries become inadequate to contain the overflow of signification. A logical impossibility, the hermaphrodite —the child and gift of Hermes—is the place where "roads parallel merge and roads contrary also" (*SL* 272). As the space of excess, the hermaphrodite is also an antispace, a container that overflows; similarly, the hermaphroditic economy circulates from gender to gender and back but ultimately occupies neither position permanently.

6. M. Keith Booker claims that "Bloom is not a transvestite at all but a transsexual" (1990, 450). The difference is important: whereas transvestites supposedly wish to assert the primacy of the phallus by first veiling the penis but then exposing it triumphantly, transsexuals want to lose it altogether, as if to embody the symbolic lack they recognize. Both, however, ultimately fetishize the phallus as the transcendent signifier. Since Bloom possesses both vulva and penis, however, he is not a full transsexual, but a hermaphrodite. Cf. Beja 1982, 262–63.

The hermaphrodite demonstrates the limitations of representation as containment, exclusion, or univocal meaning; he and she thus makes both ends meet but at the same time embodies the inadequacy of that formulation by reaching outside the binary logic that generates it. Like transvestites, hermaphrodites violate the binary structure of the economy of signification; but they mark not so much the entry into the Symbolic as the simultaneity of entry and exit. Hermaphrodites thus typify the linguistic economy of "Circe": they are simultaneously fetishes—sexchanges frozen into a single body—and a representation of sexual commerce. The hermaphrodite in this way illustrates the possibility of an economy that can circulate sex organs and yoke them together.

In a sense, the hermaphrodite also typifies the economy of prostitution. As Stephen suggests in *Stephen Hero*, one can't "consider harlots as human beings. *Scortum* and *moechus* are both neuter nouns" (192): that is, to have sexual intercourse for money is to become neuter, to become subhuman, to enact the Homeric Circe's transformation of humans into pigs. Accordingly, to be a prostitute is to have no gender. Similarly, to be a Jew in Europe is to be an ethnic hermaphrodite, an outcast with mixed group identities. In both senses Bella/o is a hermaphrodite. And yet a hermaphrodite is not a null-gendered creature but its converse, a double-sexed person. Thus the hermaphroditic figures in "Circe" are not only symbols of alienation and incomplete assimilation; they also transform the neutrality and impersonality of prostitution into a potential for transcendence or liberation. They mark not only the third space outside of the sexual transaction but the capacity for human beings to circulate among diverse genders, to acquire a variety of capacities, to thrive in an economy of excess. Whereas Bella/o's gender ambiguities exemplify his/her oppressive self-contradictions—a woman who functions economically as a man—Bloom's are liberating. He becomes the son of Hermes by being "married" to Bello; this exchange enables him to enact and expend the guilt he feels as a sexual and ethnic outsider. As hermaphrodite, Bloom weds the economic prudence, money, and commercial instincts associated with Hermes to the gift giving and sexual congress associated with Aphrodite. Expanding upon and dramatizing the sexual, economic, and political tendencies already operating in Bloom, his sexchange affirms and extends his powers of *ex*change. Indeed, Bloom's hermaphroditic circulation moves him from the economy of prostitution to the economy of heaven—where "there are no more marriages, glorified man, an androgynous angel, being a wife unto himself" (9.1050–52)—and leads him directly to his meeting with the young poet.

NECESSARY EVILS AND PRODIGAL SONS

Bloom finds Stephen Dedalus in Bella Cohen's. If Bloom is clearly seeking a son, Stephen does not seem consciously to be seeking a father. Indeed, in *Portrait*, Stephen cast aside all fathers but his self-generated artistic one and would likely reject any other father as he has his consubstantial one. Nevertheless, his dialogue with Lynch (or Lynch's cap) suggests that he recognizes either a need or a destiny in which he will encounter a surrogate father. As he develops his musical analogy about fundamentals returning to dominants, the cap mockingly interjects, "Ba! . . . Jewgreek is greekjew. Extremes meet" (15.2097–98). Despite its derisory tone, this phrase heralds the impending encounter between the Greek Dedalus—the prodigal son who expends his goods—and the Jew (and Greek) Bloom, whose Jewishness has come to signify not only his alienation but also economic behaviors and discourses from which Stephen can benefit. We have seen how Bloom's trials makes sexual and social extremes meet; Stephen's words and behavior in "Circe" also imply his awareness of the need for what Bloom represents and his desire to make extremes meet.

Another of Stephen's speeches to Lynch invokes a cluster of figures that indicate both his continuing struggle to discover his destiny and the importance of his meeting with Bloom: "What went forth to the ends of the world to traverse not itself. God, the sun, Shakespeare, a commercial traveller, having itself traversed in reality itself becomes that self. . . . which it was ineluctably preconditioned to become" (15.2117–21). In the library he similarly argued that Shakespeare "found in the world without as actual what was in his world within as possible" (9.1041). This again is the pathway to the "economy of heaven": to apprehend and discover the Other within oneself. Just as Bloom's transformations and circulations dramatize his hidden capacities, enabling him to use them or purge them, so Stephen must discover the inchoate Shakespeare—father, Jew, and economic agent—within himself. Accordingly, after uttering these words, he turns and sees Bloom (15.2142), who combines God, Shakespeare, and commercial travelers as *"Reuben J Antichrist, wandering Jew,"* bearing the *"huddled mass of his only son,"* and carrying *"promissory notes and dishonoured bills"* (15.2144–48). As Dodd and Antichrist, however, Bloom remains a usurer who cannot redeem his physical or financial offspring. Thus this apparition represents Stephen's resistance to material and spiritual redemption and Bloom's fatherhood, and his desire to sacrifice himself like the son of Dodd.

As for Dowie, so for Stephen, God is a salesman and therefore belongs in the brothel. This strange affiliation between God and whores has been introduced in earlier episodes through motifs yoking prostitution, paternity, salvation, and the economy of art. Earlier Stephen drew a parallel between salvation and prostitution when he sarcastically called Georgina Johnson, the whore on whom he spent the pound borrowed from AE, a "goddess" (15.122). Later we learn that a "commercial traveller married her and took her away with him," a Mr. Lambe from London, "who takest away the sins of our world" (15.3633–37). The British commercial traveler "rescued" the Irish whore, just as British soldiers in Nighttown claim to "protect" Ireland but treat her as a whore. But prostitutes do perform a sacrificial function: they take away sins by purging the sexual repression of an allegedly devout Irish populace. Prostituted laborers who epitomize the oppression of Irish women and workers, whores are nevertheless scorned as the *part maudite* of society. While exemplifying the Irish economy, their transactions are overtly condemned but covertly sanctioned. Like the artist and the Savior, they are scapegoats.

Bloom may be alluding to this purgative function when he calls Zoe a "necessary evil": she performs a useful, if to some distasteful, social function (15.1980; cf. 16.742). In "Scylla and Charybdis," Stephen uses the same phrase: "a father, Stephen said, . . . is a necessary evil" (9.828). This verbal connection between fathers and whores might seem merely coincidental, but it becomes significant once we consider the larger political contexts in which both prostitution and paternalism operate. This larger scheme is introduced in "Nestor" when, after Deasy claims that Jews "eat up the nation's vital strength," Stephen mentally counters by recalling Blake's "Auguries of Innocence": *"The harlot's cry from street to street / Shall weave old England's windingsheet"* (2.338; 356). Later, in "Circe," Stephen alters the allusion to read "Ireland's windingsheet" (15.4642). But he does not mean that prostitutes are "eating up the nation's vital strength"; he means that the English master is. As we have seen, Stephen views England as land of commercial travelers, of merchants who buy cheap and sell dear, unlike whores, who "sell the body but have not power to buy the soul," and thus are bad merchants who buy dear and sell cheap (16.736–38). For Stephen the British Empire is a sovereignty of successful harlots who buy both body and soul. Stephen reiterates this identification when he encounters Privates Carr and Compton, belligerent representatives of that "brutish empire," and asks where he is "least likely to meet these necessary evils" (15.4575–76). Just as Shakespeare, the English Shylock, is the artistic father whom he must simultaneously kill and embrace, so English commerce and the soldiers that protect it are Ireland's economic and political "fathers." They too exact their pounds of flesh. The soldiers are thus both whores and fathers, and Stephen eventually recognizes that he must kill this tyrannical father—the prostituted one who now resides in his own soul—to achieve liberation.

The Heavenly Father is implicated here as well. Blake's harlot's cry adumbrates Stephen's description of God as a "shout in the street" (2.386; cf. 15.2119–20), and associates harlots with God through His servants in the Catholic church. For Stephen (and Joyce), the sexual repressions of Catholicism not only create and maintain the virgin-mother-wife-whore continuum so evident in "Circe" but also maintain the social rigidity and moral hypocrisy that spread paralysis. Moreover, as "Grace" and "Wandering Rocks" plainly demonstrate, for Joyce the Roman Catholic church in Ireland is politically and economically complicitous with the English master, because it fosters a complacent and spiritually bankrupt ideology of acquiescence. In this sense, Ireland's two masters converge in the brothel, built "with bricks of religion" (*CW* 215). Whores, priests, and soldiers are all guilty of simony, of merchandising the sacred; the commodification of women and the colonization of Ireland are therefore grounded upon similar paternalistic principles. Thus, as long as Ireland is subject to England —a whore of a whore—it will weave its own windingsheet (McGee 1988, 144).

Whores, soldiers, priests, fathers: necessary evils, nets that ensnare the Irish and Stephen, whose defiance of fathers can now be read as part of a political stance against paternalism of all stripes. But the passage from Blake may also show a way to make at least one of these evils less so. Since the harlot "weaves," her labor resembles the labor of the Penelopean and Shakespearean artist who "weaves and unweaves his image" (9.378). Stephen's earlier association of salesmen or usurers and artists similarly yokes their efforts at generation and suggests that Shakespeare's Shylockian qualities inspired his greatest works; thus here the association of harlotry and artistry suggests that Stephen is attempting to liberate himself from these nets by abandoning all material ties. Whereas a "prosodite" like Beaufoy sells his powers to the highest bidder, a Penelopean writer's weaving and unweaving knit together the life and death impulses and thereby transcend material existence.

Moreover, the artist's indiscriminate acts of self-creation and self-generation mirror the promiscuous self-trafficking of the prostitute. According to Stephen, for the Shylockian Shakespeare "all events brought grist to his mill" (9.748): every experience provides raw material that the artist breeds into literary offspring. Likewise, later Bloom and Stephen spot the whore in the black straw hat, "reconnoitring on her own with the object of bringing more grist to her mill" (16.705–6). The shared metaphor of milling weds the artist's self-marrying and the whore's erotic commerce. The artist must traffick in his own life, must transubstantiate all events and experiences into the bread of art; he mints literary currency from experiential deposits. Both the artist and the whore exchange with lutulent reality —the artist by transforming it, the whore by channeling lust into commercial sluices—and perform purgation. Indeed, the artist must be a whore if he is to perform his "holy office," his role as "Katharsis-Purgative" who carries off the "filthy streams" of society" (*CW* 149–151). His material may derive from excrement, but he must incorporate these accursed portions if his productions are to be anything but sterile. Accordingly, although both artists and whores are scapegoats and laborers who weave, only artists unweave what they have woven. Accordingly, it is fitting that Stephen encounters his surrogate father, a commercial traveler, in the brothel. The exchange between Stephen and Bloom gathers these threads of paternalism, prostitution, and purgation and weaves them into the garments of liberation.

Still, Stephen seem less liberated than bent on self-destruction. If he is not selling out his art, nonetheless he is acting the prodigal son by "murdering his goods with whores" (14.276). Thus while Bloom is entertaining visions of Virag, the prodigal Stephen is visited by a series of father figures, including Artifoni (15.2501–4), Frs. Dolan and Conmee (15.3670–76), and Cardinal Stephen Simon Dedalus, who speaks the words of Stephen's consubstantial father (15.2654–91). Stephen acknowledges these patriarchs when he says, "Imitate pa. Filling my belly with husks of swine. Too much of this. I will arise and go to my" (15.2495–96; cf Luke 15:16–18). Like Stephen an exile, the biblical prodigal returned and was welcomed; but Stephen does not want to return. Even though he copies the prodigal's economic habits, he wants to rewrite the parable in his own terms. Stephen's ambivalence is further disclosed by one of the *Notesheets* for

"Circe," which alludes to the parable in Luke that immediately follows that of the Prodigal Son: "SD friends of the mammon of iniquity" (268). The Parable of the Unjust Steward, as I have shown elsewhere, is a key intertext for Joyce's scathing critique of the economic complicity of Church and State in his story "Grace."[7] Both parables concern men who choose mammon over heaven; both use economic metaphors to depict moral and spiritual conditions. More importantly, the Parable of the Unjust Steward ends with Christ's famous warning about serving two masters, a line Stephen adapts to describe his own condition of servitude at the beginning of *Ulysses* (1.639; Luke 16:13). Stephen plays the Unjust Steward by serving two masters, neither of whom will "receive [him] into everlasting dwellings" (Luke 16:9), and both of whom prevent him from making both ends meet.

Stephen's economic and spiritual ambivalence is dramatized by the appearance of two more masters, Philip Drunk and Sober, *"two Oxford dons with lawnmowers, . . . masked with Matthew Arnold's face"* (15.2512–14). As Theoharis has persuasively demonstrated (1988, 151), these twins embody Matthew Arnold's descriptions of Hellenism and Hebraism, respectively. Stephen's Rudolph, Philip Sober is "Hebraic," calculating expenditures and serving as paternal conscience: "Take a fool's advice. All is not well. Work it out with the buttend of a pencil like a good young idiot. Three pounds twelve you got, two notes, one sovereign, two crowns, if youth but knew," and lists the places where Stephen has spent his cash (15.2516–20).[8] Philip Drunk counters with "Go to hell! I paid my way," quoting Deasy on the proudest words of an Englishman (15.2522). Alas, Stephen has not only paid his way today, but also the way of several others; and yet he has not paid his way in other respects: he refuses to acknowledge his debts to creditors both literary and financial, and cannot free himself from the bondage of history as debtorship and dispossession. The two Philips again reveal the conflict between the competing impulses

7. See Osteen 1991, 85–89. Herring transcribes the entry as "SD friends of the ?manner of iniquity" (268). Given his uncertainty here, however, and the fact that these lines form a key part of a previous Joycean fiction and follow closely the other parable cited directly in "Circe," it seems plain that Herring's reading is wrong. The line should be emended to quote Luke 16:9, which reads "Make unto you friends out of the mammon of iniquity" (Douay-Rheims version; cf. *D* 173).

8. The *Notesheets* show that Joyce reviewed the financial exchange in "Nestor" before completing "Circe." One entry lists the various denominations in Stephen's wages: "2 notes (1 torn), 1 sov. 2 crowns, 2s/-" (321). Joyce's care in specifying that one note is torn reinforces my argument that the torn note is a *symbola* representing Stephen and Bloom's financial transaction as an exchange of opposite halves.

of profligacy and reserve that underpin the novel's economy. But if these twin daemons symbolize Stephen's economic schizophrenia, they also adumbrate the meeting of Greek and Jew, and thus the now imminent exchange between Stephen and Bloom, which synthesizes these conflicting strains. This formula may be too schematic: as Theoharis rightly notes (1988, 154), Stephen is plagued by Hebraism —"guilt, shame, zealous self-hatred"—as well as by the twisted Hellenism manifest in his spendthrift habits. Likewise Bloom has submitted himself to Dedalian excess in his earlier trials. Nevertheless, the episode ineluctably points to the necessity for their encounter by showing Stephen's inability to integrate his opposing economies.

As these conflicts suggest, what is at stake for both characters are matters of possession and needs. To whom does Stephen belong? Does Bloom own his wife? What value does money have for each of them? Stephen is unsure of the precise nature of the "one thing needful"; he is unclear both about what is "necessary" and what is "evil."[9] Thus if he is not in search of a father, he certainly needs one, or at least someone who can help him synthesize the miser and spendthrift, Greek and Jew, Philips Drunk and Sober. Stephen has yet to confront his psychic debts, let alone pay them. Even after the initial exchange with Bloom, which I will analyze next, Stephen remains fixated on playing the prodigal. Another invisible tyrant still plagues him—the guilt over his mother's death and his heartless treatment of her. Stephen must confront her, but cannot do so until his exchange with Bloom lays bare his spiritual needs by allowing him to strip away the symbols of material power he has been trying to lose all day.

JEWGREEK AND GREEKJEW

After Bloom gets back his potato, Bella demands payment for the three whores. Stephen, *"taking out a banknote by its corner, hands it to her"* (15.3531–32), his gingerly handling suggesting that it is the torn

---

9. The title of chapter 5 of Arnold's *Culture and Anarchy*, where he develops his definitions of Hebraism and Hellenism, is "Porro Unum Est Necessarium" ("But one thing is needful"; cf. Luke 10:42). The biblical passage he is quoting comes from Christ's words to Martha, the sister of Mary, after she complains that Mary has not helped her serve but has only sat and listened to him. Christ responds that Mary has done the one thing needful. This tale directly follows the story of the Good Samaritan, a text invoked in "Eumaeus" to describe the encounter of Stephen and Bloom. Perhaps coincidentally, a bit later in "Circe," Stephen calls his ashplant *"Nothung"*—"needful" —after Wagner's Siegfried.

note he received from Deasy. He then hands Bella a gold coin, probably a half sovereign worth ten shillings (15.3540). At this point Bella decides to take advantage of his diffidence and drunkenness and demands more money, upon which Stephen *"hands her two crowns"*— ten more shillings (15.3546). Since the men have purchased only three prostitutes, the price should be thirty shillings; but Stephen has given her forty. While the women haggle over the money, Bloom, noting the overpayment, intercedes on Stephen's behalf, laying a half sovereign on the table, taking up the pound note, and offering it back to Stephen (15.3583–92). What has happened, in fact, is that Bloom has paid his own half sovereign for one whore: perhaps this payment is only fair, since he entered Bella's with Zoe and thus might be expected to pay for her attentions. But since the younger man was prepared to pay, and since Bloom was in Nighttown only to watch over him, Bloom really owes nothing. Moreover, Stephen was about to be fleeced by the shrewd Bella. In spirit, then, Bloom's half sovereign is a gift; acting as Hermes' agent, he has passed the *moly* of potential sovereignty on to Stephen. At the same time, the half sovereign, representing both Bloom's prudence and his charity, forms the necessary countersign to Stephen's economy of expenditure; it is the needful other face of Stephen's half sovereignty. Together they blend Philip Drunk and Sober, who together form a potential sovereignty that may replace that of the British monarch whose face was portrayed on the actual half sovereigns of 1904 (Reinfeld 1969, 180). Bloom's coin makes both ends meet.

His charitable work does not stop there. After Stephen fumbles drunkenly in his pockets, Bloom suggests that he keep Stephen's money for him, upon which Stephen hands him *"all his coins"* (Bloom still has the bank note [15.3601–4]). Once again paternal duties involve financial caretaking. Bloom counts the money, which comes to one pound six and eleven, "One pound seven, say" (15.3613).[10] The broken bank note has thus passed from Stephen to Bloom; its two halves have come together in exchange. Indeed, the note's movements embody the Symbolic function of money as circulating me-

---

10. The stage direction is misleading, however, since in "Eumaeus" Stephen manages to find "some" half crowns in his pocket, one of which he lends to Corley (16.195– 96). The inconsistencies and indeterminacies in monetary amounts preclude a precise determination of Stephen's budget, but one can determine it fairly closely by subtracting the amount left from the amount Stephen says he has at the beginning of "Oxen." See Appendix A for my calculations of Stephen's budget.

dium: it passes as wages from Deasy to Stephen, who then gives it to Bella as purchase price; Bloom now takes it back as a kind of banker and, at the end of the novel, returns it to Stephen (17.957–9). When Bloom returns it, the circle is completed; the *symbola*, token of identity and transaction, has served its purpose. Stephen claims he doesn't give a "rambling damn" but has shown enough concern to realize that he can no longer handle his own money (15.3615), and Bloom offers himself as a surety, "a person who makes himself liable for another's debts" (Hyde 1983, 129).

Bloom's management of Stephen's money protects the young man from losing any more, while at the same time permitting Stephen to do what he has been trying to do all day—get rid of his cash. Paradoxically, by ridding himself of the money that represents the material ties from which he wishes to escape, Stephen reattaches himself to the physical world by attaching himself to Bloom, always firmly moored to earth. Bloom's prudence, his "Jewish" economic habits, are crucial for this relationship, because they mark Stephen's entrance into the economy he described in "Scylla and Charybdis" as necessary to artistic creation. Perhaps Stephen may eventually learn to manage this economy himself, to incorporate without Bloom's help the Shylockian qualities of usurer and debt manager. If so, he may enter the economy of heaven, become father and mother to himself and thereby regenerate himself as a Shakespeare, an artist and an economist. For now, however, the two are symbiotically related, as their shared hand injuries imply (15.3713–21). Their hands—the vehicles of their monetary exchange—are the organs of material connection, and Bloom's economic and parental functions are symbolized by "the surety of the sense of touch in [Bloom's] firm full masculine feminine passive active hand" (17.289–90). That touch of surety is the genuine touch—neither exploitative nor falsely friendly—that Stephen has been seeking throughout the day. Nevertheless, neither the transactions between the two nor their psychic purgations are yet complete: other payments must still be made.

Now that he has played the paternal role, Bloom's original economic mission in going to Nighttown is nearly complete. But his psychic economy demands a final expenditure, and his encounter with Stephen leads him to confront his cuckolding directly, rather than through such proxies as Bella Cohen. Thus he acts as footman and voyeur as he imagines Boylan's rendezvous with Molly, who now resembles the Queens of Dublin society who earlier chastised him. Boylan cavalierly tosses Bloom sixpence and hangs his hat on Bloom's

cuckold's horns (15.3763–64), after which Bloom cheers him and
Molly on (15.3815–16). Now he and Stephen gaze into the mirror
simultaneously, their hallucinations merging in an image that both
blends their psychic debts and suggests a means of payment. *"The face
of William Shakespeare, beardless, appears there, rigid in facial paralysis,
crowned by the reflection of the reindeer antlered hatrack in the hall"*
(15.3821–24). In this image the crown buried in Stephen's name is
no more than a cuckold's horns. But if Bloom is not invisible
(15.3828: the logic of dramaturgy demands that the invisible be made
visible), neither are the invisible tyrants—shame and guilt—that have
been plaguing him. Indeed, the merger of Stephen's and Bloom's
fantasy indicates the first glimmerings in Bloom that Stephen might
serve as a satisfactory replacement for Boylan. In this apparition
Bloom is simultaneously Gyges, the bearer of the ring of invisibility
who spied on the queen, and King Candaules. Nonetheless, for the
first time Bloom and Stephen are thinking together: both ends meet.

The Shakespeare apparition illustrates the merger of Stephen
and Bloom by portraying each one's weaknesses: Stephen's unfulfilled literary promise and Bloom's need for punishment and sacrifice. Thus at this moment "Shakespeare" explodes in paralytic rage,
"Weda seca whokilla farst." The garbled quotation derives from a
passage in *Hamlet* when, during the Player Queen's speech in the play-
within-the-play, Hamlet's suspicions about his mother are crystallized.
The Queen says, "None wed the second but who killed the first" (III,
ii, 190). In "Circe" these words of an ironically crowned "king" express Stephen's and Bloom's needs simultaneously: neither can move
to a new stage of life until he "kills" the tyrants that haunt him. In
other words, neither can "marry" himself to the strengths of the other
and thereby make ends meet until he masters his own masters. The
Player Queen goes on to condemn second marriages as mercenary, to
which the Player King responds that time changes obligations, and
"Most necessary 'tis that we forget / To pay ourselves what to ourselves is debt" (III, ii, 202–3). Love fades, but money lasts. The King's
words apply, with modifications, to Stephen and Bloom, whose psychic economies demand that they pay themselves what to themselves
is debt and *then* forget. The Players' speeches and the Shakespeare
apparition's garbled versions of them repeat Stephen's description of
how Shakespeare turns losses into gains by objectifying his psychic
wounds and paying them off. A cuckold himself, he nevertheless
turned that fact into artistic currency. Similarly, Stephen and Bloom
may become Shakespeare—a cuckold who gains, an artist who pays

his debts—only by coming to each other's aid. Indeed, the appearance of Shakespeare here implies that Bloom's restaging of his cuckolding has finally purged his guilt. With Stephen's spiritual aid, Bloom, like Stephen's Shakespeare, can rewrite and control his domestic drama and pay his psychic debt (Henke 1990, 119).

After the phantom's speech, *"The face of Martin Cunningham, bearded, refeatures Shakespeare's beardless face"* (15.3854–55). Cunningham (who is said to resemble Shakespeare) remains problematic. On the one hand, he performs charitable acts, helping out orphans despite his own domestic and economic problems (his drunken wife pawns the furniture), and accordingly functions as a model for Bloom, the Good Samaritan who rescues the fatherless Stephen. On the other hand, as we saw in chapter 5, Mrs. Cunningham undercuts Cunningham's idealization. Thus, as "Cunningham" gazes on her, he shouts, "Immense. Most bloody awful demirep" (15.3863). Because of his wife and his own compromised political position, Cunningham's debtorship, like Stephen's, remains "immense." And just as Stephen remains an economic sentimentalist, so Cunningham remains domestically powerless and socially compromised. But Cunningham's image does rebeard Shakespeare's face, as if to illustrate that the encounter between Stephen and Bloom may help Stephen gain maturity and help Bloom regain his sense of potency and youth. Perhaps Bloom will free Stephen from his debts; perhaps Stephen will give Bloom both a son and a friend. Indeed, Bloom's decision to follow Stephen into Nighttown has already liberated him: here he has immersed himself in the economy of excess, expenditure, and purgation that has been associated with Stephen throughout the novel. In passing through this economy of excess, Bloom gains some of Stephen's sense of abandonment. The Shakespeare apparition, then, both encapsulates the economic and psychic dilemmas of each character and depicts the potential fruits—artistic, domestic and economic—of their exchange of selves.

If Bloom now seems purged of most of his demons, Stephen still must confront his. After leading the whores in the Dance of the Hours, a dizzy Stephen confronts the ghost of his mother, who appears by metempsychosis wearing a torn bridal veil and gravemould (15.4158), as if to imply that it was her marriage—and the ill use she received during it—that caused her death. She thus fits into the feminine continuum limned throughout "Circe," in which wives are turned into lifelong prostitutes and drained of spirit by the patriarchal economy. Stephen now remorsefully pleads for the word that will rename him and free him from her tyranny: "Tell me the word, mother, if you know now. The word known to all men" (15.4192–93). He begs for the word "love" as a gift that will liberate him and at the same time reattach him to the maternal earth. But instead of giving anything to him, the specter tries to steal from him, reaching out a withered arm to touch his inmost heart (15.4220–21); this touch will steal not his money but his very life. Finally, like St. George slaying the dragon, Stephen wields his ashplant to drive the phantom away. Simultaneously creative and destructive, the blow both gives him a new name and announces his desperation. *"Nothung!"* he shouts, smashing the brothel chandelier with his stick (15.4242–43). But although Stephen believes his ashplant stands in for the broken and reforged sword with which Siegfried slays a dragon, Stephen's blow breaks only a lampshade, although it does drive the maternal ghost away.

Stephen's wielding of *Nothung* proclaims his need to reforge in the smithy of his soul the artistic destiny he so boldly announced at the end of *Portrait:* Kinch the knifeblade grows into *Nothung*, the sword. A pun on "nothing," the name signifies his realization that he must become a zero, must wipe clean his psychic ledger, in order to forge ahead, just as he reduced Shakespeare to a zero to acknowledge and pay his debt to the bard. At the same time it proclaims that he is "not-hung," not to be sacrificed for his country like the Croppy Boy, who nevertheless appears soon afterward as an image of Stephen's self-sacrifical obsession (Rabaté 1991, 93). His new name announces that he will no longer be burked, strangled by the navel cord that fastens him to mother and motherland. Ironically, in wielding his ashplant and slaying the ghost of his past, Stephen imitates the picture on the reverse side of the British half sovereign coin, which depicts St. George slaying the dragon; thus Stephen's demon-slaying reenacts a legend that glorifies the English master he seeks to destroy (Reinfeld 1969, 180).[11] He can turn that half sovereign into full sover-

---

11. As Martin points out, Stephen resembles Siegfried only slightly in most other ways (1991, 51). McGee writes that the name of *Nothung* constitutes a "parody of the proper [name] itself," because it "de-essentializes, desexualizes, the very thing it is intended to essentialize and sexualize, making Stephen into no-man, or nothing, or, to be blunt, into one who is not-hung: neither man nor woman, Stephen is nothung" (1988, 141). It is true that the name is a negative or nonname and thus describes mostly what Stephen rejects. But although the notion that Stephen becomes neuter fits my thesis about gender crossings, I see little evidence that he is any more neuter here than he has been throughout the novel. As the image of Rudy, changeling boy, Stephen does seem neuter; but Rudy is a figure of Bloom's desire, not Stephen's.

eignty only by slaying the English master who occupies his consciousness, and thereby make his blow resonate for both personal and national liberation.

"Nothung" also means "needful." In so dubbing his stick and himself, Stephen declares his *in*ability to reforge his artistic identity by himself. Inebriated, nearly broke, and homeless, he certainly needs someone, perhaps even that "necessary evil," a surrogate father. It is fortunate for him that Bloom, Odysseus *polytropos* (the "man so ready at need," according to the Butcher and Lang translation), is at hand (Senn 1984, 130). Throughout the rest of their encounter, Bloom concerns himself a great deal with what he perceives to be Stephen's needs. If his intentions generally seem honorable, nonetheless his plans often address his own needs more than Stephen's. But when Stephen rushes from the brothel and Bella again tries to recoup that ten shillings, Bloom stands up for Stephen's interests: "Ten shillings? Haven't you lifted enough off him?" (15.4278). Indeed, by picking up the ashplant and preparing to strike the shade again, Bloom acts *as* Stephen as well as for him; possessing Stephen's ashplant is a way of assuming his identity. The fusion of the two characters is thus dramatized by Bloom's "taking Stephen's part" in a dual sense; in an episode full of transvestite effects, this is the culminating one: Bloom "becomes" Stephen by dressing and performing as Stephen.

Bloom's last act in Bella Cohen's solidifies their fusion. Racing out to follow Stephen, Bloom tosses a shilling down on the table to cover the damages to the shade (15.4312). The shilling is the perfect coin to symbolize their fusion, since shillings in circulation in 1904 bore on their reverse face a heraldic emblem showing a lion atop a crown (Reinfeld 1969, 181). That is, the shilling's design combines the symbolic names of the protagonists, yoking Leopold, the lion, to *stephanos*, the crown. Their numismatic union illustrates their economic and spiritual fusion. This shilling brings the total amount of Bloom's gift to eleven shillings: if ten shillings—a half sovereign—represents the incompleteness of each character, the added sum marks the beginning of their shared sovereignty. Moreover, since the sum of ten shillings has been marked as the cost of prostitutes throughout "Circe," the added increment moves their exchange out of the prostituted economy that dominates the episode and into the realm of gift exchange. Since eleven is the number of rebirth in *Ulysses*, this sum indicates the regeneration of life out of death and denominates the price of Stephen's initial redemption. In short, eleven shillings means that both ends meet.

Bloom's financial aid to Stephen is significant in another, more theoretical, sense. Throughout "Circe" the Symbolic function of money as circulating medium has been underscored on the realistic plane as the basis of the transactions in prostitution, and on the linguistic plane as a metaphor for the episode's constantly circulating tropic exchanges. Similarly, Bloom and Stephen's financial exchange employs the Symbolic function of money in the bank note's circulation from hand to hand and back. But Bloom's gift of eleven shillings activates the other two functions of money as well. Because the money that Bloom holds for Stephen is a deposit in Bloom's personal bank, it embodies the Real function of money as a genuine store of wealth. And because the money exchange symbolizes the friendship and paternity that Bloom extends to Stephen and the value that Bloom finds in him, it functions as an ideal gold that represents not only Bloom's lost son (through the association of feces, money, and gold described in chapter 3) but also Stephen's lost spiritual assets. Thus it also manifests the Imaginary function of money as a measure of values. Bloom's gift to and exchange with Stephen breaks out of the prostituted economy, then, not only because the spirit of the encounter opposes the mercantile commerce of prostitution, but also because it freights their encounter with all the charges that money can bear. Combining the erotic charge of gift exchange and the balanced accounting of the commercial traveler, their exchange blends Aphrodite and Hermes and yields a balanced ledger. In this sense, their exchange is a prototype for all exchanges: at once gift, deposit, and balanced transaction, it creates a new entity that emerges only when giving and receiving are combined; like hermaphroditism, this exchange generates a "third phenomenon" that is neither one nor other but both (Simmel 1978, 90).

SACRIFICIAL VALUES

Stephen's expenditures have been motivated by sacrifice all day, as his interior monologue in "Wandering Rocks" suggests. Now purged of (most of) his money, Stephen undergoes a bloodless but painful encounter with British soldiers that not only plays out his own sacrificial impulses but also discloses the politics of prostitution and the economy of social value. Encountering Privates Carr and Compton, he greets them sarcastically as "guests. Uninvited," for whom "history [is] to blame" (15.4370–72). Indeed, historically, thousands of British soldiers were garrisoned in Dublin and thus were a common sight on Dublin streets, especially in the red-light district

(O'Brien 1982, 246, 117–19).[12] These privates are accompanied by Cissy Caffrey (now a whore), a grouping that implies the collaboration of political and economic exploitation: Britain has prostituted the Irish economy by limiting employment and industry, enforcing this oppression with military power. However, Joyce again depicts Irish complicity in Cissy's explanation that she is "faithful to the man that's treating me though I'm only a shilling whore" (15.4382–83) and in her question to Carr, "Amn't I with you? Amn't I your girl?" (15.4651–52). Stephen is more recalcitrant, and he translates the global designs of the British Empire into the personal economic sphere—"He wants my money and my life, though want must be his master, for some brutish empire of his. Money I haven't" (15.4568–70)—as if they were sent specifically to harass him alone. But in a sense he is right: each Irish citizen has suffered economically and existentially from the occupation. Thus the Irish, Stephen included, need less to assassinate their masters, either British or Italian, than to destroy their effects on consciousness. As Stephen remarks, tapping his brow, "But in here it is I must kill the priest and king" (15.4436–37). Throwing off the oppressors of consciousness nevertheless demands sacrifices that may give to Stephen's nation the products of his mind freed from those masters.

Stephen's sacrificial intentions summon hallucinations of other Irish victims: the Wild Goose Kevin Egan (15.4498); The Croppy Boy and his executioner, Rumbold, master barber (15.4531–58); Old Gummy Granny as the Ireland of the potato famine (15.4578–88); and Mina Purefoy, *"goddess of unreason,"* about to be sacrificed on the altar of procreation by Father Malachi O'Flynn and the Reverend Mr. Haines Love (15.4691–4706). The sacrificers—including Edward VII and the clergymen, who combine the names of Mulligan, Haines, and the Reverend Mr. Love—are all trespassers representing that "history" of oppression by the collaborative powers of Church and State. Perhaps more insidious is the way that the Irish fight not against the tyrants but instead *"exchange in amity"* blows with each other (15.4681). Like those other Irish bent on self-sacrifice, Stephen

12. The soldiers' presence had another effect: over a third of the troops stationed in the Dublin garrison in the last quarter of the nineteenth century were treated for venereal disease at one time or another (most likely contracted from prostitutes). Thus, O'Brien remarks, "the prostitutes of Dublin were doing far more than republican-minded nationalists to weaken the sinews of the Empire" (1982, 117). Weak sinews or not, British soldiers dominate the Irish in "Circe." For a more detailed account of the social aspects of prostitution in turn-of-the-century Dublin, see O'Brien 1982, 189–95.

provokes Private Carr, who strikes Stephen; the poet "collapses, falls, stunned" (15.4748–49).

The aim of sacrifice is to consecrate a victim and thereby to alter the "moral condition of the person who accomplishes it" (Hubert and Mauss 1964, 13). The person to whom the benefits accrue may be either the victim or a separate person, called the sacrifier (Hubert and Mauss 1964, 10); in the latter case the victim passes on to the sacrifier the new qualities acquired through suffering and purification. Sacrifice redeems the sacrifier by allowing the victim to pay the sacrifier's moral debts; the sacrifier returns to the community, purged of sin. Here Stephen acts as victim, but the benefits accrue both to him and to Bloom; just as Bloom has paid Stephen's debts, now Stephen acts out Bloom's role as scapegoat, thereby paying him back for his gifts. The sacrificial scene thus dramatizes on a broader and more mythic level what their financial exchange signified on an economic level. More importantly, sacrifices generate new value. According to Simmel, because true exchange exists only when each party gives up something and therefore loses another potential value, all exchange involves sacrifice (1978, 83). Value is created when a good acquires the worth of the good for which it is exchanged. Because value is created only by a rehabilitated loss, all value is "the issue of a process of sacrifice" (Simmel 1971, 48); exchange synthesizes loss and gain into a third element that combines the values of giving and receiving. Bloom's sacrifices thus empty him to receive the value that Stephen offers and represents: he loses money but receives spiritual value. Stephen sacrifices his money but gains spiritual assets and, unintentionally, a caretaker. The exchange between the two, then, generates value through reciprocity: each loses something, but value is created by recuperating the sacrifice those losses entail. Stephen must lose in order to gain; the sacrifice of his old self permits him to exchange reciprocally with Bloom and acquire the values that Bloom represents.

Sacrifice also has the broader social function of binding victim and sacrifier to their community. The victim gives something up that the community then receives through the victim's ceremonial consecration of the values he or she represents. The victim becomes a gift given in exchange for the suffering he or she has endured, which is now ritually consecrated; thus the sacrifice both purges the community and creates new values that are given back to the group. In this sense, then, "sacrifices create the social entity" (Hubert and Mauss 1964, 102) by engendering value through ritual exchange. It is logical, therefore, to read Stephen's encounter with Private Carr as an allegory of the relations between Ireland and the British Empire, in which his knockout functions as an attempt to rehabilitate the social order by self-sacrifice. But Stephen's sacrifices again merely reenact on a small scale the history of bloodshed, violence, and futile martyrdom that *Ulysses* critiques in such episodes as "Cyclops." If Stephen could instead manage the bloodless sacrifice of art, he might finally engage in fruitful reciprocal exchange with his community. If he could replace paralyzing and antiquated heroic images like the Croppy Boy with an image of art as sacrifice and labor, he might regenerate that community; in so doing, he could purge and glorify himself as well. Such sacrifices are simultaneously selfish and generous; they are both gift and contract in which both victim and community receive a fair exchange (Hubert and Mauss 1964, 100). Stephen's attempt at sacrifice thus expresses, misguidedly, Joyce's own "selfish generosity" as an attempt to generate value through loss, not only for himself, but for Ireland.

Stephen's knockout also dramatizes personal debts for Joyce. If there is to be a sacrificial victim, there must also be a Judas, and Lynch, who deserts Stephen in his time of need, fills that role. In Lynch, as we have seen, Joyce pays off his debts to Vincent Cosgrave, whom he believed had betrayed him by seducing Nora and by deserting him during a fracas similar to the one here (see *JJ* 160–61). Pointing at Lynch, Stephen intones, *"Exit Judas. Et laqueo se suspendit"* (15.4730): the betrayer also undergoes a symbolic hanging. In addition, Carr, Bennett, and Rumbold (the principals in Joyce's entanglement with Henry Carr, detailed in chapter 1) are paid their moral wages by being cast as villains in the Circean drama. Joyce balances his psychic ledger by a double-entry moral bookkeeping. Playing Shakespeare-as-Shylock, he takes his pound of flesh in literary currency.

Often, then, Joyce seems more concerned to pay off personal scores than to restore his community through artistic sacrifices. This economy is not value-generating but mere accounting. But in other respects, art is by definition sacrificial: transmuting the flesh of experience into the Word necessitates suffering and expenditure. Joyce believed that his sacrifices—including his exile from Ireland—were necessary to produce texts that disclose the relationships between individual and community. The very artistic labor that, through a carnivalization of social rituals, reveals Stephen's economic and aesthetic inadequacy and the weaknesses in Dublin's political economy, also provides a possible means of correction. Thus in writing "Circe," he again labors to engineer the economy of excess analyzed in regard to other episodes. Like those episodes, "Circe" was a difficult one to execute. In August, 1920 fairly early during its composition, Joyce wrote, " 'Circe' is giving me in all ways a great deal of worry. I have written the greater part of it four or five times. . . . Circe herself had less trouble weaving her web [*sic*] than I have with her episode" (*L* III, 15). By December he had rewritten the episode eight times (*L* III, 32). Like his characters, the author must sacrifice to generate value. But if, as Bataille contends, the author means to add to "society's store of fixed meaning," then "he can only escape the constraints imposed by social conventions of language by a willed determination to sacrifice 'all that language adds to the world' " (cited in Richman 1982, 125). The author's sacrifices are thus simultaneously creative and destructive, as his transubstantiation risks the sacrifice of meaning. Replicating the history of Irish political sacrifices and economic excess, Joyce simultaneously affirms and denies his Irish identity in his artistic sacrifices. Likewise, the reader, too, must undergo purgation and sacrifice through his or her circulation in the Circean economy of excess; such a process may generate new values and create a new community of readers.

As for Stephen's sacrifice, it is literally bloodless—Cissy asks, "Is he bleeding!" and a man answers, "No. Gone off" (15.4778–80)—but it is not Eucharistic. It also seems more comic than exalted. The vigilant Bloom stands by, holding Stephen's hat as he once did for Parnell, whom Stephen aims to replace (16.1336; 1915–18). In the nick of time appears Corny Kelleher, police tout and avatar or steward of Hermes, bearer of the dead to Hades. Fulfilling Hermes' function as patron of thieves and commercial travelers, he has escorted two "commercials" to Nighttown (15.4861). Corny's arrival on the scene is "Providential" (15.4858): his insider status functions as *moly*, an "accident of providence," a gift of Hermes (*SL* 272).[13] Kelleher's presence as Hermes' representative signifies the god's approval of Stephen and Bloom's exchanges, indicates the efficacy of the sacrifices that have brought them together and ensures their further exchanges.

---

13. The notesheets to "Circe" reinforce Kelleher's association with Hermes. Immediately following a list of Hermes' attributes—"Guide, to & from Hereafter," "god of dreams (nightcap) speed, . . . commerce, thieves," etc.—a note reads "Corn. Kell. business card sober drivers speciality" (304). Kelleher's hearses are driven by sober guides to ensure their safe passage to Hades.

Left standing guard, Bloom believes sleep is *"exactly what Stephen needs"* (15.4915–16). For the first time he purposefully touches Stephen (shaking his shoulder), and for the only time in the novel calls him by his first name (15.4922; 4927). His touch and his naming demonstrate concern and friendship. He also holds Stephen's dinged hat—his "crown"—and ashplant; Bloom's possession of Stephen's identifying markers constitutes another transvestite effect—Bloom dressing as Stephen—that dramatizes their exchange in typical Circean fashion through change of costume. Bloom has, temporarily, "become" Stephen; extremes meet through exchange. Indeed, when Bloom murmurs "in the rough sands of the sea . . . a cabletow's length from the shore . . . where the tide ebbs . . . and flows" (15.4952–53), it is as though Stephen's hat has imbued him with Stephen's poetic talent. Stephen has also filled Bloom's needs by enabling him to act out the paternal instincts that brought him to Nighttown in the first place.

At this crucial moment the fusion of Stephen's and Bloom's needs produces the final apparition—Rudy, Bloom's lost son—*"a fairy boy of eleven, a changeling, kidnapped, dressed in an Eton suit with glass shoes and a little bronze helmet, holding a book in his hand"* (15.4957–58). Most critics have read the apparition as a symbol of Bloom's fatherly feelings for Stephen and interpreted Rudy's ivory cane and book as Bloom's refiguration of Stephen's ashplant and scholarly accomplishments. Most have read his appearance as proof that Stephen and Bloom's meeting is significant and positive. Herr, however, remarks on what a "bizarrely cross-coded" figure this Rudy is and argues that he resembles the "principal boy" in early twentieth-century panto shows (1986, 176), implying that Rudy is another grotesque figure satirizing Bloom's paternal feelings and idealized vision of the upper class. Herr's reading is helpful: one must recognize the comedy and absurdity of this vision and avoid sentimentalizing it. Moreover, Rudy's *"unseeing"* gaze at Bloom (15.4964), seems to signal Bloom's awareness of the irreparability of the past and his recognition of an unbridgeable gap, not only between his past and his present but also between his own education and abilities and Stephen's.

But Rudy's strange appearance and sources in popular culture need not invalidate his positive symbolic significance. Indeed, the theatrical history buried in the stage directions confirms his positive value. As a "changeling," Rudy's role would be played by the kind of boy actor who would have played a woman's roles in Shakespeare's day. In Renaissance drama, Garber argues, changeling boys symbolize what is "never present—or, at least, never speaks" (1992, 85).

Indeed, "boy actors [themselves] . . . *are* changelings, are not only in process of change but are significations of change, and *ex*change, in and of themselves. An actor is a changeling; a boy . . . is a medium, and a counter of exchange" (Garber 1992, 92; emphasis hers). The changeling boy exemplifies the power of theater to effect transformation and exchange; similarly, the changeling boy in "Circe" represents the changes in and exchanges between Stephen and Bloom, both of whom are now changelings as well. As a changeling—something simultaneously present and absent, at once fetishized and ephemeral —Rudy perfectly betokens the relationship between Stephen and Bloom: the figure simultaneously fetishizes them and frees them from fetishization. It is both real and imaginary. Rudy is Stephen reclothed in Bloom's imagination as the prodigal returned. In this sense the ruby buttons on Rudy's suit (15.4965–66) consummate the motif of ruby rings, which have served in "Circe" as emblems of marital possession and loss; his appearance thus returns the ruby to Bloom (cf. Ungar 1989, 493). As a boy of eleven, moreover, Rudy confirms the significance of eleven as a sign of renewal. Indeed, he is the final gift of Hermes and Aphrodite, the transfiguration of Circe's prostituted economy. Like a hermaphrodite or transvestite, Rudy is "neither one thing nor the other" (18.1308); like reciprocal exchange itself, he constitutes that third phenomenon, a value that is neither one nor the other, but both. This moment—in my view the most moving in the entire novel—crystallizes the value of their exchange: Bloom has found a son, and Stephen a father. "Circe" ends, according to the Linati schema, with the "fusion of Stephen and Bloom"; Rudy embodies that fusion.

At the same time, however, he indicates the fleeting quality of their exchange and Bloom's inability to see Stephen as anything but an embodiment of his own needs. Like Rudy, Stephen will leave. A placeholder for the imaginary father/son relationship now beginning between the two protagonists, Rudy is a kind of double fantasy: he is both Bloom's fantasy of return and Stephen's fantasy of departure. Thus Rudy's appearance raises a larger question: do Stephen and Bloom really carry out meaningful exchanges with each other? Do they really gain anything new from their Circean hallucinations? Since neither seems to remember this episode, nor refers to the fantasies, is "Circe" nothing more than a long reiteration of what we already know about these characters? Several recent critics have argued that "Circe" neither purges the protagonists nor furthers their development. Rabaté, for example, remarks that "what is definitively lost with the baroque dispersion of all the motifs is the notion of psychic economy. Bloom and Stephen do not gain anything in this scene; they do not learn any deeper truth about themselves and never mention their fantasies when dialoguing after the episode" (1991, 89; cf. Herr 1986, 165). I would argue instead that "Circe" both explores and explodes the psychic and textual economies by subjecting the novel and its characters to the economy of excess. In fact, it is precisely that excess, that expenditure, that brings about their purgations. At least, then, "Circe" dramatizes for them and for us where their needs lie and through its mental theater permits each to stage his own private sacrifices and thereby objectify, if not pay, his psychic debts. The purgative moments prepare them both, but especially Bloom, for the encounter that ends this episode (and the Adventures section of the novel) and sends them towards home. Indeed, the bare fact that the protagonists are now together proves that they are not exactly "as they were at the outset" (Herr 1986, 165).

Moreover, the economic elements of "Circe" are crucial to understanding their encounter: Stephen's willingness to give his money to Bloom, the highly charged symbolic qualities involved in the exchange, and Bloom's reenactment of the connection between fatherhood and financial management all suggest that their money exchange both produces and reflects fruitful exchanges on other levels. Although it takes place within a prostituted economy, their exchange finally transcends it. Bloom's monetary aid provides a starting mechanism for their friendship and creates a material, symbolic, and imaginary bond between them. The exchange of money also embodies the changes both have undergone and the values generated by purging and paying psychic debts. Each has what the other needs: Stephen needs Bloom's material sense, his stability, his connection to the earth; Bloom needs Stephen's youthfulness, his sense of abandon, his knowledge. Each receives from the other a new value, a new essence. Nevertheless, the next two episodes demonstrate the difficulty of sustaining any exchange, no matter how charitable its initiating motives. The Nostos subjects the relationship to two kinds of alienating narratives: the first uses a bourgeois, conventional, and spurious Bloom who perceives all narratives, all money, all relationships, as counterfeit; and the second employs a hyper-rational narrator who presents art and desire as collections of objects and narrative as accounting. Thus although Bloom's meeting with Stephen does make both ends meet, synthesizing the dual strains we have discovered in Joyce and Bloom, this balanced ledger remains provisional. If

the novel is to remain true to the implied psychic, linguistic, or financial economies of "Circe" and if it is to continue to offer an authentic
account of the characters' behavior (and, indeed, of human behavior),
it must not stop here, but must occasion further circulation, further
exchanges, further returns.

10

The Money Question at the Back of Everything

> Truths are illusions about which one has forgotten that this
> is what they are; metaphors which are worn out and with-
> out sensuous power; coins which have lost their pictures,
> and now matter only as metal, no longer as coins.
> —Nietzsche (1873) 1954, 47

Eumaeus" marks the beginning of the Nostos, the return to origins.
Likewise the reader, after the dizzying transformations of "Circe,"
turns to the sixteenth episode with relief: here again is recognizably
novelistic prose, and a familiar world of sandstrewers, brooms, and
cups of coffee. As in realism, the narrator emphasizes economics as
both form and content, finding "the money question . . . at the back
of everything" (16.1114) in a dual sense: habitually employing economic terms to explain behavior, the teller also relies (perhaps unwittingly) upon homologies between money and narration in hopes of
discovering a stable economy of meaning. The reassurances these
homologies promise soon dissolve, for, beneath the appearance of
realism, beneath the narrator's bourgeois ideology and entrepreneurial plans, emerges a counternarrative that challenges conventional
economies of meaning, subverts stable identity, and undermines the
belief that money explains and stabilizes value. As part of the Nostos,
"Eumaeus" is also much concerned with origins and originality. In
this regard, too, the very homologies that seem reassuring actually
problematize the relationships among value, origins, and authenticity: here money and narratives are counterfeit; identities are genuine

forgeries; charity disguises profit making. These tensions in the economy of "Eumaeus," then, expose tensions in the concepts of originality, genuineness, ownership, and value upon which the economies of money and realism are founded. Moreover, these problematic relationships shed new light both on the relationships between the narrator and the protagonists and on the social exchanges between Stephen and Bloom.

COINING WORDS

The episodes of the *Odyssey* that correspond to "Eumaeus" foreground questions of narrative deception and disguise. In book 13, Odysseus is finally taken home by the Phaiakians, his ship laden with the treasures he has received in exchange for his colorful tales: his narratives have earned substantial returns. Profoundly asleep when he lands, the awakened Odysseus fails to recognize either Ithaca or Athena, who appears disguised as a boy and tells him where he is; asked to identify himself in return, Odysseus contrives an elaborate fiction of origins that identifies him as a wandering, ragged Cretan. As in "Cyclops," Odysseus responds to a request for identification with a lie, again implying the unreliability of narrative identification. Praising him—"you play a part as if it were your own tough skin" (Homer 1961, 239)—Athena transforms him into just such a ragged old man, thereby making his lie true. Then, in book 14, Odysseus approaches the hut of Eumaeus, his swineherd, who fails to penetrate his disguise but welcomes him anyway. Though Eumaeus is dubious of travelers' tales ("wandering men tell lies . . . for fresh clothing"; they can "work [a] story up at a moment's notice, given a shirt or cloak" [Homer 1961, 251]), he asks the Cretan to identify himself. Once again Odysseus responds with a narrative disguise, embellishing the tale he told Athena and offering a story that parallels his real history at several points. Despite his skepticism, Eumaeus credits the entire narrative—all but the true part in which the Cretan claims that Odysseus is alive and will soon return to reclaim his *oikos*. One of his stories (about receiving a cloak from Odysseus) earns the Cretan a warmer cloak. Here, then, narratives are cloaks, false skins, truthful lies that earn tellers return gifts. Narrative is a medium of exchange whose value as currency depends not upon veracity or proof of origins but upon fictional creditability. Joyce's "Eumaeus" also treats narrative as counterfeit currency, as disguise or deception; however, in Joyce's reworking of the tale, money is also subject to the deceptions inherent in narrative.

Just as the *Odyssey* portrays Odysseus' attempts to return to his place of origin, so "Eumaeus" charts the beginning of Bloom's return. For though Joyce's schema gives the "art" as "navigation," it might better be dubbed "circumnavigation," so as to refer not only to the voyages of Bloom, Odysseus, and the yarnspinning sailor Murphy (Odysseus Pseudangelos) but also to the prose style. Here paragraphs wander from their subjects only to return by incommodious vicuses of recirculation; sentences tiptoe with delicate circumlocution around sensitive subjects; clichés encircle each other in uneasy mutual orbits. The teller's circumnavigations also chart Bloom's: as Bloom considers whether "Murphy" is authentic, his mind wanders to his own travel plans (16.500–516), then to possible tours he might arrange for Molly, to prospects for vacation enterprises, and finally back to Murphy (16.600). Murphy's tales of circumnavigation occasion Bloom's mental travels, which again entertain ways of making ends meet both psychically and economically. Similarly, when the denizens of the shelter discuss Parnell, Bloom, although deeming Parnell's "return highly inadvisable" (16.1311–12), makes a return himself, remembering the same events (Parnell's adultery, fall, and the *United Ireland* incident) two different times (16.1358–1552). Unlike Bloom, the narrator of "Eumaeus" is never quite able to make ends meet, to balance the competing demands of clarity and finesse, to decide which economic ideology he espouses, or even to remember precisely what the topic was.

As if mirroring Bloom's compulsive recycling and mental circumnavigation, the narrator, like Murphy a disguised or composite figure, recycles the commonest phrases and utterances. Reusing clichés, stereotypes, and received opinions, the narrative voice aims not to be original but rather to express what everyone already knows. Straining to sound impressive, he sometimes employs a pretentious foreign and Latinate diction but elsewhere ingratiates himself to an implied audience of bourgeois novel-readers by adopting colloquial expressions and earthy proverbs. Although the narrator labors to produce Bakhtin's "ennobled discourse," which attempts to stretch a single "respectable" linguistic cloak over the diversity of social life (1981, 384–85)—his style, like his ideology, is inconsistent. Seemingly middle-class and English, the narrator nonetheless plumps for Ireland; unthinkingly spewing out stereotyped phrases, his dogged triteness produces cliché collisions that achieve a hilarious originality.

Given his desire to please, we might expect the narrator to practice a conventional realism. He fails to do so, but not, as Gerald Bruns claims, because he cannot "redeem . . . ordinary content by means of style" (1974, 364); rather, he fails because he tries too hard to redeem it. In striving for a model realism, the narrator violates most of the strategies realism uses to encourage referential reading (see H. Steele 1988, 6; and chapter 3, above). Though the world of "Eumaeus" may be "rich," the narrator impoverishes it by placing all behaviors into prearranged slots shaped by his received phrases; he undermines his capacity to transmit information about the world by depicting a plethora of lies, dubious stories, and false histories; his garrulousness and handicapped style constantly thrust him into the reader's attention. And if one of the chief functions of realism is to provide a clear description of events, here the narrator is hopelessly lame, obscuring simple events by compulsive qualifications: "it was a warm pleasant night yet wonderfully cool for the season" (16.1461). Is it warm or cool?[1] If often the language offers an embarrassment of riches, in these cases it truly "beggars description" (16.599).

Nevertheless, the narrative presence betrays a decidedly bourgeois obsession with money. Both the notesheets and the episode are highly seasoned with economic terms and phrases, some of which Karen Lawrence has discussed in her fine recent essay on the episode (1992, 367). As she observes (1992, 361), the narrator transforms even socialist and religious concepts into bourgeois platitudes, so that revolution must come on the "due instalments plan" (16.1101), and hell is run like an insurance program (16.642–43). Thus in the teller's eyes, Bloom too seems thoroughly bourgeois: he defends Jews for economic reasons (16.1124) even as he disclaims his own Jewishness; he warns Stephen against Mulligan while admiring his ability to "draw . . . a handsome fee" (16.291); he worries about robbers in this seedy part of town (16.117-26). When Bloom explains his belief that each person should have "a comfortable tidysized income" of £300 per year (16.1134)—far more than either he or Stephen earns and far more than any welfare plan could feasibly provide—it is transformed into a commonplace according to which "you can live well . . . if you work" (16.1140). Although Bloom (according to this narrator) desires to "do good and net a profit" (16.800), here Debit and Credit overwhelm his charitable impulses. The tentative and vacillating prose thus reflects Bloom's lukewarm bourgeois allegiances, which in turn exemplify the divided allegiances of the Irish middle class: attempting to serve both God and mammon, both Ireland and England, and to

---

1. Likewise, do Stephen and Bloom make a beeline or do they lag (16.100; 103)? Does Bloom give a whistle or doesn't he (16.29–30)? Does Murphy uncork or unscrew the bottle (16.927)?

synthesize nationalist idealism with an "English" pragmatic economics, they fail to satisfy either demand and only paralyze themselves in
impossible conflicts.

Curiously, although economic terms compulsively worm their
way into the apple of discourse, when the narrator is forced to mention actual cash transactions, he resorts to Latinate euphemisms such
as "pecuniary emolument" or "highly remunerative" (16.1840;
16.522), as if embarrassed openly to discuss such vulgar matters.
Though he cannot baldly talk about money, he cannot not talk about
it. Thus it is in keeping with his desperate and insecure middle-class
principles to find "the money question . . . at the back of everything"
(16.1114–15), a belief that both drives him to mercenary postures
and condemns those postures in others. And yet the episode's verbal
economy violates the narrator's expressed adherence to bourgeois
conservation. As Bell notes, his prose constantly makes "expenditure
that is too large" (1991, 115), perpetrating redundancies, wasting
words, and repeatedly saying what is "needless to say" (e.g., 16.1264).
Ironically, even as the narrator habitually defends the bourgeois values of prudent economic management, the narrative economy engages in a "squandermania" (16.87) of words that eludes such
management. Though he celebrates regulation and regularity (Lawrence 1992, 366), he cannot regulate his own prose. In terms of ideology and style, then, "Eumaeus" is not realistic but antirealistic, its
realistic facade only more thoroughly subverting the conventions it
seems so anxious to follow.

One obvious way the narrator tries to manage events is by re-
sorting to clichés, a habit that has earned much critical comment. Its
proliferating platitudes give the episode the appearance of a huge
verbal pawnshop or compost heap, a receptacle for sixteenth-hand
formulae borrowed or stolen from public discourse. The handicapped style of "Eumaeus" is a "hackneyed run" (16.1850), a limping
narrative of cobbled clichés, an unwelcome gift to the reader, a verbal
Trojan Horse.[2] The recycler of this hackneyed prose is thus himself
a hack (also derived from "hackney"), a lame stylist, a kind of lesser
Philip Beaufoy who writes only for and about money. Behind his
clichés lies an entire history of linguistic coinage, an enormous verbal
marketplace in which messages and phrases circulate, like commodi-

---

2. Lawrence (1992, 362) traces the derivation of "hackney" from a term for a
run-down horse and points out the pertinence of its other meanings for "Eumaeus":
the word also refers to a cab carriage ("Eumaeus" takes place in a cabman's shelter)
and to a prostitute (one wanders through the shelter).

ties to be bought and sold. But clichés demand no "change" from their "purchasers," instead sailing along automatically, circulating effortlessly without stopping at the brain. Thus if the teller is again one of the "intellectual debtors of society" (*Notesheets*, 395), his creditors are not single authors but rather the entire linguistic community. And if he is a hack, he is not even a very good one, because he deals in easily available merchandise, cannot keep a good inventory of his stock, and has stolen most of his wares.

Clichés are recognizable verbal formulae, tired or wornout metaphors that have lost their figurative power and become frozen into a unity, "failed aphorisms" that no longer seem pithy (Levine 1979, 118; Sabin 1987, 13, 22). Originally a printing term like its semantic kin *stereotype*, cliché was an onomatopoeic word coined to mimic the sound of a new style of mechanical printing that used a solid plate or type-metal cast taken from a form, rather than the form itself. That is, cliché or stereotyped printing uses not an original plate to make copies, but a copy of the plate; what it produces are thus copies of a copy. Metaphorically, then, clichés are mass-produced phrases, verbal coins that have circulated so long they have lost their stamp and value. As W. J. McCormack notes, clichés "stand on the frontier between language which is produced through known human agencies . . . and language which is produced by machinery" (1988, 327), and therefore display the effects of industrial capitalism on language. Mass products themselves, clichés level all discourse into collections of commonplaces and, in so doing, reconstruct subjects along lines of "type" (Lawrence 1981, 174).[3]

Clichés thus exemplify Walter Benjamin's famous observations that the age of mechanical reproduction has eliminated the "aura" of originality attached to artworks (1979, 852), thereby generating a "sense of the universal equality of things" (1979, 853). Therefore it is pointless to search for the origins of a cliché: clichés are by definition worn-out coins, terms whose origins have been lost or effaced by constant circulation.[4] And yet, even as a reproducer of clichés, the

3. For an exploration of the various "types" in "Eumaeus," see Mahaffey 1988, 173.

4. Levine contends that clichés generate the "paradoxical situation of a discourse that is totally unoriginal and yet that—because we have already heard or said it ourselves—reminds us of its origins" (1979, 113). But a user may repeat a cliché without knowing or reflecting on its origins; indeed, the repetition of clichés actually demonstrates a failure to reflect upon their origins. Clichés are precisely those phrases that lack origins, that issue from a collective linguistic warehouse that nobody owns.

narrator of "Eumaeus" is fatally flawed: by misaligning his clichés (Kenner 1987, 130), reproducing them inaccurately or heaping them up in excess, he not only manages to remind us of their origins but accidentally achieves originality. Thus, for example, when Stephen and Bloom decide to "put a good face on the matter and foot it" (16.32), the reader imagines a foot smashing someone's face, thereby restoring the original picturesqueness to phrases that have long since lost their metaphoric power. The *mis*use of clichés restores their origins. A marvelous longer example of cliché collision occurs when Bloom muses on Parnell's adulterous history:

> First it was strictly Platonic till nature intervened and an attachment sprang up between them till bit by bit matters came to a climax and the matter became the talk of the town till the staggering blow came as a welcome intelligence to not a few evildisposed, however, who were resolved upon encompassing his downfall though the thing was public property all along. . . . Since their names were coupled, though, . . . where was the particular necessity to proclaim it to the rank and file from the housetops, the fact, namely that he had shared her bedroom which came out in the witnessbox on oath when a thrill went through the packed court literally electrifying everybody in the shape of witnesses swearing to having witnessed him on such and such a particular date in the act of scrambling out of an upstairs apartment with the assistance of a ladder in night apparel, . . . a fact the weeklies . . . coined shoals of money out of. (16.1364–79)

This hackneyed run stumbles over its own feet as metaphors mix (attachments spring up, downfalls are circular), repetition fails to create balance ("matters" misplaces its plural), and sentences get dizzy with excess information (a ladder wearing a negligee escapes from a window); metonymies run amok, as someone yells "it" (unspecified) from housetops to a group of soldiers, a courtroom gets electrical power and witnesses (or their shapes) are electrocuted, and witnessboxes take oaths. Of course, the sexual circumlocutions and euphemisms betray Bloom's anxiety about adultery; his circumnavigation edges delicately around the real topic, as if commonplaces will disarm and depersonalize the pain: they didn't have sex, they merely "shared a "bedroom"; they didn't "couple," only their names did (his *P* and her *O*? His "Chas." into her "Kitty"?). No wonder "all seemed a kind of dream" (16.1401)! Inadvertently molding these shopworn terms into fresh images, the narrator resembles a verbal pawnbroker who earns a profit by recycling used goods. Strangely, the passage attains originality through the sheer barrage of commonplaces; the narrator does not produce fresh concepts but instead coins new words and phrases by reusing the inherited linguistic capitual of his community, creating (through a chrematistic verbal economy) surplus value simply by gathering worthless linguistic currency. In this passage old coinages are newly minted as counterfeit clichés.

The final line of the cited passage suggests a homology between money and narrative developed throughout the episode: both newspapers and narrators earn their keep with stories and may even "coin shoals of money" from them. Clichés and money share problems of originality and origins. According to Shell, because coins are all "ontologically equal to each other as products of the same die," the first ones "destroyed the aura of individual objects and encouraged a sense of the universal equality of things" (1978, 86). At once works of art and exchangeable objects, coins eliminated originality as a measure of economic (and numismatic value) and thereby valorized it in the aesthetic register. Clichés are thus to language what minted coins and (to extend the analogy) paper money are to economics. As for clichés so for genuine currency: originality is inimical to authenticity. Legitimate currency is intended to exemplify anonymity and authority and must be an exact copy of an original plate. Its institutional sanction derives from that lack of originality.[5] In fact, only counterfeit money is original because, even though counterfeiters aim to copy authentic currency, they never succeed entirely. The originality of counterfeits, once discovered, is felonious. Like clichés, counterfeits suppress their origins, permitting originality to seep in only through error or poor craft, just as the "Eumaeus" teller's originality arises through his ineptitude. Like a poor counterfeiter who manages to produce only obvious "originals," the narrator mints imperfect copies, counterfeits of common verbal currency.

"OBVIOUSLY BOGUS": NARRATIVE COUNTERFEITS

These homologies exist in part because, as certain nineteenth-century trompe l'oeil artists demonstrated, money is not only a subject

---

5. The contemporary artist J. S. G. Boggs, discussed later in the chapter, claims that each monetary bill is "a unique numbered edition" of a painting (cited in Weschler 1988a, 36). But actually the serial number, which is the only unique aspect of a bank note, is not part of the painting. A genuine bank note must be indistinguishable in every other respect from every other note.

for art but is itself art.[6] However, the problematics of originality expose the differences: whereas originality is necessary for aesthetic value, it destroys the exchange value of currency. Only when art goes on sale does economic value depend upon originality, which then becomes a kind of "gold standard" guaranteeing the circulation of the aesthetic economy (Johnston 1990, 10).[7] But what if the gold standard is removed? Revolutionary consequences follow. If in some respects coins and paper money depend upon different protocols—coins have some value in themselves because they are made of metal, whereas paper money is virtually worthless in itself—in terms of symbolic value both forms of currency are the same: "as money, each consists merely in the substantiation of the exchange function through a common relation of the interested parties to an objective institution" (Simmel 1978, 183). Without a gold standard, all currency rests solely upon the promise that it will be honored as a medium of circulation, which in turn is guaranteed by the institutional authority of a bank or central political power (Simmel 1978, 184). The power to coin money or print bills is thus also the power to add value to the material and labor embodied in money (Simmel 1978, 210). Without that guarantee of power, counterfeit and genuine currency are identical; as long as those who spend the money agree to accept it as such, its origins are moot. As a circulating medium (the Symbolic function of money), worthless counterfeits operate precisely the same way as genuine money and can replace it. In this sense, then, the money economy depends upon a form of faith or credit in the authenticity and power of the existing political order, a suprarational standard that resembles both the "aura" surrounding original art and religious faith (Simmel 1978, 179).

Real money claims to tell a true story. But the role of credit and belief here also suggests a homology between financial and narrative economies: both depend upon credit, on the willingness to believe in an imaginary gold standard of value and a measure of truth, which paradoxically may emerge only through the fictionality of the narrative. What kind of tale do counterfeits tell? "Counterfeit" derives

6. One of these artists, William Harnett, was arrested for counterfeiting during the apprehension of the counterfeiter nicknamed Jim the Penman (Weschler 1988b, 90). For a further account of these painters and their work, see Weschler 1988b, 88–90, and Michaels 1987, 161–64.

7. Johnston bases his remarks on Goux's insights about the Symbolic, Imaginary, and Real functions of gold in the money economy (1990, 47–48). For an illuminating discussion of the relationships between the gold standard and aesthetic representation, see Michaels 1987, 139–80.

from the Latin *contra* + *facere:* "to make in opposition or contrast to something else." Counterfeit money is therefore currency made in opposition to legitimate banking and governmental institutions. Counterfeits, then, are counter*narratives* to the authorized fictions of genuine currency; while pretending to replicate the legitimate power of governments, counterfeits actually claim that institutional guarantees are merely conventional, that one bill or coin is as good as any other. In one sense, counterfeits merely extend the revolution in economics that permitted money to depart from the gold standard: they assert that if no gold or no real metallic value stands behind currency, then value is merely a matter of community assent, of willing collective suspension of disbelief backed by force.

Counterfeit currency is a specific type of fiction. As Shell writes, "a coin as money is counterfeit when the stated place of origin does not correspond to the actual place of origin" (1982, 160). That is, counterfeit money, like Odysseus, tells a spurious story about its origins. Counterfeits efface their true origins in order to make returning impossible; instead they aim to replace these returns with financial returns. If real money presents itself as a "realistic" fiction backed by a gold standard of truth and political legitimacy, counterfeits use a fiction of origin to subvert the tales of "legitimate" currency by revealing that their "truth" and genuineness—and hence their value—are functions of narrative faith. More generally, counterfeit money confronts us with the fact that money, both "true" and counterfeit, is a fiction, a condition revealed by the work of such contemporary artists as J. S. G. Boggs. Boggs draws American bank notes; after he draws a bill, he "spends" it by persuading someone to accept it as face-value payment for a commodity or service. He then keeps both the change and the item (or token of the item) purchased, upon which art collectors pursue the "original" bills and usually pay far more than face value for them. After they bring the bill back to Boggs, he makes a completed work out of the transaction. The finished work, then, consists of the bill, the change given for the purchase he makes with his counterfeit, and the object purchased, all collected in a tableau.[8] Thus Boggs's art is not really drawing bills so much as creating narratives of economic transactions. The economist Robert Krulwich observes

8. My sources for this account are Lawrence Weschler's two articles on Boggs, who was tried (and acquitted) for counterfeiting in England. Ironically, Boggs himself was once the object of a forger/counterfeiter who drew second-rate copies of currency and tried to pass them off as "original" Boggses (Weschler 1988a, 39).

that Boggs' economic narratives illustrate "the essential nature of exchanges and money. He forces us to see . . . how it's all a fiction, . . . an act of faith" (quoted in Weschler 1988a, 44).

The work of another "artist," the second "Jim the Penman" (the "original" is discussed below), an American counterfeiter who was himself a counterfeit of the original Jim, exposes several ironies in the relationships between genuine and counterfeit money. Like his namesake a supremely talented crook, this Jim (so dubbed by the New York *Sun*, but actually a Prussian immigrant farmer named Emanuel Ninger [M. Bloom 1957, 44]) painstakingly traced his bills with a camel's hair brush, an artist's implement. So artistic were his works that when he was finally arrested in 1896 (after more than a decade of successful counterfeiting), there was a public protest, and a penmanship expert wrote to the *Sun*, observing that Ninger's works were commanding prices above their stated economic value, and proclaiming him a genius (M. Bloom 1957, 45–46). Ultimately, therefore, Ninger's counterfeits transcended their economic value, which depended upon their condition as copies, and became prized for their originality as works of art. One component of this originality was Ninger's curious refusal to copy the words "Engraved and Printed at the Bureau of Engraving & Printing," printed on every genuine American bill at the time. Asked why he didn't copy this phrase, he answered, "with devastating logic," " 'Dey didn't make dem' " (M. Bloom 1957, 44). Curiously, then, in an important sense his notes were not counterfeit at all, since their maker refused to lie about their origins. It is possible (if not probable) that Joyce knew of this notorious case, since Ninger's trial was highly publicized and Joyce's interest in the first Jim the Penman has been amply documented. In any case, the work of this artist, like that of Boggs, both exposes the fictionality of money—its reliance on a paradoxical unoriginality—and resembles the "Eumaeus" narrator's practice of borrowing from or copying coinages already in public circulation.

If counterfeits are narratives, it would seem also that twentieth-century narratives are counterfeits. The withdrawal of the gold standard for currency parallels the decline of literary realism, which depends, like the gold standard, upon a naïve version of semiosis that valorizes referential representation. As Goux shows, these changes in banking and aesthetic practices were historically synchronic, and both exemplified a revolution in attitudes toward symbolic exchange (1988, 23). Thus if the nineteenth century was the "golden age of counterfeiting" (M. Bloom 1957, 137), the early twentieth century was the golden age of counterfeit texts (Gide's novel is only the most obvious example). What is *Ulysses,* after all, but a counterfeit classic, a copy of an epic that both lacks a Ulysses and fails to live up to its face value and implied origin? In seeming to reproduce an earlier text, in repudiating originality, it becomes original; in this sense "Eumaeus," a counterfeit of a tale about counterfeit identities and exchanges, is typical of the entire novel. Twentieth-century novels such as *Ulysses* are also counternarratives, stories produced in opposition to nine-teenth-century narratives of the gold standard; they inscribe the shift in symbolic exchange also illustrated by changes in currency. These texts are counterfeits that subvert the economies of meaning assumed by realism, just as paper money revolutionized the condition of eco-nomic exchange by withdrawing its foundation in metal (cf. DiPiero 1988, 9). They expose the economy of realism as nothing more than a convention, a fiction, an act of faith. *Ulysses* is thus oppositional in a number of ways: not only does it repudiate nineteenth-century real-ism by counterfeiting it, but it also challenges the concept of symbolic exchange and mimesis upon which realism is founded. In offering itself as a counterfeit, in effect it claims that all narratives are at once original and unoriginal, genuine and counterfeit.

We have navigated rather far from the cabman's shelter, so let us return. The connections established in "Eumaeus" between money and narrative are exemplified by two incidents. The first is Stephen's encounter with "Lord" John Corley. Like Odysseus, Corley uses a story as a medium of exchange, hoping to wheedle a loan from Ste-phen by pleading that he has "not as much as a farthing to purchase a night's lodgings" (16.145). As the two talk, Bloom tries to recall Corley's suppositious genealogy and, after tortuously attempting to remember whether he is descended from nobility or kitchen help, finally wonders whether the "whole thing wasn't a complete fabrica-tion" (16.153). If Corley's noble origins are counterfeit, a dubious communal fiction, likewise his new tale of woe is "hardly deserving of much credence" either (16.174–75). Nevertheless Stephen, moved perhaps by a newfound sense of charity, perhaps by the recognition of his own likeness in Corley, or perhaps by a desire to get rid of him, lends him some money.[9] Digging in his pockets, he comes up with

9. Day rightly observes that this is "the first act of charity" we've seen from Ste-phen all day. In giving Corley a half crown, he writes, "Stephen symbolically completes the circle of Irish betrayal with an act of *agape* (1980, 14; cf. Moseley 1967, 19). While it is possible that Stephen feels genuine sympathy for Corley, the loan is congruent with the larger pattern of abandonment and expenditure we have traced in Stephen throughout this study.

"what he surmised in the dark were pennies" but which turn out to be half crowns (16.192–94). The "counterfeit" pennies are actually worth more than their "face" value, unlike Corley, who is worth less. Indeed, the man who could once extract gold sovereigns from slaveys (see "Two Gallants") with his flashy talk is now reduced to begging for small change. In any case, Corley's counterfeit tale earns actual cash; its dubious provenance is irrelevant to Stephen's act of faith in Corley's narrative currency.

The origins of Stephen's coins are, however, mysterious, since both he and we have believed he has given all his money to Bloom in Bella Cohen's. Nor do we know how many half crowns he has. But if we credit his proclamation that he begins "Oxen of the Sun" with £2 19s in his pocket, calculate the plausible prices of the rounds he bought in Burke's (see chapter 6), and assume that these half crowns are part of the larger sum rather than some other hidden treasure, we can calculate how many half crowns he has here and from there determine his budget for the day. Stephen probably has three half crowns here before giving Corley one.[10] This number has much to recommend it, not the least of which is its trinitarian symmetry with the three turds (apparently not counterfeit) excreted by the streets-weeper's horse at the end of the episode. But my narrative of origins is only a plausible fiction and depends upon several unprovable assumptions: that Stephen is telling the truth in "Oxen," that the half crowns are part of his total, and that he pays the tram fare to Nighttown. In fact, we cannot know for sure how many half crowns

10. We can assume that Stephen enters Nighttown with at least the £1 6s 11d he gives to Bloom, plus the pound he spends there. At the beginning of "Circe," then, he must have at least £2 6s 11d, minus the 2d he probably spent for his and Lynch's tram fare to get there. This would bring his total at the end of "Oxen" to £2 7s 1d. Subtracted from £2 19s, this leaves almost twelve shillings unaccounted for: too much for the two rounds he buys. The half crowns in his pocket help to explain this discrepancy. He cannot have four half crowns (4 × 2s 6d = 10s), because that would bring his total at the end of "Oxen" to £2 17s 1d, and we know he only has £2 16s 11d after the first round, which cost 2s 1d ("two bar and a wing" [14.1502–3]). It is also unlikely that he has two half crowns here, because that would mean his total cash at the end of "Oxen" comes to £2 12s 1d (£1 6s 11d given to Bloom + £1 spent at Cohen's + 2d [tram fare] + 5s [two half crowns]), which in turn means his second round would have cost 4s 10d: far too high for the number of drinks he buys. Thus he must have three half crowns here before giving one to Corley; that would bring his total at the end of "Oxen" to £2 14s 7d, making the price of the final round 2s 4d, a plausible figure, and only a little more than the cost of the first round. The slightly higher price would be attributable to the higher cost of absinthe, an "expensive . . . libation" (14.1531). See Appendix A for Stephen's Bloomsday budget.

Stephen possesses. Here again the novel subverts the economy of
realism or documentary fact. By effacing these realistic details, Joyce
again suggests that *Ulysses* is realism's counterfeit coin. Nevertheless,
the Corley episode illustrates how narrative operates as a medium of
exchange and a substitute for labor and suggests that such exchanges
occur even when both the money and narratives exchanged are
counterfeit.

The homologies between counterfeit money and counterfeit narration are perhaps best illustrated in Bloom's responses to the dubious tales of D. B. Murphy (16.337), Joyce's inexact copy of the
counterfeit Odysseus, who regales his audience with brief vignettes
about his many voyages. Sporting an unoriginal name (calling yourself Murphy "in a land of murphies is like saying [your name] is
'Noman' " [R. Ellmann 1972, 155]), Murphy is a stereotype and probably a counterfeit: the postcard meant to confirm his veracity does
the opposite, since it is addressed to an A (Antonio?) Boudin, not to
somebody named Murphy (16.489). Bloom's responses to Murphy's
stories are consistently cloaked in monetary metaphors. For example,
Murphy first claims to know a Simon Dedalus who is an expert marks-
man (a counterfeit Simon?); but Bloom can "neither make head nor
tail" of this narrative coin (16.385). After listening to Murphy, Bloom
believes he is "not likely to get a great deal of change out of such a
wily old customer" (16.625): Murphy's counterfeit narratives do not
inspire credit or bring genuine money in return. Along the way,
Murphy claims to have seen "queer" sights (16.464), which is true
since, in thieves' argot, "queer" bills are counterfeits.[11] Later Bloom
opines that there is "something spurious" about him (16.833); the
only other time "spurious" is used in *Ulysses* occurs when Bloom's
bodyguards distribute "spurious coins" during his mayoral fantasy in
"Circe" (15.1574).[12] Finally deciding that Murphy is "obviously bogus"
(16.1045)—appropriately, since "bogus" was originally the name for
a device used to make counterfeit coins—Bloom concludes that "the
lies a fellow told about himself couldn't probably hold a proverbial
candle to the wholesale whoppers other fellows coined about him"
(16.846–47). Communal counterfeits are more extravagant and more

11. Thus one notorious nineteenth-century American counterfeiter was known
as "Big Bill the Queersman" (L. Smith 1944, 86).
12. Joyce's "Notes on Business and Commerce" contain a pertinent entry. After
"spurious coin," he writes "Detection—weight and melting" (*JJA* 3:481). For Joyce,
"spurious" referred specifically to counterfeit money.

dubious than personal tales of origins. But if other people coin tales and sell them wholesale, Murphy seems content to solicit attention with his coinages. Even wholesale whoppers or counterfeit stories may operate as mediums of exchange: as a sign of his audience's interest, Murphy is provided not with a quid, or pound sterling, but the token payment of a "quid" of tobacco (16.468). Hence, while arguments that Murphy is Joyce in disguise seem as dubious as Murphy's own stories, in a sense they are right: his counterfeit tales are a paradigm for all those in the episode, including the narrator's. Murphy is an exemplary counterfeit teller, an Odyssean disguiser of origins.[13]

It seems, then, that in "Eumaeus" all narratives are counterfeits, spurious tales of dubious provenance, and therefore that the episode renders problematic all assumptions about truth value and representational authenticity. In a deeper sense, however, counterfeits rest upon a mimetic theory of representation, upon the notion that the "real" (even if it is merely the "symbolic" or "imaginary" reality of money) can be represented (Vernon 1984, 205), that cleverly faked money can be taken for real currency. That is, the idea of the counterfeit remains parasitical upon the existence (or the faith in the existence) of that which it "counters," which is by definition not counterfeit. Thus beneath the practice of counterfeiting lies a belief in the possibility of exact replication, of reproduction that would ultimately eliminate the need for representation. Ultimately, the aesthetic behind counterfeiting, like that of conservative nineteenth-century economists, is a "goldbug" aesthetic; like gold fetishism, counterfeiting seeks to withdraw entirely from the money economy paradoxically by adopting its faith in the possibility of perfect representation (Michaels 1987, 162, 165). In this sense, counterfeiting only extends the reach of the money economy.

The counterfeit thus exemplifies a conservative economy grounded upon the belief that beneath all copies lies something that is not a copy, some universal form of value. With this in mind, Baudrillard contends that the counterfeit was "the dominant scheme of

---

13. Among those who claim that Murphy is a Joyce figure are Maddox (1978, 160), Brook Thomas (1982, 136), McMichael (1991, 145), and Bell (1991, 201), who argues that Murphy is a "satiric caricature of an author," a qualification that seems more accurate. Counterfeiting may run in Murphy's family: he claims that his son, Danny, has run off to sea instead of working in a draper's where he could be "drawing easy money" (16.658–59).

the 'classical' epoch" and has been superseded in the twentieth century by simulation (1988, 135). It is no longer possible to distinguish
the counterfeit from the genuine because such recognitions depend
upon a clear distinction between the authentic and the bogus. Instead
postmodernism has generated what Johnston calls the Nietzschean or
Deleuzian schema, an economy of modulating differences rather than
of stable origins (Johnston 1990, 40; Baudrillard 1988, 139).[14] In this
economy there is no "true recognition but only creative misrecogni-
tions, since every representation is always a displacement and a disguise" (Johnston 1990, 21). Rather than counterfeits, we have only
what Baudrillard calls simulacra, "the generation of models of a real
without origin or reality; a hyperreal" (1988, 166). With the loss of
the gold standard of mimesis and truth, narratives can be understood
not as lies or counterfeits but as simulacra, mass products modeled
after other copies whose originals never existed. In this sense "Eumaeus" is not realist but "hyperrealist," its subversion of narrative
credit, identity, and truth creating an infinite regress of reproduction,
of fleeting and modulating difference. And yet most readers detect
something genuine in "Eumaeus" beneath the play of counterfeits:
perhaps a real Bloom beneath the narrator's obfuscating bourgeois
commonplaces, perhaps a realistic (if one-sided) depiction of the relationship between Stephen and Bloom, perhaps a smiling Joyce behind
the narrator's solecisms. It may be more accurate to say, then, that
"Eumaeus" oscillates between the model of the counterfeit, in which
the absence of the original or standard implies its presence (as when
the typographical error turns Bloom into "L. Boom" [16.1260]),
and the model of the hyperreal, in which no original is recuperable
(Murphy may be bogus, but we have no idea who he "really" is). Such
oscillation places the two economies in a dialogical relationship. In
any case, the episode presents a series of homologies between narrative and monetary economies that illuminate not only the nature of
fiction but also the interpretive strategies with which critics attempt to
explain it. By implying that narratives are counterfeits, "Eumaeus"
suggests that we critics are also counterfeiters: as tale-tellers who offer
as currency our explanations of origins or behavior, we exchange
discourse that imitates or counters the narrative economies represented within the text. If so, we counterfeiters must acknowledge

14. Nietzsche's argument about truth and lies, which I have used as the epigraph
for this chapter, provides the foundation for Johnston's description of simulation as
"Nietzschean." For Nietzsche, all truths are clichés.

the provisionality of our tales or risk being duped into our univocal readings, our own goldbug aesthetic.

GENUINE FORGERIES

If the nineteenth century was a golden age of counterfeiting, it also seems to have been a "golden age of forgery" (S. Cole 1956, 5), and such crimes still occupied a prominent place in the popular consciousness in 1904. Thus as Stephen and Bloom converse at cross-purposes about the word "soul," Bloom contends confusedly that many of the biblical passages in question are "genuine forgeries," like those pretenders and forgers of Shakespeare (16.781–72), one of whom, as we have seen, is Stephen himself. Genuine forgeries: this oxymoron provides another way of approaching the deceptive textual and financial economies of "Eumaeus"; indeed, forgery seems even more pertinent to the linguistic economies of "Eumaeus," because it is a more clearly textual crime than counterfeiting. Unlike counterfeiting, which aims to reproduce currency, forgery works upon checks, which are money that has already been abstracted not only from gold, but even from bank notes. Forgers defraud not only banks but also the individuals who deposit money in them. Thus whereas counterfeiting is primarily a crime against the authority of governments and institutions, forgery is essentially a crime against individuals. And if counterfeits are original pieces of currency that aim to replicate copies (i.e., "genuine" bills), in contrast forgeries are copies designed to pass as originals.[15] Most importantly, forgery is a crime of fraudulent identity, and identity is one of the principal concepts that "Eumaeus" puts to question. Like counterfeit money, however, forgeries are narratives; as Sonia Cole notes, a forgery is "a document which not only tells a lie, but tells a lie about itself" (1956, 18): a forgery misrepresents its own origins. In this sense, the Odysseus who returns home to Ithaca is himself a genuine forgery, a fraud who reveals truth through trickery. Several forgeries lie behind the tales in "Eumaeus" and further challenge and illuminate the nature of ownership, identity, textuality, and authority.

The forgery motif lurks behind the characters' foggy anecdotes and cloudy memories of Parnell. Bloom twice recollects the story of

---

15. The "Notes on Business and Commerce" contain an entry on "forgery," which reads: "Rightful owner can claim bill from acceptor and proceed against payee for conversion. Banker liable to be sued for conversion on bills real or cheque" (*JJA* 3:484).

Parnell's adultery and fall and also considers the likelihood that the shelter keeper is Fitzharris, who drove a decoy getaway cab in the Phoenix Park murders. This notorious incident occurred when a splinter group of radical Fenians stabbed Lord Frederick Cavendish, the new chief secretary of Ireland, and Thomas H. Burke, an under-secretary in Dublin Castle whom they regarded as the architect of the "coercion policy," which aimed to ensure Irish compliance with English law by restricting civil liberties (Gifford 1988, 94). In early 1886, Parnell's signature was forged on several letters in order to implicate him in the conspiracy. The Parnell forgeries were perpetrated by Richard Pigott (not Lester Piggott, as Gifford [1988, 553] has it), a seedy journalist whose newspapers were failing and who was chronically short of money. Parnell's penchant for disguise fueled the gossip: he was often "not his old self" (16.1301), going "under several aliases such as Fox and Stewart" (16.1322–23): Parnell himself was frequently a genuine forgery. "The money question" is at the back of these forgeries in at least two senses: first, the impecunious Pigott was reportedly paid over £600 for the letters (Lyons 1977, 369). Second, according to Kitty O'Shea's account, when Parnell read the forged letters in the paper, he did not get angry, but instead made a joke and then retired to spend the next few hours with his experiments in assaying gold (Abels 1966, 279; cf. Lyons 1977, 375), as if to prove that he could distinguish fact from fool's gold and earn money at the same time. Parnell was aware of the truth, the gold standard according to which the charge was counterfeit. In contrast, Pigott's testimony, in which he was caught repeating the famous error in spelling "hesitancy" that Joyce attributes to HCE in *Finnegans Wake*, departed from the gold standard. In his second day of testimony, Pigott claimed he had forged only some of the letters; one of the authentic pieces, he claimed, was "the facsimile letter from which the whole strange history derived" (Lyons 1977, 421): this one, at least, was allegedly a genuine forgery. After a searing cross-examination that utterly discredited Pigott's testimony, he fled to Spain where, as he was being apprehended, he put a gun to his mouth and killed himself (Lyons 1977, 422). Ironically, the Pigott heirs were given a different surname so that they could not be traced to the disgraced author, thereby becoming Pigott's last forgeries (Abels 1966, 302).

The son of a diehard Parnellite, Joyce knew of the Phoenix Park murders, a phantom that implicates even Parnell and his legend in the forgery theme.[16] But if Parnell measured these forgeries against

---

16. For Joyce's own account of the case, see *CW* 225.

the gold standard of truth, later assayers have been less perspicacious, as the Parnell apocrypha circulating through "Eumaeus" proves. A second legend also figures in the episode: twice, in slightly different words, Bloom recalls the incident in which Parnell returned in 1890 to recapture the newspaper *United Ireland* (which he had founded), remembering that when Parnell lost his hat in the crowd (thus literally becoming "uncrowned"), Bloom himself returned it (16.1336; 1513–16). Though this anecdote may also depart from the gold standard of "strict history" (16.1514), at least it bears some resemblance to other contemporary accounts. Katherine Tynan's version typifies the florid tone of most such accounts; she describes Parnell's face as "ghostly pale, save only that on either cheek a hectic crimson spot was glowing. His hat was off now, his hair dishevelled, the dust of conflict begrimed his well-brushed coat" (quoted in Lyons 1977, 536). Parnell's hat here traces a trajectory that presages his own later fall; like his hat, he later rose again, but only as a legend in Irish popular mythology. Despite Bloom's belief that he "broke up the type" of the newspaper (16.1501–2), Parnell could not break out of the "type" of Irish hero-ism, a pattern of betrayal and martyrdom that Joyce thought applied to himself. Thus in the "Eumaeus" accounts, Parnell seems less a recognizable person than a stereotype, a cliché, an Irish wish-fulfill-ment more "insuppressible" than the newspaper of that name. In-deed, the real Parnell bears about as much resemblance to the legends created in his name as Pigott's letters did to Parnell's own handwrit-ing; later narratives transformed Parnell into a forgery less genuine than his pseudonyms.

But to forge is not merely to fool; the first definition of the verb is simply "to make, fashion, frame or construct." A "forger" is not just a fraud or copycat but also an author. In this regard, a number of critics have noted that Stephen's triumphant vow to "forge in the smithy of my soul the uncreated conscience of my race" (*P* 253) impli-cates his artistic destiny in a pun on "forging" as theft (see, for exam-ple, Riquelme 1983, 38). Similarly, in *Ulysses* Stephen's self-making includes an element of fakery or self-dramatization that Mulligan recognizes by calling him the "loveliest mummer of them all" (1.97–98). Joyce too was a forger, signing his first story, the *Irish Homestead* version of "The Sisters," with the name Stephen Daedalus—a false name that nevertheless alluded to the identity he soon assumed in fiction. Conversely, in writing *Portrait,* Joyce "forges" the conscience of Ireland by cashing in some of his own experiences under that same alias. And Shem (whose abode is also littered with "counterfeit franks" [*FW* 183.19]) is, as we have seen, accused of uttering an "epi-

cal forged cheque on the public for his own private profit" (*FW*
181.15–16), a check that may be the book itself. Thus, as Kershner
contends, Stephen's artists are all "involved in a sort of 'forgery,' a
criminal falsification which for Joyce . . . is a necessary aspect of art"
(1978, 226). If good forgers are artists, likewise good artists are forgers, and their works are "genuine forgeries"—tales of origins whose
value is a function of their credible fraudulence.

   In his speech to Parliament about the forgeries, Parnell expressed
surprise that the *Times* would allow itself to be hoodwinked. Describing his own handwriting as cramped, he noted that, in contrast, the
letters were clearly written by a "ready penman" (quoted in Abels
1966, 280). Equally "ready" is the narrator of "Eumaeus": a stylist
never at a loss for words despite his lack of talent, he resembles Pigott
more than Parnell. Thus if Stephen's aim was to take Parnell's place
as the type of the Irish hero, in "Eumaeus" this role is usurped by a
forger. Indeed, the narrator of "Eumaeus" seems to be an early version of Shem the Penman, a producer of forgeries and counterfeits
who is himself loosely based upon a famous forger, the first Jim the
Penman. This Jim the Penman (real name: James Townsend Saward)
led a highly successful gang of London forgers in the 1840s and
1850s. The "first to make forgery an organized business, to devise
techniques to guard against discovery" that have been used ever since
(Dilnot 1930, 12), Jim was a believable storyteller and earned a good
deal of money from his forgeries, which were successful both because
of his ability to imitate others' signatures and because he shielded
himself with layers of deception, including a great many pseudonyms.[17] In a fittingly Joycean coincidence, this man of many aliases
accomplished his first forgery by cashing checks in the name of one
J. B. Doe (first name John, no doubt [Dilnot 1930, 71])! Saward was
ultimately incriminated by a letter to a comrade that fell into the
wrong hands and, like Parnell, was eventually betrayed by underlings
(Dilnot 1930, 31). In a final irony Jim the Penman, who was himself a
barrister (Dilnot 1930, 13), was not represented by counsel during his

   17. Saward would never try to cash the checks himself, instead having a hench-
man hire messengers who never knew the identity of the ringleader; as an extra
safeguard, he would have all of the parties in the transaction followed to prevent
betrayal. Some striking coincidences crop up in the case. For example, one of Jim's
accomplices went under the alias of Hunter (Dilnot 1930, 78), which was also the name
of the model for Leopold Bloom (*L* II, 168; *JJ* 230). A man who wrote his checks
strictly for money, Jim sometimes took lodgings as Mr. White in Hackney Road—a
fitting place for a hack writer.

1857 trial; though he had made "shoals of money" from his criminal activities, he could not afford an attorney for his own trial (Dilnot 1930, 78). Upon conviction, this forger was sentenced to the very Odyssean punishment of transportation for life (Dilnot 1930, 33).

Both the counterfeiter and the forger named Jim the Penman resemble the narrator, although the narrator is probably a lesser artist than either of them. Capable of penning a decent facsimile of events but not good enough to pass his work off as original, the "Eumaeus" narrator has the craft to produce only a passable forgery of novelistic style. I thus heartily approve of Bell's sobriquet "the Penman" for this narrator (1991, 112, 116). A counterfeiter of the most worthless coins of discourse and a pilferer of nearly worthless verbal currency, the Penman of "Eumaeus" engages in a form of collective intertexuality that again subverts laws of literary originality and ownership. In short, he is what Beaufoy calls Bloom—a "plagiarist"—even though he more closely resembles that disseminator of "copy," Beaufoy himself (15.822; 824).[18] A forger, the Penman also resembles Bloom, who plays the Parnellian heroic role in *Ulysses,* and who is accused of being a "forger" during his Circean trial (15.1159). As "author-journalist" (15.801), Bloom also resembles Pigott and, as forger and plagiarist, seems to fit the picture of the narrator I have been drawing in this chapter. Indeed, late in "Eumaeus," Bloom contemplates imitating Beaufoy by writing *"My Experiences,* let us say, *in a Cabman's Shelter"* (16.1231). These resemblances have led some critics (e.g., Kenner 1987, 130; Bowen 1989, 67) to conclude that the narrator is none other than Bloom himself. But as we have seen in chapter 3, Bloom's treatment of clichés is much different from the Penman's; whereas the latter heaps them up until they become, through sheer excess, original coinages, Bloom always views them skeptically, analyzing their content for buried metaphors and nonsensical implications. Unlike the Penman, a counterfeit Englishman who calls Shakespeare "our national poet" (16.782), Bloom, despite his waffling about his Jewishness, asserts his Irishness several times in *Ulysses.* The Penman

---

18. As Johnston points out, both forgery and plagiarism are instances of "doubling denied": "plagiarism denies and hides the first or original speaker of an utterance by attributing it to a second speaker; forgery denies a second speaker's doubling of an utterance by falsely attributing it to a first" (1990, 153). Or as Mallon puts it, forgery is "plagiarism's more glamorous inversion, in which the perpetrator claims not that what he hasn't produced is really his own, but that what he indeed has created is actually somebody else's" (1989, 135). To put it yet another way: plagiarists sign their own name to somebody else's work; forgers sign somebody else's name to their own work.

is therefore not Bloom but a counterfeit or forgery of Bloom—a Mr. Boom perhaps—a near copy who nevertheless departs from the original in small but noticeable ways.[19] An imitator of Bloom without his wit and irony, Jim Beaufoy-Pigott Boom cannot help but draw Bloom in his own image. He forges his Bloom by imitating his voice, by copying his signature, and in so doing creates a narrow, bourgeois Bloom whose generosity and compassion to Stephen are merely disguises for exploitation. Incapable of appreciating motives other than money, Penman Boom reinvents Bloom as a compulsive manager, a Boylanesque manipulator, a Pigott to Stephen's Parnell. To conclude, however, that this Bloom is the "real" Bloom is as mistaken as to accept the ragged Cretan's tale as the entire *Odyssey*. The Bloom of "Eumaeus" thus resembles the previous Blooms as a forgery or counterfeit resembles the "original"; hence the encounter between Stephen and Bloom, the social exchange towards which the novel has been leading, is forged in terms of mercenary motives and becomes a counternarrative or counterfeit of the version presented in "Circe," which perceives it as charity or gift exchange.

   In disguising the narrator as Bloom, Joyce plays his own variation on Odysseus' narrative disguises. In this sense *Ulysses* presents not an "essential" Bloom, but a series of fictions, of counterfeits, of forgeries that may pass for "Bloom" as long as readers accept them as the narrative medium of exchange. But any reader's Bloom will remain only a counterfeit of the various "originals" (themselves copies of a collective Odysseus) found in the text. Thus if Murphy's and Corley's tales suggest that narrative is inevitably counterfeit, the Penman's impersonation implies that all narratives are genuine forgeries, that all such representation is both fraudulent and factual, since they depart from an original that may itself be irrecoverable. Likewise, readers who traffick in these counterfeits or forgeries are inevitably themselves forgers or counterfeiters, lesser artists engaged in a fruitless attempt to mimic "original" currency that is already fraudulent. If the "true" origins of coinages and narratives are irrecoverable, then what remains is our belief in fiction. Hence our stories about *Ulysses*

---

19. McGee observes that the "Eumaeus" narrative voice "may be intended to be a recognizable forgery of Bloom's voice—in other words a bad forgery that would be one of a number of bad forgeries" in the chapter (1988, 151). But if, as we have seen, this forgery has taken in critics as astute as Kenner and Bowen, he would seem to be a rather good forger, one capable of trapping even those who examine the signatures quite closely.

are fictions that attempt to replicate and exchange with the textual currency perpetrated by that master counterfeiter and forger, Jim the Penman, alias James Joyce.

AS BAD AS OLD ANTONIO?

To begin considering how these narrative economies influence the Stephen/Bloom relationship, we must now return to the arms (or rather the chest) of Murphy. One of Murphy's tales concerns the bizarre tattoo he sports, which features "a full view of the figure 16 and a young man's sideface looking frowningly rather" (16.675–76). Itself a "portrait of the artist" (Kenner 1987, 130n), the tattoo is allegedly a picture of one Antonio, the (now deceased) Greek sailor who drew it. The lines that Murphy sings at the end of his presentation *("As bad as old Antonio, / For he left me on my ownio")* quote two songs about men—sentimentalists, and perhaps also counterfeit Antonios—who abandon their debtors and lovers (Bauerle 1982, 276, 278).[20] A number of critics have offered clever readings of the Antonio motif.[21] But its intertextual and philological history has never been satisfactorily explicated. The name is significant: as the patron saint of swineherds, St. Anthony must patronize this episode, named for Odysseus' swineherd. Because of this beatific association, the name eventually came to refer to the smallest pig in a litter: the "anthony" is the runt, the "pigott" if you will, just as "Eumaeus" contains some of the most deformed prose in *Ulysses* and is often considered the ugliest of Joyce's textual progeny. A more significant intertextual debt, however, threads its way again back to Shakespeare's *Merchant of Venice,* despite the Penman's caveat that the Antonio under discussion is "no relation to the dramatic personage of the same name" from Shakespeare (16.839–40). Given the episode's habitual use of counterfeits and forgeries, an explicit disavowal may logically be taken as an explicit allusion. And, indeed, the relation-

20. Both C. W. Murphy songs, "Oh, Oh, Antonio!" (1908) and "Has Anybody Here Seen Kelly" (1909), anachronistically appear before they were written. Not only are both cited by another Murphy; the second song also cites the first. Thus the songs are doubly implicated in the episode's exploration of counterfeiting and forgery.

21. For example, Richard Ellmann (1972, 155) contends that 16 refers to Antonio's homosexuality (with a pun on "Greek" and another on Murphy's "queer" tales); those cited above argue that the portrait depicts Murphy's role as a surrogate of Joyce; others have observed that the number refers self-reflexively to this episode, the sixteenth in the novel.

ships among Shakespeare's Antonio, his friend Bassanio, and his creditor Shylock parallel and shed light on the economic components of the budding friendship between Stephen and Bloom.[22]

Shakespeare's play contains its own counterfeiting theme. Antonio and Bassanio, the characters whose friendship is tested by Shylock's usury and Bassanio's courtship of Portia, may both be said to have "double selves," inasmuch as each is torn between the desire for justice and mercy, a conflict that grows out of their shifting roles as debtor and creditor. Even at the beginning of the play, Antonio laments that he has "much ado to know myself" (1.1.7), and he is described by friends as being like "two-headed Janus," laughing and frowning alternately like Murphy's tattoo (1.1.50–56). Portia, of course, is herself a "genuine forgery," a woman who, when disguised as a male judge, proves to be a sound arbiter.[23] Indeed, Joyce's, Homer's, and Shakespeare's texts all thematize "the seeming truth which cunning times put on / To entrap the wisest" (3.2.100–1). A successful merchant, Shakespeare's Antonio relies upon sea-borne commercial success when he acts as surety for Bassanio's debt and pledges a pound of his flesh to Shylock. Thus when Antonio's fortunes fail, Shylock is asked how he will use Antonio's flesh and answers, "to bait fish withal" (3.1.55): like Murphy's friend, who was "ate by sharks" (16.691), Shakespeare's Antonio may become a meal for fish. Both the decline in Antonio's fortunes and his relationship with the Jew Shylock would suggest that in "Eumaeus" Stephen performs Antonio's role. Thus Bloom's plans for Stephen's singing career are a Dublin equivalent of Shylock's usurious financial practices. But assigning Stephen the role of Antonio ignores other important parallels, the most significant of which is that Bloom resembles Anto-

---

22. Of course, Shakespeare was also subject to a number of forgers, one of whom, William Henry Ireland, I have already noted briefly in chapter 6. Two explicit allusions to *The Merchant of Venice* occur in "Eumaeus." The first comes when Bloom and Stephen pass Rourke's bakery and Bloom thinks "O tell me where is fancy bread" (16.58–59), a punning reference to the song sung during Bassanio's meditation on Portia's caskets (3.2.63–72). The second occurs later as Bloom, musing on the ethics of Italians, finds them "a bit too given to pothunting the harmless necessary animal of the feline persuasion" (16.869–70); Shylock, in his speech about the fickleness of affections, wonders why some cannot abide "a harmless necessary cat" (4.1.55).

23. When Bassanio courts her and chooses the lead casket, he opens it to reveal "Fair Portia's counterfeit" (3.2.116). This scene is echoed when Bloom shows Stephen Molly's photo. For an examination of the courtship of Portia in terms of coinage and usury, see Shell 1982, 56–60.

nio in acting as surety for Stephen: he pays for the damages Stephen incurs in Cohen's and holds his money for him.

Ronald Sharp argues that *The Merchant of Venice* is "utterly dominated by the giving of gifts" (1986, 122); but one could as easily say that it is dominated by debt bondage. Indeed, the play's personal and economic conflicts derive from its analysis of the distinction between gift exchange and usury. Friends lend money generously and may even offer their own lives as collateral, whereas strangers not only specify and demand repayment but take usurious interest. Thus Antonio insists that Shylock take interest on his loan to Bassanio, so that the Jew will know that they are not his friends (1.3.33–38). Shylock's usury clearly marks him as an outsider in Christian Venice. Similarly, Stephen's fortunes may now be threatened by a Jew who promises to "help" him. That is, one may read Bloom's "gift" of hospitality and money to Stephen as merely a camouflaged bribe: "to buy his favour, I extend this friendship" (1.3.169). But Antonio is not above exploiting Bassanio's feelings of indebtedness. After the disguised Portia tricks Shylock into forfeiting his bond, Antonio persuades Bassanio to give to the judge the ring he received from Portia (4.1. 449-51), even though he swore never to part with it (3.2.185–6). In effect, Antonio is asking Bassanio to sacrifice his marriage for his friendship. Accordingly, as Shell argues, Antonio is also guilty of the "spiritual usury" I have attributed to Mulligan (1982, 75).[24] The play thus brilliantly exposes the degree to which friendship and its economic corollary, gift exchange, are themselves subject to (and indeed necessitate) usurious accounting: to what degree, it asks, can human relationships be reduced to matters of debit and credit?

The question of spiritual usury is precisely the issue, as we shall see in more detail below, in interpreting Bloom's motives for rescuing Stephen. Is his offer of friendly aid merely a means of making money, of inserting himself into the circles from which he has been excluded? Or are Bloom's genuinely charitable motives distorted by an entrepreneurial narrator? Whether we cast Bloom as Antonio or as Shylock, the parallels with *The Merchant of Venice* imply that Bloom's generosity is really disguised usury: either his schemes about Stephen's singing career are the machinations of a spiritual usurer who demands com-

24. Sharp offers a competing reading, contending that "Antonio's sacrifice is not less heroic, or less a sacrifice, because of his occasional self-regard; on the contrary, it is all the more heroic, for it has been more dearly bought" (1986, 150). This assessment may be true of Bloom as well.

pensatory return for what was originally given gratis—Bloom as Antonio—or Bloom's generous acts are a Shylock's demand for a pound
of flesh, which thereby transform a gift into a debt. If Shakespeare's
play moves from debt bondage to the exchange of rings as gifts,
"Eumaeus" conversely translates Stephen and Bloom's relationship
from a gift exchange to a mercantile transaction. In a larger sense,
then, "Eumaeus" poses the possibility that the gift economy ultimately
generates the same distinction between insiders and outsiders as does
usury; that is, the underside of gift exchange is the establishment
of bonds that may be as oppressive as more obviously exploitative
commercial ones.

The other intertextual debt lying behind the Antonio/16 motif
derives from the sixteenth book listed in Bloom's library, *Soll und
Haben* (Debit and Credit), an 1855 German novel by Gustav Freytag
(17.1383). It is most obviously an example of Joyce's sense of humor:
the list of Bloom's books closely precedes Bloom's tabulation of his
own debits and credits; the author's name is a pun on *Freitag*, the
German word for Friday, the day of the week on which the Nostos
takes place, June 16 having become June 17. An enormous bestseller
in German-speaking countries, *Soll und Haben* sold almost 400,000
copies between 1915 and 1930, far more than at any other time since
its publication (Carter 1968, 328). Since Joyce was living in Zurich
during the time of the novel's greatest popularity, he would likely
have at least heard of it, whether or not he actually read the novel.
Thus it seems plausible that Joyce could have used it to draw parallels
that not only illuminate the relationship between Stephen and Bloom
but also shed light on the bourgeois ideology of "Eumaeus" and on
the connection between debts and drowning in *Ulysses*.

Soll und Haben is a *Bildungsroman* tracing the maturation of Anton
Wohlfart, whose name both implicates him in the Antonio motif and
supplies its own allegorical subtext ("Wohlfart" is one who "travels
well" or "journeys for good," rather like Bloom or Odysseus). Leaving
home after the death of his auditor father, Anton apprentices as a
clerk in the firm of Herr Schröter, who deals (fittingly enough) in
commodities such as coffee. Indeed, it is a yearly Christmas gift of
coffee from Schröter's firm to Anton's father that prompts him to
seek employment there. Since Bloom's bookmark is placed at "p. 24"
(17.1384), someone seems to have read at least these early chapters.
Page 24 of one German edition of the novel gives the family history
of the Baron Rothsattel, a nobleman whose inability to balance debits
and credits draws Anton into a futile attempt to rescue him, and into

the Polish insurrection of 1848. Recounting the relationships between father and son, page 24 describes how the baron begins the novel wealthy and complacent, unlike his father, who had to rebuild the family fortunes after his own father had squandered them. In this regard, Bloom imitates the baron's father, reconstructing the family fortunes after his own father's economic catastrophe. As the novel proceeds, the current baron reenacts that history, much as Stephen does his own family history of financial failure. Another (coincidental?) parallel to *Ulysses* and Joyce's life emerges when (just before page 24) Anton encounters the baron's daughter, a lovely young lady whose name, Lenore, is rendered in the widely available 1857 English translation as Leonora. If Joyce knew anything about the novel, he could scarcely have failed to note and exploit this blending of the names of his wife and his hero.[25]

Throughout Freytag's novel Anton's sober, industrious and well-regulated life is contrasted with those of the baron and Anton's former schoolmate, the Jewish Veitel Itzig, who had retained some loyalty to Anton because the latter had protected him from classmates' anti-Semitic attacks. As Anton's fortunes rise through thriftiness and honesty, Itzig's rise from shady financial dealings he has learned from a Gentile lawyer and from his employer, a Jewish moneylender named Hirsch Ehrenthal. Although for its day the novel's portrayal of Jews is relatively innocuous, nonetheless its characters would likely offend Jewish readers. This anti-Semitism—mitigated slightly by the portrayal of Ehrenthal's son, Bernhard, a sickly scholar whose moral probity contrasts sharply with his feeble body—may explain why the bookmark is placed at p. 24: who would want to finish a novel so biased against one's own religion or ethnic group?[26] This aspect of the novel makes its presence in Bloom's library curious,

25. The catalogue of Bloom's books does not specify an edition and, since many editions of *Soll und Haben* exist (with different pagination), it is impossible to tell which page 24 is the marked one. In all editions, however, the first chapters deal with the death of Anton's father and Anton's relationship with Veitel Itzig; even if Bloom (or Joyce) had read only that far, parallels to Bloom's life would have been apparent.

26. Most critics agree, however, that Freytag himself was not an anti-Semite. Indeed, in later years Freytag apologized for that aspect of the novel and "went out of his way to praise Jews who had made significant contributions to German culture and society" (Sammons 1969, 317; cf. Carter 1968, 326). Even Bernhard, however, despite his intelligence lacks vitality and strength and remains significantly less admirable than the best German characters in the novel (Carter 1968, 326). For a consideration of his character and its relationship to the treatment of Jews in Freytag, see Gelber 1983.

even ironic. Nevertheless, Anton Wohlfart's recurrent financial dealings with Jews and his friendship with Bernhard resemble Stephen's
incipient friendship and potential financial relationship with Bloom.
In this sense, Stephen (himself a scholar and hero of a *Bildungsroman*)
plays the role of Anton/Antonio to Bloom's Jewish businessman. In
"Eumaeus," in fact, Bloom defends Jews precisely because they are
practical and proficient at balancing debit and credit (16.1124–25).
If, in the Penman's eyes, Bloom is a usurer of those he calls his
friends, then he resembles the Itzigs and Ehrenthals of the world,
although Mr. Boom does not censure him for those practices.

   Although the novel's anti-Semitism is open to question, its jingo-
ism and celebration of bourgeois ideology are not. The Poles, for
example, are said to have no civilization because they have no middle
class, "that class which represents civilisation and progress";[27] indeed,
in many ways the novel is far more anti-Polish than anti-Semitic.
Several times Anton champions what he calls the "poetry of mercantile life" (193; 1:377) and describes commerce as a web of strands
that connects individuals together and thereby improves human life
immeasurably (140–41; 1:274–75). Freytag virtually duplicates
Bloom's bourgeois contention that revolution "never reaches anything or stops anything" (16.1100–1101) when he has Herr Schröter
say that revolution "always brings on ruin, and seldom produces anything new" (207; 1:402). The plodding, bourgeois narrative and ideology of *Soll und Haben* is thus echoed by Joyce's Freitag/Friday
narrator, the Penman of "Eumaeus." But whereas in "Eumaeus" this
ideology seems at odds with some of its other narrative practices,
Freytag's novel clearly valorizes the movement away from the romantic and toward the practical, a movement similar to that signaled by
Joyce's preference for Bloom over Stephen. In that sense, then, it
is Bloom who resembles Anton, the sober, prudent, and bourgeois
"German."

   Ulysses also shares with *Soll und Haben* a recurrent symbol for
economic failure. I have already detailed the association between
drowning and financial ruin in *Ulysses;* this connection is made repeatedly in *Soll und Haben*. Early in the novel Anton is nearly drowned by
his friend Fritz von Fink, who then rescues him (73; 1:141). Later,
Bernhard and Leonora see a peasant child drowning. Since Bernhard

---

27. Freytag, *Debit and Credit*, 197; *Soll und Haben* 1: 382–83. Hereafter I cite two
sets of page numbers parenthetically, first those of the English translation, followed by
those from German two-volume edition. Quotations are from the English translation.

cannot swim (foreshadowing his father's final bankruptcy), Leonora (like Leo Bloom a good swimmer) jumps in to save the little girl (180; 1:351–52). Most significantly, after Anton finally succeeds in bringing order to the baron's finances and returns to uncover the Jewish usurers' plot to destroy him, the novel's climax involves two drownings. Fearing that his accomplice will implicate him in the theft of the baron's mortgages, Itzig drowns his helper; then, just as he is preparing to marry Ehrenthal's daughter, Itzig's crimes are discovered. Attempting to escape, Itzig meets his own death by water, thus reenacting not only the deaths of Odysseus' crewmen but also of Murphy's Antonio (490;2:386). Although Anton cannot save the baron from the financial sharks who victimize him, it is Itzig who ultimately drowns, thus paying an appropriate symbolic penalty for his swamping of the baron.

In its relentless description of how the Baron's "friends" exploit him through legal and illegal financial machinations, in its depiction of Anton's discovery of both his vocation and his future wife (Herr Schröter's sister) by means of the poetry of commerce, and in its constant comparisons between accounting ledgers and moral accounts, *Soll und Haben*, like *The Merchant of Venice*, assesses the degree to which human relationships can be figured by tallying debits and credits. Unlike Shakespeare's play, however, Freytag's novel presents such moral accounting as a satisfactory means of maintaining both a well-regulated financial life and a healthy social and domestic life. Even if Anton Wohlfart has no sense of humor, little generosity, and absolutely no sense of irony—indeed, virtually no other quality worth mentioning other than his accounting ability—nevertheless he resembles Bloom in that his ultimate success results from his ability to make both ends meet. Just as *Soll und Haben* traces its youthful hero's involvement with and ultimate victory over "Jewish" usury, so "Eumaeus" traces the temptation Bloom feels to exercise spiritual usury on his own youthful acquaintance. Finally, in borrowing Shakespeare's and Freytag's texts for his own literary ends, Joyce again performs literary usury, making literary capital from the texts of others.

A CAPITAL OPENING

Bloom has learned the lesson of debit and credit too well, at least as he is drawn by the Penman's implement. In contrast, Stephen, who has left his father's house "to seek misfortune" (16.253), has now spent over two pounds on Bloomsday, more than half his monthly salary. Bloom rightly senses that, despite his "high educational abilities," Stephen has "no little difficulty in making both ends meet" (16.306–7): he cannot (or rather will not) balance debit and credit and seeks to escape from history through expenditure. If the Penman's Bloom oversimplifies by reducing Stephen's difficulties to "the money question," nevertheless, as I have argued throughout, Stephen's economic attitudes and behavior affect and illuminate his artistic and social paralysis.

Bloom's perception of Stephen's problems may not be purely altruistic. Early in the episode Bloom appears to take the paternal interest in Stephen for which we have been prepared throughout the novel, and inquires how much he lent to Corley. Stephen tells him, adding that Corley "needs it"; "Needs!" explodes Bloom (16.245), voicing one of the primary concerns in their relationship. What Stephen "very badly need[s]" (16.3) is constantly on Bloom's mind. Indeed, throughout the episode Bloom and the narrator invoke needs (mostly economic) to explain behavior; Bloom even offers a generalized (if confused) philosophy to summarize his plans for social welfare: "Everyone according to his needs or everyone according to his deeds" (16.247), "needs" having taken the place of "ability" in Marx's formulation (1978, 531). As if he has understood Stephen's proclamation of his name *Nothung*—Needful—in "Circe," Bloom senses that Stephen's "homelife . . . had not been all that was needful" (16.1177–78). But because of the episode's blindness to any but material wants, Bloom's assessment of what will fill those needs never reaches behind "the money question." Thus, just as Corley thinks that Stephen "hadn't a thing to do but hand out the needful" (i.e., cash) (16.181), so the Eumaean Bloom believes that what Stephen most needs is someone to hand him "the needful," which he hopes to put "in his way" (16.507; 1619). Obviously, since Stephen has been attempting to rid himself of the needful, and even of needs, throughout the novel, Bloom's moral accounting is somewhat off the mark. More importantly, the Bloom of "Eumaeus" is really concerned with his own needs, and desires as much to exploit Stephen's needs as to fill them.

The second major theme in their relationship is introduced when Stephen utters one of his gnomic pronouncements about artistic destiny. Bloom suggests that Stephen could put his talent to use by working to serve Ireland (16.1158), whereupon Stephen retorts that "Ireland must be important because it belongs to me" (16.1164–65). "What belongs" asks Bloom, a question that hovers in the background

throughout their encounter, as the narrative ideology transforms all
human relationships into matters of belonging and possession: who
owns whom? To what degree does charity create a bond of ownership?

Bloom prods Stephen to ingest the protean coffee and bun by
telling him he'll "feel a different man" (16.814), but it is Bloom who
seems the different man. Indeed, the line of "bitched type" that transforms him into "L. Boom" is another genuine forgery that underscores the Penman's mercantile mind as he redraws Bloom in his own
image, as a stereotype of the grasping merchant. In keeping with the
nautical motif, a boom is sail's spar, as well as a barrier of chain
stretched across a river either to obstruct navigation or to act as a
makeshift bridge. Just as the Penman's language is a boom or barrier
to smooth narrative navigation, so Bloom as Boom may either moor
Stephen's disappointed bridge to material reality or obstruct Stephen's successful navigation away from the "nets" of family, church
and State. As a boom or bridge, he may enable Stephen to reattach
his ends—to make both ends meet—or prevent him from doing so.
In another sense, too, Boom is an apt name for the Bloom of "Eumaeus," since it refers to a rapid and uncontrolled commercial advance, or in Joyce's own definition, a "sudden violent rise" (*JJA*
3:596). Bloom/Boom wants to manage Stephen's assets and turn them
into his own boom. Thus when Boom pays for the coffee and bun
with fourpence, the coins—"literally the last of the Mohicans"
(16.1697–98)—seem as counterfeit as Bloom's other gifts in the
episode.[28]

For the rest of the episode, Bloom attempts to justify his expenditures of money and time on young Dedalus. After considering writing
a Beaufoyesque prize "titbit," he turns to promotional schemes that
envision Stephen's talents and education as investments, commodities
with exchange value that will enable him to "command [his] price"
(16.1156) if he takes Bloom's advice about journalistic work. Even
when Bloom considers nonmonetary compensations, they are
couched in financial terms: "he felt it was his interest and duty even
to wait on and profit by the unlookedfor occasion though why he
could not exactly tell being as it was already several shillings to the
bad. . . . Still to cultivate the acquaintance of someone of no uncom-

---

28. Bloom's budget lists his "cash in hand" as 4s 9d (17.1458). Thus the narrator's
description of the coins is doubly counterfeit: they are neither Native Americans nor
the last.

mon calibre who could provide food for reflection would amply repay any small [outlay]" (16.1216–21). In the Penman's mercantile idiom, Bloom's paternal aid to Stephen is merely Bloom's "interest" (16.1216) on an act of spiritual usury; it is no more than a means of breeding financial offspring from fatherly feeling. Moreover, Stephen will pay a "duty" (16.1216) on his importation into the Bloom household; like a garden vegetable, Stephen is to be "cultivated" strictly to "provide food" for the Blooms. The narrator's ideology again transforms the friendliness and fatherliness of "Circe" into an opportunity to make profits.

This Bloom is not above using Molly as a lure, flashing a photo of her "opulent curves" to entice Stephen's prurient interest. Like Kitty O'Shea, Molly becomes a "Spanish type" (16.1426), as the episode's stereotyping ideology turns females into consumable commodities whose temperaments can be accounted for by climate. Slightly shop-soiled, the photo presents Molly as merely a more expensive version of the whore in the black straw hat, who now becomes an objective correlative for the seedier side of the narrator's (and Bloom's) entre-preneurial aims. Fittingly, since the episode is introduced by the pro-curing Corley, it also portrays Bloom as a voyeur and hanger-on—another Lenehan—a third "gallant" for whom women are belongings on show. Bloom wonders why Stephen, blessed with an "allowance" of brains, wastes his time with "profligate women who might present him with a dose to last him his lifetime," when he might be enter-tained at 7 Eccles Street and gain access to Molly, an unprofligate woman (16.1553–56). If he can entice Stephen to come home with him, perhaps Bloom can provide his own substitute for Boylan, and thereby regain "home rule" (the phrase would be appropriate to this narrator) and acquire prestige (and money) by using Stephen's tal-ents.

But even through Penman Boom's eyes, Bloom's intentions are not totally mercenary. He sympathizes with Stephen, is attracted by the "queer suddenly things he popped out with" (which may be coun-terfeits), hopes to prevent his getting "rooked" by some landlady, and feels "like his father" (or mother), planning to offer him maternal foodstuffs, eggs and milk (16.1566–71). Bloom claims that he would like to "put coin in his way" and give Stephen "a cup of Epps's cocoa and a shakedown for the night" (16.1619–21). But even here the words inspire suspicion. "Shakedown" suggests a mixture of motives: it may connote both a makeshift bed and an extorted contribution.[29]

---

29. The *OED's* first example of the latter definition dates from 1903.

Such a shakedown would more likely block than boost Stephen's progress or maturity; thus Bloom's coins would be "in his way" in more than one sense. Stephen should be wary: as Bassanio discovered, accepting a gift may forge oppressive bonds of obligation. Thus if friendship is "whatever is undertaken in the spirit of gift exchange" (Sharp 1986, 86), Bloom's gift, laden with potential ulterior motives, may, like the Trojan Horse, contain the form of the gift but lack its spirit.

If Stephen's education is a valuable commodity, so might his voice be. With this in mind Bloom begins to make "Utopian plans," including "prize titbits, up to date billing, concert tours in English watering resorts packed with hydros and seaside theatres, turning money away." Assuming that he "had his father's voice to bank his hopes on," Bloom speculates, "an opening was all was wanted" (16.1652–59). Though he echoes Artifoni's fatherly advice about a singing career, Bloom's paternal plans are themselves a form of banking, a Shylockian spiritual usury aimed at breeding profits from the "son's" gifts. Thus, after hearing Stephen sing Jeep's song about Sirens, Bloom amplifies his managerial schemes and imagines playing Boylan to Stephen's Molly:

> a phenomenally beautiful tenor voice like that, the rarest of boons, . . . could easily, if properly handled . . . , command its own price where baritones were ten a penny and procure for its fortunate possessor . . . an *entree* into fashionable houses in the best residential quarters of financial magnates in a large way of business and titled people. . . . Added to which of course would be the pecuniary emolument by no means to be sneezed at, going hand in hand with his tuition fees. Not . . . that for the sake of filthy lucre he need necessarily embrace the lyric platform as a walk in life. . . . [But] both monetarily and mentally it contained no reflection on his dignity in the smallest and it often turned in uncommonly handy to be handed a cheque at a muchneeded moment when every little helped. . . . [A]nd he had a capital opening to make a name for himself and win a high place in the city's esteem where he could command a stiff figure. . . . In fact, he had the ball at his feet and that was the very reason why the other, possessed of a remarkably sharp nose for smelling a rat of any sort, hung on to him at all. (16.1820–65)

In addition to those now familiar financial terms and cliché collisions, syntactical snafus and excess verbiage (sneezing on hands, embracing a platform as one walks on it, handy hands), what strikes the reader most strongly is the way that the passage slowly modulates from

weighing Stephen's advantages to weighing Bloom's. Even at the beginning the aspirations to rise in class are much more typical of the
Penman's Bloom than of Stephen.[30] By the time we reach the sentence
about being handed a cheque, it is no longer clear who "he" (the
recipient) is meant to be. Further down, the "capital opening" is
pretty clearly the manager's: he will capitalize on Stephen's vocal
assets and "make a name" for himself (this from a man whose own
acquaintances are not sure of his given name). Bloom will "make a
new man" of himself by adopting Stephen. By the end the narrator
bluntly states that "the other" (Bloom) hangs around Stephen only
because of the potential profits he might earn. Thus the "possessor"
of the voice slowly metamorphoses into someone the other might
possess; Stephen's boon has become Bloom's boom. All this, of course,
depends upon Stephen's moving in with the Blooms, where he would
have "heaps of time to practice literature in his spare moments";
literature would be a hobby, appropriately for the dilettantish Bloom
who surfaces here, someone who is a "bit of an artist in his spare time"
(16.1860–61; 1448–49). An "artist" in "Eumaeus" is always partly a
con-artist, someone who will "worm his way into" the "good graces"
of others (16.1831–32).

   In this portrait of the artist as forger (Bloom) and pawn (Stephen), the latter, like Murphy's tattoo, becomes a "pound of flesh," a
mere appendage that Bloom can make laugh or cry on command.
And so Bloom passes "his left arm in Stephen's right and led him on
accordingly" (16.1720–22), the latter phrase suggesting seduction or
bad faith: Bloom imitates Mulligan's early morning touch of Stephen,
just as he is also mimicking Mulligan's attempts to "touch" Stephen
for his talents and money. Thus if the encounter of the two men
dramatizes Bloom's belief in both ends meeting, here its references to
debit and credit seem to subsume charitable renewal. And yet, just as
Bloom perceives only one side of Stephen when he glances at his
"sideface" (16.1803), so the Penman's picture of Bloom exposes only
one of his faces. Carefully tracing the obverse face—the economic
man and cost analyzer—the narrator neglects to limn the reverse
face, Bloom's generous side. The result is a partially genuine forgery,
a superficially convincing but one-sided counterfeit.

---

30. Ironically, the concerts Bloom describes were ill-attended and thus unlikely
to make much money, as "A Mother" would suggest, and as O'Brien (1982, 48–49)
documents. In any case, most of them were attended, not by financial magnates, but
by middle-class ladies (O'Brien 1982, 48). Typically, then, even these "Utopian" plans
do not extend above the upper-middle class.

It is less Bloom's acts than the interpretation of them that seems crass. Judged solely by his behavior, Bloom appears only to be helping a needy acquaintance. Moreover, it is unlikely that Bloom could carry out these plans even if Stephen were willing: they are "Utopian" in that he knows (and we know) that they will go nowhere. But even if he could bring them to fruition, would Stephen be worse off? That is, the ultimate agreement (described in "Ithaca" [17.962–65]) to trade Italian lessons for singing instruction is, as Theoharis has argued, "a fair business exchange (less generous, but not for that reason sordid)" (1988, 171). And even if the connection between the two is "utterly commercial and utterly imaginary" (Bruns 1974, 383), it certainly inspires Bloom's imagination and even engages Stephen, as becomes clear at the end of the episode, when they share songs and discuss sirens. Indeed, the commercial reading of this encounter only balances the melodramatically charitable and filial version that ended "Circe." Even if Stephen is right to perceive a threat to his autonomy in Bloom's offer, nevertheless if Bloom can both "do good and net a profit," he may thereby satisfy both his own and some of Stephen's needs.

The end of the episode thus suggests a different reading from the one I have been offering so far. Stephen sings the end of Jeep's ballad, *Und alle Schiffe brücken* (16.1884), apparently a garbled translation of "all ships are wrecked" that revises it into "all ships are bridged." This "error" may be a portal of discovery: as the two approach the "railway bridge" (16.1887), they may be constructing a bridge between opposing economies, a touch that makes ends meet. The words of "The Low-Backed Car" also weave themselves into the final paragraphs, implying that the two heroes are *"to be married by Father Maher"* (16.1887–88) in a relationship in which money matters less than love: "I'd rather own that car, sir, / With Peggy by my side / Than a coach and four and gold galore / And a lady for my bride" (Bauerle 1982, 458–59). This may be yet another counterfeit, a forged marriage license; but if Stephen and Bloom are in any sense married, then theirs, like all marriages, merely combines a commercial arrangement and an emotional commitment. And if, as the "Ithaca" respondent claims, the events of "Eumaeus" are an "atonement" (17.2058), then the touch of Stephen and Bloom makes them one—it makes both ends meet. "All ships are bridged": the travelers navigate home.

Thus the Penman's relentlessly commercial rendering of their encounter, necessarily shaped by his stereotyping consciousness and bourgeois ideology, is only one possible tale. Just as he is a counterfeit or forgery of Bloom, so his fiction about the encounter is a counter-narrative that we may or may not credit. And if Stephen accepts Bloom's offer, counterfeit though it may be, then it is as good as true currency, just as counterfeits accepted as legal tender are no longer counterfeits. We may forge our own tales about them that will reflect our own ideology, or we may accept this counterfeit as exchangeable currency, as a "genuine" forgery or true fiction. What we must not do is assume that either the mercantile Bloom or the paternal Bloom is the whole Bloom; to do so is not only to erase the anthology of Blooms (from *antho,* Greek for "flower") we have already encountered—the lover, the giver of gifts, the sympathizer with expectant mothers, the courageous pacifist, the lewd voyeur—but to ignore the way that "Eumaeus" makes all such questions of authenticity and origins problematic. To buy the Penman's fiction is to accept a counterfeit unself-consciously, to practice a goldbug aesthetic of univocal representation in a text that overturns that textual economy on virtually every page. For Bloom's essential nature is elusive; to reduce him to a stereotype is to fall victim to the Penman's own counterfeiting. Like a counterfeit, however, Bloom's nature depends upon the tales that circulate about him. Our tale of their encounter may depict it as a fraud in which one party is duped by a counterfeiter or as a genuine exchange that, despite its fraudulent and exploitative elements, is no worse than any other exchange involving half-understood identities and partially obscured needs. To expect such an exchange to be "pure" of self-interest, or devoid of forged or counterfeit expectations, is a kind of Utopian thinking. In short, neither the Circean nor the Eumaean reading is sufficient; the reader of *Ulysses* must scan both its obverse and reverse sides to navigate through the narrative shoals, to make ends meet, to gain credit by engaging all aspects of its narrative economy.

11

Making Returns

Men perish because they cannot join the beginning with the end.

—Alcmaeon of Crotona,
quoted in Wheelwright, 1966, 30

NARRATIVE ACCOUNTING

The second episode of the Nostos, "Ithaca" also depicts and embodies returns—narrative, geographic, and economic. Its first half describes the conversations between Stephen and Bloom, borrowing a catechistic format from Joyce's early education. Indeed, paralleling the second episode ("Nestor"), the second-to-last episode adopts the authoritative tone of a "pedagogical examination" (Madtes 1983, 67) to provide readers with both more and less information than we need. Its seemingly learned responses often fail to answer the questions asked; it is often unclear whether the more authoritative voice is the questioner's or the answerer's. Stephen and Bloom also share and exchange the roles of teacher and student throughout the episode (Benstock 1991, 114), and many of their discussions and thoughts revolve around pedagogy or instruction: they deliberate about "jesuit education" (17.16); Bloom gives and refrains from giving "counsels" to Stephen (17.385); they remember the "educational careers" that both identify and distinguish them (17.548–54); Bloom recollects his unsuccessful "instruction" of Molly (17.698) and his successful instruction of Milly (17.910). Since for several years Joyce himself earned a livelihood from teaching, the concern with pedagogy is not surprising: in a sense, Joyce was an expert in the field.[1] More important, however, are the dynamic exchanges, the reciprocal give-and-take between student and teacher that exemplify successful social relations. At the end of their encounter, Stephen and Bloom agree to exchange lessons, their pedagogic exchanges both initiating and extending their acquaintance. Nevertheless, just as the answers and questions in the narrative catechism often fail to engage each other, so Stephen and Bloom, despite good intentions, sometimes fail to reach a meeting of the minds. Like many pedagogical relationships, theirs is provisional and only partly successful, subject to the conflict between self-interest and generosity that typifies most social and economic exchanges.

Many critics have remarked on the (pseudo-) scientific mentality of the "Ithaca" respondent, who seems to believe that all conditions are quantifiable and that pedantic catalogues and inventories can capture even internal or "spiritual" conditions. Here the narrative discourse resembles that of a science teacher eager to show off his or her knowledge. In many respects, the narrator resembles that protypical nineteenth-century scientist, that apparently "cold-blooded, desiccated, uninvolved" and neutral observer, the economist (McCloskey 1990, 138). The materialist ethos of the narrative economist in "Ithaca" objectifies that part of Bloom's mind that fetishizes prices and finds comfort in objects. Indeed, the respondent's discourse uses the two forms of narrative economists employ to mount their arguments: "curve fitting" or comparison; and "counterfactuals," or "what if" hypotheses (McCloskey 1990, 92–93). Thus the economistic ideology of "Ithaca" demands that readers use both imaginative economics (which examines the way economic systems use fictive concepts) and poetic economics (which scrutinizes the way literary texts employ economic discourse as an ordering principle [Heinzelman 1980, 11–12]) to comprehend the episode's exhaustive record of Bloom's return home.

Economists theorize about and experiment with general and abstract economic principles. At a lower level of abstraction resides the accountant. If the economist is a kind of novelist, the accountant resembles that less glamorous laborer, the "editor," whose job is not composition, but the "analysis and correlation of various figures so

---

1. For examples of Joyce's spirited but strange pedagogical gambits, see *JJ* 216–18.

that important facts about a business . . . may appear in their proper light and emphasis" (W. Cole 1921, 1, 5). Like economists, and like the "Ithaca" narrator, accountants use mathematics in their work.[2] Thus, with his penchant for classification and inventory, his obsession with discovering reciprocity and balance, and his unwillingness to theorize or generalize about his discoveries, the "Ithaca" narrator seems less an economist than an accountant. Often, however, the respondent's characteristic movements from trivial details to the widest possible perspectives lack even the accountant's capacity for discrimination. He overwhelms us with information but omits necessary facts; he rarely edits, but instead offers exhaustive lists. These traits move us even further down the ladder of economic sophistication from the accountant to the person who merely "record[s] known facts"—the bookkeeper (W. Cole 1921, 4). The narrators habitually use terms like *compensation, reciprocity, balance,* and *equilibrium* to describe Stephen and Bloom, as if all human interaction can be successfully portrayed by double-entry bookkeeping. For example, the keyless Bloom's "strategem" of climbing over the front railings is said to give him a "new stable equilibrium" (17.101); his final attainment of psychic and emotional stability is rendered in similar terms. This obsession with balance even shapes the narrative format: the catechism contains a compensatory mechanism, as each question is seemingly answered, stabilized, and closed off, as if totted on a ledger. Governed by this bookkeeping mentality, the discourse discovers balance where it may not exist and constantly seeks to stabilize circulation and achieve closure. In short, the narrative discourse of "Ithaca" is obsessed with making both ends meet. This fact seems to illustrate Joyce's claim that "Ithaca" is "in reality the end" of the novel (*L I*, 172). But it is a false end, not only because the narrator's tidy balance is spurious but also because "Ithaca" is succeeded by "Penelope," where the economy of debit and credit gives way to a ceaselessly circulating economy that synthesizes accounting with gift exchange.

In one sense, then, Bloom's budget epitomizes the episode's narrative discourse. The budget also exemplifies the episode's narrative

2. In fact, mathematics and accounting are historically related. The most influential early treatise on accounting, Luca Pacioli's 1494 textbook, *Summa de Arithmetica, Geometria, Proportioni et Proportionalita,* offers discussions of double-entry bookkeeping alongside treatments of arithmetic, algebra, and geometry (ten Have 1986, 40–41). Like Pacioli's treatise, "Ithaca" combines the the mathematical pedagogue and the bookkeeper.

tensions. One tension it manifests is that between narrative and anti-narrative, or motion and stasis, which I shall discuss below. The other tension is one we have already examined in other episodes: the conflict between realism and excess. Aiming to describe and classify the entire environment of 7 Eccles Street and thereby render the "bourgeois world in all its detail" (Litz 1974, 405), "Ithaca" implies that that world is richly worth examining. In this regard it is "the fullest possible realization of traditional realism" (Chace 1991, 895; cf. Madtes 1983, 68–69). "Ithaca" indeed fits five of the criteria of realist fiction: that the world is rich; that language can transmit information about the world; that language can copy the world but remains secondary to it; that the reader should believe the validity of that information (H. Steele 1988, 5–6). But if the goal of realism is to minimize excesses of signification, then "Ithaca," like most of the late episodes, thoroughly violates its conventions. In shaping the "Ithaca" manuscript, Joyce worked, as usual, by accretion, adding almost half of the episode after the original draft was completed (Madtes 1983, 43). The result was superfluity: in terms of plot, most of its information is superogatory.[3] If, as McCloskey notes, good "empirical work in economics . . . is like realist fiction" (1990, 31), then the "Ithaca" narrators are bad economists as well as inept storytellers, failing not only to discriminate between important and unimportant matters but also to keep the story moving. "Ithaca" again exhibits the Joycean economy of excess and, like "Cyclops" and "Circe," overwhelms the reader with its extravagant linguistic gifts (cf. Lawrence 1981, 188, 191). Just as Stephen is first charmed and then threatened by Bloom's generosity, so the reader may feel threatened by the excessive generosity of "Ithaca's" discourse.

The tensions in "Ithaca" are temporarily resolved into a provisional synthesis of narrative economies that mirrors the sympathetic but uneasy meeting between Stephen and Bloom. Its mixture of realist and antirealist, narrative and antinarrative elements embodies the encounter between the most extreme tendencies in Stephen's and Bloom's economies. That is, in "Ithaca" the impulses toward collection, cataloguing and balance—the anal-retentive economy of the miser or bookkeeper who piles up possessions and money to reinforce his identity—collides and eventually merges with that of the spend-

---

3. Monika Fludernik (1986, 92, 94) calculates that only 54.5 percent of the episode renders the plot and about 30 percent deals with "non-realistic" material. Thus the remainder might be considered "excess."

thrift who expends his or her goods as if submitting to the force of circulation itself. Thus the excesses of "Ithaca" can be read either as the epitome of "scrupulous meanness," of the bourgeois desire for accumulation and profit, or as a paradigm of the economy of expenditure, where the enormous lists function not as accumulation but as purgation, violating realism and the bourgeois economy behind it by comically and wilfully spending words to excess. Juxtaposing the economies of miser and spendthrift—the opposed impulses in Joyce's own psychic economy—"Ithaca" synthesizes them through expenditure that is also accumulation. In bringing together Bloom and Stephen, the episode also weds the opposed economic impulses that they represent.

One of Joyce's notesheets describes this phenomenon. "Extremes and means meet" (433): just as Stephen and Bloom meet and exchange, so Bloom makes a return that closes his circle of wandering. The moment of fusion is also a moment of closure. And yet, this stability remains partial and provisional, as the drive towards closure is constantly disrupted by the "imperfections"—economic, social, geometrical, and above all, human—in the episode's depiction of returns. Thus, although the economist or mathematician dismisses "magic"— whatever cannot be rationally explained—he or she cannot account for some aspects of human existence without betraying a "nostalgia" for that magic (McCloskey 1990, 108). This nostalgia, I suggest, both generates the episode's powerful sense of closure and balance and infects the apparently objective inventories of money and objects with an unmistakable sense of incompleteness. "Ithaca" offers reciprocity and balance as figures of return but at the same time reveals that such returns are never perfect.

RECIPROCAL EQUILIBRIUM?

The first half of the episode depicts the travelers' return and interactions at the Blooms'. As Bloom enters the house, Stephen sees only "a man," as if Bloom has assumed the Odyssean polytropism that simultaneously personalizes and depersonalizes him. Bloom is both glorified and belittled. Similarly, "Ithaca" is a "mathematico-astronomico-physico-mechanico-geometrico-chemico-sublimation of Bloom and Stephen" (*L* I, 164): "sublimation" means both "to raise" or "to exalt" and "to refine, purify or distill" (*OED*). Both characters are reduced and exalted by the catechism of "Ithaca"; when the narrative discourse emphasizes their similarities and glorifies them and their meeting, it is usually followed by a reduction that implies the differences between them and the provisionality of their atonement.

The opening scene, in which Bloom prepares the stove to heat cocoa, exemplifies this oscillation between expansion and reduction. Observing Bloom lighting the fire, Stephen recalls earlier kindlings, all performed by actual or surrogate parents (17.135–47). Bloom's inclusion here suggests that Stephen recognizes Bloom's parental motives and may even have begun to feel part of the Bloom family. The fire, moreover, is described with words—"pyre," "crosslaid," and "Abram's coal"—that suggest a sacrificial consecration of those familial ties (17.127, 128; Baker 1986, 287). The ritual is interrupted, however, by the famous "water-hymn," which traces its flow "From Roundwood reservoir" but never returns to the Bloom home (17.163–82). Indeed, the paragraph is really about an impediment to "flow"—a water shortage—and thus recognizes an economy of scarcity at odds with the celebratory tone of the succeeding description; it is less poetic than bourgeois, describing a violation of proper usage by the South Dublin Guardians at the expense of "solvent, sound" citizens like Bloom (17.177–82; cf. Baker 1986, 290). After that, however, in answer to an inquiry about what Bloom admires about water, the respondent offers an encyclopedic taxonomy of its properties, a list exemplifying the "comic disproportion of Cyclopian gigantism" (Benstock 1991, 101). Scarcity gives way to excess, as water is laden with Bloom's qualities and aspirations, including "variability" (17.189), "commercial significance" (17.192–93), "metamorphoses" (17.216), and "solidity" (17.220). Everysubstance and nosubstance, at once "everchanging" and "neverchanging" (17.233–34), water is both predictable and astonishing. The description reifies water into a series of discrete properties that enable the analyst better to collect it; at the same time, the extravagance of the description reflects water's capacity for changeability and expansion. This passage, then, combines the economies of containment and expenditure, as the narrative discourse interrupts the flow to inventory water's variable properties. While reducing Bloom and Stephen's encounter to an insignificant example of circulation, the passage also consecrates it with a "hymn."

What follows is a catalogue of objects in Bloom's kitchen cupboard, one of many such catalogues in the episode. These inventories represent Bloom's attempts to avoid thinking about the major event of the day (Boylan's liaison with Molly), but inevitably return to it. To counteract the "loss" of Molly, represented here by half-consumed food and cream, Bloom shares the cream, along with "Epps's massproduct, the creature cocoa," with Stephen (17.369). As many have noted, the pun on "massproduct" implies a secular communion. These "superogatory mark[s] of special hospitality" (17.359) seem more maternal than paternal (cf. Bormanis 1992, 594, 601), as the cream-filled cocoa creates a ritual of regeneration through commodities. The cocoa is also a gift and thus represents a "ritual statement . . . of social relations," a "starting, a sustaining mechanism of sociability" (Sahlins 1972, 215). The gift of cocoa functions according to the norms of generalized reciprocity, bringing the encounter into the economic arena of the family, where obligations of debt are replaced by communal sharing. It thereby typifies the process that "effects the transition from hostility to alliance, from anxiety to confidence, and from fear to friendship" (Lévi-Strauss 1969, 67–68). Moreover, if accepting a gift amounts to accepting the identity of the giver, Stephen not only accepts but incorporates Bloom when he ingests his mass product; for a moment Stephen is transubstantiated into a Bloom.

But as the catechist attempts to show their likenesses, his efforts also expose their differences. For example, in comparing their "educational careers" (part of the pedagogical motif), he "substitutes" Stephen for Bloom to create "Stoom," and Bloom for Stephen to create "Blephen" (17.549; 552). The blended names signify the exchange and fusion of identities. But the careers listed merely replicate the very different ones that Bloom and Stephen have already experienced: despite the blended names, their differences remain.[4] Nor can the catechist remain comfortable for long in an economy where obligations or benefits cannot be calculated. His accounting mentality leads him to present the exchange as debit and credit, so that Bloom's gift to Stephen becomes part of a moral ledger in which Bloom is satisfied "To have sustained no positive loss. To have brought a positive gain to others. Light to the gentiles" (17.352–53). Bloom's gifts are only part of a larger scheme of moral profit, in which benefits accrue to the giver. Similarly, although Stephen is needy, he also has "an equal and opposite power of abandonment and recuperation" (17.253): his impulse toward loss is recuperated by accounting, which perceives all conditions as part of a balance sheet.

The same tension between atonement and separation, between

4. The inventions show that Bloom's preferences for "applied science" are mainly pedagogic: his "improved scheme of kindergarten" would use educational toys such as "globemap playing balls, historically costumed dolls" (17.570–75).

gift and profit, emerges as the two compare artistic productions and aesthetic philosophies. We learn that Bloom too has written poems, the first when he was (appropriately) eleven years old (17.393), and the second at twenty-two (Stephen's current age; 17.411). The first was composed to win a prize from *Shamrock;* the second was a love poem written to Molly. The aims of the poems again typify Bloom's competing economic impulses: the first is designed to win money (profit) and the second to "win" Molly through a poetic gift that imitates Joyce's own textual gifts. Bloom's identities vary according to purpose: the profit-minded "L. Bloom," vs the intimate "POLDY" (17.400–401; 412–16). Like those of Odysseus, Bloom's literary productions both contain his identity and are his media of exchange; like those of Stephen's Shakespeare, his works weave and unweave their author's image. But neither poem satisfies Stephen's aesthetic philosophy because both are "kinetic": each is prompted by desire—the first for money, the second for Molly (*"You are mine. The world is mine"* (17.416)—and "desire urges us to possess, to go to something" (*P* 205).

However, as we have seen, Bloom's belief in the "infinite possibilities" available for advertisements with "magnetising efficacy" (17.583) does resemble Stephen's aesthetic of stasis. But whereas Bloom's "cogitations" are generally stimulated by a desire for "financial success" (17.576), for Stephen success cannot be measured by money. Indeed, if Bloom is motivated by possession, Stephen is driven by dispossession. Thus in exchange for Bloom's showcart ad, Stephen offers an epiphany that also depicts a woman writing (17.615–18) and follows it with a reprise of his Parable of the Plums. Although Bloom seems to appreciate the parable more than Stephen's journalistic auditors, he values it mostly for its imagined "possibilities of financial, social, personal and sexual success," especially if collected with other moral and "pedagogic" themes and submitted to a publication of "certified circulation and solvency" (17.646–51). Moreover, the suppression of the personal pronoun here (success for whom?) again suggests that Bloom's fusion with Stephen contains the potential for exploitation: the exchange may earn money for Bloom as well as for Stephen. The relationship between Stephen's pointedly ironic parable and Bloom's bourgeois response is thus itself parabolic: it curves from Stephen's aesthetic sense indirectly to Bloom's commercial imagination.

The two then begin to discuss the similarities between the Jews and the Irish. As they exchange letters and songs, each instructing the other in the lore of his "race," their "points of contact" (one of many geometrical terms) appear (17.745) and then "their mutual reflections merge" (17.769)—as in the Circean mirror—to consider the similar histories of the Irish and the Jews. But when the catechist inquires about the "reciprocal form" of their thoughts, a question that should prompt a description of similarities, the respondent instead alerts us to an inalienable difference: "He thought that he thought that he was a jew whereas he knew that he knew that he knew that he was not" (17.530–31). That is, although both are Irish, Bloom is a Jew and Stephen is not; moreover, each is suspicious of the other. Despite the indeterminate pronouns that seem to suggest fusion, Bloom's Jewishness, which Stephen has depicted in Shakespeare as necessary to artistic success, still divides them. Stephen's suspicion is also displayed in his song about Little Harry Hughes.

At first Bloom listens with pleasure to the song about a "schoolfellow's" encounter with a *"jew's daughter"* (17.802; 813). But when the daughter cuts off the schoolboy's *"little head"* (a symbolic castration or circumcision), he responds with "mixed feelings" (17.826; 830). Like Bloom's productions, Stephen's—a portrait of the artist as a schoolboy—contain his (disguised) identity; like the artist in Stephen's Shakespeare theory, the boy "meets himself" as a "jew" who demands self-sacrifice. Stephen's decision to sing this particular song seems odd: it is at least in questionable taste, if not a direct insult. Here Stephen seems less a spendthrift than a miser with an "avarice of emotions," a "jew" of friendship who responds to hospitality with suspicion and withdrawal. He fears that Bloom will welcome him into the family only to "immolate him, consenting" (17.837). The song responds to this perceived threat by saying, in effect, "I am wary of Jew/Greeks offering gifts, especially of women," as if Bloom were a Cyclops who eats his guests.

The Harry Hughes song also implicates third parties in the apparently two-way relationship between Stephen and Bloom. It first triggers Bloom's recollections of Milly as a "Jew's daughter" and then his memories of using his wedding gifts (as described in chapter 3) to "interest and to instruct her" (17.910) and her reciprocation in birthday gifts and admiration. These reciprocal exchanges of gifts that mark and forge kinship connections perhaps indicate that Stephen may take Milly's place as the person who bridges the rift between Molly and Poldy. But Molly is the more significant third party in this triangle: his earlier use of Molly's photo implies that Bloom is offering Stephen female companionship as well as his own; Stephen's singing of the Harry Hughes song may imply his recognition and refusal of such companionship (cf. McMichael 1991, 138).

Earlier Bloom considered "solutions" to the problem of "what to do" with his wife, which included "commercial activity," visits to male brothels, and "courses of evening instruction" (17.666–72). His attempts to educate her have been unsuccessful, because while she "gave attention with interest," she also "forgot with ease" (17.699–701). Molly's receptiveness to learning is presented as a kind of usurious loan, the "interest" on which she withdraws as the instruction becomes too demanding. But the bookkeeping narrator finds compensation for her apparent lack of aptitude in "The false apparent parallelism of all perpendicular arms of all balances, proved true by construction. The counterbalance of her proficiency of judgment regarding one person proved true by experience" (17.690–92). The second compensation means that she is astute enough to value Bloom properly. The first compensation, however, illustrates a more general principle that explains why Stephen and Bloom's two-way reciprocity is only apparently dualistic: any two perpendicular arms of a scale are actually part of an enormous triangle, the apex of which is the center of the earth (Gifford 1988, 576). Similarly, the catechist's reciprocal balance is really a false balance that depends upon Molly's invisible presence. Their relationship is actually a triad that involves Stephen with each of the Blooms in a different way: Stephen is at once a surrogate son and a possible substitute for both Bloom and Boylan. As lover and professor, Stephen will embody two of the solutions— sex and instruction—that Bloom previously sought.

With all of the plans he considers here and in "Eumaeus" circulating through his mind, Bloom proposes that Stephen spend the night with them. The plan has an elegant three-way reciprocity: Stephen would receive a place to study and a safe home; Bloom a "rejuvenation of intelligence" and "vicarious satisfaction"; Molly would acquire "correct Italian pronunciation" and a new erotic interest to replace Boylan (17.937–40). As we have seen, the offer combines charitable and self-interested motives; nonetheless, it is a fair business exchange (cf. Theoharis 1988, 174). But "promptly, inexplicably, with amicability, gratefully," Stephen declines the offer (17.955); at least for once he is grateful. He rightly fears that this domicile will become yet another net, a house from which he must disavow stewardship. The words of his refusal recall Bloom's own demurral to a similar offer from the Dedaluses twelve years earlier (17.473–76): their refusals are reciprocal. Stephen's words create a return in time that links past and present like a comet's return in space, even though it marks his departure from the Blooms'.

They do, however, agree upon a counterproposal in which Ste-

phen will give Italian lessons to Molly in exchange for voice lessons;
Bloom, now the third party to the exchange, will engage in "semistatic
and peripatetic intellectual dialogues" with Stephen (17.962–72).
This arrangement is more satisfactory for Stephen, since it discourages the exploitative potential of residing with the Blooms. In reaching this agreement, the two do achieve a meeting of the minds.
Indeed, the communicative transactions that confirm and continue
this arrangement are economic. That is, as Barbara Herrnstein Smith
argues in a different context, "its dynamics operate on, out of, and
through disparities of resources (or 'goods,' such as material property, information, skills . . .) between/among the agents and involve
risks, gains, and/or losses on . . . all sides" (1988, 102). If, as we have
seen, friendship is sometimes defined as whatever is undertaken in
the spirit of the gift (Sharp 1986, 86), it may be more properly defined as whatever parties undertake with the same intentions and with
equivalent potential losses and gains. In this sense, the geometry of
this set of exchanges reflects a friendship that bisects the continuum
running from usury to pure gift: it is an ideal "social exchange, . . .
an intermediate case between pure calculation of advantage and pure
expression of love" (Blau 1964, 112). Such exchanges create and solidify friendliness because they eschew written contracts and instead
depend upon mutual trust (Blau 1964, 113). These exchanges are
truly reciprocal: each gives and each receives, creating an entirely new
phenomenon out of their mutual relationship. Stephen and Bloom's
relationship has thus circulated from the gift-exchange model that set
Bloom and Stephen apart from the prostituted exchanges in "Circe,"
to the intimations of spiritual usury in "Eumaeus," and finally towards
this midpoint, a balanced social exchange. Extremes and means meet,
as Stephen and Bloom bisect the line of reciprocity.

Of course, there is an actual economic exchange to be completed
as well. Bloom returns, "without interest," the money Stephen put in
his care in Bella Cohen's (17.957). The broken bank note has returned, like Bloom, to its "home" with Stephen. The financial exchange both results from and permits the social exchange of
instruction and conversation; the social exchange extends and reflects
the balanced reciprocity and good faith symbolized in the economic
exchange. According to the narrator, Bloom returns the same
amount he was given. Such fully balanced exchanges, Sahlins observes, open the possibility of contracting out of a relationship (1972,
222); thus if this exchange were as perfectly reciprocal as the book-
keeper-respondent asserts, their connection could now be severed

and their narrative budget closed. But contrary to the bookkeeper's claims, Bloom actually returns a penny more (£1 7 0) than the £1 6s 11d that Stephen gave him (cf. 15.3613). It is a trivial sum, but this inverse "interest" on what Bloom later calls Stephen's "loan" (although the debt really runs in the opposite direction) unbalances the exchange and signifies the open-endedness also certified by their agreement to meet later. Kenner comments that "a bookkeeper might denominate [this amount] Usury, paid by the Jew to the Gentile: one more sly Joycean reversal of stereotypes. Bloom keeps the money about an hour and a half; the rate is about four per cent per week"; if so, the loan is not usurious (1987, 127).[5] But although at this rate the weekly interest would be far higher—closer to 30 percent than to 4 percent—Kenner's point is on target: Bloom gives Stephen more than he got. Moreover, by including interest in his return, Bloom enacts the previously analyzed Aristotelian pun on *tokos;* Bloom gives Stephen his own financial offspring as a symbol of his surrogate fatherhood. Indeed, since Edwardian maundy pennies bore a crown on their reverse faces (Reinfeld 1969, 181), Bloom's coin of "interest" finally gives Stephanos that material sign of the destiny and identity he has been seeking throughout *Ulysses*—a crown.

The added increment can be read as another gift which, added to the 11 shillings and fourpence for the coffee and bun Bloom bought in the cabman's shelter, brings Bloom's charity to Stephen to a total of 11s 5d. Or it may signify Bloom's payment for Stephen's playing the role of surrogate son; or it may be Bloom's way of keeping Stephen in his debt, and thus of encouraging his fulfillment of their future arrangement. The text provides contrary indications: the bookkeeper-narrator claims that the exchange is balanced, zeroed, and closed off, while the numbers themselves indicate that a bond remains, signified in the one penny increment. Despite the catechist's bias toward closure and balance, the text implies that relations do not end so neatly, that Bloom and Stephen may remain linked economically and spiritually.

The very next passage, indeed, illustrates the difficulties in as-

5. Kenner's figures are dubious. One penny is about .0031 of £1 6s 11d (1/323). McCarthy (1984b, 606) more accurately estimates that the interest would be "roughly 0.31% over the period of a few hours" (606). An hour and a half is approximately .0089 of a week (1/112). Thus, multiplying the penny interest on the £1 6s 11d by 112 (the number of hour-and-a-half segments in a week) would yield an approximate weekly interest (paid by Bloom to Stephen) of 112d, or 9s 4d: 34.6 percent. Now that is usury.

sessing the range of such circulations and returns. A clown "in quest of paternity" once claimed that Bloom was his father; another time Bloom marked a florin "for circulation on the waters of civic finance, for possible, circuitous or direct, return" (17.977; 983–84). The clown's quest failed; Bloom was not his son. Likewise, the florin never returned, thereby proving that money may not follow Bloom's path of circulatory return. These two counterinstances, in fact, cast doubt on the outcome of both characters' quests: like the clown, Stephen may not have found a father; while Bloom (symbolized by the florin) circulates and returns, the coin only circulates. These counterexamples also challenge our certitude about the characters' relationships. If the accountant-narrator's "curve fitting" (comparative) method temporarily yields a balanced equation, his counterfactual method generates opposite results. We cannot predict the future. Paternity fails; human circulation may be neither perfectible nor complete; returning is not the same.

These limitations on knowledge and return expose another difference between Stephen and Bloom. Whereas Stephen proceeds "syllogistically from the known to the unknown" as a "rational reagent between a micro and a macrocosm ineluctably constructed upon the incertitude of the void," Bloom proceeds "energetically from the unknown to the known through the incertitude of the void" (17.1013–15; 1019–20). Stephen has moved dialectically, leaving deposits of money and tokens of identity at each stage, defining himself by these losses. His linear trajectory now takes him into an uncertain future; indeed, his spendthrift habits have been designed to hasten this moment of uncertainty (Vernon 1984, 38). Stephen accepts the open-endedness of his freedom to lose; fully dispossessed, he may now be repossessed. Bloom, on the other hand, circulates *through* incertitude, but returns home to the "known." Unlike Stephen, who accepts incertitude, Bloom values return, repetition, familiarity. Stephen is defined by what he has given up, Bloom by what he possesses.

Even as the scientific voice of the episode attempts to eliminate the spiritual elements of the encounter, he is called back nostalgically to the "magic" he eschews, describing the night sky in poetic terms ("a heaventree of stars hung with humid nightblue fruit" [17.1039]), and tracing the infinite regresses of time and space until his bald descriptions encounter the limits of human knowledge and again confront "magic." Science (even economics or accounting) divorces itself from the human but, like a comet, is inexorably drawn back. With Molly's light acting as the apex of their triangle, once again these "exsuns" (or exsons: 17.1121) achieve reciprocity as each contemplates "the other in both mirrors of the reciprocal flesh of theirhisnothis fellowfaces" (17.1183). "Theirhisnothis," as McMichael glosses the word, "is not so much 'his' as 'this,' this one face in front of me, a face that neither atones with my concepts nor opposes them but rather disrupts what would otherwise be the sovereignty of my thoughts" (1991, 135). The face of the other is not mine. Although their "thought waves interweave" (Benstock 1991, 112), the reciprocal gaze affirms that the other's face is at once "theirhis" (both) and "nothis" (neither). True reciprocity obtains only through a voluntary agreement to bridge differences; otherwise, fusion leads to absorption, exploitation, spiritual usury, as the assets of one party become the assets of the other. For friendly exchange to exist, the inalienable difference of each party must remain inviolable.

No longer keyless, Bloom opens the door for Stephen who, repossessed of his crowns but still keyless, exits into the unknown. They take leave, "the lines of their valedictory arms, meeting at any point and forming any angle less than the sum of two right angles" (17.1222–23). Described in emotionless, geometrical terms, the handshake conjoins multiple layers of significance, fusing tropes of touch, economics, and reciprocity. Bloom again conveys his material friendship through his "surety of touch" (17.289–90); Stephen receives a touch that is neither exploitative nor niggardly. While Bloom gives Stephen a renewed connection to materiality, Stephen's touch gives to Bloom a detachment and new sense of freedom that helps him achieve his final equanimity. This "handtouch which is speech without words" (*FW* 174.10) signifies the reciprocity of their exchanges as well as their ephemerality. Resembling the Catholic symbol of the sacrament of matrimony—a picture of two right hands clasped (Webber 1971, 169)—the handshake is accompanied by the tolling of the bells in St. George's church, as if to commemorate the simultaneous wedding and divorce of complementary economic and religious identities.

In constantly drawing our attention to reciprocities that yield balance, the bookkeeper-narrator depicts the encounter between Stephen and Bloom as a social exchange that synthesizes gift giving and self-interest, a midpoint between spiritual usury and pure gift, which has brought together their disparate economic, social and personal qualities: they have exchanged information, conversation, money, and each has received something significant in return for his sacrifices. In all these senses, their exchange makes both ends meet. Although the narrator's scientific bias sometimes discovers balance and closure where they do not exist, and although Stephen's future remains uncertain, both the narrative form and the events leave us with a strong sense of completion. If this reciprocal fusion and balance is fleeting, its symbolic significance is undeniable, especially given the typically distorted exchanges in Joyce's Dublin. And if the characters remain subject to contingencies and fallibilities that continue to engender doubt about their motives and futures, their exchange—synthesizing most of the economic motifs in the novel—remains the most significant social and economic moment in *Ulysses*.

BALANCING BOOKS

With Stephen gone, Bloom undertakes a process of "divestiture" that necessitates a series of inventories (17.1479). Bloom gazes upon the possessions that embody the story of his life; he also compiles his budget and examines his books. The catalogues of Bloom's objects and money function in two opposed ways: on the one hand, they are accumulations of objects and words that testify to a bourgeois or miserly belief that possessions reassure and reinforce one's identity; on the other hand, they are a divestiture or expenditure of words and objects in preparation for a final departure. Ultimately, the narrator's tabulation of Bloom's possessions and money generates narratives of the past and future and provides reassurances that prepare character, narrator, and readers for a final equanimity.

Gazing into his mirror, Bloom notes "several inverted volumes improperly arranged," inverted because they appear in the mirror, and "improperly" because they are catalogued neither alphabetically nor topically. The narrator's imperative (a form that becomes increasingly prominent as the episode proceeds) to "catalogue" them is an attempt to establish a linguistic order in which there is "a place for everything and everything in its place" (17.1410), one that both reflects and revises Bloom's desultory attempts at cataloguing. Despite its apparent disorder, Bloom's library amounts to a fragmentary autobiography (17.1363–1407). Each book substantiates an element of his character or history: the 1886 post office directory documents his employment at Thom's; *The Child's Guide* proves his pedagogical interests (17.1368); *The Beauties of Killarney*, *When We Were Boys*, and *Laurence Bloomfield in Ireland* display his Irishness; *Philosophy of the Talmud* and *Thoughts From Spinoza* (Rudolph's book; see 11.1058) conversely reflect his father's influence and his Jewish heritage; *The Story of the Heavens* and *A Handbook of Astronomy, Three Trips to Madagascar, Voyages in China,* and *In the Track of the Sun* demonstrate his interest in celestial and terrestrial navigation and return; Sandow's exercises suggest his belief in physical renewal; Freytag's *Soll und Haben* (Debit and Credit) implies not only his similarity to the cost-accounting narrators of "Eumaeus" and "Ithaca" but also his own balancing mentality.

Bloom owns twenty-two books (two elevens) and has borrowed *The Stark-Munro Letters,* now overdue, from the Capel Street library. Nearly all of his books are pedagogical, either in intention or actual use; the geometry textbook that ends the list is also, typically, lost property. For my purposes, the most intriguing book in his library is Freytag's novel. We have already discussed how this *Bildungsroman* of commercial life illustrates the anti-Semitism Bloom faces and the mercantile ideology beneath Stephen and Bloom's relationship. The novel's title also fits my characterization of the "Ithaca" narrator as an accountant or bookkeeper. But the presence in Bloom's library of this jingoistic and moderately anti-Semitic German novel stills seems hard to account for. It seems very doubtful that Bloom could have read it; his German is poor at best: Stephen must translate for him the German song that ends "Eumaeus" (16.1817).[6] However, Bloom's father did speak and write German, if we can credit his son's memory of his suicide note (17.1885–86). Thus I would suggest that this book, like the Spinoza collection, was originally Rudolph's, and that Leopold either inherited it or was given it as a gift. A huge bestseller among the German bourgeoisie, the novel would likely have been found in the libraries of people of Rudolph's class. Indeed, his ownership of the book testifies to a rather touching attempt to assimilate into a German society that would never have fully embraced him, a Hungarian Jew. If he could not be a real German, he may have thought, at least he could own the right German books.

But Rudolph's possession of this book could scarcely have provided much comfort: as a much-traveled and incompletely assimilated Jew, he would probably have found the novel's anti-Semitic caricatures insulting; as a struggling and ultimately failed merchant and hotelier, he would have seen its success story as a symbol of his own

---

6. Stephen's German is not flawless either: witness his "mistake" with the word *Brücken* (16.1884). In Joyce's *Notesheets* we find this line: "Soll und Haben. Have you read? No!" (478). It is not clear who is speaking, but I would guess that neither Bloom nor Stephen has read it, Bloom because he couldn't, and Stephen because he wouldn't.

inadequacy and the Jewish moneylender Ehrenthal's failure as an omen of his own. If he had read it, the novel would have made him feel worse about his inability to achieve the middle-class stability and secure national identity the novel celebrates. If, however, as Carter argues, *Soll und Haben* was a book for "the intelligent schoolboy," and its stolid pro-German bourgeois ideology made it in every way a suitable "Konfirmationsgeschenk" or confirmation gift (1968, 329), then it is quite possible that Rudolph acquired the book when he converted to Protestantism (see 8.1073), or that he gave it to Leopold upon the latter's baptism as a Protestant (17.542) or high school grad-uation. It would have been one way for Rudolph to give his son "commercial advice" (17.1910)—as Leopold does with Milly—using a gift as means of instruction. Perhaps, then, *Debit and Credit* keeps its unread place on Bloom's shelf as a permanent reminder of his fa-ther's failure to balance accounts, as an example of how and how not to make both ends meet.

Despite these fragmentary intimations, the autobiography con-cealed in Bloom's books remains inchoate. Instead, the narrator's catalogue authorizes itself as the proper order simply by its existence on the page. The narrative discourse replaces the books with the list, thereby encompassing and rewriting Bloom's history as a fixed set of discrete objects. The library as catalogue thus seals off the past by reenclosing it within its own ahistorical order. In this respect the library fits Susan Stewart's description of the collection: that it "seeks a form of self-enclosure which is possible because of its ahistoricism. The collection replaces history with *classification,* with order beyond the realm of temporality" (1984, 151; emphasis hers). The goal of a collection is not to rediscover or return to origins but to efface origins and supplant them with the antinarrative of its own reified taxonomy. Thus Bloom's library is less a set of books than a set of objects that simultaneously invites and defeats narrative returns.

Other books are balanced in "Ithaca" when, perhaps stimulated by Bloom's discovery of a shilling placed in his pocket at Mrs. Sinico's funeral, the bookkeeper-catechist commands the respondent to "Compile the budget for 16 June 1904" (17.1455). This calculation of finances is perfectly appropriate for an episode that seeks the sense of an ending, since "finance" comes from the root *finer* (to end). In seeking to make ends meet, a financial ledger most of all seeks to end. The balance sheet signifies the narrator's desire for order and completeness as well as his tendency to view everything in terms of profit and loss (cf. Littleton and Yamey 1978, 7). More importantly, it illustrates the collision of narrative and antinarrative forces in "Ithaca." In one sense, a balance sheet is a story, a minimalist narrative of transactions: the ledger really names the cost of commodities, and thus the money amounts are themselves translations of physical exchanges, shorthand accounts of events. A "financial" account is thus a story with a beginning, middle, and a bottom line—an end. If narrative is an account, accounting is also a narrative. In another sense, however, a ledger is the opposite of narrative: it does not chronicle events in terms of their effect upon one another, nor does it provide transitions between scenes to produce a sense of dynamism. Rather, it reifies events into fixed entities, removing connectives and freezing exchanges into quantifiable amounts. It takes the raw materials of plot and removes both causality and (usually) chronology. Bloom's budget is thus a kind of schema of the economy of the novel that omits all values that cannot be quantified by prices and deletes all events that do not involve market exchanges. In that sense, the balance sheet is an antinarrative, an object that offers stability and fixity at the cost of circulation or narrative connection.[7] Because any budget holds true for only a brief time (W. Cole 1921, 9), however, the stability and completeness of this balance sheet are provisional. Thus the budget epitomizes the competing economic impulses at work throughout the novel: on the one hand, the desire to employ material signifiers (prices, inventories) to stabilize the world and preserve it from dangerous transformations; on the other, the economist's (and accountant's) awareness that all such entities are merely provisional symbols for the constant circulations in social interaction. Even the fixity of balance sheets is merely temporary; like coins or comets (the episode's symbol), all material things are really in motion.

Moreover, Bloom's budget (17.1467–78), like most compilations in "Ithaca," is less accurate than it seems. Even on its own terms, it is not a complete account. It omits all of Bloom's expenditures in Bella Cohen's (although it does include an unspecified tram fare that may be for his trip to Nighttown) and his expenses for the coffee and bun. One might conclude that the accountant simply leaves out all gifts,

---

7. Historically, in fact, double-entry bookkeeping (with its curt, graphic, and skeletal capsule) replaced the short narratives that had previously served as account sheets (ten Have 1986, 34). Many critics have remarked upon the static quality of "Ithaca," which resembles a series of "tableaux," of staged scenes, rather than an ongoing narrative (Litz 1974, 398; Peake 1977, 283). The tension between stasis and motion also emerges in the answerer's tendency to interrupt the action with digressive passages of reminiscence or information.

but he does tally Bloom's contribution to the Dignam fund, as well as the cost of the Banbury cakes he gave to the gulls.[8] The omission of the money he spent at Bella's may imply that Bloom's gifts to Stephen elude summary by a profit/loss formula, that balance sheets always leave remainders that escape closure and balance. Or it may simply mean that the Bloomian bookkeeper has "forgotten" about the brothel. As I have noted, Bloom spends a total of 11s 5d on Stephen and only a little more (15s 6d) for everything else. Even of the latter total, however, 9s 2d are gifts: 5s to the Dignams, 1d for Banbury cakes, 1s for *Sweets of Sin* (a gift to Molly), 2s 6d on the present to Martha (admittedly, given in expectation of a countergift), and 7d on the pig's foot and trotter that he gives to the dog in "Circe." All told, Bloom spends by far the majority of his money—£1 0s 7d out of his total Bloomsday expenditures of £1 6s 11d—on gifts.

The latter figure creates yet another balance, another strikingly symmetrical, reciprocal connection between Stephen and Bloom: Bloom's expenditures for the day (£1 6 11) are exactly the same amount as the cash Stephen gave him to hold (15.3613)![9] It is as if Stephen's "loan" repays Bloom in full for the expenditures he will make, thereby balancing their exchange. Curiously, the one penny he gives in "interest" to Stephen brings his expenditures into balance with Stephen's returned cash. But despite his greater wealth, Bloom has spent less today than Stephen. He has also earned £1 7s 6d in commission, a sum that here makes its belated first appearance in the text (17.1459). This sum also yields a hidden symmetry. We recall that in "Wandering Rocks" Boylan phones his secretary about Molly's

8. The initial version of the budget did leave out the Dignam gift, thereby more consistently omitting all gifts to offspring (Madtes 1983, 54). Benstock (1991, 134) assumes that the train ride (and fare) from Holles Street to Nighttown has been censored. The "tramfare" listed on the budget (17.1469) may be that one, since Bloom mentions a "mixup . . . at Westland row" station (15.636–37); or it might be the fare for a tram from Sandymount, where Bloom watched Gerty MacDowell, to the Holles Street hospital. At any rate, one train ride is missing here, and it is probably the one to Nighttown, since the budget also leaves out his other expenses there.

9. The sum for gifts does not include either the tram fare to get Bloom to the Holles Street hospital from Sandymount, where he was also on a charitable mission, or his tram fare to Nighttown. Both might be counted as gifts (to the Dignams and to Stephen, respectively) by a more charitable critic, which would bring the total of his gifts to £1 0s 9d. I do not count his 3d tip to Pat the waiter as a gift—it is payment for services rendered. I have arrived at the £1 6s 11d figure by adding all of Bloom's listed expenses, plus the 11s he spends at Bella's, plus the 1d "interest" on Stephen's "loan," plus the omitted 1d tram fare, either to Nighttown or to Holles Street.

tour (so far consisting solely of "Belfast and Liverpool"). He then mentions a monetary figure, "twentyseven and six" (£1 7s 6d), probably referring to Molly's fees for the dates (10.390–91). If so, then Leopold's Bloomsday earnings and Molly's prospective earnings come to precisely the same amount. This concealed symmetry again typifies the balancing impulse that pervades "Ithaca"; more importantly, it suggests an equality of earning power between the Blooms that is manifest in a "balance of power" that obtains throughout their relationship.

These symmetries notwithstanding, Bloom still has 4s 9d in cash and therefore has earned more today than he has spent, yielding a balance in his favor of 5s 4d. Although he has given many gifts, Bloom has "sustained no positive loss"; the moral ledger, as well as the financial one, is in his favor. Despite its apparent completeness and perfection, then, the "Ithaca" budget is inaccurate both financially and ethically; it does not account for all of his gifts and cannot account for his moral profit. Far from describing Bloom's economic day fully or accurately, the budget actually suggests by its omissions that social and economic life cannot be summed up by debit/credit accounts. In this sense, the budget amounts to a critical reading of *Ulysses;* others exist as well, and these must be pieced together by readers (cf. Benstock 1991, 135). Bloom's budget for the day is compiled in Appendix B.

These accounting discrepancies raise another question: who compiles the budget? Obviously it is the narrative presence whom I described as an accountant or a bookkeeper; as such, however, the compiler of the budget is either inept or dishonest, omitting expenses either out of incompetence or as part of his "editorial" function. Kenner asserts that it is also "such a version as Bloom might let Molly inspect" (1972, 23), but he would scarcely let her know about his half-crown gift to Martha. It does, however, seem to be a Bloomian budget, inasmuch as it completes the running budgets he keeps throughout the novel and generously terms his fidelity banking of Stephen's money a "loan" to himself. In a larger sense, however, the answer is this: the reader compiles and revises the budget. The reader must compile it for himself or herself in order to discover what the text omits. The reader must make returns, recalling and noting all of Bloom's expenditures today; the reader must read backwards to read forwards, uniting reading moments over time as if remembering a debt that must be paid. The reader scans Bloom's budget and tabulates his or her own economic, moral, or social profit-and-loss statement; to achieve his or her own sense of an ending, his or her own "financial" record, the reader must also become an accountant or bookkeeper, linking the beginnings and ends of the novel through his or her own labor of balance. As accountant or bookkeeper, the reader must also seek to make both ends meet. The contract between author (or text) and reader thus replicates that between Stephen and Bloom: both parties must be reciprocally engaged to bring forth the whole—and even then it remains incomplete. In that sense, the text is at once a symbol of the transaction between author and reader and, as it is rewritten by the reader, the transaction itself. The text's unity can only be forged through such textual bookkeeping, yet the account produced will always remain provisional. Like Bloom's budget, the reader's will leave gaps; the book can never be fully balanced or ended, because perfect balance would mark the end of bookkeeping, the end of reading.

A SYSTEM OF OBJECTS

The other part of Bloom's process of "divestiture" also involves investiture, as the narrative accountant compiles list after list of Bloom's possessions, both real and hoped-for. Some of them are capsule stories. For example, Molly's hankies and hosiery, hanging on "erect wooden pegs" (17.150), and the "exposed" keyboard, with its four consumed matches and cigarettes (17.1303–6), incorporate the tale of Molly's adultery. Many of the objects also seem frozen and fixed in place, as if designed to reassure their possessors of their own secure existence. For example, Bloom gazes at three "homothetic" (similar and similarly placed—i.e., triangular) objects: his marble clock (stopped at 4:46 A.M. in March 1896), his dwarf tree, and his embalmed owl. He places himself in a triangular relationship with these triangular objects: the tree "regards" the back of the owl, which in turn regards Bloom, who regards the tree. The reciprocal relationship transforms Bloom into one of the homothetic objects. These mutual perceptions seem to exemplify Marx's commodity fetishism, in which human relationships "assume the fantastic form of a relation between things" (1978, 321). Just as Bloom often finds stability and reassurance in calculating prices as fixed entities, here he regains some "tranquil" equilibrium by contemplating objects (17.1346). But these objects were all originally wedding gifts and thus for Bloom do not emerge out of the market economy; in that sense they are not commodities so much as souvenirs. Still, all three of them are dead or frozen, as if signifying that the marriage they commemorate is also paralyzed or moribund. These gifts have stopped circulating and in their reified and static dimensions epitomize the static economy of the form of "Ithaca."

A little later, the accountant inventories Bloom's first and second drawers. The first contains a farrago of diverse objects, including letters and drawings by Milly that depict Bloom as "Papli" (17.1776–78; 1792); a faded Christmas card (17.1780–83); pornographic and nonpornographic photos (17.1809–12; 1779); an ancient bazaar ticket and two coupons for the Royal Hungarian lottery (17.1790; 1808); some old Austro-Hungarian coins (17.1808); a brooch and a scarfpin belonging to his mother and his father, respectively (17.1794–96); an old Victorian stamp (17.1814); some writing materials (pilfered?) from Hely's (17.1783–87; 1806); two condoms (17.1804–5); his letters from Martha (17.1796–1801); his measurements before and after Sandow's exercises, and the now familiar Wonderworker prospectus (17.1815–39). Moretti claims that these collocations of objects embody Bloom's "unsatisfied aspiration to consumption" (1983, 188), but most of them are not consumable commodities. The Wonderworker, the lottery tickets, and the Sandow's measurements testify to Bloom's penchant for seeking renewal and to his hopes for the future, but most are mementoes or souvenirs of the past. Like the wedding gifts, these objects have come to replace the actual persons or events.

Stewart has persuasively analyzed the capacity of such souvenirs to function as brief narratives. The souvenir, she writes, "speaks to a context of origin through a language of longing, for it is not an object arising out of need or use value; it is an object arising out of the necessarily insatiable demands of nostalgia. The souvenir generates a narrative that reaches only 'behind' " (1984, 135). Like genuine and counterfeit money, these mementoes remind their owner of their origins. Fittingly appearing in the Nostos, these objects embody and incite nostalgia, a longing for return. Ultimately, then, they speak less of their own origins than of their possessor's and thus also provide a "false promise of restoration" possible only through narrative or reverie that replaces the possessor's real origin with an imaginary one (Stewart 1984, 136, 150). In that sense, these souvenirs and mementoes are, like the stories in "Eumaeus," counterfeits that tell of false origins. The very nostalgia they evoke demonstrates that those origins are lost, that the past is separate from the future. Thus the wedding gifts, for example, "contain" the wedding, but only as an event that can never be reexperienced; similarly, the old coins, stamps, and mementoes of Bloom's parents provide the only link to his family history, but their tale is necessarily fragmented, mythical, incomplete. Nevertheless, like the counterfeit stories in "Eumaeus," these fictions of objects serve a purpose: they reinforce Bloom's identity by enveloping his past within his present (Stewart 1984, 151), thereby reflecting his belief in the possibility of making both ends meet.

Bloom also entertains fantasies of an ideal future. His most elaborate one concerns his "ultimate ambition": to "possess in perpetuity" a large parcel of land with a "bungalowshaped 2 storey dwellinghouse" upon it (17.1497–1505). He will pay £60 per year on a principal of £1200—figures far beyond his current means—for this "abode of bliss" (17.1660–61). Dubbed "Flowerville" or "Bloom Cottage" (17.1580), it will boast all the modern conveniences and boost him to the landed gentry class. The Flowerville fantasy thus fulfills Bloom's desire for "home rule": he will not only own his dream house but also act as magistrate, typically following a course that lies "between undue clemency and excessive rigour" (17.1617). Both punishing property crimes and overturning the class system, he will balance extremes and right injustices. Flowerville is another of Bloom's (and the economist-narrator's) "counterfactuals," a "what if" story designed both to project Bloom into the future and to revise and glorify him. Bloom is realistic enough to recognize that he must also imagine ways of purchasing this domicile. But despite their pragmatic motivation, his get-rich-quick schemes are implausible; here the narrator reflects Bloom's nostalgia for magic, as he imagines winning huge sums on horse races by inventing a telegraph system that will inform him of the results before anyone else (17.1674–78), finding valuable stamps or jewels, discovering buried treasure (17.1679–90), or unearthing a "goldseam of inexhaustible ore" (17.1752). The accountant exaggerates Bloom's penchant for finding lost property into the kind of farfetched dreams that lull middle-class husbands to sleep. All of his schemes require "the support, by deed of gift and transfer vouchers" of "eminent financiers . . . possessing fortunes in 6 figures, amassed during a successful life, and joining capital with opportunity the thing required was done" (17.1746–51). The money question still lies at the back of Bloom's Utopian plans.

As presented in the exhaustive inventories of the "Ithaca" cataloguer, however, the Flowerville fantasy seems less a narrative than a mammoth list of commodities and furnishings (see especially 17.1520–72). Thus Jameson notes the "degree to which [Bloom's]

fantasies . . . are . . . bound up with objects" and argues that they are
"falsely subjective fantasies: here, in reality, commodities are dreaming about themselves through us" (1982, 139). It is true that the
description of Flowerville is couched in language borrowed from
"houseagents' advertisements and home-and-garden magazines"
(Peake 1977, 286): it is a kind of ultimate ad as well as a fantasy of
possession. Like those in "Eumaeus," this "ambition" seems anonymous, a fantasy of a bourgeois Everyman in which the homeowner is
just another homothetic object, another feature of the house that
owns him. Indeed, both as an imaginary place filled with things, and
as a long list of words, the Flowerville passage resembles Stewart's
description of the phenomenology of the collection. The collection is
the opposite of the souvenir: whereas the latter grows out of and
incites nostalgia, the "point of the collection is forgetting" objects'
origins (Stewart 1984, 152). Thus Bloom never imagines actually purchasing any of the objects in the house. In his dream, he collects
the objects without having to buy them: as in most collections, consumption is magically transformed into production (Stewart 1984,
158).

As with Bloom's ad designs, however, the comforts these fantasies
of possession afford are not primarily commercial; they have less do
to with profit than with pleasure, and involve not labor but magic.
Just as the miser gains "satisfaction in the complete possession of a
potentiality with no thought whatsoever about its realization" (Simmel
1950, 180), so Bloom's fantasies of possession exemplify the aesthetic
value of money—its Imaginary function as a measure of values. For
Bloom, "the strange coalescing, abstraction, and anticipation of ownership of property which constitutes the meaning of money is like
aesthetic pleasure in permitting consciousness a free play . . . and the
incorporation of all possibilities without violation or deterioration by
reality. If one defines beauty as *une promesse de bonheur,* this definition
is yet another indicator of the similarity between aesthetic attraction
and the attraction of money, because the latter lies in the promise of
the joys money makes possible" (Simmel 1950, 180). Bloom's Flowerville fantasy is simultaneously aesthetic and economic and captures
the essential polyvalence of money itself. Like a collection, this fantasy
represents the "ultimate self-referentiality and seriality of money at
the same time that [it] declares . . . independence from 'mere' money"
(Stewart 1984, 165). Thus, argues Stewart, the collection "translates
the monetary system into the system of objects. Indeed, that system
of objects is often designed to serve as a stay against the frailties of
the very monetary system from which it has sprung" (1984, 159). Like

money, a house filled with possessions is something that we might keep without spoiling, something that simultaneously resists and embodies the money economy.

The lists of Bloom's possessions also exemplify the narrative economy of "Ithaca." In one sense Bloom's dream house is another "extravagant expenditure of energy" like the enormous catalogues in "Cyclops" (Lawrence 1981, 193). The narrative spends prodigious amounts of time and space inventorying these possessions, amounts far beyond the economic demands of literary realism. And yet these lists are themselves collections. Like the objects in Flowerville, the words that describe them translate Bloom's consumption into imaginary production: they are now the product of the narrator's collaboration with Bloom. The bookkeeper-narrator's lists of Bloom's objects are not narratives; in fact, they interrupt the fantasy in which they reside by exhaustively compiling the objects within it, and the story of Bloom becomes instead a display of the accountant's skill at cataloguing. As with collections of objects, then, these collections of words operate as modes of containment and control (Stewart 1984, 159), as a kind of linguistic hoard that freezes the flux of narrative into a set of categorizable and fixed entities. Rather than testifying to enormous *expenditures*, the Flowerville collections exhibit both Bloom's and the narrator's need to accumulate. As we have already noted, however, the miser and spendthrift are merely shifting valences of a single impulse; thus by slightly adjusting the focus, one may read the mentality behind the "Ithaca" lists as the reverse face of the Cyclopian economy of expenditure. Both are extreme economies that betray an obsessive, transgressive labor meant to overturn the "sublime economy" of literary realism.

Bloom's second drawer contains more mementoes—a blurry photo of his father and grandfather, Rudolph's haggadah book (with his spectacles inside), and a postcard from the Queen's Hotel, where his father went bankrupt and died (17.1875–81)—that recall how different his father's life was from his own imagined future and thereby poignantly call him back to his origins. As if awakening to the genuine possibility of economic failure, the accountant "reduces" Bloom by "cross multiplication of reverses of fortune," producing a series of negative futures that balance the rosy ones Bloom has already imagined (17.1933). In his decline from "Poverty" to "Mendicancy" to "Destitution," Bloom "meets himself" as some of the Dubliners he has encountered today: from a "dun for the recovery of bad and doubtful debts" (the Nameless narrator of "Cyclops"), he deterioriates into a "fraudulent bankrupt" (a Ben Dollard), then into

a "sandwichman, distributor of throwaways" (the men in "Lestrygonians"), a "maimed sailor" (the beggar of "Wandering Rocks"), a "blind
stripling" ("Lestrygonians") and finally an "aged impotent disfran-
chised ratesupported moribund lunatic pauper" (17.1936–47). If
Flowerville is his dream, these are his nightmares: becoming one of
Dublin's relics of old decency. In the hands of the accountant-narrator, Bloom's credits—those fantasies of enrichment and possession—
must be balanced by debits.

But Bloom has more palpable consolations for these anxieties.
While Flowerville is an imaginary treasure, Bloom also has some real
money, graphically represented by the other documents in his second
drawer (17.1855–67). Here are two kinds of papers: those that certify
his identity and his heritage (his birth certificate; his graveplot; his
father's announcement of his name change), and those that prove his
solvency (his life insurance policy; his bank savings book; his certificate of possession of £900 worth of Canadian stock). As I have already
noted, these documents depict a man far more economically secure
than the seemingly marginal character we have come to know, and
one a good deal more prosperous than most of the Dubliners in
Ulysses. The documents are far more reliable "preservatives" against
the misfortunes he fears than the two rubber ones in his first drawer.
While the mementoes of Rudolph reach only "behind," these proofs
of Bloom's financial security guarantee a more stable future. Indeed,
the documents prove that he has taken his father's advice to take
care of pounds and pence (17.1910–11) and learned from Rudolph's
negative example. The documents once again link monetary and
physical generation, fatherhood and finances, as Rudolph's generation of Leopold has been translated into Leopold's ability to generate
money by interest and investment. These financial "offspring" provide for his physical ones: both kinds of progeny can be, and have
been, "produced and educed to maturity" (17.1964).

RETURNING EQUANIMITY

His visitor gone, his possessions catalogued, Bloom prepares
physically and emotionally for his final return. In the final pages of
"Ithaca," Bloom's temporal journeys are paired with some potential
spatial ones; both enable him to make returns. After contemplating
reasons for leaving Molly, the narrator charts a geometry of return
guided by triangles and spheres—by the "hypotenuse of the
rightangled triangle" formed by stars, and most of all by "a bispheri-
cal moon" of a "carnose negligent perambulating female" (17.1994–

98). These pages couple the Bloom domestic economy with the cosmic economies of space and time. After being advertised as lost property, he would wander "to the extreme limit of his cometary orbit" but finally, obeying the summons of recall, "return an estranged avenger, a wreaker of justice . . . with financial resources (by supposition) surpassing those of Rothschild or the silver king" (17.2012-23). Bloom would become both Odysseus slaughtering Penelope's suitors and a Shylockian Shakespeare taking revenge by generating negative returns on his enemies and positive returns on his money. Simultaneously geographic, astronomical, and financial, Bloom's returns would do more than make ends meet; they would turn an end into a new beginning.

He also makes returns in time, reciting the events of the day as rituals and enumerating the "imperfections" in his "perfect day" (17.2044–58; 2071). The imperfections are all failures to "obtain" (17.2074–78), as if one can attain perfection only by possession. But these returns in time mostly demonstrate the unobtainability of perfection: there is an "unsatisfactory equation between an exodus and return in time through reversible space and an exodus and return in space through irreversible time" (17.2025–28): returning is not the same. He may return through memory, but he cannot truly recapture the past; likewise, he may return in space but, like Odysseus, will find things changed. His decision to stay is itself a return after mental wandering, prompted by love as the spirit of the gift. As Odysseus, Bloom returns with tributes—the "Honour and gifts of strangers, the friends of Everyman. A nymph immortal, beauty, the bride of Noman" (17.2010–11)—into an erotic economy that, like the gift, "seeks always to return to its homeland; inexorably, even after being transferred hand to hand through a series of transactions" (Sahlins 1972, 153). Bloom limns the circulation of the gift economy, thereby becoming sublimated into Everyman and Noman; his returns enhance his value. The force of attraction overcomes his centrifugal desire; Molly, sometimes viewed as a possession, now becomes a gift that moors him to Ithaca.

And so he crawls into bed, but circumspectly and prudently, because it is the site where ends of the life cycle meet (17.2119–21). He achieves a final equanimity through a series of "counterfactuals": "if" he had smiled, he would have done so because he could now imagine himself sublimated into merely one of a series; recurrence and eternal return place his jealousy into perspective (17.2127–31), so that his return is but one of an infinity of returns in a cycle that may continue forever. Bloom's consolation, then, comes not from closure or stasis but from the impossibility of closure; his recognition of serial usurpation thus surpasses Homeric retributive reciprocity. He posits an infinite economy in which there is no last term but only eternal rotation, an economy also embodied in "Penelope." Ultimately Bloom's sense of justice depends not upon debit and credit but upon the recognition that such double-entry moral bookkeeping is inadequate.

Paradoxically, however, this recognition of cyclicity produces a provisional balance, as his subsequent reflections pass from envy to jealousy to abnegation to equanimity. Abnegation derives in part from his awareness that Boylan's presence is necessary for the "imminent provincial musical tour, common current expenses, net proceeds divided" (17.2172–76): Boylan will bring money. Why equanimity? Because adultery is natural, because it is much less reprehensible than a whole list of crimes (including forgery and usury [17.2184; 2188]), and most of all because it reflects a process of adaptation, of a compensation that results in a "reciprocal equilibrium" between the body and its environment (17.2192). Bloom mentally imitates Molly's adaptation, when his recognition of the universality of reciprocity and balance enables him to justify and accept what seems to be an imbalance. Just as the chapter begins with the restoration of Bloom's physical equilibrium, it ends with his achievement of a psychic equilibrium. Negative reciprocity (retribution) is replaced by the reciprocity of balance.

As if to express this newfound balance, Bloom makes both ends meet by kissing Molly's "melonsmellonous" rump (17.2243). She now plays catechist, for he must compile his own narrative accounts; as with his budget, there are omissions and distortions, but the "salient point" (both geometrically and narratively) of his account is Stephen Dedalus, about whom Molly creates her own counterfactual tales in "Penelope" (17.2269). Stephen is now the invisible third party, the third angle of the triangle that permits balance. Poldy and Molly lie head to foot, fusing into a yin-yang figure, a spherical balance of oppositions, thereby generating a dual-sexed being that fulfill's Stephen's predictions about "the economy of heaven" (9.1051–52). The novel now achieves a powerful sense of finality and closure, as Bloom, "the childman weary, the manchild in the womb" (17.2317–18), returns to origins. Both ends meet.

But even though Joyce claimed that "Ithaca" was "in reality the end" of the novel (*L* I, 172), its closure remains provisional. Just as the Blooms' apparent stasis is really a movement "through the everchanging tracks of neverchanging space" (17.2309–10), so this closure immediately opens again into the rotating economy of "Penelope." "Ithaca" is thus both end and beginning. Its final dot symbolizes this convergence (cf. Litz 1974, 404): it may represent the cosmic view of the Blooms' yin-yang, and even the dot of the earth itself, rotating and revolving; it may represent the "egg" about which the fetal Bloom mumbles as he falls asleep (17.2339); it may be Molly's anus (or its product), which lies near the fecal Bloom, who sees in it all those potentialities for renewal we have traced; or it may be a zero, both the end and the beginning of number, both nothing and infinite potential. The dot signifies that both ends meet, but only by constantly moving. In his *Notesheets*, Joyce wrote "0 produces ∞" (456): if "Ithaca" ends with a zero, it gives way to the ∞ of "Penelope," which does not so much combine beginning and ending as nullify the significance of such accounting terms.

Throughout "Ithaca" the narrative accountant's obsession with balance is destabilized by such forces as emotion, chance, and the existence of a third party beyond two-way reciprocity. Just as "Ithaca" constantly oscillates between stasis and motion, between balance and imbalance, between reciprocal friendship and reserve, so its final balance is disrupted and revised by the female discourse that succeeds it. If females function in "Ithaca" as either gift exchangers or gifts, "Penelope" exploits this condition, replacing such male economies with a female economy implicated in the infinite circulation of gift exchange.

In a variety of ways, then, "Ithaca" exhibits both a conflict between and a synthesis of the competing economies of *Ulysses:* accumulation and expenditure, realism and antirealism, economy and excess, motion and stasis, ending and beginning. If the episode seems to end in a static, closed balance, that balance is no more final than the financial balance of Bloom's budget. Its stasis invokes infinite motion, its closure another opening, its accumulation a form of expenditure, its economy an excess. While giving readers an ending that satisfies our desire not only to move linearly towards an end but also to make ends meet, it also frustrates those desires by remaining elusive and by giving way to an episode that obviates such distinctions. As "Penelope" again reveals, some surplus always escapes the ledger. The wealth of "Ithaca," indeed, derives not from its privileging of accumulation or expenditure, or from its enormously detailed lists, but from the way it provokes readers to recognize that such systems will always leave ends open.

Epilogue: Corporal Assets

> A woman's body is a corporal asset of the State: if she traffic
> with it she must sell it either as a harlot or as a married
> woman or as a working celibate or as a mistress. But a
> woman is (incidentally) a human being: and a human be-
> ing's love and freedom is not a spiritual asset of the State.
> ... A human being can exert freedom to produce or to
> accept, or love to procreate or to satisfy. Love gives and
> freedom takes.
>
> —*SH* 202–3

In a famous letter to Frank Budgen, Joyce writes that the "Penelope"
episode "turns like the huge earthball slowly surely and evenly round
and round spinning. . . . Though probably more obscene than any
preceding episode it seems to me to be perfectly sane full amoral
fertilisable untrustworthy engaging shrewd limited prudent indifferent *Weib. Ich bin der* [sic] *Fleish der stets bejaht* [I am the flesh that always
affirms]" (*L* I 170). This passage suggests two major patterns: first,
that Molly both repeats and contradicts herself, her turns and returns
becoming verbal analogues to the earth's rotation; second, that she
represents corporeality. In regard to the first, whereas Homer's Penelope unweaves by night what she weaves by day, her labor engendering a theoretically infinite deferral, Joyce's "Penelope" begins with
"Yes," unweaves it by a series of qualifications and denials, and then
reweaves it at the end in an affirmation that is also a repetition. This
web-weaving explains one of Joyce's notes: "fly = 6 legs. spider = 8"

(*Notesheets*, 499). Molly's "legs" are the eight sentences she draws from her consciousness, so that eight both represents the shape of her body and inscribes that body as language. As several writers have noted, Molly's sentences repeat in rotation: the material in the first is reiterated in the fourth, the second in the fifth, and so on.[1] In one sense, then, "Penelope" circulates within a closed economy of interlocking, repeated loops.

However, the very shape of the numeral 8 is polyvalent, since its loops may represent either infinite rotation or simple repetition; likewise, Molly's looping monologue incorporates both renewal and repetition. For example, sentences four and five focus on her early years in Gibraltar, the returns of her memory traversing the bottom loop of her 8 at the end of sentence four, which ends with the word "ashpit" (18.747). At this point Molly recalls her first lover, Harry Mulvey, and then recovers by remembering their exchanges of love gifts, thereby starting her trajectory back upward. Similarly, while "Penelope" repeats much of the material of *Ulysses*, it also marks a new beginning, its eight sentences placing us for the first time inside Molly's mind and enabling us to hear the female version of the novel. Just as Bloomsday begins at 8 A.M., so "Penelope" ends the day (and the novel) by beginning it again with a new set of eights.[2] The narrative she weaves is both the final product of *Ulysses* and a new tale.

The episode's symbol in Joyce's schema is not 8 but a reclining 8 (for a reclining body): not a numeral but the symbol of infinity. Thus, if in one sense the episode traces an economy closed off from the rest of the novel and restricted to a single mind, in another sense it embodies infinite rotation, a ceaseless, open circulation homologous with Penelope's open-ended weaving. Whereas "Ithaca" plunges towards stasis and finality, "Penelope" constantly renews itself and thus denies the possibility of conclusion. Subject to the constraints of her social existence as a female, Molly nevertheless seeks to transform finite means into infinite possibility.

The unpunctuated recirculation of Molly's linguistic economy has often been described as a "flow" typical of feminine discourse and as analogous with menstrual blood (Herr 1989, 131). For some feminist theorists this flow epitomizes the feminine linguistic economy, which "makes a gift of departure" so that "what takes place is an endless

---

1. See Card (1984, 59–63), Boyle (1974, 428), and Tolomeo (1973, 450).
2. In Christian numerology, eight is the number of new beginnings (Tolomeo 1973, 440). Molly's birthday is also September 8 (17.2275–76).

circulation of desire from one body to another" (Cixous 1981, 53). According to these analyses, feminine writing engenders an infinite economy that invokes "the possibility of a giving that doesn't take away" (Cixous 1981, 51): it is a perfect gift. Hyde similarly insists that to retain a gift is to deny the social relation that engenders its meaning; therefore a gift must always move (1983, 84). In this regard a gift is only a vehicle for the circulation of the gift economy, which is ideally an endless series of exchanges. Because of this kinetic and theoretically infinite circulation, gift exchanges flout the bourgeois or market economy that aims to stabilize interpersonal boundaries. As what Hyde calls "anarchist property," gifts are also "female property" (Hyde 1983, 84, 103): gift exchange is specifically feminine behavior in many societies, and the process itself is "feminine"—fluid and familial (Hyde 1983, 105). Inasmuch as it flows or circulates, then, "Penelope" invokes the gift economy. To apprehend the economic conditions under which Molly Bloom behaves, therefore, we must analyze her gift exchanges, both to characterize her domestic, social, and economic habits and to shed light on the economies of writing and reading suggested by those habits.

Recently Derek Attridge has challenged the view that Molly's discourse is typified by "flow." If one replaces the missing punctuation marks in "Penelope," he demonstrates, one discovers beneath the appearance of grammatical transgression a very conventional language and syntax (1989, 545–46).[3] For him the experience of reading the episode provides less a sense of flow than of labor, as the reader instinctively works to replace the missing syntactic markers and barriers (1989, 548). More important for my purposes is the related argument that if Molly's "flow" is in part an illusion of the appearance of the printed page, then her association with the fluid gift economy may also be a half-truth. It will become clear, indeed, that her economic habits and behaviors are motivated at least as much by shrewdness, frugality, and self-interest as by the fluid generosity that impels the gift economy. I want to argue that Molly's economy oscillates between, and finally synthesizes, the fluid, infinite, generous (female) economy of the gift and the linear, limited, mercenary (male) economy of profit and power. Just as her discourse is simultaneously repetitious and restorative, so her financial economy involves both gifts

---

3. In contrast, Henke insists that "Penelope" "offers a linguistic paradigm of *écriture féminine*": "fluid and feminine, deracinated and polymorphic," Molly's language is "uncontained by the limits of logocentric authority" (1990, 127, 130).

and profit. And just as the episode's omission of punctuation and transition marks implies their presence by forcing the reader to supply them, so her participation in the gift economy exposes the power relations that have relegated her to using it. Her use of gifts is a response to her own marginalization: barred from full participation in the market economy, she must define herself by her success in gaining gifts from men.

Her most effective tool in managing gifts is her own body: by withholding or granting access to it, she gains a measure of social, erotic, and economic power. This pattern leads to the second theme suggested by Joyce's letter—that Molly embodies corporeality. The epigraph from *Stephen Hero* recognizes that women are both empowered and dispossessed by their condition as assets. That is, women's "corporal assets" are forever under siege; though women own their bodies, patriarchal institutions and individuals are always seeking to dispossess them. Denied access to the symbolic order, women must either acquiesce to their condition as "asset" or currency, or combat it by adopting "male" economic and social behaviors. In her constant quest for gifts that will both certify her corporeal existence and offer hope of renewal—that is, provide both stability and change—Molly combines the self-renewing cycle of gift exchange with the balanced equilibrium of barter; evolving from her limitations, this pattern engenders an infinite economy that turns her corporal assets into self-renewing currency. Just as Joyce portrays Molly's flesh in words, so conversely her flesh also becomes an avenue to enter the symbolic order—to become words—and thus to assert her own liberation from male discourse. In short, "Penelope" embraces both power and generosity, both profit taking and gift giving.

THE BALANCE OF POWER

One of Joyce's notes to "Penelope" reads, "MB avarice" (*Notesheets* 515), indicating that he intended her to display shrewdness and even greed. She does. For example, her reaction to a sly coalman—"that noisy bugger trying to swindle me with the wrong bill he took out of his hat" (18.712–13)—demonstrates that she can be a "hard woman at a bargain" (6.518). Nor is she as lax about domestic economy as her idleness in "Calypso" would imply. Her attitude about the Mary Driscoll affair, for example, stresses her dominant role in household management: "not in my house stealing my potatoes and the oysters 2/6 per doz going out to see her aunt if you please common robbery

. . . either she or me leaves the house" (18.63–64). No doubt she was most upset not by the theft of potatoes but by the threat to her most prized possession, Poldy, and firmly asserted her proprietary rights. Yet she also condemns others for meanness. Mrs. Riordan is scorned as a skinflint who "never left us a farthing all for masses for herself and her soul greatest miser ever was actually afraid to lay out 4d for her methylated spirit" (18.6), and Larry O'Rourke seems chintzy: "at Xmas a cottage cake and a bottle of hogwash he tried to palm off as claret that he couldnt get anyone to drink God spare his spit for fear hed die of the drouth" (18.453–55). She ungenerously condemns the ungenerous and grimly protects her own property.

If Molly's economic attitudes are often contradictory, so are her views about her husband's. On the one hand, she mocks his habit of saving old magazines "to get a few pence for them" (18.600–604) and his stinginess about clothes ("if I buy a pair of old brogues itself do you like those new shoes yes how much were they" [18.469–70]). On the other hand, she praises him for having "sense enough not to squander every penny piece he earns down [his friends'] gullets" (18.1277–79) and at other moments admires his generosity to "old women and waiters and beggars" (18.16). While she worries about entrepreneurial schemes such as the "musical academy he was going to make on the first floor" (18.981), she also laments their money "all going in food and rent" (18.467) and criticizes Leopold for being an inadequate provider: "He ought to chuck that Freeman with the paltry few shillings he knocks out of it and go into an office or something where hed get regular pay or a bank where they could put him up on a throne to count the money all day" (18.503–6). Her recollection of Bloom's checkered employment history leads her to fear that he will be "coming home with the sack soon out of the Freeman too" (18.1222–26). Bloom is too frugal and Bloom has wild financial plans; Bloom saves too much and Bloom doesn't earn enough. Of course, Leopold's own economic habits (and ideas about them) oscillate; thus Molly's contradictory assessments capture his own ambivalence. In short, her views about her husband's financial habits vary, but generally oppose whatever he desires.

These conflicts are part of a larger power struggle between the Blooms. Her response to Bloom's unheard request for "his breakfast in bed with a couple of eggs" (18.1–3) exhibits this struggle, as she modulates from amused sarcasm—"he starts giving us his orders for eggs and tea and Findon haddy and hot buttered toast I suppose well have him sitting up like the king of the country" (18.932)—to disdainful resistance—"Im to be slooching around down in the kitchen to get his lordship his breakfast while hes rolled up like a mummy will I indeed" (18.1431–2)—to acquiescence disguised as warning—"Ill just give him one more chance . . . Ill throw him up his eggs and tea in the moustachecup" (18.1497; 1504). Her ambivalence emerges from her feelings of powerlessness and confinement: men can "pick and choose what they please . . . but were to be always chained up"; however, "theyre not going to be chaining me up no damn fear once I start I tell you for their stupid husbands jealousy" (18.1388–91).[4]

They also compete for their daughter's affections, a struggle complicated by Molly's mixed feelings, which shuttle between envy and maternal solicitude. On the one hand, she craves Milly's attention and feels rebuffed when it is denied: "she didnt even want me to kiss her at the Broadstone going away" (18.1047). Yet she intimates that "if there was anything wrong with her its me shed tell not him" (18.1021). She sometimes even conspires with Milly against Leopold, as when Milly broke the hand off the cherished statue of Narcissus, and Molly "got that little Italian boy to mend so that you cant see the join for 2 shillings" (18.1015). Although she envies Milly's youth—"I suppose he thinks Im finished out and laid on the shelf well Im not no nor anything like it" (18.1021–23)—like her husband she sometimes reinvigorates herself by using Milly's image. Thus in sentence six Molly considers Milly as a replica of herself: "they all look at her like me when I was her age of course any old rag looks well on you then" (18.1036–37). Molly sees her own reflection in Milly, whose image both rejuvenates her and reminds her that she cannot really recapture her youth. Thus if Milly represents to her father a pure gift of love, to her mother she is a mixed blessing.

More importantly, Molly tries to surmount male dominance by earning her own money with her singing career. One should not be misled by the smirks of Bloom's male acquaintances into assuming that Molly's vocal career is a joke. Her singing tour with some other artistes begins in Belfast in about a week (18.349; cf. 5.52), and

---

4. Although she briefly considers female government a solution to these problems in sexual politics, again she equivocates, on a single page claiming both that "you wouldnt see women going and killing one another . . . when do you ever see women rolling around drunk like they do or gambling every penny they have and losing it on horses" (18.1435–38) and that a woman is always "ready to stick her knife in you I hate that in women no wonder they treat us the way they do we are a dreadful lot of bitches" (18.1457–59).

Bloom's anxiety over Molly's affair with Boylan has been competing all day with his anticipation of the money that might accrue from this association. She too thinks of it economically, hoping that Boylan will get them a first-class carriage and buy her some gifts there (18.367; 404). Otherwise Molly's thoughts about her career reveal little aside from some of her favorite songs and her professional disdain for Fanny M'Coy (18.1268) and "Kathleen Kearney and her lot of squealers" (18.878). But many Dubliners seem to respect her talent: even the nonmusical George Lidwell, for example, recognizes that she has "a fine voice" (11.1209). Boylan has evidently begun publicizing the tour, because Jack Power already knows about it (6.212), and the witless Nosey Flynn remembers having heard about it after Bloom reminds him (8.786). It would seem, then, that Molly is respected as a singer and that Boylan is working hard as her manager.

In any case, her career has definitely advanced since the Blooms were "on the rocks" in Holles Street, when she had to sing for next to nothing at the Coffee Palace, and even resorted to selling clothes to supplement their income (11.485–95). Molly's career history is a plausible one for its time. Of the five major forms of employment for women in 1900—operators of clothing businesses; owners of food stores; lodging-house keepers and tavern owners; teachers; and musicians (Walzl 1982, 41)—Molly has worked at two of them. But since "no career was as promising for a young woman or as secure for a mature woman as music" (Walzl 1982, 42), she has chosen the most secure professional pathway. Indeed, if the figures Boylan recites on the phone to his secretary— £1 7s 6d (£2 15 for the two)—are Molly's fees for her concerts, then her earning power is excellent, especially considering that many male laborers in Dublin supported families on a pound a week (she does not earn this much every week). The symmetry between this figure and Bloom's commission for the day (17.1459) implies that the Blooms' earning power is comparable.

And yet, other textual and contextual signs give contrary signs. Walzl notes that even a "first rate [vocal] *artiste* could probably not make a decent livelihood" from singing alone (1982, 39). Moreover, since her tour consists so far of only two dates, Belfast and Liverpool (10.389–90), its success (and Boylan's managerial and publicity skills) seem less certain. Moreover, Molly has had no concerts for over a year, possibly because of her (or Boylan's) politically incorrect choice of repertoire: at her last concert she sang "The Absent-Minded Beggar," a pro-British song about the Boer war, at a time when Irish sentiment was strongly pro-Boer (18.374–76; Callow 1990, 463). These facts also presage an unsuccessful tour, although today's rehearsal of "Love's Old Sweet Song," and excerpts from *Don Giovanni* seem more promising. Given Boylan's control over her prosperity, one wonders what will happen to Molly's vocal career if she and Boylan break up. These considerations suggest that even her "own money" and career are not really in her control.

Her economic freedom is limited in other ways. For all his uxoriousness, Bloom still manages the purse strings and dictates the family's changes of residences, which are connected to his jobs (Callow 1990, 468). In one sense, too, even his apparent leniency about Boylan may merely mask his management of the affair: he gives her "freedom" but in so doing pushes her to earn money that will free him from sole responsibility for breadwinning; if her career necessitates adultery, still "part shares and part profits." Social and legal obstacles also limit Molly's options. A real Molly Bloom would not have been allowed to get a separation or to retain custody of Milly even if divorce had been possible; nor would she have had the "right to the money she earned by singing . . . nor could she have invested money or held property in her own name" (Shloss 1989, 537). Like Stephen and Bloom—indeed, like all Irish—Molly is dispossessed. Her limited autonomy is circumscribed by male individuals and institutions. Blocked from attaining full participation in the market economy, Molly is forced to seek alternative paths to power.[5]

Sometimes her knowledge of the politics and economies of erotic relationships often makes her seem quite cynical. Accepting the male view of sexuality as merchandising, she describes Bloom's liaison with Martha in appropriate commercial terms: "had a good time somewhere still she must have given him great value for his money of course he has to pay for it from her" (18.1208–10). She shrewdly recognizes that both Gerty and Martha have presented themselves as commodities, and that all the parties seem to have received "great value." In Molly's mind, Bloom has not been paying his conjugal debts, and so she is justified in looking elsewhere for compensatory rewards.[6] Recognizing the economic necessity that may drive women to such measures, however, she does not seem offended that Bloom

5. Shloss argues that Molly's "resistance to the union . . . has been reduced to insurgency" (1989, 539). While Shloss overestimates Molly's hostility to Bloom—by the end of the episode she fantasizes about reconciliation, and in many ways she remains devoted to him—in a sense she is right that Molly's management of gifts is an "act of subterfuge" (1989, 539).

6. Richard Brown notes that Joyce had read Matharan's *Casus de Matrimonio fere quingenti,* in which "the sexual act is understood as a rendering of the conjugal debt incurred in the marriage contract" (1985, 45–46).

once suggested that she "pose for a picture naked for some rich fellow in Holles street when he lost the job at Helys" (18.560–61; Devlin 1991, 76). What *Stephen Hero* laboriously expounds, Molly knows from experience: to some degree all women have been prostituted by patriarchal institutions. Thus the "Ithaca" respondent is wrong when he maintains that Molly "understood little of political complications, internal, or balance of power, external" (17.680–82). Comprehending the domestic, economic, and social constraints on her power, she still achieves a balance of power by shrewdly exercising the weapons she has.

FEMALE PROPERTY

These businesslike attitudes may mask feelings of victimization. Yet such posturing pervades her episode, which has been read as a series of poses or "star turns" that extend her stage career to the domestic realm (Herr 1989, 130; Devlin 1991, 74). Nevertheless, these poses are responses to a much older and more generalized female predicament that helps to explain both her consuming habits and her gift exchanges. If gifts are "female property," they may be so because women themselves originally functioned as female property. Lévi-Strauss has shown that in many pretechnological societies the woman herself is "the supreme gift among those that can only be obtained in the form of reciprocal gifts" (1969, 65). The exchange relationship in the marriage ceremony is not between a man and a woman but between "two groups of men, and the woman figures only as one of the objects in the exchange" (Lévi-Strauss 1969, 115). Indeed, the condition of women as supreme gifts is a cornerstone of Western institutions of property and culture, since the exchange of females establishes and maintains a distinction between exogamy and endogamy through the incest taboo. In preindustrial cultures the exchange of women does not, however, signify commodification in precisely the capitalist sense, because objects in a "primitive" gift economy are generally imbued with highly personal qualities; here "things . . . are to some extent parts of persons, and persons . . . behave in some measure as if they were things" (Mauss [1925] 1967, 11). Even in such societies, however, a distinction pertains between the givers (men) and the gifts (women) (Rubin 1975, 174). When this pattern is extended into capitalist or bourgeois societies, women become "female property"—merchandise to be used and exchanged by males. Under such conditions the only property left to the female are her "corporal assets"—the body that she must decorate and manipulate to increase its economic value—still constantly threatened by male appropriation.[7]

Thus Molly's consuming habits are directed almost entirely at commodities designed to enhance her sexual attractiveness. Most of her complaints about their lack of money or her husband's stinginess are responses to the limitations on her capacity to assert power through clothing: "Ive no clothes at all . . . 3 [outfits] whats that for any woman" (18.470–72); "sure you cant get on in this world without style . . . the men wont look at you and women try to walk on you because they know youve no man" (18.466–74). Her clothes are alternately liberating and constraining. She wishes someone would buy her "one of those kidfitting corsets . . . advertised cheap in the Gentlewoman with elastic gores on the hips . . . what did they say they give a delightful figure line 11/6 obviating that unsightly broad appearance across the lower back to reduce flesh" (18.446–49). And yet such clothes make her feel "all staysed up" so that she "cant do a blessed thing in them" (18.628–29).[8] Resisting male dominion over women, Molly nevertheless partially accepts the male fictions about women found in ads. However, when she asked Bloom to purchase the lotion that "made my skin like new" (18.459), it was not because it was advertised as such but because it works. Molly's ambivalence about ads reveals her skillful management of erotic commerce. She realizes that advertising is male discourse about women but takes advantage of this mind-set by advertising herself ("youd want to print it up on a big poster for them" [18.706–7]) as a valuable commodity. In fact,

7. The epigraph from *Stephen Hero* remains ambiguous not only because it is difficult to determine Stephen's attitude towards the condition he describes but also because his description elides the distinction between use value and exchange value. Since the use value of any good is not truly economic unless it is convertible into a quantity of some other good (as a book might be bought for cash or traded for bread), a woman cannot really exchange her body without its becoming abstracted from its corporal reality (its use value as a sexual object) and phenomenalized into an exchange value. Thus, as Irigaray points out, a woman as commodity is "divided into two irreconcilable 'bodies': her 'natural' body and her socially valued, exchangeable body, which is a particularly mimetic expression of masculine values" (1985, 180).

8. The "reduction" of female flesh by corsets seems to represent male attempts to "reduce" female power, first by making female bodies into commodities and then by appropriating that last commodity and bringing it under strict control. However, Valerie Steele (1985, 161–91) has shown that it was males who led the revolt against restrictive undergarments, fearing damaging effects on female reproductive capabilities and hence on property rights.

her consumption of clothing and accessories is never a passive acquiescence to male images of women but has quite specific erotic and economic aims: to retake control of her body and relationships by directing her own erotic scenarios.[9]

Jennifer Wicke similarly argues that Molly's consumption evinces not oppression but self-direction: when she shops, she is doing "cognitive analytic work," her "requisite contribution to the domestic economy" (1991, 751, 755).[10] Most of the clothes Molly buys are designed to fit into specific scenes—both erotic and economic—that she hopes to shape like a theatrical impresario. For example, she envisions a scene of erotic revenge on Poldy in which she'll put on her "best shift and drawers let him have a good eyeful out of that to make his micky stand for him" (18.1508–10). Or she imagines a skit involving herself and Stephen for which she'd "have to get a nice pair of red slippers like those Turks . . . used to sell" (18.1494–95). Similarly, she recognizes that her new role as adulteress also demands new garments: "if its to go on I want at least two other good chemises" (18.438). Sometimes the lovers seem to be no more than costumes or props, as when Boylan is described as "a change in a way not to be always and ever wearing the same old hat" (18.83–84). For Molly clothes are first of all costumes, and her myriad roles in these minidramas reveal a woman as polytropic as her husband. Her consumption may therefore be, as Wicke asserts, another form of labor that coexists with and mirrors her other performances, but it is labor with quite specific goals: to create a picture of herself or of femininity, and to act out scripts that, though written by men, are directed by herself. Perhaps most importantly, her consuming carves out an alternate route to economic power via an erotic commerce that responds to male authority by exercising the female power to procure commodities as gifts.

9. Both Mahaffey (1988, 160), who claims that Molly is "blinded by the fictions created by clothes," and Henke, who contends that she is "duped by advertising panaceas" (1990, 141), misread Molly's strategies. Her management of her assets is in fact quite canny and not a bit "blind."

10. Wicke overstates the case when she claims that shopping is for Molly "a terrifying labor of scrutiny and frustration" (1991, 756); it is more often an exhilarating adventure, as her plans for grocery shopping and for accompanying Boylan in Belfast imply: "it would be exciting going round with him shopping buying those things in a new city" (18.406–7). Wicke's description more closely fits Gerty MacDowell, whose limited prospects for sexual and economic fulfillment are inextricably tied to consuming; this raises the stakes and makes shopping exceedingly difficult and quite terrifying.

In one sense, Joyce's Penelope resembles Homer's, who extorts "presents in order to recover some of the financial losses [the suitors'] lengthy banquet has caused" (Herring, "Penelope," in *Notesheets*, 67). Thus one of Joyce's notes reads "Pen wheedles present" (*Notesheets*, 494). But whereas the Homeric Penelope extracts bridal gifts to maintain the established order in Odysseus' absence (Foley 1984, 61), Joyce's Penelope views gifts as tangible evidence of the competition between the sexes (and between males) and therefore uses them to subvert the patriarchal order. We have already seen how Boylan encodes his image of himself and Molly in his gifts of meat, fruit, and wine; in accepting his gift, Molly accepts that image as at least one of her identities. We have also discussed how Bloom's gift, the pornographic book *Sweets of Sin,* inscribes both his and Molly's fetishized, well-clothed roles in the adulterous triangle and at the same time enables him to objectify his jealousy and manage it. But these gifts and the ones described below are effective only if Molly agrees to accept them. If a woman can wrest control of her own body, she may achieve at least the circumscribed "freedom" to "take" that Stephen describes in *Stephen Hero.* Thus when she muses that Boylan "could buy me a nice present up in Belfast after what I gave him theyve lovely linen up there or one of those nice kimono things" (18.403), she is describing a straightforward erotic exchange—her body for presents—that ultimately suggests she is no man's property. By managing gifts as capital, Molly tries to turn her corporal assets to profit. Accepting the male view of herself as a commodity, she turns this limited economy into a limited autonomy. In placing herself in circulation, she transforms the male economy into a female economy; managing gifts and herself as currency, she forces men to "spend" both sexually and economically. By the end of *Ulysses,* indeed, female property is transformed into the opposite of property—a gift that subjects itself to ceaseless exchange and that can never be fully owned, but at least is managed by the female. Likewise, in the economy of the text, "Penelope" becomes the final gift.

In the past Bloom has presented her with diverse reflections of their identities: Lord Byron's poems (Bloom as Byronic lover; 18.185); a watch (18.345—as much for him as for her); and eight big poppies (18.329) for her birthday (and presumably because she is a "Flower of the mountain" [18.1602]). Today he has bought (or rather, not yet bought) the lotion and soap that become associated with Molly as one leaf of *moly.* Bloom also seems to conceive of Stephen Dedalus as a possible gift to Molly, even though his presentation of her photo in "Eumaeus" implies that *she* is the gift (she wonders why he didn't "make him a present of it altogether and me as well" [18.1304–5; cf. McMichael 1991, 188]). But though she entertains erotic fantasies involving a Stephen who has little in common with the unwashed bard we know (she imagines that he is "clean" [18.13256]!), and though she fantasizes about his body, she, like her husband, soon turns him into a vehicle to attain notoriety (and a rise in class), complete with Margate vacations and scandalous stories in the paper (18.1364–66). Stephen thus emerges as another item for her to consume (almost literally so, since she fantasizes about performing fellatio on him [18.1352–53), a kitsch commodity like the Blooms' statue of Narcissus (18.1346–49). By the end of her monologue, moreover, he has stirred her maternal feelings as much as her libido ("his poor mother wouldnt like that if she was alive ruining himself for life" [18.1454]). Thus she weaves and unweaves Stephen's image to fulfill her fluctuating needs. This imaginary Stephen does function as a gift, as Molly's fantasies revitalize and rejuvenate her. But Stephen is gone, and probably lucky to be. Molly's quasi-maternal schemes issue from her loneliness, and although Boylan has satisfied her desire to be physically "filled up," she would look to Stephen to fill her emotional and intellectual needs. In missing connections with Molly, Stephen has escaped being incorporated into her home and body—and has thus flown by another potential net woven by a Penelope who is also a Calypso.

Molly yearns more for material gifts than such complicated human ones. The three objects that figure in most gift exchanges in "Penelope" (and in *Ulysses* as a whole) are flowers, rings, and letters. Many characters assume that flowers are always gifts. Molly, for example, assumes that Boylan's carnation was a present from some other woman, rather than his own purchase (18.125). Gerty MacDowell fantasizes about flowery gifts—a "ruched teacosy with embroidered floral design for [Father Conroy] as a present" (13.460–62)— and imagines presents as part of her idealized courtship ritual, perhaps because the picture of "halcyon days" she has pinned up in her outhouse depicts a "young gentleman . . . offering a bunch of flowers to his ladylove" (13.336). Molly also says that she loves flowers—"Id love to have the whole place swimming in roses God of heaven theres nothing like nature (18.1557)—and recalls having received a flowered apron from Poldy (18.1546), and flowers from her first lover, Lt. Mulvey, who crushed some on her bosom (18.778). But as Attridge (1989, 560) points out, most of the flowers she thinks about are "cultural artifacts"—wallpaper, house decorations, songs—not natural blooms. When she thinks of decorating 7 Eccles Street with flowers, moreover, she envisions buying them herself, not receiving them as favors. Perhaps the eight big poppies Molly once received from Bloom are "impressionistic tokens of the female genitalia" (Henke 1990, 134), but it seems more likely that such gifts encode *his* image and incorporate her into that image as a "bloom" (Henke 1990, 160). In fact, flowers are not ideal gifts in *Ulysses;* on the contrary, they are usually associated with the most self-deluded characters (e.g., Gerty's fantasies), with trite or insincere expressions of love (e.g., Martha's pressed flower), or with conventional scenes such as the "Eumaeus" Penman's prediction of Stephen's courtship of the nonexistent Miss Ferguson: "complimentpaying and walking out leading up to fond lovers' ways and flowers and chocs" (16.1564–65). Flowers seem more appropriate to these less interesting avatars of Bloom—the Boom of Eumaeus, Henry Flower—than to genuine erotic commerce, and typify them at their most lugubrious and "lovelorn" (15.146; 11.301).

The most significant deficiency of flowers, however, and the best reason they do not epitomize the perfect gift is precisely what makes them lovely—their ephemerality. Flowers cannot in themselves represent the gift-exchange circuit because they cannot be passed on. Once they are given they stay put, decay, and die. In contrast, Molly's other most desirable gifts—rings and loveletters—formally capture the endless exchanges that identify gift exchange as a unique economic system: the circular shape of the ring itself represents the gift-exchange circuit, and loveletters can be exchanged as long as the post (and desire) exists—theoretically forever. Thus even though Molly's famous final words as she recalls making love with Bloom describe her body as a "flower of the mountain" (18.1576), the words have power because they have circulated through the loop of her memory. That is, her final words are a gift to herself, a self-addressed loveletter that has passed through the double ring of memory and returns again and again, each time making her feel renewed. This memory acts as a gift not because it concerns flowers, but because of its regenerative circulation.

Though Boylan and Bloom have each given her gifts, neither has recently given her what she really wants—a genuine loveletter (Boylan's recent letter "wasnt much" [18.735]). Since her lovers no longer write to her, she has been forced to post messages to herself (18.698–99); lacking recent missives, Molly thinks about the letters she received in past years. She thus recalls Mulvey's letter as "the

first" (18.748) but laments that he failed to continue the correspondence when he went to India. This memory, coming at the beginning
of sentence five, marks the commencement of her upward swing out
of the "ashpit." These recollections of letters provide a way of making
returns, of regenerating her, and thus themselves function as gifts.
For Molly letters represent an erotic, feminine discourse comparable
to (and substitutable for) the male discourse of advertising: whereas
Wonderworker might "make a new man of [Bloom] and life worth
living" (17.1829), Molly believes a genuine loveletter would make a
new woman of her, because it would "fill up [her] whole day and life"
and enable her to see "a new world" (18.735–39; cf. Mahaffey 1988,
175; Gordon 1981, 126, 128).[11] A loveletter unites giver and recipient
in a verbal embrace. The lover's identity is transmitted in written
form, then returned and reincorporated by the reader, who then
sends back her own image, reborn but not reified. The words "put
some heart up into" the correspondents (18.733) by involving both
donor and recipient in the circulation of eros. And unlike orgasms,
loveletters last. Thus Molly fondly recalls Poldy's writing letters "every
morning . . . sometimes twice a day I liked the way he made love . . .
then I wrote the night he kissed my heart" (18.327–30). His letters
(written gifts) reinforced *her* identity rather than his, eventually uniting both through an exchange of words that married their spiritual
and corporal assets. The loveletter is thus a true gift that knits donor
and recipient: the writer gives his or her heart, and the reader's heart
is given back and rejuvenated.

Molly also recalls a "mad crazy" letter from Poldy in which he
wrote that "everything connected with your glorious Body everything
underlined that comes from it is a thing of beauty and of joy [*sic*] for
ever" (18.1176–78). Appearing in sentence seven, this letter consummates a short section that strikingly outlines the psychoanalytic associations between feces and filthy lucre. The passage (18.1149–80)
considers doctors, discharges and charges, as Molly assesses the
money doctors make (18.1157), recollects the physician's direction
that she do the "one thing gold" (i.e., defecate: 18.1161), her own
examination of Milly's stools for worms (18.1168), and the physician's
fee (one guinea: 18.1169). Poldy seems also to perceive her fecal

---

11. She also recalls the notes she received from Hester Stanhope, which sometimes accompanied gifts of dresses or books (18.612–14; 652). These too are loveletters (18.623), although their erotic component is latent rather than overt.

"discharges" as valuable merchandise, as "gold turds" (*Notesheets*, 491) and thus echoes the Freudian description of the psychic economy in which feces are first gifts, then money. Bloom's coprophilic correspondence, moreover, resembles that of his creator, whose notorious, erotically scatological 1909 loveletters to Nora similarly betray a fascination with Nora's "brown part," as Molly calls it, as well as with the product—the gift—of that part (*SL* 184–86, 190–92; see also chapter 1, above). As we have seen, for Joyce gifts, letters, and feces are part of a single symbolic economy.

The movement from gift to money is also inscribed in Molly's shrewd plans to use Bloom's anal obsession as an economic tool. If he wants to "kiss [her] bottom," she thinks, she'll "bulge it out right in his face as large as life he can stick his tongue 7 miles up my hole as hes there my brown part then Ill tell him I want £1 or perhaps 30/-Ill tell him I want to buy underclothes then if he gives me that well he wont be too bad I dont want to soak it all out of him like other women do I could often have written out a fine cheque for myself and write his name on it for a couple of pounds a few times he forgot to lock it up besides he wont spend it" (18.1521–27). Her fecal gift will earn her filthy lucre, thereby turning her corporal (and copral) assets into genuine currency—gold turds indeed. In this instance she turns the erotic and excremental gift economy into an opportunity for a limited economic sovereignty. If Bloom will not "spend" (in either sense), then she will do it for him. More generally, these excremental associations are appropriate to the novel's final episode: just as women are the excluded members of a patriarchal society, so excrement is the cursed and excluded product of the body. Molly's cunning plans to use her feces to earn money, however, imply that these "end products" also "bear the seeds of a new beginning" (Tucker 1984, 155), just as "Penelope," the book's last episode, is at the same time a new narrative and a denial of the possibility of endings, both an end and an opening (McGee 1988, 187). Full of returns and embodying the circuit of memory symbolized by exchanges of missives, "Penelope" is another "commodious vicus of recirculation" (*FW* 3.2). With her memories of the past launching her into the future, with her excremental language, and with her ability to turn losses into gains, Molly, like Poldy, makes both ends meet.

In addition to new chemises and a present in Belfast, Molly plans to extract some other gifts from Boylan: "if I only had a ring with the stone for my month a nice aquamarine Ill stick him for one and a gold bracelet" (18.261). Just as they induced each other to "spend" sexually this afternoon, she will now induce him to spend money; after all, "hes not a marrying man so somebody better get it out of him" (18.411–12). She hopes to use the ring, usually a symbol of union, as a mark of her independence from Bloom; even though the ring would be a gift from Boylan, it would commemorate *her* birth and thus reinforce her identity, not his. As female property, the ring would mark her new condition as owner of her own property—herself. Employed as a symbol of the commodification of women in "Circe," rings are also here commodities exchanged for feminine corporal assets. But here they are also genuine symbols of love and its economic corollary, gift exchange.

Partly this association with gifts is a result of Molly's fond memories of rings: in addition to a letter, she once received from Mulvey a "clumsy Claddagh ring" (18.866). His gift of a loveletter began their affair, creating a return through space by post; then the gift of a ring marked its end and symbolized his hoped-for return in time. But a gift cannot be hoarded; it must be passed on. Thus she did not keep it but gave it to her next lover, Lt. Gardner, when he went to fight in the Boer War (18.867). If, as Hyde insists, the perfect gift is a "copula, a band, by which the several are knit into one" (1983, 153), then any ring given as a love or wedding gift perfectly symbolizes both its own social and erotic function (unification) and the circular pattern of gift exchanges in general, which must move from one party to another and back and may continue endlessly. The circular shape of the ring thus represents not only Molly's return in memory but also the cyclic trajectory of the gift economy. Like a heart, the perfect gift generates circulation and moves under an Odyssean obligation to return to its source (Hyde 1983, 138).

The Claddagh ring is ideal in another respect. A traditional symbol of Galway, the ring is described elsewhere by Joyce as "decorated with the king's crest: two joined hands supporting a crowned heart" (*CW* 234). Like a loveletter, the gift of a Claddagh ring "puts some heart" into its recipient by picturing the heart of the donor. It thus represents not only its own possible circulation but, with its engraving of joined hands, also the yoking of the lovers created when it is given. Moreover, if Molly's Claddagh ring was a "gimmal" Fede ring, its "two ends" could also be "joined, the hands clasping and interlocking" (Cumpiano 1989, 50). Such a ring would replicate the shape of Molly's double-ring-shaped monologue. In any case, the Claddagh ring has united two affairs, its circulation mirroring the symbol of the episode in which it is described: ∞.[12] The role of the ring in Molly's recollection, then, revises its deployment elsewhere in the novel as an emblem of male domination and instead exemplifies her vision of the perfect gift—that which rejuvenates and liberates both donor and recipient and at the same time weds them. In this sense rings are both ideal gifts and ideal symbols of gift exchange.

Still, Molly's scheme to obtain a ring from Boylan seems quite mercenary, and she conceives of the ring as a kind of payment for her body. She must react to the fact that, despite her ability to manipulate her lovers for gifts, she remains dependent upon males and their presents for her sense of self-worth; after all, she can scarcely give presents to herself. Thus while she has a wedding ring (18.408), neither her husband nor Boylan has yet offered her a new ring to foster or symbolize her desired rebirth. Bloom has instead brought her *Ruby: the Pride of the Ring*, associated with female objectification. Accordingly, there remains a sense in which her manipulation of the gift economy is a sign of her oppression and inability to enter the symbolic economies of the marketplace. Nevertheless, Molly's transformation of an economic limitation into limited freedom manifests a skill as impressive as her husband's; her oscillation between hard-eyed shrewdness and heart-filling generosity mirrors Bloom's economic and emotional ambivalence.

LOVE GIVES AND FREEDOM TAKES

The last three sentences of "Penelope"—also the last three sentences of *Ulysses*—demonstrate one of the strongest tendencies of the Blooms and the text in which they exist: the need and capacity to connect ends and beginnings. As it nears its nominal end, "Penelope" becomes increasingly obsessed with renewal, and Molly entertains most of her thoughts about Milly (sentence six) and Stephen (sentences seven and eight) just before her final return in the last forty lines. Near the end of her monologue, she echoes Bloom's ecstatic

---

12. Cumpiano (1989, 48–49). recounts the invention of the Claddagh ring, the Spanish-Irish history of which is congruent with Molly's history. The design is attributed to one Richard Joyce (!), a Galway artificer who, on his way to the West Indies in 1675, was kidnapped and sold as a slave to a Turkish goldsmith, who then taught him his craft. After the accession of William III in 1689, Joyce was freed and returned to Galway. This Joyce's story contrasts with the stories of those other seafarers, Mulvey and Gardner, who left Penelope but never returned to her. Even the conception of the ring, then, contains a tale of departure, circulation, and return.

and regenerative memory of the seedcake exchange on Howth: "the day I got him to propose to me yes first I gave him the bit of seedcake out of my mouth . . . yes 16 years ago my God after that long kiss I near lost my breath yes he said I was a flower of the mountain yes so we are flowers all a womans body yes that was one true thing he said in his life . . . yes that was why I liked him because I saw he understood or felt what a woman is and I knew I could always get round him" (18.1573-80). Here the erotic component of erotic commerce finally seems to overwhelm the commercial side. Like Bloom, who returns to Molly at the end of his journey, Molly returns to Bloom at the end of her mental circumnavigation.

The memory of the seedcake exchange also consummates the series of kisses that have punctuated the episode. Molly earlier describes kisses in terms that resemble Stephen's (and Joyce's) descriptions of the moment of epiphany: "theres nothing like a kiss long and hot down to your soul almost paralyzes you" (18.106). A kiss freezes time, exposing the moment and revealing its essence. It "paralyzes," a word now used in a way that illustrates precisely what so many of Joyce's *Dubliners* characters lack: true intimacy. Taking my cue from Sheldon Brivic, who defines kissing as an "expensive gift," and "the gift of tongue" (1991, 188, 185), I want to reiterate my argument that the seedcake exchange is a powerful image of mutual gift giving. For Molly, as for her husband, this moment constitutes perfect reciprocity. The kiss demands that one offer oneself and accept the gift of the other; it is a double loop in which each individual is subsumed into the unity of reciprocity. Such gifts create a third space similar to that defined by Simmel as characteristic of balanced exchanges. As Brivic writes, "the identities affirmed by these kisses are not those of discrete individuals, but of circuits of interchange" (1991, 191). The mutual kiss is erotic commerce, manifesting the ceaselessly circulating gift economy. The kiss is owned by both and neither; in it each person is at once rejuvenated individually and liberated from the self and submerged into the process of exchange: "She kissed me. I was kissed. . . . Kissed, she kissed me" (8.915–16). Thus Molly also remembers her first meaningful kiss from Bloom as a gift of the heart: "the night he kissed my heart at Dolphins barn I couldnt describe it simply makes you feel like nothing on earth" (18.330). The gift of tongue is beyond words. As it earlier did for Bloom, for Molly the memory of powerful erotic commerce regenerates her by reviving the feeling of expansion that it brought sixteen years ago.

And yet, even during this sublime moment, Molly's love and generosity are tinged with self-interest: "I knew I could always get round him." For her, "a womans body" is the greatest gift one can give, but it is also a "corporal asset" to be wielded shrewdly. Her view of erotic commerce thus remains partly commercial, even though she recognizes that such commerce demands that one give the self. Recalling how she gave herself freely sixteen years ago, she filters the memory of the event through her pragmatic mature consciousness. Molly's use of her corporal assets thus resembles the selfishly generous gift economy described by Richard Rowan in *Exiles:* "It is yours then forever when you have given it. It is yours always. That is to give" (56). In giving herself to Bloom and then to Boylan, Molly paradoxically retains control of her corporal assets, because within her assent lies the possibility that she will withhold. In giving her assets she proclaims that they are hers—only hers—to give and thereby establishes her own freedom. She simultaneously gives and takes. The monologue, which rises to a breathless climax of assent as she tenders herself to a man, nevertheless simultaneously announces that only *she* can say "yes," and that after the ecstasy subsides, the power struggle will continue. What she owns, finally, is her own body; in giving it but always retaining the choice of withholding it, she ensures that her property remains at least partly female.

During the rhapsodic moment on Howth, Molly recognizes another quality in Bloom that she herself manifests: the ability to feel what the other sex "is." Likewise, twice in the last three sentences she imagines being a man (18.1146; 1379–82). As Herr and Devlin have shown, Molly's androgyny is another aspect of her theatricality. Devlin notes that many of Molly's "female" characteristics are "actorly"— parodic and exaggerated—and therefore that she might be conceived as "both a female male impersonator and a female female impersonator" who adopts the traits of both genders (1991, 85; cf. Herr 1989, 135). Obviously, in one sense Molly is a female impersonation, since her words are scripted by a male, James Joyce, who is therefore engaging in a form of verbal transvestism or transsexualism. In this sense "Penelope" is Joyce's own "Molly house," which, we recall, is a place where males cross-dress as women. Moreover, because "Penelope" grows out of Joyce's encounter with women and constitutes part of the textual gift that *Ulysses* became, it is in some respects aimed to a specifically female audience. As we saw in chapter 1, Joyce gave his texts to women as both payments (for Harriet Shaw Weaver, and for Sylvia Beach) and gifts (for Nora). As a gift "Penelope" is not merely a male impersonating a female, but rather a loveletter in which the author submits himself to feminine discourse. Describing loveletters as liberating erotic gifts, "Penelope" is Joyce's loveletter both to Nora and to his ideal (and actual) readers. The episode is therefore a supplement that revises the entire preceding text and yet lies outside of it; it affirms female discourse and the gift as the indispensable countersign (*SL* 278) to the male economy of acquisition and property but at the same time confirms what has preceded it by returning to Bloom. Just as Ulysses ends with Molly's memory of the gift of herself, Joyce gives himself to his readers as a woman. That is, Joyce not only gives to his readers as women but gives himself as a woman to his readers.[13]

As a woman with an eye for profit but lacking economic autonomy, and as someone obsessed with extracting gifts as tokens of erotic attraction, Molly yokes male and female economies. Her Penelopean economy weds Hermes, the thief and god of commerce, to Aphrodite, the goddess of love. Like "Nausicaa," then, "Penelope" generates a discourse that is economically and erotically hermaphroditic; it is so both because of her creator's willingness to inhabit the feminine economy and because of Molly's own transformational capacity. In turning a limitation into a means of power, in locating herself within a gift economy and then managing it with a skill that makes her gifts both more and less than gifts, Molly contrives a new economy that is neither solely feminine nor masculine but both at once. In this economy "the boundaries between the genders, or sex and excrement, or word and flesh, succumb to impudent and restless violations" (M. Ellmann 1982, 88). Some theorists would describe even this violation of gender as feminine because it both emerges from oppression and generates what Irigaray calls "ceaseless exchanges" (1985, 31). In this sense the feminine economy denotes whatever is "improper," whatever subverts the concept of "proper"-ty: objects and words are not retained but given and circulated.

But if defined as an ongoing process of circulation and the power of transformation, this economy is not strictly feminine. It is even more radical: in recognizing that exchanges may subvert even the categories of gender and sex, and permit—even require—sexchange, Molly's economy challenges definitions of femininity. Her semiotic economy constitutes that "third space" which I have identified with

___

13. Restuccia's argument (1989, 155) that Joyce's style merely "masquerades as *écriture feminine*" ignores the degree to which "femininity" is always partly a costume. Moreover, even masquerades may transgress gender boundaries.

the hermaphrodite. Rather than erecting boundaries, it offers a system of modulating differences. Thus what "Penelope" most strongly affirms is its own provisionality. It does so by certifying and embodying the human capacity to transgress the restricted economies of balance and duality and to generate a ceaselessly circulating series of identities, behaviors, roles. In its constant circulation and rotation, Molly turns her limitations of language and opportunity into a Penelopean web that unweaves distinctions and oppositions almost as soon as it weaves them. Thus her final words transcend the novel's sense of closure, creating a rotating structure that continually returns us to its beginnings, an economy at once complete and open-ended. The body-in-words of "Penelope" makes 8 into ∞, thereby transforming "both ends meet" from a bourgeois formula for balancing accounts into a celebration of the exchanges and possibilities in a potentially infinite economy. This hermaphroditic, boundless economy may be the text's own *moly*, Hermes' final gift.

The economy of reading "Penelope" also partakes of that gift. Molly's monologue presents another consciousness the reader must occupy and incorporate, just as he or she has passed through the myriad narrators that have previously composed the body of *Ulysses*. Lying outside the closed, balanced economy of the time-bound cosmos of *Ulysses*, "Penelope" becomes the gift that draws text, author, and readers into a single body outside of time. It thus creates a textual gift, that "link by which the several are knit into one" (Hyde 1983, 153). This gift economy is itself Homeric: Vico tells us that Homer's name derives from "*homou*, together, plus *eirein*, to link" (1968, 318). Joyce's gift of *Ulysses* glosses Vico's imaginative etymology, as the author links together the many narrators, and in so doing encourages the reader to replicate that unifying gesture. As in the copula formed by gift exchange, reading *Ulysses* makes the reader a Homer, "the one who links." Like Molly, the reader is both giver and receiver. Just as gifts "make one body of many" (Hyde 1983, 66) by instigating exchanges of the identities encoded in the gifts, "Penelope" incorporates the reader into the body of the text, enabling him *and* her to regenerate his *and* her own spiritual and corporal assets through intercourse with its words. Thus the reader of *Ulysses* receives a large gift that demands a large return: like Molly and Nora, the reader recreates him- *and* herself by accepting the gift of a book.

Joyce's gift, however, is also propelled by expenditure and excess. Because "Penelope" (like most of *Ulysses*) is anarchist property or antiproperty, it also frustrates the reciprocal and extravagant gift of the reader's attention and devotion. As one moves backward and forward throughout the novel in reading "Penelope," one constantly reshapes one's responses to the text, linking moments in time in a way that mirrors Molly's movements. The reader's returns strive to reunite the beginnings and ends of the text, to make both ends meet. But this is never a closed economy: some gaps will remain open, and the reader's desire for completion will be disappointed. In demolishing the authoritarian position of the author as sole creator and instead encouraging—even demanding—equal participation by the reader, *Ulysses* constantly forces readers to revise their habits of reading. To read *Ulysses* is thus to be part of a larger economy of transformation, as one's sense of self is continually challenged by a text that ceaselessly alters the terms of its narrative contract. To read *Ulysses* is therefore to participate in the very exchanges—those violations of balance, gender, and identity—that it depicts. Engendered by weaving and unweaving, this Penelopean economy also turns the reader into a Penelope—now figured as a hermaphrodite—a replica of Stephen's Shakespearean artist who weaves and unweaves his and her image in the economy of heaven. Joyce's final gift, then, bestows the book's corporal and spiritual assets upon the reader, who is challenged to add to and then return them. Affirming and then overturning the economy of balance in its gift-driven, rotating infinity, "Penelope" embodies Joyce's gift of a book and passes this gift to his readers. If the reader can accept Joyce's challenging gift, then he *and* she may not only make both ends meet but also transcend the very idea of ending.

Appendixes
Works Cited
Index

Stephen's Bloomsday Budget

Each entry is listed in order of appearance, with the episode and line number of its occurrence given to the right of the amount.

DEBIT:

	£	s	d	
Loan: Mulligan	0	0	2	(1.724; not part of wages)
Tram fare	0	0	1	(between "Nestor" and "Proteus")
Telegram: Mulligan	0	1	.5	(before 9.550)
Drinks	0	11	11.5	(between "Aeolus" and "Oxen"; 9.535)
Drinks (Burke's)	0	2	1	(14.1502–3)
Drinks	0	2	4	(around 14.1535; not shown paying)
Tram fare	0	0	2	(from Holles St. to Nighttown)
Bella Cohen's	1	0	0	(15.3540–84)
Loan: Leo. Bloom	1	6	11	(15.3604): Subtotal: £3 4s 8d.
Loan: Corley	0	2	6	(16.195–96)

[3-7-2]

Balance:	1-16-10	
	£5- 4- 0	

CREDIT:

	£	s	d	
Wages received	3	12	0	(2.209–24)
Loan refunded (Leo Bloom)	1	6	11	(17.957–59)
Interest	0	0	1	(17.958)
Cash in hand	0	5	0	(three half-crowns in "Eumaeus" minus loan to Corley)

£5- 4- 0

Stephen's total expenses for Bloomsday: £3-7-2 minus £1-7-0 equals £2-0-2.

Cash in hand leaving chez Bloom: £1-7-0 plus 5s, which equals £1 12s.

Bloom's Revised Budget

Entries are listed in order of appearance, with episode and line numbers given to the right of the amount. Cf 17.1456–78.

DEBIT:

	£	s	d	
1 Pork kidney	0	0	3	(4.182)
1 Copy *Freeman's J.*	0	0	1	(5.49)
1 Bath and grat.	0	1	6	(between "Lotus-Eaters" and "Hades")
Tram fare	0	0	1	(from Leinster St. to Irishtown: between "Lotus-Eaters" and "Hades")
In Mem. Patk Dignam	0	5	0	(10.974; remitted in "Hades")
2 Banbury cakes	0	0	1	(8.74)
1 Lunch	0	0	7	(8.776)
1 Renewal fee for bk.	0	1	0	(around 10.641: payment not shown)
1 Packet paper etc.	0	0	2	(11.306–8)
1 Postal order & stamp	0	2	8	(11.868)
1 Dinner and tip	0	2	0	(11.1003)
Tram fare	0	0	1	(From house of mourning to Sandymount; between "Cyclops" and "Nausicaa")
Tram fare	0	0	1	(From Holles St. to Nighttown)
1 Pig's foot	0	0	4	(15.155–59)
1 Sheep's trotter	0	0	3	(15.155–59)
1 Cake chocolate	0	1	0	(15.144)
1 Sq. soda bread	0	0	4	(15.144)
Gift: Stephen D.	0	10	0	(15.3583–84)
Repair to lamp	0	1	0	(15.4312)
1 Coffee and bun	0	0	4	(16.1697–98)
Return of loan (SD)	1	6	11	(17.957–59)
Interest on loan	0	0	1	(17.957–57)
Balance:	0	5	4	

£2-19- 2

CREDIT:

	£	s	d	
Cash in Hand	0	4	9	(17.1457; cf 16.1697)
Commission rec'd.	1	7	6	("Aeolus"; not shown; cf. 10.392)
Loan (SD)	1	6	11	(15.3604)

£2-19- 2

Bloom's total expenses for June 16 are £1-6-11 (the same sum as Stephen's "loan").

Cash in hand plus earnings equals £1 12s 3d: that is, threepence more than Stephen's total.

Works Cited

Abbott, H. Porter. 1967. "The Importance of Martin Cunningham." *JJQ* 5: 47–52.

Abels, Jules. 1966. *The Parnell Tragedy*. New York: Macmillan.

Adams, Robert M. 1962. *Surface and Symbol: The Consistency of James Joyce's Ulysses*. New York: Oxford Univ. Press.

———. 1974. "Hades." In Hart and Hayman, 91–114.

Ahearn, Edward. 1989. *Marx and Modern Fiction*. New Haven: Yale Univ. Press.

Anthony, P. D. 1983. *John Ruskin's Labour*. Cambridge: Cambridge Univ. Press.

Aristotle. 1940. *Politics*. Translated H. Rackham. Cambridge, Mass.: Harvard Univ. Press.

———. 1980. *The Nicomachean Ethics*. Translated, with an introduction, by David Ross. New York: Oxford Univ. Press.

Atherton, J. S. 1974. "The Oxen of the Sun." In Hart and Hayman, 313–39.

Attridge, Derek. 1989. "Molly's Flow: The Writing of 'Penelope' and the Question of Women's Language." *Modern Fiction Studies* 35: 543–65.

Austin, Linda M. 1989. "Labor, Money and the Currency of Words in *Fors Clavigera*." *ELH* 56: 209–27.

Bacon, Francis. 1937. *Essays, Advancement of Learning, New Atlantis and Other Pieces*. Edited by Richard Foster Jones. New York: Odyssey.

———. 1944. *The Advancement of Learning and Novum Organum*. New York: Willey.

Baker, Harold D. 1986. "Rite of Passage: 'Ithaca,' Style and the Structure of *Ulysses*." *JJQ* 23: 277–97.

Bakhtin, M. M. 1965. *Rabelais and His World*. Translated by Helene Iswolsky. Cambridge, Mass.: MIT Press.

———. 1981. *The Dialogic Imagination: Four Essays*. Translated by Caryl Emerson and Michael Holquist and edited by Michael Holquist. Austin: Univ. of Texas Press.

Barthel, Diane. 1988. *Putting On Appearances: Gender and Advertising.* Philadelphia: Temple Univ. Press.

Barthes, Roland. 1974. *S/Z.* Translated by Richard Miller. New York: Hill and Wang.

Bataille, Georges. 1985. "The Notion of Expenditure." In *Visions of Excess: Selected Writings 1927–1939*, translated by Allan Stoekl, with Carl R. Lovitt and Donald M. Leslie, Jr., and edited by Allan Stoekl. Minneapolis: Univ. of Minnesota Press.

———. 1988. *The Accursed Share.* Translated by Robert Hurley. New York: Zone.

Baudrillard, Jean. 1988. *Selected Writings.* Edited and introduced by Mark Poster. Stanford: Stanford Univ. Press.

Bauerle, Ruth, ed. 1982. *The James Joyce Songbook.* New York: Garland.

———, ed. 1993. *Picking Up Airs: Hearing the Music in Joyce's Text.* Urbana and Chicago: Univ. of Illinois Press.

Bazargan, Susan. 1985. "Oxen of the Sun: Maternity, Language, and History." *JJQ* 22: 271–80.

Beach, Sylvia. 1980. *Shakespeare and Company.* Reprint, Lincoln: Univ. of Nebraska Press.

Beja, Morris. 1982. "The Joyce of Sex: Sexual Relationships in *Ulysses.*" In *The Seventh of Joyce*, edited by Bernard Benstock, 255–68. Bloomington: Indiana Univ. Press.

Bell, Robert H. 1991. *Jocoserious Joyce: The Fate of Folly in* Ulysses. Ithaca: Cornell Univ. Press.

Benjamin, Walter. 1979. "The Work of Art in the Age of Mechanical Reproduction." 2d ed. In *Film Theory and Criticism*, edited by Gerald Mast and Marshall Cohen, 847–70. New York: Oxford Univ. Press.

Benstock, Bernard. 1974. "Telemachus." In Hart and Hayman, 1–16.

———. 1988. "The £ S. d. of *Dubliners.*" *Twentieth Century Literature* 34: 191–210.

———. 1991. *Narrative Con/Texts in* Ulysses. Urbana and Chicago: Univ. of Illinois Press.

Berry, Wendell. 1987. *Home Economics.* San Francisco: North Point Press.

Blau, Peter M. 1964. *Exchange and Power in Social Life.* New York: Wiley.

Bloom, Harold. 1973. *The Anxiety of Influence.* New York: Oxford Univ. Press.

Bloom, Murray Teigh. 1957. *Money of Their Own: The Great Counterfeiters.* New York: Scribner's.

Bogart, Leo. 1967. *Strategy in Advertising.* New York: Harcourt.

Booker, M. Keith. 1990. "The Baby in the Bathwater: Joyce, Gilbert and Feminist Criticism." *Texas Studies in Literature and Language* 32: 446–67.

Bormanis, John. 1992. " 'in the first bloom of her new motherhood': The Appropriation of the Maternal and the Representation of Mothering in *Ulysses.*" *JJQ* 29: 593–606.

Bowen, Zack. 1974. *Musical Allusions in the Works of James Joyce: Early Poetry Through* Ulysses. Albany: State University of New York Press.

————. 1989. Ulysses *as a Comic Novel.* Syracuse: Syracuse Univ. Press.

Boyle, Robert, S.J. 1965. "A Note on Reuben J. Dodd as 'a dirty Jew.'" *JJQ* 3: 64–66.

————. 1974. "Penelope." In Hart and Hayman, 407–33.

Brivic, Sheldon. 1980. *Joyce Between Freud and Jung.* Port Washington, N.Y.: Kennikat.

————. 1985. *Joyce the Creator.* Madison: Univ. of Wisconsin Press.

————. 1991. *The Veil of Signs: Joyce, Lacan and Perception.* Urbana and Chicago: Univ. of Illinois Press.

Brown, Norman O. 1947. *Hermes the Thief.* Madison: Univ. of Wisconsin Press.

————. 1959. *Life Against Death: The Psychoanalytical Meaning of History.* Middletown, Conn.: Wesleyan Univ. Press.

Brown, Richard. 1985. *James Joyce and Sexuality.* Cambridge: Cambridge Univ. Press.

Bruns, Gerald L. 1974. "Eumaeus." In Hart and Hayman, 363–83.

Budgen, Frank. 1960. *James Joyce and the Making of* Ulysses. Reprint, Bloomington: Indiana Univ. Press.

Caesar, Terry P. 1989. "Joycing Parody." *JJQ* 26: 227–37.

Callow, Heather Cook. 1990. "'Marion of the Bountiful Bosoms': Molly Bloom and the Nightmare of History." *Twentieth Century Literature* 36: 464–76.

Card, James Van Dyck. 1984. *Anatomy of Penelope.* Rutherford, N.J.: Fairleigh Dickinson Univ. Press.

Carlyle, Thomas. N.d. *Past and Present.* New York: Frank F. Lovell.

Carter, T. E. 1968. "Freytag's *Soll und Haben;* A Liberal National Manifesto as a Best-Seller." *German Life and Letters* 21, no. 4 (July): 320–29.

Chace, William M. 1991. "Historical Realism: An Eco." *JJQ* 28: 889–901.

Cheng, Vincent J. 1991. "White Horse, Dark Horse: Joyce's Allhorse of Another Color." In *Joyce Studies Annual 1991,* edited by Thomas F. Staley, 101–28. Austin: Univ. of Texas Press.

Cixous, Helene. 1981. "Castration or Decapitation?" Translated by Annette Kuhn. *Signs: The Journal of Women in Culture and Society* 7: 41–55.

Cole, Sonia. 1956. *Counterfeit.* New York: Abelard-Schuman.

Cole, William Morse. 1921. *The Fundamentals of Accounting.* Boston: Houghton Mifflin.

Cope, Jackson I. 1974. "Sirens." In Hart and Hayman, 217–42.

Cornford, Francis M. [1912] 1957. *From Religion to Philosophy: A Study in the Origins of Western Speculation.* Reprint, New York: Harper.

Crosby, Christina. 1991. "Money Changes Everything." Paper read at Midwest Modern Language Association Convention, Chicago, November, 1991.

Cullen, L. M. 1987. *An Economic History of Ireland Since 1660.* 2d ed. London: Batsford.

Culler, Jonathan. 1981. *The Pursuit of Signs: Semiotics, Literature, Deconstruction.* Ithaca: Cornell Univ. Press.

Cumpiano, Marion. 1989. "Joyce's *Finnegan's* [sic] *Wake.*" *The Explicator* 48: 48–51.

Day, Robert Adams. 1980. "Joyce's Gnomon, Lenehan and the Persistence of an Image." *Novel* 14: 5–19.

Derrida, Jacques. 1978. *Writing and Difference.* Translated by Alan Bass. Chicago: Univ. of Chicago Press.

———. 1982. *Margins of Philosophy.* Translated by Alan Bass. Chicago: Univ. of Chicago Press.

———. 1984. "Two Words for Joyce." In *Post-Structuralist Joyce: Essays from the French,* edited by Derek Attridge and Daniel Ferrer, 45–59. Cambridge: Cambridge Univ. Press.

———. 1988. "*Ulysses* Gramophone: Hear say yes in Joyce." Translated by Shari Benstock. In *James Joyce: The Augmented Ninth,* edited by Bernard Benstock. 27–75. Syracuse: Syracuse Univ. Press.

Devlin, Kimberly J. 1991. "Pretending in 'Penelope': Masquerade, Mimicry, and Molly Bloom." *Novel* 25: 71–89.

de Vries, Leonard. 1968. *Victorian Advertisements.* Philadelphia: Lippincott.

Dick, Susan. 1981. "Tom Kernan and the Retrospective Arrangement." *JJQ* 18: 147–59.

Dilnot, George. 1930. *The Trial of Jim the Penman.* London: Geoffrey Bles.

DiPiero, Thomas. 1988. "Buying into Fiction." *Diacritics* 18, no. 2: 2–14.

Draper, Roger. 1986. "The Faithless Shepherd." *New York Review of Books,* June 26, 14–18.

Eco, Umberto. 1982. *The Aesthetics of Chaosmos: The Middle Ages of James Joyce.* Translated by Ellen Esrock. Tulsa: University of Tulsa Monograph Series.

Ellmann, Maud. 1982. "Polytropic Man: Paternity, Identity and Naming in *The Odyssey* and *A Portrait of the Artist as a Young Man.*" In *James Joyce: New Perspectives,* edited by Colin MacCabe, 73–104. Bloomington: Indiana Univ. Press.

Ellmann, Richard. 1972. *Ulysses on the Liffey.* New York: Oxford Univ. Press.

———. 1977. *The Consciousness of Joyce.* New York: Oxford Univ. Press.

Epstein, E. L. 1974. "Nestor." In Hart and Hayman, 17–28.

Finley, M. I. 1954. *The World of Odysseus.* New York: Viking.

Fludernik, Monika. 1987. " 'Ithaca'—An Essay in Non-Narrativity." In *International Perspectives on James Joyce,* edited by Gottlieb Gaiser, 88–105. Troy, N.Y.: Whitston.

Fogel, Daniel Mark. 1990. *Covert Relations: James Joyce, Virginia Woolf and Henry James.* Charlottesville: University Press of Virginia.

Foley, Helene P. 1984. " 'Reverse Similes' and Sex Roles in the *Odyssey.*" In *Women in the Ancient World: The "Arethusa" Papers,* edited by John Peradotto and J. P. Sullivan, 59–78. Albany: State University of New York Press.

Foucault, Michel. 1979. "What Is an Author?" In *Textual Strategies: Perspectives in Post-Structuralist Criticism,* edited by Josue V. Harari, 141–60. Ithaca: Cornell Univ. Press.

French, Marilyn. 1976. *The Book as World: James Joyce's* Ulysses. Cambridge, Mass.: Harvard Univ. Press.

Freud, Sigmund. [1905] 1960. *Jokes and Their Relation to the Unconscious.* Translated by James Strachey. London: Hogarth Press.

———. "Character and Anal Erotism." [1908] 1959. In *Collected Papers,* vol. 2, translated by Joan Riviere, 45–50. New York: Basic.

———. [1913] 1959. "The Predisposition to Obsessional Neurosis." In *Collected Papers,* vol. 2, 122–32.

———. [1916] 1959. "On the Transformation of Instincts with Special Reference to Anal Erotism." In *Collected Papers,* vol. 2, 164–71.

———. [1924] 1959. "The Economic Problem in Masochism." In *Collected Papers,* vol. 2, 255–68.

———. [1930] 1982. *Civilization and Its Discontents.* Translated by Joan Riviere, revised and edited by James Strachey. London: Hogarth Press.

Freytag, Gustav. [1855] 1895. *Soll und Haben.* 2 vols. Leipzig: S. Hirzel.

———. 1857. *Debit and Credit.* Translated by Mrs. Malcolm. London: Richard Bentley.

Frow, John. 1990. "Intertextuality and ontology." In *Intertextuality: theories and practices,* edited by Michael Worton and Judith Still. Manchester and New York: Manchester Univ. Press.

Garber, Marjorie. 1992. *Vested Interests: Cross-Dressing and Cultural Anxiety.* New York: Routledge.

Gelber, Mark H. 1983. "An Alternate Reading of the Role of the Jewish Scholar in Gustav Freytag's *Soll und Haben." Germanic Review* 58: 83–88.

Gifford, Don, with Robert J. Seidman. 1988. Ulysses *Annotated: Notes for James Joyce's* Ulysses. Rev. and exp. ed. Berkeley: Univ. of California Press.

Glasheen, Adaline. 1974. "Calypso." In Hart and Hayman, 51–70.

Gordon, John. 1981. *James Joyce's Metamorphoses.* Dublin: Gill and Macmillan.

———. 1991. "Obeying the Boss in 'Oxen of the Sun.'" *ELH* 58: 233–59.

Gose, Elliot B., Jr. 1980. *The Transformation Process in Joyce's* Ulysses. Toronto: Univ. of Toronto Press.

Gouldner, Alvin W. 1960. "The Norm of Reciprocity: A Preliminary Statement." *American Sociological Review* 25: 161–78.

Goux, Jean-Joseph. 1988. "Banking on Signs." *Diacritics* 18, no. 2: 15–25.

———. 1990. *Symbolic Economies: After Marx and Freud.* Translated by Jennifer Curtiss Gage. Ithaca: Cornell Univ. Press.

Groden, Michael. 1977. Ulysses *in Progress.* Princeton: Princeton Univ. Press.

Hart, Clive. 1974. "Wandering Rocks." In Hart and Hayman, 181–216.

Hartsock, Nancy C. M. 1983. *Money, Sex and Power: Toward a Feminist Historical Materialism.* New York and London: Longman.

Haug, W. F. [1971] 1986. *Critique of Commodity Aesthetics: Appearance, Sexuality and Advertising in Capitalist Society.* Translated by Robert Bock. Minneapolis: Univ. of Minnesota Press.

Hayman, David. 1974. "Cyclops." In Hart and Hayman, 243–75.

Heinzelman, Kurt. 1980. *The Economics of the Imagination*. Amherst: Univ. of Massachusetts Press.

Henke, Suzette A. 1978. *Joyce's Moraculous Sindbook: A Study of* Ulysses. Columbus: Ohio State Univ. Press.

———. 1990. *James Joyce and the Politics of Desire*. New York: Routledge.

Henke, Suzette A., and Elaine Unkeless, eds. 1982. *Women In Joyce*. Urbana: Univ. of Illinois Press.

Herr, Cheryl. 1986. *Joyce's Anatomy of Culture*. Urbana: Univ. of Illinois Press.

———. 1987. "Art and Life, Nature and Culture, *Ulysses*." In *Joyce's* Ulysses: *The Larger Perspective*, edited by Robert D. Newman and Weldon Thornton, 19–38. Newark: Univ. of Delaware Press.

———. 1989. " 'Penelope' as Period Piece." *Novel* 22: 130–42.

Herring, Phillip F. 1989. "James Joyce and Gift Exchange." *LIT: Literature Interpretation, Theory* 1: 85–97.

Hindley, Diana, and Geoffrey Hindley. 1972. *Advertising in Victorian England 1837–1901*. London: Wayland.

Hoberman, Gerald. 1982. *The Art of Coins and Their Photography*. London: Spink and Son; New York: Abrams.

Hoey, Allen. 1988. "The Name on the Coin: Metaphor, Metonymy, and Money." *Diacritics* 18, no. 2: 26–37.

Homans, George C. 1958. "Social Behavior as Exchange." *American Journal of Sociology* 63: 597–606.

Homer. 1961. *The Odyssey*. Translated by Robert Fitzgerald. New York: Doubleday.

Hornik, Marcel. 1959. "Leopold Bloom = Candaules." Pamphlet. Oxford: Lincombe Lodge Research Library.

Hubert, Henri, and Marcel Mauss. 1964. *Sacrifice: Its Nature and Function*. Translated by W. D. Halls. Chicago: Univ. of Chicago Press.

Hyde, Lewis. 1983. *The Gift: Imagination and the Erotic Life of Property*. New York: Random House.

Irigaray, Luce. 1985. *This Sex Which Is Not One*. Translated by Catherine Porter with Carolyn Burke. Ithaca: Cornell Univ. Press.

Iser, Wolfgang. 1978. *The Act of Reading: A Theory of Aesthetic Response*. Baltimore: Johns Hopkins Univ. Press.

James, Henry. 1908. *The Spoils of Poynton*. New York: Scribner's.

Jameson, Fredric. 1970. "Seriality in Modern Literature." *Bucknell Review* 18: 64–80.

———. 1982. *"Ulysses* in History." In *James Joyce and Modern Literature*, edited by W. J. McCormack and Alistair Stead, 126–41. London: Routledge and Kegan Paul.

Janusko, Robert. 1983. *Sources and Structures of James Joyce's "Oxen."* Ann Arbor: UMI Research Press.

Jhally, Sut. 1987. *The Codes of Advertising*. New York: St. Martin's.

Johnston, John. 1990. *Carnival of Repetition: Gaddis's* The Recognitions *and Postmodern Theory*. Philadelphia: Univ. of Pennsylvania Press.

Joyce, James. 1964. "Daniel Defoe." Pamphlet (Italian). Edited and translated from the Italian by Joseph Prescott. Buffalo: Buffalo Studies.

————. 1971. *Readings.* 3 cassettes. *Ulysses,* read by James Joyce. Cassette 1, side 2. Caedmon.

Joyce, Stanislaus. 1971. *The Complete Dublin Diary of Stanislaus Joyce.* Edited by George H. Healey. Ithaca: Cornell Univ. Press.

Kaye, Julian B. 1957. "Simony, the Three Simons, and Joycean Myth." In *A James Joyce Miscellany,* edited by Marvin Magalener, 20–36. New York: James Joyce Society.

Kearney, Colbert. 1989. "The Joycead." In *Coping With Joyce: Essays from the Copenhagen Symposium,* edited by Morris Beja and Shari Benstock, 55–72. Columbus: Ohio State Univ. Press.

Kempf, Roger. 1976. "James Job Joyce." *Moeurs: Ethnologie et Fiction.* Paris: Editions du Seuil.

Kenner, Hugh. 1956. *Dublin's Joyce.* Bloomington: Indiana Univ. Press.

————. 1972. "Molly's Masterstroke." *JJQ* 10: 19–28.

————. 1974. "Circe." In Hart and Hayman, 341–62.

————. 1978. *Joyce's Voices.* Berkeley: Univ. of California Press.

————. 1983. *A Colder Eye: The Modern Irish Writers.* New York: Penguin.

————. 1986. "Beaufoy's Masterplaster." *JJQ* 24: 11–18.

————. 1987. *Ulysses.* Rev. ed. Baltimore: Johns Hopkins Univ. Press.

Kershner, R. B., Jr. 1978. "Artist, Critic and Performer: Wilde and Joyce on Shakespeare." *Texas Studies in Literature and Language* 20: 216–29.

————. 1989. *Joyce, Bakhtin and Popular Literature: Chronicles of Disorder.* Chapel Hill: Univ. of North Carolina Press.

Kierkegaard, Soren. 1954. *Fear and Trembling and The Sickness Unto Death.* Translated by Walter Lowrie. Princeton: Princeton Univ. Press.

Knapp, James F. 1988. *Literary Modernism and the Transformation of Work.* Evanston, Ill.: Northwestern Univ. Press.

Knuth, A. M. L. 1976. *The Wink of the Word: A Study of James Joyce's Phatic Communication.* Amsterdam: Rodopi.

Lambridis, Helle. 1976. *Empedocles: A Philosophical Investigation.* University, Ala.: Univ. of Alabama Press.

Law, Jules David. 1989. "Simulation, Pluralism and the Politics of Everyday Life." In *Coping With Joyce: Essays From the Copenhagen Symposium,* edited by Morris Beja and Shari Benstock, 195–205. Columbus: Ohio State Univ. Press.

Lawrence, Karen R. 1981. *The Odyssey of Style in* Ulysses. Princeton: Princeton Univ. Press.

————. 1987. "Paternity, the Legal Fiction." In *Joyce's* Ulysses: *the Larger Perspective,* edited by Robert D. Newman and Weldon Thornton, 89–97. Newark: Univ. of Delaware Press.

————. 1992. " 'Beggaring Description': Politics and Style in Joyce's 'Eumaeus.' " *Modern Fiction Studies* 38: 355–76.

Leonard, Garry M. 1991. "Women on the Market: Commodity Culture, 'Femininity,' and 'Those Lovely Seaside Girls' in Joyce's *Ulysses.*" In *Joyce Studies Annual 1991*, edited by Thomas F. Staley, 27–68. Austin: Univ. of Texas Press.

Levine, Jennifer Schiffer. 1979. "Originality and Repetition in *Ulysses* and *Finnegans Wake.*" *PMLA* 94: 106–20.

Lévi-Strauss, Claude. 1969. *The Elementary Structures of Kinship.* Rev. ed. Translated by James Harle Bell, John Richard von Sturmer, and Rodney Needham. New York: Beacon.

Littleton, A. C., and B. S. Yamey, eds. 1978. *Studies in the History of Accounting.* Reprint, New York: Arno.

Litz, A. Walton. 1974. "Ithaca." In Hart and Hayman, 385–405.

Lodge, David. 1977. *The Modes of Modern Writing: Metaphor, Metonymy and the Typology of Modern Literature.* London: Edward Arnold.

Lowe-Evans, Mary. 1989. *Crimes Against Fecundity: Joyce and Population Control.* Syracuse: Syracuse Univ. Press.

Lyons, F. S. L. 1977. *Charles Stewart Parnell.* New York: Oxford Univ. Press.

MacCabe, Colin. 1978. *James Joyce and the Revolution of the Word.* London: Macmillan.

Maddox, James H., Jr. 1978. *Joyce's* Ulysses *and the Assault Upon Character.* Brunswick, N.J.: Rutgers Univ. Press.

———. 1987. "Mockery in *Ulysses.*" In *Joyce's* Ulysses: *The Larger Perspective,* edited by Robert D. Newman and Weldon Thornton, 141–56. Newark: Univ. of Delaware Press.

Madtes, Richard. 1983. *The "Ithaca" Chapter of Joyce's* Ulysses. Ann Arbor: UMI Research Press.

Mahaffey, Vicki. 1988. *Reauthorizing Joyce.* Cambridge: Cambridge Univ. Press.

Mair, John. 1938. *The Fourth Forger: William Ireland and the Shakespeare Papers.* London: Cobden-Sanderson.

Mallon, Thomas. 1989. *Stolen Words: Forays Into the Origins and Ravages of Plagiarism.* New York: Ticknor and Fields.

Mandell, Maurice I. 1984. *Advertising.* 4th ed. Englewood Cliffs, N.J.: Prentice-Hall.

Manganiello, Dominic. 1980. *Joyce's Politics.* London: Routledge and Kegan Paul.

Martin, Timothy. 1991. *Joyce and Wagner: A Study of Influence.* Cambridge: Cambridge Univ. Press.

Marx, Karl, and Friedrich Engels. 1978. *The Marx-Engels Reader.* Edited by Robert C. Tucker. 2d ed. New York: Norton.

Mauss, Marcel. [1925] 1967. *The Gift: Forms and Functions of Exchange in Archaic Societies.* Translated by Ian Cunnison. New York: Norton.

McArthur, Murray. 1988. *Stolen Writings: Blake's* Milton, *Joyce's* Ulysses *and the Nature of Influence.* Ann Arbor: UMI Research Press.

McCarthy, Patrick A. 1984a. "The Case of Reuben J. Dodd." *JJQ* 21: 169–74.

―――. 1984b. "Joyce's Unreliable Catechist: Mathematics and the Narration of 'Ithaca.' " *ELH* 51: 605–18.

McCloskey, Donald N. 1990. *If You're So Smart: The Narrative of Economic Expertise.* Chicago: Univ. of Chicago Press.

McCormack, W. J. 1988. "James Joyce, Cliché, and the Irish Language." In *James Joyce: The Augmented Ninth,* edited by Bernard Benstock, 323–35. Syracuse: Syracuse Univ. Press.

McGee, Patrick. 1988. *Paperspace: Style as Ideology in Joyce's* Ulysses. Lincoln: Univ. of Nebraska Press.

McMichael, James. 1991. Ulysses *and Justice.* Princeton: Princeton Univ. Press.

Meredith, George. 1961. *The Ordeal of Richard Feverel.* New York: Signet.

Michaels, Walter Benn. 1987. *The Gold Standard and the Logic of Naturalism: American Literature at the Turn of the Century.* Berkeley: Univ. of California Press.

Moore, George Foot. 1925. *Metempsychosis.* Cambridge, Mass.: Harvard Univ. Press.

Moretti, Franco. 1983. *Signs Taken for Wonders: Essays in the Sociology of Literary Forms.* Translated by Susan Fischer, David Forgacs, and David Miller. London: New Left Books.

Moseley, Virginia M. 1967. *Joyce and the Bible.* DeKalb: Northern Illinois Univ. Press.

Moshenberg, Daniel. 1988. "The Capital Couple: Speculating on *Ulysses.*" *JJQ* 25: 333–47.

―――. 1991. "What shouts in the street: 1904, 1922, 1990." *JJQ* 28: 809–18.

Newman, Robert D. 1987. *"Transformatio Coniunctionis:* Alchemy in *Ulysses."* In *Joyce's* Ulysses: *The Larger Perspective,* edited by Robert D. Newman and Weldon Thornton, 168–86. Newark: Univ. of Delaware Press.

Nietzsche, Friedrich. [1873] 1954. "On Truth and Lie in an Extra-Moral Sense." In *The Portable Nietzsche,* edited by Walter Kaufmann, 42–47. New York: Viking.

―――. [1887] 1956. *The Birth of Tragedy and The Genealogy of Morals.* Translated by Francis Golffing. New York: Doubleday.

O'Brien, Joseph V. 1982. *"Dear, Dirty Dublin": A City in Distress, 1899–1916.* Berkeley: Univ. of California Press.

O'Farrell, Patrick. 1975. *England and Ireland Since 1800.* London: Oxford Univ. Press.

Opie, Robert. 1985. *Rule Britannia: Trading on the British Image.* New York and Middlesex: Viking.

O'Shea, Michael J. 1986. *James Joyce and Heraldry.* Albany: State University of New York Press.

Osteen, Mark. 1991. "Serving Two Masters: Economics and Figures of Power in Joyce's 'Grace.' " *Twentieth Century Literature* 37: 76–92.

―――. 1995. "The Treasure-House of Language: Managing Symbolic Economies in Joyce's *Portrait."* Forthcoming in *Studies in the Novel.*

Pat [Patrick Kenny]. 1907. *Economics for Irishmen.* Dublin: Maunsel.

Peake, C. H. 1977. *James Joyce: The Citizen and the Artist.* Stanford: Stanford Univ. Press.

Pearl, Cyril. 1969. *Dublin in Bloomtime: The City James Joyce Knew.* London: Angus and Robertson.

Pecora, Vincent P. 1986. " 'The Dead' and the Generosity of the Word." *PMLA* 101: 233–45.

Pierce, David. 1992. *James Joyce's Ireland.* New Haven: Yale Univ. Press.

Plato. 1961. *Republic.* Translated by Paul Shorey. In *The Collected Dialogues of Plato,* edited by Edith Hamilton and Huntington Cairns. Princeton: Princeton Univ. Press.

Power, Arthur. 1974. *Conversations with James Joyce.* Chicago: Univ. of Chicago Press.

Power, Henriette Lazaridis. 1993. "Pantomime Songs and the Limits of Narrative in *Ulysses.*" In *Picking Up Airs: Hearing the Music in Joyce's Text,* edited by Ruth Bauerle, 53–66. Urbana: Univ. of Illinois Press.

Rabaté, Jean-Michel. 1991. *James Joyce, Authorized Reader.* Baltimore: Johns Hopkins Univ. Press.

Raleigh, John Henry. 1977. *The Chronicle of Leopold and Molly Bloom:* Ulysses *as Narrative.* Berkeley: Univ. of California Press.

Redfield, James. 1983. "The Economic Man." In *Approaches to Homer,* edited by Carl A. Rubino and Cynthia W. Shelmerdine, 218–47. Austin: Univ. of Texas Press.

Reinfeld, Fred. 1969. *Catalogue of the World's Most Popular Coins.* Revised by Burton Hobson. Garden City, N.Y.: Doubleday.

Restuccia, Frances L. 1984. "Transubstantiating *Ulysses.*" *JJQ* 21: 329–40.

———. 1989. *Joyce and the Law of the Father.* New Haven: Yale Univ. Press.

Richards, Thomas. 1990. *The Commodity Culture of Victorian England: Advertising and Spectacle, 1851–1914.* Stanford: Stanford Univ. Press.

Richman, Michèle. 1982. *Reading Georges Bataille: Beyond the Gift.* Baltimore: Johns Hopkins Univ. Press.

Riffaterre, Michael. 1978. *Semiotics of Poetry.* Bloomington: Indiana Univ. Press.

———. 1980. "Syllepsis." *Critical Inquiry* 6: 625–38.

———. 1990a. "Compulsory reader response: the intertextual drive." In *Intertextuality: Theories and Practices,* edited by Michael Worton and Judith Still, 56–78. Manchester and New York: Manchester Univ. Press.

———. 1990b. *Fictional Truth.* Baltimore: Johns Hopkins Univ. Press.

Riquelme, John Paul. 1983. *Teller and Tale in Joyce's Fiction: Oscillating Perspectives.* Baltimore: Johns Hopkins Univ. Press.

Rossi-Landi, Ferruccio. 1975. *Linguistics and Economics.* The Hague: Mouton.

Rubin, Gayle. 1975. "The Traffic in Women: Notes on the 'Political Economy' of Sex." In *Toward an Anthropology of Women,* edited by Rayna R. Reiter. 157–210. New York and London: Monthly Review Press.

Ruskin, John. 1903–12. *The Library Edition of the Works of John Ruskin.* Edited by E. T. Cook and Alexander Wedderburn. 39 vols. London: George Allen.

Sabin, Margery. 1987. *The Dialect of the Tribe: Speech and Community in Modern Fiction.* New York: Oxford Univ. Press.

Sahlins, Marshall. 1972. *Stone Age Economics.* Chicago: Aldine.

Sammons, Jeffrey L. 1969. "The Evaluation of Freytag's *Soll und Haben.*" *German Life and Letters* 22, no. 4 (July): 315–24.

Scholes, Robert. 1992. *In Search of James Joyce.* Urbana and Chicago: Univ. of Illinois Press.

Schudson, Michael. 1984. *Advertising, the Uneasy Persuasion: Its Dubious Impact on American Society.* New York: Basic.

Schwartz, Barry. 1967. "The Social Psychology of the Gift." *American Journal of Sociology* 73: 1–11.

Scott, Bonnie Kime. 1984. *Joyce and Feminism.* Bloomington: Indiana Univ. Press.

———. 1991. "Riding the 'vicociclometer': Women and Cycles of History in Joyce." *JJQ* 28: 827–39.

Seidel, Michael. 1976. *Epic Geography: James Joyce's Ulysses.* Princeton: Princeton Univ. Press.

Senn, Fritz. 1980. "Scareotypes: On Some Trenchant Renditions in *Ulysses.*" *Modern British Literature* 5: 22–28.

———. 1984. *Joyce's Dislocutions: Essays on Reading as Translation.* Edited by John Paul Riquelme. Baltimore: Johns Hopkins Univ. Press.

———. 1989a. "Joyce the Verb." In *Coping With Joyce: Essays from the Copenhagen Symposium,* edited by Morris Beja and Shari Benstock, 25–54. Columbus: Ohio State Univ. Press.

———. 1989b. "Ovidian Roots of Gigantism in Joyce's *Ulysses.*" *Journal of Modern Literature* 25: 561–77.

———. 1991. "Joycean Provections." In *Joycean Occasions: Essays from the Milwaukee James Joyce Conference,* edited by Janet E. Dunleavy, Melvin J. Friedman, and Michael Patrick Gillespie, 171–94. Newark: Univ. of Delaware Press.

Shapiro, Stephen A. 1964. "Leopold Bloom and Gulley Jimson: The Economics of Survival." *Twentieth Century Literature* 10: 3–11.

Sharp, Ronald A. 1986. *Friendship and Literature: Spirit and Form.* Durham: Duke Univ. Press.

Shechner, Mark. 1974. *Joyce in Nighttown: A Psychoanalytic Inquiry into Ulysses.* Berkeley: Univ. of California Press.

Shell, Marc. 1978. *The Economy of Literature.* Baltimore: Johns Hopkins Univ. Press.

———. 1982. *Money, Language and Thought: Literary and Philosophical Economies from the Medieval to the Modern Era.* Berkeley: Univ. of California Press.

Sherburne, J. S. 1972. *John Ruskin, or the Ambiguities of Abundance.* Cambridge, Mass: Harvard Univ. Press.

Shloss, Carol. 1989. "Molly's Resistance to the Union: Marriage and Colonialism in Dublin, 1904." *Modern Fiction Studies* 35: 507–16.

Sicari, Stephen. 1990. "Bloom in Purgatory: 'Sirens' and *Purgatorio II.*" *Twentieth Century Literature* 36: 477–88.

Simmel, Georg. 1950. *The Sociology of Georg Simmel.* Edited, translated, and with an introduction by Kurt H. Wolff. New York: Free Press.

———. 1971. *On Individuality and Social Forms: Selected Writings.* Edited by Donald N. Levine. Chicago: Univ. of Chicago Press.

———. 1978. *The Philosophy of Money.* Translated by Tom Bottomore and David Frisby. New York: Routledge.

Sims, Peter. 1989. "A Pocket Guide to *Ulysses.*" *JJQ* 26: 239–58.

Singer, Kurt. 1958. "Oikonomia: An Inquiry Into Beginnings of Economic Thought and Language." *Kyklos* 11: 29–54.

Skeat, Walter M. 1935. *An Etymological Dictionary of the English Language.* Oxford: Clarendon Press.

Smith, Barbara Herrnstein. 1988. *Contingencies of Value: Alternative Perspectives for Critical Theory.* Cambridge, Mass.: Harvard Univ. Press.

Smith, Craig. 1991. "Twilight in Dublin: A Look at Joyce's 'Nausicaa.' " *JJQ* 28: 631–35.

Smith, Kenneth. 1951. *The Malthusian Controversy.* London: Routledge.

Smith, Laurence Dwight. 1944. *Counterfeiting: Crime Against the People.* New York: Norton.

Somerville, Jane. 1975. "Money in *Dubliners.*" *Studies in Short Fiction* 12: 109–16.

Steele, H. Meili. 1988. *Realism and the Drama of Reference: Strategies of Representation in Balzac, Flaubert and James.* University Park: Pennsylvania State Univ. Press.

Steele, Valerie. 1985. *Fashion and Eroticism: Ideals of Feminine Beauty from the Victorian Era to the Jazz Age.* New York: Oxford Univ. Press.

Stern, J. P. 1973. *On Realism.* London and Boston: Routledge.

Stewart, Susan. 1984. *On Longing: Narratives of the Miniature, the Gigantic, the Souvenir, the Collection.* Baltimore: Johns Hopkins Univ. Press.

Stoller, Robert J. 1985. *Observing the Erotic Imagination.* New Haven: Yale Univ. Press.

Sultan, Stanley. 1987. *Eliot, Joyce and Company.* New York: Oxford Univ. Press.

ten Have, O. 1986. *The History of Accountancy.* 2d ed. Translated by A. van Seventer. Palo Alto, Calif.: Bay Books.

Theoharis, Theoharis Constantine. 1988. *Joyce's* Ulysses: *An Anatomy of the Soul.* Chapel Hill: Univ. of North Carolina Press.

Thomas, Brook. 1982. *James Joyce's* Ulysses: *A Book of Many Happy Returns.* Baton Rouge: Lousiana State Univ. Press.

Thom's Official Directory of the United Kingdom of Great Britain and Ireland for the Year 1904. 1904. Dublin: Alexander Thom.

Thornton, Weldon. 1987. "Voices and Values in *Ulysses.*" In *Joyce's* Ulysses: *The Larger Perspective,* edited by Robert D. Newman and Weldon Thornton, 244–70. Newark: Univ. of Delaware Press.

Tolomeo, Diane. 1973. "The Final Octagon of *Ulysses.*" *JJQ* 10: 439–54.

Tomkinson, Neil. 1965. "Bloom's Job." *JJQ* 2: 103–107.

Topia, André. 1984. "The matrix and the echo: Intertextuality in *Ulysses.*" In *Post-Structuralist Joyce: Essays from the French,* edited by Derek Attridge and Daniel Ferrer, 103–25. Cambridge: Cambridge Univ. Press.

Torchiana, Donald T. 1986. *Backgrounds for Joyce's* Dubliners. Boston: Allen & Unwin.

Tucker, Lindsey. 1984. *Stephen and Bloom at Life's Feast: Alimentary Symbolism and the Creative Process in James Joyce's* Ulysses. Columbus: Ohio State Univ. Press.

Ungar, Andras P. 1989. "Among the Hapsburgs: Arthur Griffith, Stephen Dedalus, and the Myth of Bloom." *Twentieth Century Literature* 35: 480–501.

Valente, Joseph. 1988. "The Politics of Joyce's Polyphony." In *New Alliances in Joyce Studies: "When it's Aped to Foul a Delfian,"* edited by Bonnie Kime Scott, 56–69. Newark: Univ. of Delaware Press.

Van Caspel, Paul. 1986. *Bloomers on the Liffey: Eisegetical Readings of Joyce's* Ulysses. Baltimore: Johns Hopkins Univ. Press.

Vernon, John. 1984. *Money and Fiction: Literary Realism in the Nineteenth and Early Twentieth Centuries.* Ithaca: Cornell Univ. Press.

Vico, Giambattista. 1968. *The New Science of Giambattista Vico.* Translated by Thomas Goddard Bergin and Max Harold Fisch. Ithaca: Cornell Univ. Press.

Vlastos, Gregory. 1947. "Equality and Justice in Early Greek Cosmologies." *Classical Philology* 42: 156–78.

Voelker, Joe, and Thomas Arner. 1990. "Bloomian Pantomime: J. A. Dowie and the 'Messianic Scene.' " *JJQ* 27: 283–91.

Walzl, Florence L. 1982. *"Dubliners:* Women in Irish Society." In *Women in Joyce,* edited by Suzette Henke and Elaine Unkeless, 32–53. Urbana: Univ. of Illinois Press.

Webber, F. R. 1971. *Church Symbolism.* 2d ed. Detroit: Gale.

Weir, David. 1991. "Sophomore Plum(p)s for Old Man Moses." *JJQ* 28: 657–61.

Wenke, John. 1980. "Charity: The Measure of Morality in 'Wandering Rocks.' " *Eire-Ireland:* 100–113.

Weschler, Lawrence. 1988a. "Value: I—A Fool's Question." *New Yorker,* Jan. 18: 33–56.

———. 1988b. "Value: II—Category Confusion." *New Yorker,* Jan. 25: 88–98.

Wheelwright, Philip, ed. 1966. *The PreSocratics.* Indianapolis: Odyssey.

Wicke, Jennifer A. 1988. *Advertising Fictions: Literature, Advertisement and Social Reading.* New York: Columbia Univ. Press.

———. 1991. " 'Who's She When She's At Home?' / Molly Bloom and the Work of Consumption." *JJQ* 28: 749–63.

Wilde, Oscar. 1969. *The Artist as Critic: Critical Writings of Oscar Wilde.* Edited by Richard Ellmann. New York: Random House.

Williams, Raymond. 1980. "Advertising: The Magic System." *Problems in Materialism and Culture*. London: Verso. 170–95.

Williams, Trevor L. 1991. "Demystifying the Power of the Given: The 'Telemachus' Episode of *Ulysses*." *Twentieth Century Literature* 37: 38–53.

Williamson, Judith. 1978. *Decoding Advertisements: Ideology and Meaning in Advertising*. London: Boyars.

Wright, David G. 1991. *Ironies of* Ulysses. Savage, Md.: Barnes and Noble.

Yeats, William Butler. 1965. *The Autobiography of William Butler Yeats*. New York: Macmillan.

Index

Richard Fallis, *Series Editor*

Irish Studies presents a wide range of books interpreting important aspects of Irish life and culture to scholarly and general audiences. The richness and complexity of the Irish experience, past and present, deserve broad understanding and careful analysis. For this reason, an important purpose of the series is to offer a forum to scholars interested in Ireland, its history, and culture. Irish literature is a special concern in the series, but works from the perspectives of the fine arts, history, and the social sciences are also welcome, as are studies that take multidisciplinary approaches.

Selected titles in the series include: